LITERACY

Helping Children Construct Meaning

Second Edition

J. David Cooper

Ball State University

with an introduction by

Kathryn H. Au

Houghton Mifflin Company ■ **Boston** **Toronto**

Dallas   Geneva, Illinois   Palo Alto   Princeton, New Jersey

To Isabelle Cooper
Mother, Friend, Supporter

Senior Sponsoring Editor: Loretta Wolozin
Development Editor: Susan Yanchus
Senior Project Editor: Rosemary Winfield
Senior Production/Design Coordinator: Renee Le Verrier
Senior Manufacturing Coordinator: Holly Schuster
Marketing Manager: Rebecca Dudley

Cover design by Perennial Design.
Front cover art by Jerry Williams, grade 1, McGilvra Elementary School. Back cover art by Benton, grade 1.

Photo credits for photographs reprinted from *Mummies, Tombs, and Treasure* by Lila Perl: pages 171 and 172, reproduced courtesy of the Cairo Museum from Grafton Elliott Smith, "The Royal Mummies," *General Catalogue of the Egyptian Antiquities of the Cairo Museum* (Cairo: Service des Antiquités de l'Egypte, 1912); page 173, reproduced by courtesy of the Trustees of the British Museum; page 175, Egyptian Ministry of Information.

Page 29, excerpt from Graeme Base, *The Eleventh Hour*. Published in 1989 by Harry N. Abrams, Incorporated, New York. Copyright © Doublebase Pty, Ltd., 1988. All rights reserved. Reprinted by permission of Harry N. Abrams, Incorporated and Penguin Books Australia, Ltd.

Page 72, reprint of Juanita Havill, *Jamaica Tag-Along*. Text copyright © 1989 by Juanita Havill. Illustrations copyright © 1989 by Anne Sibley O'Brien. Reprinted by permission of Houghton Mifflin Co. All rights reserved.

Page 170, excerpt from Lila Perl, *Mummies, Tombs, and Treasure*. Text copyright © 1987 by Lila Perl. Drawings copyright © 1987 by Erika Weihs. Reprinted by permission of Clarion Books, a Houghton Mifflin Company imprint. All rights reserved.

Page 243, reprint of Allen Say, *The Bicycle Man*. Copyright © 1982 by Allen Say. Reprinted by permission of Houghton Mifflin Co. All rights reserved.

Page 293, excerpt from T. L. Harris and R. E. Hodges, *A Dictionary of Reading and Related Terms* (Newark, DE: International Reading Association, 1981). Reprinted with permission of the International Reading Association.

Page 329, reprint of Dorothy Butler, *My Brown Bear Barney*, illustrated by Elizabeth Fuller. Copyright © 1988 by Dorothy Butler. Reprinted by permission of Greenwillow Books, a division of William Morrow & Company, Inc. and Reed Publishing (NZ), Ltd.

Library of Congress Catalog Card Number 92-72264

ISBN 0-395-64782-7

23456789-RT-96 95 94 93

Contents

5 ▪ Identifying Words as an Aid to Constructing Meaning   274

6 ▪ Responding and the Construction of Meaning   345

7 ▪ Writing and the Construction of Meaning   398

8 ■ Modeling Strategies for Constructing Meaning   456

9 ■ Constructing Meaning Across the Curriculum   496

10 ▪ Assessment and Evaluation in the Literacy-Centered Classroom   **544**

Preface

Helping all children become literate is one of the most exciting and rewarding adventures one can have! This adventure is a major component of the teacher's job. *Literacy: Helping Children Construct Meaning,* Second Edition, was written to support preservice and inservice teachers in learning to help children develop literacy effectively.

Background

This book reflects the dramatic changes in our understanding of literacy that have taken place in recent years. The first edition of the text, *Improving Reading Comprehension* (1986), was written at a time when we were just learning how to use much of the new knowledge gained from research on comprehension. Since then we have broadened our understanding to realize that we must think about comprehension within the context of literacy—reading, writing, speaking, and listening—with thinking an integral part of each.

What does this understanding mean for teachers? We know that children and young adults develop literacy by having many "real" literacy experiences that are supported by the teacher and their peers. For example, some children in a class might read the beautiful new book *My Great Aunt Arizona* (Houston, 1992) with partners while others read it with the teacher. Following the reading, they could form small discussion groups to talk about their favorite parts or other points of interest; during these discussion groups the teacher models, prompts, participates, and observes. This is the natural process of how children construct meanings. To be effective, teachers need to know how to help students learn to construct meaning for themselves.

Revisions in This Edition

The second edition of this text addresses the process of developing literacy, the interaction between learners' prior knowledge and their experiences, and the teacher's role in bringing these elements together. It explains and develops the constructive nature of constructing meaning. Because the text covers so much new ground it was given a new title—*Literacy: Helping Children Construct Meaning*—to reflect what educators have learned and what educators know we must do to help students develop literacy and their abilities to construct meaning.

The structure of the text provides teachers a unique approach to preparing for a literature-based classroom. This structure grew out of the strengths of the first edition, whose framework incorporated samples of literature and lessons that modeled the process of "how to teach" comprehension. Preservice and inservice teachers responded so enthusiastically to this situational guidance that it became the springboard for the second edition's new "Literacy Lessons" and thematic unit plans.

In the revision, many aspects of the modeling framework were rethought and broadened to make it more flexible and practical for teachers using a whole-language philosophy in their classrooms. To give just a few examples, there are numerous minilessons, self-reflective commentaries on why particular strategies are effective, and charts to summarize the many parts of a complete literacy program. This text can be used as a textbook in a college course, but also as a handbook that teachers will want to keep as a reference as they develop their own strategies for helping students construct meaning and develop literacy.

The Literacy Program

The central feature of *Literacy: Helping Children Construct Meaning*, Second Edition is a literacy program whose focus is on interactive learning. It develops this program in several ways:

- The text presents and develops a model for creating a literacy program in a school or classroom that includes three interrelated parts—*motivation, independent reading and writing,* and *instruction in reading and writing.*
- Complete unadapted literature is included in the text to model the process of developing literacy lessons. The literacy lesson concept is easy to use with any type of literature at any level. Sample literacy lessons and minilessons are presented for each whole piece of literature.
- Each chapter of the book discusses strategies and procedures that have been effective with all students including second language learners and students with special needs.
- Each chapter also contains a graphic organizer preview, an opening vignette to model constructivist teaching in action, a summary, bibliographies of professional references and children's books, and suggested additional readings.

Organization and Scope of the Text

The ten chapters of the book provide comprehensive coverage of topics important in helping teachers learn to help children construct meaning:

Chapter 1, "Understanding Literacy Learning and Constructing Meaning," provides background on the changing views of comprehension, literacy and literacy learning, emergent literacy, language acquisition, prior knowledge, and schema theory. It introduces principles for guiding the construction of meaning.

Chapter 2, "Developing a Literacy Program," shows how thematic units, literacy lessons, and minilessons fit into this program. It discusses the concept of scaffolded instruction. The story *The Bicycle Man* by Allen Say is the basis for the sample Literacy Lesson in this chapter.

Chapter 3, "Activating and Developing Prior Knowledge," presents background material supporting the importance of schema and prior knowledge for literacy development. It suggests strategies for helping students achieve independence in activating their own prior knowledge. *Mummies, Tombs, and Treasure* by Lila Perl is the basis for a sample literacy lesson focusing on prior knowledge activation.

Chapter 4, "Vocabulary Development in the Literacy Program," focuses on how students develop vocabulary and emphasizes strategies leading to student independence. *Jamaica Tag-along* by Juanita Havill is the basis of a literacy lesson involving vocabulary.

Chapter 5, "Identifying Words as an Aid to Constructing Meaning," develops the idea that identifying words is a means to the end of constructing meaning, and presents shared reading as one way to develop the ability to identify words. It also demonstrates how reading and writing can be used to practice meaningful word identification. *My Brown Bear Barney* by Dorothy Butler is used as the basis for a Literacy Lesson on meaningful word identification.

Chapter 6, "Responding and the Construction of Meaning," shows how responding to literature leads to the development of students' abilities to construct meaning and presents techniques and strategies—from journals to literature circles—to support responding.

Chapter 7, "Writing and the Construction of Meaning," focuses on how to promote and support writing within the literacy program. It gives a detailed description of the Writing Workshop as a way to getting students enthusiastic about writing.

Chapter 8, Modeling Strategies for Constructing Meaning," models for teachers how to model strategies for students, and discusses five strategies supported by research.

Chapter 9, "Constructing Meaning Across the Curriculum," applies many concepts developed in earlier chapters to the entire curriculum, and gives a plan for developing cross-curricular thematic units.

Chapter 10, "Assessment and Evaluation in the Literacy-Centered Classroom," focuses on assessment as an integral part of instruction and suggests guidelines and techniques for developing portfolios.

Instructor's Resource Manual

The Instructor's Resource Manual that accompanies this text contains numerous additional ideas for modeling constructivist teaching and sparking students' interest in literature-based approaches. The Instructor's Resource Manual was developed in conjunction with Dr. Nancy D. Kiger of the University of Central Florida. For each chapter of the text, the manual provides organizing tools such as chapter outlines and summaries; questions and activities to encourage class discussion and active learning; and pedagogical aids such as transparency masters to reinforce key concepts in the text. The manual was developed as a flexible tool to complement individual instructors' unique teaching styles.

Acknowledgments

This text is a reflection of my continuing efforts to understand how children develop literacy and to help teachers develop this understanding. The thousands of teachers and children with whom I have worked during the last seven years and some of the finest research the field has produced have helped me to more clearly formulate my own thinking about literacy learning.

There are many people who have supported me in writing this text. Nancy Sargeant, vice president and editorial director, Houghton Mifflin Company, made it possible for me to have the time to conceptualize this text. Vicki McLain (professor, Kennesaw State College), Susan E. Page (consultant and author), and Michael D. Robinson (classroom teacher) reacted to the initial manuscript and gave invaluable suggestions. Kathy Au (researcher and author) raised questions and made suggestions that helped me to clearly present many new ideas for teachers. Nancy Kiger (professor, University of Central Florida, author, and editor) reviewed the manuscript for content and clarity in its initial and final drafts and helped to make the ideas clearer for readers; Nancy gave literally hundreds of hours of her own time to this task. Brenda Stone Anderson (my right hand) typed and retyped manuscript, designed charts, posters, and graphs, and made the manuscript look great. Merryl Maleska Wilbur (former Houghton Mifflin developmental editor) helped to develop the original text, and Loretta Wolozin (senior sponsoring editor, Houghton Mifflin) saw and supported the need for a text of this type. Susan Yanchus (development editor, Houghton Mifflin) gave invaluable insights and suggestions about ways to improve my manuscript. Rosemary Winfield (production editor, Houghton Mifflin) saw the manuscript through production, resulting in a teacher-friendly, reader-friendly design.

Special thanks and appreciation go to C. Michael Shaw, executive vice president; John T. Ridley, publisher; and Loretta Wolozin, sponsoring editor, all of Houghton Mifflin, for their efforts and support in resolving problems related to including full pieces of unadapted literature in this text. They know and understand how important it is for teachers to learn to use literature effectively.

A big thanks goes to the many teachers and children who have provided me with samples of work, most without names. These pieces help to illustrate many of the concepts developed in this text.

The manuscript was also reviewed by college and university professors from across the country. The following gave valuable suggestions that led to an improved text:

Janice A. Dole, University of Utah

Barbara Edwards, University of North Carolina, Charlotte

William A. Henk, Pennsylvania State University

Joan Nelson Herber, SUNY Binghamton

Ellen Jampole, SUNY Cortland

Barbara G. Lyman, University of Delaware

Richard Robinson, University of Missouri

Katherine M. Seeley, Western Michigan University

Timothy C. Standal, University of Washington

William Valmont, University of Arizona

John Wolinski, Salisbury State University

Throughout this text I have stressed one consistent belief—*children and young adults learn to read and write by reading and writing with support from more experienced individuals.* As I complete this text and reflect on what I have written, I believe this more than ever. I am even more convinced of this when I read a note a kindergarten child wrote to her principal which said:

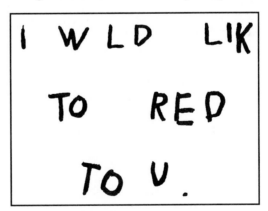

You, too, will have your own stories to share that will be testimonials to your convictions and beliefs.

J. David Cooper

August 1992

Introduction

Near the end of the past school year, while visiting a first-grade class, I noticed that Tiffany had finished the draft of a new story. When I asked if she would read it to me, she did so in a confident voice. Her story began in a matter-of-fact way, by describing how she and her family got into the car and drove to the beach. At the beach she went swimming, was engulfed by a big wave, and would have drowned had her father not been nearby. Later her uncle took the family out in his boat, and she surprised everyone by reeling in a big fish.

"Wow," I said. "So much happened in just one day."

Tiffany gazed at me with an air of superiority. "I wrote *fiction*," she said.

I hope that I can be excused for my ignorance. It wasn't long ago that writing in the primary grades meant little more than handwriting and copying from the board. Most educators did not dream that first graders could be composing fiction. Similarly, reading meant little more than sounding out words and reading aloud. Tiffany and her classmates can do a lot more than read aloud. They have read books by a dozen different authors, and they can tell you if they prefer Joy Cowley or Mercer Mayer, and why. They have opinions, and they have confidence in themselves as readers and as writers.

A remarkable transformation is taking place in classrooms throughout our nation. The field of reading and language arts is in a state of transition, moving from transmission approaches emphasizing skills toward transactional, process, and whole language approaches emphasizing the purposeful uses of language and literacy. In classrooms where transactional approaches have taken hold, teachers recognize the importance of guiding children to construct meaning when reading and writing. When children recognize that reading and writing are both processes of constructing meaning from text, they often come to understand literacy as Tiffany and her classmates do. These children do not just go through the motions of reading and writing. They write for their own purposes with a sense of audience, and they read enthusiastically for their own purposes.

The challenge, as I see it, is to make the kind of instruction and classroom environment Tiffany experienced available to all students. This is a tremendous challenge, because transactional approaches require a high level of expertise on the part of the teacher. Most preservice teachers, as well as inservice teachers, have had few opportunities to experience transactional approaches in their own education. Thus, while many teachers find the philosophy of transactional, process, and whole language approaches appealing, they often falter when it comes to bringing the philosophy to life in their own classrooms.

Literacy: Helping Children Construct Meaning deals with the practical realities faced by teachers in the classroom and addresses the concerns, even fears, that many teachers are voicing in this period of transition. J. David Cooper brings to this book a wealth of experience gained through working with hundreds of teachers throughout the United States and through teaching in elementary classrooms himself and the gifts of explaining complex, abstract concepts in plain English and spelling out practical implications.

In my opinion, what sets this book apart is that it seeks the middle ground and is progressive without being faddish. In the rush to embrace transactional approaches, or any new educational approaches for that matter, we show a tendency to throw the baby out with the bathwater. In the case of transactional approaches, I have noticed this tendency in two areas in particular. These are unintended, yet real, outcomes in many schools where teachers are exploring transactional approaches.

First, there is a rejection of systematic, teacher-led instruction, in the mistaken belief that, if the right environment is provided, children will magically teach themselves to read and write. In this book David highlights the role of the teacher and the teacher's responsibility for planning and providing lessons within the context of authentic literacy activities. David believes in providing children with the opportunity to construct their own meanings and to make discoveries, but he insists that teachers be prepared to model, guide, demonstrate, and otherwise instruct children.

Second, there is a denial of the importance of strategies and skills. There is no doubt in my mind that, in the past, we broke reading and writing down into too many little skills and spent too much time on the instruction of these skills in isolation. Yet the present danger is that teachers will hesitate to teach children the very skills and strategies that will enable them to become effective readers and writers. David shows how teachers may avoid this trap by teaching specific skills and strategies in the context of real reading and writing, so that children see the utility of these skills and strategies.

My experiences with Tiffany and her teacher, as well as with many other students and teachers, have convinced me of the promise of transactional approaches. This book reflects a view David and I share: that this promise can only be fulfilled if we respect and carry with us what seems strongest in both the old and the new.

Kathryn H. Au

August 1992

LITERACY

**Helping Children
Construct Meaning**

Understanding Literacy Learning and Constructing Meaning

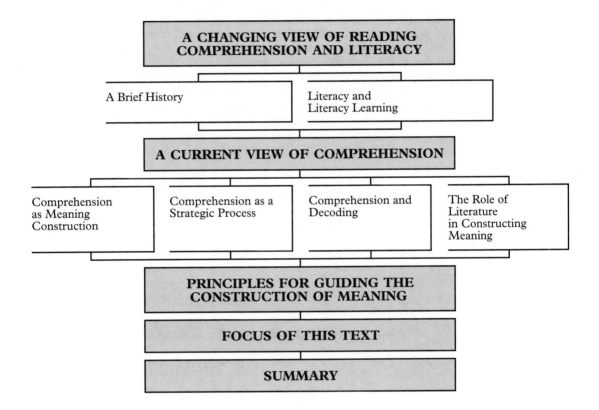

A CHANGING VIEW OF READING COMPREHENSION AND LITERACY

A Brief History

Literacy and Literacy Learning

A CURRENT VIEW OF COMPREHENSION

Comprehension as Meaning Construction

Comprehension as a Strategic Process

Comprehension and Decoding

The Role of Literature in Constructing Meaning

PRINCIPLES FOR GUIDING THE CONSTRUCTION OF MEANING

FOCUS OF THIS TEXT

SUMMARY

A *brief look at how some fourth graders are working with the book Flossie and the Fox (McKissack, 1986) will help us begin to think about what happens in classrooms to help students develop their abilities to construct meaning. Flossie and the Fox is a wonderful book written in dialect about a little African American girl from the south and how she outsmarts a fox.*

Fourth-graders Eddie, Andrew, Lisa, Christina, Jose, Terri, and Gil were each huddled in their own special place in the classroom reading the book Flossie and the Fox (McKissack, 1986). When Lisa finished the book, she wrote in her journal how she felt about Flossie. When Gil finished, he drew a picture of his favorite part of the story and wrote, "Flossie is soo-o-o smart!!!" As each reader finished the book, journal writing began.

Soon Mrs. Miller asked for everyone who was reading Flossie and the Fox to meet in a discussion group. On the wall hung a chart like the one shown below. The students began by sharing their personal responses from their journals. Everyone was so eager to share that Mrs. Miller had to encourage them to take turns.

Our Predictions About
Flossie and the Fox

1. *The fox is going to eat Flossie's eggs.*
2. *Flossie is going to trick the fox.*
3. *A fox is smart. I think the fox will trick Flossie.*

After the students shared their personal responses, Mrs. Miller asked, "How did we do with our predictions?" Students discussed which predictions had been confirmed in their reading of Flossie and which had not. For example, Terri said that she found out right away that what she had predicted didn't happen.

Mrs. Miller then asked the children whether the first prediction on the chart had been confirmed. Three students said it had not, but the others were not sure. Terri suggested, "We could look back in our books to see if it was true." After several students responded, Mrs. Miller directed the group to page 9. She asked them to think about the first prediction as she read aloud the page. Then she modeled the thinking involved in evaluating predictions by saying, "This section begins to tell me that Flossie is not going to be tricked by the fox. This leads me to believe that our first prediction may not be confirmed. In fact, it leads me to think I should change the original prediction that we made because I have gotten more information about Flossie and how she thinks."

A discussion followed focusing on predictions and how they change as one gathers more information during reading. After all the predictions were discussed, Mrs. Miller asked the group what they would like to do with the story now that they had finished it. Lisa, Jose, Gil, and Eddie wanted to take parts and make a play. The others wanted to add examples of Flossie's dialect to the class language wall (part of the class language project that Mrs. Miller had started to help children develop an appreciation and understanding of different dialects and cultures).

THESE FOURTH-GRADERS and their teacher were developing literacy. The book being discussed was an original work, not one that was adapted or rewritten. The group had previewed the story of Flossie and the fox and had predicted what they thought would happen. They then revisited the story to think about how their predictions had been confirmed or changed as they read. When Mrs. Miller realized that students were having difficulty with one prediction, she used a think-aloud process to model how she might have changed her thinking about the first prediction. The students then discussed how each prediction had been confirmed, changed, or rejected.

These students made authentic, personal responses to *Flossie and the Fox*; they responded to the story by doing the types of things one usually does naturally or socially after reading a story. That is, they did not just answer workbook questions, a form of response that occurs only in school. Mrs. Miller encouraged the children to choose their own forms of response, just as real readers do in real life. Finally, the students decided what they wanted to do with this story after they had completed it.

The scene described in Mrs. Miller's room is being repeated more and more in classrooms throughout the country:

- Students read original works of literature.
- Reading and writing activities are developed and used together.
- Personal, creative responses are encouraged and respected.
- Students and teacher work together to formulate an understanding of the book.
- If needed, the teacher uses various strategies in a natural and unobtrusive manner to promote better comprehension during discussions.
- The teacher is concerned about creating positive attitudes and maintaining a high degree of motivation.

Contrast Mrs. Miller's classroom with the one more commonly seen when the first edition of this text (Cooper, 1986) was written:

- The teacher taught the group a reading skill. Sometimes the skill was modeled using passages of text.
- Students then practiced the skill on a worksheet or in a workbook.

- Students read stories that had been adapted to conform to a particular readability formula.
- Students answered questions about the story on worksheets; then they usually discussed the story.
- Students then usually completed more skill activities.

Comparing and contrasting these two classrooms shows how the world of reading instruction is changing. Classroom teachers, reading specialists, and researchers have learned a great deal about how children and young adults learn to read and write, or become literate. Much of this information has been known for many years (Huey, 1908), but we are now beginning to apply it to classrooms. Only recently have conditions in public education, attitudes of educators, and newer research findings really supported the movement from a very skills-centered approach to reading and writing instruction to a more holistic approach that focuses on reading and writing as full processes that support each other.

A CHANGING VIEW OF READING COMPREHENSION AND LITERACY

Since before the turn of the century (Huey, 1908; Robinson, Faraone, Hittleman, and Unruh, 1990; Smith, 1965), educators and psychologists have noted the importance of comprehension as a part of reading and have tried to understand what really happens when a reader comprehends. Though this interest has intensified in recent years, the process of comprehension itself has not changed. As Roser points out, "Whatever children and adults did as they read in ancient Egypt, Greece, or Rome, and whatever they do today in order to derive or apply meaning to print, is the same" (1984, p. 48). But two things have changed: our understanding of how comprehension takes place and the literacy demands of society. In today's technological world, there is an escalating need for literate, critical thinkers who can fully participate in society.

A Brief History

Emphasis on Decoding

During the 1960s and 1970s, a number of reading specialists believed that reading comprehension was an end product of decoding (Fries, 1962); if students could name the words, comprehension would occur automatically. This basic belief became the foundation for a series of reading texts that are still in use in some parts of the country (Fries et al., 1966). However, as teachers placed greater emphasis on decoding, they found that many students still did not understand what they read; comprehension was *not* taking place automatically.

Educators then began to believe that perhaps teachers were asking the wrong types of questions. Because teachers asked predominantly literal questions, students were not being challenged to use their inferential and critical reading and thinking abilities. So the emphasis in reading instruction shifted, and teachers began asking students a greater variety of questions at differing levels according to some taxonomy, such as the Barrett Taxonomy of Reading Comprehension (Clymer, 1968). (On a *literal* level, one sees exactly what is stated in the text; on an *inferential* level, one uses text clues to make predictions and draw conclusions; on a *critical* level, one evaluates the text.) However, it wasn't long before teachers began to realize that they were asking questions primarily as a means of checking comprehension, not teaching it, and were focusing heavily on questions at the literal level. This view was supported by research on the use of questions in classroom practices and in basal readers (Durkin, 1978, 1981a). Current thinking supports teachers using questions as prompts to focus students' attention on the important aspects of a text (Beck & McKeown, 1981; Shake & Allington, 1985) that elicit both literal and inferential levels of thought (Sadow, 1982). However, asking questions alone is still not teaching.

Comprehension "Skills"

During the late 1960s, 1970s, and early 1980s educators began to believe that the best way to develop comprehension was to identify a set of discrete skills called "comprehension skills" (Otto et al., 1977). The focus of reading instruction in many classrooms then became the teaching and practicing of each individual skill, even though previous researchers and educators had questioned the efficacy of these practices (Goodman, 1965).

Numerous studies have attempted to identify the skills of reading comprehension (Davis, 1944, 1968, 1972; Spearritt, 1972; Thorndike, 1973), but an examination of their results reveals that they did not consistently identify the same skills. The only skill that appeared in three of five such studies was identification of word meanings; all other skills were found in no more than two of the five studies.

Rosenshine (1980), in a review of professional literature concerning the skill issue in reading comprehension, drew the following conclusions:

1. *It is difficult to confidently put forth any set of discrete comprehension skills.*
2. *Comprehension skills are simply not taught in a hierarchical fashion.*
3. *It is not clear whether all, or even any, of the skill exercises in reading comprehension are essential or necessary. (p. 552)*

Thus research does not clearly support the identification of any set of comprehension skills; nor is there specific evidence that teaching students main-idea, sequence, cause-and-effect, or other skills will make them better comprehenders. This, along with other evidence presented in this chapter, leads one to conclude that comprehension is *not* a set of discrete skills.

A Transactional Approach

During the 1970s and 1980s, researchers in education, psychology, and linguistics began to theorize about how a reader comprehends and then attempted to verify certain aspects of their theories through research (Anderson & Pearson, 1984; Smith, 1971; Spiro, 1979). Many researchers returned to the early works of Dewey and Rosenblatt to look for new theories and answers (Goodman, 1989). Rosenblatt was the first person to indicate that reading was a transaction between the reader and the text; she established the belief that readers have the right to, and do, establish their own meanings (Rosenblatt, 1938/1983, 1978).

The research and theories of the 1970s and 1980s broadened the thinking of many educators, causing them to focus on a literacy perspective rather than the isolated elements of reading, writing, speaking, listening, and thinking. The work of the Russian psychologist Vygotsky (1978) has provided a basis for the concept that children learn by being supported by adults and peers. At the same time, the idea was established that children learn language holistically rather than in parts and pieces (Halliday, 1975). Today the work of these researchers and others has led educators to focus on comprehension in the broad perspective of *literacy learning* (Clay, 1979, 1982, 1985; Teale & Sulzby, 1986).

Literacy and Literacy Learning

Literacy is the ability to read and write (Teale & Sulzby, 1986, p. xix). In the broader sense, literacy involves all of the language arts—reading, writing, speaking, and listening—with thinking being a part of each of these elements. As Wells (1990) states, "To be fully literate is to have the disposition to engage appropriately with texts of different types in order to empower action, feeling, and thinking in the context of purposeful social activity" (p. 14).

When thinking about helping students develop or grow into literacy, it is important to remember that reading, writing, speaking, listening, and thinking do not develop as separate components and should not be taught as separate subjects. Actually, all aspects of literacy develop simultaneously and inter- actively (Freeman & Hatch, 1989; Strickland, 1990). Children learn to read and write by simply reading, writing, and responding to their reading and writing (Pappas & Brown, 1987). Thus literacy develops as students encounter many authentic or real literacy experiences in which they are able to approximate the real tasks of literacy (Cambourne, 1988). *In other words, children learn to*

Figure 1-1   Sample of a Kindergartner's Writing

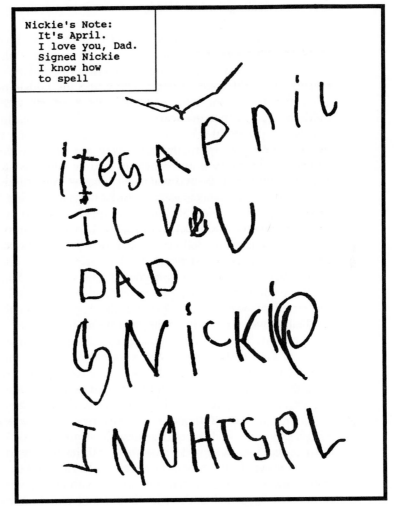

read, write, speak, listen, and think by having real opportunities to read, write, speak, listen, and think as opposed to completing contrived exercises that involve marking, circling, and underlining.

For example, the young child who writes a note as illustrated in Figure 1-1 is having an authentic, or real, literacy experience. She is learning to form letters and to construct and convey meaning. This child is developing a major understanding about the functions of print (to convey meaning) as well as about the forms or conventions of print (to form letters, to construct sentences).

Her attempt to write a note is her approximation, her trial, of a complete note. As she continues to have such experiences, she will get more feedback and her approximations will come closer and closer to a more accepted form of note writing.

Going through approximations such as these is exactly how we all learn anything. Think back to when you learned to ride a bicycle. You had seen other people ride a bike, so you had models to emulate. You probably began by getting on the bike and trying to make the pedals move while someone held on to you or the bike. (This was a part of the scaffold or support that children need as they are learning. Gradually, the scaffolding is taken away [Mason & Au, 1990].) You knew what real bike riding was supposed to be, but your first few approximations were not perfect. You continued to get feedback from yourself and others each time you tried to ride the bike, and each approximation allowed you to test another hypothesis that you had about bike riding; your mistakes were essential to your learning (Cambourne, 1988). Gradually, over a period of time, your approximations came closer and closer to skillful bike riding, until you finally achieved your task and rode off alone!

Literacy learning follows similar patterns: learners go through various approximations as they strive to develop their own literacy (Cambourne, 1988; Wells, 1990). Think about how you became a reader. Someone probably read to you or you saw or heard others read, so you had models of reading. When you found a book or story that you liked, you began to pretend to read it. Gradually, over a period of time, you began to associate ideas with each page and the print. Through repeated approximations over many years, you became a reader. Your early attempts were not perfect: it was through your partial or incomplete approximations and repeated contacts with "real reading" provided through models from adults and peers that you grew into literacy and became a reader. Even before this, you had already developed some of your abilities to listen, speak, and think in this manner. This oversimplification of the complex process of literacy learning illustrates the type of process that all learners undergo as they develop their abilities to construct meaning.

These conclusions about how literacy learning takes place have developed over many years of research and study. Although many of them have been recognized by noted authorities in reading and literacy learning for years (Huey, 1908), they have become more fully understood in recent years with research in emergent literacy, language acquisition, and schema theory.

Emergent Literacy

The Old View.   For years, educators talked about "reading readiness," *which is not the view supported in this text.* The basic set of beliefs underlying the readiness concept have been succinctly described by Teale and Sulzby (1986):

1. *Instruction in reading can only begin efficiently when children have mastered a set of basic skills prerequisite to reading. The most important skills predict subsequent achievement most strongly.*

2. *The area of instructional concern is reading. It is implied that composing and other aspects of writing (except for letter formation—or handwriting) should be delayed until children learn to read.*

3. *Sequenced mastery of skills forms the basis of reading as a subject to be taught; instruction focuses almost exclusively on the formal aspects of reading and generally ignores the functional uses of reading.*

4. *What went on before formal instruction is irrelevant, so long as sufficient teaching and practice presented in a logical sequence are provided when instruction begins.*

5. *Children all pass through a scope and sequence of readiness and reading skills, and their progress up this hierarchy should be carefully monitored by periodic formal testing. (p. xiii)*

The New View.   This concept of reading readiness went virtually unchallenged until the mid-1960s, when Durkin's (1966) classic study, *Children Who Read Early*, showed that it was simply not viable. This study was followed by investigations into language acquisition and the literacy habits of young children (Clay, 1967) that led to the formation of the concept known as emergent (emerging) literacy (Clay, 1967; Teale & Sulzby, 1986).

Emergent literacy is the idea that children grow into reading and writing with no real beginning or ending point, that reading and writing develop concurrently and interrelatedly and according to no right sequence or order (Strickland, 1990; Teale & Sulzby, 1986). Instead, learners are always emerging. Moreover, this process begins long before children enter school—through the activities and experiences in their everyday lives and through their interactions with peers and adults (Goodman, 1986; Harste, Woodward & Burke, 1984; Heath, 1983; Sulzby, 1985). Literacy learning involves all elements of the communication process—reading, writing, speaking, listening, and thinking. Quite simply, children develop their ability to comprehend by sharing books that are meaningful to them with peers and adults.

Language Acquisition

As described so far, the process of acquiring language is continuous and unending: each of us continues to acquire new aspects of language through our interactions and experiences. Therefore, language acquisition is first and foremost a social process (Cook-Gumprez, 1986; Wells, 1990). Taylor and Dorsey-Gaines (1988), in their award-winning book *Growing Up Literate*, report that inner-city families "use literacy for a wide variety of purposes (social, technical and *aesthetic* purposes), for a wide variety of audiences, and in a wide variety of situations" (p. 202). Thus all children come to school with a language base, and this base may or may not match the base on which the school is trying to build. Since it has been clearly established that there is a strong connection between oral language and reading (Cazden, 1972; Loban, 1963; Menyuk, 1984; Ruddell, 1963), it is important for schools to build literacy experiences around whatever language a child has developed. *All children have the right to develop their literacy from the language base that they bring to school.*

There are many theories of language acquisition. *Nativists* believe that children acquire language innately without practice or reinforcement (Chomsky, 1965; Lenneberg, 1967; McNeil, 1970). Those who hold the *cognitive development* point of view stress that children acquire language through their various activities (Piaget & Inhelder, 1969). Vygotsky, mentioned earlier, presents a concept known as *a zone of proximal development* (1978), which is a range in which a child can perform a task only with the help of an adult. In this theory, therefore, adult interaction is critical to language acquisition.

Halliday (1975) views language acquisition as an active process in which children try out their language and make approximations of real language. We should therefore accept errors during literacy development, because it is through these approximations that children gradually develop their perfected forms of language.

All of these theories contribute to our understanding of how children acquire language. Basically, we know that children acquire language

1. When they have a need that is meaningful and real;
2. Through interactions with peers and adults;
3. By making approximations of real language;
4. At varying rates and in various stages even though they all go through similar phases of development.

This understanding then provides us with a solid basis on which to develop a literacy program that fosters comprehension development. At no time during children's acquisition of oral language do they stop to learn an isolated part or piece of language. From the outset, the process is whole, meaningful, supportive, and continuous.

Prior Knowledge, Schemata, Background, and Comprehension

Another area that has contributed to our improved understanding of literacy learning and reading comprehension is schema and schema theory. Schemata (plural of *schema*) are structures that represent the generic concepts stored in our memory (Rumelhart, 1980). Schema theory explains how these structures are formed and related to one another as we develop knowledge.

Children develop schemata through experiences. If readers have had no experience or limited experience with a given topic, they will have no schemata or insufficient schemata to recall, and comprehension will be limited or impossible. Many studies on comprehension, schemata, and background have shown that prior knowledge greatly influences comprehension (Adams & Bertram, 1980; Durkin, 1981b; Pearson et al., 1979). (The terms *prior knowledge* and *background* are used interchangeably by researchers and educators.) Readers' backgrounds seem to have a greater influence on the comprehension of implied information than directly stated information, probably because they understand implied information only when they can relate it to their prior knowledge and experiences.

The process of comprehension depends on the reader's schemata. The more nearly those schemata match the schemata intended by the author, the easier it is to comprehend the text. An example will help illustrate this point.

Example 1.1

Read the following paragraph:

Andrew was having a great time at his birthday party. He was playing games and opening presents. When it came time to blow out the candles on the cake, he blew and blew but they would not go out. As soon as he thought he had blown out the candles, they would light up again.

To comprehend this paragraph, you must have a schema about birthday parties. However, if that schema does not include anything about trick candles, you will not be able to understand what has happened to Andrew. From the information in the paragraph, you can tell that Andrew was having a birthday party—the text stated this—and your schema for birthday parties helps you formulate and understand most of what was taking place at the party. However, to understand what type of candles were on Andrew's cake you must rely even more heavily on your schema, because the text does not tell you what kind of candles they were. Therefore, to fully comprehend this paragraph you have to use both your schema and clues from the text.

Readers use their schemata and clues from the text in varying amounts as they comprehend (Spiro, 1979). If readers used only their schemata to comprehend, no two individuals would ever agree about the information in what they read. Alternatively, if readers used only clues from the text to comprehend, all readers would agree that a given selection had the same meaning (Strange, 1980). Clearly neither of these conditions is true. In fact, effective comprehenders use an *interactive* process, both relying heavily on their schemata and obtaining information from the text. Even though these two processes appear to occur simultaneously, it is the reader's schemata that provide the structure needed to associate meaning with text (Anderson & Pearson, 1984).

In summary, schemata are the categories of knowledge (concepts, information, ideas) that are formed in readers' minds through real or vicarious experiences. As reading comprehension occurs, readers relate the ideas from the text to their acquired or prior knowledge—their schemata. If they do not already have schemata for a particular topic or concept, they may form a new schema for that topic if enough information is provided. As they construct new knowledge by relating new information to already stored information, their schemata continuously expand. (Schema theory will be discussed further in Chapter 3.)

A CURRENT VIEW OF COMPREHENSION

In light of what we have learned over the past several decades, we can now formulate a better definition of reading comprehension. Comprehension is a strategic process by which readers construct or assign meaning to a text by using the clues in the text and their own prior knowledge. In the broad sense this is also a definition of reading, since reading is comprehending, or the construction of meaning. This meaning comes primarily from our own existing knowledge.

Two major perspectives should help us understand the process of comprehension more clearly and lead to the formulation of appropriate learning experiences that foster comprehension growth: comprehension as meaning construction and comprehension as a strategic process.

Comprehension as Constructing Meaning

Comprehension is a process by which the reader constructs or assigns meaning by interacting with the text (Anderson & Pearson, 1984). Reading and writing are both constructive processes that are mutually supportive (Pearson & Tierney, 1984; Tierney & Shanahan, 1991).

The understanding that readers achieve during reading comes from their accumulated experiences (prior knowledge), experiences that are triggered as they identify the author's words, sentences, and paragraphs. Although readers do not need to be able to orally decode every word on a page, they must be able to use the variety of cues provided in printed text to decode words. The interaction or transaction (Rosenblatt, 1938/1983) between the reader and the text is the foundation of comprehension. In the process of comprehending, readers relate the new information presented by the author to old information stored in their mind (schemata); this process is the process of comprehending.

Let's consider an example.

Example 1.2

> **Read the following sentence:**
>
> The lazy, old cat spent his whole day curled up asleep by the fireplace.

What did you think about when you read this sentence? You probably had no difficulty comprehending it. Maybe you immediately pictured in your mind an old cat that you had seen, known, or heard about. Using your schemata about cats, you may have thought of all the qualities and characteristics of this cat and could picture it asleep by the warm fire. Although the writer of this sentence intended to convey a certain meaning to you, the reader, the exact meaning that you constructed related to the knowledge, information, feelings, and attitudes about cats that you have in your mind. You constructed your meaning from within your experiences (Pearson & Tierney, 1984). It is this interaction between the reader and the text that is the process of comprehending. As Anderson and Pearson (1984) note, "To say that one has comprehended a text is to say that she has found a mental 'home' for the information in the text, or else that she has modified an existing mental home in order to accommodate that new information" (p. 255).

To comprehend the written word, readers must be able to (1) understand how an author has structured or organized the ideas and information presented in the text, and (2) relate the ideas and information from the text to ideas or information stored in their mind (schemata). By doing these two things, they interact with the text to construct meaning. That is exactly what you did as you read the sentence about the cat. *The meaning that the reader constructs or assigns does not come from the printed page; it comes from the reader's own experiences that are triggered or activated by the ideas the author presents.*

Of course, readers are usually presented with more material to read than a single sentence. As they proceed through the text, they gain additional information, which in turn activates other ideas from their schemata and helps them construct further meaning. An example will help to illustrate how this process works.

Example 1.3

> **Read the following two sentences:**
>
> I ran quickly through the tunnel trying to escape my captors. As I rounded a turn, the ground seemed to disappear beneath me.

What did you think of as you read these two sentences? You probably gained some idea that the paragraph is about someone who is in trouble. You probably pictured a person running through a tunnel. At this point, you can't be sure what the writer means by the ground disappearing. You have constructed your meaning for the two sentences, but your understanding seems incomplete. Now read the complete paragraph to see what happens to the meaning you constructed.

Example 1.4

> I ran quickly through the tunnel trying to escape my captors. As I rounded a turn, the ground seemed to disappear beneath me. I seemed to fall for hours. Just as I saw the ground approaching, a voice called, "Wake up! It's time for breakfast."

After reading the complete paragraph, your understanding of what is happening has changed because new information from the author has helped you construct a different meaning.

To summarize, as readers gather additional information from the text, they relate that information to the information stored in their memory and in this way construct meaning. No matter how long or short the text, the process occurs in the same manner.

Comprehension as a Strategic Process

Comprehension can also be viewed as a strategic process in which readers adjust their reading to suit their purpose and the type of text that they are reading. (Anderson, Hiebert, Scott & Wilkinson, 1985). Both processes—constructing meaning and strategic adjustment—operate simultaneously. Strategic readers are also able to monitor their thinking while reading.

Each time you read you have a purpose. If you are reading for fun and enjoyment, you will read differently than if you are reading to study for a test or to follow the directions for putting together a toy. Strategic readers are also able to adjust their reading to the type of text at hand. The book *Inspirations: Stories About Women Artists* (Sills, 1989) is likely to be approached differently than *Ronald Morgan Goes to Bat* (Giff, 1988), which is a humorous story about a young boy learning to play baseball.

Part of this process of adjustment is understanding the organization of the text, or what is known as *text structure*. There are two basic types of text structure: narrative and expository. *Narrative text* tells a story and is the type usually found in short stories and novels. *Expository text* provides information and facts and is the type usually found in textbooks, informational books, and directions or instructions for doing something (often referred to as procedural text). Text structure will be discussed more fully in Chapter 3.

Teachers have known for many years that students do not read science material in the same way that they read a story. Narrative and expository writings are organized differently, each with their own particular vocabulary and concepts. Thus readers must use their comprehension processes differently when reading these different types of text. Indeed, there is evidence that teaching students strategies for focusing on text structure will enhance their comprehension (Beach & Appleman, 1984; Taylor & Beach, 1984). Mason and Au (1990) refer to this as teaching readers to apply different types of knowledge as they read.

Strategic readers are also able to use their metacognitive processes while reading. *Metacognition,* which refers to the knowledge and control that students have over their own thinking and learning activities (Brown, 1980), appears to involve two basic components (Baker & Brown, 1984):

1. Awareness of the processes and skills needed to complete a task successfully
2. The ability to tell whether one is performing a task correctly and to make corrections during the task if needed, a process termed cognitive monitoring or comprehension monitoring.

Both aspects of metacognition play an important role in reading comprehension. Although the research does not indicate absolutely that teaching metacognitive processes will make readers better comprehenders, there is sufficient evidence to support incorporating these aspects into modeling strategies (Mier, 1984; Pearson & Dole, 1987; Schmitt, 1990).

Comprehension and Decoding

Effective comprehenders have the ability to identify words automatically (Adams, 1990; Perfetti, 1985); however, they do not have to be able to identify every word or know the meaning of every word in a text to understand it. Nagy, in summarizing the research on how many unknown words a student can handle in a text, points out that readers may be able to "tolerate text in which as many as 15 percent of the words are not fully known." He goes on to conclude that "students do not have to know *all* of the words in a text to read it with a high level of comprehension" (Nagy, 1988, p. 29).

Traditionally, the term *decoding* has been used to describe the process of identifying words without emphasizing their meaning. Decoding, however, is the ability to get the intended meaning from a printed message by analyzing the graphic symbols. Since identifying words is a means to this end, learning any system of identification (context, phonics, structural analysis) helps in constructing meaning. In other words, the goal of any literacy experience is always the construction of meaning.

Throughout the history of education educators have debated the role of word identification, and especially phonics, in reading instruction (Chall, 1967, 1983; Flesch, 1955, 1981). This debate has ranged from political controversy to rage and anger. The most recent attempt to bring clarity and sanity to the controversy has been Adams's book *Beginning to Read: Thinking and Learning About Print* (1990), a scholarly, technical work that has been summarized into a shorter piece by Stahl, Osborn, and Lehr (1990). But even this most recent work has met with controversy (Weaver, 1990). Moreover, it is important that educators do not mistakenly use these works to support the teaching of isolated phonics, which is contrary to what we know about how children develop literacy (Strickland & Cullinan, 1990).

The most powerful statement made in the summary of Adams's book comes just before the conclusions:

> *The research reviewed in this book gives ample evidence that we do, indeed, know a great deal about beginning reading. Yet the divisiveness over code-emphasis versus meaning-emphasis rages on. Isn't it time to stop bickering about which is more important? Isn't it time that we recognized that written text has both form and function? To read, children must learn to deal with both, and we must help them. (Stahl, Osborn & Lehr, 1990, p. 123)*

Effective, skilled readers must know how to identify words. However, based on the evidence that children learn to read and write by reading and writing, it is the premise of this text that children learn phonics and other aspects of word identification by being immersed in the reading of meaningful texts. These texts are read aloud to children, and then children are encouraged to share and repeat them. From the outset children focus on meaning: they develop their ability to construct meaning and to identify words simultaneously. Children *do not* first learn to identify words and then to comprehend what they are reading.

The meaningful texts for early reading experiences should be highly predictable in terms of rhyme and sound patterns and plot. These texts might include such books as *Sheep in a Jeep* (Shaw, 1986), *The Three Billy Goats Gruff* (Galdone, 1973), or *There's a Wocket in My Pocket* (Seuss, 1974). Through repeated read-alouds, the sound elements are modeled for children, who are then encouraged to spell words as they think they are spelled (invented spelling or temporary spelling). These types of learning experiences promote natural literacy learning and lead to effective comprehension. The body of research supporting the effectiveness of such techniques continues to accumulate (Bridge, Winograd & Haley, 1983; Cohen, 1968; Ribowsky, 1985; Tunnell & Jacobs, 1989).

The basic premise of this text is that effective comprehenders must know how to identify words, and this identification results in the construction of meaning. Children develop their abilities to use various decoding strategies, including phonics, through reading and writing. Chapter 5 will discuss this area in more detail.

The Role of Literature in Constructing Meaning

Throughout this text all discussions about literature refer to stories, informational texts, and articles in their original form. In other words, the texts of "real" or "authentic" literature have not been rewritten to make them conform to some readability procedure or to any other guidelines to control their difficulty. The language is the original language of the author. Routman (1988, pp. 22–23) gives an excellent example showing what happened to Ann McGovern's story *Too Much Noise* when it was rewritten for a readability-controlled basal reader:

Original

> *A long time ago there was an old man.*
> *His name was Peter, and he lived in an old, old house.*
> *The bed creaked.*
> *The floor squeaked.*
> *Outside, the wind blew the leaves through the trees.*
> *The leaves fell on the roof. Swish. Swish.*
> *The tea kettle whistled. Hiss. Hiss.*
> *"Too noisy," said Peter.*

Rewritten Version

> *Peter was an old man*
> *Who lived in an old, old house.*
> *There was too much noise in Peter's house.*
> *The bed made noise.*
> *The door made noise.*
> *And the window made noise.*
> *Peter didn't like all that noise.*

What differences do you notice when you compare the two texts?

Many teachers continue to ask these questions: "Why use real literature in the literacy program as opposed to stories and materials that have been written to fit a grade-level text?" "What are the values of using real literature for helping children develop their literacy abilities?" The answers to both of these questions revolve around three main points:

1. Real literature is motivating, captivating, and engaging for students of all ages.
2. Real literature provides learners a natural base for developing and expanding their language.
3. Real literature is easier to read and understand than text that has been developed to conform to grade-level standards.

Real Literature Motivates, Captivates, and Engages

A major part of helping children develop their ability to construct meaning is to keep them motivated and excited about learning. The use of real literature has that power. For example, the young preschooler finds a favorite book and asks someone to read it again and again. Whether it is Dr. Seuss's *Green Eggs and Ham* (1960) or Margaret Wise Brown's *Goodnight Moon* (1947), that child is motivated, captivated, and engaged in learning and the love of literature. This young child is experiencing a book that has natural language and is not written to conform to given grade-level standards. In reality, literature has no grade level. It is, in part, how literature is approached that makes it easy or difficult for students to read and experience it and to construct meaning.

This same motivation can be created in classrooms by placing real literature at the core of literacy learning. Studies have shown that in classrooms where real literature is used, children are motivated to read stories again and again and to read them with "passionate attention" (Sanders, 1987). It is this type of engagement that is needed by all learners to help them construct meaning. It might be created by using Julie Brinckloe's *Fireflies!* (1985) or Betsy Byars's *The Summer of the Swans* (1970). As Louise Rosenblatt (1938/1983) concludes:

> When there is active participation in literature—the reader living through, reflecting on, and criticizing his own responses to text—there will be many kinds of benefits. We can call this "growth in ability to share discriminatingly in the possibilities of language as it is used in literature." But this means also the development of the imagination: the ability to escape from the limitations of time, place and environment, the capacity to envisage alternatives in ways of life and in moral and social choices, the sensitivity to thought and feeling and needs of other personalities. (pp. 290–291)

Real Literature Provides Natural Language

Real literature also provides children with models of natural language that continually help them develop and expand their own language structures (Sawyer, 1987). This expansion is the foundation for all meaning construction. Real literature provides opportunities to experience many language structures and an ever-increasing vocabulary. The beauty of language expressed in words and through the art of magnificent illustrations gives students the basis for expanding their language, their experiences, and their schemata, the foundation for constructing meaning. Texts that have been created to conform to grade-level standards are unable to accomplish this goal in the same way (Huck, 1991).

Real Literature Is Easy to Understand and Read

Many children come to school with a sense of story (Applebee, 1978), especially if they have been read to regularly. They understand the predictability and patterns in texts. Therefore, it only seems logical that school experiences should begin by building on this knowledge. However, many texts, especially those used for early reading instruction, are not predictable and do not rely on a logical story structure. *Becoming a Nation of Readers* notes, "Many stories for the early grades do not have a predictable structure. In fact many of these selections do not actually tell a story" (Anderson, Hiebert, Scott & Wilkinson, 1985, p. 66). The use of real literature as a basis for literacy learning will capitalize on what most students know when they come to school and will expand those existing structures. Even beginning readers can learn to read successfully by reading such books as *Skip to My Lou* (Westcott, 1989) or *My Brown Bear Barney* (Butler, 1988). (See Chapter 5 for more discussion of beginning readers and writers.)

The use of rewritten texts (like the sample shown on page 17) often confuses children and causes them not to understand or enjoy the story (Routman, 1988). In fact, research has shown that when texts are rewritten to conform to grade-level standards or a readability formula, they are frequently more difficult for students to read (Simons & Ammon, 1989).

In summary, real literature is critical to successfully developing students' abilities to construct meaning. It helps to create an atmosphere that motivates, captivates, and engages all children in active learning by giving them meaningful texts so that they can learn to read by reading. As Charlotte Huck (1989) notes, "We don't achieve literacy and then give children literature; we achieve literacy *through* literature" (p. 258). Literature not only provides a natural base for developing an oral language; it also capitalizes on the knowledge that children bring to school and is easier for them to read and understand than are texts created to meet grade-level standards. Real literature creates the fun and excitement needed for successful learning. "If teachers would see themselves first as purveyors of pleasure rather than instructors in skill, they may find that skill will flourish where pleasure has been cultivated" (Fader, in Routman, 1982, p. 22).

PRINCIPLES FOR GUIDING
THE CONSTRUCTION OF MEANING

Constructing meaning is the ultimate goal of all literacy instruction. This chapter has developed a basic point of view about comprehension and literacy learning that results in four principles for guiding literacy development (see Table 1.1).

Table 1-1   Principles for Guiding the Construction of Meaning

1. Reading, writing, speaking, listening, and thinking develop simultaneously as learners grow into literacy.
2. Individuals learn to read and write by reading, writing, and responding to their reading and writing.
3. Prior knowledge and background are major elements in one's ability to construct meaning.
4. Comprehension is the process of constructing meaning by relating ideas from a text to one's prior knowledge and background.

---

1. *Reading, writing, speaking, listening, and thinking develop simultaneously as learners grow into literacy.* The research on literacy learning, emergent literacy, and language acquisition clearly shows that all aspects of the language arts develop together as learners become literate. Therefore, the major focus of instruction should be the development of activities that promote the authentic use of reading, writing, speaking, listening, and thinking using real literature as the basis for learning. These are the types of activities that will promote students' abilities to construct meaning.

2. *Individuals learn to read and write by reading, writing, and responding to their reading and writing.* No evidence supports the idea that readers and writers develop by being taught discrete skills. Readers and writers become readers and writers by reading and writing. Through opportunities to respond to their reading and writing and to share their reading and writing with others, learners develop the skills and strategies of successful readers and writers. The opportunities to approximate real reading and writing help learners develop their abilities to read and write. This concept of learning parallels the way in which children acquire oral language (Halliday, 1975).

3. *Prior knowledge and background are major elements in one's ability to construct meaning.* The theory and research about prior knowledge, schemata, and background knowledge clearly support the principle that background influences the ability to construct meaning. The literacy program must incorporate instructional procedures that help learners activate or develop and relate that background to what they read as well as what they write.

4. *Comprehension is the process of constructing meaning by relating ideas from a text to one's prior knowledge and background.* Helping learners construct meaning involves helping them to focus on the relevant features of a text and to relate those features to their prior experiences. This includes using real literature, which provides students with models of different types of text. Since the construction of meaning is a personal process, each reader will develop his or her own meanings from any text that is read.

Author's note.

These four principles form the basis for all of the ideas for developing literacy that are presented in the remainder of this book. Teachers who use these ideas to guide their thinking about comprehension development from a literacy perspective will be the most effective teachers in the schools of the future.

FOCUS OF THIS TEXT

Literacy: Helping Children Construct Meaning is written for preservice and inservice classroom teachers and reading specialists. Two major themes are developed throughout this text:

1. Understanding the process of constructing meaning from a literacy perspective
2. Creating interactive, child-centered classrooms that facilitate the construction of meaning from a literacy perspective

The remaining chapters in this book will help you further develop the knowledge and skills needed to support students in developing their ability to construct meaning:

- Chapter 2 develops the concept of a literacy program focusing on the classroom as a community of learners.
- Chapter 3 discusses the role of prior knowledge and background and presents strategies and procedures for helping students become independent in activating their prior knowledge for any literacy experience.
- Chapter 4 focuses on the role of vocabulary in the construction of meaning.
- Chapter 5 develops some of the basic understandings needed to help students learn to identify words.
- Chapter 6 focuses on how to use responding to literature as part of helping students develop their ability to construct meaning.
- Chapter 7 emphasizes the role of writing.
- Chapter 8 presents a detailed discussion of modeling.
- Chapter 9 pulls together many of the concepts developed in the first eight chapters and relates them to the construction of meaning across the curriculum.
- Chapter 10 presents ideas for dealing with assessment in the classroom literacy program.

SUMMARY

Reading instruction is changing. More and more teachers are having students read "real literature" and respond to the texts in a variety of ways. It is through these responses that readers and writers develop their ability to construct meaning.

Educators have changed their views of reading comprehension; it is no longer thought of as getting meaning from the page or as a set of discrete skills. It is the process of constructing meaning by interacting with a text. The changes that are taking place in classrooms and in our thinking about comprehension have resulted from three major areas of study and research on literacy and literacy learning: emergent literacy, language acquisition, and prior knowledge, schemata, and background.

Reading is inseparable from literacy. Literacy includes all aspects of language—reading, writing, speaking, listening, and thinking—which develop concurrently and interrelatedly as children grow into literacy. Therefore, constructing meaning must be viewed in this broader perspective of literacy learning.

Readers and writers become readers and writers by reading and writing. By having many opportunities to experience real reading and writing, children develop their abilities to read and write by approximating real reading and writing. This process is exactly the same process that children go through in acquiring language.

The reader's schemata are the basic categories of knowledge stored in the mind. These schemata, which are a part of the reader's prior knowledge, develop and change as a result of experiences. Schemata form the basis on which the reader and writer constructs meaning.

As a result of current research, comprehension is now seen as a strategic process of constructing meaning. Effective comprehenders must be able to identify words, but the end result of word identification is constructing meaning. It is not necessary for a reader to pronounce or know the meaning of every word on a page to read it with a high degree of comprehension.

The use of real literature is important in developing students' abilities to construct meaning. Real literature is more motivating, easier, and fun to read than literature that has been altered to control its difficulty.

There are four basic principles that should guide you as you support children in learning to construct meaning:

1. Reading, writing, speaking, listening, and thinking develop simultaneously as learners grow into literacy.
2. Individuals learn to read and write by reading, writing, and responding to their reading and writing.
3. Prior knowledge and background are major elements in one's ability to construct meaning.
4. Comprehension is the process of constructing meaning by relating ideas from a text to one's prior knowledge and background.

Children's Books

Brinckloe, J. (1985). *Fireflies!* New York: Macmillan.
Brown, M. W. (1947). *Goodnight moon.* New York: Harper.
Butler, D. (1988). *My brown bear Barney.* Auckland, New Zealand: Reed Methuen.

Byars, B. (1970). *The summer of the swans.* New York: Viking Penguin.
Galdone, P. (1973). *The three billy goats gruff.* New York: Clarion.
Giff, P. R. (1988). *Ronald Morgan goes to bat.* New York: Viking Kestrel.
McKissack, P. C. (1986). *Flossie and the fox.* New York: Dial Books.
Seuss, D. (1960). *Green eggs and ham.* New York: Beginner Books, Random House.
Seuss, D. (1974). *There's a wocket in my pocket.* New York: Random House.
Shaw, N. (1986). *Sheep in a jeep.* Boston: Houghton Mifflin.
Sills, L. (1989). *Inspirations: Stories about women artists.* Niles, IL: Albert Whitman.
Westcott, N. B. (1989). *Skip to my Lou.* Boston: Little, Brown.

For Additional Reading

Morrow, L. M. (1989). *Literacy development in the early years: Helping children read and write.* Englewood Cliffs, NJ: Prentice-Hall.
Strickland, D. S., & Morrow, L. M. (Eds.). (1989). *Emerging literacy: Young children learn to read and write.* Newark, DE: IRA.

References

Adams, M., & Bertram, B. (1980). *Background knowledge and reading comprehension.* Reading Education Report No. 13. Urbana: Center for the Study of Reading, University of Illinois. (ERIC Document Reproduction Service ED 181 431).
Adams, M. J. (1990). *Beginning to read: Thinking and learning about print.* Cambridge, MA: MIT Press.
Anderson, R. C., Hiebert, E. H., Scott, J. A., & Wilkinson, I. A. G. (1985). *Becoming a nation of readers: The report of the Commission on Reading.* Washington, DC: National Institute of Education.
Anderson, R. C., & Pearson, P. D. (1984). A schema-theoretic view of basic processes in reading comprehension. In P. D. Pearson (Ed.), *Handbook of reading research* (pp. 255–291). New York: Longman.
Applebee, A. N. (1978). *The child's concept of story: Ages two to seventeen.* Chicago: University of Chicago Press.
Baker, L., & Brown, A. L. (1984). Cognitive monitoring in reading. In J. Flood (Ed.), *Understanding reading comprehension* (pp. 21–44). Newark, DE: International Reading Association.
Beach, R., & Appleman, D. (1984). Reading strategies for expository and literary text types. In A. C. Purves & O. Niles (Eds.), *Becoming readers in a complex society* (pp. 115–143). Eighty-third Yearbook of the National Society of Education. Chicago: University of Chicago Press.
Beck, I., & McKeown, M. (1981). Developing questions that promote comprehension: The story map. *Language Arts, 58,* 913–918.
Bridge, C., Winograd, P. N., & Haley, D. (1983). Using predictable materials vs. preprimers to teach beginning sight words. *Reading Teacher, 36*(9), 884–891.
Brown, A. L. (1980). Metacognitive development and reading. In R. J. Spiro, B. C. Bruce & W. F. Brewer (Eds.), *Theoretical issues in reading comprehension* (pp. 453–481). Hillsdale, NJ: Lawrence Erlbaum.

Cambourne, B. (1988). *The whole story: Natural learning and the acquisition of literacy in the classroom.* New York: Aston-Scholastic.

Cazden, C. (1972). *Child language and education.* New York: Holt, Rinehart and Winston.

Chall, J. S. (1967). *Learning to read: The great debate.* New York: McGraw-Hill.

Chall, J. S. (1983). *Learning to read: The great debate* (rev. ed.). New York: McGraw-Hill.

Chomsky, C. (1965). *Aspects of the theory of syntax.* Cambridge, MA: MIT Press.

Clay, M. M. (1967). The reading behavior of five-year-old children: A research report. *New Zealand Journal of Educational Studies, 2,* 11–31.

Clay, M. M. (1979). *Reading: The patterning of complex behavior* (2nd ed.). Auckland, New Zealand: Heinemann.

Clay, M. M. (1982). *Observing young readers: Selected papers.* Exeter, NH: Heinemann.

Clay, M. M. (1985). *The early detection of reading difficulties* (3rd ed.). Auckland, New Zealand: Heinemann.

Clymer, T. (1968). What is "reading"? Some current concepts. In H. M. Robinson (Ed.), *Innovation and change in reading instruction.* Sixty-seventh Yearbook of the National Society for the Study of Education. Chicago: University of Chicago Press.

Cohen, D. (1968). The effect of literature on vocabulary and reading achievement. *Elementary English, 45,* 209–213.

Cook-Gumprez, J. (Ed.). (1986). *The social construction of literacy.* Cambridge: Cambridge University Press.

Cooper, J. D. (1986). *Improving reading comprehension.* Boston: Houghton Mifflin.

Davis, F. B. (1944). Fundamental factors of comprehension in reading. *Psychometrika, 9*(3), 185–197.

Davis, F. B. (1968). Research in comprehension in reading. *Reading Research Quarterly, 3*(4), 499–544.

Davis, F. B. (1972). Psychometric research on comprehension in reading. *Reading Research Quarterly, 7,* 628–678.

Durkin, D. (1966). *Children who read early.* New York: Teachers College Press.

Durkin, D. (1978). What classroom observations reveal about reading comprehension instruction. *Reading Research Quarterly, 14*(4), 481–533.

Durkin, D. (1981a). Reading comprehension instruction in five basal reader series. *Reading Research Quarterly, 16*(4), 515–544.

Durkin, D. (1981b). What is the value of the new interest in reading comprehension? *Language Arts, 58*(1), 23–43.

Flesch, R. (1955). *Why Johnny can't read.* New York: Harper and Row.

Flesch, R. (1981). *Why Johnny still can't read.* New York: Harper and Row.

Freeman, E. B., & Hatch, J. A. (1989). Emergent literacy: Reconceptualizing kindergarten practice. *Childhood Education, 66*(1), 21–24.

Fries, C. (1962). *Linguistics and reading.* New York: Holt, Rinehart and Winston.

Fries, C., et al. (1966). *Merrill linguistic readers.* Columbus, OH: Merrill.

Goodman, K. S. (1965). A linguistic study of cues and miscues in reading. *Elementary English, 42,* 639–643.

Goodman, Y. (1986). Children coming to know literacy. In W. H. Teal & E. Sulzby (Eds.), *Emergent literacy: Reading and writing* (pp. 1–14). Norwood, NJ: Ablex.

Goodman, Y. M. (1989). Roots of the whole language movement. *Elementary School Journal, 90*(2), 113–127.

Halliday, M. A. K. (1975). *Learning how to mean.* New York: Elsevier North-Holland.

Harste, J. C., Woodward, V. A., & Burke, C. L. (1984). *Language stories and literacy lessons.* Portsmouth, NH: Heinemann.

Heath, S. B. (1983). *Ways with words.* Cambridge: Cambridge University Press.

Huck, C. S. (1989). No wider than the heart is wide. In J. Hickman & B. E. Cullinan (Eds.), *Children's literature in the classroom: Weaving Charlotte's web* (pp. 252–262). Needham Heights, MA: Christopher-Gordon.

Huck, C. S. (1991). Literature in the whole language classroom. In K. S. Goodman, L. B. Bird & Y. M. Goodman (Eds.), *The whole language catalog* (p. 188). Santa Rosa, CA: American School Publishers.

Huey, E. B. (1908/1968). *The psychology and pedagogy of reading.* Cambridge, MA: MIT Press.

Lenneberg, E. (1967). *Biological foundations of language.* New York: Wiley.

Loban, W. D. (1963). *The language of elementary school children.* Champaign, IL: National Council of Teachers of English.

McNeil, D. (1970). *The acquisition of language: The study of developmental psycholinguistics.* New York: Harper & Row.

Mason, J. M., & Au, K. H. (1990). *Reading instruction for today* (2nd ed.). Glenview, IL: Scott, Foresman.

Menyuk, P. (1984). Language development and reading. In J. Flood (Ed.), *Understanding comprehension* (pp. 101–121). Newark, DE: International Reading Association.

Mier, M. (1984). Comprehension monitoring in the elementary classroom. *Reading Teacher, 37*(8), 770–774.

Nagy, W. E. (1988). *Teaching vocabulary to improve reading comprehension.* Newark, DE/Urbana, IL: IRA/NCTE.

Otto, W., et al. (1977). *The Wisconsin design for reading skill development: Comprehension.* Minneapolis, MN: NCS Educational Systems.

Pappas, C., & Brown, E. (1987). Learning how to read by reading: Learning how to extend the functional potential of language. *Research in the Teaching of English, 21,* 160–184.

Pearson, P. D., et al. (1979). *The effect of background knowledge on young children's comprehension of explicit and implicit information.* Champaign, IL: Center for the Study of Reading, University of Illinois.

Pearson, P. D., & Dole, J. A. (1987). Explicit comprehension instruction: A review of research and a new conceptualization of instruction. *Elementary School Journal, 88*(2), 151–165.

Pearson, P. D., & Tierney, R. J. (1984). On becoming a thoughtful reader: Learning to read like a writer. In A. C. Purves & O. Niles (Eds.), *Becoming readers in a complex society* (pp. 144–173). Eighty-third Yearbook of the National Society of the Study of Education. Chicago: University of Chicago Press.

Perfetti, C. (1985). *Reading ability.* New York: Oxford University Press.

Piaget, J., & Inhelder, B. (1969). *The psychology of the child.* New York: Basic Books.

Ribowsky, H. (1985). *The effects of a code emphasis approach and a whole language approach upon emergent literacy of kindergarten children.* Unpublished paper presented at the National Reading Conference.

Robinson, H. A., Faraone, V., Hittleman, D. R., & Unruh, E. (1990). In J. Fitzgerald (Ed.), *Reading comprehension instruction 1783–1987: A review of trends and research.* Newark, DE: International Reading Association.

Rosenblatt, L. (1938/1983). *Literature as exploration.* New York: Modern Language Association.

Rosenblatt, L. (1978). *The reader, the text and the poem.* Carbondale: Southern Illinois University Press.

Rosenshine, B. V. (1980). Skill hierarchies in reading comprehension. In R. J. Spiro et al. (Eds.), *Theoretical issues in reading comprehension* (pp. 535–554). Hillsdale, NJ: Lawrence Erlbaum.

Roser, N. L. (1984). Teaching and testing reading comprehension: An historical perspective on instructional research and practices. In J. Flood (Ed.), *Promoting reading comprehension* (pp. 48–60). Newark, DE: International Reading Association.

Routman, R. (1988). *Transitions: From literature to literacy.* Portsmouth, NH: Heinemann.

Ruddell, R. B. (1963). The effect of the similarity of oral and written patterns of language structure on reading comprehension. *Elementary English, 42,* 403–410.

Rumelhart, D. E. (1980). Schemata: The building blocks of cognition. In R. J. Spiro et al. (Eds.), *Theoretical issues in reading comprehension* (pp. 33–58). Hillsdale, NJ: Lawrence Erlbaum.

Sadow, M. (1982). The use of story grammar in the design of questions. *Reading Teacher, 35,* 518–522.

Sanders, M. (1987). Literacy as "passionate attention." *Language Arts, 64,* 619–633.

Sawyer, W. (1987). Literature and literacy: A review of research. *Language Arts, 64*(1), 33–39.

Schmitt, M. C. (1990). A questionnaire to measure children's awareness of strategic reading processes. *Reading Teacher, 43*(7), 454–461.

Shake, M., & Allington, R. (1985). Where do teacher's questions come from? *Reading Teacher, 38,* 434–438.

Simons, H., & Ammon, P. (1989). Child knowledge and primerese text: Mismatches and miscues. *Research in the Teaching of English, 23*(4), 380–398.

Smith, F. (1971). *Understanding reading.* New York: Holt, Rinehart and Winston.

Smith, N. B. (1965). *American reading instruction.* Newark, DE: International Reading Association.

Spearritt, D. (1972). Identification of subskills of reading comprehension by maximum likelihood factor analysis. *Reading Research Quarterly, 8,* 92–111.

Spiro, R. J. (1979). *Etiology of comprehension style.* Champaign, IL: Center for the Study of Reading, University of Illinois.

Stahl, S. A., Osborn, J., & Lehr, F. (1990). *Beginning to read: Thinking and learning about print, by M. Adams, A Summary.* Champaign, IL: Center for the Study of Reading.

Strange, M. (1980). Instructional implications of a conceptual theory of reading comprehension. *Reading Teacher, 33*(4), 391–397.

Strickland, D. S. (1990). Emergent literacy: How young children learn to read and write. *Educational Leadership, 47*(6), 18–23.

Strickland, D., & Cullinan, B. (1990). Afterword. In M. J. Adams, *Beginning to read: Thinking and learning about print* (pp. 426–433). Cambridge: MIT Press.

Sulzby, E. (1985). Kindergartners as writers and readers. In M. Farr (Ed.), *Advances in writing research* (Vol. 1). Norwood, NJ: Ablex.

Taylor, B. M., & Beach, R. W. (1984). Effects of text structure instruction on middle-grade students' comprehension and production of expository text. *Reading Research Quarterly, 19*(2), 147–161.

Taylor, D., & Dorsey-Gaines, C. (1988). *Growing up literate.* Portsmouth, NH: Heinemann.

Teale, W. H., & Sulzby, E. (1986). *Emergent literacy.* Norwood, NJ: Ablex.

Thorndike, R. L. (1973). Reading as reasoning. *Reading Research Quarterly, 9,* 135–147.

Tierney, R. J., & Shanahan, T. (1991). Research on the reading-writing relationship: Interactions, transactions, and outcomes. In R. Barr, M. L. Kamil, P. Mosenthal & P. D. Pearson (Eds.), *Handbook of reading research* (Vol. 2, pp. 246–280). White Plains, NY: Longman.

Tunnell, M. O., & Jacobs, J. S. (1989). Using real books: Research findings on literature based instruction. *Reading Teacher, 42*(7), 470–477.

Vygotsky, L. S. (1978). *Mind in society.* Cambridge, MA: Harvard University Press.

Weaver, C. (1990). Weighing claims of "phonics first" advocates. *Education Week,* March 28, p. 32.

Wells, G. (1990). Creating the conditions to encourage literate thinking. *Educational Leadership, 47*(6), 13–17.

Developing a
Literacy Program

2

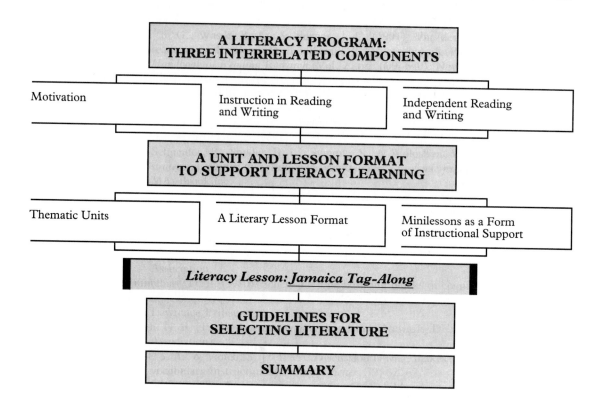

**A LITERACY PROGRAM:
THREE INTERRELATED COMPONENTS**

Motivation

Instruction in Reading
and Writing

Independent Reading
and Writing

**A UNIT AND LESSON FORMAT
TO SUPPORT LITERACY LEARNING**

Thematic Units

A Literary Lesson Format

Minilessons as a Form
of Instructional Support

Literacy Lesson: Jamaica Tag-Along

**GUIDELINES FOR
SELECTING LITERATURE**

SUMMARY

*L*et's begin by looking at how Graeme Base invites readers into his magnificent mystery, The Eleventh Hour (Base, 1988):

A book is read, a story ends, a telling tale is told.

But who can say what mysteries a single page may hold?

A maze of hidden codes and clues, a clock at every turn,

And only time will tell what other secrets you may learn . . .

In The Eleventh Hour (Base, 1988), the story of Horace's eleventh birthday party, someone has stolen the feast that Horace had prepared for his guests. As the celebration draws to a close, the guests are surprised to discover that even though the feast has been stolen, Horace has hidden the birthday cake in another place. However, the mystery is not solved. The book concludes:

Then, as they sat and ate their lunch, there came one last surprise,

When Horace asked for everyone to kindly close their eyes.

And there it was—the Birthday Cake!

The Guests all clapped and cheered.

He'd kept it in the kitchen, and it hadn't disappeared!

And so they picnicked on the lawn until the evening fell,

And everyone left satisfied—the day had finished well.

But in the end, although the thief was someone they all knew,

*They never found out who it was that stole the feast—can you?**

BEAUTIFUL BOOKS SUCH AS *The Eleventh Hour* are the basis for successful literacy learning. By reading and responding to such books, children can approximate real reading and writing and continue their literacy growth (Huck, 1989). However, simply exposing students to wonderful books will not in and of itself make them better readers and writers. As Wells (1990) says, "Children learn most effectively through participation in meaningful, joint activities in which

*Reprinted from the book *The Eleventh Hour* by Graeme Base. Published in 1989 by Harry N. Abrams Incorporated, New York. Copyright © Doublebase Pty Ltd, 1988. All rights reserved.

their performance is assisted and guided by a more competent member of the culture" (p. 15). To this end, Chapter 2 will help you develop

1. a clear concept of a *literacy program.*
2. a flexible thematic unit plan and *literacy lesson format supported by minilessons* that will work throughout the literacy program.

Both formats, the literacy program and the literacy lesson supported with minilessons, will help you see the importance of long-range planning and understand how to carry it out more effectively.

A LITERACY PROGRAM: THREE INTERRELATED COMPONENTS

Teachers should develop a concept of a literacy program and should know how the components of this program work together. In recent years, many teachers have thought of their published textbooks or basal readers as their reading program (Winograd, Wixson, & Lipson, 1989). But *published textbooks do not constitute a program,* even though some of them may be appropriate resources. What then is a literacy program?

A program is a plan for getting something done. A literacy program, therefore, is a plan for supporting children as they develop their ability to read, write, speak, listen, and think or grow into literacy. Figure 2.1 shows the three interrelated components of a literacy program for the classroom and/ or school:

1. • Motivation
2. • Instruction in reading and writing
3. • Independent reading and writing

These three components continually interact with one another in the dynamic, literacy-centered classroom. When one observes such a classroom, one will not (and should not) see them as isolated elements, even though their presence will be evident as the children engage in authentic reading and writing.

I. MOTIVATION

Motivation, the act of providing an incentive or reason for doing something, is the key to learning or doing anything successfully. When individuals are highly motivated and the experiences they are having are meaningful and purposeful for them, they learn more readily (Holdaway, 1979). "*Motivation* requires initiating, sustaining, and directing students' enthusiasm and persever-ance in the pursuit of curricular goals" (Roehler & Duffy, 1991, p. 886).

Figure 2.1   A Literacy Program

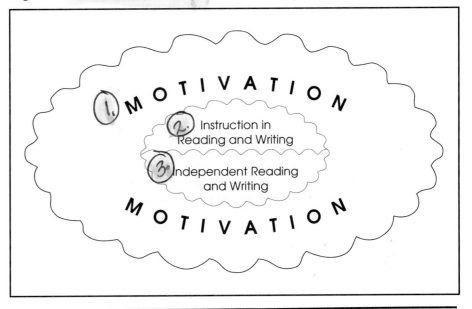

Sometimes motivation comes from within students; at other times it is fostered by the teacher, other students, or experiences. Motivation is *not a single activity* that a teacher conducts; it involves a complex set of ongoing attitudes and activities that occur in the classroom environment and that lead to the creation of a community of learners, including the teacher, who are excited about reading and writing and want to learn. Within this environment, students take ownership for their learning: that is, they come to feel that they have the right to choose what they want to learn and to manage that learning in cooperation with their peers and teacher. Motivation, in the literacy program, is crucial to creating authentic learning experiences that promote positive attitudes about reading and writing and sustain keen interests and enthusiasm.

A. A Literate Environment

One begins to build motivation by creating a literate classroom environment that is rich in language and print. Such an environment stimulates authentic learning and promotes the concept of the class as a community of persons who are learning together. This type of environment, which is basic to every classroom at every grade level, provides part of the motivation needed to encourage all learners to want to construct meaning.

The literate environment should include a variety of different areas or centers, each with a specific focus. The contents, organization, and arrangement of these areas will vary from classroom to classroom and from grade level to grade level. *It is most important to place these special areas where they will be readily accessible to the children.* Often this should be in the center of the room (Harste, Woodward, & Burke, 1984), but in many classrooms space is at a premium and this will not be possible. Therefore, you will need to think how to arrange these special areas to make the best use of your available space. Limited space need not be a deterrent to creating a literate environment.

The areas or centers in the classroom should include the following:

1. *Library Area*

The major purpose of this area is to promote and support independent reading (see page 55). It should include many books of varying levels and interests, magazines, and newspapers, all organized and displayed in an attractive way. To promote the concept of the children as both readers and writers, this area should also include books that have been "published" by the students themselves (see Chapter 7 on publishing).

The collection of books in the library area should be changed or added to frequently. Books may be borrowed from the school library, local library, or bookmobile; brought in by children; or donated by parents or community groups.

The library area should have some appropriate seating, such as an old rocker, beanbag chairs, a bathtub with pillows, or tables and chairs. There should also be a bulletin board where book jackets might be displayed or children might display an advertisement for their favorite book. For example, a child who has just finished reading *The Cricket in Times Square* (Selden, 1960) might want to make a poster to advertise and sell the book to other children.

If your school has a central library staffed with a librarian, media specialist, or some other type of support person, you will want to work with this person as you create your classroom library area. It is important to view the school library as an extension of the classroom library, since both it and the librarian are valuable resources for your program. For example, the librarian can help you select books (see page 95) and plan units, and the school library should become a place where students can come and go freely to select books and other resources.

2. *Writing and Publishing Area*

The writing area is the place where you promote writing and display some of the children's writing. It should have tables and chairs and some of the tools for writing, including paper (unlined for beginners), pencils, markers, crayons, scissors, and tape. If possible, there might be an old typewriter, or even better, a computer with the appropriate word-processing program for your grade level. Some of the more popular software programs include the following:

⭐ *Magic Slate*
Sunburst Communication
39 Washington Avenue
Pleasantville, NY 10570

⭐ *Kidwriter*
Spinaker Software Corporation
One Kendall Square
Cambridge, MA 02139

⭐ *Apple Works 3.0*
Claus Corporation
Box 58168
Santa Clara, CA 95052

⭐ *Primary Editor Plus*
IBM Corporation
P.O. Box 132-W
Boca Raton, FL 33429

⭐ *The Children's Writing and Publishing Center, 2-8*
Learning Company
6493 Kaiser Drive
Fremont, CA 94555

The writing area should also have a place where each child can store writing ideas and products. This might be an individual file folder or some type of box for each child.

To help children publish their books, you should include in this area materials for making book jackets, such as old wallpaper books, cardboard, construction paper, yarn, and brads. For more discussion of writing and the use of the writing area, see Chapter 7.

3. Listening and Viewing Area

This area should contain a listening post with headphones, a tape recorder, and/or a compact disc player. There should be tapes of books and stories to which students might listen as well as blank tapes for students to record their own stories. For viewing, the area needs a filmstrip viewer. Many schools now have video players and recorders, making it possible to use the educational videos that are becoming available.

4. Sharing Area

An important part of learning to construct meaning is sharing what you have read or written and approximating authentic reading and writing experiences (Holdaway, 1979). For this reason, children need a place to get together to share what they are reading and writing. This area should include tables and chairs or other comfortable seating, and some places for students to display some of the products they have developed. The author's chair (see page 58) might be kept in this area.

5. Creative Arts Area

Drama, art, and music are important to children as they respond to their reading and writing and share it with others. Therefore, there should be some area that includes puppets and items that might be used for costumes and props for giving plays, retelling stories, or giving Readers Theater performances. (For a discussion of the Readers Theater, see Chapter 6 and "For Additional Reading" at the conclusion of this chapter.)

A portion of this area could have materials for painting, drawing, paper sculpture, or other art activities. If space is available, a separate area may be developed for art. Some simple musical instruments should also be available, such as a recorder, autoharp, or xylophone. Using music with pieces of literature such as *Ben's Trumpet* (Isadora, 1979) and *Song and Dance Man* (Ackerman, 1988) is appropriate at many different grade levels (Lamme, 1990). A teacher does not have to be musically inclined to help children carry out many of these activities.

6. Group Meeting Area

You will also need an area where you can meet with small groups for discussions and instruction. This might contain a chalkboard, overhead projector, and other materials such as books and charts that you will need for teaching.

7. Display Area

Displays of items related to topics of study, art pieces, photographs, and posters all help to motivate students and expand their backgrounds. The area for such displays should be changed frequently and should include material brought in by students. For example, a class reading or listening to *Where the Red Fern Grows* (Rawls, 1961) might create a display of photographs of pets that have meant a great deal to them, as Old Dan and Little Ann meant to Billy.

Figure 2.2   A Checklist for Evaluating the Classroom Literate Environment

Checklist

1. Do I have the following areas or combinations of areas in my
   classroom?   Yes | No

   - Library area   ___ | ___
   - Writing and publishing area   ___ | ___
   - Listening and viewing area   ___ | ___
   - Sharing area   ___ | ___
   - Creative arts area   ___ | ___
   - Group meeting area   ___ | ___
   - Display area   ___ | ___

2. Do I change or improve areas within reasonable time frames?   ___ | ___
3. Do students utilize certain areas more than others?   ___ | ___

   Which ones? _____

   _____

4. Areas that I need to add: _____

   _____

   _____

5. Areas that I need to improve or change: _____

   _____

   _____

A literate environment is an important aspect of motivation within the literacy program. It is a vital part of developing oral language, expanding prior knowledge, and creating an atmosphere that promotes opportunities for authentic reading and writing experiences that children are able to share with all members of the classroom community. Figure 2.2 presents a checklist that can be used to evaluate the literate environment in your classroom.

B. Reading Aloud to Children

Another important motivating element is reading aloud to children. When teachers read aloud a favorite book such as *The Best Town in the World* (Baylor, 1982), they convey their love and excitement for both reading and learning. Such reading is considered by some to be "the single most important activity for building the knowledge required for eventual success in reading" (Anderson,

Hiebert, Scott, & Wilkinson, 1985, p. 23). Indeed, research has shown that preschool children who learn to read on their own generally have had an adult who has read to them repeatedly (Durkin, 1966; Clark, 1976). The overall value and importance of reading aloud to children at home have been clearly documented (Strickland & Taylor, 1989). As teachers, we should therefore encourage all parents to read to their children as much as possible.

The value of reading aloud to children as a part of the classroom program has also been verified (McCormick, 1977). Not only does it help to motivate students, but it also provides a basis for expanding oral language and prior knowledge (Feitelson, Kita & Goldstein, 1986), especially for those children who have not had these experiences at home. Reading aloud also influences children's writings (Dressel, 1990). When children actually hear a great variety of stories, they reflect many story features in their own writing. For example, the children's writing presented in Figure 2.3 has been influenced by the story pattern and structure in *Brown Bear, Brown Bear* (Martin, 1967). Similar influences can be seen in the writings of older students as they encounter many more experiences with literature (Dressel, 1990).

Certainly there is no substitute for reading to children at home; however, classroom read-aloud periods can provide some of the same benefits (Strickland & Taylor, 1989; Taylor & Strickland, 1986). The following are some guidelines that should be helpful as you plan the read-aloud periods in your classroom:

1. • *Read aloud every day.* Select a consistent time so that children will look forward to it. Many teachers prefer to read aloud first thing in the morning because it gets the day off to a positive start. If there are a few extra unexpected minutes throughout the day, use them for extra read-aloud time.

2. • *Have a comfortable, inviting place in the classroom for reading aloud.* Use the library area if it is large enough, and use a favorite or special chair such as a rocker.

3. • *Select books that both you and the children will enjoy.* Some books may relate to specific themes or topics of study, but they do not have to. If you find that you have selected a book that the class is not enjoying, stop reading it and take some time to discuss why you have stopped. You should also vary the types of books you read, and be sure to include some poetry, since children of all ages enjoy poetry that rhymes and has humor (Terry, 1974; Thomas, 1989). Two favorite poets of most children are Shel Silverstein and Jack Prelutsky. Some of their best-known works are shown below:

Where the Sidewalk Ends (Silverstein, 1974)

A Light in the Attic (Silverstein, 1981)

The New Kid on the Block (Prelutsky, 1984)

Ride a Purple Pelican (Prelutsky, 1986)

Tyrannosaurus Was a Beast (Prelutsky, 1988)

Figure 2.3a   Sample of Child's Writing Influenced by the Story Pattern from *Brown Bear, Brown Bear* (Martin, 1967)

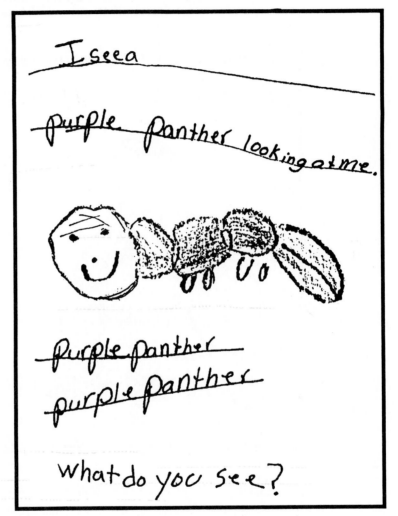

Figure 2.3b   Sample of Child's Writing Influenced by the Story Pattern from *Brown Bear, Brown Bear* (Martin, 1967)

I see a Violet Vampire looking at me !

Violet Vampire- Violet Vampire What do you see?

Poems of A. Nonny Mouse (Prelutsky, 1989)

Beneath a Blue Umbrella (Prelutsky, 1990)

Something Big Has Been Here (Prelutsky, 1990)

There are also many good anthologies that include poetry by many authors as well as by single authors. You might want to consider the following:

★ *A New Treasury of Children's Poetry: Old Favorites and New Discoveries* (Cole, 1984)

★ *Random House Book of Poetry for Children* (Prelutsky, 1983)

★ *The Poetry of Black America: Anthology of the 20th Century* (Adoff, 1973)

★ *A Child's Garden of Verses* (Stevenson, 1885/1981)

④ • *Read with expression and feeling.* Make the book come alive for children. Trelease (1989) suggests adding a real-life dimension to your read-alouds; for example, if you are reading *Blueberries for Sal* (McCloskey, 1948), have a bowl of fresh blueberries for children to taste.

⑤ • *Allow time for discussion during and after each read-aloud period.* If students have questions during reading, take time to discuss them, and use the discussion to talk about favorite parts, feelings, or reactions. Also be sure to share your own thoughts about a book or story.

⑥ • *Above all, don't allow the discussion to become a time to "test" children on the book.* Direct the discussion so that children get to share their thoughts but also stay on the topic.

⑦ • *Allow students to write or draw as they listen.* Some may find it easier to pay attention if they are allowed to write or draw while they are listening. Of course, they should not be completing work assignments at this time.

★ *The New Read-Aloud Handbook* (Trelease, 1989) and ★ *For Reading Out Loud: A Guide to Sharing Books with Children* (Kimmel & Segal, 1983) might be helpful in planning read-aloud periods (see "For Additional Reading").

C Attitudes and Expectations of Teachers

The third aspect of motivation involves the attitudes and expectations of the teacher. The teacher who is enthusiastic and positive about reading, writing, and learning and who conveys these feelings to the students does a great deal to motivate. If you believe that all students can learn and share these feelings both directly and indirectly, you set up expectations for success for all students (Wigfield & Asher, 1984). Brophy (1986) argues that one of the most important aspects of motivation is modeling learning as a rewarding, fulfilling activity. If children know you expect that they can learn, they are likely to learn more effectively. Thus this kind of attitude on your part will help them succeed daily, with each success contributing further to motivation.

Good →

Communication with Parents

Finally, communication with parents is an important part of motivating students (Vukelich, 1984). If you send home newsletters and have school meetings where parents are invited to attend, you keep parents involved and informed about what you are doing in the classroom, which in turn helps to create and maintain a higher degree of motivation for learning. By communicating with parents, you can help them know the importance of supporting their children in many positive ways. This support, in turn, leads to better motivation.

In summary, motivation involves initiating, sustaining, and directing students' enthusiasm and perseverance in the pursuit of curricular goals (Roehler & Duffy, 1991). It includes creating a literate environment, reading aloud to students, modeling a positive attitude, and communicating with parents. Motivation and all of its related aspects permeate and influence all elements of the literacy program: they are not limited to one activity or set of activities.

INSTRUCTION IN READING AND WRITING

The second component in the literacy program is instruction. Arriving at a definition of instruction is neither easy nor simple (Durkin, 1990), and debate over what constitutes instruction has existed for some time (Hodges, 1980). Nevertheless having a definition of instruction is critical to creating a literacy program.

Durkin (1990) says, "Instruction refers to what someone or something does or says that has the potential to teach one or more individuals what they do not know, do not understand, or cannot do" (p. 472). Roehler and Duffy (1991) define instruction as the intentional actions taken by a teacher to develop specified curricular outcomes. Au (in press) defines instruction as helping the student to become interested and involved in a meaningful activity, then providing the student with the support needed to successfully complete the activity" (manuscript, p. 3–13). Each of these definitions fits the concept of literacy learning developed in Chapter 1. Recall two of the four basic principles for guiding comprehension development presented in that chapter:

1. Reading, writing, speaking, listening, and thinking develop simultaneously as learners grow into literacy.
2. Individuals learn to read and write by reading, writing, and responding to their reading and writing.

Within the framework of this text, instruction is viewed as anything that is done intentionally within the classroom to promote the construction of meaning. Instructional activities may include such things as the following:

- Groups of students working together to read and respond to a piece of literature
- Questions posed by a peer or teacher to prompt an individual discussing a book
- Specific lessons or minilessons developed by the teacher
- Projects completed by students

(A.) The Role of the Teacher

The teacher may create the circumstances and conditions within the classroom that let instruction take place or may work together with students to plan instructional activities. In many instances, teachers may direct the activities. In lessons or minilessons, they may use *modeling;* that is, they may show or demonstrate for students how to use the processes of reading or writing or how to use particular strategies that might be helpful in constructing meaning. For example, when teachers read a story to the class, they are modeling reading; when they write a group story with the class, they are modeling writing. Many times, modeling involves the use of "think-alouds," sessions in which teachers share the thought processes they have gone through in formulating the meaning of a text (Clark, 1984; Meichenbaum, 1985). For a detailed discussion of modeling and sample lessons using "think-alouds," see Chapter 8.

In other instances, the teacher may set up an activity where students work together on a task. This is known as *cooperative learning.* The teacher observes the activity while students are working and provides directive support through questions and/or suggestions. (For further reading on cooperative learning, see "For Additional Reading.")

Instruction also involves opportunities for students to respond to their reading and writing. *Responding* is the essence of what literacy is all about—constructing personal meanings (Rosenblatt, 1938/1983; 1978). It includes activities such as reacting to, talking about, or doing something appropriate with a piece of literature that has been read or listened to or a story that has been written. For example, after having written a mystery, a student might want to read it aloud to some classmates or have it read and reacted to by others. Students who have read a piece such as *Bridge to Terabithia* (Paterson, 1977) might respond to it by getting together in a group or literature circle for a discussion. Such responding must be authentic in that it must be the type of activity one naturally does with reading and writing; it may take place before, during, or after students read or write. For example:

- *Before reading:* Students might look at a book and predict what will happen in it. This is the beginning of responding.
- *During reading:* As students are reading, they might have a reaction to a particular character and write a note about it in their journal.

• *After reading:* Because students loved the book they read, they may select another book by the same author or may choose to retell the story to someone else.

From an instructional point of view, the teacher's role is to plan and support the activities and experiences that encourage responding. Teachers should include lessons that involve reading many kinds of books, all the time prompting students to respond in ways of their own choosing or directing them by offering suggestions for the type of response they might make. Posting a reading response chart such as the one on page 59 is one way to accomplish this.

Instruction begins with the reading of literature in a variety of ways. The support provided by the teacher while students are involved in any aspect of reading or writing can be thought of as *scaffolding* (Collins, Brown, & Newman, 1986). This might be questioning that helps students understand what they have read or modeling to show students how to think through a particular piece of text or to learn a strategy. As students become more and more competent, the teacher begins to remove the scaffolding and provides less and less support. This is what Pearson (1985) calls the gradual release of responsibility. In other words, the teacher gradually gives more responsibility to the students. This process can be observed in any learning situation. For example, young children who learned to read before going to school learned in this way: first someone read to them, and then gradually that person read less and less and the children read more and more.

Instruction may be planned or unplanned (Durkin, 1990), and both types are necessary. However, once you have learned how to provide quality planned instruction, you are more likely to be comfortable seizing the "teachable moment," responding spontaneously to a situation that arises unexpectedly during a lesson or activity. For example, suppose the children have read *Today Was a Terrible Day* (Giff, 1980). In the discussion that follows, you realize that several children do not understand why Ronald Morgan is feeling so unhappy in school. Therefore, you begin by directing them to the first unhappy incident when Ronald Morgan dropped his pencil. By questioning and discussing, you are able to help the children see how the event of dropping the pencil and Miss Tyler's response made Ronald sad and unhappy. You continue through the story, looking at all events that take place in this way. Not only are you taking into account the "teachable moment," but you are also providing the support or scaffold, when it is needed, to help the children construct meaning.

Reading and Writing as Modes of Instruction

A basic premise of this text, as already stressed, is that children learn to read and write by reading and writing (Smith, 1983). Therefore, reading and writing are the actual modes or forms of instruction through which the skills and strategies of reading and writing develop. In other words, as Walmsley and Walp (1990, p. 258) put it, this is a "skills-through-application approach."

1. Modes of Reading

A piece of literature may be accessed or read by students in a variety of ways, depending on their reading abilities and current levels of performance as well as the complexity of the literature being read. No one mode is exclusively for the at-risk reader or the advanced reader. Rather, decisions as to which mode should be used in a given lesson or instructional situation should be made by the teacher and/or students on the basis of the literature, the students' reading abilities, and the particular lesson or situation. The primary concern for you as the teacher is to be aware of each of the possible ways to approach reading and when, why, and how to use them. Five reading modes will be discussed—independent reading, cooperative reading, teacher-guided reading, shared reading, and reading aloud.

a. Independent Reading.   During independent reading students read an entire selection by themselves. As a mode of instruction, independent reading should not be confused with the independent, self-selected (voluntary) reading portion of the literacy program discussed later in this chapter (see page 89). Since independent reading involves the least support possible, it is used when students have sufficient ability to read a piece of literature without any support from the teacher or peers. *All students, at all levels, need to have instructional experiences in independent reading.* It is well known that at-risk learners frequently get few, if any, opportunities to read whole pieces of quality literature independently (Allington, 1977, 1983).

b. Cooperative Reading.   Cooperative reading uses the principles of cooperative learning (Slavin, 1990). Pairs of students or triads take turns reading portions of a piece of literature aloud to each other or silently and then stop to discuss what they have read. The students then predict what they think will happen next and continue reading the next portion of the text silently and stop for discussion. This pattern continues until the book or selection is finished. Cooperative reading is sometimes called buddy reading, partner reading, or paired reading (Tierney, Readence, & Dishner, 1990). It should be used when students need *some support* and are not quite able to handle an entire selection independently. The following guidelines, based in part on the successful reciprocal teaching model (Palincsar & Brown, 1986), should be helpful for using cooperative reading in your classroom. You may want to model this process for your students.

Guidelines for Cooperative Reading

1. *Preview and predict.* Have the students look through the text and examine the illustrations and/or pictures; ask them to read the beginning portion of the text and predict what they think will happen or what they will learn.
2. *Read orally or silently.*

   Oral version
   _____

   - *Skim silently.* Each student skims the text silently before beginning oral reading.
   - *Read orally.* One student reads aloud the first part of the text while the other or others follow along.
   - *Discuss, respond, and check predictions.* The students stop and retell and/or discuss what was read. They talk about whether they have verified or need to change their overall predictions.
   - *Predict and read.* The students then predict what they think might happen or what they might learn in the next section. The second student then reads aloud the next section. This pattern continues until the selection is completed.

   Silent version
   _____

   - *Read.* Each student reads the same portion of text silently, keeping in mind the predictions made.
   - *Discuss, respond, and check predictions.* The students stop and retell or summarize what they have read. They tell how they feel about what they have read or what they have learned, and they talk about whether their overall predictions were verified and/or need to be changed.
   - *Predict and read.* The students then predict what they think will happen next or what they will learn. They continue reading the next section silently. This pattern is followed until the entire piece has been completed.

3. *Summarize and respond.* After completing the entire selection, the students summarize what they have read. They respond by discussing how they feel about what they have read and deciding what they might do with it (tell someone about it; write their own summaries; use art to share what they read, and so forth).

When using cooperative reading, students may take turns reading a sentence, paragraph, or page. Be sure that they are allowed to pass when their turn comes if they do not feel prepared to read the text.

Ⓒ Teacher-Guided Reading.   In this mode of reading, the teacher carefully guides or directs students through the silent reading of a piece of literature by asking them a question or helping them formulate a question that they then try to answer as they read the designated section of text. Sometimes the teacher helps students make these predictions. At the conclusion of each section, the students stop and discuss with the teacher the answer to the question or their predictions, as well as other points. At each stopping point, the teacher allows and encourages students to respond to what they have read.

Teacher-guided reading is used when students need a great deal of support in constructing meaning from the text, either because of the complexity of the text or because of the students' abilities. This approach also allows the teacher to adjust the support or scaffold according to students' needs. For example, suppose your students are reading *Matilda* (Dahl, 1988) and you are guiding them through the first chapter, "The Reader of Books." After reading the first portion of the chapter you realize that the students do not have the appropriate or sufficient background needed to construct meaning from it. For example, your students cannot relate to a child who can go to school reading as well as Matilda does. Therefore, you introduce into the discussion the background points they need. This is the type of unplanned instruction that uses the teachable moment. *The lesson scenario might go as follows. Use the annotations in parentheses to help you see what is happening.*

(Relates prior knowledge to first chapter.)

Teacher:	We have previewed the book *Matilda* and know that it is about a little girl who is gifted. We are now ready to read the first chapter. Who can find it in the book and read the title?
Sammy:	"The Reader of Books."

(Get students to think about what might happen.)

Teacher:	What do you think that title tells you about Matilda?
Megan:	She might read books.
Beth Ann:	I think the teacher reads books.
Teacher:	Let's turn through the chapter and look at the illustrations that Quentin Blake, the illustrator, drew. What does Matilda seem to be doing?
Tara:	She's reading lots of books.
Sammy:	It looks like she is in the library.
Juro:	Maybe she just looks at the pictures. She's so young to read.

(Guides students to predict. Helps students set purpose for reading.)

Teacher:	What would you predict is going to happen in this chapter?
Sammy:	Matilda is going to read a lot of books.
Juro:	Matilda is a little girl, but she reads a bunch of books.
Teacher:	(Records predictions on chalkboard.) Let's read pages 7, 8, and 9 to see if either of these predictions is correct. (Students read.)

(Teacher follows up by having students check predictions. This is all a part of the scaffolding.)

Teacher: Were either of our predictions confirmed?

Larry: No. The author just told us that some parents think their kids are geniuses.

(Support students in clarifying.)

Teacher: Did he mean the kids really are geniuses?

Juro: No. Parents just think they are.

Teacher: How can you tell that Roald Dahl is making fun of these types of parents?

Analise: Because of the funny things he would write about the kids.

Teacher: Like what?

Beth Ann: He said he would write that Maximillian is a total washout and that he hopes there is a family business for him.

Sammy: That's funny.

Teacher: Why?

Sammy: Because it just is. Maximillian must be lazy or dumb.

Megan: No, he isn't. Roald Dahl is just being funny.

(Helping students see how authors motivate readers.)

Teacher: Do you think he is trying to get us interested in his book?

Most students: Yes.

(Encouraging personal response.)

Teacher: How did these pages make you feel?

Larry: They were kind of funny.

Beth Ann: Sad. I hope a teacher wouldn't really write those things.

(Supporting students in thinking about their predictions.)

Teacher: Do you think we should change your predictions?

Juro: No, we haven't read enough yet.

(Supporting students in having a purpose for reading.)

Teacher: Let's read pages 10 and 11 and think about our predictions.

(Follow-up on purpose for reading.)

Larry: She's smart.

Juro: She's a little kid.

Analise: Her mother and dad don't like her.

Juro: That's sad.

Teacher: It is sad. Why do you think they feel that way?

Sammy: Because she is so smart and wants to read.

Teacher: Are there books for her to read?

Beth Ann: No. Just one on cooking.

(Supporting students in keeping predictions in mind and setting their own purpose for reading.)

Teacher:	Have we learned whether our predictions are true?
Megan:	No, but maybe Matilda is going to the library.

(Supporting students to read to check the predictions they have made. Begins to help students monitor their own reading.

Teacher:	Let's read and find out. Read pages 12 through the top of page 15.
	(Students read.)
Teacher:	What did she do?
Juro:	She went to the library. Her dad wouldn't get her any books.
Teacher:	Were our predictions true?
Analise:	Yes, she read all the children's books.

(Teacher provides a purpose for reading.)

Teacher:	Let's read pages 15, 16, 17, and to the end of the last full paragraph on 18 to see if she reads anything else.
	(Students read.)

(Follow-up on purpose for reading.)

Teacher:	What did she read next?
Larry:	I think she read some books, but I never heard of them.

(Students' responses show they don't know the books.)

Tony:	Me either!
Teacher:	The books listed on page 18 are novels that adults usually read.
Megan:	That's why I don't know 'em.
Teacher:	Maybe your parents might read some of these books.
Beth Ann:	Not mine!

(Teachable moment! Build concept of novel.)

Teacher:	What is a novel?
Sammy:	Is it a story?
Teacher:	Yes. What else can you tell me about a novel?
Juro:	Is this book a novel?
Megan:	Does a novel have chapters?
Teacher:	Yes, it does. *Matilda* is a novel like the ones listed on page 18.
Juro:	Is a novel true?
Teacher:	No. A novel is what we call fiction. There are many types of fiction. We'll talk about those later. Let's go on with our discussion.
Teacher:	Was Matilda taking her books home to read?
Sammy:	No.

Teacher:	Why not?
Analise:	I'll bet she was afraid of her dad.
Larry:	No, she wasn't.
Teacher:	Why do you think that, Larry?
Larry:	She just didn't seem to be afraid of him. I'm not afraid of my dad.

(Helps students set own purpose by predicting.)

Teacher:	What would you predict she's going to do about her books?
Juro:	Read them in the library.
Analise:	Maybe she'll take them home.

(Draws students back to the chapter and focuses them on their predictions.)

Teacher:	Let's finish the chapter and see if our predictions are true. (Students read.)

(Follow up on purpose.)

Teacher:	What did Matilda do about getting books to read?
Sammy:	She started taking them home from the library.
Teacher:	What did she do with her books?
Juro:	She took a trip.
Teacher:	Did she really go on a trip?
Megan:	No. She just read stories about places.
Teacher:	How did you think this book might take us other places?
Tony:	We don't know much about English schools. This'll be like a trip.
Teacher:	Does anyone have any questions?

(Students don't understand.)

Beth Ann:	What is Bovril or Ovaltine?
Teacher:	Does anyone know?
Most students:	No.

(Begin to use teachable moment.)

Teacher:	Any clues?
Analise:	It must be something you drink or eat. It says she took a hot drink to her room.
Teacher:	Ovaltine is like hot chocolate.

(Encourages more personal response and gets students thinking about the remainder of the book.)

Teacher:	How does this chapter make you feel about Matilda? Think about this. Before we start the next chapter, you can share your thoughts about your feelings for Matilda.

Because of its flexibility, guided reading is a very powerful tool; you can provide more support for students at the beginning of the reading and can gradually release the responsibility to students as the reading progresses. In this process, you control the amount of support through (1) the types of questions you ask before reading and during discussion, (2) the amount of text you have students read, and (3) the type of discussion held between reading sessions. When more support is needed, you can direct the discussion; then, as you give students more responsibility, they may carry out and direct the discussion with a partner.

Throughout teacher-guided reading, be aware of the role of questions. Simply asking children about what they have read is not going to teach them how to construct meaning (Durkin, 1978, 1981; Herber & Nelson, 1975). However, we do know that the questions asked during guided reading can help if they are of the appropriate types (Beck, 1984; Beck, Omanson & McKeown, 1982). Good questions meet the following criteria:

- Questions posed *before* reading should lead students to the important ideas in the text. In narrative text, they should focus on the setting of the story (time and place), the major characters, the story problem, the action, the resolution, and the overall moral or theme. In expository text, they should focus on the main ideas. For example:

     Narrative text: Who are the two important characters that are introduced in the story, and what do they do?

     Expository text: What is the first important thing that we learn about plants?

- Questions used *during* discussion *between* the reading of sections should pull together ideas brought out in reading and should help build relationships among ideas. For example:

     Narrative text: Who were the two characters? What did you learn about them and how they usually work together?

     Expository text: What was the first important thing you found out about plants? How is this likely to help people?

- Questions should be asked in an order that follows the order of the text.

By using these guidelines, you will help students develop what Beck calls an overall mental picture of the text being read (Beck, 1984). An example illustrating the use of teacher-guided reading can be found in the literacy lesson on page 71.

A monitoring guide can be used independently by students who still need structured support during reading. Sometimes called a study guide by content-area teachers, this is a sheet that poses questions and gives activities that carefully guide students through the reading of the text. Although often used in content classes, it can be used in reading any text. Figure 2.4 shows a portion of a monitoring guide that could be used by students reading the first chapter of *Matilda* (Dahl, 1988).

Figure 2.4   Portion of a Monitoring Guide

Monitoring Guide for *Matilda*

by Roald Dahl, illustrated by Quentin Blake
Chapter 1, "The Reader of Books," pages 7–21

Previewing and Predicting
- Try to get an idea about this chapter
  - Look at the illustrations
  - Read page 7
- Write your prediction about what you think will happen in this chapter:

  _____

  _____

Reading Pages 7–11
- Now read pages 7–11 to see if your prediction was verified. Maybe you will want to change your prediction. As you read, make notes about any thoughts you have about the chapter.

- Notes: _____

  _____

After Reading Pages 7–11
- What did you learn about your prediction?

  _____

  _____

- Complete this chart showing what you learned about Matilda. Add other ovals if you need them.

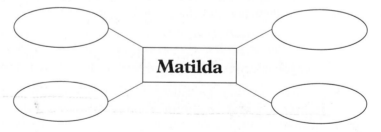

d. **Shared Reading.**   Holdaway (1979) developed a procedure known as the "shared book experience" for introducing beginners to reading by using favorite stories, rhymes, and poems. In this procedure, the teacher reads aloud a story and then invites children to join in when they feel comfortable. Stories are read several times, and children are given many opportunities to respond through writing, art, drama, discussion, and so forth. In Holdaway's early description of this procedure, some of the children's favorite books were enlarged for group study; this is the basis for the "big book" concept used by many teachers.

Shared reading provides very strong support for learners. It allows for the modeling of real reading and accounts for the ways in which "natural readers" have learned to read by being read to, reading along with an adult or older peer, and ultimately reading on their own. Although shared reading can be used for beginning reading, it can also be used with students who are encountering difficulty with learning at any level. For a detailed discussion and a sample lesson on how to use shared reading, see Chapter 5.

e. **Reading Aloud.**   Sometimes the best way to help children understand a particular piece of literature is to first read it aloud and discuss it with them. This type of reading helps to activate already acquired knowledge and to develop background vocabulary and concepts; it also is a way to model real reading.

Reading literature aloud for instructional purposes (not to be confused with reading aloud for motivation, as discussed earlier) provides very strong teacher support for students. It is used when a particular piece of literature has many difficult concepts or words, would be hard for students to decode, or is difficult to follow. After the teacher has read a piece aloud, students may then read it under the teacher's guidance, cooperatively, or independently.

f. **Combinations of Reading Modes.**   Table 2.1 summarizes the five modes of reading that have been discussed. These modes offer varying levels of support for students, and many times it is appropriate to combine several at once. For example, if your students are reading a short story or a chapter in a book, you might begin by reading aloud the first portion of a chapter and discussing it with them. Next, you might put students into pairs and have them do the oral version of cooperative reading, that is, read along with each other. Finally, you might complete the chapter by having each student read a small portion of the text independently; in this way each would also have the opportunity to read alone. This combined instructional reading strategy can be called *read aloud, read along, read alone.* Notice that by combining these forms of reading you are providing a scaffold for learning that gradually releases some responsibility to the students. At the same time you have activated prior knowledge, developed background, and modeled real reading rather than a discrete or isolated skill. For more on this strategy, see Chapter 5.

Table 2.1   Modes of Reading

Mode	Description	When to Use
1. Independent reading	Students read text alone without support, usually silently.	When students are likely to have no difficulty with the text or are highly motivated about the text or text topic.
2. Cooperative reading	Students read with a partner or partners, either orally or silently.	When students' abilities show need for some support. May also be done just for fun.
3. Teacher-guided reading	Teacher talks and walks students through sections of text with questions and student predictions.	When text or students' abilities show need for much support. May be used for variety.
4. Shared reading	Teacher reads aloud as students see the text. Students chime in when they are ready to do so.	When students need a great deal of support for reading. Often used with beginning readers.
5. Reading aloud	Teacher reads aloud text. Students usually do not have a copy of the text.	Used when text is too difficult, when background needs to be developed, for fun or for variety.

Remember that you can create different combinations as you work to meet the differing needs of your students in relation to the literature they are reading. You should also give them the opportunity to select their own mode of reading (see page 66). Finally, you may vary the mode of reading just to add fun and variety to your instruction.

Modes of Writing

Throughout the literacy program students will also be writing in response to literature (see Chapter 6) and for other purposes. When they write, they will frequently do process writing; that is, they follow the same steps used by effective writers (Graves, 1983; Hillocks, 1987): selecting the topic, drafting, revising, proofreading, and publishing. These five steps and process writing are discussed in detail in Chapter 7.

There are three basic modes of writing that may be used as a part of instruction and learning: independent, collaborative, and shared.

(a.) **Independent Writing.**   Independent writing is what students do when they write alone. It assumes that students are able to develop their product with little or no support from any other source.

(b.) **Collaborative Writing.**   When students write collaboratively, they work with a partner or partners on a single product, often taking turns doing the actual writing. This mode of writing (comparable to the cooperative reading mode) gives students support by letting them work together and share ideas. It is often a good way to support the writer who is unmotivated.

(c.) **Shared Writing.**   Just as there is shared reading, so there can also be shared writing (McKenzie, 1985). In this activity, you and your students work together to write a group story on the chalkboard, a chart, or the overhead projector, following the steps of process writing. In the beginning you might do the actual writing, but as you progress different students might take turns writing parts of the story. You may also choose to build into the story problems that you know students are having in their own writing. In this way you can model a particular aspect of grammar or spelling for a group of students without pointing out those problems in their writing. At the same time, you are also modeling the full process of writing and can share the thinking processes involved in the construction of meaning.

Figure 2.5 shows a sample shared writing of a story about camping in the revising stage. Shared writing can be used when you think students need a large amount of support to help them expand their writing abilities. It is a powerful vehicle for developing minilessons to help students overcome problems in writing at all grade levels.

(d.) **Combinations of Writing Modes.**   Table 2.2 summarizes the three modes of writing that have been discussed. You may use these modes with any students at any grade level, and you may also find that you want to combine them. For example, you may begin a product with shared writing and move to collaborative or independent writing, depending on the amount of support you feel that students need. Keep in mind that *all students* at *all levels* need to have the experience of independent writing in order to develop independence. You will need to vary the modes of writing you use with students in light of their needs and growth stage.

Figure 2.5   Sample of a Shared Writing Experience

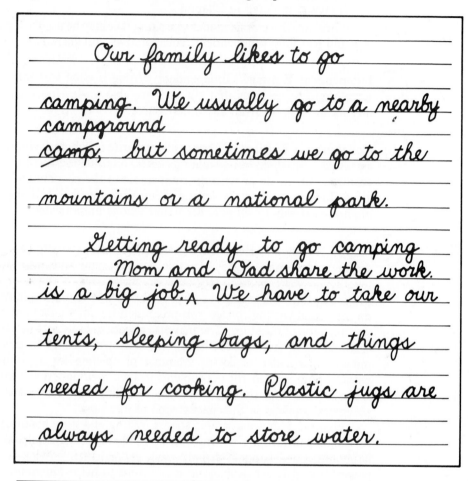

Our family likes to go camping. We usually go to a nearby ~~campground camp~~, but sometimes we go to the mountains or a national park.

Getting ready to go camping is a big job. ^Mom and Dad share the work. We have to take our tents, sleeping bags, and things needed for cooking. Plastic jugs are always needed to store water.

Just as you can give students choices of reading modes, you can also give them the opportunity to select the mode of writing they use. For example, you might suggest that students write a story independently or collaboratively. As with reading, students will select the mode of writing that most appropriately meets their current needs.

In summary, the instructional component of reading and writing in the literacy program can be viewed as anything that is done intentionally in the classroom to support students in learning to construct meaning. It involves

Table 2.2   Modes of Writing

Mode	Description	When to Use
Independent	Students write alone.	Students need little or no support.
Collaborative	Students write with a partner or partners on a single product.	Students need some support in their writing.
Shared	The group or class writes together, usually working with the teacher or a peer as leader.	Students need a large amount of support in their writing or you see the need to focus on a particular writing convention.

many activities, such as using different modes of reading and writing, responding to literature, lessons, or minilessons that involve modeling, and engaging in various projects. The teacher creates the circumstances and conditions for all of these activities to occur. Instruction can be thought of as a scaffold that is gradually removed as children gain competence in reading and writing; however, when the need arises, the scaffold or instruction can and should be brought back.

III INDEPENDENT READING AND WRITING

The third component of the literacy program is independent or voluntary reading and writing. *Every day, in every classroom* where the focus is on helping students develop the ability to construct meaning, students should have time for *self-selected reading* and *self-initiated writing.*

Time for Reading and Writing

Research consistently supports the importance of giving students time for independent reading (Anderson, Wilson & Fielding, 1988; Elley & Mangubhai, 1983; Fielding, Wilson & Anderson, 1986; Morrow, 1987; Taylor, Frye & Maruyama, 1990). Existing evidence indicates that independent reading

- *enhances their reading comprehension.*
- *provides them with a wide range of background knowledge.*
- *accounts for one-third or more of their vocabulary growth.*

* *promotes reading as a* lifelong activity. *(Center for the Study of Reading, n.d., p. 1)*

Similarly, researchers have verified the importance of extended writing as the major way in which students develop their ability to use grammar and learn to spell (Anderson et al., 1985; Hillocks, 1987). Independent reading and writing help make literacy learning an exciting process and also provide students with many authentic experiences—the basis for all literacy learning. Existing research offers guidelines and suggestions that should help teachers create and maintain this component in their classroom (Anderson et al., 1988; Graves, 1983; Graves & Hansen, 1983; Morrow & Weinstein, 1982, 1986; Taylor et al., 1990).

The amount of time for independent reading and writing needs to be given serious consideration when planning the literacy program. Research evidence suggests some guidelines to follow for independent reading (Anderson et al., 1985; Taylor et al., 1990) but offers little or no guidance for the amount of time for independent writing.

Becoming a Nation of Readers: The Report of the Commission on Reading (Anderson et al., 1985) suggests that two hours of independent reading per week should be expected of children by the time they are in third or fourth grade; this would include both in- and out-of-school reading. However, a more recent study suggests that in-school independent reading may be more significant than out-of-school reading, *even though both are important* (Taylor et al., 1990). Taylor et al. found that an average of 16 minutes per day of independent reading in school for fifth and sixth graders was significantly related to their reading growth; the out-of-school reading time was approximately 15 minutes per day.

Independent reading and writing are important because children are learning to do what we want them to do—*read* and *write*. They are thinking and expanding their schema and prior knowledge, which is the basis for their literacy learning. In the process, they are developing and using what Clay (1985) calls a self-improving system.

B. Guidelines for Planning Independent Reading and Writing

In light of existing research findings and good classroom practices, several guidelines should be considered in planning the independent reading and writing component of the literacy program:

* Create a program that will promote both in-school and out-of-school independent reading and writing.
* Begin the program in kindergarten. Ideally, good reading habits will have been modeled for children before this time through at-home read-aloud opportunities; even if this has not happened, this will be a good beginning.
* Allow 10 to 15 minutes per day for independent in-school reading from

kindergarten through grade 2. Allow approximately 20 to 30 minutes per day for independent writing.

- In grades 3 through 6, increase the amount of time for in-school independent reading to 15 to 20 minutes per day. Provide 30 to 45 minutes per day for independent writing.
- Above grade 6, continue to increase the amount of independent reading and writing. Because of changes in school structure at these levels, this time may need to be provided in several different classes.
- Be flexible about the amounts of time devoted to independent reading and writing. Gradually build up the time. When independent reading and writing are going well in class, extend the time if possible.
- Have designated periods or times for independent reading and writing. These do not have to be back to back.
- Give your independent reading and writing periods names that are appealing to the students, such as USSR—Uninterrupted Sustained Silent Reading, SQUIRT—Sustained Quiet Uninterrupted Reading Time, DEAR—Drop Everything And Read, or WART—Writing And Reading Time.
- Encourage students to share what they have read or written during their independent reading and writing time. Make this a pleasant experience that will encourage them to want to participate, but do not demand sharing.
- During independent reading and writing time, *you should also be reading and writing.* This provides an adult model and says that you also value these activities. During sharing, you should also share what you have read and written. Sharing can take place in pairs or small groups.

There are many exciting ways to promote and encourage independent reading and writing. Many times, however, teachers overlook this important aspect of the literacy program, for a number of reasons:

- *Not important.* Clearly, the research we have discussed shows that this is not true.
- *Must learn the skills first.* Everything discussed in this text so far shows that this is not the case.
- *Not enough time.* Research shows how important this area really is. Therefore, we must make enough time.
- *Not enough books in my room.* Even though some classrooms may have limited resources, these can be built. Use the school library, public library, book clubs and book club bonuses, students' books brought in from home, and so forth.
- *Students will read at home.* This may or may not happen. Recall that some researchers are saying that in-school independent reading time may be more important than out-of-school time (Taylor et al., 1990).

Ⓒ Suggested Activities

The following activities are just a few ways to develop and support independent reading and writing as a part of your literacy program.

Journals. Have students make a reading journal in which they keep track of the books they have read. Suggest that they include the title, author, and date completed. Then have them record how they have responded to the book. A reading response chart similar to the one presented in Figure 2.6 is a good way to encourage personal responses to reading. Charts should be changed frequently and should always include the "Other" category to get students to create their own response activities. For a detailed discussion of journals and response charts, see Chapter 6.

Records of Books Read or Time Spent Reading. Use other types of reading records to help students see the amount of reading they are doing. For example, use a thermometer like the ones pictured in Figure 2.7 to have students keep track of books read or the number of minutes spent reading independently at home and at school.

Author's Chair and Reader's Chair. Designate a chair where students who have written something and are ready to share it can sit as they read it to a group or the whole class. This is known as the author's chair and is a very effective way to encourage students to share what they have written (Graves & Hansen, 1983). Another chair, designated the reader's chair, can be the place where students sit when they have a story or book that they would like to read, retell, or just talk about with a partner or group.

Home Reading and Writing Programs. Programs that promote and encourage independent reading and writing at home are important to the success of the literacy program. These can range from a simple system in which children take home a favorite book that they have read in school to read aloud to a family member, to more elaborate programs.

One simple system for encouraging at-home reading can consist of having books in plastic bags that children take home to read on their own or to a family member. The person to whom the book has been read then completes a certificate to be returned to school. (If the child reads the book alone, some designated person still fills in the certificate.) Figure 2.8 shows a sample completed certificate for the book *The Secret in the Matchbox* (Willis, 1988). When the certificate is returned to the school, the child is recognized for the accomplishment and the certificate is placed in her or his reading folder. You can devise your own variation of this type of program. For example, Farris (1987) has created a successful at-home reading program using magazines that were sent home with activities to promote family reading.

Figure 2.6   Sample Reading Response Chart

READING RESPONSE CHART

1 Enter in your journal
  - Title
  - Author
  - Date completed

2 Select a way to respond
  - Talk with a friend about your book.
  - Write in your journal about your favorite character. Tell why.
  - Read your favorite part to a friend.
  - <u>Other</u>: You decide what you want to do.

Similar programs can be used to promote at-home independent writing. Reutzel and Fawson (1990) have created "The Traveling Tales Backpack," which contains materials for writing with suggestions for getting students to write their own stories at home. Table 2.3 shows the materials included in the backpack. Many teachers have used a similar idea with a briefcase. Linda Vaile, a first-grade teacher from Green Bay, Wisconsin, puts writing materials in an old briefcase and makes it a special event for children to take it home to do independent writing. Students take turns carrying the briefcase home and sharing their writing when they return to the class.

Figure 2.7   Sample Reading Thermometer

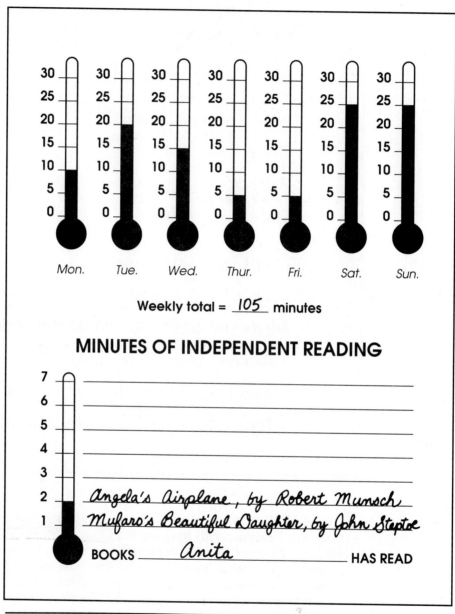

Weekly total = _105_ minutes

MINUTES OF INDEPENDENT READING

BOOKS ___ *Anita* ___ HAS READ

Angela's Airplane, by Robert Munsch
Mufaro's Beautiful Daughter, by John Steptoe

Figure 2.8   Certificate Verifying Home Reading

Home Reading Certificate

This verifies that __Troy Brown__

read __The Secret in the Matchbox__

(__X__ *aloud to* __Angela__ / ____ *alone*)

on __December 17, 1990__ .

__Angela Brown__

__Sister__

You can encourage independent reading and writing at school and at home in a variety of ways. A combination of procedures and activities should be used to keep motivation high. Whatever techniques are used, they should motivate and reward individuals themselves rather than compare individuals to one another.

In summary, independent reading and writing constitute an important part of the literacy program. These activities should take place in school and at home. For the in-school program, the amount of time should range from a minimum of 10 minutes per day in kindergarten to a minimum of 20 minutes per day in sixth grade for independent reading. Writing time should range from 20 to 45 minutes per day. Many different techniques should be used and should be changed frequently to motivate and support independent reading and writing.

This section of Chapter 2 has developed the concept of the literacy program. This program includes motivation, instruction in reading and writing, and independent reading and writing. These three components interact with each other continuously. By making sure that you have them present in your

Table 2.3 Contents of the Traveling Tales Backpack

Plain unlined paper	Small stapler
Lined paper	Staples
Construction paper—multiple colors	Brass fasteners
Drawing paper	Card stock
Poster paper	Hole punch
Crayons	Yarn
Watercolors	Wallpaper for book covers
Water-base markers	Glue stick
Colored pencils	Tape
Pencils	Paper clips
Felt-tip pens	Ruler
Felt-tip calligraphy pens	Letter stencils
Scissors	

Source: Reutzel & Fawson (1990).

classroom and/or school, you develop a program that helps students develop their ability to comprehend or construct meaning, promotes and fosters student ownership of literacy learning, and builds a love for reading and writing. The remainder of this chapter will focus on developing a unit and lesson format for use in the literacy program.

A UNIT AND LESSON FORMAT TO SUPPORT LITERACY LEARNING

In order to plan the appropriate instruction to help your students grow and develop in their abilities to comprehend and construct meaning, you need some type of format to help you organize what you do. This section will present

- a simple, easy-to-use thematic unit plan.
- a literacy lesson format that can be used alone or throughout the thematic unit.
- a minilesson concept and format that can be used to support literacy lessons as needed.

Table 2.4   Thematic Unit Outcomes from Selected Grade Levels

Theme	Grade Level	Constructing Meaning Outcome	Attitudes and Habits Outcome
Friendship	Kindergarten	Use events from stories and own experiences to make predictions about friendship.	Share favorite stories about friends with others and talk about the importance of friendship.
Folktales	Grade 1	Understand how folktales use sequence of events and repetitive language.	Choose a favorite folktale to share.
Byrd Baylor (author theme)	Grade 3	Understand how an author develops characters in realistic stories.	Independently read and share books by another favorite author.
Outer space	Grade 5	Generate and answer own questions about outer space.	Develop an appreciation for space exploration.
Adventure writing	Grade 7	Understand how characters respond to various tests of courage in adventure.	Develop an appreciation for adventure literature.

(A) Thematic Units

Definition

A thematic unit is a framework based on a particular topic, idea, author, or genre. Each unit has outcomes or goals that specify what you want students to accomplish as a result of the unit experiences and lessons. One way to think about the unit outcomes is to consider them in terms of the two overall goals of literacy learning: constructing meaning and developing positive attitudes and habits. Constructing meaning is what this text is all about; this overall goal or outcome tells you what understanding(s) you expect your students to accomplish as a result of reading the literature in a unit. Attitudes and habits are the feelings, beliefs, and routines related to reading and writing that you hope students develop through the unit experiences. Table 2.4 presents some sample unit outcomes for thematic units from various grade levels.

Thematic units usually consist of several pieces of literature around which the lessons and experiences are developed. These themes may involve a number of curricular areas, such as science, art, music, or math, even though the focus of the unit is developing the ability to read and write. (See Chapter 9 for a detailed discussion of planning cross-curricular units.) For example, a thematic unit on understanding families and family relationships might include books such as *Number the Stars* (Lowry, 1989) and *Where the Red Fern Grows* (Rawls, 1961). Though very different, both stories show how the relationships and feelings within families are revealed under different circumstances.

The theme plan consists of three parts:

- *Introducing the thematic unit:* This portion of the unit activates and assesses prior knowledge for the theme and develops any additional background needed to understand it. At this time you let students know what they will do during the unit and have them participate in deciding what they would like to accomplish.
- *Lessons and activities:* These are the specific experiences of the unit developed around each piece of literature.
- *Closing the thematic unit:* This section consists of activities that pull together the major learnings in the unit and allow children to share and celebrate their successes.

There are several advantages to using a thematic unit plan.

1. By incorporating several different pieces of literature focused on a common theme, you enable students to thoroughly account for and develop their prior knowledge and background on a particular subject, which is an essential part of meaning construction (Paris, Wasik, & Turner, 1991).
2. The thematic unit allows for a variety of experiences and lessons that promote literacy learning as an active, constructive process, which in turn fosters the community of learners concept (Pappas, Kiefer, & Levstik, 1990).
3. The unit plan allows the teacher to provide differing levels of support (or scaffolds for learning) based on a common body of literature for the class; this, in turn, makes the classroom a community for learning, a place where all children can learn and have similar experiences and successes.
4. All students are getting a great deal of practice with reading and writing through independent activities.

Lessons need to be planned around each of the pieces of literature included in each unit. The next section will focus on how to develop these specific lessons and activities.

A Literacy Lesson Format

Various formats have been suggested for lesson plans to guide children in learning to read. These include the DRTA—Directed Reading Thinking Activity (Stauffer, 1969), the DRA—Directed Reading Activity (Harris &

Sipay, 1985; Burns, Roe & Ross, 1988), the DRL—Directed Reading Lesson (Cooper, 1986; Cooper, Warncke, Shipman & Ramstad, 1979), and others. Although these plans differ somewhat, they are similar in that they focus primarily on reading. The lesson format that follows focuses on both reading and writing and helps the teacher and students relate both activities as integrated literacy learning processes. It has three simple parts: introducing the literature, reading and responding to the literature, and extending the literature.

1. Introducing the Literature

When each piece of literature is introduced, two things must happen:

1. Students' prior knowledge must be activated and assessed, and pertinent additional background must be developed. *Sometimes* this may include the development of key concept vocabulary.
2. Students must develop their purpose(s) for reading.

These two things are accomplished in a variety of ways and with differing levels of teacher support, depending on the literature and the students' needs. Sometimes you might want to teach a few words that are key to understanding the literature. Or you might use artwork: for example, if students in a second-grade class are going to read *The Art Lesson* (de Paola, 1989), you might have them preview the story by looking at the pictures and discussing what they think the book will be about. Their purpose for reading then becomes seeing whether or not their predictions will be verified. Throughout, you provide support according to their needs. Many times you may incorporate writing into this phase of the lesson; for example, you may have students do a "quick write" to activate prior knowledge or to write predictions that will be checked during and after reading.

2. Reading and Responding to the Literature

Reading and responding to literature take place concurrently; that is, students respond while they are reading as well as after they have read.

Different pieces of literature will need to be read using different modes of reading (see page 43 for modes of reading), depending on the literature and the abilities of the students. Beginning readers and writers and those having difficulty learning need more teacher support than those who are making effective progress. Moreover, some pieces of literature are more complex than others and require more teacher support even for students who are progressing well.

The primary focus of this part of the lesson is reading and getting to know the piece of literature. While students are reading, they should be helped and reminded to monitor their reading by asking themselves whether what they are reading makes sense; if it does not, they should know and use appropriate strategies to help overcome the problem and construct meaning. (See Chapter 8 on modeling strategies for reading.) This aspect of metacognitive development is a vital part of constructing meaning and comprehension (Paris et al., 1991).

It is not necessary for you to always select the mode of reading that students will use. This decision can and should be made, in part, by the students. When students are given the opportunity to choose their own modes of reading, they select ones that are most appropriate for their own needs and take greater ownership of their learning.

When responding to the literature, students need to do something: *think about it, talk about it, write about it, or do something creative with it involving art, music, or drama.* Responses should be personal and creative because construction of meaning is an individual matter. However, one important activity is summarizing what was read. Again, some students and some pieces of literature will require more teacher support than others. By observing carefully how students respond, you can determine whether they need additional support or minilessons that go directly back to the literature (see page 68 on minilessons).

Let's suppose your class is now ready to read *The Art Lesson* (de Paola, 1989). This book seems easy enough for all students in your class to read it independently. However, you offer them the option of reading it independently or cooperatively. You remind students to check if their predictions were verified or changed as they read, and encourage them to make running notes about their feelings or reactions in their journals. After-reading responses could involve getting into small groups to retell the story and share their favorite parts. From the responses, you may discover that some students do not understand why Tomie was upset about the art lessons. You then go back to the book and model how Tomie's expectations for art lessons had been built up and how he became disappointed in school. This could be done by developing a chart like the one shown in Figure 2.9.

③ *Extending the Literature*

Extending the literature means encouraging students to use what they have learned in various appropriate ways or in different curricular areas such as science, social studies, art, music, writing. The teaching of writing may be tied directly to the literature by having the literature serve as a model for a certain type of writing. For example, a natural writing extension for *The Art Lesson* is writing a story. Of course, you would vary the mode of writing according to students' needs. (See page 53 for modes of writing. Chapter 7 contains more about writing and the writing process.)

This simple, easy-to-use literacy lesson is flexible and can be used throughout all grades. Adjustments and variations are made in accordance

Figure 2.9   Chart Modeling Tomie's Disappointment in *The Art Lesson* (de Paola, 1989)

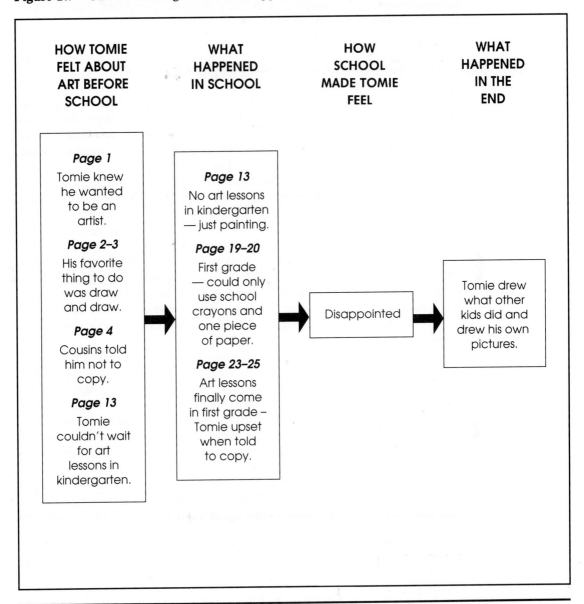

with the developmental levels of the students, the literature being read, and the needs of the individual students. Table 2.5 summarizes the parts of the literacy lesson, and a sample lesson using *Jamaica Tag-Along* (Havill, 1989) appears on page 71 of this chapter.

Minilessons as a Form of Instructional Support

Throughout all literacy lessons that you develop, you will need to provide different levels of support to help students experience literature. Sometimes this will be provided when *introducing* the literature, sometimes while students are reading and responding, and sometimes as they are extending the literature. Support will be provided in many forms and in many ways.

For students who need additional directed support in learning to construct meaning, you can use minilessons that go directly back to the literature or to the students' own writing to model the construction of meaning, a skill, or a strategy. These minilessons may take place before, during, or after reading or writing. However, you determine the need for a minilesson by how students read and respond to the literature or how they write and respond to their writing: in other words, remember that *the core of all learning focuses on the literature,* not on specific skills. Thus the minilessons should only be used to more directly model a skill or strategy if the students' reading and writing show that the need exists. Figure 2.10 shows how all of these elements fit together.

Minilessons may be informal and unplanned. For example, suppose your students are reading *Mufaro's Beautiful Daughters* (Steptoe, 1987). As they are responding and discussing the fairy tale, you realize that they have not understood that the snake, hungry little boy, and old woman are all the same person, the king, Nyoka. You immediately go back to the story and have them locate the places where each character appeared and show them that these are all the king who has changed himself into these characters. This is a minilesson that takes place immediately when the "teachable moment" arises.

Minilessons may also be more formal and more carefully and thoroughly planned. In any case, they should *always go back to the literature being read and/ or a sample of writing for examples and modeling.* A typical planned minilesson would incorporate the following steps:

1. *Introduction:* Let the students know what they will learn and relate it to the literature or their writing.
2. *Teacher modeling:* Model the element being taught using the literature or writing to show examples. Incorporate think-alouds as needed. (See page 41 for an earlier discussion of think-alouds, as well as Chapter 8.)
3. *Student modeling and guided practice:* Guide students in modeling and using what is being taught by finding other examples of what they have learned in the literature or in their writing.

Table 2.5   Summary of the Literacy Lesson

Lesson Part	Purposes	Remarks
Introducing	Activate and assess prior knowledge and develop background Help students set purposes for reading	The amount of teacher support provided will depend both on the literature and on the students' needs. Sometimes the support will include development of key concepts and vocabulary. Activities used will incorporate reading, writing, speaking, listening, and thinking.
Reading and Responding	Read and have access to the entire selection Do something creative and personal during and/or after reading the selection Summarize what has been read	The mode for reading the selection is determined by students' needs and the literature. This portion of the lesson focuses on the personal construction of meaning. By observing students' responses, you will be able to determine the need for additional support or minilessons using the literature as the vehicle for instruction.
Extending	Use the understandings and ideas gained from the literature Use the literature as a model for writing	Extension of the literature will utilize the knowledge gained in many creative ways or in other curricular areas. Writing may be taught using the literature as a model for the *type* of writing being developed. (See Chapter 7 on writing.)

4. *Summarizing and reflecting:* Help students to summarize what they have learned and talk about how and when they might use it.

The follow-up for the minilesson should include the following:

1. *Independent practice:* Have students read or write using what has been taught.
2. *Application:* Give students repeated opportunities to use or apply what they have learned immediately in other reading and writing experiences.
3. *Reflecting about use:* After students have had several opportunities to apply what was taught, encourage them to talk about how they have used what they have learned and what they might do to improve it.

Figure 2.10   Model of Reading and Writing with Minilessons

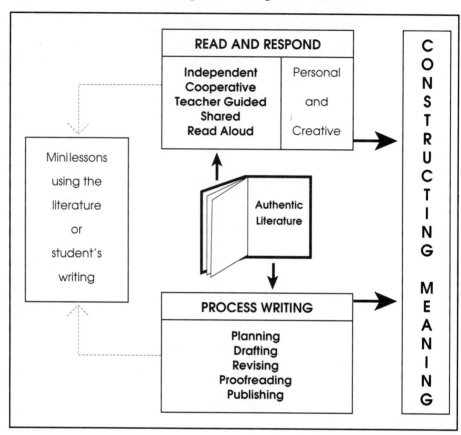

Research shows that directed lessons such as the type being suggested here do help some students learn to read and write (Pearson & Dole, 1987). Again, they are not discrete skill lessons, and they should be used only when the need for more directed support is clearly called for as evidenced by problems in the students' reading and writing. These lessons should always go back to the literature or sample of writing for examples of what is being taught, and all practice and application should be in the form of reading and writing, not filling blanks, marking, circling, or underlining on a worksheet. A minilesson is given as a part of the literacy lesson in the next section of this chapter. (Minilessons are discussed in more detail in Chapter 8.)

Literacy Lesson

Jamaica Tag-Along

This section presents a sample literacy lesson and minilesson based on the discussions on pages 62–70 of this chapter and the book *Jamaica Tag-Along* (Havill, 1989), a delightful story about a little girl who wants to tag along with her older brother and who realizes she is treating a little boy on the playground like her older brother has treated her. Juanita Havill has also written another book about Jamaica entitled *Jamaica's Find* (1986); children love both books because they can so easily relate to Jamaica and her problems.

The literacy lesson plan presented here has been used with children and illustrates the concepts and ideas about literacy learning developed throughout this text. Many of its ideas have been discussed in the first two chapters, but some will be discussed later. The plan for *Jamaica Tag-Along* would be suitable for a thematic unit on growing up, which might be used in late first grade or early second grade. The "notes" presented throughout the plan explain why each activity was selected and give references to sections of this text that explain the rationale behind what was done. The minilesson on inferencing on page 64 should be used only if students have demonstrated a need for such support.

Before Reading the Plans

1. **Think about what you have learned about constructing meaning and literacy learning.**
2. **Review the parts of a literacy lesson (page 62) and of a minilesson (page 68).**
3. **Read *Jamaica Tag-Along* to determine the problem, action, and outcome in the story.**

While Reading the Plan

1. **Think about the literacy lesson plan and how the parts were carried out.**
2. **Think about why each part was done as it was. Note any questions you might have.**
3. **Think of other ways you might have developed this lesson.**
4. **Think about which activities would help you know when to use the minilesson.**

Jamaica ran to the kitchen to answer the phone. But her brother got there first.

"It's for me," Ossie said.

Jamaica stayed and listened to him talk.

"Sure," Ossie said. "I'll meet you at the court."

Jamaica
Tag-Along

Juanita Havill

Illustrations by Anne Sibley O'Brien

Ossie got his basketball from the closet. "I'm going to shoot baskets with Buzz."

"Can I come, too?" Jamaica said. "I don't have anything to do."

"Ah, Jamaica, call up your own friends."

"Everybody is busy today."

"I don't want you tagging along."

"I don't want to tag along," Jamaica said. "I just want to play basketball with you and Buzz."

"You're not old enough. We want to play serious ball."

Ossie dribbled his basketball down the sidewalk.
Jamaica followed at a distance on her bike.
Buzz was already at the school court, shooting baskets with Jed and Maurice.
She parked her bike by the bushes and crept to the corner of the school building to watch.

That's not fair, Jamaica thought. Maurice is shorter than I am.
Pom, pa-pom, pa-pom, pom, pom.
The boys started playing, Ossie and Jed against Buzz and Maurice.

Jamaica sneaked to the edge of the court.

Maurice missed a shot and the ball came bouncing toward her. Jamaica jumped. "I've got the ball," she yelled.

"Jamaica!" Ossie was so surprised he tripped over Buzz. They both fell down.

Jamaica dribbled to the basket and tossed the ball. It whirled around the rim and flew out.

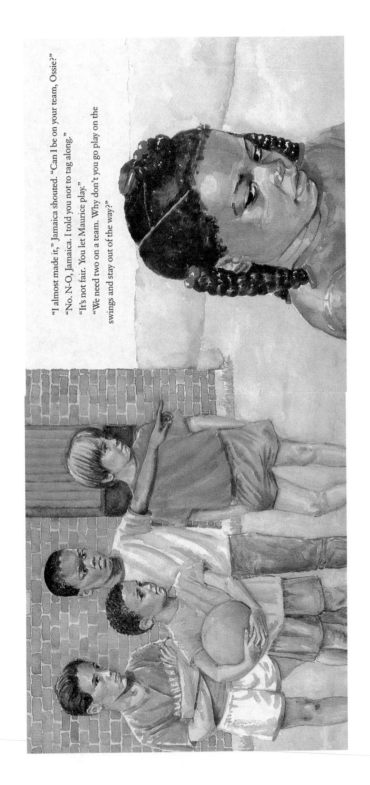

"I almost made it," Jamaica shouted. "Can I be on your team, Ossie?"

"No. N-O, Jamaica. I told you not to tag along."

"It's not fair. You let Maurice play."

"We need two on a team. Why don't you go play on the swings and stay out of the way?"

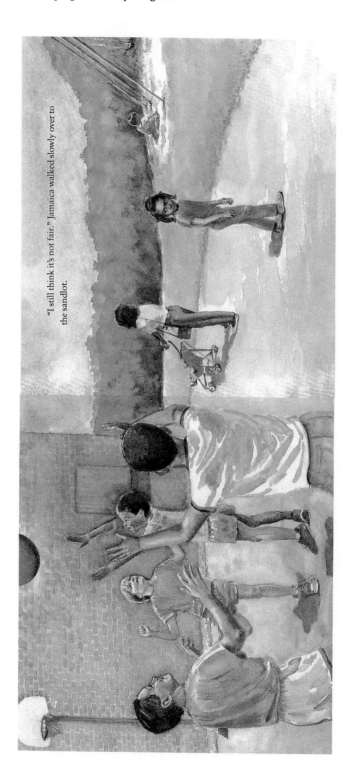

"I still think it's not fair." Jamaica walked slowly over to the sandlot.

She started to swing, but a little boy kept walking in front of her. His mom should keep him out of the way, Jamaica thought. She looked up and saw a woman pushing a baby back and forth in a stroller.

Jamaica sat down in the sand and began to dig. She made a big pile with the wet sand from underneath. She scooped sand from the mound to form a wall.

"Berto help," said the little boy. He sprinkled dry sand on the walls.

"Don't," said Jamaica. "You'll just mess it up." Jamaica turned her back.

She piled the wet sand high. She made a castle with towers. She dug a ditch around the wall.

Jamaica turned to see if Berto was still there. He stood watching. Then he tried to step over the ditch, and his foot smashed the wall.

"Stay away from my castle," Jamaica said.

"Berto," the woman pushing the stroller said, "leave this girl alone. Big kids don't like to be bothered by little kids."

"That's what my brother always says," Jamaica said. She started to repair the castle. Then she thought, but I don't like my brother to say that. It hurts my feelings.

Jamaica smoothed the wall. "See, Berto, like that. You can help me make a bigger castle if you're very careful."

Jamaica and Berto made a giant castle. They put water from the drinking fountain in the moat.

"Wow," Ossie said when the game was over and the other boys went home. "Need some help?"

"If you want to," Jamaica said.

Jamaica, Berto, and Ossie worked together on the castle.

Jamaica didn't even mind if Ossie tagged along.

*Literacy
Lesson
continued*

Literacy Lesson Plan

Thematic unit title: Growing Up

Level: Late first or early second grade

Unit focus:

Attitudes and habits: Respond in self-selected ways to stories about growing up.

Constructing meaning: Understand how we learn and change from our experiences.

Strategies and skills focus: Story prediction strategy
Inferencing
Writing a story

Introducing *Jamaica Tag-Along*

ACTIVITY	PROCEDURE	NOTES
Brainstorming about experiences	Invite children to get into groups of three to compile lists of problems they have had with older brothers or sisters. Encourage them to talk about how they felt in these situations. Make a class summary chart.	Activates pertinent prior knowledge and gets children thinking about the central problem. Students for whom this lesson is planned do not need vocabulary instruction before reading.

Problems with Older Brothers and Sisters	How We Feel

| Previewing *Jamaica Tag-Along*

Strategy: story map prediction | Show the book *Jamaica Tag-Along*. Read the title, author, and illustrator. Have children look through the book to see what they think will happen. | The story map prediction strategy chart helps students see how to predict. The chart and the discussion help support them as they begin to construct meaning. Predictions |

Literacy Lesson continued

ACTIVITY	PROCEDURE	NOTES

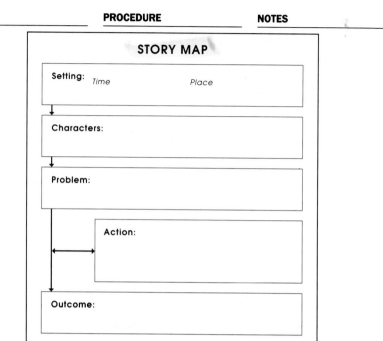

Show the story map prediction strategy chart, and remind children that they have used it before. Briefly review definitions of setting, characters, and problem in a story.

Ask children to predict the setting, characters, and problem. Record group predictions. (For children who have difficulty predicting, model how to make predictions about setting; then have children predict the other parts.)

become the purpose for reading. For a discussion of the story map prediction strategy, see Chapters 3 and 8.

Literacy Lesson continued

Reading and Responding to *Jamaica Tag-Along*

ACTIVITY	PROCEDURE	NOTES
Student selection of reading mode	Suggest that this story might be read in two ways—independently and with teacher support (teacher-guided/ independent reading). Encourage students to select the way they prefer.	Gives students choices and helps them take part in meeting their own needs. (Some may need suggestions on which way to read the story.)
Independent reading (for children who select to read this independently)	Have them read it to verify their predictions.	Most of my children can read this book independently because it is easy enough for them to understand.
Making notes and responding while reading independently	Remind children to make notes and respond in their journals as they read, if they choose to do so.	This will encourage natural responding.
Teacher-guided/ independent reading (for children who select it)	Guide children who select this mode through part of the story and then have them read the remainder independently. Direct them through three parts of the story to verify the predictions they made: pages 1–2, 3–9, and 10–17.	The different modes of reading provide varied levels of support to meet individual needs.
	Discussion questions: pages 1–2: Who were the characters we met? Where is this story taking place?	Helps children construct meaning by checking their predictions, building a mental map of the story, and responding personally as they read.
	Predicting: What do you think Ossie is going to do? Why?	Helps children develop their ability to monitor by continuously making, verifying, and changing predictions.

*Literacy
Lesson
continued*

ACTIVITY	PROCEDURE	NOTES
	pages 3–9: Were your predictions correct? What is the problem in this story? How do you feel about Jamaica and Ossie right now?	Checks predictions and brings out story problem. Predictions help students to relate their own knowledge to the reading and to monitor their reading.
	Predicting: How do you think the boys will treat Jamaica now? Why	
	pages 10–17: Was your prediction correct about how the boys would treat Jamaica? Who did Jamaica meet? How did Jamaica react to Berto when he tried to help her?	Checks predictions and brings out story action.
	Predicting: What do you think will happen in the remainder of the story?	Sets purpose for reading remainder of story.
	pages 18–28: Have children read remainder of story independently to see if their predictions are verified.	
Children-selected responses	Display the after-reading response chart and ask children to select how they wish to respond in their journals. Children may share their responses in the discussion circles.	Allow all children to respond in the manner that is best for them. Ideas are on the chart. For a discussion of the importance of responding to literature, see page 66 and Chapter 6.

After Reading Response Chart

1. Enter in your journal
   • Title
   • Author
   • Response
2. Select a way to respond
   • Write about your favorite character. Tell why you picked this character.
   • Draw a picture about your favorite part. Write about it.
   • Decide what you can do to respond.

Literacy Lesson continued

ACTIVITY	PROCEDURE	NOTES
Literature discussion circles	Divide the class into literature discussion circles. Display the discussion circle chart and go over the procedures before children begin.	Literature discussion circles (or literature circles) are another form of responding to literature. The chart guides children and thus helps structure this experience. See Chapter 6 for a further discussion of literature circles.

Discussion Circle Chart: Story Prediction

1. Talk about the predictions made before reading. Check the story prediction chart.
2. Retell the story. Follow the parts on the story prediction chart.
3. Share your response with the group.

ACTIVITY	PROCEDURE	NOTES
	As the children work, move from group to group to monitor and support the activity.	Observe how well children can make predictions and inferences. For children who need extra support with inferencing, use the minilesson on inferencing (see end of this plan). For a discussion of minilessons, see page 68. For a discussion of observing, see Chapter 10.
Whole-Group Discussion: Summarizing the story and checking the unit focus	Hold a class discussion to summarize the points covered on the discussion circle chart.

Conclude by having children talk about what Jamaica and Ossie may have learned from this experience.

Have children relate Jamaica's experiences to their own. | |

Literacy
Lesson
continued

ACTIVITY	PROCEDURE	NOTES
Extending *Jamaica Tag-Along*		
Theme mural on growing and changing	Some children may add panels to the theme mural on growing up. Each child can draw a picture about how Jamaica and/or Ossie changed and can then write a caption to their picture.	Allows children to construct personal meaning in another way. Helps to continue to pull together the theme.
Process writing: Writing a story, brainstorming	Begin story writing by having children brainstorm to compile a list of possible topics for a story that they will write during this theme unit. Writing will be continued throughout the unit.	This is a very strong example of a good story. The use of the prediction strategy will have helped children focus on the elements of a story. For more discussion of process writing, see Chapter 7.

Minilesson on Inferencing

Thematic unit: Growing Up

Book: *Jamaica Tag-Along*

Focus: Using story clues to make inferences

When to Use: Use only when children have demonstrated through responding that they need more directed support on constructing meaning in this book and inferencing.

ACTIVITY	PROCEDURE	NOTES
Introduction: let children know what they will learn	Tell children that sometimes authors give you a clue to what they mean without really saying it. (Give example from a story children know.) In this lesson, they will revisit Jamaica to look at how the author has done this.	It is important to let children know what they will learn. This focuses their attention and gives them a purpose for the lesson. The term *inferencing* may be used. See page 68 for a discussion of minilessons.

Literacy Lesson continued

ACTIVITY	PROCEDURE	NOTES
Teacher modeling of inferencing	Ask children to discuss how Jamaica felt in the story. Have children open their books to pages 6–7 and to follow along as you read the pages aloud. Then *think aloud* with children:	Modeling using the literature that has already been read gives children a meaningful starting point. For a discussion of modeling, see page 41 and Chapter 8. If more than one modeling experience is needed, use the next two pages differently than planned.

> *Think Aloud:*
>
> "These pages tell me that Jamaica really wants to play with the older boys. She is getting upset because Maurice is shorter than she is. I use the author's clues and my own knowledge to begin to figure this out. The story doesn't say this directly."

ACTIVITY	PROCEDURE	NOTES
Student modeling and guided practice	page 8: Have children read this page to tell how the boys feel about Jamaica. Then ask them to explain how they were able to tell. Did the author say it?	This activity begins to release the responsibility for inferencing to the children. Some may need several examples.
Summarizing and reflecting on how to inference	Help children summarize what they have learned about inferencing: Did the author tell you everything about Jamaica? How were you able to figure out that the boys were getting upset with Jamaica? When do you think you will use this strategy?	Children need to summarize in their own words what they have learned. Guiding them with questions is a good way to do this. It is important to get children to put into their own words what they have done and when they might use it. This helps to create better conditions for transfer to other books they will read.

Literacy Lesson continued

ACTIVITY	PROCEDURE	NOTES
Independent practice using inferencing	Using the story clues chart, ask children to go through the remainder of the book to locate other places where they used story clues to learn something that the author didn't say directly.	This type of practice puts the process of inferencing in meaningful text and continues to release the responsibility of inferencing to the children. See page 42 on the importance of releasing responsibility.

Story Clues		
Page	**Clue**	**What Was Learned**
--	---------------	------------------------
	---------------	------------------------
	-----	------------------------

	Summarize the activity after children have completed it.	
Application of inferencing	In the next book in the theme, ask children to look for clues that authors give to suggest things they don't really say. Have them be ready to share these places and explain how they could tell what was meant.	Application of this process in reading is important. If children have difficulty using it, further modeling will be needed.

After Reading the Plan

1. **Review and discuss the plan with some of your peers who have also studied it.**
2. **Select a piece of literature that you know well and develop a literacy lesson plan of your own. Share your plan with some of your peers and discuss it.**

GUIDELINES FOR SELECTING LITERATURE

Selecting the appropriate literature for the literacy program is both a critical and challenging decision, but it can be fun and rewarding if you have some guidelines in mind for carrying it out.

What constitutes "good literature" is a much-debated topic (Goodman & Goodman, 1991). Although this judgment is generally a personal matter, it is possible to select a variety of quality literature for your students. Since there are thousands of new books published annually, literature selection is an ongoing process that should involve you, other teachers, the librarian or media specialist, students, parents, and other interested persons.

There are four basic criteria to consider in selecting literature: developmental appropriateness, student appeal, literary quality, and cultural and social authenticity.

Ⓐ Developmental Appropriateness

For years, selections for reading instruction have been based on their readability as determined by one of several formulae that yield a grade-level score. However, serious questions have been raised about the validity of such formulae (Klare, 1984; Weaver & Kintsch, 1991). In addition to lacking validity, such prescriptions actually cause problems (Routman, 1988; Simons & Ammon, 1989): the literature is in essence destroyed, watered down, or made more difficult by such procedures; moreover, when the natural language patterns are altered and controlled vocabulary is used, the reader does not have the appropriate clues to read the text with ease and fluency.

Remember that beginning learners (kindergarten, first, and second grade) need highly predictable literature that offers the richness, rhyme, and pattern of the language (Bridge, Winograd, & Haley, 1983; Goodman & Goodman, 1991). For example, the book *Mary Wore Her Red Dress and Henry Wore His Green Sneakers* (Peek, 1985) has a predictable language pattern:

> *Mary wore her red dress, red dress, red dress,*
> *Mary wore her red dress all day long.*
>
> *Henry wore his green sneakers, green sneakers, green sneakers,*
> *Henry wore his green sneakers all day long.*
> *[and so forth]*

Bridge et al. (1983) have identified seven patterns of predictability in literature:

1. Phrase or sentence repeated (example: *Mary Wore Her Red Dress and Henry Wore His Green Sneakers*, Peek, 1985)
2. Repetitive-cumulative pattern in which a word, phrase, or sentence is repeated (example: *Nobody Listens to Andrew*, Guilfoile, 1957)

3. Rhyming patterns (example: *Sheep in a Jeep*, Shaw, 1986)
4. Familiar cultural sequences, cardinal and ordinal numbers (example: *Over in the Meadow*, Keats, 1971)
5. Familiar cultural sequences, alphabet (example: *Dr. Seuss's A B C*, Seuss, 1963)
6. Familiar cultural sequences, days, months, colors (example: *Monday, Monday, I Like Monday*, Martin, 1970)
7. Predictable plots (example: *Mr. Gumpy's Outing*, Burningham, 1970)

These patterns should be considered when selecting literature for the beginning levels. The more difficulty children are having learning to read and write, the more highly predictable the literature needs to be.

To determine the developmental appropriateness of a book beyond the beginning reading levels, look at the concepts and general complexity of the text. Are the concepts ones your students will know? Have they had experience with them? Is the text written in a style that is clear and easy to understand for students of the age you are teaching? These are the types of questions that can guide your selection.

The general nature of the guidelines just described may prompt you to think that deciding on developmental appropriateness is a very arbitrary process. However, recall that literature has no grade level. Therefore, there is no one single grade for which a book may be assumed to be absolutely appropriate. Rather, a book may be used in different ways at different grade levels. For example, *Ira Says Goodbye* (Waber, 1988) may be read aloud to children in kindergarten but may be read independently by second or third graders. This is why lists of recommended reading developed by various states give grade spans for books. Sample entries from the California listing (*Recommended Readings*, 1986) suggest some grade-level ranges for several books:

Gag, Wanda
    Millions of Cats   K–2

Hutchins, Pat
    Rosie's Walk   K–6

Kellogg, Steven
    Island of the Skog   3–4

Miles, Miska
    Annie and the Old One   2–8

Student Appeal

This may well be one of the most important aspects to consider in selecting literature for the literacy program. The books selected need to appeal to students, captivate their imaginations, and entice them to want to read more and more. Appeal may best be determined by the students themselves. However, when you cannot consult with each student, you should consider such sources as *"Children's Choices"* and *"Young Adults' Choices"* published early in the fall of each year in *The Reading Teacher* and *The Journal of Reading*, publications of the International Reading Association. These listings present favorite books voted on by children and young adults. There is also a listing of teachers' choices published annually in *The Reading Teacher*. You may want to consider earlier editions of all these listings.

Literary Quality

The books you select should be of high literary quality. Watch for elements of plot, characterization, setting, theme, style, and point of view that create memorable stories. You may want to read Norton's (1991) chapter "Evaluating and Selecting Literature for Children" listed in the section "For Additional Reading" for a detailed discussion of how high-quality literature incorporates these elements.

Determining the literary quality of books is a large task for a busy teacher. The following sources can help you evaluate new books as they become available:

The WEB, published four times a year, describes how books on specific topics may be used in the classroom. Published by Martha L. King Center for Language and Literacy, The Ohio State University, 29 Woodruff Avenue, Columbus, OH 43210-1177.

The Horn Book Magazine reviews books from many perspectives. Write to The Horn Book Magazine, Park Square Building, 31 St. James Avenue, Boston, MA 02116.

The New Advocate provides articles and book reviews. Published four times a year by Christopher-Gordon Publishers, Inc., 480 Washington Street, Norwood, MA 02062.

Book Links presents reviews of books that have been grouped by thematic areas. Published bimonthly by the American Library Association, 50 East Huron Street, Chicago, IL 60611.

In addition, the following professional journals review literature in each edition:

The Reading Teacher (elementary), published by the International Reading Association

The Journal of Reading (middle school and junior high school), published by the International Reading Association

Language Arts (elementary), published by the National Council of Teachers of English

---

Table 2.6   Criteria for Selecting Reading Materials

When considering reading materials, the following criteria need to be addressed:

1. Literary quality—this will always be personal. Individual readers need to develop their own criteria.
2. Authentic social or cultural significance—this includes the truth value, validity, and honesty of the reading material; knowledge that is most accepted by scientists; concerns for ethnic diversity and stereotyping; and a sense that the material fits pragmatically what is known in the social and cultural world.
3. Cohesion and coherence—the way in which the text hangs together.
4. Illustrations—illustrations help to create a context and add an extra meaning dimension to the written text.
5. Teaching possibilities—the many opportunities to use the materials to support the rest of the curriculum.
6. Psychological possibilities—a wide range of materials to serve many different interests and purposes.

Source: Goodman & Goodman (1991).

Cultural and Social Authenticity

The literature selected for the literacy program must include selections that are both culturally and socially authentic. "Through multicultural literature, children of the majority culture learn to respect values and contributions of people in other parts of the world. . . . The wide range of multicultural themes also helps children develop an understanding of social change" (Norton, 1991, p. 531). In essence, reading and writing about a variety of real cultural and social situations helps students develop an appreciation and understanding of how persons from a variety of cultures and social settings live and work together. Such books as *The Patchwork Quilt* (Flournoy, 1985), *Hawk, I'm Your Brother* (Baylor, 1976), *Felita* (Mohr, 1979), and *The Rainbow People* (Yep, 1989) are examples of the types of literature that should be a part of every literacy program. You may also want to read Norton's chapter on multicultural literature listed in "For Additional Reading." For other guidelines on selecting literature, see Tables 2.6 and 2.7.

Another source for literature is a basal series. Over the past few years, basals have been highly criticized for both their content and their instructional suggestions (Goodman, Freeman, Murphy & Shannon, 1988). Although many of the criticisms have been valid, many related more to how basals were used than to what was in them, and publishers have now begun to look more critically at what goes into such texts. In fact, many publishers now incorporate authentic, unadapted literature into their series and resources. When selecting

Table 2.7   Selecting Books for Reading Programs

Does the story have charm, magic, impact, and appeal?

- Will the children demand that the book be reread, or will they revisit it by themselves?
- Will chunks of language and meaning resurface at later times?
- What is the book's lasting appeal?
- Will the book stand repeated readings?

Is the idea worthwhile?

- Does the author's message have merit for its own sake? (Many stories contain a moral, but morals should be inherent in the story and not presented as a reason for the reading.)
- Is the idea worth the time and effort spent on the reading?
- Does the story say something new, or, if a familiar theme, does it offer a new view?

Are the story's shape and structure appropriate?

- Does the shape and structure help to carry the reader through the story?
- Does the story have a beginning, a middle, and an identifiable climax with an acceptable resolution?
- Does the story create its own pace?
- How has the author linked the episodes?
- What gaps is the reader required to fill?
- How does the author signal a change of pace, mood, or action.

Is the language effective?

- Does the language suit the theme and the characters?
- Does the language spark the child's imagination, and inspire thought?
- Are there memorable phrases and/or sentences?
- Do the characters act and speak naturally?
- Does the author use book language to heighten the story's shape?
- How much does the author leave to the reader's imagination?

Is the story authentic?

- Is the story credible to the reader?
- Does it avoid condescensions, stereotyping, and inaccuracy?
- Does the author fulfill the promises engendered by the title, theme, and story shape?
- Will it lead the child into further reading and learning?

Do the illustrations help the reader gain meaning from the text?

- Are they appropriate for the theme and characters?
- Do they make the meaning of the text clearer?
- Do the illustrations reflect the mood of the story and give rise to feelings and emotions?
- Do they complement the text, rather than compete with it?

Table 2.7   Selecting Books for Reading Programs (Cont.)

Is the format of the book appropriate?

- Do the book's size and its shape suit the content and the reader, or do they merely fit a series format?
- Do the typeface and size, spacing, and line breaks match the reader's stage of reading development?

Source: From M. Mooney, *Developing Lifelong Readers.* Wellington, NZ, Ministry of Education, 1988. Reprinted by permission.

---

a basal series, therefore, you should apply the same criteria that have been suggested for selecting books. In addition, you should keep the following points in mind:

- The literature should be authentic and unadapted. It should not be rewritten to conform to a readability score.
- The basal is a resource, not a recipe book. Choose the pieces of literature that are best for your students. *You do not have to use all the selections provided.*

Selecting literature is a big job, but by using some of the suggestions given here, you will make the task more manageable.

SUMMARY

This chapter has developed two important frameworks: The literacy program, and a thematic unit plan supported by literacy lessons and minilessons. The literacy program has three important parts—motivation, instruction in reading and writing, and independent reading and writing. These three components interact in helping children learn to construct meaning and grow into literacy.

A thematic unit and literacy lesson format were suggested as a way of planning and organizing instruction throughout the literacy program. In each literacy lesson, a work of literature is introduced, read and responded to, and finally extended in some way. Different modes of reading and writing are used throughout the lessons to vary support for students as needed. Within the framework of the literacy lesson, minilessons can be used to more directly model strategies and the processes of constructing meaning. A literacy lesson for *Jamaica Tag-Along* with a minilesson on inferencing was presented, and criteria for selecting literature for thematic units and literacy lessons were suggested.

Children's Books

Ackerman, K. (1988). *Song and dance man.* New York: Knopf.

Adoff, A. (Ed.). (1973). *The poetry of black America: Anthology of the 20th century.* New York: Harper and Row.

Base, G. (1988). *The eleventh hour.* New York: Harry N. Abrams.

Baylor, B. (1976). *Hawk, I'm your brother.* New York: Scribner's.

Baylor, B. (1982). *The best town in the world.* New York: Scribner's.

Burningham, J. (1970). *Mr. Gumpy's outing.* London: Henry Holt.

Cole, J. (Ed.). (1984). *A new treasury of children's poetry: Old favorites and new discoveries.* New York: Doubleday.

Dahl, R. (1988). *Matilda.* London: Jonathon Cape.

de Paola, T. (1989). *The art lesson.* New York: G. P. Putnam.

Flournoy, V. (1985). *The patchwork quilt.* New York: Dial.

Giff, P. R. (1980). *Today was a terrible day.* New York: Viking.

Giff, P. R. (1988). *Ronald Morgan goes to bat.* New York: Viking Kestrel.

Guilfoile, E. (1957). *Nobody listens to Andrew.* Cleveland: Modern Curriculum Press.

Havill, J. (1986). *Jamaica's find.* Boston: Houghton Mifflin.

Havill, J. (1989). *Jamaica Tag-Along.* Boston: Houghton Mifflin.

Isadora, R. (1979). *Ben's trumpet.* New York: Greenwillow Books.

Keats, E. J. (1971). *Over in the meadow.* New York: Scholastic.

Lowry, L. (1989). *Number the stars.* Boston: Houghton Mifflin.

McCloskey, R. (1948). *Blueberries for Sal.* New York: Viking.

Martin, B., Jr. (1967). *Brown bear, brown bear.* New York: Henry Holt.

Martin, B. (1970). *Monday, Monday, I like Monday.* New York: Holt, Rinehart and Winston.

Mohr, N. (1979). *Felita.* New York: Dial.

Munsch, R. (1983). *Angela's airplane.* Toronto: Annick Press.

Paterson, K. (1977). *Bridge to Terabithia.* New York: Crowell.

Peek, M. (1985). *Mary wore her red dress and Henry wore his green sneakers.* New York: Clarion.

Prelutsky, J. (Ed.). (1983). *Random House book of poetry for children.* New York: Random House.

Prelutsky, J. (1984). *The new kid on the block.* New York: Greenwillow Books.

Prelutsky, J. (1986). *Ride a purple pelican.* New York: Greenwillow Books.

Prelutsky, J. (1988). *Tyrannosaurus was a beast.* New York: Greenwillow Books.

Prelutsky, J. (1989). *Poems of A. Nonny Mouse.* New York: Knopf.

Prelutsky, J. (1990). *Beneath a blue umbrella.* New York: Greenwillow Books.

Prelutsky, J. (1990). *Something big has been here.* New York: Greenwillow Books.

Rawls, W. (1961). *Where the red fern grows.* New York: Bantam.

Seldon, G. (1960). *The cricket in Times Square.* New York: Dell.

Seuss, D. (1963). *Dr. Seuss's A B C.* New York: Random House.

Shaw, N. (1986). *Sheep in a jeep.* Boston: Houghton Mifflin.

Silverstein, S. (1974). *Where the sidewalk ends.* New York: Harper and Row.

Silverstein, S. (1981). *A light in the attic.* New York: Harper & Row.

Steptoe, J. (1987). *Mufaro's beautiful daughters: An African tale.* New York: Scholastic.

Stevenson, R. L. (1885/1981). *A child's garden of verses.* New York: Checkerboard Press, a Division of Macmillan.

Waber, B. (1988). *Ira says goodbye*. Boston: Houghton Mifflin.

Willis, V. (1988). *The secret in the matchbox*. New York: Farrar, Straus & Giroux.

Yep, L. (1989). *The rainbow people*. New York: Harper and Row.

For Additional Reading

Educational Leadership. (1990). Volume 47, Number 4. Entire issue on cooperative learning.

Johnson, D. W., Johnson, R. T., & Holubec, E. (1988). *Cooperation in the classroom*. Edina, MN: Interaction Book Company.

Kimmel, M. M., & Segal, E. (1983). *For reading out loud: A guide to sharing books with children*. New York: Delacorte.

Norton, D. E. (1991). Evaluating and selecting literature for children. In *Through the eyes of a child: An introduction to children's literature* (3rd ed.) (pp. 83–126). New York: Macmillan.

Norton, D. E. (1991). Multicultural literature. In *Through the eyes of a child: An introduction to children's literature* (3rd ed.) (pp. 529–605). New York: Macmillan.

Pearson, P. D. (1985). Changing the face of reading comprehension instruction. *Reading Teacher, 38*, 724–738.

Sloyer, S. (1982). *Readers theatre: Story dramatization in the classroom*. Urbana, IL: National Council of Teachers of English.

Tierney, R. J., Readence, J. E., & Dishner, E. K. (1990). Readers theater. In *Reading strategies and practices: A compendium* (3rd ed.) (pp. 190–195). Boston: Allyn and Bacon.

Trelease, J. (1989). *The new read-aloud handbook*. New York: Penguin.

Walmsley, S. A., & Walp, T. P. (1990). Integrating literature and composing into the language arts curriculum: Philosophy and practice. *Elementary School Journal, 90*(3), 251–274.

References

Allington, R. L. (1977). If they don't read much, how they ever gonna get good? *Journal of Reading, 21*, 57–61.

Allington, R. L. (1983). The reading instruction provided readers of differing reading abilities. *Elementary School Journal, 83*, 548–559.

Anderson, R. C., Hiebert, E. H., Scott, J. A., & Wilkinson, I. A. G. (1985). *Becoming a nation of readers: The report of the Commission on Reading*. Washington, DC: National Institute of Education.

Anderson, R. C., Wilson, P. T., & Fielding, L. G. (1988). Growth in reading and how children spend their time outside of school. *Reading Research Quarterly, 23*(3), 285–303.

Au, K. H. (in press). *Literacy instruction in multicultural settings*.

Beck, I. (1984). Developing comprehension: The impact of the directed reading lesson. In R. C. Anderson, J. Osborn & R. J. Tierney (Eds.), *Learning to read in American schools: Basal readers and content texts* (pp. 3–20). Hillsdale, NJ: Lawrence Erlbaum.

Beck, I. L., Omanson, R. C., & McKeown, M. G. (1982). An instructional redesign of reading lessons: Effects on comprehension. *Reading Research Quarterly, 17*(4), 462–481.

Bridge, C., Winograd, P. N., & Haley, D. (1983). Using predictable materials vs. preprimers to teach beginning sight words. *Reading Teacher, 36*(9), 884–891.

Brophy, J. (1986). *Socializing student motivation to learn.* Research Series No. 169. East Lansing: Michigan State University, Institute for Research on Teaching.

Burns, P. C., Roe, B. D., & Ross, E. P. (1988). *Teaching reading in today's elementary schools* (4th ed.). Boston: Houghton Mifflin.

Center for the Study of Reading. (n.d.). *Suggestions for classroom: Teachers and independent reading.* Urbana: Center for the Study of Reading, University of Illinois.

Children's choices for 1991. (1991). *Reading Teacher, 45,* 128–139.

Clark, C. M. (1984). Teacher planning and reading comprehension. In G. G. Duffy, L. K. Roehler & J. Mason (Eds.), *Comprehension instruction: Perspectives and suggestions* (pp. 58–70). New York: Longman.

Clark, M. M. (1976). *Young fluent readers.* London: Heinemann.

Clay, M. M. (1985). *The early detection of reading difficulties* (3rd ed.). Auckland, New Zealand: Heinemann.

Collins, A., Brown, J. S., & Newman, S. E. (1986). *Cognitive apprenticeship: Teaching the craft of reading, writing and mathematics.* Report No. 6459. Cambridge, MA: BNN Laboratories.

Cooper, J. D. (1986). *Improving reading comprehension.* Boston: Houghton Mifflin.

Cooper, J. D., Warncke, E., Ramstad, P. A., & Shipman, D. (1979). *The what and how of reading instruction.* Columbus: Merrill.

Dressel, J. H. (1990). The effects of listening to and discussing different qualities of children's literature on the narrative writing of fifth graders. *Research in the Teaching of English, 24,* 397–414.

Durkin, D. (1966). *Children who read early.* New York: Teachers College Press.

Durkin, D. (1978). What classroom observations reveal about reading comprehension instruction. *Reading Research Quarterly, 14*(4), 481–533.

Durkin, D. (1981). Reading comprehension instruction in five basal reader series. *Reading Research Quarterly, 16*(4), 515–544.

Durkin, D. (1990). Dolores Durkin speaks on instruction. *Reading Teacher, 43,* 472–476.

Elley, W. B., & Mangubhai, F. (1983). The impact of reading on second language learning. *Reading Research Quarterly, 19*(1), 53–67.

Farris, P. (1987). Promoting family reading through magazine packs. *Reading Teacher, 40,* 825–826.

Feitelson, D., Kita, B., & Goldstein, Z. (1986). Effects of listening to stories on first graders' comprehension and use of language. *Research in the Teaching of English, 20,* 339–356.

Fielding, L. G., Wilson, P. T., & Anderson, R. C. (1986). A new focus on free reading: The role of tradebooks in reading instruction. In T. E. Raphael (Ed.), *Contexts of school-based literacy* (pp. 149–160). New York: Random House.

Goodman, K. S., Freeman, Y. S., Murphy, S., & Shannon, P. (1988). *Report card on basal readers.* New York: Richard C. Owen.

Goodman, K., & Goodman, Y. (1991). Consumer beware! Selecting materials for whole language readers. In K. S. Goodman, L. B. Bird, & Y. M. Goodman (Eds.), *The whole language catalog* (p. 119). Santa Rosa, CA: American School Publishers.

Graves, D. H. (1983). *Writing: Teachers and children at work.* Exeter, NH: Heinemann.

Graves, D., & Hansen, J. (1983). The author's chair. *Language Arts, 60,* 176–182.

Harris, A. J., & Sipay, E. R. (1985). *How to increase reading ability* (8th ed.). New York: Longman.

Harste, J. C., Woodward, V. A., & Burke, C. L. (1984). *Language stories and literacy lessons.* Portsmouth, NH: Heinemann.

Herber, H. L., & Nelson, J. (1975). Questioning is not the answer. *Journal of Reading, 18,* 512–517.

Hillocks, G., Jr. (1987). Synthesis of research on teaching writing. *Educational Leadership, 45,* 71–82.

Hodges, C. A. (1980). Toward a broader definition of comprehension instruction. *Reading Research Quarterly, 15*(2), 299–306.

Holdaway, D. (1979). *The foundation of literacy.* Sydney: Ashton Scholastic, distributed by Heinemann, Portsmouth, NH.

Huck, C. S. (1989). No wider than the heart is wide. In J. Hickman & B. E. Cullinan (Eds.), *Children's literature in the classroom: Weaving Charlotte's web* (pp. 252–262). Needham Heights, MA: Christopher-Gordon.

Klare, G. R. (1984). Readability. In P. D. Pearson (Ed.), *Handbook of reading research* (pp. 681–744). New York: Longman.

Lamme, L. L. (1990). Exploring the world of music through picture books. *Reading Teacher, 44,* 294–300.

McCormick, S. (1977). Should you read aloud to your children? *Language Arts, 54,* 139–143.

McKenzie, M. (1985). *Shared writing. Language matters.* London: Inner London Educational Authority.

Meichenbaum, D. (1985). Teaching thinking: A cognitive behavioral perspective. In S. Chapman, J. Segal, & R. Glaser (Eds.), *Thinking and learning skills: Current research and open questions* (Vol. 2, pp. 407–426). Hillsdale, NJ: Lawrence Erlbaum.

Mooney, M. (1991). Selecting books for use in reading programs. In K. S. Goodman, L. B. Bird, & Y. M. Goodman (Eds.), *The whole language catalog* (p. 121). Santa Rosa, CA: American School Publishers.

Morrow, L. M. (1987). Promoting voluntary reading: The effects of an inner city program in summer day care centers. *Reading Teacher, 41,* 266–274.

Morrow, L. M., & Weinstein, C. S. (1982). Increasing children's use of literature through program and physical design changes. *Elementary School Journal, 83,* 131–137.

Morrow, L. M., & Weinstein, C. S. (1986). Encouraging voluntary reading: The impact of a literature program on children's use of library centers. *Reading Research Quarterly, 21,* 330–346.

Norton, D. E. (1991). *Through the eyes of a child—An introduction to children's literature* (3rd ed.). New York: Macmillan.

Palincsar, A. S., & Brown, A. L. (1986). Interactive teaching to promote independent learning from text. *Reading Teacher, 39*(8), 771–777.

Pappas, C. C., Kiefer, B. Z., Levstik, L. S. (1990). *An integrated language perspective in the elementary school: Theory into action.* New York: Longman.

Paris, S. G., Wasik, B. A., & Turner, J. C. (1991). The development of strategic readers. In R. Barr, M. L. Kamil, P. Mosenthal, & P. D. Pearson (Eds.), *Handbook of reading research* (Vol. 2, pp. 609–640). New York: Longman.

Pearson, P. D. (1985). Changing the face of reading comprehension instruction. *Reading Teacher, 38*, 724–738.

Pearson, P. D., & Dole, J. A. (1987). Explicit comprehension instruction: A review of research and a new conceptualization of instruction. *Elementary School Journal, 88*(2), 151–165.

Recommended readings in literature—Kindergarten through grade eight. (1986). Sacramento: California State Department of Education.

Reutzel, D. R., & Fawson, P. C. (1990). Traveling tales: Connecting parents and children through writing. *Reading Teacher, 44*, 222–227.

Roehler, L. R., & Duffy, G. G. (1991). Teacher's instructional actions. In R. Barr, M. L. Kamil, P. Mosenthal, & P. D. Pearson (Eds.), *Handbook of reading research* (Vol. 2, pp. 861–883). New York: Longman.

Rosenblatt, L. (1938/1983). *Literature as exploration.* New York: Modern Language Association.

Rosenblatt, L. (1978). *The reader, the text and the poem.* Carbondale: Southern Illinois University Press.

Routman, R. (1988). *Transitions: From literature to literacy.* Portsmouth, NH: Heinemann.

Simons, H., & Ammon, P. (1989). Child knowledge and primerese text: Mismatches and miscues. *Research in the Teaching of English, 23*(4), 380–398.

Slavin, R. E. (1990). *Cooperative learning: Theory, research and practice.* Englewood Cliffs, NJ: Prentice-Hall.

Smith, F. (1983). *Essays into literacy.* Portsmouth, NH: Heinemann.

Stauffer, R. G. (1969). *Teaching reading as a thinking process.* New York: Harper & Row.

Strickland, D. S., & Taylor, D. (1989). Family storybook reading: Implications for children, families, and curriculum. In D. S. Strickland & L. M. Morrow (Eds.), *Emerging literacy: Young children learn to read and write* (pp. 27–34). Newark, DE: International Reading Association.

Taylor, B. M., Frye, B. J., & Maruyama, G. M. (1990). Time spent reading and reading growth. *American Educational Research Journal, 27*(2), 351–362.

Taylor, D., & Strickland, D. S. (1986). *Family storybook reading.* Portsmouth, NH: Heinemann.

Teacher's choices for 1991. (1991). *Reading Teacher, 45*, 213–220.

Terry, A. (1974). *Children's poetry preferences: A national survey of upper elementary grades.* Urbana, IL: National Council of Teachers of English.

Thomas, R. L. (1989). Knowing poetry: Choosing poetry for children. In J. Hichman & B. E. Cullinan (Eds.), *Children's literature in the classroom: Weaving Charlotte's web* (pp. 161–172). Needham Heights, MA: Christopher-Gordon.

Tierney, R. J., Readence, J. E., & Dishner, E. K. (1990). *Reading strategies and practices: A compendium* (3rd ed.). Boston: Allyn and Bacon.

Trelease, J. (1989). *The new read-aloud handbook.* New York: Penguin.

Vukelich, C. (1984). Parents' role in the reading process: A review of practical suggestions and ways to communicate with parents. *Reading Teacher, 37,* 472–477.

Walmsley, S. A., & Walp, T. P. (1990). Integrating literature and composing into the language arts curriculum: Philosophy and practice. *Elementary School Journal, 90*(3), 251–274.

Weaver, C. S., III, & Kintsch, W. (1991). Expository text. In R. Barr, M. L. Kamil, P. Mosenthal, & P. D. Pearson (Eds.), *Handbook of reading research* (Vol. 2, pp. 230–245). New York: Longman.

Wells, G. (1990). Creating the conditions to encourage literate thinking. *Educational Leadership, 47*(6), 13–17.

Activating and Developing Prior Knowledge

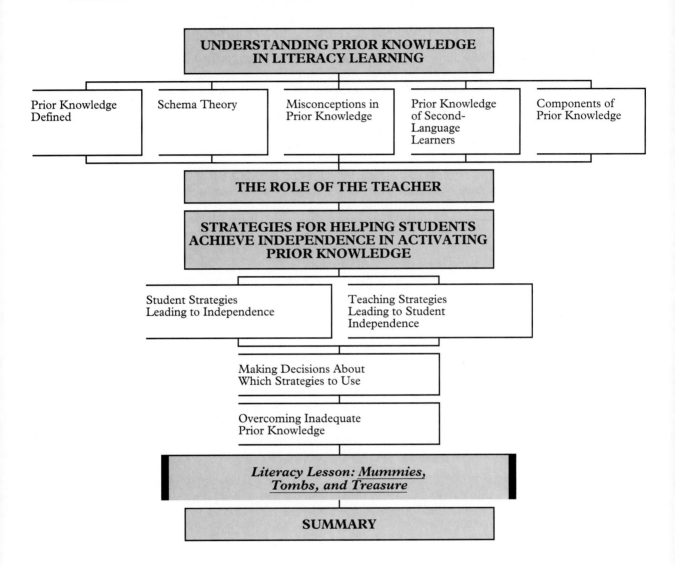

UNDERSTANDING PRIOR KNOWLEDGE
IN LITERACY LEARNING

Prior Knowledge Defined

Schema Theory

Misconceptions in Prior Knowledge

Prior Knowledge of Second-Language Learners

Components of Prior Knowledge

THE ROLE OF THE TEACHER

STRATEGIES FOR HELPING STUDENTS
ACHIEVE INDEPENDENCE IN ACTIVATING
PRIOR KNOWLEDGE

Student Strategies Leading to Independence

Teaching Strategies Leading to Student Independence

Making Decisions About Which Strategies to Use

Overcoming Inadequate Prior Knowledge

Literacy Lesson: Mummies, Tombs, and Treasure

SUMMARY

L et's drop in on a classroom where the teacher is actively engaging students in beginning a unit on Abraham Lincoln.

Mr. Willett had given his class 5 minutes to write what they knew about Abraham Lincoln. Displaying a chart labeled K-W-L (Figure 3.1), he then told the class they were going to begin a thematic unit on Abraham Lincoln. To get started, they were going to use the strategy known as K-W-L to think about what they knew about Lincoln and what they would like to learn about him.

The class was then divided into small groups and asked to use the paragraphs they had written as a basis for brainstorming ideas to go in the "know" column of the K-W-L chart. After about 5 minutes of small-group discussion, Mr. Willett brought the entire group together to summarize what they had listed. One student served as recorder and listed on the chalkboard the points given by various class members.

Mr. Willett could tell by the students' responses that most of them knew a great deal about Lincoln, but he could also tell that some had very little or erroneous knowledge that needed to be expanded and/or corrected.

IN THIS EXAMPLE, Mr. Willett was activating his class's prior knowledge before starting the theme on Abraham Lincoln. Through his observations, he was able to assess how much the students knew and to determine what additional background he needed to develop before introducing the first book that they would read, the Newbery Award winner, *Lincoln: A Photobiography* (Freedman, 1987). Mr. Willett used four different techniques for activating prior knowledge: a quick writing exercise, brainstorming, the K-W-L strategy (Ogle, 1986), and small- and large-group discussion. *All of these strategies will be discussed in detail later in this chapter.*

The importance of prior knowledge to successful literacy learning was established in Chapter 1. Chapter 3 will examine this area in more detail and will focus on techniques and strategies that help students activate and develop their prior knowledge in thematic units and literacy lessons. Throughout this chapter, two major points will be stressed:

- *Purpose*: Students must have a purpose for reading and writing; in part, this purpose is created by activating and developing prior knowledge.
- *Independence*: Students must become independent in activating their own prior knowledge if they are to construct meaning effectively.

All strategies presented in this chapter lead to these two goals.

Figure 3.1 K-W-L Strategy Chart

K	W	L
What we *know* about Abraham Lincoln	What we *want* to learn about Lincoln	What we *learned* about Lincoln

UNDERSTANDING PRIOR KNOWLEDGE IN LITERACY LEARNING

Research over the past two decades has clearly established that the process of constructing meaning through reading, writing, speaking, and listening is based on the prior knowledge that individuals bring to the situation (Adams & Bertram, 1980; Anderson & Pearson, 1984). Tierney and Cunningham (1984) concluded after reviewing extensive research that "intervention research has supported the existence of a causal relationship between background knowledge and comprehension" (p. 612). Similar conclusions have been drawn by more recent researchers, even though there are still many unanswered questions about prior knowledge and literacy learning (Barr, Kamil, Mosenthal, & Pearson, 1991). As was noted in Chapter 1, researchers and educators use the terms *prior knowledge, background, background knowledge or information,* and *world knowledge* interchangeably; in this text the term *prior knowledge* will be used when referring to all of these areas.

Prior Knowledge Defined

The concept of prior knowledge is not new to educators. For many years, it has been recommended that teachers ensure that readers have the appropriate background for reading a given selection because it was felt that such background enhanced learning (Smith, 1965). Essentially, prior knowledge is "the sum of a person's previous learning and development; experience; . . . experiences which precede a learning situation, story, etc." (Harris & Hodges,

1981, p. 29). The information that Mr. Willett gained from his students through quick writing, discussion, and the use of K-W-L constituted their prior knowledge about Abraham Lincoln.

Schema Theory

Our understanding of the importance of prior knowledge in literacy learning has been developed through research based on schema theory, which was introduced in Chapter 1. Schema theory (plural *schemata*) is based on the assumption that individuals develop a cognitive structure of knowledge in their minds (Bartlett, 1932; Rumelhart, 1980). As individuals experience the world, they add new information to their schemata, which are divided into various interrelated categories. One way to picture this more concretely is to think of the mind as a large system of file folders. As new knowledge and information are gained, the mind creates a new file folder or schema or adds the information to an existing schema (Anderson & Pearson, 1984; Rumelhart, 1980). Then, as individuals develop and expand their schemata, they construct meaning by drawing from various schemata and by building connections between them; that is, they make inferences (Anderson & Pearson, 1984). This process goes on continuously while anyone is engaged in literacy tasks. An example will illustrate how the experience of reading expands one's schemata.

Example 3.1

> You are going to read a magazine article about the pleasures of automobile racing. The first thing you do as you begin to read is think about automobile racing and what you know about it. In so doing, you are activating your schemata for automobile racing, which may have been formed over many years of experience. If your schemata for automobile racing include positive, pleasant ideas, you will read the article differently than if they include negative, unpleasant ideas. If you have no schema or very limited schemata for automobile racing, you will begin to form a schema as you read the article, and you will relate the information you gain to any other schemata you have about cars. For example, you may have a schema that relates auto racing to danger; if you read an article about how training reduces the risks or dangers, you may form a new and broadened schema. Throughout the process of reading, you constantly take the information gained from the text and relate it to an existing schema, thus expanding that schema, or you form a new schema (see Figure 3.2).

Schema theory contends that individuals understand what they read only as it relates to what they already know. Anderson, Reynolds, Schallert, and Goetz (1977) demonstrated this very clearly through their research. They asked

Figure 3.2   Reader Interacting with the Text to Activate and Expand Schema

students in an educational psychology class and students in a weightlifting class to read the following passage and tell what they thought it was about. Read this passage for yourself and see what you think:

> *Rocky slowly got up from the mat and planned his escape. He hesitated a moment and thought. Things were not going well. What bothered him the most was being held, especially since the charge against him had been weak. He considered his present situation. The lock that held him was strong but he thought he could break it. He knew, however, that his timing had to be perfect. Rocky was aware that it was because of his early roughness that he had been penalized so severely—much too severely from his point of view. The situation was becoming frustrating; the pressure had been grinding on him far too long. He was being ridden unmercifully. Rocky was getting angry now. He felt he was ready to make his move. He knew that his success or failure depended on what he did in the next few seconds. (p. 372)*

What was the focus of this paragraph? What topic came to your mind as you read? The educational psychology students tended to interpret the passage as a prison escape, whereas the weightlifting students interpreted it in relation to a wrestling match. This research bears out the premise of schema theory and shows that individuals construct meanings in light of their prior knowledge and interests. This adds additional support to the powerful premise that the construction of meaning is an individual and personal matter (Rosenblatt, 1938/1983).

Schema theory and the research carried out within this framework clearly show that prior knowledge is an important element in the process of constructing meaning. Research in emergent literacy further supports this conclusion (Sulzby, 1989). For in-depth reading on schema theory, see "For Additional Reading" at the conclusion of this chapter.

Misconceptions in Prior Knowledge

Although research has documented the significance of prior knowledge in students' abilities to construct meaning, there is also evidence that some students bring incomplete or erroneous ideas to certain learning tasks. When this happens, of course, these misconceptions can interfere with meaning construction (Driver & Erickson, 1983; Lipson, 1982, 1983), and numerous researchers have attempted to look at how this happens (Alvermann, Smith & Readence, 1985; Dole & Smith, 1989; Hynd & Alvermann, 1986; Pace, Marshall, Horowitz, Lipson & Lucido, 1989). In all instances, they found that an individual's interpretation of the text was definitely influenced by erroneous or incomplete prior knowledge. Various attempts to alter or change the students' misconceptions have met with some success (Alvermann & Hynd, 1987; Dole & Smith, 1989; Maria, 1988). Although most of this research has been conducted using scientific material, it is assumed that misconceptions can interfere with the construction of meaning in narrative and expository texts as well. Strategies for overcoming misconceptions will be discussed later in this chapter.

Prior Knowledge of Second-Language Learners

In classrooms throughout the country, many children are learning English as a second language; such children are often referred to as ESL (English as a Second Language) students or LEP (Limited English Proficiency) students. More recently, they have been called Students Acquiring English because that is what they are actually doing and this label has a more positive connotation.

Regardless of the term used, these are all students whose native language is not English. Some may have learned to read in their native language. For example, a Hispanic child may have learned to speak and read first in Spanish. It has been shown that second-language learners are able to learn to read in their native language and English at the same time (Barrera, 1983). They develop literacy and the ability to construct meaning through essentially the same process as first-language learners, the only differences being those of language structure, knowledge of the language, and cultural prior knowledge (Weber, 1991). Since second-language learners have an extensive base of prior knowledge that has not been developed around English and the cultural traditions of English, special attenion needs to be given to their prior knowledge.

Rigg and Allen (1989) have given five principles regarding the literacy development of second-language learners.

1. *People who are learning another language are, first of all, people.*
2. *Learning a language means learning to do the things you want to do with people who speak that language.*
3. *A person's second language, like the first, develops globally, not linearly.*
4. *Language develops best in a variety of rich contexts.*
5. *Literacy is part of language, so writing and reading develop alongside speaking and listening. (p. viii)*

You will notice that these principles do not differ significantly from what has already been said about helping all students learn to construct meaning. Second-language learners bring their own language and prior knowledge to the classroom, which we must build on and expand. As Rigg and Allen (1989) conclude, "We should offer our second-language students a rich bath of language, not a string of language beads, one bead at a time" (p. xi). For further reading on this topic, see Rigg and Allen (1989) and Au (in press) listed under "For Additional Reading" at the end of this chapter.

What exactly does all of this mean for you as a teacher? Given the vast quantity of research related to schema theory and prior knowledge, you need to keep the following points in mind as you develop and conduct your literacy program:

- Prior knowledge is crucial to the successful construction of meaning for *all* learners.
- Some students will have incomplete or erroneous prior knowledge related to a topic; it is therefore important to assess a student's state of knowledge, if possible, before any learning experience.
- When students have erroneous or incomplete prior knowledge, it is possible to alter it and help them construct meaning more successfully.

The remainder of this chapter will focus on how to support students in achieving independence in activating their own prior knowledge.

Components of Prior Knowledge

Within the literacy program, prior knowledge needs to be thought of in two ways: as overall prior knowledge and as text-specific or topic-specific prior knowledge.

Figure 3.3 Overall Prior Knowledge Development

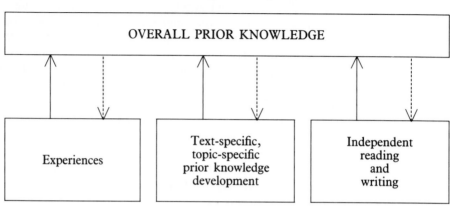

Overall prior knowledge is the entire base of knowledge that students possess. It develops as a result of all their accumulated experiences both in and out of school, such as being read to, taking trips, watching television, or seeing movies. Since this development is facilitated by extensive reading and writing, the *independent reading and writing* component of the literacy program is critical for expanding this knowledge base (Center for the Study of Reading, n.d.). The more students read and write, the more extensive prior knowledge they have, which in turn improves their ability to construct meaning. (For a detailed discussion of independent reading and writing, see Chapter 2.)

Text-specific or *topic-specific prior knowledge* is the specific information needed for a particular theme or experience. For example, if students are going to read *The Boys' War* (Murphy, 1990), a book about the Civil War and the experiences of the young boys who fought in it, they will need specific information about the Civil War itself as well as knowledge about the structure of this type of text. Development of text-specific or topic-specific prior knowledge along with independent reading and writing and many other experiences expands students' overall prior knowledge and gives them a stronger base to use in constructing meaning (see Figure 3.3).

There are two major components of text-specific or topic-specific prior knowledge that you need to be concerned about as you develop thematic units and literacy lessons: knowledge about the type of text—understanding that a story has certain elements—and knowledge about the topic—for example, having some knowledge about mountains before reading a book on mountains. Both play an important role in helping students construct meaning (Paris, Wasik, & Turner, 1991).

Figure 3.4 A Story Grammar

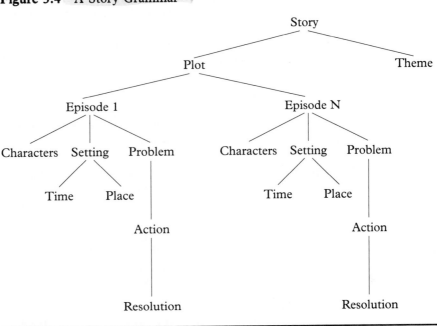

Knowledge About the Text

As you will recall from Chapter 1, there are two basic types of text—narrative and expository. Since students need some knowledge about both types of text, it is important for you to have some basic understanding about them.

Narrative Texts. Narrative texts tell a story and are organized into a sequential pattern that includes a beginning, a middle, and an end. Within this pattern, any given narrative may be composed of several different episodes, each consisting of characters, a setting, a problem, action, and a resolution of the problem (the outcome). These elements are the story's grammar or basic plan. Figure 3.4 illustrates how they fit together, with episode N representing any number of episodes that might be included in the story. Such a graphic representation is called a story map, of which there are many different forms (Freedle, 1979). The exact map for a story depends on the story's structure.

The *theme* of a story is the basic idea—stated or unstated—about which the whole story is written. In good literature the theme is most often unstated, requiring the reader to infer it. The *plot* is the way in which the story is organized; it is made up of episodes. The *setting* is the place and time at which the story occurs. The *characters* are the people or animals who carry out the action in a story. The *problem* is the situation or situations that initiate or lead to other events in the story. Finally, the *action* is what happens as a result of the problem; it is composed of events that lead to the solution of the problem, which is called the *resolution* or outcome.

Let's consider a story that you are likely to know—"The Three Pigs"—to illustrate the elements of narrative text. A story map of "The Three Pigs" is shown in Figure 3.5. As you can see by studying this map, you need only the essential elements to understand the story. Each episode leads to the next, leading the reader to the overall understanding, or the theme, of the story. Notice that three of the episodes have essentially the same problem, but the third ends with a different resolution.

Expository Texts.   Expository texts present information organized around main ideas. These are the types of materials commonly found in informational books, textbooks, newspapers, and magazines. Students generally have more difficulty reading expository texts than narrative texts because they have had less experience with them and because these texts do not follow a set beginning-middle-end pattern; instead, how the information is organized depends on its type and purpose. There are five frequently used patterns of expository writing (Meyer, 1975; Meyer & Freedle, 1984):

- *Description* presents information about a particular topic or gives characteristics of the topic. Unlike the other types of expository text structure, descriptive passages do not provide readers with clue words to aid in comprehension; therefore, readers must use the basic strategies they have learned for noting details and selecting the important information from the passage. However, the structure of descriptive passages can help the reader anticipate the type of content that is likely to follow.
- *Collection* presents a number of ideas or descriptions in a related group. Since the writer is presenting lists of related points, this structure is often called a listing or sequence, and the author frequently uses clue words such as *first, second, next,* and *finally* to introduce the points. When reading this type of passage, readers must be able to infer the relationship between the listed points and the overall topic. In this process, it is important to note details and to identify the sequence of ideas in the passage.
- The *causation*, or cause-effect, type of expository structure presents ideas so that a causal relationship is either stated or implied. This structure is frequently used in science, social studies, and mathematics textbooks and in newspaper and magazine articles. The author often uses such clue words and phrases as *therefore, consequently, because, as a result of, since,* or *the reasons for.* When reading text with this type of structure, the reader must be able to identify the elements that are being related and either recognize or infer the cause-effect relationships.
- The *response* structure presents a problem, question, or remark followed by a solution, answer, or reply. This type of structure is often used in

Figure 3.5 Story Map of "The Three Pigs"

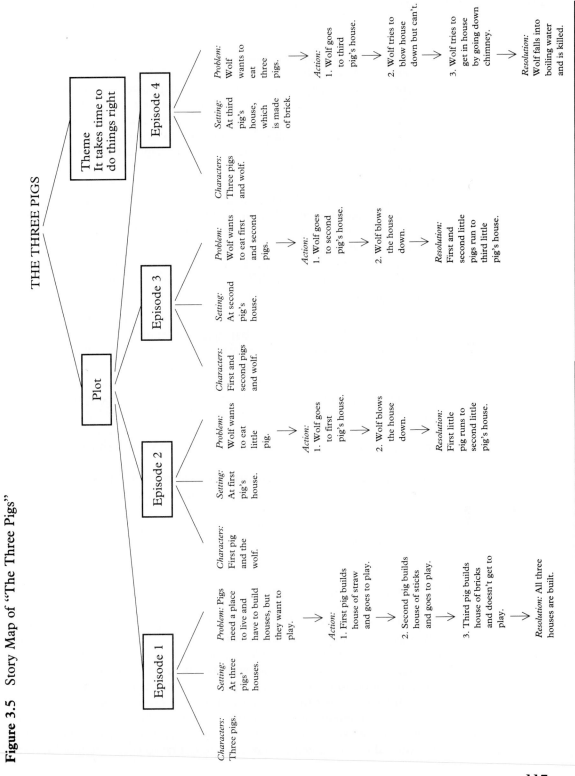

mathematics, science, and social studies. Sometimes (as in mathematics) the author presents the problem but the reader is expected to provide the solution. The author may use clue words and phrases such as *the problem is*, *the question is*, *one reason for the problem*, *a solution*, or *one answer is*, but these do not always appear. When an author does not clearly identify the problem, the reader must look for clues to help clarify it. Then, after identifying a problem, the reader should anticipate that a solution will follow.

- *Comparison* requires the reader to note the likenesses and differences between two or more objects or ideas. This type of structure is frequently found in social studies and science texts, and the author uses clue words and phrases such as *like*, *unlike*, *resemble*, *different from*, *same as*, *alike*, or *similar to* to make comparisons. When reading comparison structures, the reader must be able to recognize the objects or ideas being compared and the points of similarity or difference between and among them. Often these will not be directly stated.

Table 3.1 presents an example of each of the five types of expository text structure. Remember, however, that one paragraph is not sufficient to determine the overall structure of a particular text. Moreover, within a given expository text, several of these structures may be present.

Students do not need to understand all of the technical elements of narrative text or the different types of expository texts. However, they do need to know *enough about text structure to know the basic differences between narrative and expository texts and to realize how this will help them construct meaning*. This knowledge is gained through experiences with reading and writing and through minilessons, if needed.

This limited knowledge of text structure will assist you in helping students activate the appropriate type of prior knowledge (discussed in the remainder of this chapter); it will also help you identify which words are key to understanding a selection (see Chapter 4) and the types of questions to ask when you use teacher-guided reading (see Chapter 2).

Knowledge About the Topic

The second component of text-specific or topic-specific prior knowledge is knowledge about the topic of the theme or book to be read, which includes the key concepts or ideas relative to the topic and key terminolgy. This knowledge must be activated along with knowledge of text structure if it is to be effective in improving students' abilities to construct meaning.

If you were reading the book *Ronald Morgan Goes to Bat* (Giff, 1988), at first glance you might think that the prior knowledge that needed to be activated was knowledge of baseball, but this book is narrative. The problem is that Ronald really wanted to play baseball but he couldn't catch or hit, even

Table 3.1 Examples of Expository Text Structures

Expository Structure	*Example*
Description	The tiger is the master of the Indian jungle. It stalks its prey in deadly silence. For half an hour or more, it carefully watches and then slowly, placing one foot softly in front of the other, closes in.
Collection	As master of the Indian jungle, the male tiger plays many roles. First, he is the hunter of prey who stalks in deadly silence. He is the beauty of the jungle, an expert at doing nothing in order to rest to be ready for his hunt. Finally, the lord of the jungle is the active seeker of mates, who begins his mating with a nuzzle but ends with a roar.
Causation or cause-effect	We observed the tiger from our vehicle as it stalked the herd of deer. As a result of the slight noise from our running camera, the tiger turned and knew we were there. This didn't stop it from returning to its intended prey. Slowly and carefully it moved forward, not making a sound. The deer were initially unaware of its presence, but because of the shifting winds they caught the tiger's scent. This was enough to scare them away.
Response, problem-solution, question-answer, or remark-reply	One problem to be resolved in tiger watching is transportation. How is it possible for observers to get close enough to a tiger without scaring it away or being attacked? Nature has helped solve this problem by making the tiger and the elephant friends. It is possible for an elephant carrying several people to get very near a tiger without even being noticed. If it weren't for this natural friendship, tiger watching would be virtually impossible.
Comparison	The power of the great tiger is like that of no other animal in the jungle. With one steady lunge, it can destroy its prey, seemingly without any effort at all. Unlike other predators, the tiger basks in the sun after an attack in order to prepare for its next kill. The actions of the tiger resemble those of no other animal in the Indian jungle.

though he was enthusiastic about the game. The prior knowledge activation that is most likely to improve students' abilities to construct meaning from this text must focus on what it's like to really want to do something even though one is not very good at it. This is what Beck (1984) refers to as schema-directed prior knowledge development. If the students had been preparing to read an expository text about baseball, the focus of the prior knowledge activation and development would have been the main ideas of the book, probably ideas related to the game of baseball. Strictly topical prior knowledge activation and development without consideration of the actual structure of the text does not improve students' abilities to construct meaning (Beck, Omanson & McKeown, 1982).

The prior knowledge needs for narrative text are determined by the story line. The needs for expository text are determined by the topic, main ideas, and structure of the text.

Suppose your students were going to read an article entitled "Birds in Winter," about the survival of birds during a blizzard. In order to construct meaning from this article, students must understand the concepts of *survival* and *blizzard*. Study examples 3.2 and 3.3 to see the correct and incorrect ways of activating prior knowledge to help students more effectively construct meaning as they read the article.

Example 3.2

Correct Method of Activating Prior Knowledge (schema directed to help reader relate background to the selection)

Today we are going to read the article "Birds in Winter." Before we read it, I want you to think about some important ideas that will help you understand what you read. From the title, what would you say this article is going to be about? (Record student responses; discuss them.) This article is about how birds survive during a blizzard. (Relate the students' predictions to surviving in a blizzard.) What is a blizzard? (Students respond. Write a sentence on the chalkboard that contains the word *blizzard*, and discuss its meaning.) What does it mean to survive in a blizzard? What kind of problems might birds have surviving during a blizzard? Discuss these questions; list students' responses on the board and discuss them. Add your own points to the discussion. Conclude the discussion by developing a list of points about how birds survive in a blizzard, for example:

1. A blizzard is a bad snowstorm with high winds.
2. Birds could have many problems surviving in a blizzard. These could include

   getting food.
   not freezing to death.
   having water to drink.
   having a place to sleep that is protected from the wind.

Notice that the discussion in Example 3.3 is topical and general. It does not include background development related to the main point or key concepts of the article. The discussion in the first example, in contrast, clearly requires

Example 3.3

> **Incorrect Method of Activating Prior Knowledge (typical of what has been found in basal readers)**
>
> Today we are going to read the article "Birds in Winter." Have you ever seen birds during the winter? What kinds of birds do you usually see in winter? How do birds get food in winter? (The discussion continues in this manner.)

students to use whatever past experiences or schemata they have developed about birds and winter to make predictions. The teacher develops what students already know by relating that information to the concepts of *survival* and *blizzard*. Key-concept vocabulary is developed within the context of the background development. Finally, the teacher guides the students in summarizing the key points from the background development activity to make sure that they have a schema for reading the article that relates directly to its main point.

THE ROLE OF THE TEACHER

When you are using thematic units and literacy lessons within the literacy program, it is important for you to think about two things in relation to prior knowledge:

1. What prior knowledge probably needs to be activated and/or developed for the overall theme, for each book that is to be read during the theme, and for writing that is to be done?
2. How independent are your students in using strategies to activate their own prior knowledge?

To make the first decision effectively, you must consider three elements: (1) the theme goals, (2) the theme topic, and (3) the literature.

You begin by considering what you want your students to accomplish in relation to the theme. This constitutes your theme goals related to students' attitudes and habits and their ability to construct meaning. (See Chapter 2 for a discussion of goals for thematic units.)

Next, you think about the topic of the theme. What are the big ideas or concepts that students need to understand? For example, if you are starting a theme on science fiction, do students know what science fiction is, and have they had prior experiences with it?

Then you think about each book to be read in your chosen theme. Are the books narrative or expository? What is the story line for the narratives? What are the main ideas of the expository texts? Making these decisions will help you determine the prior knowledge that is most likely to help students effectively construct meaning.

To judge the students' independence, you must think about them in relation to the theme goals, the topic, the literature to be read, and their ability to use various strategies. You can make this assessment by observing your students and by using the strategies and techniques suggested in the next section of this chapter. It is not necessary to make the assessment of students' prior knowledge something separate from instruction. *Good instruction incorporates assessment, and every instructional activity can also be used for assessment.* Therefore, the assessment of prior knowledge becomes a natural part of instruction.

Holmes and Roser (1987) have identified and compared five different techniques for assessing prior knowledge during instruction:

- *Free recall*: "Tell me what you know about _____."
- *Word association*: "When you hear the words *thief, stolen,* and *detective,* what do you think of?"
- *Recognition*: Display the following key terms (phrases or sentences may be used) and ask students to tell which they think may be related to the book they are about to read, *The Polar Express* (Van Allsburg, 1985): *train, North Pole, wagon, train, conductor, sand, snow.*
- *Structured question*: In preparation for reading the book *Martin Luther King, Jr.: Free at Last* (Adler, 1986), ask students a set of prepared questions that will help you assess prior knowledge: "Who was Martin Luther King, Jr.?" "What was Martin Luther King's concern in life?" "How did Martin Luther King try to reach his goal in life?"
- *Unstructured discussion*: "We are going to read about outer space. What do you know about it?"

Holmes and Roser (1987) found the last procedure, unstructured discussion, to be *least effective and useful* for assessing prior knowledge. Note that each of these techniques is designed to activate as well as assess prior knowledge; assessment is discussed in more detail in Chapter 10.

One issue that concerns most teachers is how to assess and develop each individual student's prior knowledge when working with many students at the same time. It may not be possible to know everything about every student's prior knowledge of a particular theme, but you can get a good sense of what the group knows and the group's level of independence by using the types of teaching strategies suggested in the next section and by helping students develop independence in activating their own prior knowledge. The sample lesson presented at the conclusion of this chapter illustrates the process of selecting prior knowledge for a theme and for one book. You might want to look at that lesson now before completing the remainder of the chapter to get an overview of how the lesson functions (see page 169).

STRATEGIES FOR HELPING STUDENTS ACHIEVE INDEPENDENCE IN ACTIVATING PRIOR KNOWLEDGE

Studies support the idea that prior knowledge activation and development can improve the construction of meaning for students, but they do not give us any clear and absolute guidelines to follow in exactly how to do this (Langer, 1981, 1984; Tierney & Cunningham, 1984). There are many ways to help learners become more strategic and independent readers (Paris, Wasik & Turner, 1991). Within the framework of the thematic unit and literacy lesson, there are three places where prior knowledge activation and development might occur:

1. When introducing the theme, at which time the focus is on the broad concepts and ideas needed to understand the theme
2. When each piece of literature is introduced within the lessons
3. Throughout the theme when you observe that certain students need more prior knowledge to better understand what they are reading or writing

This section of the chapter will present student and teaching strategies that can be used to activate and develop prior knowledge in various places throughout the thematic unit. A strategy is a plan selected deliberately to accomplish a particular goal (Paris, Lipson & Wixson, 1983; Paris, Wasik & Turner, 1991). When students reach the point where they can use a strategy automatically, they have achieved independence in its use. A student strategy is one that students can use on their own to construct meaning. A teaching strategy is a plan or activity that can be used by the teacher to accomplish a desired outcome.

Student Strategies Leading to Independence

Two basic strategies that students can use to activate their prior knowledge and to set their own purposes for reading are preview and predict and K-W-L. Table 3.2 presents an overview of these strategies and indicates when they should be used.

Preview and Predict

Description.   Preview and predict combines the processes of previewing and predicting, both of which have been shown to be effective in helping students construct meaning. (Graves & Cooke, 1980; Graves, Cooke & LaBerge, 1983; Fielding, Anderson & Pearson, 1990; Hansen, 1981). Students look over the material to be read and then predict what they think will happen (narrative text) or what they will learn (expository text). This is the first step of

---

Table 3.2 Student Strategies for Activating and Developing Prior Knowledge

Strategy	Type of Text	Comments
Preview and predict	Narrative or expository	For all students; variations may be used to increase motivation and interest in using the strategy.
• Story map prediction	Narrative	
• Preview and self-question	Expository	
K-W-L	Expository	For all students; good for introducing a thematic unit.

---

inferencing, which is ongoing in the process of constructing meaning. After completing the reading, students decide whether or not their predictions have been confirmed, verified, or changed.

Procedures.   Students begin by reading the title of what they are going to read. Then they look at the pictures or illustrations to get a sense of what is going to be covered. They also need to decide whether this is a story or informational text. Using their prior knowledge and the information gained from their preview, students then predict what will happen or what they will learn. For beginning readers and primary children, the preview should be very simple, focusing on the title and illustrations. Middle-grade and junior-high and middle-school students can do more sophisticated previews by reading the first few paragraphs of the text and/or captions under the illustrations.

After completing the preview, students read to see if their predictions are verified. It is important to stress that predictions are not necessarily all right or all wrong; students will be constantly thinking about their predictions and changing them as they read (or monitoring their reading). See Chapter 8 for a discussion of monitoring strategies.

One effective way to help students learn and remember to use this as well as other strategies is to display a strategy poster (Paris, Cross & Lipson, 1984). Figure 3.6 presents a strategy poster for preview and predict. The wording on the poster should be adjusted for different grade levels. All strategies must be modeled if they are to be learned effectively (Pressley et al., 1990). Modeling is discussed in detail in Chapter 8.

When to Use.   Research has shown that the preview and predict strategy is effective with narrative text, but it can also be used with expository text. As students begin to use the strategy independently, be sure to distinguish between

Figure 3.6   Poster for Preview and Predict Strategy

the two types of text. Preview and predict is most effective when you think that students have some knowledge of the topic. With second-language learners or students having difficulty constructing meaning, this strategy works better under the teacher's direction and/or in combination with another strategy for activating prior knowledge. A limited amount of research has suggested that, generally speaking, any type of previewing strategy is more effective in helping students recall story information when it is carried out with teacher guidance (Neuman, 1988). This is most likely to be true when students are just beginning to learn the strategy.

Assessment Value.   By observing students' responses during the preview and predict process, you should be able to tell the status of their prior knowledge before reading a text. From this information you can decide on the need for additional prior knowledge development activities.

Discussion.   The preview and predict strategy will help students activate their prior knowledge and set their own purposes for reading. The real power of this strategy will come when students use it on their own. However, students may not see its importance and refuse to use it. Therefore, as you teach this strategy, it is critical to discuss and show students its importance. This is most likely to happen through repeated successful opportunities to use the strategy. The preview portion of the strategy may be used alone.

One variation of preview and predict is story map prediction, which is specifically for narrative texts. Training in the use of story maps has been shown to be effective in helping students improve their comprehension (Pressley et al., 1990). Figure 3.7 presents a strategy poster for story map prediction.

Beginning students should focus on one or two elements of the story map in making their predictions. As they become more sophisticated, they can focus on more elements. In all instances, it is better not to try to have students predict all the action in a story because this is usually not possible from an initial preview; furthermore, if it could be done, there would be little point to reading the story.

Another variation, preview and self-question, is designed to use with expository texts. Again, students preview the text and pose questions they think they can answer in their reading. Figure 3.8 presents a strategy poster for preview and self-question, which is similar to the question-generating strategy discussed in Chapter 8.

K-W-L Strategy

Description.   K-W-L is another strategy for activating students' prior knowledge and helping them determine their purpose for reading expository texts. It requires students to focus on three questions, two before they read and one

Figure 3.7 Poster for Story Map Prediction Strategy

STORY MAP PREDICTION

BEFORE READING

1. This is a story. What can I learn about the parts of the story by previewing?

STORY MAP

Setting: _Time_ _Place_

Characters:

Problem:

Action:

Outcome:

2. I predict...

DURING READING

3. Am I confirming my predictions? Do I need to change my predictions?

AFTER READING

4. What were the parts of the story? Were my predictions verified or changed?

Figure 3.8   Poster for Preview and Self-Question Strategy

Figure 3.9   K-W-L Strategy Sheet

K-W-L Strategy

1. K—What I *know*	W—What I *want* to find out	L—What I *learned* and still need to learn

2. Categories of information I expect to use

A.   E.
B.   F.
C.   G.
D.

after they read: What I *know* (K), What I *want* to learn (W), and What I *learned* and still need to learn (L). This strategy, developed by Ogle (1986), is the one that Mr. Willett was using at the beginning of this chapter. The two questions before reading help students activate their prior knowledge and set their purposes for reading by raising questions that they want to answer. The driving force behind this strategy is the students and their ideas and questions.

Procedures.   Each student has a worksheet like the one shown in Figure 3.9. For the first two steps, the teacher leads students in a discussion of the topic relative to the book they are going to read. During the last step, students write down their answers to the questions posed before reading.

1. *Step K—What I know* begins by students brainstorming what they know about the topic. In keeping with the need to have schema-directed prior knowledge activation and development, the teacher selects a topic specifically related to the main ideas and key concepts of the material students will read. Ogle (1986) states the following:

   > When the class will read about sea turtles, use the words *sea turtles* as the stimulus, not "What do you know about animals in the sea?" or "Have you ever been to the ocean?" A general discussion of enjoyable experiences on the beach may never elicit the pertinent schemata. . . . If there appears to be little knowledge of sea turtles in your students' experiences, then ask the next more general question, "What do you know about turtles?" (p. 565)

   Students record what they know on their worksheet and add to it as they share their ideas. Meanwhile, the teacher should also record these ideas on a larger version of the worksheet on the chalkboard, chart, or overhead projector. In order to broaden and deepen students' thinking during the discussion, Ogle suggests that the teacher ask students such questions as "Where did you learn that?" or "How might you prove it?" When disagreement occurs, students must look for answers in the reading. If they seem to have little knowledge about the topic, ask more specific questions to draw out what information they do have.

The second part of the brainstorming involves the identification of *categories of information* that might be found in the material they will read. The teacher might ask students to look over their list of what they know to see if any of the items fit into categories of information that might be found in their reading: for example, "foods turtles eat" or "use of sea turtles by man." Throughout all this brainstorming, interest and excitement increase as students begin to raise many questions.

2. *Step W—What I want to learn* is a natural outgrowth of step K. As students continue to share ideas, areas of uncertainty or lack of knowledge will arise, and you can then help them turn these into questions that may be answered by reading the text. As the discussion continues, students may think of other questions about sea turtles. Record all questions on the group chart. Just before the students are ready to read, ask them to write several questions on their worksheet that *they* want answered. This step helps student set their purpose for reading. If the text that students are to read is long or complex, you may preview it with them before they read to help them get a sense of it. Sometimes you will want to have students read the text in parts, depending on the text and the students' abilities.

3. *Step L—What I learned* requires students to write the answers to their questions after reading; this helps them determine which questions they still need to answer or if they have additional questions. It also helps to take students beyond the reading of a single selection.

The following transcript of a lesson involving K-W-L shows the type of interaction that takes place (Ogle, 1986, pp. 567–569). The italicized annotations have been added by this author to draw attention to what is happening in the lesson.

(Starting the K-step. Teacher also helps students relate to information they already have.)

Teacher: Today we're going to read another article about animals. This one is about a special kind of spider—the Black Widow. Before we begin the article, let's think about what we already know about Black Widows. Or if you aren't familiar with this kind of spider, think about some things you know about spiders in general, and we can then see if those are also true for the Black Widow. (Teacher writes *Black Widow spider* on the board and waits while students think about their knowledge of spiders. Next she elicits ideas from children and writes their contributions on the board.)

(Students interact.)

Tony: Spiders have six legs.

Susan: They eat other insects.

Eddie: I think they're big and dangerous spiders.

(Teacher directs and deepens thinking.)

Teacher: Can you add more about what you mean when you say they're big and dangerous?

Eddie: They, they, I think they eat other spiders. I think people are afraid of them, too.

Steph: They spin nests or webs to catch other insects in.

Tom: My cousin got stung by one once and almost died.

(Teacher focuses responses.)

Teacher: You mean they can be dangerous to people?

Tom: Yah, my cousin had to go to the hospital.

(Teacher draws in other students.)

Teacher: Does anyone else know more about the Black Widow? Tammy?

Tammy: I don't think they live around here. I've never heard of anyone being stung by one.

Teacher: Where do Black Widows live? Does anyone know? (She waits.) What else do we know about spiders?

John: I think I saw a TV show about them once. They have a special mark on their back. I think it's a blue triangle or circle, or something like that. If people look, they can tell if the spider's a Black Widow or not.

Teacher: Does anyone else recall anything more about the way they look? (She waits.) Look at what we've already said about these spiders. Can you think of other information we should add?

John: I think they kill their babies or men spiders. I'm not sure which.

(Teacher focuses students to begin to think about sources of information.)

Teacher: Do you remember where you learned that?

John: I think I read an article once.

(Beginning to think about questions.)

Teacher: OK, let's add that to our list. Remember, everything on the list we aren't sure of we can double check when we read.

(Teacher directly focuses on categories of information.)

Teacher: Anything more you think we should know about these spiders? (She waits.) OK, before we read this article let's think awhile about the kinds or categories of information that are likely to be included. Look at the list of things we already know or have questions about. Which of the categories of information have we already mentioned?

Peter: We mentioned how they look.

(Teacher informally models the concept of categories of information.)

Teacher: Yes, we said they're big and have six legs. And someone said they think Black Widows have a colored mark on them. Good, description is one of the main categories of information we want to learn about when we read about animals or insects. What other categories of information have we mentioned that should be included?

Anna: Where they live; but we aren't sure.

Teacher: Good, we should find out where they live. What other kinds of information should we expect to learn from the article? Think about what kinds of information we've learned from other articles about animals.

Diane: We want to know what kind of homes they make.

Raul: What do they eat?

Andy: How they protect themselves.

Cara: How do they have babies? How many do they have?

(Focus shifts to more questions to be answered.)

Teacher: Good thinking. Are there other categories of information we expect to learn about? (She waits.) We've thought about what we already know and what kinds of information we're likely to learn from an article on Black Widow spiders. Now what are some of the questions we want to have answered? I know we had some things we weren't sure about, like where these spiders live. What are some of the things you'd like to find out when we read?

Cara: I want to know how many baby spiders get born.

Rico: Do Black Widows really hurt people? I never heard of that, and my dad knows a lot about spiders.

Andy: Why are they called Black Widows? What's a widow?

(Students identify their own specific questions.)

Teacher: Good question! Does anyone know what a widow is? Why would this spider be called a "Black Widow"? (After eliciting questions from several students, the teacher asks each child to write their own questions on their worksheet.) What are the questions you are most interested in having answered? Write them down now. As you read, look for the answers and jot them down on your worksheet as you go, or other information you don't want to forget. (The students read the article.)

(Teacher encourages personal response to the article and gets students to think about what they have learned.)

Teacher: How did you like this article? What did you learn?

Raul: The Black Widow eats her husband and sometimes her babies. Yuck! I don't think I like that kind of spider!

Steph: They can live here—it says they live in all parts of the United States.

Andy: They can be recognized by an hourglass that is red or yellow on the abdomen.

(Focus on vocabulary development and expansion.)

Teacher: What is another word for *abdomen*? (She waits.) Sara, please look up the word *abdomen*. Let's find out where the hourglass shape is located. While Sara is looking the word up, let's check what we learned against the questions we wanted answered. Are there some questions that didn't get answered? What more do we want to know?

(The discussion continues in this manner.)

When to Use.   As has already been noted, K-W-L should be used with expository texts. Even though the research using this strategy has involved students in the middle grades, it could be used with students at any level. Primary children and students experiencing difficulty constructing meaning may need a more simplified version focusing just on the K-W-L without thinking about sources of information. This strategy is a good way to initiate a thematic unit because it sets students up to continue to read several selections on a given topic. It is also useful when reading chapters in textbooks such as science, social studies, or health.

All students will profit from using this strategy; because it is so interactive, it gives students many opportunities to learn from each other. K-W-L is especially strong for second-language learners and students experiencing difficulty constructing meaning because it immerses them into a natural discussion and offers a strong scaffold provided by teacher support and student interaction. Sometimes it will be necessary to incorporate other teaching strategies such as previewing and the use of concrete materials to further develop prior knowledge.

Assessment Value.   K-W-L affords many opportunities to assess students' prior knowledge during all three steps. During the K and W steps, you can tell whether students have prior knowledge relative to the topic and how accurate it is. During the L step, you can tell whether students have gained new knowledge and how well they have integrated that knowledge with what they already know.

Discussion.   K-W-L is based on a sound theoretical research base (Ogle, 1986). However, additional research evaluating its effectiveness is still needed.

It is necessary to model the use of the strategy for students in its initial stages. (See Chapter 8.) Repeated opportunities to use the strategy under teacher direction are important.

K-W-L can become an independent student strategy after students have had much experience with it. Even though it was designed as a teaching strategy, students can use it as an independent study strategy working alone

Figure 3.10   K-W-L Strategy Poster

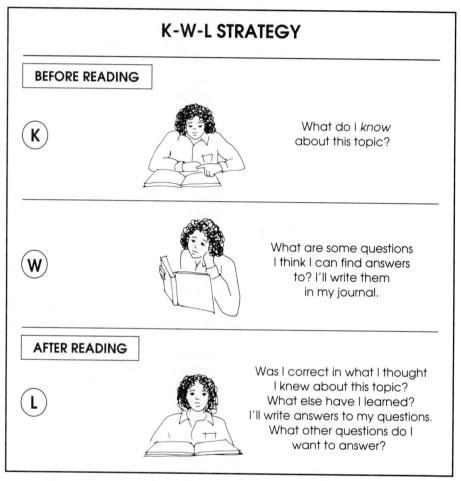

or cooperatively. A poster like the one shown in Figure 3.10 can be displayed to help students achieve independence in using this strategy.

Both student strategies presented, preview and predict and K-W-L, are sound approaches to helping students construct meaning. They foster student ownership of learning and promote and support meaning construction by helping students take what they know and relate it to what they are reading, writing, or thinking. As students become independent in using both strategies, they will be able to call up their own prior knowledge and set their own purpose(s) for reading and writing.

Teaching Strategies Leading to Student Independence

As you will recall, a teaching strategy is a plan or technique that can be used by the teacher (or a student assuming the role of teacher) to accomplish a desired outcome, whereas a student strategy, as discussed earlier, is a plan that students can employ independently to help them more effectively construct meaning. With all the talk about strategies during the last decade, there has not always been a clear distinction drawn between teaching strategies and student strategies.

This section discusses eleven teaching strategies in terms of their value for supporting students in *becoming independent* in activating their prior knowledge and setting their purpose(s) for reading. Table 3.3 describes when to use these strategies. Remember that your goal should always be to move students toward independence as quickly as possible.

Discussions

Description. Discussion is one of the most widely used strategies for activating students' prior knowledge before reading or writing. However, much of what is done in the name of discussion is nothing more than the teacher assessing students' comprehension (Durkin, 1978, 1981) or conducting a recitation period (Dillon, 1984). Such unstructured discussions have been found to be ineffective in activating appropriate prior knowledge (Holmes & Roser, 1987).

A discussion is an interactive procedure whereby the teacher and students talk about a given topic; it is not simply the teacher telling students a body of information. According to Alvermann, Dillon, and O'Brien (1987), discussions must meet three criteria:

- *Discussants should put forth multiple points of view and stand ready to change their minds about the matter under discussion;*
- *students should interact with one another as well as with the teacher;*
- *and the interaction should exceed the typical two or three word phrase units common to recitation lessons. (p. 7)*

Procedures.   Conducting an effective discussion for activating and developing prior knowledge before reading requires careful planning on the part of the teacher as well as on-the-spot decisions during the discussion. The following guidelines should be helpful in carrying out this process:

1. *Review the text that is to be read.* Determine the story line or main ideas to help you decide what key background concepts are needed to comprehend the text. Make certain that your focus is on more than the topic of the text. For example, if your class is going to read the expository text *Monarch Butterfly* (Gibbons, 1989), focus your discussion on what

Table 3.3 Teaching Strategies for Activating and Developing Prior Knowledge

Strategy	Type of Text	Comments
Discussions	Narrative or expository	For all students.
Brainstorming	Narrative or expository	Use when students have some knowledge of topic; for all students.
Quick writing	Narrative or expository	For all students; often needs to be combined with other strategies.
Semantic mapping	Most effective with expository; can be used with narrative	For all students; gives a visual picture of concepts.
Prequestioning and purpose setting	Narrative and expository	For beginning learners or those having difficulty; usually combined with other strategies.
Anticipation guides	Best with expository; may be used with narrative	Useful for overcoming misconceptions in prior knowledge. For all students.
Structured previews	Narrative or expository	Especially for second-language learners or students experiencing difficulty constructing meaning.
Reading aloud to students	Narrative or expository	Good to use when students have limited or erroneous prior knowledge; for all students, especially second-language learners.
Role playing	Narrative; sometimes expository, especially in social studies	For students needing more concrete prior knowledge development.
Projects	Narrative or expository	For all students; develops long-term prior knowledge throughout a theme.
Concrete materials and real experiences	Narrative or expository	For students with limited prior knowledge.

students know about monarch butterflies (or if nothing is known, butterflies) and their life cycle. If, on the other hand, your students are reading the story (narrative) *Imogene's Antlers* (Small, 1985), the discussion should focus on how they might react if they had a strange or unusual circumstance occur in their lives.

2. *Ask questions that require students to respond with more than* yes *or* no. Questions should require students to elaborate and explain their answers. Teachers who are just learning to lead a discussion should write out the questions in advance to be sure that they require more than *yes* or *no* responses. The suggested guidelines for discussions in teacher's manuals to basal readers, content texts, or story plans that accompany trade books can be used to help formulate the discussion plan.

3. *Encourage students to raise their own questions about the topic or about other students' answers.* It is a good idea for the teacher to model such behavior and tell students that they can ask similar questions of the teacher or other students. (See Chapter 8 on modeling.)

4. *Call on individual students to answer questions; don't always wait for volunteers to answer.* We want to encourage maximum participation by all students, even those who are sometimes reluctant to respond. Calling on individual students helps to encourage those who need extra support in responding.

5. *When calling on individual students to answer questions, ask the question before calling on the student.* This practice encourages everyone to listen and encourages all members of the group to participate.

6. *After asking a question, give students sufficient time to answer.* Teachers frequently do not give students enough "wait time" to think about their answers. The exact amount of time varies from situation to situation.

7. *Participate in the discussion and model good questioning and question-responding behavior.* Encourage students to ask questions in a discussion in the same manner you do.

8. *Keep the discussion focused on the topic* and don't allow it to drag on for an unnecessarily long time, losing students' attention. A short, lively discussion is better and more motivating than one that is too lengthy.

9. *Conclude the discussion by having students summarize the points that were made.* Provide guidance as needed, but don't simply tell students what was covered. For the discussion to be of value to them, they must be able to internalize and verbalize the points that were developed.

Discussions may be planned for the whole class or small groups. Sometimes it is good to begin with small-group discussions and then use the whole-class format to pull together the ideas discussed in each group. This is a natural way to lead to a summary and to involve all students in a more interactive lesson. In either instance, the nine guidelines suggested above still apply. It is also a good idea to develop with students a set of guidelines or suggestions to be followed during discussions. Figure 3.11 presents a sample set of guidelines developed by a group of fifth graders and their teacher.

Figure 3.11   Sample Discussion Guidelines Developed by One Fifth-Grade Class

Our Discussion Guidelines

1. Stick to the topic.
2. Pay attention to the person talking.
3. Ask questions about ideas given.
4. Give everyone a chance to participate.
5. Think about what is being said.
6. Try not to interrupt others.

When to Use.   Discussion is a teaching strategy that can be used with any group at any time for activating and developing prior knowledge. When your students have limited or incorrect knowledge about the topic or seem generally to have difficulty constructing meaning, it is a good idea to combine discussion with other strategies to make prior knowledge activation and development more concrete. In many cases, students are developing more prior knowledge than they are activating. For example, if a group has limited prior knowledge about frogs, they will profit from a discussion combined with photographs, a film, or a filmstrip on frogs. To help students move toward independence, encourage them to take the lead in small-group discussions. Cooperative learning is effective in achieving this goal.

Assessment Value.   Discussion is an excellent way to assess the state of students' prior knowledge; however, it must not be unstructured (Holmes & Roser, 1987). Through the responses students give and the ways in which they interact with each other, you will be able to tell what they know and what their misconceptions are.

Discussion.   As a teaching strategy, discussion is a powerful technique for activating and developing prior knowledge. However, it is also effective for other purposes, such as helping students construct their own meanings by responding to reading and by writing. Chapters 6 and 7 will focus on the use of discussion in these other ways. For more about discussion, see "For Additional Reading" at the conclusion of this chapter.

An important factor in using discussion is knowing the cultural rules that guide the entire process of asking and answering questions. Mason and Au (1990) point out that these unwritten rules affect the way children from different cultures participate and respond in discussions. For example, they found that Hawaiian children responded best when the teacher asked a question and the children were allowed to respond if they had something to say. Several children spoke at once, and the teacher then repeated the highest-quality response for the group. Mason and Au point out that this pattern reflects the Hawaiian emphasis on the group rather than the individual (pp. 49–50). You will find that other cultural groups may also vary in how they respond to traditional classroom practices.

Your job is to be sensitive to the various cultures represented in your classroom and to try to match your teaching strategies and procedures to fit not only the students' language base but also their cultural values. This is true, of course, for all teaching strategies.

Brainstorming

Description.   Brainstorming requires students to tell all that they know about a particular topic or idea. This begins to activate their prior knowledge about that idea or topic.

Procedures.   Students can work individually or in pairs. They first are asked to generate all of the ideas they have for a particular topic and then to share their ideas with the group. The teacher lists the ideas on the chalkboard, and then the teacher and students discuss them. By hearing others' ideas, students activate additional information they have stored in their memories or learn new information. The following steps indicate one way a brainstorming activity may be carried out.

1. Provide students, individually or in pairs, with cards on which they can record information.
2. Tell students that they are to write on the cards any words, ideas, or phrases that they know about the given topic. Provide a time limit for the activity, and tell students not to be concerned about spelling.
3. After students have completed the activity, have them read their lists aloud to the group as you record their ideas on the chalkboard or overhead projector.
4. Discuss the information recorded, pointing out ideas that are directly related to the selection students are going to read. If incorrect information is on the list, you may want to leave it there until after reading; through discussion and responding, students may correct themselves. However, if the error is significant and is likely to interfere with meaning construction, discuss it at this point. Don't just refuse a student's ideas and not include them on the list.
5. Direct the discussion of the ideas generated by the students to the story line or main ideas of the selection. Conclude the discussion by helping the students set a purpose for reading or give them a purpose for reading.

When to Use.   Brainstorming should be used when you feel that students have some knowledge of the topic to be discussed. It is useful as an opening activity for a thematic unit or for reading a story or informational text. For example, if your sixth graders are about to begin the book *Cousins* (Hamilton, 1990), you could use brainstorming to have them think about what might happen when there are conflicts between cousins in a family.

The following script shows how a teacher used brainstorming to introduce an article about whales.

(Teacher focuses the brainstorming.)

Teacher: Today, we are going to read an article about whales and why they are in trouble. I want you to write on this card all the things you can think of about whales. Don't worry about spelling. (The ideas of two students were pictured on the accompanying cards. After a few minutes, the teacher asked the students to stop writing.)

Ted

Whales are mammals.
Whales live in the ocean.
These are killer whales.
Whales can talk.

Elsie

fish
big
eat people

Teacher: I want each of you to read what you have written on your card, and I will write your ideas on the board. (The teacher listed all the students' ideas on the board, accepting all responses from each student. When students had the same responses, the teacher recorded the idea only once.)

(Students are looking for incorrect information.)

Teacher: Let's look at our list of ideas to see if there is anything that is incorrect.

Whales are mammals

Whales live in the ocean

There are killer whales

Whales can talk

Fish

Big

Eat people

Can be made into oil

Can be eaten

Are hunted by fishermen

Student: Whales aren't fish.

Teacher: Whales are sort of like fish because they live in the ocean; they look like fish, but they are much bigger than most fish. We also know that whales are not fish. We will learn why in our reading. (The teacher removed *fish* from the list.)

Teacher: You know that dinosaurs once lived on the earth, but they are no longer around. For many reasons, we don't have dinosaurs. The same thing is happening to whales. Look at this list of characteristics of whales to see if you can identify any reasons why whales might be in trouble or in danger of disappearing. (The students responded. The teacher then discussed their answers. The teacher identified those items the students missed.)

Teacher: We are going to read the article entitled "Disappearing Whales." Based on the information that we have just discussed about whales and why they might be in danger of disappearing, what do you think would be a good thing for us to think about or look for as we read?

Student: Maybe we could look to see if our reasons about why whales disappear are right and maybe we can find some others.

(Setting a purpose for reading.)

Teacher: That's a good idea. (The teacher wrote the student's response on the board and had students read the article silently, telling them that they would later discuss the article based on that purpose.)

Assessment Value.   Brainstorming is an excellent way to assess students' prior knowledge. As you could see in the dialogue presented above, the teacher was able to identify and *begin* to correct errors in students' prior knowledge about whales.

Discussion.   Many times when teachers are using brainstorming, they let the ideas get too far out of focus for the topic or idea being considered. It is important that you keep the brainstorming focused without controlling it. You will also find that brainstorming works well when you follow small-group discussion with a whole-class discussion. If students have a limited amount of knowledge of the subject, the small-group activity is usually more effective because it enables them to learn from each other.

Brainstorming, like the other strategies presented in this chapter, is often better if used in conjunction with another strategy, such as preview and predict or purpose setting. Not only will you more effectively meet individual needs, but you will also keep interest high by varying your teaching strategies.

Quick Writing

Description.   The relationships between reading and writing have been stressed throughout this text. Writing has been shown to be an effective way to activate prior knowledge before students read (Marino, Gould & Haas, 1985; Moore, Readence & Rickleman, 1989). Quick writing is structured by the teacher and is done in a brief amount of time.

Procedures.   The procedures to follow are very general because the specific steps to employ will depend on the selection being read and what is to be written. The following guidelines should be helpful:

1. *Select what you want students to write about.* This should be something that relates directly to the story line or main ideas in the text. For example, if students are going to read *The Stupids Have a Ball* (Allard & Marshall, 1978), you might ask them to pretend they are a person who does everything the opposite of normal, telling funny things that might happen to them. Since the characters in this story do just that, this activity would begin to get students thinking along these lines. Quick writing can focus on a character, on the story problem, or on the major topic developed in an expository text.
2. *Have students write.* Allow students a brief amount of time to complete the writing (3 to 5 minutes). Encourage them not to be concerned about spelling or grammar, since these papers are not to be evaluated and graded.
3. *Invite students to share what they have written.* During this time, direct students in a discussion of all of the ideas shared, focusing them on the story line or main ideas in the selection.

4. *Help students formulate a purpose for reading.* For example, after writing about being a strange person who does the opposite of everything in life, they can then read *The Stupids Have a Ball* to see how the Stupids are like the characters they have written about.

When to Use.   Writing can be used as soon as students begin to be able to write and express their ideas. If you know that students have limited prior knowledge relative to the topic, it would be best to use some other technique that would more concretely develop the concepts and ideas needed. Second-language learners in most instances should have an activity that introduces key words and phrases prior to writing; discussion combined with more concrete materials such as pictures would accomplish this goal.

Assessment Value.   Although writing is a valuable way to assess students' prior knowledge, you must be cautious about drawing conclusions from a student's response to a written task without comparing it to an oral sample. Students may be hampered by limited writing skills or a dislike for writing, leading the teacher to conclude erroneously that the student has limited prior knowledge. A good rule to follow is to make no firm conclusion about a student's prior knowledge on the basis of a single sample *from any source*. It is always wise to look at two or more samples from different sources such as writing and discussion or brainstorming and discussion.

Discussion: Writing is an important element in the overall process of constructing meaning, and helps students build the connections between reading and writing. However, quick writing does not replace the process writing or response writing that takes place through the literacy lesson, independent writing, and writer's workshop. For more discussion of writing, see Chapter 7.

Semantic Mapping

Description.   Pearson and Johnson (1978) describe a strategy called semantic mapping that can be used to help students activate and develop prior knowledge by seeing the relationships in a given topic. A semantic map is a visual representation of a particular concept. Ovals are used to represent the concepts, and lines with arrows and words written above them represent the relationships. The relationships depicted on a map can be *class* (pine trees), *example* (White Pine), or *property* (needles). Figure 3.12 shows a semantic map for pine trees that was created with a group of third graders preparing to read a science article about the uses of pine trees.

Procedures.   There are many different ways to use semantic mapping. The first set of guidelines that follows is more structured and directed by the

Figure 3.12   Semantic Map for Pine Trees

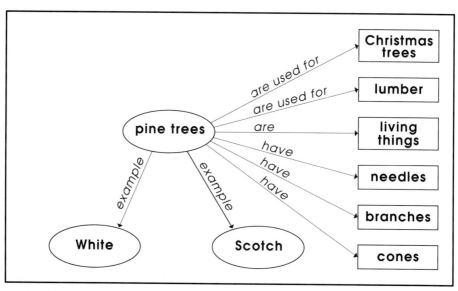

teacher; the second set, although teacher directed, incorporates brainstorming followed by grouping and labeling of concepts. The second set uses many of the ideas suggested by Taba (1967) many years ago, as described by McNeil (1987); the Taba lesson was known as List-Group-Label and was suggested for social studies but can be used in many more situations.

Guidelines 1

1. Write the major concept being discussed on the chalkboard or overhead and draw an oval around it. (In Figure 3.12 the concept is pine trees.)
2. Ask students to think of words to describe the topic (such as pine trees). Write those words in boxes and link them with arrows to the main concept oval. Write words and phrases above the arrows such as *have* or *are used for* to indicate the relationship between the main concept and the boxed words.
3. Ask students to give some examples of the topic and write these in ovals with arrows indicating examples.

Guidelines 2

1. Present the concept to be discussed by placing it in an oval on the chalkboard or overhead.

Figure 3.13   Semantic Map Developed Using Guidelines

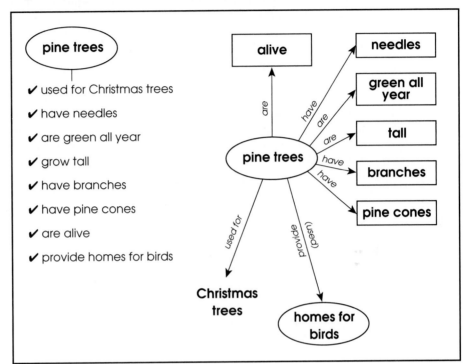

2. Ask students to brainstorm all of the words or ideas that they can think of related to the concept. If necessary, probe with questions to get additional information.
3. Guide students in grouping the words or ideas to create the semantic map for the concept. Use different shapes to depict the different categories of information—rectangles for uses or descriptions, circles for examples, and squares for other types of information. Figure 3.13 shows how this process worked with a different group of third graders following the second set of guidelines.

There is no one right way to develop a semantic map. The words written on the arrows to show relationships will vary according to the topic being discussed.

When to Use.   Semantic mapping is most effective when used with expository texts. It can also be used with narratives, but you must be certain that the concept used for activating prior knowledge is central to the story line.

Semantic mapping can be used with all students; it helps them visually see the relationships between the ideas being discussed. Second-language learners and students with limited prior knowledge may respond best when the second set of guidelines is used because they then start more globally and move to categorizing. When using this strategy, you should always keep the activity focused on the central ideas in the text; otherwise, it is likely to lead students in directions that will not improve their construction of meaning.

Semantic mapping is a good procedure to follow when students are going to read several books or selections related to the same topic. The teacher and students can start the map before students begin the reading and can add to it as they gain new background information from their reading. In this way, students will clearly see that reading helps build background for further reading. After they have completed their reading, they can return to the map to make additions or changes.

Assessment Value.   As you use semantic mapping with students, you are able to assess their understandings of various concepts and relationships. This procedure helps you see how students are thinking by giving you insights into the relationships and categories they suggest.

Discussion.   Semantic mapping has also been suggested for many other uses in helping students construct meaning; these include summarizing the text, expanding their vocabulary, and writing (Noyce & Christie, 1989; Stahl & Vancil, 1986; Weisberg & Balajthy, 1985).

A variation of the semantic mapping strategy is semantic webbing, in which students generate ideas and/or words related to a given topic and then talk about how these ideas are related; lines are drawn showing these relationships. Figure 3.14 shows a semantic web created with a group of students to activate their knowledge about what it is like to be the oldest child in a family. Although webbing can be used this way, I have found that it is a better strategy for expanding vocabulary because it often takes students too far afield from the text when used to activate their prior knowledge. Webbing is also a good way to brainstorm for writing. Semantic mapping will be discussed in more detail in Chapter 4.

Prequestioning and Purpose Setting

Description.   Another way to activate students' prior knowledge before reading is to ask a question or give them a topic to think about that will continue to focus their attention as they read. Such procedures have been shown to be effective in activating students' prior knowledge and in improving their ability to construct meaning (Tierney & Cunningham, 1984).

Figure 3.14   Semantic Web

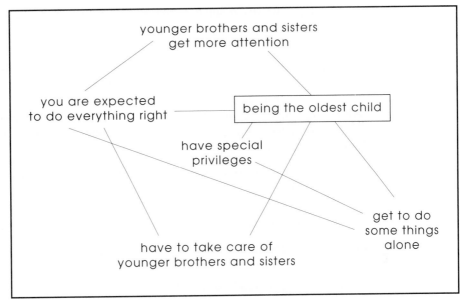

Procedures.   The following are some simple guidelines that should be used flexibly with various reading tasks.

1. Examine the text that is to be read. Determine the story line or main ideas.
2. On the basis of your examination, decide what prior knowledge students are likely to need to construct meaning.
3. Formulate a question or questions or a statement of purpose for students to think about before reading. These should focus students on the big ideas in the text rather than on some obscure, insignificant details.

Recall the article "Birds in Winter" that was discussed earlier. The focus of that article was on the survival of birds during a blizzard, and the main point was that birds often have to depend on humans to survive under extreme winter conditions. The following prequestions would be useful for this article:

How do the problems faced by the birds in this article compare to the problems you have seen birds experience during bad winter storms?

On the basis of the article "Birds in Winter" and on your own experience, why do you think it is important for people to help birds during winter storms?

The following would be an appropriate purpose-setting statement for this article:

> You have discussed some of the problems that birds can have surviving in winter. Read this article to find out if there are other reasons why birds have difficulty surviving in blizzards.

Notice that the only real difference between this purpose statement and the questions is the form in which the purpose is stated.

The following prequestions would not be appropriate for this article because they focus on specific points and do not direct the reader's attention to the overall text. Furthermore, these questions do not require readers to draw extensively from their prior knowledge:

> What two birds have the greatest difficulty surviving during blizzard conditions?

> What three reasons are stated by the author to justify why people should help birds during blizzards?

The second question is better than the first but still fails to direct the reader to relate prior knowledge to the text.

4. Have students read the text to answer the question or to accomplish the purpose given.
5. After reading, return to the question or purpose statement to see if students have achieved their goals and to discuss what they found. Research has demonstrated that returning to check the purpose for reading is important in helping students construct meaning (White, 1981).

When to Use.   This strategy should be used when students are just beginning to learn to construct meaning and cannot yet formulate their own purposes or prequestions or when the text is extremely difficult. Keep in mind, however, that your goal is to get students to assume greater responsibility and ownership for their learning. Therefore, you will not help students by overrelying on this strategy. Since your real goal should be to get them to use the independent strategies discussed in the first portion of this chapter, you should usually combine prequestions and purpose statements with other strategies such as discussion or brainstorming to activate prior knowledge. It is always important for students to have a purpose in mind for their reading.

Assessment Value.   Prequestions and purpose statements are not as helpful as other strategies in assessing students' immediate prior knowledge relative to a topic or idea. Their assessment value comes after reading, when students respond and show how well they have constructed meaning.

Discussion.   Prequestions and purpose statements are an effective strategy for providing the scaffold for learning that some students need, and you will find that you frequently use them when you employ the teacher-guided reading mode discussed in Chapter 2. One variation is to put them in monitoring guides or study guides (discussed in Chapter 2). These will be discussed more in Chapter 9.

Anticipation Guides

Description.   An anticipation guide is a series of statements about a particular text that students are going to read. Students indicate whether they agree or disagree with the statements before reading and return to them after reading to do the same. This strategy, developed by Readence, Bean, and Baldwin (1981, 1985, 1989), is designed to activate prior knowledge and to give students a purpose for reading.

Procedures.   Readence, Bean, and Baldwin (1981, 1985, 1989) suggest eight steps in constructing and using anticipation guides.

1. *Identify major concepts.* Review the text to identify the major concepts or main ideas to be learned.
2. *Determine students' prior knowledge of these concepts.* Drawing on your experiences with your students, think about what they know about these concepts or ideas. This will help you decide what statements you want to write.
3. *Create statements.* Using the information gained from steps 1 and 2, write out four to eight statements for students to react to that relate to the concepts to be learned and the students' prior knowledge. The exact number of statements depends on the amount of text to be read, the number of concepts in the text, and the age of the students. The statements should reflect information about which students have some knowledge but not complete knowledge. They should not be just a true-false type of check. Some good statements for a chapter on food and nutrition might be the following:
   1. *An apple a day keeps the doctor away.*
   2. *If you wish to live a long life, be a vegetarian.*
   3. *Three square meals a day will satisfy all your body's nutritional needs.*
   4. *Calories make you fat. (Tierney, Readence & Dishner, 1990, p. 48)*
4. *Decide on the statement order and presentation mode.* Order the statements in a sequence that follows the text, inserting spaces where students can respond. Create a set of directions. Finally, decide whether the guide is to be presented individually or in a group mode such as the chalkboard or overhead.
5. *Present the guide.* Present the guide to students and tell them that they are to react to each statement by indicating whether they agree or disagree with it. Tell them that they will share their responses with the group.

Figure 3.15   Anticipation Guide for Social Studies

Chapter 6, Transportation

Directions: Read each statement. Before reading, mark *A* for agree or *D* for disagree. Do the same after reading.

Before Reading		*After Reading*
_____	1. Travel has not changed much in the last 25 years.	_____
_____	2. The car is still the best way to travel.	_____
_____	3. The safest way to travel is by air.	_____
_____	4. Large cities need to have more parking garages for increased population.	_____
_____	5. Cars should be banned from the central business district of large cities.	_____

6. *Discuss each statement briefly.* Encourage students to share their opinions and tell why they feel as they do. You can tally the total responses to each item.

7. *Direct students to read the text.* Have students read the text, keeping their opinions in mind. As they read they should think about how the text relates to the statements on the guide.

8. *Conduct a follow-up discussion.* First ask students to respond to each statement in light of what they have read. Then they should discuss the statements, focusing on what has been learned and how their opinions and ideas have changed. Figure 3.15 presents a sample anticipation guide for a social studies chapter on transportation.

When to Use.   Anticipation guides may be used for any students at any level. They are generally more useful for expository texts but may also be used with narrative texts. Figure 3.16 presents a guide to be used with *Today Was a Terrible Day* (Giff, 1980).

This type of strategy is effective when students have misconceptions in prior knowledge; by interacting with the text and comparing opinions with what was learned from reading, students are likely to change their misconceptions.

Assessment Value.   This is an excellent diagnostic tool. By looking at and listening to students' responses, you can tell the state of their prior knowledge and can easily recognize their misconceptions. Then, by looking at the after-reading responses, you can tell whether those misconceptions have changed.

Figure 3.16   Anticipation Guide for *Today Was a Terrible Day* (Giff, 1980)

Today Was a Terrible Day

Write *A* for agree or *D* for disagree after each statement below.

1. Kids who get into trouble at school don't care what others think of them.

   _____

2. You shouldn't be friends with people who get into trouble at school.

   _____

3. Teachers don't like kids who get into trouble at school.

   _____

4. Kids who get into trouble at school don't like their teachers.

   _____

5. Kids who have trouble learning to read are dumb.

   _____

Source: Sample Anticipation Guide for *Today Was a Terrible Day* (Giff, 1980) developed by Molly McLaurin, I.S. Klein, and D. Klein, Texas. Used by permission of the author.

Discussion.   The construction of the anticipation guide is very important and sometimes challenging. The statements must require students to think; they should not be of the list of true-false variety. The theory underlying this strategy is very solid. However, since I am unaware of any controlled research using this strategy, it should be used with this precaution in mind.

Structured Previews

Description.   The value of previewing a text before reading was discussed earlier in this chapter, but some students may need to have the previewing process structured more carefully before they can construct meaning. A structured preview is carefully guided by the teacher and often involves some type of graphic display of information to help students see the ideas that are forthcoming in the text and how they are organized. The concept behind this teaching strategy is based on research showing that students' prior knowledge needs to be directed toward the story line (Beck, 1984; Beck, Omanson & McKeown, 1982). To be helpful to students, this process needs teacher guidance (Neuman, 1988).

Procedures.   The procedures for conducting a structured preview are different for narrative texts and for expository texts, though there are similarities between the two.

Figure 3.17   Story Map for Structured Preview

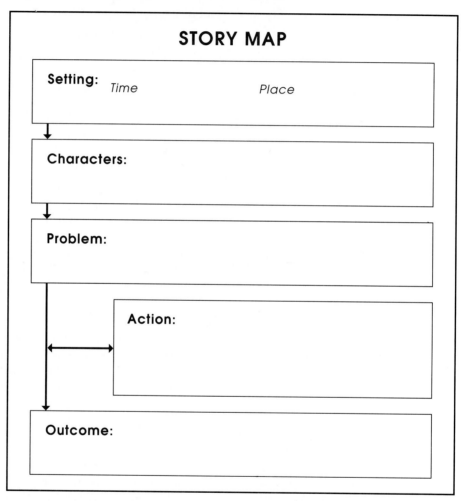

Narrative Structured Preview

1. Look through the book to get a sense of the story line. Identify the setting, characters, problem, action, and outcome.
2. Formulate questions or statements that will direct students to read the title and the opening paragraph or two (depending on the level), and look at the first few illustrations. Have students share what they learn.
3. Display the story map (see Figure 3.17) and discuss with students the elements in the story. For beginning learners and those having difficulty

constructing meaning, focus on only one or two elements and include other elements when additional stories are read.

4. Ask students to predict what they can about the story elements from their preview. Make certain that your questions and directions continually help students focus on the story line instead of the general topic of the story.

5. Have students read the story silently in its entirety or in sections as needed. Then return to the story map to help them see whether their predictions were verified or changed. Have students work with you to complete the story map.

The steps involved in the structured preview must always be adjusted to fit the story content, illustrations, and level. The primary focus of the preview should always be to get students to begin to think about the particular story problem and relate what they already know to it. If your third-grade students are going to read *Wilfrid Gordon McDonald Partridge* (Fox, 1985; shown in Figure 3.18), a book about how a young boy helps an elderly woman in an old people's home get her memory back, you begin the structured preview by having children look at the cover and tell who they think this book is going to be about. Next, by looking through the first three or four pages, you ask children to talk about old people's homes and the types of things that might be problems for people in them, focusing on the idea that some people forget things as they get older. You then complete the preview by presenting the story map and asking children to predict the characters and the possible problem in the story. Again, the exact structure of the preview should be adjusted to your students' needs.

Expository Structured Preview

The narrative structured preview has a fairly definite pattern because all narrative texts have the same basic structure. The expository structured preview is much less definite because such expository text has varying text structures. Therefore, you will need to adapt the following guidelines to fit the structure of the text your students are reading.

1. Review the text to determine the main ideas. Try to identify a graphic organizer that will help students see how the information fits together. For example, if the text has three main ideas, the graphic organizer might be like the one shown in Figure 3.19. However, many texts do not lend themselves to such a neat outline, and you may not always be able to have a graphic organizer.

2. Formulate questions and statements to use in helping students preview the text by reading the title, looking at the illustrations and captions throughout (depending on the grade level), and reading subheads, if provided.

3. Guide students through a preview of the text, having them begin to predict the type of information they will learn.

Figure 3.18   Cover for *Wilfrid Gordon McDonald Partridge*

Wilfrid Gordon McDonald Partridge
Written by Mem Fox   Illustrated by Julie Vivas

Source: Fox (1985). Used by permission of Kane/Miller Book Publishers, Brooklyn, NY.

4. Present the graphic organizer and tell students that the ideas in this text are organized in this pattern.
5. Have students read the text in its entirety or in sections as needed to look for the main ideas depicted in your organizer. As they become more sophisticated readers, they can also identify the information that supports the main ideas.

Conducting a structured preview for expository texts means that you must pay close attention to how the main ideas are presented in the text. For example,

Figure 3.19 Graphic Organizer Showing Three Main Ideas in an Expository Text

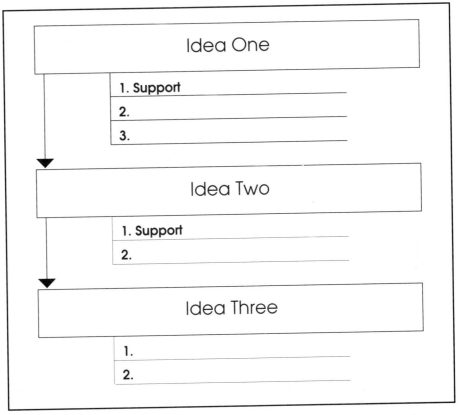

if your second graders are going to read *Fiesta!* (Behrens, 1978), you should note that this work has only one main idea with many facts given about it. Figure 3.20 shows how this idea with its supporting facts might be depicted. When conducting your preview, you should only present the basic outline of the graphic organizer, telling students that they will learn one big idea about fiesta and six areas of information about what happens during fiesta. This type of structured preview activates prior knowledge about the topic and also gives students a framework to use in thinking about how the information is organized.

When to Use.   Structured previews are good to use at a number of different times:

- When the text is particularly difficult
- When students are second-language learners

Figure 3.20   Graphic Organizer for Structured Preview of *Fiesta!*

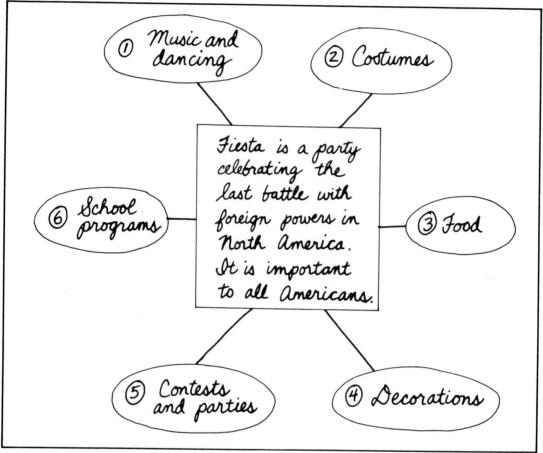

- When students are having difficulty constructing meaning
- When you know students have limited prior knowledge about the topic or with the type of text

Assessment Value.   Students' responses during the preview session will help you determine the status of their prior knowledge and what they are gaining from the preview. Since the preview is so teacher directed, it may not afford as many open opportunities for you to see exactly what students know and are thinking. You would select this strategy because you know that your students need this type of scaffold.

Discussion.   The use of structured previews and graphic or semantic organizers is not new (Pehrsson & Robinson, 1985), and they can be very helpful to students in both reading and writing. However, teachers sometimes make things too complicated for students and don't really help them improve their ability to construct meaning. Therefore, you should always keep your structured previews as simple as possible, making certain that any graphic organizers used *do* help students see how the text is organized. The structured preview may be combined with many of the other strategies discussed in this chapter.

Reading Aloud to Students

Description.   The importance of reading aloud to students was well established in Chapter 2 (Anderson, Hiebert, Scott & Wilkinson, 1985; Dressel, 1990; Feitelson, Kita & Goldstein, 1986). In this strategy the reading is specific to a thematic topic or selection.

Procedures.

Reading Aloud Background Material

This strategy can be carried out using the following guidelines:

1. Select a book, article, or other background material that relates to the topic or selection.
2. Introduce the material to the students by telling them what it is about and why you are reading it to them.
3. Give students a purpose for listening to the material. For example, have them listen to identify some important idea or concept or to retell an important part of the story. As an alternative, you can also ask them to make predictions about what they expect to learn as they listen.
4. After the read-aloud, discuss the material by checking the purpose for which students were to listen or discuss whether predictions were confirmed. This procedure is similar to the Structured Listening Activity recommended by Choate and Rakes (1987).

Reading Aloud a Portion of a Selection

Guidelines for using this strategy are as follows:

1. Decide on the story or article students are going to read.
2. Identify how much of the initial part of the selection you are going to read aloud.
3. Introduce the selection and give students a purpose for listening.
4. Read aloud the section selected.
5. Discuss the portion read aloud, being sure to check the purpose given for listening.

6. Have students predict what they think will happen or what they will learn in the remainder of the text.
7. Have students read to check their predictions.
8. Discuss the entire selection, focusing on whether students' predictions were verified.
9. Have students respond to the selection in their own way.

This second read-aloud strategy can be varied by having the teacher read aloud part of the text and alternating these sessions with students reading cooperatively or independently. The amount of reading aloud the teacher does should be dependent on the students' needs and the text. This is a variation of the read aloud, read along, read alone strategy discussed in Chapter 2.

When to Use.   The read-aloud strategy is an excellent one to use when you know that students have limited or erroneous prior knowledge. It is also good for second-language learners because it helps to develop oral language.

Assessment Value.   By reading aloud to students, you can tell generally how they comprehend through listening. It is more difficult to use the read-aloud strategy as a way to assess students' specific prior knowledge. You can tell how well they remember and organize ideas without being concerned about decoding or their abilities to figure out words.

Discussion.   Reading aloud is an excellent way to build students' background and increase motivation, and it should not be overlooked as a significant strategy for helping *all* students develop their ability to construct meaning. Reading aloud is also useful in building prior knowledge for writing.

Role Playing

Description.   Role playing involves students in taking parts and acting out a situation. The purpose of this strategy is to get students to think about a problem or circumstance and bring their prior knowledge to bear on it.

Procedures.   Role playing can be fun, but it requires careful planning to make it a valuable experience for prior knowledge activation.

1. Select the book you want students to read. Determine the story line.
2. Select a situation that would be easy and fun for children to role-play. Make sure that it relates to the story line but does not give away the story.
3. Describe the situation to the children. Divide them into small groups to decide on parts and to determine how they will act out their situation.
4. Have each group perform and discuss the situations, focusing the discussion on the book to be read, not an evaluation of the performance.
5. Have students read the book to compare their experience with that of the book.

Suppose that your sixth graders are going to read *Wayside School Is Falling Down* (Sachar, 1989), a hilarious book about the adventures of children in Louis Sachar's imaginary school. You could ask children to role-play the strangest and funniest thing that they could imagine happening in school. As each group performs, you then discuss the incident, leading the children to focus on the book by directing them to see how their experiences compare with those of the Erics and other children in Wayside School.

When to Use.   Role playing is a good strategy to use for students who need more concrete experiences for activating their prior knowledge. Often second-language learners will be able to relate and interact with their peers in a role-playing situation when they are reluctant to talk out individually in an open discussion. Although role playing is often used with narrative texts, it may also be useful with expository texts, especially social studies.

Assessment Value.   The opportunity to observe students in a role-playing situation is excellent. You can get a sense of their prior knowledge as well as the way they think and solve problems. For more discussion about observations, see Chapter 10.

Discussion.   Too often prior knowledge activation is handled only through discussion. Remember that many children enjoy role playing and are more likely to be themselves and use what they actually know in this activity. At the same time, some students may be too shy to participate, in which case you may consider using simple puppetry to accomplish the same purpose.

Projects

Description.   A project is a task that someone undertakes to achieve a particular goal; it is usually long term in nature, and because of its goal, you can tell when it is completed (Ward, 1988). For example, students might construct a model of an Indian village during a thematic unit on Indians of the Southwest. This project would be long term in that it would be completed throughout the thematic unit and would focus continuously not only on activating prior knowledge but also on integrating new knowledge with prior knowledge.

Procedures.   Using projects in the classroom is not difficult; the important thing is to have a plan for carrying them out. The following guidelines should be helpful:

1. *Identify the project.* Decide what the project will be; usually it will relate to a particular theme or area being studied. Some possible projects might include the following:
   - Making a birdhouse

- Developing a family tree
- Constructing a simple machine
- Writing a book comparing the characters of a particular author

You may select the project that you want students to carry out; however, students often have their own ideas and should be encouraged to use them. This helps to foster students' ownership in their learning and increases motivation.

2. *Select resources.* Decide what resources you want students to use—library, encyclopedia, books, interviews, and so on. As students improve their ability to construct meaning, they will be able to identify the resources they need for themselves.

3. *Make a plan to carry out the project.* Both you and the students need a plan. It should include what they will do and when they will do it, thus giving both you and them a way to monitor the project.

4. *Plan how to share the project.* It is important for students to share their projects because interaction with peers is a part of their authentic learning experience. Therefore, they need to have an idea of how they will do this. Will sharing take place through a book that is developed, a display, a show, or some other means?

To be of value to students, projects must be clearly focused. Having a plan will help to make this happen. A project sheet like the one shown in Figure 3.21 should help you with this planning and monitoring process.

When to Use.   Projects may be used with any students at any grade or age level, as long as they match the students' abilities and work habits. Since projects involve developing and integrating long-term prior knowledge over a thematic unit, they are not the most efficient way to activate and develop prior knowledge before reading a particular text.

Assessment Value.   All of the activities that take place during a project can help you determine the status of students' prior knowledge by observing how they respond. However, because of the long-term and independent nature of projects, they don't lend themselves to easy observation of activities. They do, however, provide authentic experiences that will show what students know as well as what they can do.

Discussion.   The use of projects does much more than activate prior knowledge. It is also a way for students to have many kinds of authentic experiences that help them learn new strategies and skills and gain new information. Projects often create the need for students to read and do research. They help students integrate new knowledge with old knowledge, learn to work cooperatively and independently, develop critical thinking, and learn new skills and strategies. Students may do projects independently or in groups,

Figure 3.21   Project Planning and Monitoring Sheet

Project Plan

I. Project, Title, and Focus

_____

_____

II. Resources to Be Used

_____   _____

_____   _____

_____   _____

III. Action Steps

_____ _Step_ _____   _Date Completed_

1. _____   _____

_____

2. _____   _____

_____

3. _____   _____

_____

IV. Sharing Plans

_____

_____

_____

depending on their purposes. In all cases, they should be encouraged to select and plan their own projects through the use of a theme project chart like the one shown in Figure 3.22.

You must be cautious when you use this strategy. Sometimes students get so caught up in completing a project that it replaces most, if not all, of the reading and writing that they should be doing.

Figure 3.22   Theme Project Chart

Projects for the Fairy Tale Theme

1. Write your own fairy tale.
2. Create a diorama of your favorite fairy tale.
3. Make a collection of favorite fairy tales.
4. Plan your own project. You decide what you would like to do in this unit.

Concrete Materials and Real Experiences

Description.   Often the best way to activate and develop students' prior knowledge is to use concrete materials and real experiences. These could include pictures, films, filmstrips, videos, field trips, or classroom planned experiences. For example, a classroom science experiment involving treating three plants differently—one gets water and no light, one gets light and no water, and one gets water and light—would be a good way to develop prior knowledge before starting a theme on plants or on air and water.

Procedures.   The only procedures to follow are to be sure that the materials or experiences actually help in activating and developing prior knowledge that is relevant to the theme, the text to be read, or the writing experience. Sometimes videos, films, and filmstrips take students in a direction that is not necessarily relevant to the situation at hand. Therefore, make your decisions carefully, always being sure that what you are using really helps to accomplish your intended goal—helping students more effectively construct meaning.

When to Use.   Concrete materials and real experiences are most important when students lack prior knowledge on a particular topic. Second-language learners and children who come to school with limited background often need this type of support. It is also useful whenever a topic new to all students needs to be introduced.

Assessment Value.   Since concrete materials and real experiences are used to *develop* prior knowledge, they will have limited assessment value. However, as in all learning experiences, students' responses will give you an indication of what they know and what they are learning.

Discussion.   Sometimes real experiences in classrooms do not seem to have a clear connection to the instruction. Therefore, you should always introduce field trips, films and videos, or classroom experiences by letting children know the purpose of the experience. After the experience is completed, you and the students should talk about what was learned and how it relates to the topic or theme being covered. For example, in preparation for a thematic unit on wild animals, students should make predictions about certain animals before going to the zoo. Then they can discuss which predictions were confirmed and summarize what they learned about the animals. This knowledge will help them as they work in this unit.

Making Decisions About Which Strategies to Use

Thirteen different strategies—two student strategies and eleven teaching strategies—with variations have been presented and discussed. Each strategy has as its primary focus activation and/or development of prior knowledge, leading students to set their purpose for reading. As the teacher, you must continuously make decisions about which strategies to use in thematic units and literacy lessons.

Each learning situation is different. Some lessons will call for combining several strategies, and others will require only one strategy. Some will require heavy teacher support, others almost none. The following guidelines should help you decide which strategies to use and when to use them:

Motivation and Interest

The amount of student motivation and interest for a topic or book will directly influence the amount of prior knowledge activation and development needed. Usually students who select their own topics or their own books are either very highly motivated or have good prior knowledge about the topic. If they are highly motivated to read or write about a certain topic but they have little prior knowledge about it, they will need support in developing this knowledge. Those who know a great deal about the topic will need little or no support in activating or developing their prior knowledge.

It is important to consider students' needs in planning prior knowledge activation. The quickest way to destroy a reading or writing experience is to have students do dozens of activities before they ever get to do what they really want to do—*read* or *write*. When prior knowledge is not activated before a reading or writing experience, you should observe during the experience to see if it is needed. Even when you select the books students read, the amount of student motivation and interest should guide you in deciding how much prior knowledge you need to activate.

The Text

The type of text (narrative or expository) and its difficulty must also be considered when deciding which strategies to use. With narrative text, you should focus on the story line; for expository text, focus on the main ideas.

When topics or texts have complex concepts, ideas, or structures, more prior knowledge activation will be needed, and some strategies will be more useful than others. Refer back to Tables 3.2 and 3.3 (pages 124 and 136) for a summary of when to use the student and teaching strategies presented in this chapter.

Student Needs and Level of Independence

A major consideration in deciding how much prior knowledge development is needed for a thematic unit or selection is the students themselves. As you become familiar with your students, you will know which ones need the most prior knowledge support. Students who have achieved independence will need no support, but keep in mind that this need will change from situation to situation. Again, refer to Tables 3.2 and 3.3 for guidance.

Lesson Variety

A final factor to consider is lesson variety. Using the same strategies over and over again becomes boring to both you and the students. Vary your strategies to keep interest and motivation for learning high.

Overcoming Inadequate Prior Knowledge

Students who experience difficulties in constructing meaning often have limited or erroneous prior knowledge (Lipson, 1984). These students often need *more* prior knowledge development that is *directed specifically to the reading or writing task* that they are expected to perform. All of the strategies presented in this chapter can be used to help in these circumstances, but they need to be approached systematically and somewhat differently than for other students.

Limited Prior Knowledge

All students come to school with prior knowledge; however, it may not match what the school community expects them to have. If they lack experience with the world in general and with literacy events, they may have had limited life experiences or may not have been read to at home. Or they may come from homes where the concept and motivation for literacy learning are different from that of the school (Taylor & Dorsey-Gaines, 1988). Regardless of the circumstances, *it is our goal to help them take whatever prior knowledge they bring to school and expand and build on it.*

Within the framework of the literacy program, there are many opportunities to expand students' world knowledge and knowledge and experience with literacy events. You must do this systematically, always emphasizing the value of each individual and what he or she brings to school. The following suggestions should be helpful in planning classroom experiences that will help expand students' prior knowledge.

Sharing and Talking.   Create many opportunities for students to share and talk about their own experiences and background. This places importance on what they bring to school and says, "What you know is good and of value." Opportunities for these experiences can be provided in opening morning exercises, sharing times, or throughout the day when appropriate. Students of all ages like the opportunity to talk about what is important to them.

Sharing should also give students time to talk about books they have read or things they have written. This is a good time to make use of the author's chair or reader's chair discussed in Chapter 2.

Read-Aloud Time.   Reading aloud to children is one of the best ways to broaden their prior knowledge and language experiences. If children have not been read to at home, this activity is even more significant in school. See Chapter 2 for guidelines on reading aloud to students.

Independent Reading and Writing Time.   Reading and writing expand students' prior knowledge. Therefore, students who have limited prior knowledge need *more time to read and write independently*. Give the independent reading and writing component of your literacy program more significance. See Chapter 2 for suggestions.

Plan Lessons and Experiences to Develop Prior Knowledge.   Use the strategies suggested in this chapter and those you learn from other sources to systematically develop prior knowledge when you start a new theme, when students read a selection, or when they begin a writing experience. Use the literacy lesson format presented in Chapter 2 with the strategies that lend themselves to more concretely developing prior knowledge for students.

Students who have limited prior knowledge often need continued support throughout their reading lesson to develop and relate this knowledge to what they read. Two lesson formats that emphasize the development of prior knowledge throughout the lesson have been suggested by school-based researchers: the Experience-Text-Relationship (E-T-R) format for narrative text (Au, 1979) and the Concept-Text-Application (C-T-A) format for expository text (Wong & Au, 1985). These lessons are similar in design to the literacy lesson format suggested in Chapter 2. The following guidelines should help you in using them:

1. *Experience-Text-Relationship Lesson format (E-T-R)*

     Teacher planning: Review the story that students are to read; identify the story line and important elements. Decide how you can directly relate these ideas to students' experiences, and look for natural places where you can divide the story into segments for students to read. See Chapter 2 on teacher-guided reading.

Experience—E: Begin by discussing the topic of the story generally, relating it to students' backgrounds. Then move the discussion to the story specifically, using a picture from the story if appropriate. Have students predict what they think will happen, and then have them read the first segment to see if their predictions were verified. Also, tell students to begin to identify the story characters, setting, and problem.

Text—T: After the first segment has been read, stop to talk about it: Were predictions verified? What new information was learned? Have children predict what they think will happen in the next segment, and continue this pattern until the story is completed. If the story takes several days to read, assign independent work that requires students to write about the story.

Relationship—R: When the story is completed, ask students questions that require them to relate what they have learned to their own experiences: "What would you have done in this situation?" "How does this story compare to others you have read that have a similar problem?"

2. *Concept-Text-Application Lesson format (C-T-A)*

Teacher planning: Preview the text that is to be read to identify the main ideas. Try to create a visual structure that will help students see the information (see the expository structured preview guidelines on page 153). Select any key-concept words that need to be taught (see Chapter 4 for preteaching vocabulary). Look for natural places to divide the text into segments for reading.

Concept—C: Get children interested in the text by asking them questions such as "Do you believe in _____?" "How do you feel about _____?" Then ask specific questions that focus on the concepts and vocabulary in the text: "What is a _____?" "Tell me what you know about _____." Assess your students' knowledge through these types of questions and provide the needed instruction to develop their background, concepts, and vocabulary.

Text—T: Give students a question to answer as they read the first segment of text. Then, after the reading is completed, have them answer the question. Present your visual display and begin to have students help to fill in the information. Continue reading in this way until the text is completed, assessing background and vocabulary needs and providing instruction as needed.

Application—A: After reading, have students summarize the entire text orally, referring to the visual structure used throughout the reading. Then have them complete some type of follow-up where they use the information in writing, in an oral presentation, or in a short project. For example, students might make a quick bulletin board display, write a pretend newspaper article, or give a short talk to other members of the class.

In summary, helping students overcome limited prior knowledge requires a systematic effort on your part. It begins by valuing what students bring to school and proceeds by providing the types of opportunities that support expanding and developing prior knowledge. The strategies and techniques for doing this are basically the same as for all students; however, they must be more systematically applied in these situations.

Misconceptions in Prior Knowledge

Correcting misconceptions or erroneous prior knowledge is a time-consuming task that is not always done successfully. Research does indicate, however, that it is possible to make these corrections and improve students' abilities to construct meaning (Alvermann & Hynd, 1987; Alvermann, Smith & Readence, 1985; Dole & Smith, 1989; Hynd & Alvermann, 1986; Maria, 1988). Although research presents no hard-and-fast guidelines, it does give some suggestions that lead to the following guidelines:

Activate and Assess Prior Knowledge.   First you must find out what students know and/or think about the topic, using many of the strategies discussed in this chapter. As students respond, you will want to assess their knowledge, noting misconceptions or errors.

Decide on the Best Time for Correcting the Error or Misconception.   This is not an easy decision to make. Research suggests that changing students' misconceptions involves much more than correcting inaccuracies before reading. It is a long-term process that takes place through reading and writing over a period of time. Minor errors or misconceptions may be corrected before reading, but more serious ones will need to be viewed in the long-term process of instruction. Brainstorming and discussion may be natural strategies for correcting minor misconceptions (Flood & Lapp, 1988) before reading. However, Maria (1990) cautions that too much focus on correcting errors or misconceptions before reading may deter students from wanting to read.

Select the Strategies to Be Used.   Whereas all the strategies discussed in this chapter might be useful in correcting minor misconceptions, those that involve more long-term thinking processes are more likely to be effective in

Figure 3.23   Thinksheet Based on Dole and Smith (1989) Research

Matter Unit Thinksheet

Central Questions	① Everyday Ideas I Know or Believe	② Scientific Ideas from My Textbook	③ Text Ideas Same as Everyday Ideas	④ Text Added Information	⑤ Text Conflicted with Everyday Ideas	⑥ Text Was Confusing
1. What are objects made of?						
2. What happens when water freezes/ evapo- rates?						
3. What happens when a nail rusts?						

overcoming more deep-rooted misconceptions. One such strategy is the anticipation guide presented on page 149.

Another strategy designed and used in research specifically for the purpose of correcting misconceptions in prior knowledge is the "thinksheet" (Dole & Smith, 1989; Maria, 1988). Figure 3.23 presents a sample thinksheet that employs the Prior Knowledge Monitoring and Integrating (PKMI) strategy, which works as follows:

1. Introduce the topic and have a general discussion about it.
2. Present the thinksheet and have students record their ideas in column ①.
3. During reading, have students complete column ② and place a check in the appropriate column (③–⑥).
4. After reading, have students discuss their thinking about the central questions and what they learned from reading.

PKMI was effective in changing fifth-grade students' thinking about a text (Dole & Smith, 1989); however, much more research is needed before this strategy can be considered completely viable.

Research on the role of misconceptions in prior knowledge and the construction of meaning is just beginning to accumulate. Although the guidelines presented here are certainly supported by the limited amount of research that exists, you should be on the lookout for new information in this area.

Literacy Lesson

Mummies, Tombs, and Treasure

This chapter has focused on strategies for activating and developing prior knowledge and on how to use these strategies in thematic units and literacy lessons. At the conclusion of Chapter 2, you read a literacy lesson for narrative text, *Jamaica Tag-Along* (Havill, 1989). In that lesson, two strategies were utilized when introducing the book to activate and develop prior knowledge—brainstorming (a teaching strategy), and story map prediction (a student strategy). You might want to look back at that lesson now to see how those strategies were used.

The following lesson focuses on introducing the theme and introducing one of the books to be read during the theme. You will be able to see how global prior knowledge is activated and developed when introducing the theme and how text-specific prior knowledge is activated and developed for the first chapter.

This portion of the sample unit is based on a thematic unit plan on "ancient Egypt" designed for fifth, sixth, or seventh graders in which one of the books to be read is *Mummies, Tombs, and Treasure* (Perl, 1987). The sample presented here focuses on introducing the theme and gives a literacy lesson for the first chapter in the book.

Before Reading the Plan

1. **Think about what you have learned about prior knowledge activation and development.**
2. **Recall the parts of a thematic unit plan and a literacy lesson. (See Chapter 2 if you need to review.)**
3. **Read "The First Egyptian Mummies," Chapter 1 of *Mummies, Tombs, and Treasure* (Perl, 1987).**
4. **Read and study the teacher preparation section to see how I decided which prior knowledge to activate for the theme and the literacy lesson.**

While Reading the Plan

1. **Notice how prior knowledge was activated and developed for this theme and lesson.**
2. **Think about why each strategy was used. Note any questions that you have.**
3. **Think of other ways that you might have activated and developed prior knowledge for this theme and lesson.**

MUMMIES, TOMBS, AND TREASURE
Secrets of Ancient Egypt

BY LILA PERL

Illustrated with photographs · Drawings by Erika Weihs

CLARION BOOKS

Contents

1

The First Egyptian Mummies

What is a mummy, and why do we find mummies so fascinating? We've all heard of old-time horror movies with names like *The Mummy's Hand*, *The Mummy's Ghost*, and *The Mummy's Tomb*. And then there is "the mummy's curse." Even today there are people who believe that anyone who has ever gone near a mummy will meet with sudden misfortune.

Yet a mummy is nothing more than a dead body, either human or animal. Perhaps the reason mummies fill some of us with fear and fire up our imaginations is that they are so lifelike. Many Egyptian mummies are thousands of years old. But they still have their hair, their fingernails and toenails, and even their eyelashes. Their flesh and their features are well preserved. In looking at photographs taken when these mummies were discovered, in recent times, we can tell them apart and recognize their faces.

A mummy, of course, is a dead body that has been

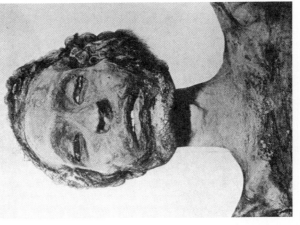

The 3000-year-old mummy of an ancient Egyptian priest

sues of once-living things, returning them to nature in other forms.

But sometimes nature springs a surprise or two on us. One such surprise took place long ago in the vast North African desert country of Egypt. Before the beginning of recorded history — perhaps seven or eight thousand years ago — people began to settle on the banks of the Nile River, which runs through the Egyptian desert. The ribbons of well-watered land that bordered the Nile provided precious soil for growing food crops. So, in selecting a place to bury their dead, the Egyptian farming people avoided the river shore. They chose instead the hot, barren sands that lay beyond it.

The people dug small shallow graves. Usually they buried their dead in a crouched position. They placed them on their sides with their knees drawn up to their chests. That way their bodies took up as little space as possible.

The Egyptians hoped that in some magical way the dead were not really dead. Perhaps their spirits lay beneath the sand along with their limp, unclothed bodies. Perhaps a spirit might wish to eat or drink just as the living did. So the families of the dead included some clay pots of food and jars of water in the shallow pit graves. And sometimes they added a man's favorite tool or spear of sharpened stone, a woman's beads of shell or bone, or a child's toy.

Then the family covered the grave with sand and piled some rocks on top of it. The rocks helped to mark the grave. They also made it difficult for jackals and other wild animals of the desert to reach the body inside it.

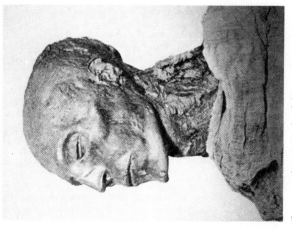

The mummy of King Seti I, who ruled Egypt 3,300 years ago

preserved — either accidentally by nature or on purpose by humans. Without preservation, dead animal matter usually decays very quickly. This is true of plant matter, too. A dead bird or cat, a piece of rotting fruit, can show us some of the stages of decay. Decay is caused by bacteria. These microscopic organisms break down the tis-

The hot dry sand of the shallow unlined graves did an amazing thing: it preserved the bodies of the early Egyptians wonderfully well. Moisture helps bacteria in bringing about decay. And the human body contains about seventy-five percent water. By rapidly absorbing the body's moisture, the hot sand acted as a natural preservative. The skin and other organs dried instead of decaying, and the first Egyptian mummies were born!

Similar accidents of nature have taken place in other parts of the world. But the early Egyptians had no way of knowing about those.

We know today, for example, that bodies can be naturally preserved by dry cold as well as by dry heat. In Siberia in northern Asia, woolly mammoths — huge prehistoric animals that resembled hairy elephants — have been found well preserved in ice. Their mummified bodies are at least ten thousand years old, for that is when the last of the mammoths died out.

Dry cold has also preserved the bodies of the Incas of Peru. The people of that far-reaching Indian empire lived in the high Andes Mountains of South America. Until they were conquered by Spanish explorers about five hundred years ago, they placed their dead in rock shelters. They arranged the bodies in a sitting position with knees drawn up, and bound them into bundles, wrapped in cloth, grass, and fur. In the dry, crisp mountain air, the Inca dead were soon transformed into mummies.

The early Egyptians must have been pleased when they somehow discovered the naturally mummified bodies of their dead. Soon they looked for ways to improve their graves. They lined the burial pits with straw

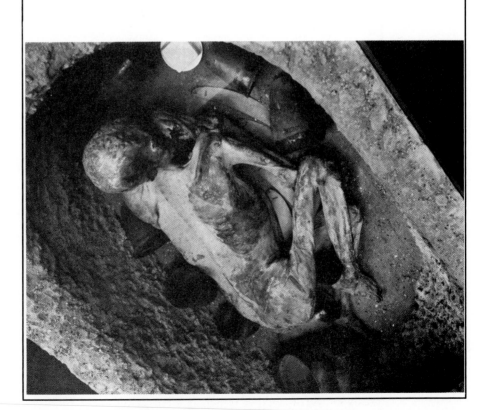

A naturally preserved mummy, with fingernails, toenails, and a few locks of reddish hair, found in a shallow desert grave

5

matting or with animal skins. And, as time went on, they added a crude floor and walls of sun-dried bricks. The bricks were made of chopped straw and mud, and were molded by hand. Some burial chambers even had ceilings of rough wooden beams. Such graves were costly because wood was very scarce in Egypt, a land with few trees.

The Nile farmers were becoming more prosperous, though. Each year when the river flooded its banks, it deposited a rich layer of mud and renewed the fertility of the soil. The farmers dug a network of irrigation ditches. This brought water into their fields so that there would be enough moisture throughout the growing season. Rain almost never fell in the Egyptian desert.

As the population living along the Nile grew, life became less simple. Village governments had to be formed to keep careful records of the lush farmland known as the "black land." (The desert, by contrast, was called the "red land.") The village officials measured property boundaries, oversaw the digging of irrigation canals, noted the amount of grain that was stored from each year's harvest, and started collecting taxes from the Nile villagers. Soon the villages were organized into bigger regions, or provinces, and finally into two kingdoms — Upper Egypt and Lower Egypt.

Then, about five thousand years ago, all of Egypt came under the rule of a single king. He was known as the "lord of the two lands." The year in which Upper Egypt and Lower Egypt were united was about 3100 B.C., and the name of the first king was Menes [MEN-eez].

It is always confusing to learn that Upper Egypt is really the southern part of the country and Lower Egypt the northern part. This is because the Nile River flows from south to north, carrying the waters of melting snows and jungle rains from the mountains and forests of central Africa. So Upper Egypt is "upriver" from Lower Egypt.

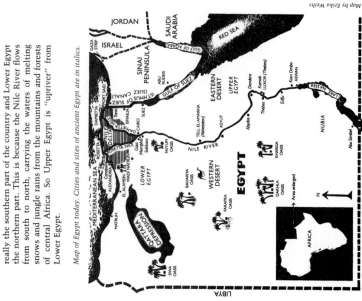

Map of Egypt today. Cities and sites of ancient Egypt are in italics.

Map by Erika Welsh

6

A wooden statue of an Egyptian king wearing the short white kilt and the white crown of Upper Egypt

UPPER EGYPT LOWER EGYPT DOUBLE CROWN

The crown of Upper Egypt, the crown of Lower Egypt, and the double crown of the "two lands"

The new king wore an interesting crown. It combined the old pear-shaped white crown of Upper Egypt and the boxy red crown of Lower Egypt; one set atop the other. This headdress was known as the "double crown." It was an important symbol of the joining of the two parts of the country.

Now that Egypt had become a great kingdom, what was going to happen to its powerful ruler when he died? He certainly could not be buried naked in a shallow desert grave, not even one that was lined with brick and roofed with wood. A great king needed a proper coffin of wood or even stone.

So, while commoners continued to be buried in the old way, kings and their queens, and other nobles were more carefully prepared for burial. Instead of being left unclothed, their bodies were wrapped in strips of linen, the same cloth that Egyptians wore throughout their lives. Linen was woven from flax, which was grown along the Nile. Cotton was unknown in Egypt at the time, and wool was too coarse, itchy, and hot. Many people considered it "unclean."

But, unlike the short white linen kilt worn by men or the long, close-fitting linen dress worn by women, the clothing of the dead consisted of tightly wound bandages. And to protect the body even further, the Egyptians poured warm resin over the layers of bandages until they were well soaked. Resin was an oily, sticky extract that came from certain plants. Because it did not dissolve in water and hardened to a varnish-like finish, the Egyptians figured it would keep the body dry.

Then they placed the body in a tightly closed coffin and buried it deeper than the ordinary pit grave. Because the early kings and queens were laid to rest with valuable jewelry and other treasures, the Egyptians wanted to be sure that the grave goods would be safe from both animals and humans.

But the new royal burials turned out to be a horrible mistake. Locked into their layers of bandages and sealed in their thick-walled coffins, the bodies of the rulers rapidly decayed from within. The hot, dry sand that would have mummified them was shut out.

The Egyptians learned of this when grave robbers tunneled deep beneath the desert sands and broke open the coffins to steal the royal treasures. All that remained inside the stiff coating of bandages was a heap of bones.

There was no mummy, no likeness of the dead person at all!

Clearly, the Egyptians had to find a better way of making mummies. Nature had shown them one way to do it. But they wanted grander burials, more secure and impressive tombs. Above all they wanted mummies that were as well preserved, or even better, than those that were buried directly in the sand.

The Egyptians of the newly formed kingdom would have to find some other method for transforming their dead into lifelike and long-lasting mummies.

*Literacy
Lesson
continued*

Teacher Preparation

This theme was selected because it has high student appeal and is a topic of study usually found in grades 5, 6, or 7. Preparation for this theme proceeded in the following way:

1. I selected books for the theme. *Mummies, Tombs, and Treasure* (Perl, 1987) would be read by all students, and other books would be self-selected from the school library.
2. I then identified my major outcomes in terms of attitudes and habits and constructing meaning:
   - *Attitudes and habits*: Develop an appreciation of influences from the past on the present.
   - *Constructing meaning*: Understand how previous civilizations have influenced our lives today.

   I decided that strategies and skills focus would be on the following:
   - Preview and self-question
   - Summarizing information from different sources
   - Using library resources

   This theme and text naturally lend themselves to focusing on these areas.

3. Next, I thought about the major background concepts that students needed to have for a theme on ancient Egypt. I concluded that they needed to know where it was, when it existed, and what the climate was like.
4. I then read the book *Mummies, Tombs, and Treasure* (Perl, 1987) and determined that the first chapter has two main ideas with a strong cause-effect structure.

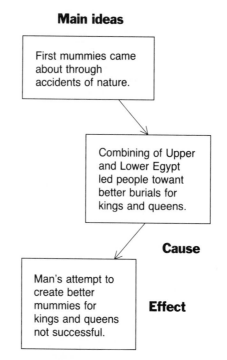

This graphic organizer would help students see the structure in the first chapter and prepare them for the remainder of the book.

5. Next, I reviewed Chapter 1 to see if there was any key-concept vocabulary related to the main ideas. Four words seemed important—*mummy*, *bacteria*, *decay*, and *coffin*. *Mummy* and *bacteria* were defined in the text, and students would know *decay* from their experiences with teeth and *coffin* from their television experiences. Therefore, I decided not to preteach any vocabulary. Vocabulary would be the focus of an extension activity after reading, if needed.

6. Finally, I decided that I would use the following teaching strategies to introduce the theme:

   • *Brainstorming and discussion* (using a photograph of a mummy and a map): This would help bring out what students knew and give them a general idea of where Egypt is. The discussion would be focused and directed.

   • *Anticipation guide*: This would help students think about what they believed before the unit and see how that changed after the unit.

   • *Project*: Students would plan a project during the theme. This would help them integrate what they were learning. They would use the book we were reading together, as well as self-selected books from the library. The project might be a report, display, or some other idea chosen by students.

*Literacy
Lesson
continued*

For the first literacy lesson, I decided to use a structured preview because this would give students a sense of how the book was organized and would help them think about constructing meaning as they read. I also planned to use the preview and self-question strategy because it is appropriate for expository text and I wanted students to continue to become more independent in activating their prior knowledge and setting their purpose for reading.

Thematic Unit and Literacy Lesson Plan

Thematic unit title: Ancient Egypt

Level: Grades 5, 6, or 7

Unit focus:

Attitudes and habits: Develop an appreciation of influences from the past on the present.

Meaning construction: Understand how previous civilizations have influenced our lives today.

Strategies and skills focus: Preview and self-question
         Summarizing information from
          different sources
         Using library resources

Introducing the Theme

ACTIVITY	PROCEDURE	NOTES
Brainstorming and discussion about Egypt	Show students mummy photograph and ask them where they think this is from. Discuss ideas.	Motivates students. Activates global prior knowledge. Gives me a chance to assess prior knowledge.
	Divide class into small groups and invite students to share what they know about ancient Egypt.	
	Bring class together and discuss what is known, focusing on	
	• where Egypt is.	
	• what it is like (desert).	
	• when it existed.	

Literacy Lesson continued

ACTIVITY	PROCEDURE	NOTES
	Display a map and have students locate Egypt; continue discussion focused around above points.	
Anticipation guide	Tell students that they will be learning a lot about ancient Egypt. Distribute the anticipation guide and ask students to read each statement and indicate whether they agree or disagree. Students will return to this after the unit is completed.	Continues to activate prior knowledge. Focuses students' thinking on the unit outcomes. Will allow students to see how their knowledge and beliefs change during the unit.

Ancient Egypt

Before the Unit		*After the Unit*
_____	1. All that we know about burial was learned from the mummies.	_____
_____	2. Studying history is not a good idea.	_____
_____	3. Not many treasures of the past exist today.	_____
_____	4. What we know today is based only on new scientific discoveries.	_____

ACTIVITY	PROCEDURE	NOTES
Introducing the theme project	Tell students that during the theme they will be doing a project on Egypt. They can pick a suggested one or design their own. Students can decide on their project after reading a chapter or two in the book *Mummies*.	Provides a way for students to integrate new knowledge with what they already know.

Literacy Lesson continued

ACTIVITY	PROCEDURE	NOTES

Possible Projects

1. Write a book about Egypt.
2. Make a miniature mummy.
3. Create visual display showing how things from Egypt have influenced our lives.
4. Conduct a television news show about discoveries in ancient Egypt.
5. You decide. Plan your own project.

	Discuss selecting other books from the library to use for the project. Encourage students to share their ideas.	Begins to focus on using library resources. This will continue later in the unit.

Introducing *Mummies, Tombs, and Treasure*

Using preview and self-question strategy	Display the preview and self-question poster (see page 128). Have students preview *Mummies, Tombs, and Treasure* and list questions in their journal they would like to answer while reading this book. Encourage them to make notes about each question as they read.	Activates prior knowledge related specifically to the book and makes students take responsibility for their own learning by having them raise questions they want answered; these become their purpose for reading. Students have learned to use this strategy in previous units. If more modeling is needed, provide it here (see Chapter 8).
Structured preview of Chapter 1, "The First Egyptian Mummies"	Invite students to locate Chapter 1 and read the title and captions for each illustration. Ask students what they think they will learn in this chapter. Discuss briefly.	The structured preview activates and develops prior knowledge specific to the chapter. I decided to use this because I felt this class needed this type of support in beginning the book.

*Literacy
Lesson
continued*

ACTIVITY	PROCEDURE	NOTES
	Display the graphic organizer for Chapter 1. Discuss with students that this chapter has two main ideas and a cause-effect organization.	

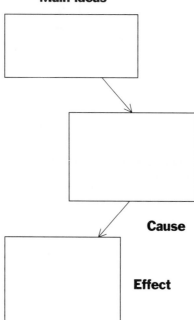

Main ideas

Cause

Effect

**Reading and Responding to
"The First Egyptian Mummies"**

Independent reading	Have students read the chapter, looking for information that will help them answer their questions.	Because of the structured preview and the interest and easiness of the text, students will be able to read this chapter independently.

*Literacy
Lesson
continued*

ACTIVITY	PROCEDURE	NOTES
Making journal notes	Remind them to note any words in their journals they want to discuss and to think about completing the graphic organizer when they have finished their reading.	
Discussion partners	Have students meet with a partner to talk about what they learned and how they felt about this chapter.	Encourages personal response and allows students to construct their own meanings.
Whole-class discussion	Summarize partners' discussions.	Allows to get a sense of students' responses.
Completing the graphic organizer chart	Display the graphic organizer chart. Ask students to help complete the chart. Discuss the two main ideas and the cause-effect structure.	This experience will help students formulate main ideas and see how certain events cause other things to happen. If students have difficulty with this, I will model how I would identify these points (see Chapter 8 on modeling).
Discussing journal notes and vocabulary	Invite students to share any notes or words they wrote in their journals. Ask them to look at their original list of questions to see if they can answer any of them yet.	Allows a way to teach any words causing difficulty; also, a good assessment opportunity to identify students who will need more support while reading the remainder of this book.

Extending "The First Egyptian Mummies"

Students are likely to be excited about getting on with the reading of this book; therefore, no additional activities are planned, and students will read the remainder of the book independently. We will stop for discussion after every two chapters or more frequently if needed. If some students need teacher support (determined through responses to Chapter 1), I will meet with them in small groups and guide their reading and/or have them do cooperative reading. The project will be started after students have read several chapters; then meetings in the library will be planned. Throughout the reading of this book, I will conduct

Literacy
Lesson
continued

conferences with students to give them needed support in constructing meaning. See Chapters 6 and 7 for information on conferencing.

After Reading the Plan

1. Review and discuss the plan with some of your peers who have read it, focusing on how prior knowledge was activated and developed throughout the lesson.
2. Assume that you have a group of students who need much more prior knowledge development for the book *Mummies, Tombs, and Treasure*. Work out a plan showing how you will do this for Chapter 1.

SUMMARY

This chapter has focused on the importance of activating and developing prior knowledge for the effective construction of meaning. It has included information about how to use prior knowledge to help all students develop their ability to construct meaning. Second-language learners, students with limited prior knowledge, and students with misconceptions need special support. Thirteen strategies, two student strategies and eleven teaching strategies, were described with emphasis on how and when to use them. *The ultimate goal of the literacy program is to get students to use strategies independently and to call up their own prior knowledge in order to determine their purpose for reading.* A sample lesson illustrating the process the teacher goes through in planning a lesson focusing on prior knowledge was presented.

Children's Books

Adler, D. A. (1986). *Martin Luther King, Jr.: Free at last*. New York: Holiday House.
Allard, H., & Marshall, J. (1978). *The Stupids have a ball*. Boston: Houghton Mifflin.
Behrens, J. (1978). *Fiesta!* Chicago: Childrens Press.
Fox, M. (1985). *Wilfrid Gordon McDonald Partridge*. New York: Kane/Miller.
Freedman, R. (1987). *Lincoln: A photobiography*. New York: Clarion.
Gibbons, G. (1989). *Monarch butterfly*. New York: Holiday House.
Giff, P. R. (1980). *Today was a terrible day*. New York: Viking.
Giff, P. R. (1988). *Ronald Morgan goes to bat*. New York: Viking Kestrel.
Hamilton, V. (1990). *Cousins*. New York: Philomel.
Murphy, J. (1990). *The boy's war*. New York: Clarion.
Perl, L. (1987). *Mummies, tombs, and treasure*. New York: Clarion.
Sachar, L. (1989). *Wayside School is falling down*. New York: Lothrop, Lee & Shepard.
Small, D. (1985). *Imogene's antlers*. New York: Crown.
Van Allsburg, C. (1985). *The polar express*. Boston: Houghton Mifflin.

For Additional Reading

Alvermann, D. E., Dillon, D. R., & O'Brien, D. G. (1987). *Using discussion to promote reading comprehension*. Newark, DE: International Reading Association.

Anderson, R. C., & Pearson, P. D. (1984). A schema-theoretic view of basic processes in reading comprehension. In P. D. Pearson (Ed.), *Handbook of reading research* (pp. 255–291). New York: Longman.

Au, K. H. (in press). *Literacy instruction in multicultural settings*.

Graesser, A., Golding, J. M., & Long, D. L. (1991). Narrative representation and comprehension. In R. Barr, M. L. Kamil, P. Mosenthal & P. D. Pearson (Eds.), *Handbook of reading research* (Vol. 2, pp. 171–205). New York: Longman.

Rigg, P., & Allen, V. G. (1989). *When they don't all speak English*. Urbana, IL: National Council of Teachers of English.

Weaver, C. A., III, & Kintsch, W. (1991). Expository text. In R. Barr, M. L. Kamil, P. Mosenthal & P. D. Pearson (Eds.), *Handbook of reading research* (Vol. 2, pp. 230–245). New York: Longman.

References

Adams, M., & Bertram, B. (1980). *Background knowledge and reading comprehension*. Reading Education Report No. 13. Urbana: Center for the Study for Reading, University of Illinois. (ERIC Document Reproduction Service ED 181 431).

Alvermann, D. E., Dillon, D. R., & O'Brien, D. G. (1987). *Using discussion to promote reading comprehension*. Newark, DE: International Reading Association.

Alvermann, D. E., & Hynd, C. R. (1987, December). *Overcoming misconceptions in science: An on-line study of prior knowledge activation*. Paper presented at the meeting of the National Reading Conference, St. Petersburg, FL.

Alvermann, D. E., Smith, L. C., & Readence, J. E. (1985). Prior knowledge activation and the comprehension of compatible and incompatible text. *Reading Research Quarterly, 20*, 420–436.

Anderson, R. C., Hiebert, E. H., Scott, J. A., & Wilkinson, I. A. G. (1985). *Becoming a nation of readers*. Champaign, IL: Center for the Study of Reading, University of Illinois.

Anderson, R. C., & Pearson, P. D. (1984). A schema-theoretic view of basic processes in reading comprehension. In P. D. Pearson (Ed.), *Handbook of reading research* (pp. 255–291). New York: Longman.

Anderson, R. C., Reynolds, R. E., Schallert, D. L., & Goetz, E. T. (1977). Frameworks for comprehending discourse. *American Educational Research Journal, 14*, 367–381.

Au, K. H. (1979). Using the experience-text-relationship method with minority children. *Reading Teacher, 32*, 677–679.

Au, K. H. (in press). *Literacy instruction in multicultural settings*.

Barr, R., Kamil, M. L., Mosenthal, P., & Pearson, P. D. (1991). *Handbook of reading research* (Vol. 2). New York: Longman.

Barrera, R. B. (1983). Bilingual reading in the primary grades: Some questionable views and practices. In T. H. Escobedo (Ed.), *Early childhood bilingual education* (pp. 164–184). New York: Teachers College Press.

Bartlett, F. C. (1932). *Remembering*. Cambridge: Cambridge University Press.

Beck, I. (1984). Developing comprehension: The impact of the directed reading lesson. In R. C. Anderson, J. Osborn & R. J. Tierney (Eds.), *Learning to read in American schools: Basal readers and content texts* (pp. 3–20). Hillsdale, NJ: Lawrence Erlbaum.

Beck, I. L., Omanson, R. C., & McKeown, M. G. (1982). An instructional redesign of reading lessons: Effects on comprehension. *Reading Research Quarterly, 17*(4), 462–481.

Center for the Study of Reading. (n.d.). *Suggestions for classroom: Teachers and independent reading*. Urbana: Center for the Study of Reading, University of Illinois.

Choate, J. S., & Rakes, T. A. (1987). The structured listening activity: A model for improving listening comprehension. *Reading Teacher, 41*, 194–200.

Dillon, J. T. (1984). Research on questioning and discussion. *Educational Leadership, 42*, 50–56.

Dole, J. A., & Smith, E. L. (1989). Prior knowledge and learning from science text: An instructional study. In the Thirty-eighth Yearbook of the National Reading Conference, *Cognitive and social perspectives for literacy research and instruction* (pp. 345–352). Chicago: National Reading Conference.

Dressel, J. H. (1990). The effects of listening to and discussing different qualities of children's literature on the narrative writing of fifth graders. *Research in the Teaching of English, 24*, 397–414.

Driver, R., & Erickson, G. (1983). Theories in action: Some theoretical and empirical issues in the study of students' conceptual frameworks in science. *Studies in Science Education, 10*, 37–60.

Durkin, D. (1978). What classroom observations reveal about reading comprehension instruction. *Reading Research Quarterly, 14*(4), 481–533.

Durkin, D. (1981). Reading comprehension instruction in five basal reader series. *Reading Research Quarterly, 16*(4), 515–544.

Feitelson, D., Kita, B., & Goldstein, Z. (1986). Effects of listening to stories on first graders' comprehension and use of language. *Research in the Teaching of English, 20*, 339–356.

Fielding, L. G., Anderson, R. C., & Pearson, P. D. (1990). *How discussion questions influence children's story understanding*. Tech. Report No. 490. Urbana: Center for the Study of Reading, University of Illinois.

Flood, J., & Lapp, D. (1988). Conceptual mapping strategies for information texts. *Reading Teacher, 41*, 780–783.

Freedle, R. P. (1979). *New Directions in discourse processing*. Hillsdale, NJ: Lawrence Erlbaum.

Graves, M. F., & Cooke, C. L. (1980). Effects of previewing difficult short stories for high school students. *Research on Reading in Secondary Schools, 6*, 28–54.

Graves, M. F., Cooke, C. L., & LaBerge, H. J. (1983). Effects of previewing difficult and short stories on low-ability junior high school students' comprehension, recall and attitude. *Reading Research Quarterly, 18*, 262–276.

Hansen, J. (1981). The effects of inference training and practice on young children's reading comprehension. *Reading Research Quarterly, 16*, 391–417.

Harris, T. L., & Hodges, R. E. (1981). *A dictionary of reading and related terms*. Newark, DE: International Reading Association.

Holmes, B. C., & Roser, N. L. (1987). Five ways to assess readers' prior knowledge. *Reading Teacher, 40*, 646–649.

Hynd, C. R., & Alvermann, D. E. (1986). Prior knowledge activation in refutation and non-refutation text. In J. A. Niles & R. V. Lalik (Eds.), the Thirty-fifth Yearbook of the National Reading Conference, *Solving problems in literacy: Learners, teachers, and researchers* (pp. 55–60). Rochester, NY: National Reading Conference.

Langer, J. (1981). From theory to practice: A prereading plan. *Journal of Reading, 25*, 152–156a.

Langer, J. (1984). Examining background knowledge and text comprehension. *Reading Research Quarterly, 19*, 468–481.

Lipson, M. Y. (1982). Learning new information from text. The role of prior knowledge and reading ability. *Journal of Reading Behavior, 14*, 243–261.

Lipson, M. Y. (1983). The influence of religious affiliation on children's memory for text information. *Reading Research Quarterly, 18*, 448–457.

Lipson, M. Y. (1984). Some unexpected issues in prior knowledge and comprehension. *Reading Teacher, 37*, 760–764.

Maria, K. (1988, December). *Helping fifth graders learn with science text.* Paper presented at the meeting of the National Reading Conference, Tucson, AZ.

Maria, K. (1990). *Reading comprehension interaction: Strategies and issues.* Parkton, MD: York Press.

Marino, J. L., Gould, S. M., & Haas, L. W. (1985). The effect of writing as a prereading activity on delayed recall of narrative text. *Elementary School Journal, 86*, 199–205.

Mason, J. M., & Au, K. H. (1990). *Reading instruction for today* (2nd ed.). Glenview, IL: Scott, Foresman.

McNeil, J. D. (1987). *Reading comprehension: New directions for classroom practice* (2nd ed.). Glenview, IL: Scott Foresman.

Meyer, B. J. F. (1975). *The organization of prose and its effects on memory.* Amsterdam: The Hague North-Holland Press.

Meyer, B. J. F., & Freedle, R. O. (1984). Effects of discourse type on recall. *American Educational Research Journal, 21*, 121–143.

Moore, D. W., Readence, J. E., & Rickelman, R. J. (1989). *Prereading activities for content area reading and learning* (2nd ed.). Newark, DE: International Reading Association.

Neuman, S. (1988). Enhancing children's comprehension through previewing. In J. E. Readence & R. J. Baldwin (Eds.), The Thirty-seventh Yearbook for the National Reading Conference, *Dialogues in literacy research* (pp. 219–224). Chicago: National Reading Conference.

Noyce, R. M., & Christie, J. F. (1989). *Integrating reading and writing instruction in grades K–8.* Boston: Allyn and Bacon.

Ogle, D. M. (1986). K-W-L: A teaching model that develops active reading of expository text. *Reading Teacher, 39*(6), 564–570.

Pace, A. J., Marshall, N., Horowitz, R., Lipson, M. Y., and Lucido, P. (1989). When prior knowledge doesn't facilitate text comprehension: An examination of some of the issues. In the Thirty-eighth Yearbook of the National Reading Conference, *Cognitive and social perspectives for literacy research and instruction* (pp. 213–224). Chicago: National Reading Conference.

Paris, S. G., Cross, D. R., & Lipson, M. Y. (1984). Informed strategies for learning: A program to improve children's reading awareness and comprehension. *Journal of Educational Psychology, 76,* 1239–1252.

Paris, S. G., Lipson, M. Y., & Wixson, K. K. (1983). Becoming a strategic reader. *Contemporary Educational Psychology, 8,* 293–316.

Paris, S. G., Wasik, B. A., & Turner, J. C. (1991). The development of strategic readers. In R. Barr, M. L. Kamil, P. Mosenthal, & P. D. Pearson (Eds.), *Handbook of Reading Research* (Vol. 2, pp. 609–640). New York: Longman.

Pearson, P. D., & Johnson, D. D. (1978). *Teaching reading comprehension.* New York: Holt, Rinehart and Winston.

Pehrsson, R. S., & Robinson, H. A. (1985). *The semantic organizer approach to writing and reading instruction.* Rockville, MD: Aspen Systems Corporation.

Pressley, M., Burkell, J., Cariglia-Bull, T., Lysynchuck, L., McGoldrick, J. A., Schneider, B., Snyder, B. L., Symons, S., & Woloshyn, V. E. (1990). *Cognitive strategy instruction that really improves children's academic performance.* Cambridge, MA: Brookline.

Readence, J. E., Bean, T. W., & Baldwin, R. S. (1981, 1985, 1989). *Content area reading: An integrated approach.* Dubuque, IA: Kendall/Hunt.

Rigg, P., & Allen, V. G. (1989). *When they don't all speak English.* Urbana, IL: National Council of Teachers of English.

Rosenblatt, L. (1938/1983). *Literature as exploration.* New York: Modern Language Association.

Rumelhart, D. E. (1980). Schemata: The building blocks of cognition. In R. J. Spiro et al. (Eds.), *Theoretical issues in reading comprehension* (pp. 33–58). Hillsdale, NJ: Lawrence Erlbaum.

Smith, N. B. (1965). *American reading instruction.* Newark, DE: International Reading Association.

Stahl, S. A., & Vancil, S. J. (1986). Discussion is what makes semantic maps work in vocabulary instruction. *Reading Teacher, 39,* 62–67.

Sulzby, E. (1989). Assessment of writing and of children's language while writing. In L. Morrow & J. Smith (Eds.), *The role of assessment and measurement in early literacy instruction* (pp. 83–109). Englewood Cliffs, NJ: Prentice-Hall.

Taba, H. (1967). *Teacher's handbook for elementary school social studies.* Reading, MA: Addison-Wesley.

Taylor, D., & Dorsey-Gaines, C. (1988). *Growing up literate.* Portsmouth, NH: Heinemann.

Tierney, R. J., & Cunningham, J. W. (1984). Research on teaching reading comprehension. In P. D. Pearson (Ed.), *Handbook of reading research* (pp. 609–655). New York: Longman.

Tierney, R. J., Readence, J. E., & Dishner, E. K. (1990). Reader's theater. In *Reading strategies and practices: A compendium* (3rd ed.) (pp. 190–195). Boston: Allyn and Bacon.

Ward, G. (1988). *I've got a project on . . .* Australia: Primary English Teaching Association, distributed by Heinemann, Portsmouth, NH.

Weber, R. (1991). Language diversity and reading in American society. In R. Barr, M. L. Kamil, P. Mosenthal, & P. D. Pearson (Eds.), *Handbook of reading research* (pp. 97–119). New York: Longman.

Weisberg, R. K., & Balajthy, E. (1985, December). *Effects of semantic mapping training on disabled readers' summarizing and recognition of expository text structure.* Paper presented at the National Reading Conference, San Diego, CA.

White, R. E. (1981). The effects of organizational themes and adjunct placements on children's prose learning: A developmental perspective. *Dissertation Abstracts International, 42,* 2042A-2043A. (University Microfilms No. 81-25, 038).

Wong, J. W., & Au, K. H. (1985). The concept-text-application approach: Helping elementary students comprehend expository text. *Reading Teacher, 38,* 612–618.

Vocabulary Development in the Literacy Program

4

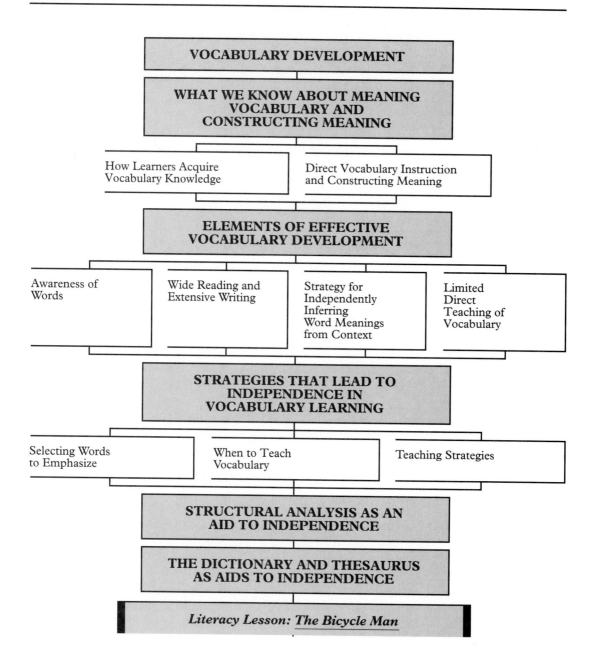

VOCABULARY DEVELOPMENT

WHAT WE KNOW ABOUT MEANING VOCABULARY AND CONSTRUCTING MEANING

How Learners Acquire Vocabulary Knowledge

Direct Vocabulary Instruction and Constructing Meaning

ELEMENTS OF EFFECTIVE VOCABULARY DEVELOPMENT

Awareness of Words

Wide Reading and Extensive Writing

Strategy for Independently Inferring Word Meanings from Context

Limited Direct Teaching of Vocabulary

STRATEGIES THAT LEAD TO INDEPENDENCE IN VOCABULARY LEARNING

Selecting Words to Emphasize

When to Teach Vocabulary

Teaching Strategies

STRUCTURAL ANALYSIS AS AN AID TO INDEPENDENCE

THE DICTIONARY AND THESAURUS AS AIDS TO INDEPENDENCE

Literacy Lesson: The Bicycle Man

Figure 4.1 "Never Mince Words with a Shark" by Jack Prelutsky (1984)

Never Mince Words with a Shark

You may quarrel with centipedes, quibble with seals,
declaim to a duck in the park,
engage in disputes with cantankerous coots,
but never mince words with a shark.

You may rant at an anteater, banter with eels,
and haggle with gaggles of geese,
heap verbal abuse on a monkey or moose,
but a shark you had best leave in peace.

You may argue with otters, make speeches to teals,
and lecture at length to a shrew,
but a shark will deflate your attempts at debate,
and before you are done, you are through.

Source: "Never Mince Words with a Shark" from *The New Kid on the Block* by Jack Prelutsky. Copyright © 1984 by Jack Prelutsky. Reprinted by permission of Greenwillow Books, a division of William Morrow & Company, Inc. and William Heinemann Ltd.

READING POETRY SUCH as "Never Mince Words with a Shark" (Prelutsky, 1984) (Figure 4.1) and other literature rich in language is one of the ways children develop their vocabularies. Chapter 3 dealt with the importance of activating and developing prior knowledge; as we shall see, vocabulary is an integral part of this knowledge. This chapter will focus on strategies and techniques for developing vocabulary that continuously promote the integration of new knowledge with old knowledge and that lead to the active construction of meaning.

VOCABULARY DEVELOPMENT

As readers develop vocabulary, they learn two aspects about words: recognition and meaning (Chall, 1987); these two vocabularies, however, *are not* separate from each other. Children's *recognition vocabulary* consists of that body of words that they are able to pronounce or read orally. Beginning literacy learners focus much of their attention on recognizing words (Chall, 1987) even though their primary focus is on meaning. Children's *meaning vocabulary* is that body of words whose meanings they understand and can use. *Recognition and meaning vocabularies develop simultaneously as students learn to read and write.*

Students' recognition vocabulary ultimately becomes sight vocabulary, or words that they are able to read instantly and use in constructing meaning. Beginning readers and writers rapidly build such vocabularies through reading and writing experiences. Chapter 5 will focus on how readers and writers develop their ability to identify words and to develop a recognition vocabulary; this chapter will concentrate on what we know about meaning vocabulary and strategies to foster its growth.

WHAT WE KNOW ABOUT MEANING VOCABULARY AND CONSTRUCTING MEANING

Vocabulary is a reflection of an individual's knowledge and *concepts* in a particular area. For example, a person knowledgeable about music will understand and use the words *meter*, *clef*, and *timbre* in ways that reflect musical knowledge, and an avid gardener will know and use terms such as *perennial*, *deciduous*, and *Gaillardia*.

The study of vocabulary has been of interest to researchers and educators for many years (Beck & McKeown, 1991). It has been clearly established that there is a strong relationship between the knowledge of word meanings (vocabulary) and reading comprehension (Anderson & Freebody, 1981; Davis, 1971; Johnston, 1981). The strength of this relationship has led educators to recommend that students be taught crucial word meanings before reading selections (Tierney & Cunningham, 1984). However, the wisdom of this procedure and others related to the teaching of vocabulary to improve comprehension has been questioned and challenged by more recent researchers (Nagy, 1988). *There is a great deal more to improving an individual's ability to construct meaning than just teaching a few words before a selection is read.* Two significant issues will be addressed to help you more fully understand the strong relationship that exists between vocabulary knowledge and comprehension: (1) How do learners acquire vocabulary knowledge? and (2) Does instruction in vocabulary lead to improved comprehension?

How Learners Acquire Vocabulary Knowledge

Studies of the size of children's vocabularies have given varying estimates for various grade levels (Loban, 1963; Lorge & Chall, 1963; Nagy & Anderson, 1984; Seashore, 1947). The discrepancies may have resulted from researchers using different definitions for what constituted a word, different concepts of what it means to know a word, and different bodies of words used to represent English (Beck & McKeown, 1991). In light of these problems, researchers have concluded that the early estimates of vocabulary size are much too low (Nagy & Anderson, 1984). It is sufficient to conclude that students in school know many words. A reasonable estimate based on current research places the *average* high school senior's vocabulary at approximately forty thousand words (Nagy & Herman, 1987). When the figures on vocabulary size are compared from year to year, it appears that students must learn twenty-seven hundred to three thousand new words per year (Beck & McKeown, 1991; Nagy & Herman, 1987), or approximately seven new words per day, in order to achieve this forty-thousand average by the time they are seniors in high school. Table 4.1 presents a table from Nagy and Herman (1987) summarizing this research.

The question, then, is how students acquire this astounding vocabulary. There are several plausible answers—through reading and/or listening to a wide variety of texts and/or through the direct instruction of word meanings. Extensive research on both of these points of view (Beck & McKeown, 1991; McKeown & Curtis, 1987; Nagy, 1988) leads to four major positions on how students acquire vocabulary (Beck & McKeown, 1991):

1. Students develop vocabulary knowledge through wide reading (Nagy & Herman, 1987).
2. Students learn vocabulary from context but need instruction about context in order to use it effectively (Jenkins, Stein & Wysocki, 1984; Sternberg, 1987).
3. Students are often hindered as much as they are helped by context. Therefore, they should be encouraged to use the dictionary as an aid in acquiring word meanings (Schatz & Baldwin, 1986).
4. Students can also profit from direct instruction in vocabulary (Beck, McKeown & Omanson, 1987; Graves, 1986, 1987; Stahl & Fairbanks, 1986).

Table 4.1   Summary of Research Showing Vocabulary Size and Growth

| Author | Estimated Word Stock of English | Original Figures | | | Recalibrated Figures[a] | | |
		Grade 3	Grade 12	Average Annual Growth	Grade 3	Grade 12	Average Annual Growth
Dupuy (1974)	12,300	2,000	7,800	644	4,016	38,457	3,827
Brandenburg (1918)	28,000	5,429	14,975	1,061	7,705	32,290	2,732
Kirkpatrick (1891, 1907)	28,000	6,620	17,600	1,220	10,004	41,517	3,501
M.K. Smith (1941)	166,247	25,500	47,000	2,389	23,672	40,789	1,902
Cuff (1930)	35,000	7,425	21,840	1,602	9,834	42,685	3,650

Source: From Nagy and Herman, "Summary of Research Showing Vocabulary Size and Growth," in Margaret C. McKeown and Mary E. Curtis, eds., *The Nature of Vocabulary Acquisition,* copyright © 1987 Lawrence Erlbaum Associates. Used with permission.

a. Recalibrated figures for grades 3 and 12 were arrived at by the following formula:

$$R = V*(1 + ((V/N)*((88,533/N) - 1)))$$

where R is the revised estimate of absolute vocabulary size, V is the author's original estimate of absolute vocabulary size, N is the total word stock of the language as represented by the dictionary or corpus used by the original author, and 88,533 is the total number of distinct word families estimated to exist in printed school English by Nagy and Anderson (1984). This formula attempts to capture the fact that the size of the estimated word stock of English (N) becomes more of a limiting factor as the size of a person's vocabulary (V) increases.

Given the strength of the research supporting these four positions and my own experience with children, I believe that we must consider all of these as viable ways for students to acquire vocabulary. The strength of the research behind the argument supporting wide reading as a means of improving both vocabulary and overall reading is very powerful and must be taken seriously (Fielding, Wilson & Anderson, 1986; Nagy & Herman, 1987). This is part of the rationale for having an independent reading and writing component as part of the literacy program (see Chapter 2). But while students are reading widely, they need to become independent in inferring word meanings; therefore, helping them develop an independent strategy for doing this through the use of context, the dictionary, and structural analysis will serve them well. Finally, *some students under some circumstances* may profit from the direct teaching of vocabulary; however, direct teaching is not as powerful in achieving overall growth in vocabulary and comprehension as is wide reading (Nagy & Herman, 1987). What we know about direct teaching of vocabulary must be examined carefully to determine how and when we should do it.

Direct Vocabulary Instruction and Constructing Meaning

As was noted earlier, it has been a long-standing practice to teach students words that are perceived as crucial for understanding a selection before reading. This practice has been justified on the basis of the extensive body of research showing a strong correlation between the knowledge of word meanings and comprehension. There are two important questions that must be considered when thinking about the direct teaching of vocabulary: (1) Does the direct teaching of vocabulary improve comprehension? and (2) If direct teaching is used, how and when should it be done?

Direct Vocabulary Teaching and Improved Comprehension

The goal of teaching students vocabulary has been to improve their overall comprehension. Early studies in this area had mixed results; some found that direct teaching did improve overall comprehension, whereas others found that such teaching only improved the knowledge of the specific words taught and had little or no effect on overall comprehension (Jenkins & Pany, 1981; Mezynski, 1983). However, more recent studies have found that the direct teaching of selected words results in small but significant improvements in comprehension (McKeown, Beck, Omanson & Pople, 1985; Stahl, 1983; Weiss, Mangrum & Liabre, 1986; Wixson, 1986). The determining factors seem to have been how the words were taught.

How and When Direct Teaching Is Effective

The direct teaching of vocabulary refers to those types of activities in which information about the meanings of words is made directly available to students; this may range from very strong teacher-led lessons to weaker forms of instruction such as looking up words in a dictionary (Beck & McKeown, 1991). In some studies, effective instruction appears to have had several important qualities:

1. *Only a few words central to the content of the story or informational text were taught* (Beck, Perfetti & McKeown, 1982; Wixson, 1986). In other words, the random teaching of any unknown word does not help students improve their comprehension. The words must be key-concept words.
2. *Words were taught in meaningful contexts that conveyed the particular meaning relevant to the text* (Gipe, 1978–1979; Nagy & Herman, 1987). Since words

have multiple meanings, teaching a meaning that does not fit the material to be read is fruitless for students and may even hinder overall comprehension.

3. *The teaching of vocabulary was integrated with the activation and development of prior knowledge.* Vocabulary is a specialized version of prior knowledge (Nagy & Herman, 1987). In all studies that were successful in improving comprehension by teaching vocabulary, the words taught were in some way related to the student's prior knowledge.

4. *Teachers taught words thoroughly by offering students rich and varied information about them* (Beck et al., 1987; Nagy & Herman, 1987). Simply presenting definitions is not sufficient to teach students words; the words must be related to one another and to students' experiences. When possible, they were grouped into topical or semantic categories (Stevens, 1982).

5. *Students were exposed to a word many times* (Nagy & Herman, 1987). Knowledge of word meanings is gained in increments through many experiences. Therefore, words must be used in a variety of situations, such as writing and reading, to help students achieve ownership of them.

6. *Students were actively involved in the process of learning the words* (Beck et al., 1987; Nagy & Herman, 1987). Students were not passive learners just being told information or definitions. They verbalized what they had learned and related it to their own lives.

However, although the research reveals these consistent characteristics of effective teaching, *it does not show that there is any one best method for achieving these qualities* (Beck & McKeown, 1991). Rather, a variety of techniques should be used for such instruction.

Another question about direct vocabulary teaching is when to provide it—before reading, during reading, or after reading. Blachowicz (1987) found that most vocabulary instruction takes place before reading. However, researchers recommend that teachers teach vocabulary before, during, and/or after reading depending on the text to be read and the students involved (Beck, McKeown, McCaslin & Burkes, 1979).

Many researchers have looked at the effects of preteaching vocabulary on students' overall comprehension (McKeown et al., 1985; Stahl, 1983; Weiss et al., 1986; Wixson, 1986). Although they all obtained positive results, they did not compare their preteaching with the effects of vocabulary instruction provided during or after reading instruction. One researcher, Memory (1990), did look at the placement of vocabulary instruction using ninth-grade biology students, twelfth-grade government students, and twelfth-grade economics students. Students were taught technical terms at different times before, during, or after reading. Memory concluded that "this investigation failed to identify one time for teaching difficult technical terms in content area classes that is more effective than others if the objective is the learning of definitions"

(p. 52). However, the teaching of definitions is not the goal of vocabulary instruction. Moreover, it must be remembered that this conclusion was reached for high school students reading expository texts. As Tierney and Cunningham (1984) state, "These conclusions lead us to question the practice of cursorily introducing new word meanings before having students read. This practice is probably only justified when just one or two crucial words are taught at some depth" (p. 612).

Finally, a question must be raised about the direct and isolated teaching of vocabulary-related skills such as using context clues, prefixes, suffixes, base words, and the dictionary, which are aimed at helping students achieve independence in vocabulary learning. The research in these areas has yielded mixed results (Beck & McKeown, 1991; Graves, 1987; Pressley et al., 1990). Therefore, it must be concluded that such teaching is of limited value in improving students' abilities to construct meaning.

In summary, we know a great deal about how students acquire meaning vocabulary and how it is related to the improvement of comprehension:

- Students acquire approximately forty thousand word meanings by the time they are in high school; they do this at an average rate of twenty-seven hundred to three thousand words per year, or seven words per day.
- Vocabulary is acquired through wide reading and varied experiences with texts, use of context, use of the dictionary, and direct teaching, but wide reading appears to be the most powerful method.
- Direct teaching of vocabulary only improves comprehension when a few key words are thoroughly taught in meaningful contexts; the words must be related to the students' prior knowledge in ways that actively involve the students in learning, and multiple exposures are needed.

For in-depth reading on vocabulary development and comprehension, see "For Additional Reading" at the conclusion of this chapter.

ELEMENTS OF EFFECTIVE VOCABULARY DEVELOPMENT

As a teacher, you are responsible for implementing the literacy program in your classroom. Recall that this program should include motivation, independent reading and writing, and instruction in reading and writing; this concept of a literacy program is based on the premise that children learn to read and write by reading and writing. Throughout this process students will vary in their need for support from their teacher and peers.

Effective vocabulary development takes place within the literacy program. On the basis of the research summarized thus far, we can conclude that it includes four important elements: awareness of words, wide reading and extensive writing, learning strategies for independently inferring word meanings from context, and *limited* direct teaching of vocabulary and vocabulary related skills.

Awareness of Words

Most vocabulary learning occurs independently (Graves, 1987). Considering the large number of words that students encounter and the need to learn them, it is obvious that all of these words cannot be taught. Therefore, we must make students aware of learning words and create an intrinsic motivation and interest so that they will learn words independently.

Being aware of and interested in words helps students develop "ownership" of them. This happens when students see how a word relates to their overall background (Beck, 1984). Students develop networks of words and their relationships through repeated experiences with the words in their reading and writing and through activities specifically designed to help them build relationships among words. Thus first encounters with a word may help students learn its meaning, but it is repeated use that develops ownership. Vocabulary learning is an incremental process; we know more about the meaning of a word after each encounter with it. As readers develop ownership of words, they relate them to their existing schemata and develop new schemata, thus cementing the ownership.

The atmosphere in a classroom where authentic literacy experiences take place promotes this awareness and ownership of words. By making students aware of and interested in learning words, you will provide the support that helps them expand their schemata and create new ones. Many different types of activities will help to promote this awareness. Notice how all of the following suggestions are integral parts of reading and writing or extensions of reading and writing:

Noting Words in Journals

As students keep journals, have them make personal lists of words that are of interest to them or that they would like to discuss with a group, a peer, or you. Direct students to look for words that interest or puzzle them rather than have them simply identify all the words they do not know. This places the focus of such activities on what students can do and makes it a positive learning experience. For more information on use of journals, see Chapter 6.

Reading Aloud

The value of reading aloud to students was discussed in Chapter 2. This is an excellent way to make students aware of words and to expand their oral vocabulary, which is the foundation for all other vocabulary learning. As you are reading aloud a book like *Anastasia Krupnik* (Lowry, 1979), stop periodically and discuss words like *Hubbard Squash*, *ostentatious*, or other words that might be interesting, unusual, or fun for children to think about. Books that are especially written to focus on certain types of words can be read aloud before students read them independently. Some examples are *Delivery Van: Words for Town and Country* (Maestro & Maestro, 1990), *Taxi: A Book of City Words* (Maestro & Maestro, 1989), *The Weighty Word Book* (Levitt, Burger & Guralnick, 1985), and *Murfles and Wink-a-Peeps* (Sperling, 1985). For your own reference, you might want to have available a book about word histories, such as *Word Mysteries and Histories* (Editors of the American Heritage Dictionary, 1986).

Discussion Circles

After students have finished reading a book, encourage them to get together in discussion circles to respond to the book and talk about words of interest. Even when all students have not read the same book, they enjoy sharing funny or unusual words from what they have read. (See Chapter 6 for a discussion of literature circles or discussion circles.) This motivates other children to want to read the book and to become more interested in learning about words.

Word Banks, Word Files, and Word Books

These devices are the students' personal files of words they have learned or are interested in learning. The words can be taken from books read, from areas of study such as science, from interest areas, from writing, and other sources, such as newspapers. Each word is either put on a card or written in a word book with a sentence the student has written using the word and relating it to prior knowledge. For example, a student might write the following sentence for the word *periodic*: "In my class, we have *periodic* tests in math two or three times a month." At the primary levels, the word bank idea is motivational because words and sentences can be written on cards shaped like coins and dropped into banks made of plastic bottles, boxes, or other containers. Students can then "withdraw" words from the bank and review them frequently. Students should always be encouraged to use the banked words in their writing.

Writing

One of the best ways to make students aware of words and to promote ownership is to encourage them to write. Through the use of shared writing and minilessons, you can help children be conscious of using a variety of words and more descriptive words. Whenever students use words in their writing, you can be sure they have started to take ownership of them. (See Chapter 7 on writing.)

Word Expansion Activities

After several students have read the same book or worked together in a unit on the same topic, they can use such activities as word maps. semantic maps, semantic feature analysis, or webbing to play with the words of interest to them. These activities will be discussed later in this chapter.

Bulletin Boards or Word Walls

Bulletin boards developed by students displaying words of interest or words on a particular topic, or word walls with lists of these words, also promote awareness and ownership. Students can then be encouraged to use the words from the bulletin board or wall in their writing.

All of these activities are based on the students' reading and writing. Words are not studied in isolation apart from meaningful contexts. The constant focus of these experiences is relating new knowledge to old, constantly expanding students' schemata. The benefits of awareness and ownership activities are far-reaching. They promote independence in word learning and motivate students to want to learn more about words.

Wide Reading and Extensive Writing

"Increasing the volume of students' reading is the single most important thing a teacher can do to promote large-scale vocabulary growth" (Nagy, 1988, p. 32). Writing in conjunction with reading and writing alone engages students in much more thoughtful learning and improves their ability to construct meaning (Tierney & Shanahan, 1991). Therefore, it is critical to promote wide, independent reading and self-initiated writing. Reading provides models of rich language that help students learn many new words, and writing provides an authentic reason for students to use those words and develop ownership of them. Because these two processes are so closely related and interrelated, they are mutually supportive.

Chapter 2 discussed extensively the importance of the independent reading and writing component of the literacy program. Children *must be* encouraged to read self-selected books and to do self-initiated writing on a daily basis. This must be viewed as a significant component of the literacy program and not be something that is done when there is "extra time" or done outside of class. Recall that some researchers are suggesting that *in-school independent reading time may even be more important to improving students' abilities to construct meaning than out-of-school reading time* (Taylor, Frye & Maruyama, 1990).

In addition to the ideas suggested in Chapter 2, you should also try the following:

Book Displays

Have exciting and colorful displays of your favorite books and new books. Take a few minutes to read or tell a little about the book—just enough to "get the kids hooked" into wanting to read it. Encourage the students to place books they have read in the display and give a very brief comment about them. This transfers much of the ownership for learning to the students and makes them active participants.

Discussions of Interesting Words

Periodically invite children (or parents, custodian, and so forth) to talk about interesting or humorous words from books they have read or things they have written. By sharing the sentence in which a word appears and telling others what they think it means, children learn to apply all aspects of vocabulary learning to independent reading and writing. Such words can be placed on a class word wall for all students to use.

Many of the ideas suggested for promoting word awareness can also be used to help promote vocabulary development during independent reading and writing.

Strategy for Independently Inferring Word Meanings from Context

A necessary part of effective vocabulary development is teaching students a strategy for independently inferring word meanings (Calfee & Drum, 1986; Graves, 1987; Paris, Lipson & Wixson, 1983). If students are doing extensive wide reading and they come to an unknown word, they need a plan for trying to determine its meaning. Getting students to use such a strategy is not easy but is well worth the time and effort.

The student strategy presented here is based on the suggestions of Calfee and Drum (1986) and Graves (1987) and on my own experiences with students. You will need to adjust the steps to meet the varying grade levels of your students:

1. When you come to a word you do not know, read to the end of the sentence or paragraph to decide if the word is important to your understanding. If it is unimportant, read on.
2. If the word is important, reread the sentence or paragraph containing the word. Try context to infer the meaning.
3. If context doesn't help, look for base words, prefixes, or suffixes that you recognize.
4. Use what you know about phonics to try to pronounce the word. Is it a word you have heard?
5. If you still don't know the word, use the dictionary or ask someone for help.
6. Once you think you know the meaning, reread the text to be sure it makes sense.

Students should be taught these steps in accordance with their level of maturity in reading. For example, a beginning reader might only have enough maturity to focus on a very simplified version of each step. Figure 4.2 shows a strategy poster that might be used with primary-grade children, and Figure 4.3 shows one that could be used with intermediate or higher grades. When students are learning this strategy, they should help in verbalizing the statements that go on the strategy poster; in this way, the strategy becomes theirs. They should then be reminded to refer to the poster and use the strategy as they are reading. As was noted in Chapter 2, you must model strategies thoroughly and give students repeated opportunities to use them (see Chapter 8 on modeling).

Limited Direct Teaching of Vocabulary

The final element of effective vocabulary development is the limited direct teaching of words and word-related skills. Given the mixed results of the research on direct teaching of vocabulary cited earlier (see page 195), it is simply not reasonable to consider this the major source for vocabulary learning for students. With the extensive number of words in the language to be learned, it is not possible to teach them one by one. Furthermore, vocabulary research shows that the direct teaching of vocabulary often helps students learn the words but does not improve comprehension.

Despite the strong research evidence that the direct teaching of vocabulary is of little value in helping students improve their meaning construction, many teachers have persisted in following this practice. The question is WHY?

Figure 4.2 Primary-Grade Strategy Poster for Inferring Word Meanings

BE A WORD DETECTIVE

When I Come to a Word That Causes Me Trouble...

1. I should read on to the end of the sentence or paragraph.

2. Look for word parts I know.

3. Try to figure it out from the letter sounds.

4. Ask someone or look it up in the dictionary.

There are a number of reasons why this practice has held on for so long, *but these reasons are no longer valid.*

- Educators did not thoroughly understand the process of comprehension. They believed that the meaning in a text resided in individual words. Therefore, they erroneously assumed that the direct teaching of words would improve comprehension. *Now we know that comprehension is a process of constructing meaning by using one's prior knowledge and interacting with the text.* Learning the meanings of separate individual words has a very small relationship to this overall process. This new knowledge is slowly becoming available to more and more teachers.

- Educators (and publishers of basal readers) believed that the teaching of words before a selection was read improved comprehension for students

Figure 4.3 Intermediate- and Middle-School Strategy Poster for Inferring Word Meanings

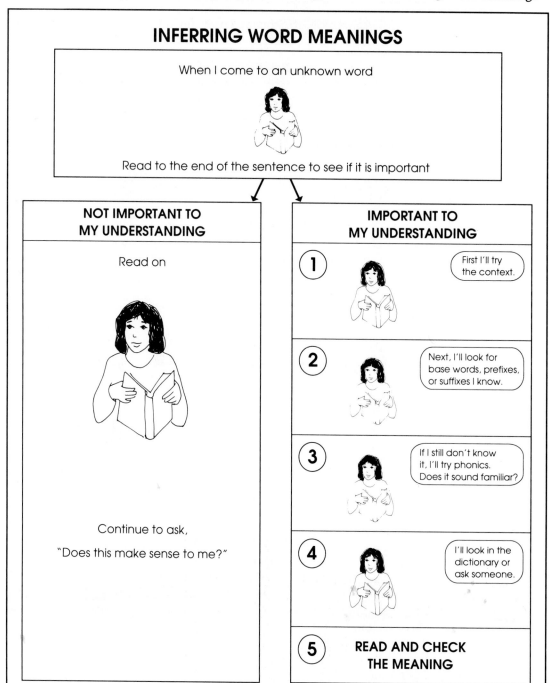

even though there was not a strong research base for this practice. *Now that there is a strong research base showing that this practice is of limited value in improving comprehension, and then only under certain circumstances, educators are beginning to let go of this practice.*

- Teachers did not know what to do in place of direct vocabulary teaching. *Now we know that there are many teaching strategies that help students become independent vocabulary learners and support them in developing an extensive meaning vocabulary.* These include independent reading and writing and strategies like the use of word maps and vocabulary self-collection discussed later in this chapter.

Direct teaching of vocabulary *may lead to improved comprehension only when the following conditions are met:*

- A *few* key words are thoroughly taught in meaningful context.
- Words are related to the students' prior knowledge in ways that actively involve them in learning.
- Students are given multiple exposures to the words.

The few words that are taught can be used by the teacher to model the process of learning word meanings. The direct teaching of vocabulary-related skills, such as the use of context clues, prefixes, suffixes, base words, and the dictionary, should *occupy a very small proportion* (if any) of instructional time; incidental teaching at point of use or need may be of more value. Again, *it is more advantageous for students to spend their time reading and writing.*

STRATEGIES THAT LEAD TO INDEPENDENCE IN VOCABULARY LEARNING

Although wide reading and extensive writing are the primary ways through which students develop their vocabulary knowledge, it is possible to use certain strategies and techniques that will help students become independent in their vocabulary learning and their ability to construct meaning.

Carr and Wixson (1986) give four guidelines for evaluating vocabulary instruction, all of which are based on the research conclusions discussed earlier:

1. *Instruction should help students relate new vocabulary to their background knowledge.* Since vocabulary is a specialized part of prior knowledge, students are more likely to improve their meaning construction when they do this.
2. *Instruction should help students develop extensive word knowledge.* Just learning a definition is not learning a word (Nagy & Herman, 1987). To really learn a word and develop ownership, students must relate it to other concepts and words that they know (Beck, 1984).

3. *Instruction should provide for active student involvement in learning new vocabulary*. Student-centered activities are most effective in helping students understand a word. For example, the teacher should have students take the lead in crafting their own sentences rather than simply giving them sentences.

4. *Instruction should develop students' strategies for acquiring new vocabulary independently*. Because of the large number of words in our language, students must be able to learn many words on their own. The student strategy for inferring word meanings presented earlier is one way to promote this type of learning. The types of teaching strategies and techniques used by the teacher also influence students' abilities to learn words independently.

All of the teaching strategies for vocabulary instruction suggested here meet these criteria. As the teacher, you must constantly decide which words to teach, when to teach these words, and which strategies to use for teaching. *Remember, however, that the bulk of vocabulary learning is going to take place through wide reading and self-initiated writing.*

Selecting Words to Emphasize

When selecting the words that you will focus on during a literacy lesson, you must consider two factors: the text and the students. The process for selecting vocabulary is similar to the process suggested in Chapter 3 for identifying prior knowledge. Figure 4.4 summarizes the decisions involved in vocabulary teaching. The first five of these decisions will be discussed below; the remaining two decisions will be discussed in the next two sections of the chapter.

1. *Review the text to identify the story line(s) or main ideas.* This information will give you a framework for identifying the important ideas in the text, which will be your basis for selecting the words for direct teaching. As was discussed in Chapters 2 and 3, this knowledge is also important in helping you select the prior knowledge that needs to be activated or developed and in deciding what questions to ask if you use guided reading. Therefore, creating a story map for narrative text or a graphic organizer for an expository text will be very helpful as you work throughout a thematic unit.

2. *Compile a list of words related to the story line(s) or main ideas.* By looking at your story map or graphic organizer, you can see the important ideas in the story or informational text and can then select words that are important or crucial to understanding the selection—these are your key-concept words. For example, recall the sample lesson presented at the conclusion of Chapter 3 (see page 169). The graphic organizer for the first chapter in *Mummies, Tombs, and Treasure* (Perl, 1987) helped me identify four key-concept words that seemed important to the chapter—*mummy, bacteria, decay,* and *coffin.*

Figure 4.4 Decisions to Make About Vocabulary Teaching

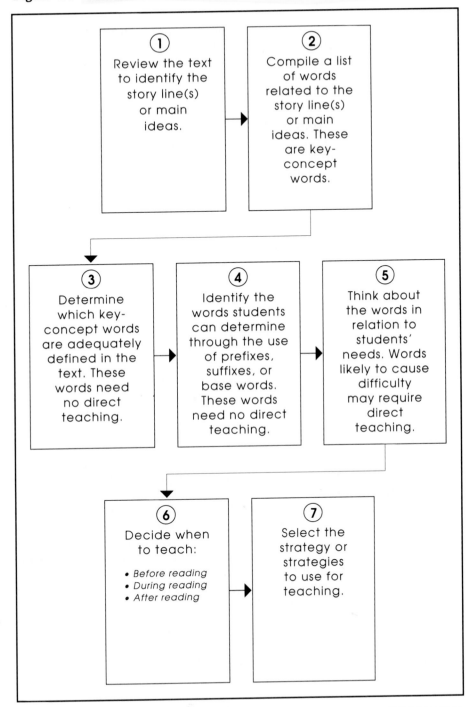

Sometimes it is easier to carry out this process with expository text such as *Mummies, Tombs, and Treasure* than with narrative text. However, it can also be done using narrative text as long as the story line is used and the terms selected focus on the problem and action within the story (Wixson, 1986). The sample lesson at the conclusion of the present chapter will illustrate this complete process using a narrative text.

3. *Determine which key-concept words are adequately defined in the text.* Some of these will be defined through context and some by direct definition. Further, pronunciation guides and footnotes may be given for words that are not likely to be in the students' oral vocabularies and prior knowledge. A word usually does not have to be directly taught if the text contains adequate clues to its meaning and pronunciation, but sometimes you may want to focus on such words after reading as a way of expanding vocabulary. Recall the lesson presented at the conclusion of Chapter 3; two of the words (*mummy* and *bacteria*) were defined directly in the context and were not taught directly before reading.

4. *Identify words students can determine through the use of prefixes, suffixes, root words, or base words.* Some of the key-concept words remaining on the list will include structural elements that students can use to determine pronunciation and meaning. If they can use these elements, the words containing them will not need to be taught directly. None of the words in the lesson at the end of Chapter 3 fit into this category.

5. *Think about words in relation to students' needs. Words likely to cause difficulty may require direct teaching.* Finally, think about the words remaining on the list. If any of them are likely to be in students' prior knowledge, they do not have to be taught directly. Again, you might want to focus on these words after reading as a means of expanding students' vocabularies.

The words remaining on the list are those that may require direct teaching. They are unknown from students' prior knowledge and are unlikely to be learned independently through the use of context and/or structural analysis. The number of words remaining on the list should be two or three. If it is larger, you will probably want to consider using guided reading and divide the reading of the selection into sections so that you can only teach two or three words before reading. Keep in mind that research supports teaching only a *few*, if any, key words before reading as a means of improving comprehension (Beck, Perfetti & McKeown, 1982; Tierney & Cunningham, 1984; Wixson, 1986).

Now that you have identified the words that need direct teaching, you must decide when and how they should be taught. A lesson illustrating this complete process for a narrative text is presented at the conclusion of this chapter (see page 242).

When to Teach Vocabulary

The research discussed earlier in this chapter shows that there is no one best time to teach vocabulary. It may be developed before, during, or after reading, depending on a number of factors. Therefore, you must make decisions in relation to each instructional situation. Some students may need vocabulary support throughout their reading, and others may need no support. In the lesson at the end of Chapter 3 (page 169), I chose not to teach any words before reading because the text defined the key words or students knew them from their experiences; also, I did not feel that the students needed the support of preteaching vocabulary. Let's look at the conditions under which vocabulary should be taught before, during, and after reading.

Before Reading

Vocabulary instruction should be provided before reading in the following situations:

1. • Students are experiencing difficulty in constructing meaning and seem to have limited prior knowledge of any kind, including vocabulary. They might be second-language learners, learning-disabled students, or students who are generally experiencing difficulty with comprehension.

2. • There are words in the text to be read that are *clearly* a part of the prior knowledge that is needed to understand the text and you are confident that students do not know these terms.

3. • The text to be read has unusually difficult concepts; even though your students do not normally need vocabulary support before reading, it might be good to provide it in these situations. For example, suppose your third graders really want to read *The Mouse Rap* (Myers, 1990), which is somewhat developmentally above their age level. Therefore, before reading the book you introduce some of the words and concepts that you feel are beyond their knowledge and experience.

4. • When students have previewed the text they are going to read and have identified words that *they feel* they need to know to understand the text. Sometimes this is a good way to identify words that students really do need to know. If they are bothered by a word, even if it is unimportant to understanding the text, it may still interfere with their overall meaning construction. Through direct teaching before reading, you can help them see that knowing this word (or every word) is not important to their overall understanding of a text. However, you have to exercise caution when deciding to teach vocabulary before reading based on student self-selection because you could end up devoting too much time to words that really are not important to understanding the material.

During Reading

Vocabulary support during reading is usually provided for students who are in need of overall teacher support through guided reading. These are likely to be students who are experiencing difficulty in constructing meaning or who are reading a text that has particularly difficult concepts. When you are using guided reading with students (see Chapter 2), you may often find that it is more appropriate to deal with words and concepts at the beginning or end of each segment of reading rather than try to teach too many words before reading. Vocabulary support during reading has the advantage of giving students immediate opportunities to use the words.

In addition, during reading many teachers in grades 4 and above have children note interesting or unknown words in their journals. The children then bring these words to discussion groups and they are used by the teacher as the basis for vocabulary instruction. Teachers usually find that these are the same words they would have selected for instruction themselves.

After Reading

Vocabulary instruction after reading has two primary purposes:

- To help students clarify the meanings of any words that may have been of interest to them during reading or that may have caused them difficulty.
- To expand students' vocabularies by having them focus on interesting words that are related to the text that was read. For example, if first graders have read *Roundabout Cozy Cottage* (Graham, 1987), you might want to use the text and illustrations to expand their vocabularies about terms around the house. *Johnny Tremain* (Forbes, 1971), on the other hand, provides many places throughout the text to help intermediate-grade students see how an author uses rich, descriptive language. Focusing on some of these passages would be a good way to expand vocabulary and also relate the importance of descriptive language to writing.

The decisions about when to provide vocabulary instruction and support must be based on students' needs and the nature of the text; *sometimes no instruction will be necessary*. Table 4.2 summarizes these considerations in relation to the possible times to teach vocabulary.

Teaching Strategies

The final decision that you must make is *how* to teach vocabulary directly (see Figure 4.4, page 207). Many different strategies can be used in this process; there is no one best method (Beck & McKeown, 1991). However, the

Table 4.2 When to Provide Vocabulary Instruction

Factors to Consider	Vocabulary Instruction		
	Before Reading	*During Reading*	*After Reading*
Student considerations	*Any* students are experiencing difficulty constructing meaning. Students have previewed text and identified words they want to know.	Students are receiving guided reading support.	Students have identified words of interest or that cause difficulty. Students need to expand vocabularies.
Text considerations	Text has words that are definitely keys to understanding. Text has unusually difficult concepts.	There are words that are keys to understanding text and are likely to cause students difficulty in constructing meaning.	Text has good opportunities for expanding vocabularies.

procedures used must help students improve their ability to construct meaning and not just to learn isolated words. Therefore, the strategies and techniques for supporting vocabulary development presented here are ones that help students relate new knowledge to old knowledge, actively involve students in the process of learning, help students thoroughly learn words, and support students in the process of learning to use their own strategy or strategies for independently inferring word meanings. *The ultimate goal of all vocabulary development is to help students become independent learners who have strategies for inferring the meanings of unknown words when they encounter them in reading;* further, these students will have extensive vocabulary knowledge that they are able to use in constructing meaning through reading and writing.

Table 4.3 presents an overview of seven different teaching strategies that can be used as a part of literacy lessons to help students gain independence in vocabulary learning. They should not be used to develop isolated vocabulary lessons separate from reading and writing. The format for discussing each strategy focuses on description, procedures, when to use, assessment value, and discussion.

Table 4.3   Overview of Vocabulary Teaching Strategies That Promote Student Independence

Strategy	Purpose	When to Use	Comments
Concept of definition (word maps)	Help students become independent word learners by teaching elements of a good definition	Middle elementary and above Expository texts	Good support for strategy for independently inferring word meanings
Semantic mapping	Integrate prior knowledge and vocabulary learning	Before or after reading All texts	Develops in-depth word knowledge
Semantic feature analysis	Develop word knowledge by comparing words	Before or after reading Expository text and some narratives	Often more effective after reading
Hierarchical and linear arrays	Develop word relationships	After reading All texts	Encourages students to compare and contrast words
Preview in context	Use text context to develop word meanings	Before reading All texts	*Must have text* with good context clues
Contextual redefinition	Use context to determine word meaning	Before reading All texts	Useful when texts do not provide strong context clues
Vocabulary self-collection	Help students learn self-selected words	After reading All texts	Makes students responsible for own vocabulary learning

Concept of Definition Procedure (Word Maps)

Description.   Schwartz and Raphael (1985) describe a strategy known as the concept of definition procedure, more commonly called a word map strategy because it employs the use of a word map.

Figure 4.5   Basic Concept of the Word Map

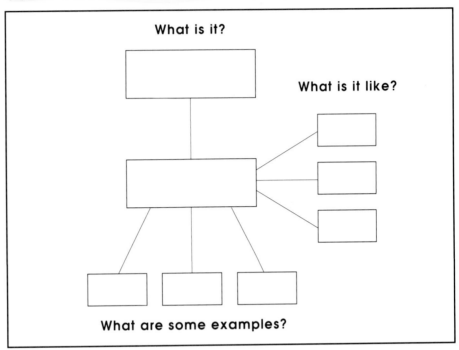

Source: Robert M. Schwartz and Taffy E. Raphael, "Concept of Definition: A Key to Improving Students' Vocabulary," *Reading Teacher*, November 1985, pp. 198–203. Reprinted with permission of Robert M. Schwartz and the International Reading Association.

The purpose of the concept of definition procedure is to help students in the middle grades and above gain control of the vocabulary acquisition process by teaching them the type of information that makes up a definition and how to use context clues and background knowledge to increase their understanding of words. This is done by using a word map (see Figure 4.5) that helps students visually depict the elements of a given concept. Each concept is composed of three types of information:

1. Class: *What is it?*
2. Properties that distinguish the concept from others: *What is it like?*
3. Example of the concept: *What are some examples?*

Figure 4.6 shows a completed word map for the concept *ice cream.*

Procedures.   Schwartz and Raphael (1985) suggest that this strategy can be taught to students in four lessons. The following procedures were adapted from their guidelines.

Figure 4.6   Completed Word Map for *Ice Cream*

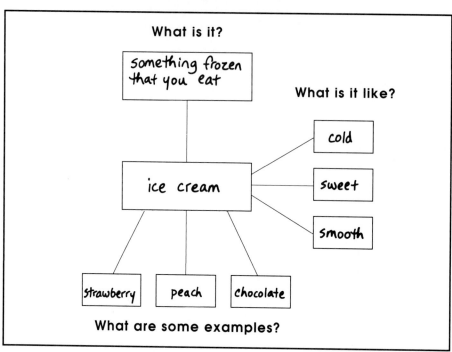

Lesson 1

1. Prepare for the lesson by selecting three or more concepts that children already know and by developing a list of information about each; include class, at least three properties, and at least three examples. A sample list for *ice cream* is shown below:

   ice cream
   chocolate
   cold
   dessert
   strawberry
   frozen
   sweet
   peach
   smooth

2. Begin by discussing the importance of being able to accurately determine word meanings in order to better comprehend texts. Tell students that the strategy they will be learning during the next four lessons will help them tell whether or not they really know the meaning of a word.
3. Present students with the structure of a word map (Figure 4.5). Tell them that this map is a picture of the three things that really let us know when we understand a word. Go over each part with them.
4. Using the lists prepared for the three concepts, have students help you complete a word map for two of the concepts.
5. After they have completed the two word maps with you, have them work with a partner to complete the third. Have students share their work and discuss it.
6. Next have students select a concept of their own to map, independently or with a partner.
7. Finally, have them write a definition for one of the concepts developed during the lesson. The definition for ice cream might be as follows:

> *A dessert that is a frozen, sweet food that you eat. It is cold. Some examples of ice cream are chocolate, strawberry, and peach.*

Lesson 2

1. Prepare for the lesson by locating or writing several sample passages that give complete information on the concepts to be discussed (class, at least three properties, at least three examples). Content textbooks are often a good source for these passages. A sample passage for the concept *flowers* might read as follows:

> *Flowers*
>
> *Have you ever thought about plants and how they reproduce? Flowers are the parts of seed-bearing plants that help to make this happen. You may think that flowers are just pretty to look at or nice to smell. But they are important to making more plants. Each flower has special parts. You probably have noticed only the petals. Look more closely. Flowers have other important parts such as the pistil and the stamen. Look at some of your favorite flowers such as the tulip, rose, or daisy to see if you can find these parts.*

2. Present the passages along with the word map. Tell them that they are to read each passage and complete the word map.
3. After they have completed the word maps, have students give oral or written definitions for the concepts presented.
4. Once students seem to understand the concept of the word map, tell them that it is not necessary to limit properties and examples to three items.

Lesson 3

1. Prepare for this lesson by writing or locating several passages that are less complete in their definitions than those used in lesson 2.
2. Direct students in reading the passages and completing the word maps as they did in lesson 2. If they do not see that the information provided in the passages is incomplete, help them see this by asking such questions as "Does the passage tell you what _____ is like?" or "Does the passage give any examples of _____?"
3. Have students use other sources and their own prior knowledge to complete the word maps.
4. Complete the lesson by guiding students to the conclusion that texts do not always give complete definitions.

Lesson 4

1. Prepare for this lesson by writing or locating several more passages with incomplete contextual information for several concepts. Write incomplete definitions for the concept, leaving out one or more of the parts of the definition as developed through the use of the word map. An incomplete definition might read as follows:

   A musician is a man who plays an instrument. He is very talented.

2. Tell students that the purpose of this lesson is for them to use what they have learned from developing word maps to decide whether some definitions are complete or incomplete.
3. Have students read the passages and evaluate the definitions for their completeness. Tell them to write the information that is missing from the definitions.
4. Conclude the lesson by discussing with students how they were able to tell that the definitions were incomplete. Discuss how they should use this type of thinking any time they are reading and come to words they don't know.

It may be necessary to repeat one or more of these lessons several times for review purposes before students can use this procedure independently.

When to Use. Research for the concept of definition procedure has been conducted using fourth and eight graders. It appears to work best with students in the intermediate and higher grades with expository texts. Maria (1990) also reports that it is effective with at-risk students in the upper elementary grades.

This strategy can be used in four lessons throughout a thematic unit to help students develop the understandings needed to apply the concepts in later units. The four lessons are likely to be more meaningful if they are placed after the reading of selections.

You may also use the word map portion of the lessons as a means of thoroughly developing the meanings of several related words before or after the reading of a selection or at the beginning of a particular theme. For example, if you are beginning a thematic unit on space travel, you might use the word map activity to develop concepts such as *astronaut*, *space shuttle*, *rocket*, and *pilot*. When developing closely related terms, include questioning like that used in the rich vocabulary instruction program reported by Beck and her colleagues (Beck, McCaslin, & McKeown, 1980; Beck et al., 1987; Beck et al., 1982). Probe relationships by asking such questions as "Is an *astronaut* the same as a *pilot*?" and "Do *pilots* fly *rockets*?"

Assessment Value.   You can learn two things about your students as they are learning and using this strategy: their ability to determine unknown word meanings and their prior knowledge of the concepts being developed. Schwartz and Raphael (1985) report that students who have been taught this strategy are more aware of what to do to figure out the meaning of a new word. When asked how to do this, students "indicated they would ask themselves questions and think about what they already knew. In contrast, the students without this instruction tended to answer, 'I would look it up' " (pp. 203–204).

You can determine students' knowledge and understanding of the particular concepts being developed through their responses to the structured portions of the lessons and through their answers when they generate their own words for word maps and definitions. If you are using the word map concept to develop related terms, you can tell by the responses that students give to your probing questions whether they really understand the terms.

Discussion.   The concept of definition procedure is excellent for preparing students to use the student strategy for independently inferring word meanings (see page 202). By using this procedure, you help students develop a concept of what they must know to understand a word and begin to think about the sources within the text that might help them define a word; that is, this strategy promotes the integration of existing prior knowledge with new knowledge. However, it requires heavy initial teacher support and guidance, and it does not work with all words; for example, it works with nouns but not with verbs.

Since many words have similar properties, Schwartz (1988) has expanded the word map concept to include the idea of comparisons. Figure 4.7 presents one such revised version. The teacher and students place a word similar to the main concept in the comparison box and discuss how this word and the main word have common properties. This procedure helps students become more precise in thinking about the properties they identify for the main concept and also helps students to further integrate knowledge within their schemata. Figure 4.8 shows a completed word map for *desert* using the revised map plan.

As was mentioned earlier, the word map portion of the concept of definition strategy is also very useful for developing vocabulary for a given

Figure 4.7   Basic Concept of Definition Map, Revised

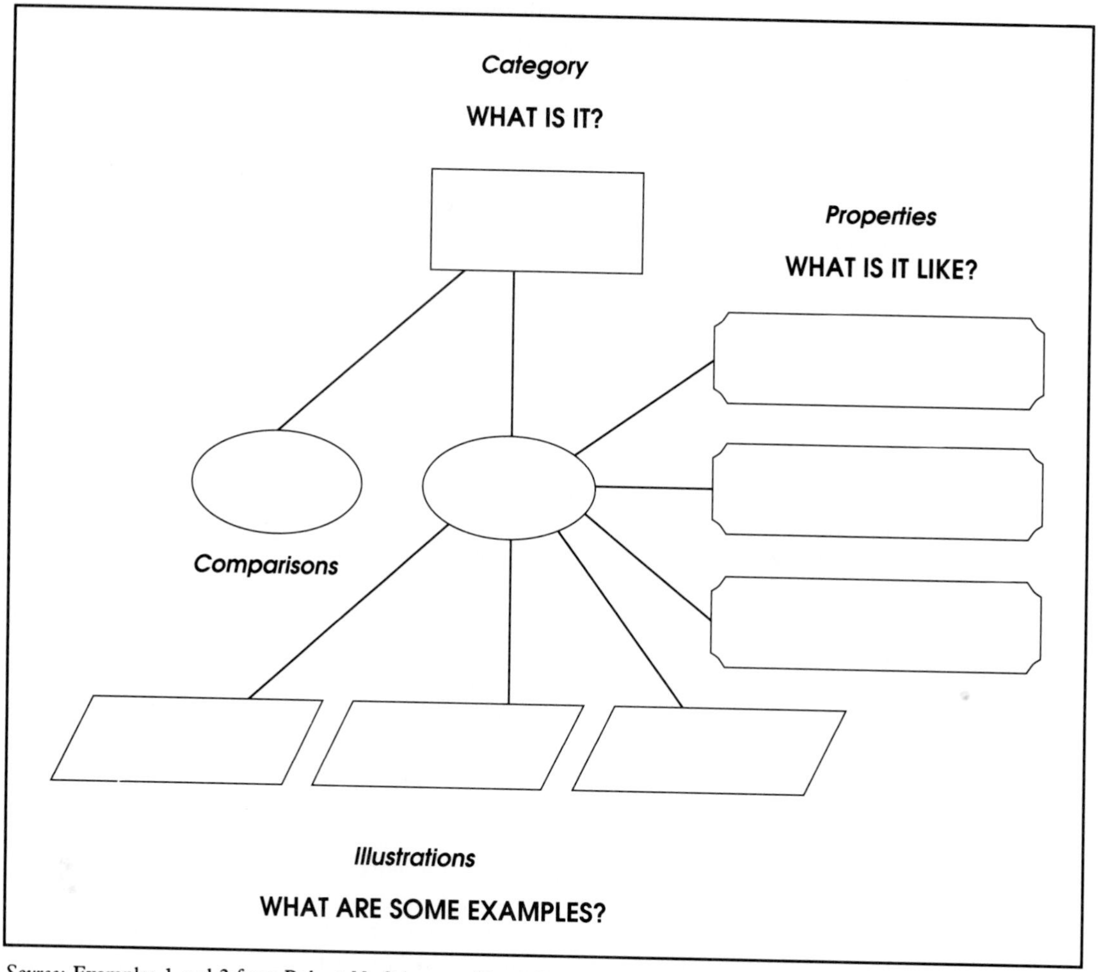

Category

WHAT IS IT?

Properties

WHAT IS IT LIKE?

Comparisons

Illustrations

WHAT ARE SOME EXAMPLES?

Source: Examples 1 and 2 from Robert M. Schwartz, "Learning to Learn Vocabulary in Content Area Textbooks," *Journal of Reading*, November 1988, pp. 108–118. Reprinted with permission of Robert M. Schwartz and the International Reading Association.

thematic unit or selection. It may be effectively used throughout a unit to help students develop deeper understandings of the words they have encountered, and it can also be effectively incorporated into content-area instruction. Be careful, however, that making word maps does not become the goal of the activity, which *must always remain the development of vocabulary knowledge to improve the construction of meaning* and independence in word learning.

Figure 4.8   Completed Word Map for *Desert*

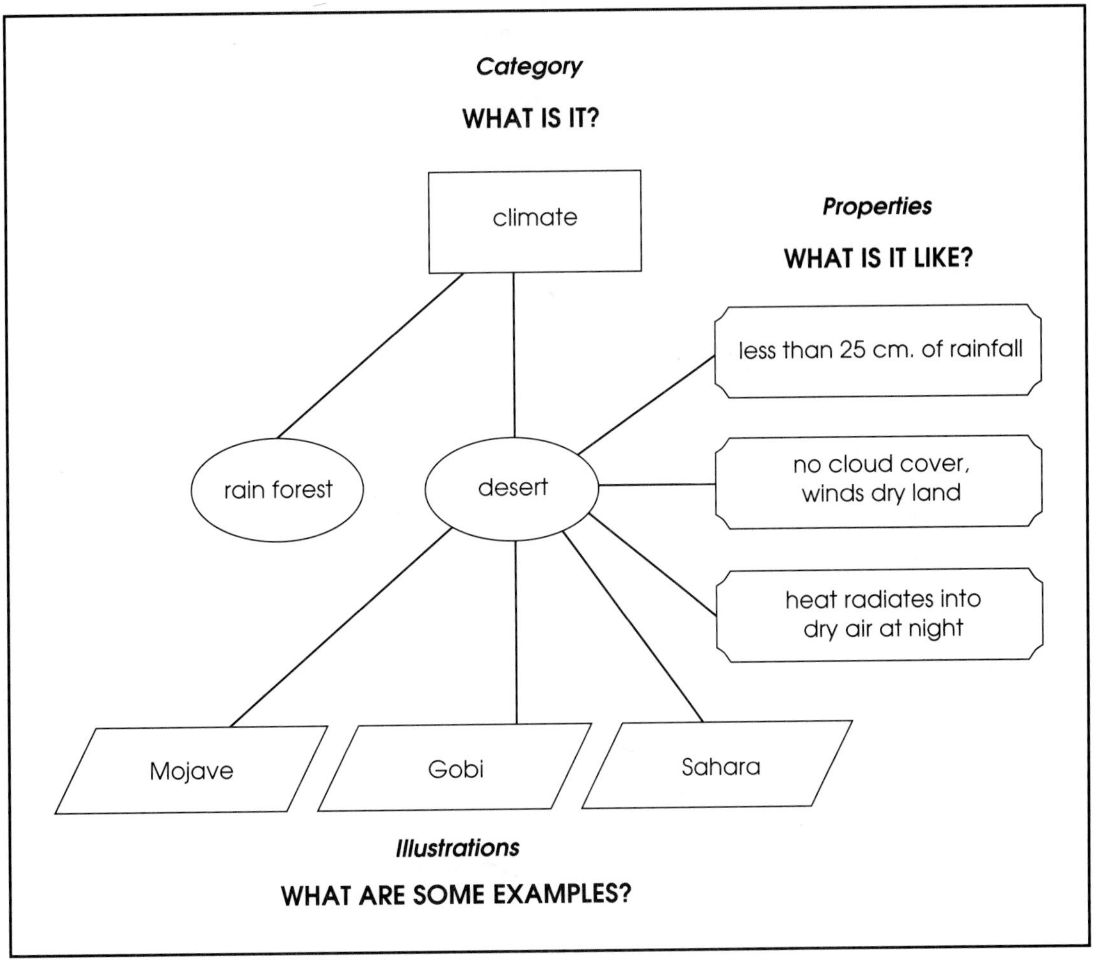

Category

WHAT IS IT?

climate

Properties

WHAT IS IT LIKE?

less than 25 cm. of rainfall

rain forest

desert

no cloud cover,
winds dry land

heat radiates into
dry air at night

Mojave   Gobi   Sahara

Illustrations

WHAT ARE SOME EXAMPLES?

Source: Examples 1 and 2 from Robert M. Schwartz, "Learning to Learn Vocabulary in Content Area Textbooks," *Journal of Reading*, November 1988, pp. 108–118. Reprinted with permission of Robert M. Schwartz and the International Reading Association.

Semantic Mapping

Semantic mapping, discussed in detail in Chapter 3 (see pages 143–146) as an excellent strategy for activating and developing prior knowledge, uses a mapping strategy similar to the word map used in the concept of definition instruction just discussed. It can be used before reading and then expanded after reading to integrate students' new knowledge into their prior knowledge.

Semantic mapping is a time-consuming procedure. Therefore, when you use it before reading, you must be certain that you have selected key-concept words for the text to be read. It is often better to use it after reading to expand vocabulary and to pull together concepts that students already possess.

Semantic mapping has many variations and uses; it is a good way to brainstorm for writing (see Chapter 7). For a detailed look at ideas for using semantic mapping, see Heimlich and Pittelman (1986) listed in "For Additional Reading" at the conclusion of this chapter.

Semantic Feature Analysis

Description. With this procedure, students develop vocabulary and learn important concepts by looking at how a group of related words differ and how they are alike (Johnson & Pearson, 1984). Figure 4.9 shows how some first-grade students and their teacher set up a semantic feature analysis grid after they had completed a unit on gardening. They then discussed each word, indicating what they knew about the word in relation to each characteristic. This strategy has been very effective in helping students develop vocabulary and learn to construct meaning (Anders & Bos, 1986).

Procedures. Use the following procedures to develop semantic feature grids:

1. Select a category or class of words (such as vegetables).
2. List items that fall into this category down the left side of the grid.
3. List features that some of the items have in common across the top of the grid.
4. Put pluses (+), minuses (−), and question marks (?) in the squares of the grid to indicate whether the items in the category have the feature under consideration. Discuss each item, making sure that students understand that some items are sometimes characterized by a feature, sometimes not. For example, for the grid in Figure 4.9, the teacher should be sure students understand that the tomato can be both green and red but is usually cooked when green.
5. Add additional words and features to the grid.
6. Complete the grid and discuss each word.

The process should be repeated many times using different categories, moving from the concrete to the abstract. The teacher should encourage students to continuously look for new words to add to the grids. Students can keep grid sheets in folders or notebooks and can add to them throughout the year.

After completing a semantic feature grid, students should examine the pattern of pluses and minuses to determine how the words are alike and how they are different. Question marks should serve as a basis for further research to clarify understanding of the word. This strategy will help students to expand their vocabularies as well as to refine the meanings of words they already know.

Figure 4.9   Semantic Feature Analysis Grid

Vegetables	Green	Have Peelings	Eat Raw	Seeds
Potatoes	−	+	+	?
Carrots	−	+	+	−
Tomatoes	− +	+	− +	+
Broccoli	+	?	+ '	−
Squash	+ −	+	+	+
Cabbage	+	−	+	−

When to Use.   Semantic feature analysis may be used before or after reading to develop vocabulary, but it is often more effectively used after reading as a means of expanding vocabulary. It is usually most helpful with expository texts but may also be used with some narrative texts. Finally, it is an excellent way for students to develop understanding in various content areas.

In addition to developing vocabulary, semantic feature analysis is very effective for reinforcing vocabulary and related concepts in content textbooks (Stieglitz & Stieglitz, 1981). It may be used to review chapters before tests or to pull together concepts in concluding a thematic unit for students at all levels. For younger students, semantic feature grids using very simple categories and features can be developed as oral language activities.

Assessment Value.   As students develop semantic feature grids, you will be able to assess their prior knowledge in relation to the category and words being discussed. Students' responses will help you assess their understandings of word relationships as well as their thinking abilities.

Discussion.   Semantic feature analysis is one of the strategies that concentrates on helping students build relationships among concepts. Although concept of definition instruction and semantic mapping also do this, they are not as effective as feature analysis. The strength of this strategy comes when students are actively involved in the process of constructing the grids and discussing them. This, along with cooperative learning, is an excellent way to foster active participation in the process of learning.

Nagy (1988) suggests that the Venn diagram is another way to apply semantic feature analysis in the classroom. Figure 4.10 presents a blank Venn diagram. In these diagrams, two things are compared, the properties of each individual item are listed down the sides of the circles, and the properties common to both are listed in the intersection. For in-depth reading on semantic feature analysis, see Pittelman, Heimlich, Berglund, and French (1991) in "For Additional Reading."

Figure 4.10   Blank Venn Diagram

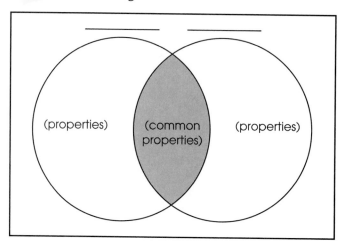

Hierarchical and Linear Arrays

Description.   Words sometimes have hierarchical relationships, for example, the names of scientific organisms (Nagy, 1988). Therefore, a hierarchical array like that shown in Figure 4.11 can be constructed to help students develop an understanding of these relationships. The exact structure of the array will depend on the concepts being analyzed.

At other times, words have a linear relationship, for example, *good, better, best; tepid, hot, scalding.* A linear array like the one shown in Figure 4.12 can be used to show this relationship. The use of both hierarchical and linear arrays helps students learn to think independently about word relationships and to develop concepts.

Procedures.   The following procedures can be used in developing hierarchical or linear arrays with students:

1. Select a concept or group of words from literature or from students' writing for study.
2. Begin by showing students the type of array that will be constructed.
3. Guide students in constructing the array. Discuss the relationship between the words as the array is developed.

After students have had considerable experience with arrays, they can select the words for study and decide the type of array they will use. You can also use the array as a means of activating students' prior knowledge; for example, if you are going to study the places people live, you can begin with the basic

Figure 4.11 Hierarchical Array

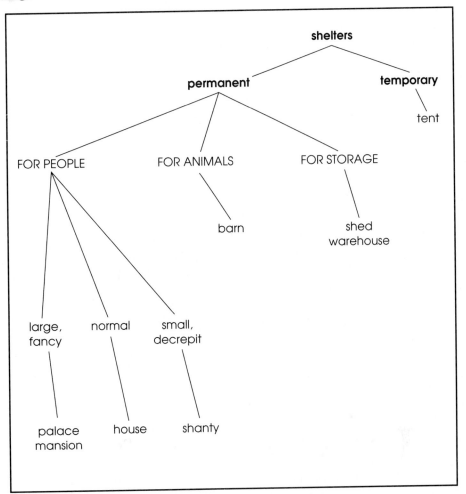

Source: William Nagy, *Teaching vocabulary to improve reading comprehension*, 1988. Used with permission of the author.

framework of the array presented in Figure 4.11 and ask students to generate the information. As the unit progresses, students can add to or change the array.

When to Use. Arrays are best to use after reading to help students expand their vocabularies. The visual aspect of arrays is good for helping at-risk learners or second-language learners more concretely see the relationships among words.

Figure 4.12   Linear Array

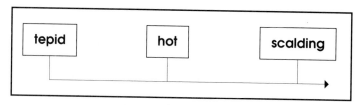

Assessment Value.   Students' responses during the development of arrays will help you assess their prior knowledge and their ability to develop relationships.

Discussion.   The value of arrays is that they encourage students to compare and contrast words (Blachowicz, 1986). Blachowicz suggests several variations called semantic gradients and concept ladders.

Another variation of the hierarchial array is the "thinking tree" (Kirby & Kuykendall, 1985, as discussed in Nagy, 1988). Figure 4.13 presents an example of a thinking tree activity. Students begin by working alone to think of types of transportation and problems associated with one specific type of transportation, cars. They then think about problems associated with other forms of transportation. Finally, they work with a partner or small group to develop other thinking trees for an area of invention. This activity may also be applied to more abstract terms such as *freedom* (see the partial example in Figure 4.14).

Preview in Context

Description.   The preview in context strategy, developed by Readence, Bean, and Baldwin (1981, 1985, 1989), does just what the title says—previews words in context. With this strategy, the teacher guides students to use the context and their prior knowledge to determine the meanings of a selected set of words.

Procedures.   The following four steps are involved in using this strategy.

1. *Prepare.* Select the words to be taught in accordance with the procedures suggested earlier in this chapter (see page 207). These must be key-concept words, and there must *not be more than two or three to teach*. Identify passages within the text that contain strong context clues for the term to

Figure 4.13   A Thinking Tree Activity

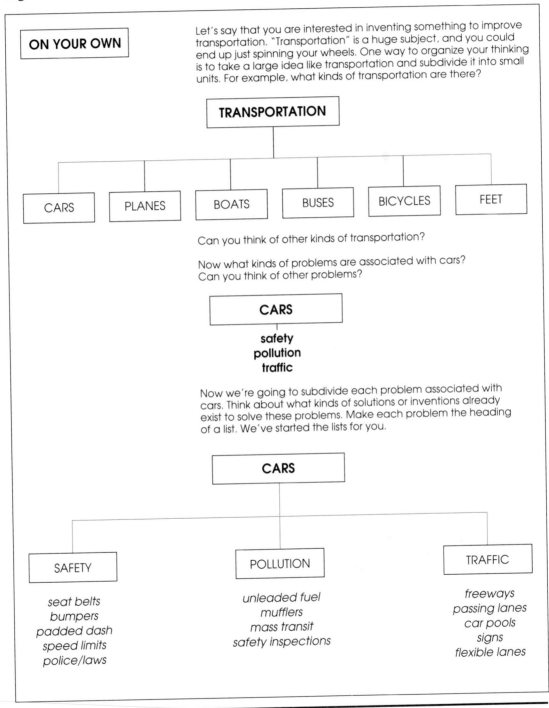

ON YOUR OWN

Let's say that you are interested in inventing something to improve transportation. "Transportation" is a huge subject, and you could end up just spinning your wheels. One way to organize your thinking is to take a large idea like transportation and subdivide it into small units. For example, what kinds of transportation are there?

TRANSPORTATION

CARS   PLANES   BOATS   BUSES   BICYCLES   FEET

Can you think of other kinds of transportation?

Now what kinds of problems are associated with cars?
Can you think of other problems?

CARS

safety
pollution
traffic

Now we're going to subdivide each problem associated with cars. Think about what kinds of solutions or inventions already exist to solve these problems. Make each problem the heading of a list. We've started the lists for you.

CARS

SAFETY

seat belts
bumpers
padded dash
speed limits
police/laws

POLLUTION

unleaded fuel
mufflers
mass transit
safety inspections

TRAFFIC

freeways
passing lanes
car pools
signs
flexible lanes

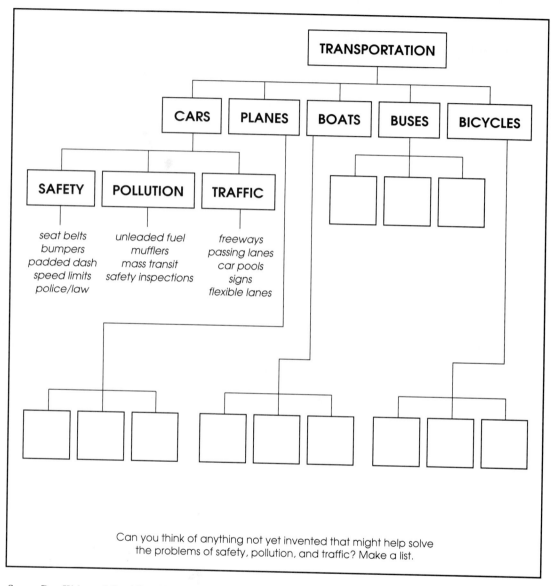

Can you think of anything not yet invented that might help solve
the problems of safety, pollution, and traffic? Make a list.

Source: Dan Kirby and Carol Kuy Kendall, *Thinking Through Language, Book One.* Copyright © 1985 by
the National Council of Teachers of English. Reprinted with permission.

Figure 4.13, continued

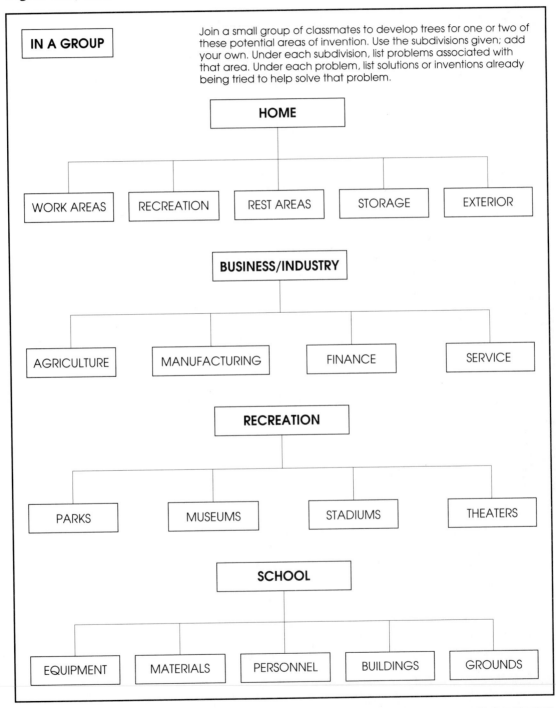

Figure 4.14 Partial Thinking Tree for *Freedom*

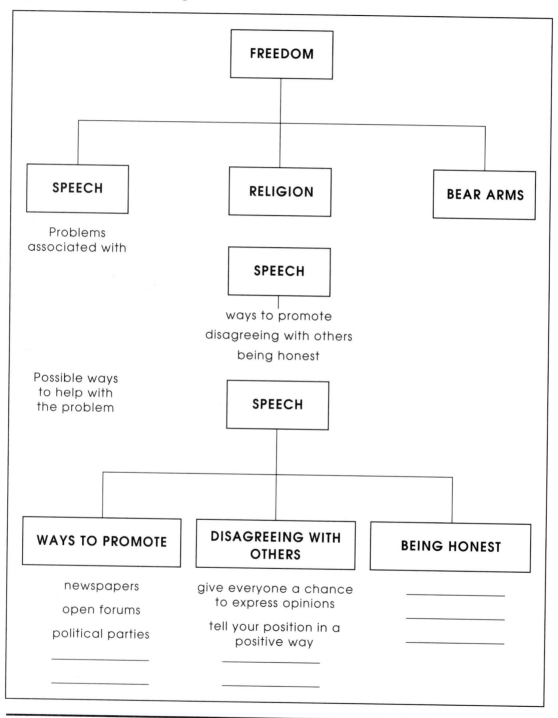

be taught. For example purposes, we will focus on teaching *decay* and use the following passage from *Mummies, Tombs, and Treasure* (Perl, 1987).

> *Without preservation, dead animal matter usually decays very quickly. This is true of plant matter, too. A dead bird or cat, a piece of rotting fruit, can show the stages of decay. Decay is caused by bacteria. (p. 2)*

2. *Establish the context.* The word and the context are presented to the students; the passage is read aloud as students follow along. Then students reread it silently.

3. *Specify the word meaning.* You must now talk students toward a definition of the word under study. By asking them questions, you encourage them to use their prior knowledge and clues in the text to arrive at a meaning for the word. An example of this type of questioning follows:

Teacher: What does this text tell you about the word *decay*?

Student: That dead animals decay.

Teacher: What happens to them when they decay?

Student: They rot.

Teacher: How could you tell from this text that decay means to rot?

Student: By what it says about rotting fruit.

4. *Expand the word meaning.* After students have a basic understanding of the word, try to deepen their understanding by discussing synonyms, antonyms, other contexts, or other examples where the word might be used. The purpose of these activities is to expand students' knowledge of the word. If students have access to a dictionary or a thesaurus, they could use them. The discussion might go as follows:

Teacher: Can you think of other things that decay?

Student: Teeth. I get cavities sometimes.

Teacher: How do we prevent decay?

Student: Put something on things that keep them from decaying.

Teacher: Like what?

Student: Fluoride keeps your teeth from decaying.

Teacher: What about dead things? How do we keep them from decaying?

Student: You embalm dead people.

Teacher: So the fluid used for embalming preserves things or keeps them from decaying. Can you think of words that mean the same as decay?

Student 1: rot.

Student 2: spoil.

After the words have been taught, students should be encouraged to place the words in their word banks or notebooks.

When to Use.   Preview in context is a strategy to use before reading, but it must be used *only* when the context for the word is strong. It is appropriate for all students at all grade levels but not for students who have limited prior knowledge.

Assessment Value.   As students respond in the discussions, you are able to tell the extent of their prior knowledge and their ability to use context clues.

Discussion.   The preview in context strategy is simple and easy to use. However, it is often difficult to identify contexts that contain enough clues to help students infer word meanings. Nagy (1988) points out that "context may look quite helpful if one already knows what the word means, but it seldom supplies adequate information for the person who has no other knowledge about the meaning of the word" (p. 7).

The strength in this strategy comes through the intensive discussion between the teacher and students, which deepens students' understanding. Therefore, it is important for you to be able to skillfully direct the discussion with your students.

Contextual Redefinition

Description.   Texts frequently do not provide sufficient context for students to determine the meaning of an unknown word (Schatz & Baldwin, 1986). Contextual redefinition helps students more effectively use context by presenting them with *sufficient context* before reading and showing them how to use the clues to *make informed guesses* about a word's meaning (Cunningham, Cunningham, & Arthur, 1981).

Procedures.   The following five-step procedure for using contextual redefinition was adapted from Tierney, Readence, and Dishner (1990):

1. *Select unfamiliar words.* Using the procedures suggested earlier in this chapter, select two or three words to be pretaught. For this example, *hippophargy* and *carapace* will be used.
2. *Write a sentence.* Write a sentence or more with sufficient clues provided for the meaning of the word to be taught. Try to use different types of context clues, such as direct definition, synonyms, and comparison/contrast. If the text has sufficient context clues for the word in question, use it. Here are two sample sentences:

   > The drought had been so long and severe that the cattle had died. Only the horses survived. Yet the natives were so hungry that they had to resort to *hippophagy* to avoid starvation.

   > Without its *carapace*, a turtle is subject to certain death from its enemies or the elements.

3. *Present the words in isolation.* Using the chalkboard or overhead projector, present the words in isolation and ask students to pronounce the words or pronounce them for them. Then encourage students to provide a definition for each word. Wild guesses may occur; this is part of the learning process. Encourage students to come to a consensus about the meaning of each word.
4. *Present the words in context.* Using the contexts prepared for the lesson, present each word and have students read the contexts aloud or read them for them. As students discuss each word, have them come to a consensus about its meaning. Encourage guessing from the clues; in this way, at-risk students are able to participate. To help students become more attuned to the value of context, ask them to discuss the differences between trying to define the words in context and in isolation.
5. *Use a dictionary for verification.* Discuss the dictionary definition and compare it to the one developed by the students. Then compare the differences between the definitions given for isolated words and the words in context.

When to Use.   The contextual redefinition strategy is used to teach totally *new* words before reading. It is appropriate for all students who possess some skill in using the dictionary and is especially useful when the text does not provide context that will help students infer the meanings of the words selected for preteaching. Students who are having difficulty learning to construct meaning and second-language learners may profit from the use of this strategy.

Assessment Value.   You can assess students' prior knowledge by their responses in guessing definitions in isolation and in context. The use of the context samples will let you know how well students are able to use context. Finally, dictionary verification will give you opportunities to see how effectively students use the dictionary.

Discussion.   Although some researchers have found that the use of context sentences is an effective way to teach students vocabulary (Gipe, 1978–1979), many questions have been raised about the value of such procedures, as was noted in the discussion of the preview in context strategy (Nagy, 1988). However, when the words to be pretaught are *carefully selected, kept to a minimum of two or three,* and *thoroughly taught,* there *may be* some value to preteaching for improving comprehension (Tierney & Cunningham, 1984; Wixson, 1986). Therefore, the keys to effectively using preview in context and contextual redefinition are careful word selection and thorough discussion of them in the process of teaching. It must also be remembered that students need repeated encounters with the words through reading and writing to develop ownership of them.

Vocabulary Self-Collection

Description.   This strategy (Haggard, 1982, 1986) places the responsibility for learning words on the students. After a reading experience, students select a word that they think the entire class should study. They are also encouraged to select additional words for their own personal study. This strategy has the advantages of being interactive and being based on authentic reading experiences.

Procedures.   The following procedures are based on Haggard's suggestions (1986):

1. *Select words for study.* After students have read a story or informational text, ask them to review it and select one word for class study. They may do this as individuals, partners, or teams. You as teacher should also select one word for study so that you are an active learning partner and gain some influence in the process. Encourage students to select words that seem important or interesting.
2. *Compile and define the words.* Ask each student or group to give the word selected for study and the definition of the word that was determined from context. List each word on the chalkboard or overhead with the definition, including your word as well. Use the dictionary to verify or complete definitions as needed, and encourage all students to participate in this process. With the students, agree on a final list of words and definitions.
3. *Finalize the list.* With the students, review the list to eliminate duplications, words that seem unrelated to the story or topic of study, and words that students just don't want to study. Agree on a reasonable number (three to five) for the final list, and have students put the words and definitions in their vocabulary notebooks or journals. Some may choose to record words eliminated from the class list in their personal list. When they write the words in their journal, ask them to write a sentence demonstrating the use of the word in their own life or showing their understanding of it.
4. *Use and extend the words.* Encourage students to use the words in their writing and to look for them in other books they read. Plan activities that reinforce the words, such as semantic maps, semantic feature analysis, and arrays.

These procedures are based on the concept of vocabulary development after reading, but you can adapt them to before reading by having students preview the text and select words that they think are going to be important for study.

When to Use.   This strategy may be used with both narrative and expository texts and with all students at any grade level. When students do not have sufficient skill to use the dictionary, the teacher will need to provide the definitions.

Assessment Value.   This strategy gives you many opportunities to assess students' word knowledge. When they select words for study and give definitions from context, you can assess their use of context clues. As they participate in expanding definitions given by other students, you can determine the extent of their prior knowledge.

Discussion.   Vocabulary self-collection has many appealing features: it is easy to implement, is interactive, is based on authentic reading experiences, and is very versatile. Although the limited research on this strategy was carried out with college students (Haggard, 1986) and there is no empirical evidence of its use with elementary or secondary students, it should not be discarded for this reason.

Vocabulary self-collection lends itself to the concept that children learn to read and write by reading and writing. By selecting their own words, students become active participants in their own process of learning and also learn to see the classroom as a community of learners. Some teachers may worry that students will not select important words, but it should be remembered that when the teacher participates in the process the students and teacher become partners in learning. Moreover, there is no guarantee that words selected by the teacher will be any more readily learned by students than will self-selected words. This strategy respects the students as learners and incorporates all of the ideas about authentic learning that have been stressed throughout this text.

Seven strategies for developing vocabulary have been discussed. All of them help students become independent vocabulary learners and constructors of meaning, and each meets the criteria for effective vocabulary instruction developed throughout this chapter. Three of the strategies focus on the use of context and on developing in-depth word knowledge: concept of definition, preview in context, and contextual redefinition. Two stress word relationships: semantic feature analysis and hierarchical and linear arrays. Semantic mapping focuses on in-depth knowledge and word relationships, and vocabulary self-collection focuses on self-selection of words to study and on using context and the dictionary to determine word meanings. All of these strategies require continual integration of new knowledge with old knowledge. Of course, no one strategy alone can meet the needs of all students and all learning situations, and *no one strategy or no combination of strategies is as powerful for developing vocabulary as wide reading and extensive writing*. Nevertheless, when *used judiciously* in combination with wide reading and extensive writing, these strategies should give students the experiences needed to develop strong vocabularies and to improve their meaning construction.

STRUCTURAL ANALYSIS AS AN AID TO INDEPENDENCE

Recall that it was stated earlier in this chapter that the goal of vocabulary development was for students to achieve independence in word learning because the number of words to be learned was too great for them to be taught individually. It was suggested that the way to achieve this independence was by making students aware of words and by helping them develop a strategy for independently inferring word meanings (see page 202). One of the things that students are encouraged to do when using this strategy is to look for structural elements within the word that might help them determine its meaning. However, it must be kept in mind that the teaching of structural elements is of limited value and must be done only under certain circumstances (see page 215).

As has been stated repeatedly throughout this text, students learn skills such as the use of structural elements through reading and writing. As they are going through this process, they often require the support of the teacher. This support may be provided through direct vocabulary teaching strategies or through minilessons that go back to the students' reading or writing material to focus directly or incidentally on a particular skill such as structural analysis.

Structural analysis is the study of meaningful word parts. It may help students as they learn to recognize words (pronunciation) and as they determine the meanings of words. The following elements are usually considered part of structural analysis:

- *Base words:* Meaningful linguistic units that can stand alone and contain no smaller meaningful parts; also called free morphemes (re*sell: sell* is the base word).
- *Root words:* Words from which other words are derived; usually the derivational word is from another language and is a bound morpheme— it cannot stand alone (*scribble* comes from the Latin root *scribere*, meaning "to write"). Teachers frequently use the terms *base word* and *root word* synonymously, but they are not the same.
- *Prefixes:* Units of meaning that can be added to the beginnings of base words or root words to change their meanings; these are bound morphemes and cannot stand alone (*un*happy: *un* is the prefix meaning "not").
- *Suffixes:* Units of meaning that can be added to the ends of base or root words to change their meanings; these are bound morphemes (tear*ful: ful* is the suffix meaning "full of").
- *Inflectional endings:* Word parts that can be added to the ends of root or base words to change their case, gender, number, tense, or form; these are bound morphemes (boy*'s:* possessive case; steward*ess:* gender; tree*s:* number; walk*ed:* tense; funni*est:* form). Sometimes inflectional endings are called suffixes.

- *Compound words:* Two or more base words that have been combined to form a new word with a meaning that is related to each base word (*run + way = runway*).
- *Contractions:* Shortened forms of two words in which a letter or letters have been replaced by an apostrophe (*do + not = don't; girl + is = girl's*).

Students will become familiar with compound words and contractions through their reading and writing experiences, and for most students simply showing them what these are as reading and writing takes place is usually sufficient. In some instances, however, students may need more directed support using the minilesson as discussed in Chapter 2; but even when this is required, the lesson *always goes back to the literature* to help students see how the compound or contraction was used in context. For example, if your students have just completed reading *Aunt Flossie's Hats (and Crab Cakes Later)* (Howard, 1991) and you noticed that they were having trouble figuring out compound words or contractions, you could use this story as the basis for a minilesson involving the following simple steps:

1. Go back to the story (revisit it) to identify a compound word or contraction. Read the section containing it aloud to students as they follow along. Ask them if they notice anything special about the compound or contraction.
2. Define *compound* or *contraction*. Point out another example; then point out words that are not examples.
3. Direct students to read a page where another example exists. Ask them to find the compound word or contraction.
4. Make a chart of other examples that students are able to find.
5. Conclude the lesson by discussing with students how they should use this new knowledge in reading and writing.
6. As students read and write, you may need to do periodic reviews.

Aunt Flossie's Hats (and Crab Cakes Later) is particularly good for this experience because it contains numerous examples of both compounds and contractions such as *afternoons, hatboxes, here's, she's,* and so forth.

Knowledge of the remaining elements of structural analysis also develops through reading and writing. The addition of prefixes and suffixes to words accounts for a large number of words for students in grade 4 and above (Nagy & Anderson, 1984). However, the prefixes and suffixes encountered have variant meanings, which makes it difficult for students to see a pattern (Graves, 1987). If you have to provide a minilesson, it is important to know which prefixes and suffixes to focus on and how to construct your lesson (for guidelines, see Graves, 1987; Nagy & Anderson, 1984; White, Sowell, & Yanagihara, 1989).

White, Sowell, and Yanagihara (1989) determined, on the basis of frequency of occurrence, that there are nine prefixes and ten suffixes of sufficient use to students to merit instruction (see Table 4.4). They also determined that knowing the prefixes listed would account for 76 percent of

Table 4.4 Prefixes and Suffixes That Merit Instruction

Prefixes		*Suffixes*	
un- dis- *in-, im-* *non-* ir- ⎤ ⎬ ⎦	meaning "not": *unhappy,* *disrespectful,* *inactive,* *impossible,* *nonresistant,* *irresponsible*	-s, -es	plural: *girls* tense: *jumps*
re-	meaning "back or again": *revisit*	-ed	tense *jumped*
		-ing	tense *jumping*
un- dis- ⎤ ⎬ ⎦	meaning "do the opposite of": *untie,* *disassemble*	-ly	meaning "like" *sisterly*
in-, im-	meaning "in or into": *indoors*	-er, -or	meaning "one who performs a specialized action": *swimmer; er-* used to form comparative degree with adjectives: *darker*
en-, em-	meaning "into or within": *entangle*	-tion, -ion, -ation, -ition, ⎤ ⎬ ⎦	meaning "action": *absorption*
over-	meaning "too much": *overdose*	-able, -ible	meaning "susceptible, capable, worth": *debatable*
mis-	meaning "wrong": *misspell*	-al, -ial	meaning "of or relating to": *parental*
		-y	meaning "consisting of or inclined toward": *sleepy*
		-ness	meaning "state, quality, condition, or degree": *brightness*

*Accounts for nearly 50 percent of all prefixed words (Graves, 1987).

Source: Based on White, Sowell, and Yanagihara (1989).

prefixed words and knowing the suffixes would account for 85 percent of suffixed words. Graves (1987) reported that knowing just four prefixes (*un- in-* [not], *dis-, non-*) would account for nearly 50 percent of all prefixed words. Therefore, in planning minilesson support focusing on word parts, you should give greatest attention to the nine prefixes and ten suffixes listed in Table 4.4.

In addition to knowing which prefixes and suffixes are the most beneficial for students, you must also be aware of some of the pitfalls of using prefixes as an aid to word meaning (White et al., 1989); there are three to keep in mind:

1. Prefixes are not consistent in their meaning; for example, *un-*, *dis-*, *re-*, and *in-* each have two meanings.
2. False analysis with prefixes often occurs. For example, removing *in* from *intrigue* leaves no recognizable base word. With prefixes *re-*, *in-*, and *dis-* there is a high risk of false analysis.
3. Looking only at word parts may mislead the reader in determining the word's true meaning. For example, *unassuming* means "modest" instead of "not supposing."

If you are aware of these possible pitfalls and know how often the affixes occur, *you can plan* minilessons that help students who demonstrate the need for such support. The following suggestions were adapted from White et al. (1989).

Minilessons Using Prefixes

A series of six lessons is suggested, which would be taught following experiences with literature that provide examples of prefixes.

- *Lesson 1:* Define and teach the concept of a prefix. Create a chart like the following:

> Prefix
> 1. – A group of letters that go in front of a word (*un-*)
> 2. – Changes the meaning of a word (*kind – unkind*)
> 3. – When you peel it off, a word must be left. (ⓤⓝkind)

Use examples and nonexamples to teach point 3 (*unkind*, example; *uncle*, nonexample).

- *Lesson 2:* Negative meanings of *un-* and *dis-*. Prepare sentences containing prefixed words. Because many prefixed words have suffixes, use familiar base words containing suffixes as well as prefixes. Have students read the sentence looking for a prefixed word, and then have them "peel off" the prefix, looking for the base word. The following sample sentence could be used:

  John didn't come home when he was told; he disobeyed his father.

Lesson dialogue might go as follows:

Teacher: What does obey mean?

(Students reply.)

Teacher: So what does *dis-* mean here?

(Students reply.)

Teacher: And *disobeyed* means what?

(Students reply.)

Teacher: Does this make sense?

(Students reply.)

Teacher: You should always check to see that the meaning makes sense.

(Students reply.)

Teacher: Now let's look at a word where *dis-* is not a prefix. *Discover—* does this word mean "something that is not a cover"? Let's check the dictionary.

Sentences for the lessons can be written by the teacher or taken from literature that has been read. After each lesson, students should be encouraged and reminded to use their knowledge about prefixes to determine the meanings of unknown words as they use the strategy for inferring word meanings. The remaining four lessons follow this pattern and focus on the following prefixes:

- *Lesson 3:* Prefixes *in-, im-, ir-,* and *non-,* meaning "not."
- *Lesson 4:* Prefix *re-,* meaning "again or back."
- *Lesson 5:* Alternate meanings of *un-, dis-, in-,* and *im-.*
- *Lesson 6:* Prefixes *en-, em-, over-,* and *mis-.*

Minilessons Using Suffixes

Suffixes (or inflectional endings) tend to have abstract meanings. Therefore, instruction should focus on removing the suffix and identifying the base word. The following lessons are recommended:

- *Lesson 1:* Teach the concept of suffixes (or inflectional endings) as was done in lesson 1 on prefixes.

- *Lesson 2:* Teach *-s/es*, *-ed*, and *-ing* with no spelling changes. Show students the suffixed word, and have them identify the suffix and define the base word (examples: *boxes, talking, lasted*).
- *Lessons 3–5:* Focus on three major spelling changes that occur using suffixes:

    Consonant doubling: *begged, thinner, funny*
    Change from *y* to *i*: *flies, worried, reliable*
    Deleted silent *e*: *saved, rider, believable*

Follow the same pattern as suggested for lesson 2 but discuss the spelling change that has occurred. The suffixes used should be drawn from the list suggested in Table 4.4.

- *Lesson 6:* Suffixes that change the part of speech—*ly, er, -ion, -able, -al, -y,* and *-ness.* Again, follow the same pattern as with the other lessons. More than one lesson might be needed for this category of suffixes.

The exact grade levels for teaching prefixes and suffixes is really dependent upon students' needs. However, it is recommended that the first three prefix lessons and the first five suffix lessons be completed by the end of grade 4. All instruction should be completed by the end of grade 5.

White et al. (1989) report favorable results with students who were taught lessons similar to those described above. They stress that "the goal of prefix and suffix instruction is *use* of word-part clues to derive the meaning of unfamiliar words" (p. 307). Even in a literature-centered classroom, they feel that a "reasonable" amount of direct teaching helps students learn to use an independent strategy for inferring word meanings.

THE DICTIONARY AND THESAURUS AS AIDS TO INDEPENDENCE

Two final areas of knowledge that students must have in order to use the strategy for independently inferring word meanings and achieving independence in vocabulary learning are the use of the dictionary and the thesaurus (Graves, 1987). The dictionary is an aid for reading, writing, and spelling. The thesaurus is more valuable for writing.

Using a Dictionary

The dictionary is an invaluable tool for determining both the pronunciations and meanings of words. It is especially useful when students have tried all other skills and have still not determined the meaning or pronunciation of an unknown word. Unfortunately, the way students are often exposed to the dictionary is a turnoff to them. Therefore, there are some "don'ts" about the dictionary that you should keep in mind:

- *Don't* give students lists of isolated words to look up and define. Words out of context have no meaning, and students will not know which definition to select. Furthermore, this type of activity becomes dull and boring and is not good instruction.
- *Don't* use the dictionary as a means of punishment. Too many teachers turn to the dictionary to punish students by having them copy pages. Who would ever want to see a dictionary again?
- *Don't* require that every word on each week's spelling list be looked up in the dictionary and defined. This becomes a deadly, useless activity.
- *Don't* teach phonetic respelling except in relation to determining the pronunciation of words in the dictionary.

The *"don'ts"* for teaching use of the dictionary can be balanced with some positive *"dos"*:

- *Do* let students know that you, the teacher, often turn to the dictionary to check the spelling, pronunciation, and meanings of words.
- *Do* teach students how to use a dictionary.
- *Do* show students how to make use of a dictionary in their reading and writing.
- *Do* show students how to use a dictionary in all content areas.

The use of the dictionary must be taught in a manner that will leave students with positive attitudes. The teaching should begin in kindergarten and proceed through the primary grades until students know and understand the components of the dictionary and can use them effectively. The following sequence should guide the use of the dictionary, which should be developed through meaningful experiences, not isolated skill lessons.

1. Use picture dictionaries to introduce the concept of the dictionary in kindergarten and first grade. Have students learn to locate words in the dictionaries, and teach them to make picture dictionaries of their own.
2. As soon as students have some knowledge of the alphabet, teach them how words are arranged in the dictionary. Give them practice in locating words.
3. Show students how words in the first half of the alphabet fall in the first half of the dictionary, and words in the second half fall in the second half. Point out how, with this knowledge, students can save time by not having to turn through lots of extra pages.
4. Introduce the concept of phonetic respelling in relation to the pronunciation key, and show students how this key can help them figure out pronunciations.
5. Teach students to locate the meanings of words by using guide words; point out that the dictionary lists more than one meaning for some words.

6. Finish teaching students how to locate words alphabetically, showing them how words are alphabetized not just through the first letter but through the second, third, fourth, and subsequent letters.
7. Have students learn to select the correct dictionary definition for multiple-meaning words that are presented in written context.
8. Teach the special symbols used in dictionaries, such as *n* for noun, *v* for verb, and *sing.* for singular.
9. Show students all the other types of information that can be found in the dictionary, including lists of synonyms, an atlas, and geographic listings.
10. Provide students with experiences using many different dictionaries and glossaries.

Once students have learned the basics of using the dictionary, it can become a part of their strategy for independently inferring word meanings.

Using a Thesaurus

A thesaurus, such as *Roget's Thesaurus* (1965), is a dictionary of synonyms and antonyms and is very useful in helping readers and writers locate synonyms and antonyms as well as subtle shades of meaning for words. Teachers can introduce elementary-grade students to the use of the thesaurus with *Words to Use: A Junior Thesaurus* (Drysdale, 1971).

It is much easier to learn to use a thesaurus than a dictionary. Once students know how to alphabetize and have learned the concepts of synonyms and antonyms, the rest is quite easy. They must be taught how the thesaurus is organized, how to locate a word, and how to read the synonym or antonym entries. Students should be shown how writers use the thesaurus to locate words that they want to change in their writing to avoid repetition.

After students have learned to use the thesaurus, encourage them to use it as a means of improving their writing. One very effective way to do this is through minilessons during the writing workshop, where you demonstrate the use of the thesaurus in a group-written story. Again, students learn best by simply *writing.* (See Chapter 7.)

*Literacy
Lesson*

The Bicycle Man

This lesson illustrates the concepts of vocabulary development using a delightful book, *The Bicycle Man* (Say, 1982). You will see how words were selected for direct teaching and how the decisions were made about when and how to teach vocabulary. The plan uses the literacy lesson concept presented in Chapter 2.

Before Reading the Plan

1. **Think about what you have learned about vocabulary development from this chapter. Review any portions that you may have forgotten or that may have been unclear.**
2. **Recall the parts of the literacy lesson plan. (See Chapter 2 if you need review.)**
3. **Read *The Bicycle Man* (Say, 1982).**
4. **Read and study the "Teacher Preparation" section to see the decision making that was involved in planning the vocabulary activities for this book.**

While Reading the Plan

1. **Notice how vocabulary is developed throughout the plan and how the emphasis is on helping students achieve independence in vocabulary learning.**
2. **Think about why these particular procedures and strategies are used. Consider other strategies that you might have chosen.**

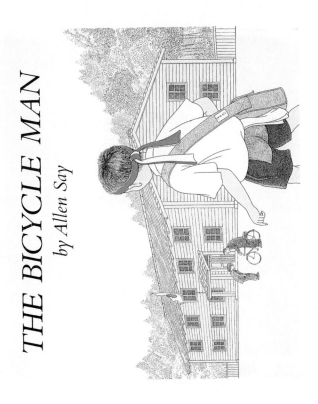

THE BICYCLE MAN

by Allen Say

When I was a small boy I went to a school in the south island of Japan. The schoolhouse stood halfway up a tall green mountain. It was made of wood and the wood was gray with age. When a strong wind blew, the trees made the sound of waves and the building creaked like an old sailing ship. From the playground we could see the town, the ships in the harbor, the shining sea.

One fine spring day we had our sportsday. All the children and teachers were out in the playground long before the first bell rang.

"Did everybody remember to bring a headband?" asked Mrs. Morita. She was our first-grade teacher. Eagerly we showed her our headbands. They were red on one side and white on the other.

"Remember, we're on the red team," she told us.

We swept the playground with all the brooms in the school.
We tied colored flags and streamers to bamboo poles. We drew
white lines on the ground with powdered chalk.

Our parents came carrying tiered lunch boxes and kettles filled
with tea. They spread their straw mats and sat around the oval
track.

When everything was ready Mrs. Morita rang the bell. It was nine o'clock. The principal stood on the platform and said, "Parents, children, my fellow teachers, let us remember that we are gathered here in the spirit of sportsmanship. Whether we win or lose, let us enjoy ourselves."

We cheered and clapped our hands.

The youngest children were the first to race. We lined up six at a time at the starting line.

"Ready, set, go!" Mr. Oka, the art teacher, boomed at us. We first graders leaped out and dashed around the track. Parents and teachers ran alongside of us, yelling encouragement. The older children waved flags and headbands and shouted at the top of their lungs until the mountain echoed the noise like rumbling thunder.

The winners went up to the judges' table and received prizes from the principal. The prizes were wrapped in white paper and tied with gold threads. Inside, there were oranges and rice cakes and pencils.

By the time the sixth graders finished running it was lunchtime. And that was the best part of the sportsday. My mother had cooked for two days preparing the good things to eat. The layers of lacquered boxes held pickled melon rinds and egg rolls, spiced rice and fish cakes. There were apples and peaches and sweets of all sorts.

teachers paired up and tied their ankles together with headbands and hopped around the oval. We screamed with delight when they stumbled and fell on top of one another.

We were cheering Mrs. Morita and someone's father when a hush fell on the playground. We stopped moving and talking and stared toward the gate.

In the afternoon we had the tug of war and piggyback races. After that the grown-ups had a race of their own. Parents and

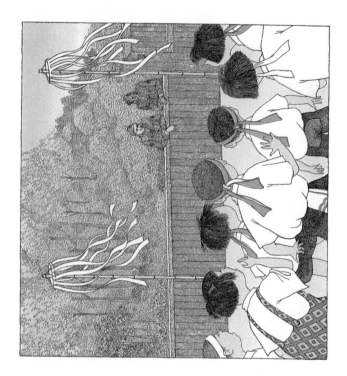

Two strangers were leaning over the fence and watching us. They were American soldiers. One of them was a white man with bright hair like fire, and the other man had a face as black as the earth. They wore dark uniforms with neckties, soft caps on their heads, and red stripes on their sleeves. They had no guns.

"Look how black he is!"

"Look at the red hair!" we whispered.

The war had been over for only a short while, not even one year. American soldiers had a base in the harbor but we had never seen them in our mountain. I felt afraid.

The foreigners smiled and waved at us. When the black man cleared the fence and came toward us we all drew back and stared. He was the tallest man I had ever seen. And his clothes! Such sharp creases! And his shoes shone like polished metal.

The soldier walked in huge strides toward the school entrance where the principal's bicycle stood. He pointed at the bicycle and turned to the judges' table. The principal stood up slowly.

"He wants the bicycle," someone said.

"Maybe he doesn't know what it is."

"No, he wants to ride it."

The principal walked up to the American and bowed. He looked like a small boy greeting a giant. The tall man gave a deep bow, almost bumping heads with the principal. We started to giggle.

We watched them talk to each other with their hands. The principal pointed at the bicycle, then at the man, and nodded. Yes, you are welcome to ride my bicycle, he seemed to say. The soldier put the palms of his hands together and smiled.

The man took the bicycle by the handlebar, kicked up the stand, and rolled it out to the center of the playground. He motioned to us to make room, and then called his friend.

The other American was nearly as tall as the black man. He took off his cap and saluted us with a big bow. We giggled and bowed back. The strangers spoke to each other and nodded.

Suddenly the rider yanked on the handlebar and lifted the front wheel off the ground.

"Oh, look!" we stirred.

"How can he ride like that?"

"What an athlete!" said the art teacher.

The black man took off his jacket and handed it to the white man. Then he hoisted a long leg over the bicycle and began to pedal it round and round in a widening circle. His friend waved the jacket like a flag and cheered him to go faster.

Then he rode backwards!

He sat on the bicycle with his body turned around. He had to twist his neck to see where he was going. He worked his long arms and legs like a huge dancing spider. We howled with wonder.

The red-haired man was the ringmaster. He ran alongside of the bicycle and shouted encouragement. The rider went round and round, with only one wheel, zigzagging this way and that. We were amazed.

he could. Then he let go.

The bicycle shot forward with great speed. The rider stood up on the pedals and, leaning on the handlebar, put both his feet up

The man rode backwards, then forwards, twirling the front wheel like a spinning gyroscope. He shouted something to the ringmaster who grasped the carrier and began to push as fast as

on the carrier! He was in the air. His cap flew off and his necktie fluttered in the wind. He seemed to be flying free, cruising like an enormous dragonfly. "Oh, oh!" we exclaimed and gasped in turn.

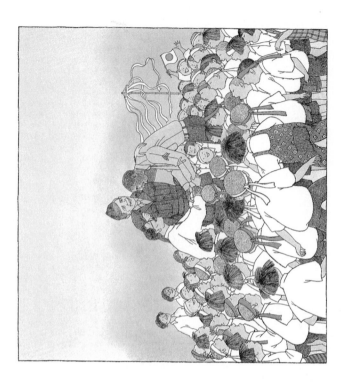

When the bicycle finally came to a stop the playground roared with wild clapping of hands and shouting. The rider panted, heaving and laughing. The ringmaster rushed up to him and lifted him in a bear hug. We mobbed around them, jumping and yelling.

The principal struggled through the crowd and the black man reached out to him. They gripped each other's arms like old friends.

The principal raised his arms to quiet us down. He took the soldiers' hands and led them to the platform. There he whispered something to Mrs. Morita and she brought him the largest box from the prize table.

The principal stood on the platform and held out the box to the Americans. He looked like the emperor awarding a great champion.

The bicycle rider received the gift with both hands and lifted it high above his head. Then he turned to the crowd.

"Ari-ga-tow, ari-ga-tow," he said. "Thank you, thank you."
The whole school bowed to him, and shouted for joy.
The Americans put their caps on and walked out the gate with their prize. They went down the mountain, arm in arm, waving and laughing. We followed them with our eyes, until they disappeared around the bend in the road.

*Literacy
Lesson
continued*

Teacher Preparation

The literacy lesson for *The Bicycle Man* (Say, 1982) was developed for a class of third graders who were making good progress in developing their literacy. They often had difficulty with comprehension but were beginning to develop more independence. This book was one that I wanted the entire class to experience. There was a great deal of independent reading and self-initiated writing in this class, and the students' vocabularies were expanding because of the extensive reading and writing and the emphasis on vocabulary. My preparation for this lesson proceeded as follows:

1. I read *The Bicycle Man* and wrote out a rough story map for it:
   - *Setting:* Japanese school after World War II.
   - *Characters:* Main—person telling the story (I), Mr. and Mrs. Morita (principal and teacher), red-headed soldier, black soldier. Secondary— Mr. Oka (art teacher).
   - *Problem:* Japanese people are afraid of the American soldiers (inferred, p. 17).
   - *Action:* (1) Students prepare the school grounds for a sportsday. (2) Parents arrive with lunch boxes and kettles of food. (3) Principal, Mr. Morita, begins sportsday with a speech about sportsmanship. (4) Children have races and prizes are given to winners. (5) Children and parents have lunch. (6) Games after lunch include parents and teachers; everyone is having fun. (7) Two soldiers arrive; one has red hair and the other soldier is black. (8) Soldiers seem very tall to children; children and adults are frightened of soldiers. (9) Black soldier wants to ride principal's bike. (10) Black soldier does tricks on bicycle and delights everyone. (11) Principal awards black soldier biggest prize.
   - *Outcome:* Everyone seems less afraid of American soldiers.
   - *Theme:* Getting to know someone helps in understanding them.

2. Next, I reviewed the story with the story map in mind to identify the key-concept words. (See page 206 for a discussion of selecting words for direct teaching.) I concluded that there were five words that were directly related to understanding the story: *sportsday, sportsmanship, foreigners, emperor,* and *champion*.

3. I then thought about these words in relation to the text and the students for whom the lesson was being prepared. I concluded that most of these students would know *emperor* because we had read *The Emperor's New Clothes* (Andersen, 1982) and *champion* because of all the emphasis on football and basketball champions in our district. *Sportsday* and *sportsmanship* are words children can figure out easily if they don't know them; they can use the context, knowledge of compound words and suffixes, and their own prior knowledge. I decided that *foreigners* was the only word that needed to be developed before reading.

Literacy
Lesson
continued

4. I decided to use three strategies throughout this lesson:
   - *Semantic mapping* for teaching *foreigners*. This strategy would help activate prior knowledge and integrate vocabulary teaching with that process (see page 219).
   - *Preview and predict* for weaving together vocabulary teaching with prior knowledge activation and purpose setting. This would work well with the preview in context strategy.
   - *Vocabulary self-collection strategy* (see page 232) for extending vocabulary after reading.

5. Finally, I decided to give students two choices for their mode of reading (see Chapter 2): cooperative and independent. I selected these two because some students need the support they can get from a partner and others prefer to read independently. I would be free to move around the class to offer individual support as needed, and I would begin by reading aloud a portion of the story.

Introducing *The Bicycle Man*

ACTIVITY	PROCEDURE	NOTES
Previewing the story	Have students get into small groups to preview the story to see what they think it will be about. Discuss group responses with the whole class.	Affords an opportunity to assess students' prior knowledge and see if there is other vocabulary and background needed.
Semantic mapping for *foreigners*	Place the word *foreigners* on the chalkboard. Tell students that *The Bicycle Man* is about foreigners, and ask them to work with a partner to brainstorm all the words they can think of related to *foreigners*. If they don't know any examples, make some suggestions and have them use the dictionary. List student responses on the board and guide students in grouping the words and constructing the semantic map.	Activates prior knowledge and develops a key-concept word at the same time. (See Chapter 3 and page 219 for a discussion of semantic mapping.)

Literacy Lesson continued

ACTIVITY	PROCEDURE	NOTES

During discussion, stress that people are often afraid of people or things they don't know.

ACTIVITY	PROCEDURE	NOTES
Making predictions: Using preview and predict	Ask students to predict what they think will happen in this story.	Flows naturally from all activities that have been done.
	Refer students to the preview and predict poster, if needed.	See Chapter 3.
	Have students record predictions in their journals.	Sets purpose for reading.

Reading and Responding to
The Bicycle Man

ACTIVITY	PROCEDURE	NOTES
Teacher read-aloud	Read aloud the first two pages as students follow along.	Gives the whole class the support they sometimes need to get started reading.
	Stop and ask students what they think is going to happen. Discuss whether they want to change any predictions.	

*Literacy
Lesson
continued*

ACTIVITY	PROCEDURE	NOTES
	Encourage students to make changes in their predictions.	Continues active process of predicting and confirming.
Making journal notes	Remind students to note any words or ideas they want to talk about in their journals.	Supports the process of responding during reading.
Student-selected mode of reading Cooperative (oral or silent) Independent	Have students select the mode of reading they want to use for the remainder of the story.	Gives students a choice in meeting their own needs. See Chapter 2 on modes of reading.
	Remind students to continue to see if their predictions were confirmed or changed.	Continues focus on reading for a purpose. As students read, observe each pair or trio; stop and ask questions or prompt those who need extra help.
Individual written responses	After they complete the story, ask students to write about it in their journals. Display the following response chart for those who need more support:	Gives all students a chance for personal response. See Chapter 5 on responding.

Responding to The Bicycle Man

Choose *one*.
Write about:
- What you learned from this story
- How this story made you feel
- The part you liked best—why?
- What you want to say about this story

ACTIVITY	PROCEDURE	NOTES
Whole-class discussion: Checking predictions Sharing responses Thinking critically	Ask students to review their predictions to note whether they were verified or changed.	Pulls together story for all students.

Literacy Lesson continued

ACTIVITY	PROCEDURE	NOTES
	Ask volunteers to share their responses to the story.	
	Conclude the discussion by asking students to talk about the following points: Who learned lessons in this story and why? Why was this an important experience for the Japanese people and the American soldiers in this story?	Promotes critical thinking.

Extending *The Bicycle Man*

Using the vocabulary self-collection strategy	Divide students into groups of three, and have each group select one word that they found most interesting or important to the story. Tell them to locate the word in the story and try to define it.	Gets students involved in becoming independent word learners. Focuses on using context and prior knowledge.
	Have each group share their word. Compile a list with definitions.	
	Contribute a word for the list (example: *lacquered boxes*).	The teacher is part of the group and should therefore contribute a word.
	Verify the definitions using the dictionary.	
	Review the list with students; have them select five to seven words for study.	
	Have selected words and definitions placed in journals.	

*Literacy
Lesson
continued*

ACTIVITY	PROCEDURE	NOTES
	Encourage students to select any other words from the list for their own study and enter them in their journal.	Puts more responsibility for learning on the students.
Self-selected activities	Invite students to select one activity they would like to pursue with a small group: (1) Make a book about Japan, (2) plan a sportsday, or (3) make a friendship chain (a paper chain with names of students who are friends, telling why they are friends).	Extends reading, giving students choices in meeting their own needs. Promotes problem solving and thinking as well as making use of the book read. May be a long-term activity that continues while other books are being read.

Example:

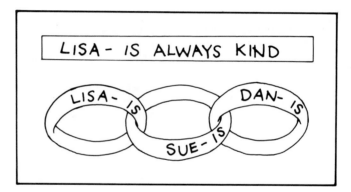

After Reading the Lesson

1. **Get together with someone else who has read the plan and discuss it. What would you have changed and why?**
2. **Assume that you are going to use this book with more advanced students. Work with a partner to revise the plan for those students.**
3. **Meet with a partner to discuss how you might use this book to develop a more extensive unit focusing more on social studies, science, and math (see Chapter 9).**

A FINAL WORD ABOUT VOCABULARY

Learning vocabulary is a natural part of reading and writing. The more exciting reading and writing experiences children have, the more they will encounter our wonderful language. It is through these experiences that children's vocabularies grow: it is through the excitement and fun of reading and writing that they learn to read and write!

SUMMARY

Students develop two reading vocabularies, recognition and meaning. This chapter has focused on meaning vocabulary and what we know about how it grows and how it is learned.

Effective vocabulary development includes helping students become aware of words, wide reading and extensive writing, learning a strategy for independently inferring word meanings, and *limited* direct teaching of vocabulary and vocabulary related skills. *The ultimate goal of all vocabulary development is for students to become independent word learners.*

This chapter has presented suggestions and guidelines for supporting effective vocabulary growth. A strategy for independently inferring word meanings was suggested, as well as seven strategies for direct teaching of vocabulary. Throughout the chapter, however, the main focus has been that students learn vocabulary through wide reading and extensive writing.

Children's Books

Andersen, H. C. (1983). *The emperor's new clothes.* New York: Harper and Row.
Forbes, E. (1971). *Johnny Tremain.* New York: Dell.
Graham, F. (illus.). (1987). *Roundabout cozy cottage.* New York: Grosset & Dunlap.
Howard, E. F. (1991). *Aunt Flossie's hats (and crab cakes later).* New York: Clarion.
Levitt, P. M., Burger, D. A., & Guralnick, E. S. (1985). *The weighty word book.* Longmont, CO: Bookmakers Guild.
Lowry, L. (1979). *Anastasia Krupnik.* Boston: Houghton Mifflin.
Maestro, B., & Maestro, G. (1989). *Taxi: A book of city words.* New York: Clarion.
Maestro, B., & Maestro, G. (1990). *Delivery van: Words for town and country.* New York: Clarion.
Myers, W. D. (1990). *The mouse rap.* New York: Harper & Row.
Perl, L. (1987). *Mummies, tombs, and treasure.* New York: Clarion.
Prelutsky, J. (1984). Never mince words with a shark. In J. Prelutsky, *The new kid on the block* (p. 89). New York: Greenwillow Books.
Say, A. (1982). *The bicycle man.* Boston: Houghton Mifflin.
Sperling, S. K. (1985). *Murfles and wink-a-peeps: Funny old words for kids.* New York: Clarkson N. Potter.

For Additional Reading

Heimlich, J. E., & Pittelman, S. D. (1986). *Semantic mapping: Classroom applications.* Newark, DE: International Reading Association.

Nagy, W. E. (1988). *Teaching vocabulary to improve reading comprehension.* Newark, DE/Urbana, IL: IRA/NCTE.

Pittelman, S. D., Heimlich, J. E., Berglund, R. L., & French, M. P. (1991). *Semantic feature analysis: Classroom applications.* Newark, DE: International Reading Association.

References

Anders, P., & Bos, C. (1986). Semantic feature analysis: An interactive strategy for vocabulary development and text comprehension. *Journal of Reading, 29,* 610–616.

Anderson, R. C., & Freebody, P. (1981). Vocabulary knowledge. In J. T. Guthrie (Ed.), *Comprehension and teaching: Research reviews.* Newark, DE: International Reading Association.

Beck, I. (1984). Developing comprehension: The impact of the directed reading lesson. In R. C. Anderson, J. Osborn & R. J. Tierney (Eds.), *Learning to read in American schools: Basal readers and content texts* (pp. 3–20). Hillsdale, NJ: Lawrence Erlbaum.

Beck, I., McCaslin, M., & McKeown, M. (1980). *The rationale and design of a program to teach vocabulary to fourth-grade students.* Pittsburgh: University of Pittsburgh, Learning Research and Development Center.

Beck, I., & McKeown, M. (1991). Conditions of vocabulary acquisition. In R. Barr, M. L. Kamil, P. Mosenthal & P. D. Pearson (Eds.), *Handbook of reading research* (Vol. 2, pp. 789–814). New York: Longman.

Beck, I. L., McKeown, M. G., McCaslin, E. S., & Burkes, A. M. (1979). *Instructional dimension that may affect reading comprehension: Examples from two commercial reading programs.* Pittsburgh: University of Pittsburgh, Learning Research and Development Center.

Beck, I. L., McKeown, M. G., & Omanson, R. C. (1987). The effects and uses of diverse vocabulary instructional techniques. In M. G. McKeown & M. E. Curtis (Eds.), *The nature of vocabulary acquisition.* Hillsdale, NJ: Lawrence Erlbaum.

Beck, I. L., Perfetti, C. A., & McKeown, M. G. (1982). Effects of long-term vocabulary instruction on lexical access and reading comprehension. *Journal of Educational Psychology, 74,* 506–521.

Blachowicz, C. L. Z. (1986). Making connections: Alternatives to the vocabulary notebook. *Journal of Reading, 29,* 643–649.

Blachowicz, C. Z. (1987). Vocabulary instruction: What goes on in the classroom? *Reading Teacher, 2,* 132–137.

Bradenburg, G. (1918). Psychological aspects of language. *Journal of Educational Psychology, 9,* 313–332.

Calfee, R. C., & Drum, P. A. (1986). Research on teaching reading. In M. C. Wittrock (Eds.), *Handbook of research on reading* (3rd ed.) (pp. 804–849). New York: Macmillan.

Carr, E., & Wixson, K. K. (1986). Guidelines for evaluating vocabulary instruction. *Journal of Reading, 29,* 588–595.

Chall, J. S. (1987). Two vocabularies for reading: Recognition and meaning. In M. G. McKeown & M. E. Curtis (Eds.), *The nature of vocabulary acquisition* (pp. 7–17). Hillsdale, NJ: Lawrence Erlbaum.

Cuff, N. (1930). Vocabulary tests. *Journal of Educational Psychology, 21,* 212–220.

Cunningham, J. W., Cunningham, P. M., & Arthur, S. U. (1981). *Middle and secondary school reading.* New York: Longman.

Davis, F. (1971). Psychometric research in reading comprehension. In F. Davis (Ed.), *Literature of research in reading with emphasis on models.* Brunswick, NJ: Rutgers University Press.

Drysdale, P. (1971). *Words to use: A junior thesaurus.* New York: William H. Sadlier.

Dupuy, H. (1974). *The rationale, development and standardization of a basic word vocabulary test.* Washington, DC: U.S. Government Printing Office (DHEW Publication No. HRA 74-1334).

Editors of the American Heritage Dictionary (1986). *Word mysteries and histories.* Boston: Houghton Mifflin.

Fielding, L. G., Wilson, P. T., & Anderson, R. C. (1986). A new focus on free reading: The role of tradebooks in reading instruction. In T. E. Raphael (Ed.), *Contexts of school-based literacy* (pp. 149–160). New York: Random House.

Gipe, J. P. (1978–1979). Investigating techniques for teaching word meanings. *Reading Research Quarterly, 14,* 624–644.

Graves, M. F. (1986). Vocabulary learning and instruction. *Review of Research in Education, 13,* 91–128.

Graves, M. F. (1987). The roles of instruction in fostering vocabulary development. In M. G. McKeown & M. E. Curtis (Eds.), *The nature of vocabulary acquisition* (pp. 165–184). Hillsdale, NJ: Lawrence Erlbaum.

Haggard, M. R. (1982). The vocabulary self-collection strategy: An active approach to word learning. *Journal of Reading, 27,* 203–207.

Haggard, M. R. (1986). The vocabulary self-collection strategy: Using student interest and world knowledge to enhance vocabulary growth. *Journal of Reading, 29,* 634–642.

Jenkins, J. R., & Pany, D. (1981). Instructional variables in reading comprehension. In J. T. Guthrie (Ed.), *Comprehension and teaching: Research reviews.* Newark, DE: International Reading Association.

Jenkins, J., Stein, M., & Wysocki, K. (1984). Learning vocabulary through reading. *American Education Research Journal, 21,* 767–788.

Johnson, D. D., & Pearson, P. D. (1984). *Teaching reading vocabulary* (2nd ed.). New York: Holt, Rinehart and Winston.

Johnston, P. (1981). *Prior knowledge and reading comprehension test bias.* Unpublished doctoral dissertation, University of Illinois, Champaign.

Kirby, D., & Kuykendall, C. (1985). *Thinking through language, Book one.* Urbana, IL: National Council of Teachers of English.

Kirkpatrick, E. (1981). The number of words in an ordinary vocabulary. *Science, 18,* 107–108.

Kirkpatrick, E. (1907). Vocabulary test. *Popular Science Monthly, 70,* 157–164.

Loban, W. D. (1963). *The language of elementary school children.* Champaign, IL: National Council of Teachers of English.

Lorge, I., & Chall, J. S. (1963). Estimating the size of vocabularies of children and adults: An analysis of methodological issues. *Journal of Experimental Education, 32*, 147–157.

McKeown, M. G., Beck, I. L., Omanson, R. C., & Pople, M. T. (1985). Some effects of the nature and frequency of vocabulary instruction on the knowledge and use of words. *Reading Research Quarterly, 20*(5), 522–535.

McKeown, M. G., & Curtis, M. E. (1987). *The nature of vocabulary acquisition*. Hillsdale, NJ: Lawrence Erlbaum.

Maria, K. (1990). *Reading comprehension instruction: Strategies and issues.* Parkton, MD: York.

Memory, D. M. (1990). Teaching technical vocabulary: Before, during or after the reading assignment. *Journal of Reading Behavior, 22*, 39–53.

Mezynski, K. (1983). Issues concerning the acquisition of knowledge: Effects of vocabulary training on reading comprehension. *Review of Educational Research, 53*, 253–279.

Nagy, W. E. (1988). *Teaching vocabulary to improve reading comprehension.* Newark, DE/Urbana, IL: IRA/NCTE.

Nagy, W. E., & Anderson, R. C. (1984). How many words are there in printed school English? *Reading Research Quarterly, 19*, 304–330.

Nagy, W. E., & Herman, P. A. (1987). Breadth and depth of vocabulary knowledge: Implications for acquisition and instruction. In M. G. McKeown & M. E. Curtis (Eds.), *The nature of vocabulary acquisition* (pp. 19–35). Hillsdale, NJ: Lawrence Erlbaum.

Paris, S. G., Lipson, M. Y., & Wixson, K. K. (1983). Becoming a strategic reader. *Contemporary Educational Psychology, 8*, 293–316.

Pressley, M., Burkell, J., Cariglia-Bull, T., Lysynchuck, L., McGoldrick, J. A., Schneider, B., Snyder, B. L., Symons, S., & Woloshyn, V. E. (1990). *Cognitive strategy instruction that really improves children's academic performance.* Cambridge, MA: Brookline.

Readence, J. E., Bean, T. W., & Baldwin, R. S. (1981, 1985, 1989). *Content area reading: An integrated approach.* Dubuque, IA: Kendall/Hunt.

Roget, P. (1965). *St. Martin's edition of the original Roget's Thesaurus of English Words and Phrases.* New York: St. Martin's.

Schatz, E. K., & Baldwin, R. S. (1986). Context clues are unreliable predictors of word meanings. *Reading Research Quarterly, 21*, 439–453.

Schwartz, R. (1988). Learning to learn vocabulary in content area textbooks. *Journal of Reading, 32*, 108–118.

Schwartz, R. M., & Raphael, T. E. (1985). Concept of definition: A key to improving students' vocabulary. *The Reading Teacher, 39*, 198–203.

Seashore, R. H. (1947). How many words do children know? *Packet, 2*, 3–17.

Smith, M. K. (1941). Measurement of the size of general English vocabulary through the elementary grades and high school. *Genetic Psychology Monographs, 24*, 311–345.

Stahl, S. A. (1983). Differential word knowledge and reading comprehension. *Journal of Reading Behavior, 15*, 33–50.

Stahl, S. A., & Fairbanks, M. M. (1986). The effects of vocabulary instruction: A model-based meta-analysis. *Review of Educational Research, 56*, 72–110.

Sternberg, R. J. (1987). Most vocabulary is learned from context. In M. G. McKeown & M. E. Curtis (Eds.), *The nature of vocabulary acquisition* (pp. 89–105). Hillsdale, NJ: Lawrence Erlbaum.

Stevens, K. C. (1982). Can we improve reading by teaching background information? *Journal of Reading, 25,* 326–329.

Stieglitz, E. L., & Stieglitz, U. S. (1981). SAVOR the word to reinforce vocabulary in the content areas. *Journal of Reading, 25,* 46–51.

Taylor, B. M., Frye, B. J., & Maruyama, G. M. (1990). Time spent reading and reading growth. *American Educational Research Journal, 27*(2), 351–362.

Tierney, R. J., & Cunningham, J. W. (1984). Research on teaching reading comprehension. In P. D. Pearson (Ed.), *Handbook of reading research* (pp. 609–655). New York: Longman.

Tierney, R. J., Readence, J. E., & Dishner, E. K. (1990). *Reading strategies and practices: A compendium* (3rd ed.). Boston: Allyn and Bacon.

Tierney, R. J., & Shanahan, T. (1991). Research on the reading-writing relationship: Interactions, transactions, and outcomes. In R. Barr, M. L. Kamil, P. Mosenthal & P. D. Pearson (Eds.), *Handbook of reading research* (Vol. 2, pp. 246–280). White Plains, NY: Longman.

Weiss, A. S., Mangrum, C. T., & Liabre, M. M. (1986). Differential effects of differing vocabulary presentations. *Reading Research and Instruction, 25,* 265–276.

White, T. G., Sowell, J., & Yanagihara, A. (1989). Teaching elementary students to use word-part clues. *The Reading Teacher, 42,* 302–308.

Wixson, K. K. (1986). Vocabulary instruction and children's comprehension of basal stories. *Reading Research Quarterly, 21,* 317–329.

Identifying Words as an Aid to Constructing Meaning

5

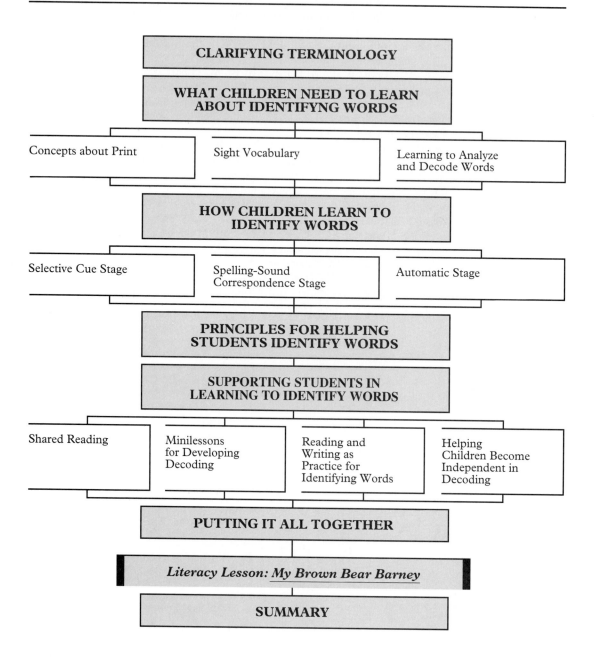

CLARIFYING TERMINOLOGY

WHAT CHILDREN NEED TO LEARN ABOUT IDENTIFYNG WORDS

Concepts about Print

Sight Vocabulary

Learning to Analyze and Decode Words

HOW CHILDREN LEARN TO IDENTIFY WORDS

Selective Cue Stage

Spelling-Sound Correspondence Stage

Automatic Stage

PRINCIPLES FOR HELPING STUDENTS IDENTIFY WORDS

SUPPORTING STUDENTS IN LEARNING TO IDENTIFY WORDS

Shared Reading

Minilessons for Developing Decoding

Reading and Writing as Practice for Identifying Words

Helping Children Become Independent in Decoding

PUTTING IT ALL TOGETHER

Literacy Lesson: My Brown Bear Barney

SUMMARY

Although effective constructors of meaning can identify words automatically (Perfetti, 1985), the ability to identify words is not a prerequisite to or separate from the ability to construct meaning. A visit to Mr. Sharpe's first- and second-grade classroom should give you some insights into how this process develops in readers and writers.

Mr. Sharpe and his students were rereading aloud the book *The Lady with the Alligator Purse* (Westcott, 1988). As Mr. Sharpe read, the children chimed in: "Miss Lucy had a baby, / His name was Tiny Tim. . . ." After reading the whole book, the boys and girls talked about their favorite parts and found pages to show what they were talking about. Luanda said, "I like the pizza page" and showed the page where they are eating pizza in the bed. Mr. Sharpe encouraged all children to talk and respond.

After the discussion, Mr. Sharpe turned to the first page and said, "Let's reread this page together"—"Miss Lucy had a baby, His name was Tiny Tim." All the children joined in.

"What was the baby's name?" The children responded, "Tiny Tim." Mr. Sharpe wrote the name on the chalkboard and asked, "What is the beginning letter of the baby's name?" Several children responded, "t." Mr. Sharpe underlined the "t" and asked, "What sound does this stand for?" "Tuh," responded several group members. He repeated the sound and asked the group to repeat it with him. He said, "We are going to talk about the t sound today because we have had trouble using it in our writing."

"Does anyone in our class have a name that begins with the sound 't' stands for?" As the children called out names, he listed them under Tiny Tim. He then asked different children to come and underline the "t" and to give the sound it stood for:

<u>T</u>iny <u>T</u>im

<u>T</u>erry

<u>T</u>homas

<u>T</u>anish

<u>t</u>eacher

One child said, "Lisa." Instead of telling the child she was wrong, Mr. Sharpe listed the name to the side of Tiny Tim and said, "Let's compare these two names. Which one begins with 't'?"—"Tiny Tim." "Which one begins with 'l'?"—"Lisa."—"Are these the same letter?"—"No."—"Let's look at our lists on the wall to see if we have one where Lisa's name will fit."

The children did not find a list for "I" because it had not been discussed yet. Mr. Sharpe tore off a long strip of paper, wrote Lisa at the top, and underlined the "L". He said, "We will talk about this letter later."

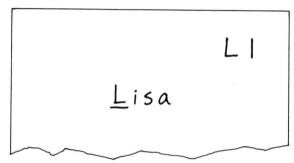

Mr. Sharpe returned to the list of "t" words, reread it with the children, and said, "When we read or spell words with a 't,' what sound will it stand for?"— "Tuh." "Right," he said. He repeated "tuh" and asked the children to repeat it with him.

"Were there other characters in our story besides Tiny Tim?"—"Yes."—"Who were they?" The children named some of the other characters. Mr. Sharpe then said, "Let's reread our story together to see if we missed any characters." The children quickly reread the book and added one more name to their list. Mr. Sharpe asked them to tell who their favorite character was and why. He then asked them to select their favorite character, draw his or her picture, and write the character's name under the picture.

While the children were drawing and writing, we asked Mr. Sharpe what he planned to do next. He replied, "I will ask the children to share their pictures and identify all the ones of Tiny Tim; these will be placed on the 't' chart to help children remember the sound."—"What if no one draws a picture of Tiny Tim?"— "We will discuss the situation and ask someone to draw a picture of Tiny Tim. However, I must tell you that this rarely happens."

"Why did you focus on 't' today?" we asked. "Because I've noticed that many of the children are not spelling words that begin with 't' correctly in their writing. Also, I have found that children like the Tiny Tim example as a model for the 't' sound."

"When will the children practice this phonic element?"—"As they read stories over the next few days, I will call their attention to words that begin with 't' and have them find them in the stories. When we write our responses to stories and write our own stories I will remind them to use what they have learned about letters and sounds. Reading and writing are the best practice for learning phonics!"

THIS ENTIRE CLASSROOM experience lasted less than 15 minutes. Before we discuss what took place, look back through the scene and make notes about what happened, thinking about how Mr. Sharpe was supporting these first and second graders in learning to identify words. Then compare your notes with the discussion that follows.

Mr. Sharpe's classroom was a literacy-centered classroom. His children were reading and writing together. Look at how the activities in this classroom were supporting these children in learning to construct meaning and in learning to identify words.

- *The focus was first on meaning.* Identifying favorite parts of their book was a meaningful experience for all these children. Focusing on meaning first is the way in which children have developed their use of oral language (Halliday, 1975). Therefore, it is logical to follow this same pattern in learning to read and write.
- *The example for the sound being taught was drawn from a story that all the children had experienced.* Words that the children had read were used as models for the sound that Mr. Sharpe wanted to teach.
- *Mr. Sharpe first clearly modeled the sound and then asked the children to find the letter standing for the sound and give the sound.* When he asked them to underline the *t* and give the sound "tuh," he was helping students associate the sound with its symbol. Mr. Sharpe was teaching a minilesson as a part of reading.
- *Children's approximations for the sound were accepted and used as a part of the teaching.* When the name *Lisa* was called out, it was used for comparing sounds and held for later work.
- *Charts modeling sounds were developed with the children and placed around the room for reference.* The "Tiny Tim" chart with students' drawings served as a model for students to use as they read and write.
- *Mr. Sharpe kept the focus on meaning construction.* By rereading the story and identifying favorite characters, the children were continuing to focus on meaning.
- *Practice for the phonic element* t *was done through reading and writing.* This type of practice kept the phonic element in meaningful contexts. It did not allow or encourage isolated practice of sounds such as circling pictures or isolated words that begin with the sound.
- *The time for teaching the sound for* t *was determined primarily by the demonstrated needs of the students.* In this case, Mr. Sharpe had seen the need in students' writing (note that he was assessing during instruction). He did not rely on some predetermined scope and sequence of skills because he knew that children do not learn the sounds in any predetermined order (Teale & Sulzby, 1986).

In this chapter, we will focus on how to help children learn to identify words as an aid to meaning construction in a literacy-centered classroom. It was noted in Chapter 1 that this entire area of word identification has been filled with controversy throughout the history of education (Adams, 1990; Chall, 1967; Chall, 1983; Juel, 1991). No attempt will be made here to debate or present the various points of view expressed in the research. Rather, this chapter will attempt to draw some viable conclusions based on the existing research. The discussion will focus on four areas: (1) what children must learn about identification of words, (2) how children learn to identify words, (3) principles for developing word identification in a literacy-centered classroom, and (4) how to support students in learning to identify words. However, before these four points are addressed, we must clarify some terms related to identifying words.

CLARIFYING TERMINOLOGY

Educators have used many different terms when discussing students' abilities to identify words: *decoding, encoding, recoding, word analysis, word identification, word recognition, sight word,* and *high-frequency word.* It will be helpful to have a clear definition of each of these terms in order to deal with the various points of view that you will encounter in your teaching career and to look at this topic more carefully in this chapter. Table 5.1 presents definitions taken from the *Dictionary of Reading Terms* (Harris & Hodges, 1981).

Notice that technically *decoding, word identification,* and *word recognition* all produce meaning, even though most authorities use the term *decoding* to label the process for simple identification, that is, to refer to a student's ability to "sound out," analyze, or give the oral equivalent for words with no emphasis on meaning. *Encoding* is writing (and spelling) or speaking. *Recoding* is oral reading with no emphasis on meaning.

Sight word is another term that causes much confusion. A *sight word* is one that is recognized immediately or instantly without analysis. Other terms used are *sight vocabulary, recognition vocabulary,* (see Chapter 4), or *instant recognition vocabulary.* A *sight word* may also be one that is taught as a whole word. It may be a word that cannot be phonetically or structurally analyzed, such as *the,* or a word that students have not acquired the necessary skills to analyze. Emphasis on sight words is sometimes called the *sight word approach* or the *whole word approach.* Technically, however, *any word* may be taught as a whole word.

High-frequency words are ones that are repeated frequently in material. There are many different listings of such words (Dolch, 1936; Johnson, 1971; Mason & Au, 1990). Although they are usually taught as sight words for reading, they are usually more effectively learned through writing. This subject will be discussed more thoroughly later in this chapter (see page 280).

Throughout this text the terms *decoding* and *word identification* are used interchangeably because these are commonly accepted terms. These terms refer to students' ability to produce the oral equivalent for a word *as well as* to construct or assign meaning for the word.

Table 5.1   Definitions of Reading Terms

Decode	To change communication signals into messages; especially, to get the intended meaning from an analysis of the spoken or graphic symbols of a familiar language, as *decode a word in one's mother tongue. Note:* To learn to read, one must learn the conventional code in which something is written in order to decode the written message. In reading practice, this term is used primarily to refer to word identification rather than to higher units of meaning.
Encode	To change a message into symbols, as *encode oral language into writing, encode an idea into words,* or *encode a physical law into mathematical symbols.*
Recode	To change information from one code into another, as *recode writing into oral speech. Note:* No necessary assumption about meaning is made in this process: *The reader recodes the coded graphic input as phonological or oral output.*
Word analysis	1. *Usually, the analysis of words into their constituent letters.* . . . 2. Phonic and structural analysis 3. *sight vocabulary, phonics, structural analysis, context clues, and dictionary skills.* . . .
Word identification	The process of determining the pronunciation and some degree of meaning of an unknown word.
Word recognition	The process of determining the pronunciation and some degree of meaning of any word in written or printed form.
Sight word	1. A word that is immediately recognized as a whole and does not require word analysis for identification 2. A word taught as a whole word.
High-frequency word	1. A word that appears many more times than others in ordinary reading material; examples are *as, in, of,* and *the.* Also called a service word.

Source: Harris and Hodges (1981).

WHAT CHILDREN NEED TO LEARN ABOUT IDENTIFYING WORDS

Adams (1990) uses an analogy to show how the system that supports our ability to read is much like a car. She likens the words on a page to the gas in the car—"no gas, no driving" (p. 3). But she also notes that gas alone does not make the car go, just as words alone (or identifying words alone) do not make reading and writing. This analogy can be extended to the broad perspective of literacy developed in this text. Learning to deal with the words in reading and writing is part of developing literacy, but it is not the ultimate goal, which is meaning construction. Learning to deal with words in writing and reading is a necessary part of developing this ability.

In order to learn to identify words and construct meaning, children must develop concepts about print, recognize many words instantly and automatically, and learn how to analyze words that they do not recognize instantly by using the various cues in the text. Each of these areas is discussed in the following sections.

Concepts About Print

If children are to learn to identify words as an aid to constructing meaning, they must first develop some concepts about print. Clay (1985) divides these concepts into four categories—*books, sentences, words,* and *letters* (see Table 5.2).

Children must learn that books convey meaning through print. In this process they also need to know the left-right, top-bottom orientation on a page as well as facts about the book such as the cover, title, author, illustrator, beginning, and ending.

Students must also develop some understanding of the sentences on the page. They need to recognize a sentence, know that it represents a spoken message, and be able to tell the beginning and ending by recognizing the capital letters and the end punctuation. They also need some understanding of other forms of punctuation, such as quotation marks.

It is important for students to develop the concept of a word and know that each word is composed of letters and that these letters have order. Part of the learning that must take place includes knowing the difference between capital and lower-case letters.

Although many children come to school with these concepts of print, some do not, so it may be necessary for you to help some children understand print. Remember that word identification begins with book experiences, not lessons on letters. These might include reading aloud to children, providing many opportunities to see and experience print in favorite stories, posters, and so forth, and shared reading and writing experiences (discussed in detail on page 286).

Sight Vocabulary

The ultimate goal for the reader is to develop a large sight vocabulary that can aid in constructing meaning. As you read materials, you do not have to analyze most of the words you encounter: they are simply part of the stock of words that you recognize and understand instantly and automatically. Through repeated reading experiences over time you have developed automaticity with most words you read (LaBerge & Samuels, 1976). This is an important aspect of developing your ability to construct meaning.

High-frequency words (sometimes called basic sight words) are also a part of your sight vocabulary. Throughout the history of reading instruction, there have been numerous attempts to identify specific lists of these words. The most well-known list was identified by Dolch (1936), and others have generated

Table 5.2   Concepts of Print

Books

- Cover
- Title, author, illustrator
- Beginning, ending
- Left/right orientation
- Top/bottom orientation
- Print tells story, not pictures

Sentences

- Identifies sentence
- Beginning, ending
- Capital letter at beginning
- Punctuation, period, comma, question mark, quotations, exclamation

Words

- Identifies words (knows that *day* is word; does not say it)

Letters

- Letter order
- Capital and lower case

Source: Based on Clay (1985).

more up-to-date lists (Johnson, 1971). All of these lists contain words like *is, the, was,* and so forth: words that tie our language together but that are very abstract and often difficult for children to learn to read. These are also the last types of words that children internalize into their oral languge (Cazden, 1972; Malstrom, 1977). Therefore, they will not be the first kinds of words students will learn to read.

Beginning readers and even more mature readers often encounter words that they do not recognize instantly—that are not sight words for them. Therefore, readers need to learn strategies that will help them decode these words by using the cues in the text. As one's sight vocabulary grows, there is less frequent need for these strategies. However, even mature readers need them occasionally.

Learning to Analyze and Decode Words

Once children have developed the concept of a word, they must be able to translate the printed letters into sounds. This involves being able to hear the sounds and to know when a word is different because it is composed of different sounds. This understanding is what has been termed phonemic awareness (Juel, 1991).

Phonemes are the speech sounds of a language. They carry no meaning. For example, the word *hat* is composed of three phonemes /h/, /a/, /t/. The word *day* is composed of two phonemes /d/, /ay/. The letters that represent phonemes are known as graphemes. The word *hat* has three phonemes and three graphemes. The word *day* has two phonemes and two graphemes (two letters constitute the second grapheme).

Phonemic awareness appears to help children learn the letter-sound correspondences needed to read and spell words and researchers have found that this awareness is one of the best predictors of later success in reading (Juel, 1988; Juel, Griffith, & Gough, 1986; Lomax & McGee, 1987). It has been found that training in phonemic awareness improves students' ability to read and to spell words (Ball & Blachman, 1991; Lundberg, Frost, & Petersen, 1988). Although our understanding of phonemic awareness is not complete, it appears that our current level of reserach knowledge is sufficient to justify it as a part of what children must learn to become efficient and automatic readers and spellers of words (Adams, 1990; Juel, 1991).

Phonemic awareness appears to have different levels of difficulty, ranging from dealing with rhyming words to being able to segment phonemes and manipulate them to make new words—for example, identifying the beginning sound in *ride* and using it to change the beginning sound in *cat* to make *rat* (Adams, 1990). Phonemic awareness should be developed within the context of reading and writing. For more in-depth reading on this topic, see Griffith and Olson (1992) listed under "For Additional Reading."

Students must know the letter-sound correspondences and be able to use them (along with the other cues in text) to analyze and deode words that they do not recognize instantly. This knowledge is what most people call phonics. It involves learning such things as consonants (*b, r, t, m*, and so forth), vowels and vowel patterns (*a, e, i, o, u, y, oa, ea, ay*), blends (for example, *br, cl, spr*), digraphs (for example, *sh, th, wh, ch, ph*), and diphthongs (for example, *oi, oy*). (*Note:* If you do not have some knowledge of the basic phonic elements, you will need to learn these in order to support students as they learn to read and write. See Mason and Au, 1990, listed under "For Additional Reading.") Children must also learn to use the structural elements that carry meaning, such as prefixes, suffixes, and inflectional endings (see Chapter 4).

Students must learn to use the letter-sound correspondences plus other text cues to develop their own strategies for decoding unknown words. These other text cues fall into two categories: *semantic*, using the meaning constructed from the text, and *syntactic*, using the structure of the language and knowledge of how words go together. All such cues are usually called context cues. Efficient decoders use multiple strategies to identify words (Clay, 1985); they do not depend on just *one* strategy.

Even though readers develop their own strategies for identifying words, it is possible to help them by modeling some steps to follow when they encounter an unknown word. See the word detective strategy and the strategy for inferring word meanings discussed in Chapter 4.

In summary, to become effective constructors of meaning, students must develop concepts about print, build an extensive sight vocabulary, and learn to decode words that they do not recognize instantly by using text cues. The decoding process involves developing phonemic awareness, learning letter-sound correspondences, learning to use context clues, and developing strategies for using these elements together.

HOW CHILDREN LEARN TO IDENTIFY WORDS

The extensive research on how children learn to identify words gives some clues about how this process takes place but does not give us definitive answers (Adams, 1990; Juel, 1991; Mason, Herman, & Au, 1991). The process starts at birth, and the oral language base that children develop in their early years becomes the foundation for them to learn to decode words.

As students develop their ability to decode words, it appears that they go through some systematic stages, though there is still debate about the exact nature of the stages. Juel (1991) concludes from an extensive review of research that these stages are the selective cue stage, the spelling-sound correspondence stage, and the automatic stage.

Selective Cue Stage

During this stage children learn about print and its functions. This means knowing that print conveys meaning and can be used for a variety of purposes, including informing, communicating, and entertaining.

Students develop all such knowledge by being read to and by having language interaction with peers and adults. Through repeated reading and writing experiences, they begin to move through this selective cue stage. Many children come to school with this stage well developed, but others need a large amount of support: they must be read to, see things labeled, have opportunities to participate in developing group stories (language experience and shared writing), and participate in shared reading.

Spelling-Sound Correspondence Stage

During this stage, students develop phonemic awareness, learn letter-sound correspondences, and begin to develop strategies for using text clues along with letter-sound correspondences to analyze and decode words. As they learn to use letter-sound correspondences, they also begin to use analogy to figure out an unknown word (Gaskins et al., 1988). (Example: I come to the word *ring,* which I do not know. I think it looks like *sing,* but it has a different beginning. I might use the analogy of *sing* to *ring* and what I know about letter-sound correspondences to determine that the word is *ring.* In other words, I am comparing and contrasting words that I know with words that I don't know.) By comparing the parts of an unknown word with a known word, children are able to begin to identify multisyllabic words, using, in part, their knowledge of structural analysis (see Chapter 4). However, students can only begin to use analogy after they have some ability to use the letter-sound correspondences (Ehri & Robbins, 1992).

These aspects of learning to decode are developed by such activities as hearing and reciting nursery rhymes, being read to, having shared reading experiences with an adult or more mature peer during which attention is drawn to the letter-sound correspondences, and being encouraged to write and use invented (or temporary) spellings. (See Chapter 7 for more discussion of invented spelling.) As students begin to develop their knowledge of letter-sound correspondences, they need an enormous number of repeated reading and writing experiences so that they can use these correspondences over and over until they begin to use them automatically (Samuels, Schermer & Reinking, 1992).

Automatic Stage

Though we do not thoroughly understand what happens during the automatic stage (Juel, 1991), we do know that learners develop the ability to decode and recognize words automatically and extend their knowledge of decoding to multisyllabic words. Essentially what we must do is *keep students reading and writing* by having *many* real reading and writing experiences that continually focus on the construction of meaning.

For more detailed discussion about the technical aspects of word identification and decoding, see Stahl, Osborn, and Lehr (1990). You might also want to read *Looking Closely* (Mills, O'Keefe & Stephens, 1992) for a thorough description of word identification in a literacy-centered classroom. Both books are listed under "For Additional Reading."

PRINCIPLES FOR HELPING STUDENTS IDENTIFY WORDS

The following principles should help to guide you as you plan literacy experiences for your students. Even though you may be focusing more heavily on one aspect, such as learning to identify and decode words, each lesson or experience may also help children learn many things simultaneously.

1. *Begin all instruction with meaningful text experiences.* Use rhymes, poems, songs, and books as the starting point for helping students learn to identify words. These texts should be highly predictable in terms of rhyme and sound patterns. By reading them aloud to children and having children read them along with you (see discussion of shared reading later in this chapter), you will help children develop concepts about print, phonemic awareness, and letter-sound correspondences. When these texts are read to or with children, the primary focus should be on constructing meaning.

2. *Children's needs and the texts being read should determine the word identification element being supported or emphasized.* We know that children do not learn letter-sound correspondences in any one particular sequence (Teale & Sulzby, 1986). Therefore, the correspondences to be taught should be based on needs children demonstrate through their reading and writing and/or on the texts being read. For example, suppose a child writes the following and reads it aloud to you:

    Te baby dg a ppe
    (The baby dog is a puppy.)

    You can tell that this child knows the consonant letter-sound correspondences for *b, d, g,* and *p* pretty well, but she needs support in learning the short medial vowel sound correspondences. This does not mean that she needs a lesson on vowel sounds. Rather, she needs to have more experience with books that illustrate these sounds so that you can point them out to her as she reads. You might use a book like *Hop on Pop* (Seuss, 1963) for this purpose.

    If you are using a book with letter-sound correspondences that your students have not yet learned to use, you might choose to focus on those elements as a part of your literacy lessons. For example, *Yertle the Turtle* (Seuss, 1950) presents a good opportunity to focus on *r*-controlled vowels.

3. *Model the element of word identification being emphasized using the texts children are reading.* Whatever letter-sound correspondence you are helping children learn should be modeled by drawing examples from the text, building on the experience which the children have already had. For example, if your children have read *Each Peach Pear Plum* (Ahlberg, 1978), you could focus on *p* (peach, pear), use context and rhyming to predict (Three Bears are hunting, I spy Baby ___Bunting___), change initial consonants to make new words (hill, Jill), and so forth.

4. *Practice in word identification comes through repeated reading and writing.* One of the best types of practice for gaining automaticity or fluency in word identification is repeated reading of many easy texts (Samuels et al., 1992). Encouraging children to write and use invented or temporary spellings also provides important practice in word identification and creates an authentic need for children to learn high-frequency words and learn to spell.

5. *Allow and encourage children to take risks as they read, trying words before you tell them what they are.* It is unrealistic to expect "perfect" oral reading

from beginning readers. Therefore, when children are reading aloud, do not stop them or give them clues every time they come to an unknown word or misread a word. Rather, let them try the word and have the chance to figure it out from the meanings that they construct. Suppose a child reads the following from the book *Noise* (Cowley, 1987):

"Julie had the radio on. Yukka-dukka, yukka-dukka, yukka-dukka, Yah! Yah! Yah!"

"Off write the radio. Off write the stereo."

A few seconds later the child says, "I meant 'went' the radio." This child was rereading and developing a strategy for identifying words. She was taking risks because her teacher allowed, encouraged, and supported her. (Example from student Toni White, age 7, and teacher Kathy Vernon from Irwin Avenue Open Elementary, as presented by Ricki Morell in *The Charlotte Observer*, Charlotte, North Carolina, 1992).

The following section of this chapter will show you how to apply these principles and support students in learning to identify words and construct meaning.

SUPPORTING STUDENTS IN LEARNING TO IDENTIFY WORDS

As you plan literacy lessons and experiences to help students learn to identify words, keep in mind what you have learned about how students develop these abilities. Beginning literacy learners (emerging learners) will require more and different support than those who have already moved into more reading and writing (transition learners). Teach children how to identify words by integrating reading and writing so they will learn to read words and spell words at the same time.

This section examines four ways to help children develop their ability to identify words, with the primary focus always being on constructing meaning. We will discuss shared reading, minilessons with a literature base, practice through reading and writing, and strategies to promote independence.

Shared Reading

The mode of reading known as shared reading (introduced in Chapter 2) or the "shared book experience" was developed by Holdaway (1979) as a means of introducing beginners (kindergarten, first, second, third grades) to reading using favorite books, rhymes, and poems. This is an excellent technique for helping children learn to identify words because it always maintains the focus on meaning. Shared reading may also be adapted and used with older students (see page 304). With this procedure the teacher models reading for students by reading aloud a book or other text and ultimately inviting them to join in.

Shared reading is a sound instructional technique that uses implicit and explicit modeling (see Chapter 8) in the natural process of reading. It is based on the extensive research that shows that young children learn their oral language through the natural process of talking, listening, and interacting with the various language models they have in their environments (Clay, 1991). These studies found that young children who learned to read at home before they went to school generally learned by having their favorite books read aloud to them again and again (Baghban, 1984; Bissex, 1980). Holdaway's (1979) procedure capitalizes on the natural learning processes of youngsters and builds on their natural curiosity to help them grow into literacy. Numerous researchers have used this procedure to successfully teach beginning reading to students of varying ability levels and backgrounds (Bridge, Winograd, & Haley, 1983; Harlin, 1990; Ribowsky, 1985).

Purposes for Reading and Rereading Books

Shared reading builds on children's natural desire to read and reread favorite books. However, Au (1991) suggests that such reading is not just random rereading. Rather, each time a book is reread with the teacher, it should be for a different purpose to extend, refine, and deepen the child's abilities to read and construct meaning. There are at least five major purposes for reading and rereading texts; even when emphasizing one of these purposes, however, always focus on meaning construction.

1. *Interest and fun:* The primary reason for young children to read a book is to enjoy it. Therefore, the *first reading of any book* should be to get children to enjoy it and be excited about it. During this reading you talk about the illustrations, characters, things that happen in the story, what you like, and so forth. Books may be reread many times for this purpose. In fact, this is the primary reason that most children choose to reread any book.
2. *Develop comprehension:* This purpose deepens the child's understanding of the book. You begin by rereading the book to the group, inviting children to join in, and directing them to think about characters, events, certain actions, or outcomes. After this reading, you encourage the children to respond to the story in a way that reveals whether they have understood it. For example, if you and your children have reread *This Old Man* (Jones, 1990), you might ask them to retell what the old man played each time.
3. *Develop concepts about print:* This includes their understandings about books, sentences, words, and letters, as discussed earlier in this chapter. For example, if you are rereading *Teeny Tiny* (Bennett, 1986) and you are on the page shown in Figure 5.1, you can briefly talk about the capital *O*

Figure 5.1   First Page of *Teeny Tiny*

Once upon a time there was a
teeny tiny woman who lived
in a teeny tiny house
in a teeny tiny village.

Source: Page from *Teeny Tiny*, text copyright © 1985 by Jill Bennett. Illustration © 1985 by Tomie dePaola. Reprinted by permission of G. P. Putnam's Sons.

in *Once* and the period at the end of the sentence. These very brief comments can be thought of as informal minilessons.

4. *Explore language:* By exploring interesting or unusual language patterns, you will help children develop a greater appreciation for language. They will learn about language structure and cues that will help them construct meaning. When reading *This Is the Bear and the Picnic Lunch* (Hayes, 1988), you might explore the language pattern as shown in the two pages in Figure 5.2:

This is the _____

who _____.

This pattern can serve as a basis for having children write a new story. One first grader wrote:

> This is the pig
> who got two big.

He then drew a picture of a huge pig and colored him bright red. This process is known as text innovation, in which children use the story pattern as a basis for writing (see page 300 for more discussion of text innovation).

Exploring language may also involve talking with children about words that rhyme, unusual vocabulary, descriptive words, or just the way an author says something.

5. *Decoding:* A final reason for reading and rereading books is to help children learn to decode words using the various cues provided in the language—context, structure (prefixes, suffixes, inflectional endings), and phonics.

A part of the scaffolding needed for children learning to decode is rereading texts with numerous examples of the decoding element they need to learn. Some specific techniques are discussed on page 295. If your children have read and sung *Willoughby, Wallaby, Woo* (Raffi, 1980; see Figure 5.3), a logical consonant to focus on during one rereading would be *w*. Children can find all the *w* words in the song and think of other words that begin like *Willoughby* and *Wallaby*. You can list them on a chart and encourage children to use them in their writing. This type of minilesson within the context of reading helps children learn to use phonics and other decoding cues.

The number of times you reread a book should depend largely on the children's interest and what you have determined as their needs from observing them during shared and repeated readings. If children have little or no interest in a book, there is really no value in rereading it; therefore, drop it and move on to another book.

The repeated reading of books over several days, weeks, or even months deepens children's understandings of them (Yaden, 1988). Each rereading provides practice and reinforcement of the skills that children must learn to identify words. Writing must also be included with the repeated readings.

As you plan shared reading lessons, you may find that you read and reread books for several purposes at the same time. For example, you may be rereading for both comprehension and exploring language. Sometimes rereading may be done just for practice and fun. The important point to remember is that each rereading has a purpose.

Figure 5.2   First Two Pages from *This Is the Bear and the Picnic Lunch*

Source: From *This Is the Bear and the Picnic Lunch* by Sarah Hayes, illustrated by Helen Craig. Text © 1988 by Sarah Hayes. Illustrations © 1988 by Helen Craig. Reprinted by permission of Little, Brown and Company USA and Walker Books Limited, London.

Procedures for Shared and Repeated Readings

The procedures presented here for shared and repeated readings are based primarily on the research of Holdaway (1979) and my work with children and teachers. For help in learning to use this procedure, see Barrett (1982), Bullock and Bullock (1988), and Peetoom (1986) listed under "For Additional Reading."

When planning lessons for shared reading, you can use the literacy lesson format discussed in Chapter 2. The parts of this lesson are introducing, reading and responding, and extending. The following procedures are *very flexible* and should be adapted and adjusted to meet your children's needs. A complete

Figure 5.3   Song Focusing on the Consonant *w*

WILLOUGHBY, WALLABY, WOO

Willoughby, Wallaby, Wee,
An elephant sat on me.
Willoughby, Wallaby, Woo,
An elephant sat on you.

Willoughby, Wallaby, Wustin,
An elephant sat on Justin.
Willoughby, Wallaby, Wania,
An elephant sat on Tania.

Source: Raffi (1980), p. 92. From "Willoughby Wallaby Woo" © 1974 by Dennis Lee. Used by permission.

sample lesson for shared reading using the book *My Brown Bear Barney* (Butler, 1988) is presented on page 313.

Example 5.1

Procedures for Shared and Repeated Readings

Materials Needed

- One copy of the book to be read in little or big book form
- Multiple copies of the book for later use

Introducing the Book

1. Gather the children around you in a comfortable location where they can all see the book.

Example 5.1
continued

2. Show the book cover; read the title, author, and illustrator. Discuss each.
3. Get children excited about the book by discussing the cover and some of the pages in the book, but don't use so many pages that the entire story is given away. This activity helps to motivate children to want to read the book and encourages them to activate and develop their prior knowledge.
4. Invite children to predict what they think will happen in the story. If they have difficulty, model predicting by "thinking aloud" to show them how you would do it. Record the predictions on the chalkboard or chart for later reference. As your children gain more experience, you can formally introduce the preview and predict strategy using the poster presented in Chapter 3. The entire process for introducing the book should take no longer than 3 to 6 minutes under most circumstances.

Reading and Responding to the Book

1. Read the book aloud to the children, holding it so that they can see each page. Many teachers use an easel for this purpose. As you read, run your hand or a pointer along under each line of print to help children develop a sense of left-to-right orientation, speech-to-print match, and other concepts of print. If some children wish to join in, encourage them to do so. However, for an initial reading, many children will just listen.
2. Continue reading the book, stopping at points of interest to briefly discuss the story or to respond to children's reactions. Progress through the entire book rather quickly to give children a complete sense of the story.
3. At the conclusion of the reading, encourage children to respond briefly to the book. Such questions as the following may be used as prompts:

   "Were your predictions right?"

   "What did you like in this story?"

   "What was your favorite part?"

   "What made you happy (or sad)?"

   "Who was your favorite character? Why?"

4. Return to the book, rereading the story page by page and inviting children to chime in. Many will feel comfortable doing this right away, but others may not join in until another day. After the second reading, many children will say, "Let's read it again." This is especially true for books, songs, or rhymes that are lots of fun. You will have to be the judge of whether it is appropriate at this time; however, under most circumstances, when children are excited and want to read, you should read.

Example 5.1
continued

5. After you have read the book again, children should then respond to it. The types of responses should include such things as the following:

   - Talking with a friend about a favorite part
   - Retelling the story to a partner
   - Drawing a picture about the story and writing a word or sentence about it
   - Drawing and writing about a favorite character
   - Writing a list of favorite characters.

To help children become comfortable with the idea of making decisions about responding, you may want to give them a couple of choices initially and then add more over time.

Many of the ideas suggested in Chapter 6 on responding are appropriate to use here. The amount of time devoted to reading and responding will be from 10 to 20 minutes, depending on the book and the children.

Extending the Book

Extending is really another response with more focus on creativity and choice. You may want to wait until children have read a book several times before extending it or wait until they have read several books within a thematic unit and combine them for extension activities.

Creative expression is the primary focus of extension activities. Holdaway (1979) suggests that these activities can be individual or group and may include such things as painting, group murals, construction projects, making masks for drama or puppetry, or writing. They may also include Readers' Theater, retelling or dramatizing for a friend or another group, drawing, or music-related activities. In all of these extension activities, children are using what they are learning in authentic situations that help them develop the ability to construct meaning.

This plan for shared reading is very flexible. As you use it, you will develop the style and technique appropriate for you and your children. Table 5.3 summarizes the basic elements of the shared reading procedure around the literacy lesson concept.

Each rereading or repeated reading should be thought of as being done for one of the purposes discussed on pages 287–289. Throughout the year, children often ask to read one of their favorite books from the beginning of the year. One first-grade teacher said, "I'm so tired of *Brown Bear, Brown Bear* (Martin, 1967) and *Mary Wore Her Red Dress and Henry Wore His Green Sneakers* (Peek, 1985) because the children are still asking to read them in May; they just love those books and never get tired of them."

Each time a repeated reading is carried out, you are continuing to model for children. At the same time, you are scaffolding your instruction by transferring more and more responsibility to the children. Although each repeated reading may seem to be just fun for the children, it carries

Example 5.1 continued

Table 5.3   Shared Reading Using the Literacy Lesson Concept

Lesson Component	Description	Time	Comments
Introducing	Present book; discuss cover, author, illustrator. Predict what might take place.	3–6 minutes	Activates and develops prior knowledge Helps children set purpose for reading
Reading and responding	Read aloud book to children, running hand under text. Invite children to join in. Reread book several times. Have children respond to the book.	10–20 minutes	Models reading and meaning construction
Extending	Develops creative activities using the book.	Depends on activities done	Makes use of knowledge in creative and authentic experiences

very important responsibilities for learning. The following suggestions should be helpful:

1. Invite children to recall the title and what the book was about. Prompt and support them if needed.
2. Tell children why they are rereading the book with statements like the following:

   "As we reread this book, let's think about who the important characters are." (comprehension)

   "In our story today, notice how the author repeats lines over and over." (explore language)

   "Today as we reread one of our favorite stories, let's notice how the author used the same sounds in words over and over to make our story funny." (decoding)

3. Quickly reread the entire book, inviting children to join in. Continue to run your hand under the text as you read or use a pointer to track along under each line. Many children will chime right in. Keeping your purpose for rereading in mind, go back through the book, rereading a page or several pages at a time and encouraging children to chime in as you read. Talk about each section of rereading, focusing on your purpose. For example:

Example 5.1 continued

Purpose: Comprehension
Prompt: "Who are the important characters in our story so far?"

Purpose: Explore language
Prompt: "What words did the author use over and over again?"

Purpose: Decoding
Prompt: "What letters and sounds did our author use over and over to make our story funny?"

4. After completing the rereading of the book, have children complete a response activity that again draws their attention to the purpose. For example:

Purpose: Comprehension
Possible response: Dramatize your favorite character.

Purpose: Explore language
Possible response: Write a group story using the story pattern. For example, after reading *Brown Bear, Brown Bear* (Martin, 1967), have children help write a story using the pattern:

- "Brown Bear, Brown Bear, What do you see?"

  "I see a redbird looking at me."

- "Redbird, Redbird, What do you see?"

  "I see a _____ _____ looking at me."

- "_____ _____, _____ _____, What do you see?"

  "I see a _____ _____ looking at me."

  This response may also be done individually.

Purpose: Decoding
Possible response: Make a list of the words that have the sound repeated. Encourage children to write their own stories using some of these and other words.

Techniques to Use with Shared Reading

The following sections discuss seven techniques, which can be divided into two broad categories—during reading (pointing, masking, and cloze activities) and after reading (pocket charts, word walls, and text innovations). Minilessons may take place during reading or after reading.

Pointing.   Holdaway (1979) indicates that children must learn that there is a one-to-one relationship between the spoken word and the written word. Since they must also learn letter-sound relationships, it is important to point to each word as it is read during shared reading. You may do this with your hand or with some type of pointer. Holdaway suggests that this should be done carefully

Figure 5.4   A Device for Masking and Framing During Shared Reading

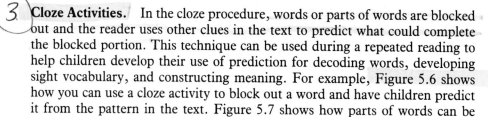

and meticulously, especially in the beginning stages. You don't want to read the books word by word, but you do want children to see the relationship between the spoken and written word. This technique also helps children develop their concepts about print. As they mature in their reading, it can be dropped.

    Masking.   If you want children to focus on a particular word or a part of a word, a good way to do this is by using a frame or sliding frame like the one shown in Figure 5.4 to mask and frame the word or word part (Holdaway, 1979). This device is made with heavy tagboard and a slide, as illustrated in Figure 5.5. Usually masking and framing takes place during repeated readings and not during the initial reading. For example, if you are rereading a story to focus on decoding, you can use the masking frame to draw attention to and talk about a particular letter-sound relationship. You might frame a word that begins with a particular sound and ask children to find or think of other words that begin with that sound.

The masking-framing device can also be used after a story has been read to have children go back into the story to locate certain words. This is a good way to help children develop their sight vocabularies.

Cloze Activities.   In the cloze procedure, words or parts of words are blocked out and the reader uses other clues in the text to predict what could complete the blocked portion. This technique can be used during a repeated reading to help children develop their use of prediction for decoding words, developing sight vocabulary, and constructing meaning. For example, Figure 5.6 shows how you can use a cloze activity to block out a word and have children predict it from the pattern in the text. Figure 5.7 shows how parts of words can be

Figure 5.5   Construction of a Masking-Framing Device

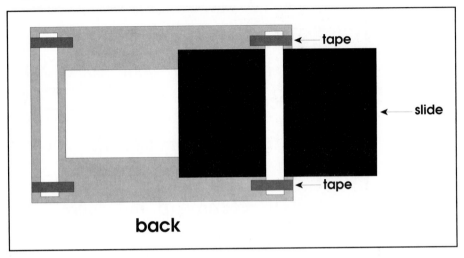

Figure 5.6   Using a Cloze Activity

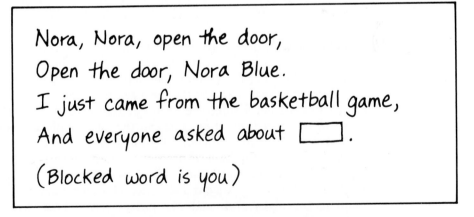

Source: From *Everyone Asked About You*, copyright © 1990 by Theodore Faro Gross. Reprinted by permission of Philomel Books.

Figure 5.7   Using a Cloze Activity to Focus on Beginning Sounds

"Jillian, Jillian, Jillian Jiggs!
It looks like your room has
been lived in by p⬚!
"Later. I promise. As soon as
I'm through,
I'll clean up my room. I
promise. I d⬚."
(masked words are pigs and do)

Source: Jillian Jiggs, copyright © 1985 by Phoebe Gilman. Reprinted by permission of Scholastic, Canada Ltd., 123 Newkirk Road, Richmond Hill, Ontario L4C 3G5.

blocked to have children focus on the use of beginning sounds. The masking-framing device suggested above may be used with cloze activities.

4. **Pocket Charts.**   Pocket charts are large, heavy paper, cloth, or plastic charts that have pockets where words or sentences may be placed. They are an excellent tool for helping children develop their ability to construct meaning after a story has been read, and they also increase children's sight vocabularies. All the words from a story can be printed on cards, or sentences from the story can be printed on strips. You can then have children rebuild the story using the words or the sentence strips. Figure 5.8 shows a pocket chart on which a page from the book *Possum Come a-Knockin'* (Van Laan, 1990) has been rebuilt. Pocket charts can also be used for developing many different activities with stories. A good source for ideas for using this device can be found in the McCracken and McCracken (1986) book listed under "For Additional Reading."

Figure 5.8   Pocket Chart

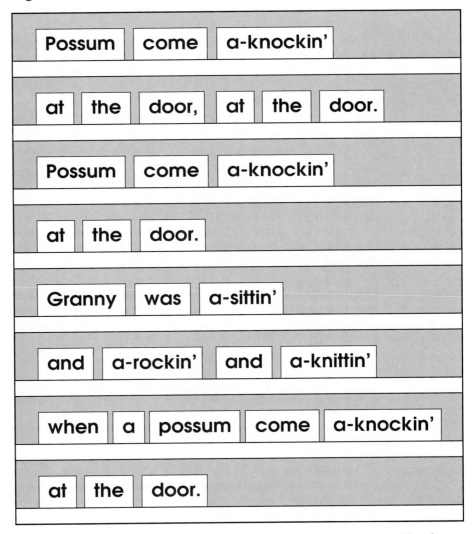

Source: From Nancy Van Laan, *Possum Come a-Knockin'*, copyright © 1990, Alfred A. Knopf. Reprinted by permission.

Word Walls.   A word wall or word chart is a listing of words that are of interest to students; ones that follow a particular pattern in their beginning sounds, vowel sounds, or endings; or words on a particular topic. These charts can be placed on the wall or on bulletin boards for reference during writing. Word walls are an excellent way to tie writing and reading together and to reinforce vocabulary. They can be used with all writing, reading, and learning activities. Children may also keep their own individual word banks or books.

Text Innovations and Writing.   Another important strategy is known as text innovation (Holdaway, 1979), in which children use the pattern in the text to create their own text under the direction of the teacher or alone. This process is used when you want children to explore the language of the book they have read. It develops and reinforces vocabulary, letter-sound associations, spelling, and language usage. However, only books that have interesting, repetitive patterns are appropriate for text innovations. This may be done as a response to reading or as an extension of reading. A first-grade class wrote the group story shown in Figure 5.9 with their teacher after having read *Possum Come a-Knockin'* (Van Laan, 1990). They had also just completed a unit on pigs and had read *Oink* (Geisert, 1991) and *Pigs* (Munsch, 1989).

Minilessons.   Minilessons, as discussed previously, are short lessons with a specific focus. For some students, you may find it necessary to focus on a particular letter-sound correspondence or set of high-frequency words as a part of the repeated readings of books. In fact, each rereading can be thought of as a minilesson with a specific purpose. During the minilesson, you use the literature to model the decoding element or elements on which you want to focus. A detailed discussion of minilessons is presented on page 306.

Materials for Shared Reading

The materials used for shared reading should be stories, books, articles, songs, and poems that excite children and captivate their imaginations (Holdaway, 1986). Many of these materials should have simple story lines or ideas presented in a predictable and/or repetitive pattern. (Chapter 2 presented seven different categories of predictable literature.) Others will simply be wonderful books that children will enjoy reading so much that they will want to read them again and again.

When using shared reading with youngsters in the beginning or emerging stages of reading and writing, books should be highly predictable, such as *There Was an Old Lady Who Swallowed a Fly* (Adams, 1973), *The Grouchy Ladybug* (Carle, 1977), or *The Lady with the Alligator Purse* (Westcott, 1988). If the children with whom you are working are having difficulty learning to decode words, the books should be highly predictable in terms of rhyme and sound patterns; books like *Drummer Hoff* (Emberley, 1967) or *Fire! Fire! Said*

Figure 5.9   Text Innovation Written After Reading *Possum Come a-Knockin'*

Piggy come a-oinkin';
At the pen, at the pen.
Piggy come a-oinkin';
At the pen.

Daddy was a-sloppin';
At the pen, at the pen.
Daddy was a-sloppin';
At the pen.

Source: Based on Van Laan (1990).

Mrs. McGuire (Martin, 1970) meet this criterion. Many listings of predictable books and other books for shared reading are available, and new ones are published frequently (Bridge, 1986, 1989; Bridge et al., 1983; Rhodes, 1981; Tompkins & Webler, 1983; Trachtenburg, 1990). An extensive listing of some of my favorite books for beginning shared reading is given at the end of this chapter.

Some of the books you use for shared reading may be in the form of a "big book," an enlarged version that can be seen by a group of children all at once. Holdaway (1979) enlarged the books that were students' favorites for group study, and the children then helped to illustrate them. Many different publishing companies produce "big books" for classroom use. With this technique, you can model reading to a larger group of students at the same time. Meanwhile, students are able to practice their reading on their own with their little book versions. Many times children will also enjoy sitting on the floor and practicing from the big book. Of course, although it is nice to have big books and usually more effective to model reading for a larger group of students, it is not necessary to have them to do shared reading. If you need a big book for a class favorite, you and the children can make it. Print the text on large sheets of paper and have the children do the illustrations.

In summary, the materials to be used for shared reading with beginners should be ones that are likely to captivate, excite, and interest children; that have clear, simple story lines or ideas; that have repetitive, predictable patterns; and that may include both big and little book versions.

What to Expect During the Initial Phases of Shared Reading

Teachers who use shared reading for the first time usually ask, "What can I expect when using this instructional model?" Knowing the answer to this question will help you use shared reading more smoothly.

Children will memorize stories, songs, and rhymes.   Since so many of the books used for shared reading have catchy, rhythmic patterns, children will memorize and chant them without even looking at the text. Teachers often say, "They're looking at the ceiling and singing the words. They aren't reading." This is *normal behavior* in children being taught to read (Baghban, 1984; Bissex, 1980). Through this memorizing, children develop sight vocabulary as well as a sense of language and the ability to construct meaning.

Children will not be able to identify every word in isolation from the texts they are reading.   Again, this is *normal behavior*, especially with abstract, high-frequency words. In shared reading, children are being immersed in many rich reading as well as writing experiences, and gradually they will learn to recognize all words, including high-frequency words. Teachers often want to put words on cards and drill students on them, but *this is not the way children develop their oral vocabularies, and it is not the way they are going to develop reading vocabularies*.

Children will want to reread certain books many times.   Just as young children at home have their favorite storybooks that they want to hear again and again, so children using shared reading will have favorites. This is *normal behavior*. These books are apt to have strong repetitive rhymes. Remember that this natural curiosity and desire for repetition is the basis of natural learning and shared reading.

Children gradually learn to decode unknown words.   Through the repeated readings of books and opportunities to write and explore language patterns, children gradually develop independence in decoding. At first, they will memorize many words, but they soon start to transfer those to new texts and at the same time begin to analyze and decode unknown words. It is *normal behavior* for children to first memorize words and then gradually develop their decoding abilities. This is the beginning of their independence in reading.

A Daily Plan for Shared Reading

Children who learn to read naturally are immersed in a language-rich, print-rich environment (Cambourne, 1988), and this type of immersion must occur for all beginning readers (Holdaway, 1979). Since children learn at a rapid pace, they need a daily schedule that supports this pace. Holdaway (1979) states it very clearly:

> *We had never realized before how much young children can absorb in a few seconds. Attention problems only arise when there is not enough going on. We keep a very snappy pace. Then if some children get behind, they soon tune in. We've given up calling for attention and admonishing those who are distracted; they* are *so because nothing interesting is going on at that moment. And if we break the spirit of the session to admonish one child,* all *of the children are likely to become distracted. So if attention flags, we crack on the pace. The result is amazing. (pp. 73–74)*

The suggested daily plan presented here is based on Holdaway's (1979) concept of a fast-paced daily lesson with high involvement and activity. As I have worked with teachers using this plan throughout the country, I have found it works very well from kindergarten through second grade. In second grade, some teachers begin to shift to the reading workshop concept because they are using a wider range of reading modes and depend less on shared reading for the whole group.

The plan presented below takes from 55 to 90 minutes, depending on your schedule and the needs of your children. It should be used as a flexible plan consisting of the following parts:

Opening Activity (3–5 minutes; sometimes called tune-in or warm-up). The purpose of this activity is to get children warmed up and ready to go. It consists of reading a chant, rhyme, or poem, or singing a song in shared fashion. This may be a new piece or one children have read or heard before. This beginning activity each day should be motivating for children.

Reread a Favorite Story (5–10 minutes). This is usually a book selected by the children because they like it, though it may also be selected by the teacher. It may be in big book or standard form. In this and other repeated readings, you are rereading for interest and fun but also to improve meaning construction.

Language Study Using or Extending the Book (10–15 minutes). The activities that take place here may range from text innovations exploring the book's language to vocabulary or phonics study. During these activities children further develop their reading and writing skills.

Read a New Book (15–20 minutes). A new book is introduced and read following the basic procedure for shared reading.

Independent Reading (10–15 minutes).   During this time children reread the new book or any other book they choose. They may read alone, with a partner, or with a group. Often they play the role of teacher and conduct shared reading with their peers.

Creative Activities (10–20 minutes).   This is the time when children work alone or together on projects and extension activities stemming from books that they have read. These activities may include painting, mural making, clay work, drama, puppetry, and many other activities.

Sharing (3–5 minutes).   This is the period of time that cements the class as a community of learners. Children briefly share and talk about their reading and related projects.

This plan allows children to have experiences with a minimum of two books per lesson and accommodates the shared reading plan. It is a flexible plan that gives them rich and successful literacy experiences.

Using Shared Reading Beyond the Beginning Literacy Levels

Up to this point, shared reading has been described as a procedure for teaching beginning literacy learners, primarily in kindergarten, first, and second grade. By the time many children reach the end of first grade and second grade, they are beginning to use other modes of reading, such as cooperative and independent reading (see Chapter 2), but some will continue to need the modeling and scaffolding provided by shared reading well into the third grade. Therefore, you should continue to think of shared reading as a viable instructional option beyond the beginning literacy level.

You will find that as children grow into literacy beyond the beginning levels, you will need to vary the type of reading they do according to two factors: (1) the complexity of the texts they are reading and (2) how effectively they are learning to construct meaning. When the text is very complex and/or children are having difficulty constructing meaning, shared reading may often be used as a part of their instructional support. Children who encounter difficulty constructing meaning are discussed in more detail in Chapter 10.

An extension of shared reading introduced in Chapter 2 is the read aloud, read along, read alone strategy, which involves three parts:

1. *Read aloud:* The teacher reads aloud the text while students follow along. This provides modeling and background for the text.
2. *Read along:* Students read along or follow along as the teacher continues to read the text (thus continuing the modeling process). Students may work cooperatively in pairs.

3. *Read alone:* Students read some portion of the text on their own. By this time they have had sufficient modeling and support to make them successful with the read-alone portion of the text.

The read aloud, read along, read alone strategy is an excellent one to use with any texts for students needing stronger scaffolding to help them construct meaning. It is especially good to use with chapter books or content-area texts.

Since this strategy is very flexible, you can vary it to meet students' needs in a variety of ways. For example, suppose you have a group of fifth graders who are having difficulty constructing meaning in a particular novel. To help them understand that novel, you decide to apply this strategy to the first chapter. This is how your plan might look:

1. Introduce the novel.
2. Read aloud the first few pages of Chapter 1. Briefly discuss it with students.
3. Give students copies of the novel. Have them read along silently as you read aloud the next few pages. Discuss the chapter up to this point, and then ask students to predict how they think it might end.
4. Have students read alone the last two pages of the chapter. Then discuss the entire chapter and have students predict what they think might happen in the second chapter.

At this point you need to decide how to handle Chapter 2. Should you increase or decrease the amount of read aloud, read along, read alone? This is a plan for modeling and scaffolding that allows you to meet individual needs. Since the obvious goal is to get students to read independently, you need to gradually remove the support provided through read aloud and read along and have students read alone. Of course, this process will occur gradually and will vary from text to text and from situation to situation. Table 5.4 summarizes the steps of this strategy.

In summary, shared reading is an instructional model for developing the ability of beginning literacy learners to construct meaning and learn to identify words through reading. It is based on research showing how children naturally develop their literacy abilities. With shared reading, the teacher models reading by reading aloud books, rhymes, poems, and songs and inviting children to chime in when they are comfortable in doing do. Materials are reread several times for different purposes to capitalize on the natural process of children wanting to listen to or read favorite books again and again. Shared reading and the activities associated with it help children develop all of the needed skills in meaning construction, including knowledge about print, vocabulary, and phonics and other decoding abilities. Shared reading requires a fast-paced, interactive daily schedule that immerses children in reading and writing. It is also a viable strategy to use with students having difficulty constructing meaning beyond the beginning literacy level. A variation of this strategy is read aloud, read along, read alone.

Table 5.4 Read Aloud, Read Along, Read Alone Strategy

Strategy Component	Procedure	Comments
Read aloud	Teacher reads aloud portion of text.	Models reading. Activates prior knowledge and develops background. Vary amount read according to student need.
Read along	Students read along (orally or silently) as teacher continues to read aloud.	Continues modeling and background. May also be done as cooperative reading. Vary amount read according to student needs.
Read alone	Students read portion of text alone.	Always have students read a portion alone. Gradually increase the amount read alone to achieve independence.

When to use:
  With texts that are complex
  When students are having difficulty constructing meaning

Minilessons for Developing Decoding

Another way to support students who are learning to identify words is to use the minilesson concept presented in Chapter 2. *Minilessons should always be embedded in the reading of literature or should return to the literature after it has been read.* These lessons may be used to develop phonemic awareness, letter-sound correspondences, use of context clues, and high-frequency words. In all cases, the literature provides the model for the element being taught. For many children, repeated reading and responding to literature will be sufficient to develop their ability to identify words. However, some students will need the support of lessons that directly draw their attention to a particular letter-sound association or high-frequency word. Minilessons may be used in combination with any mode of reading to provide students support.

Minilessons for Developing Letter-Sound Correspondences

Trachtenburg (1990) has suggested a plan for using literature to enhance the learning of phonics, and many of the ideas presented here are similar to those she suggests. The following guidelines should be helpful in planning minilessons for developing letter-sound correspondences.

Read literature containing examples of the letter-sound correspondences to be learned.   If your students need to learn particular letter-sound correspondences such as blends or prefixes, choose a piece of literature that provides several examples of this element. Use the literacy lesson format and focus on constructing meaning. For example, the humorous book *Clean Your Room, Harvey Moon!* (Cummings, 1991) contains many examples for the consonant *m*. But first students can read it to simply enjoy and respond to the way Harvey cleans his room.

Draw a model for the element from the literature.   After children have read and enjoyed the literature, take an example from the text to illustrate the letter-sound to be taught. Have children reread the example, and then point out the correspondence to them. Say the word that illustrates the letter-sound, have children repeat the word, say the sound for the element being taught, and have the children repeat it. Contrary to what many teachers have believed, there is no evidence that isolating the sound is harmful to children learning to decode words as long as it is done in moderation and within the context of reading (Anderson, Hiebert, Scott & Wilkinson, 1985; Beck & Juel, 1992; Johnson & Bauman, 1984). With *Clean Your Room, Harvey Moon!* (Cummings, 1991), have children reread page 1 aloud with you:

> *On Saturday morning at ten to nine*
> *Harvey Moon was eating toast,*
> *Waiting for the cartoon show*
> *That he enjoyed the most.*

Ask children to locate and read all the words that begin with *m*. List the words on the chalkboard, read the words, have children repeat the words, point out the consonant *m*, and give the sound for the letter—"muh." Ask children to repeat the sound. Also, note the capital and lower case *M,m*.

Identify other examples of words containing the letter-sound.   If the text being used has other examples of the letter-sound being taught, ask children to find them, reread the sentence containing the element, and then compile a list of the examples on the chalkboard or a chart. If you feel that more examples are needed, ask children to give other words that they know containing the letter-sound.

Ask children to help you select one word that can serve as their model for the sound, preferably a word that can be illustrated. Place the word on a chart with the children's illustration for future reference. For example, in *Clean Your Room, Harvey Moon!* (Cummings, 1991), have children locate words beginning with *m* throughout the text, read them, and note the sound for *m*. Then invite children to select a word that they could use to help them remember the *m* sound, reminding them that it needs to be one that can be pictured. They might choose *messy, morning, Moon,* or many others. Most children usually select *Harvey Moon* because they think his name is funny. Have children draw a picture and make a chart like the one shown in Figure 5.10 to display in the room. Place several children's drawings on the chart.

Figure 5.10   Poster for Modeling the *m* Sound

Reread the text containing the examples of the letter-sound.   Return to the text that has served as a model for the letter-sound and have children reread it together orally. Discuss the text, and then have children find the letter-sound under discussion. In *Clean Your Room, Harvey Moon!* (Cummings, 1991) they will find such words as *most, man, mother, Mom, marched,* and so forth.

Read other texts containing the letter-sound.   During the days that follow the lesson, as children are reading, call their attention to texts containing the letter-sound. After each text has been read and enjoyed, ask children questions that will draw their attention to the letter-sound and will let you know whether they have learned the sound. For example, if your children are reading *If You Give a Moose a Muffin* (Numeroff, 1991), ask questions such as "What did the little boy use to make the muffins?" (muffin mix) or "What did the moose do with the sheet?" (clean up the mess).

Give children many texts that contain the letter-sounds being taught, and encourage children to read them repeatedly, alone or with a partner, *to help build fluency and automaticity* (Samuels et al., 1992). *The repeated reading of many texts containing the letter-sounds being taught provides the type of phonics practice that is meaningful and beneficial to children learning to identify words and construct meaning.* You might use such books as *If You Give a Mouse a Cookie* (Numeroff, 1985) or *Five Little Monkeys Jumping on the Bed* (Christelow, 1989).

Encourage children to use the letter-sound in their writing. As children are learning the letter-sound, encourage them to use the sound to help them spell words in their writing, referring them to the charts for examples. Look for evidence that the children are using the letter-sounds in their invented spellings. If you are dealing with a common spelling pattern such as a short, medial vowel (*bat, cup*), or an ending (*-ing*), you should point this out to students. In this way you will integrate spelling and help children focus on consistent spelling patterns.

This minilesson pattern may be adjusted to focus on phonemic awareness, context clues, and sight vocabulary, including high-frequency words. Use the same basic lesson pattern with the following modifications.

For phonemic awareness, during rereadings focus attention on rhyming words (*cap, map*), words that have the same beginning sound (*fish, fox*), or words that have the same phonogram and have been made by changing the beginning sound (*flag, brag, drag*).

For context clues, mask words in stories and have children try to identify what the word would be. As they progress in this ability, mask only parts of the words, encouraging the use of context and letter-sound correspondences.

For sight vocabulary development, after reading a book have children find self-selected and teacher-selected words in the text. Have them frame the word and then reread the sentence containing the word. Encourage children to add words of their own choosing to their word banks or word books.

Minilessons may also be very informal: for example, you might draw children's attention to a letter-sound pattern during one of the repeated readings. In fact, these more informal lessons are often more effective because they keep the skill in context.

It may take many reading experiences for students to learn to identify words. For example, if you teach a minilesson focusing on several consonant sounds, you will need to follow this lesson with repeated reading experiences with books containing words with the sounds as well as more minilessons. Many of the minilessons may be much more informal than your initial lesson.

Reading and Writing as Practice for Identifying Words

The best way to have children practice using what they have learned about identifying words (letter-sound correspondences, strategies for analyzing words, sight words, including high-frequency words) is through reading and writing.

Reading Practice

As children are learning letter-sounds, continue selecting (or having them select) wonderful books to read. Books like *Hop on Pop* (Seuss, 1963), *Green Eggs and Ham* (Seuss, 1960), *Sheep in a Jeep* (Shaw, 1986), *Sheep on a Ship* (Shaw, 1989), and *Sheep in a Shop* (Shaw, 1991), just to name a few, are all good examples of books that can provide children with practice in constructing meaning and in using various letter-sound correspondences and high-frequency words. You will need at least one copy of the book for each two students.

Introduce the book to the children, and have them read it silently and/or orally with a partner. Invite children to discuss the story and share their reactions. If you ask volunteers to read aloud favorite parts, you can see how well the children are using their decoding abilities. Encourage them to read and reread these books again and again, and let them select their favorites for rereading. Encourage them to do things with their books, such as share them with other children in their class or another class, draw about them, act them out, or read them onto a tape recorder.

If children appear to be having difficulty learning certain letter-sounds and/or high-frequency words, follow up with a minilesson using a book that provides models for the difficult elements. First use shared reading to introduce the book for interest and fun, focusing on constructing meaning. Then have them reread it for decoding. Finally, use your minilesson to focus on the elements causing difficulty.

Writing Practice

Every time children write, regardless of its purpose, they are practicing using letter-sound correspondences and high-frequency words. Writing gives children real reasons to spell (Gentry, 1987) and to learn high-frequency words.

When children write, they should be encouraged to use *invented spelling*— that is, to spell words the way they think they sound in their initial draft without worrying about correctness. A better term for this type of spelling might be *temporary* because it says to everyone concerned (teachers, parents, administrators) that this type of spelling is going to give way to correctness. Research has shown that invented spelling helps children learn to spell as well as to use phonics as a way of analyzing words (Adams, 1990; Clarke, 1988). Thinking that children and young adults learn to spell by memorizing a list of words totally ignores what we know about how children learn this important convention of writing (Hodges, 1991).

Traditionally, teachers have expected children to master high-frequency words such as *the, is, are, was,* and so forth by reading them in a story. But because these words are so abstract, children usually have difficulty remembering them. Therefore, teachers have made flash cards to drill students on the words. However, such drills have no meaning for children and are of

Figure 5.11   Shared Writing for Practicing Reading and Spelling *ch*

Chuckie Chicken

Chuckie Chicken lived behind the old church. He chased the children around the church yard when they came to play. The children yelled, "Chuckie, Chuckie, Chuckie." Chuckie chased and chased. The children knew that all Chuckie wanted was some of their chocolate candy. Chuckie got chocolate and stopped the chase.

little or no value in helping them learn the words; furthermore, it is usually possible to construct meaning when reading even if the children do not know the high-frequency words. For example, what does the following sentence with high-frequency words missing mean to you?

_____ *day* _____ *sunny* _____ *warm.*

You probably said, "The day was sunny and warm." Certainly, the high-frequency words would have helped you, but they were not essential to your construction of meaning. Writing, on the other hand, creates a real need for learning these high-frequency words.

There are several ways to use writing as reinforcement and practice for identifying and learning to spell words:

- *Remind students to use letter-sound correspondences in writing.* As children learn various letter-sounds, remind them to use them in spelling words as they write. Encourage children to refer to the charts that have been made as models for letter-sound correspondences.
- *Use letter-sound correspondences and high-frequency words in shared writing.* When you do shared writing (see Chapter 2), build in the letter-sound correspondences and high-frequency words that have been learned. This encourages students to read them and gives them a chance to see you model their use in writing. Figure 5.11 shows a sample of shared writing

Figure 5.12   Word Wall Showing High-Frequency Words to Be Used in Writing

Our Writing Helpers

is —   Mary _is_ happy.

the —   _The_ big dog is on _the_ chair.

in —   The hat is _in_ the box.

said —   Lin Su _said_, "Please help me."

was —   The sun _was_ very bright.

It —   _It_ is my turn to play.

that a first-grade teacher wrote with his class about an imaginary bird called Chuckie Chicken. This story incorporated several words containing *ch* because the children had learned it in one of the books they had read.

- *Display lists of high-frequency words for children to use during writing.* As high-frequency words are encountered in reading, prepare lists of these words and post them on word walls, as shown in Figure 5.12. It is generally better to show them both in isolation and in a phrase or short sentence to help children remember how the word is used in the language. Each time children write, encourage and remind them to use the words in their writing.

Helping Children Become Independent in Decoding

As children develop their ability to identify words, they need support in building strategies for becoming independent in this process. Although continued reading and writing practice is important, some children profit from being given a set of steps for this purpose. The word detective strategy introduced in Chapter 4 is one effective approach (review page 201). As children are learning to identify words, introduce this strategy gradually, adjusting the poster (Chapter 4, page 203) to the elements they have learned.

During reading, you can model all such strategies and remind children to use them as they read.

You should also keep in mind that many children develop their own strategies for identifying words by reading, writing, and making discoveries about language. Do not expect all children to rigidly use this or any strategy.

PULLING IT ALL TOGETHER

How do you put all of these ideas together and plan appropriate learning experiences for children? You must remember that there is *no one absolute* way to do this. Rather, you must constantly keep in mind all the principles about how children learn to construct meaning and to identify words. Above all else, remember that children learn to read and write by reading and writing. Figure 5.13 on page 314 shows a sequence that should help summarize all of the ideas in this chapter.

Literacy Lesson

My Brown Bear Barney

This lesson was developed for a group of first graders involved in thematic unit entitled "Teddy Bears." The main book to be read using shared reading was *My Brown Bear Barney* (Butler, 1988). Three other books were also part of the unit: *Ira Sleeps Over* (Waber, 1972) was used as a shared read-aloud book, *Bear in Mind: A Book of Bear Poems* (Goldstein, 1989) was used for read-alouds and chants throughout the unit, and *The Velveteen Rabbit* (Williams, 1983) was used as a class read-aloud book. The lessons used shared reading as the basic instructional model and followed the literacy lesson (see Chapter 2) format used in other lessons in this text. Each daily schedule followed a pattern similar to that discussed earlier in this chapter (see pages 303–304).

Before Reading the Plan
1. Consider what you have learned about shared reading. Review any parts of the chapter that were not clear to you. Talk with a peer about it.
2. Read the text for *My Brown Bear Barney* (Butler, 1988).
3. Study the "Teacher Preparation" section to see the planning and decision-making process that went into the development of this lesson.

While Reading the Plan
1. Notice how shared reading was carried out to provide repeated readings for different purposes and for learning to identify words.
2. Think about how you would have changed this lesson.

Figure 5.13 Sequence for Helping Children Develop Word Identification

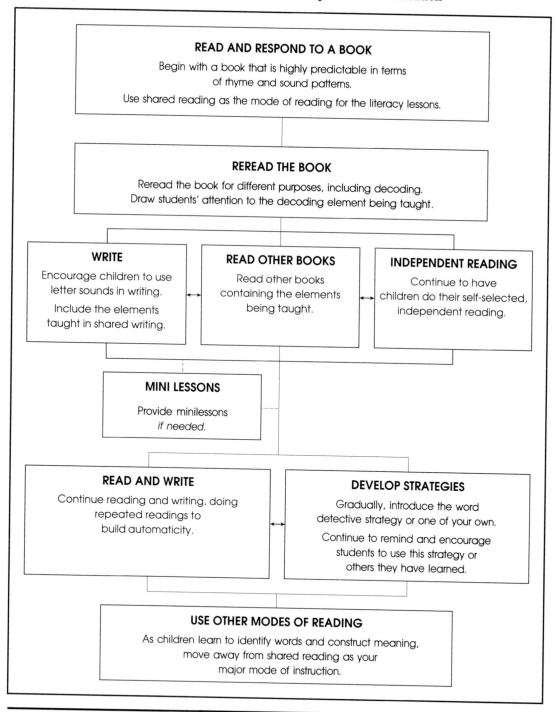

When I go shopping, I take . . .

MY BROWN
BEAR BARNEY

By Dorothy Butler
Illustrated by Elizabeth Fuller

and my brown bear Barney.

my mother, my little brother, my yellow basket,
my red umbrella

my bike, our old dog Charlie, two apples from our tree,
my boots

When I play with my friend Fred,
I take . . .

When I go gardening, I take . . . .

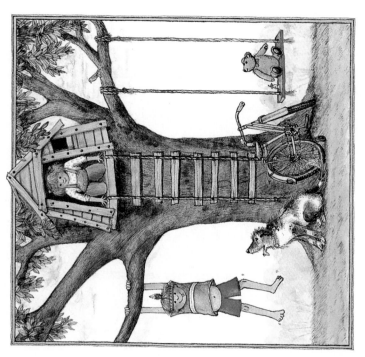

and my brown bear Barney.

and my brown bear Barney.

my father, my straw hat, my wheelbarrow, my spade

my mother, my father, my little brother, special things to eat, my sunglasses

When I go to the beach, I take . . .

When I go to my grandmother's,
I take . . . .

and my brown bear Barney.

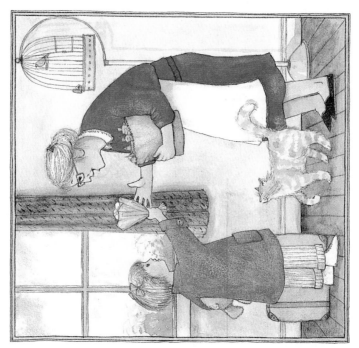

and my brown bear Barney.

my pajamas in a suitcase, a flower in green paper,
a tasty tidbit for her cat, some carrots from my garden

a good book or two, our old dog Charlie,
an apple for the morning, my big silver flashlight

When I go to bed, I take . . .

When I go to school, next year or the next,
I'll take . . . .

and my brown bear Barney.

But not my brown bear Barney.
My mother says that bears don't go to school.

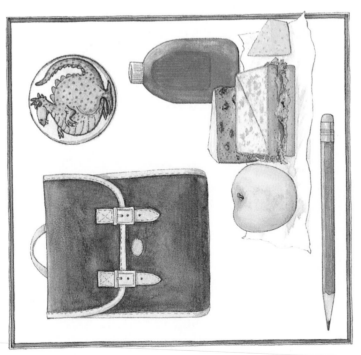

a new school bag, some lunch, my dinosaur badge and
a pencil with an eraser on the end.

We'll see about that!

*Literacy
Lesson
continued*

Teacher Preparation

This plan was developed for a first-grade class of twenty-three students. My preparation and decision making about the lessons went as follows:

1. After having talked with the children about their interests, I decided with them that we should have a unit called "Teddy Bears" because almost every one had a teddy bear and they loved talking about them.

2. I put ten different books about bears in the library center and noticed which books children picked up and examined. (These came from the school library, the public library, and my own collection.) Because there was so much interest in *My Brown Bear Barney* (Butler, 1988) and *Ira Sleeps Over* (Waber, 1972), I decided to use them. *My Brown Bear Barney* is a predictable, repeated patterned book that seemed to fit with the way my children were learning to read. *Ira Sleeps Over* is also a book about how a child finds comfort with his teddy bear. I had a copy of *Bear in Mind: A Book of Bear Poems* (Goldstein, 1989) that has good poems for chanting and opening the lessons. *The Velveteen Rabbit* (Williams, 1983) is also good for reading aloud during this unit.

3. I obtained a big book for *My Brown Bear Barney* (Butler, 1991) plus fifteen small book versions.

4. I reread both *My Brown Bear Barney* and *Ira Sleeps Over* to get a sense of the story lines. I then read and marked the poems I wanted to use as chants.

5. As I read *My Brown Bear Barney*, I noticed that in nineteen places the consonant *b* was used in the initial position (*bear* and *Barney* were each used six times; *basket*, *boots*, *beach*, *book*, *bag*, *badge*, and *bears* each once). Since my children were getting good at using consonants and context to decode words, this book would provide the practice they needed.

6. I decided that my major outcomes for this unit would be as follows:

   - *Constructing meaning:* Use important story clues to understand that favorite things often make one comfortable.
   - *Attitudes and habits:* Have fun reading, writing, and sharing books and stories about teddy bears.

   In addition to these outcomes and the many literacy skills and strategies that would develop as a result of these lessons, I wanted to focus attention on three skills: (1) making inferences, (2) reinforcing the use of context and the consonant *b* to decode words, and (3) continuing to expand recognition and meaning vocabulary.

7. I planned for this unit to last for seven to ten days, depending on student interests and responses.

   The following sample presents only the introduction for the theme and the lessons for *My Brown Bear Barney*.

*Literacy
Lesson
continued*

Introducing the Theme "Teddy Bears"

ACTIVITY	PROCEDURE	NOTES
Talking about real and make-believe bears	Remind children of their interest in reading about bears. Invite them to talk about real bears and make-believe bears, and encourage them to tell the difference.	Activates prior knowledge for the theme.
Shared writing: making a chart about make-believe bears	Tell children that in this unit they are going to be reading and hearing about some make-believe bears.	Focuses students' thinking on the types of bears they will be reading and hearing about.
	Direct a discussion, getting children to tell what they know about make-believe bears. Record their ideas on a chart. Here are some prompts, if needed: Name some make-believe bears you know. What things do make-believe bears do? Where have you seen or heard about make-believe bears? How do you feel about your favorite bear? A partial chart may look like this:	Models writing for children and continues to activate prior knowledge.

Make-Believe Bears
• Teddy bears
• Some talk
• Have names like Stinky

| Making a make-believe bear book | Invite children to draw a picture of their favorite make-believe bear or one they would like to know or have. | Connects reading and writing. Helps to focus children on the types of bears they will be reading and writing about. |

*Literacy
Lesson
continued*

ACTIVITY	PROCEDURE	NOTES

Encourage them to write about their bear; remind them to spell as they think things sound.

Invite children to share their pictures and read what they have written.

Compile bear pictures into a class book. Have children draw little bear

> Our
> Make - Believe
> Bears

pictures to put on the cover. Place the book in the library center for all to read.

Tell children that they will read and listen to some wonderful bear stories.

**Introducing My Brown
Bear Barney
(First Reading—For Interest
and Fun)**

Opening activity:
Chanting a poem

Display the poem from Goldstein's book (1989, p. 26) on a chart.

Read the poem aloud to children, pointing to the words. Invite them to chant it with you.

Warms students up for the lesson and activates prior knowledge.

*Literacy
Lesson
continued*

ACTIVITY	PROCEDURE	NOTES

MY TEDDY BEAR *

A teddy bear is a faithful friend.
You can pick him up at either end.
His fur is the color of breakfast toast,
And he's always there when you
need him most.

Marchette Chute

ACTIVITY	PROCEDURE	NOTES
Talking about *My Brown Bear Barney* and making predictions	Show students the book; read title, author, and illustrator. Discuss the cover, focusing on the character (little girl). Turn through first two or three pages and continue discussing pictures. Ask children to tell what they think is going to happen in this book. Record predictions on a chart. Tell students you will return to those at the end of the book.	Continues prior knowledge development for the book and creates excitement for reading. Helps children have a purpose as they read.

**Reading and Responding to
My Brown Bear Barney
(First Reading—For Interest
and Fun)**

Reading the story for interest and fun	Place the big book so that children can see it. Read each page aloud, pointing to the words.	Models reading.

*Source: From *Rhymes About Us* by Marchette Chute. Published 1974 by E.P. Dutton. Copyright © 1974 by Marchette Chute. Reprinted by permission of Elizabeth Chute.

Literacy Lesson continued

ACTIVITY	PROCEDURE	NOTES
	Reread the story, talking about the illustrations as you go. Invite children to chime in.	
Responding to the story: Talking about things children liked or thought were funny	Invite children to share their reactions to the story. (See if anyone has seen the bear in the little girl's backpack on the last page.)	Promotes personal responses and construction of meaning. Lets me know how well students understand.
Writing and drawing about the story	Ask children to write about their favorite thing in the story and draw a picture to go with it.	Ties together reading and writing. Focuses on constructing meaning.

**Rereading and Responding to
My Brown Bear Barney
Second Reading—
For Comprehension
(Usually the Next Day)**

ACTIVITY	PROCEDURE	NOTES
Recalling *My Brown Bear Barney*	Show children the big book and ask them to recall the story. Ask them to tell some of the specific things the little girl took with her each place she went. List them on the chalkboard.	Produces familiarity with the story.
	Ask children to discuss why the little girl always took Barney with her.	
Setting a purpose for reading	Tell children, as they reread the book, to note if they recalled all the things the little girl took with her.	Focuses attention during rereading.
Reading the story to note important story information	Read the story aloud, inviting children to chime in.	Focuses on using story clues to make inferences.

*Literacy
Lesson
continued*

ACTIVITY	PROCEDURE	NOTES
	Reread the story, inviting children to join in but stopping after each page for them to find in the picture each item the little girl took with her and also the word for it in the text.	
	On the last page, ask children what they think the little girl has done and why (has taken bear to school because she is so attached to it).	
	Reread the story, having children chime in or read after you. Continue pointing to words.	
Shared writing: Making a list	Ask children to recall the places where the little girl went and the things she took. Have them refer to the list made earlier and add items to it. Write the items on a chart.	

Places Little Girl Went	Things She Took
shopping	mother, little brother, yellow basket, red umbrella, brown bear Barney

*Literacy
Lesson
continued*

ACTIVITY	PROCEDURE	NOTES
	Rereading and Responding to *My Brown Bear Barney* Third Reading— To Explore Language (Another Day)	
Rereading to note the story pattern	Display the book and ask children to recall what the little girl did.	Children should know story well enough that they can begin rereading without further prior knowledge.
	Reread the story, inviting children to chime in.	
	Reread each page, asking children to identify the repeated pattern: When I go to _____, I take _____, _____, _____, and my _____.	Helps children understand the repetitive language.
Responding: Writing individual stories	Display the story pattern. Ask children to tell what favorite thing they always take with them.	Helps children construct meaning by innovating on the text.
	I tell children that I always take my favorite book with me—then write an example of my story.	Provides teacher modeling.

When I go out to eat,
I always take a friend,
my money, and my
favorite book.

Literacy Lesson continued

ACTIVITY	PROCEDURE	NOTES
	Ask children to write their stories using the pattern from *My Brown Bear Barney*.	
Making and sharing books	Have children make their stories into little books.	Develops construction of meaning.
	Encourage children to share their stories.	Develops a sense of community.

> **Rereading and Responding to**
> ***My Brown Bear Barney***
> **Fourth Reading—To Develop**
> **Decoding; Using Context and the**
> **Consonant *b* (Another Day)**

Preparation: Prepare the book for a cloze activity by using the framing device on page 296 or by placing removable adhesive papers over all but the *b* in the following words: *Bear, Barney, basket, boots, beach, book, bag, badge,* and *bears*.

ACTIVITY	PROCEDURE	NOTES
Rereading *My Brown Bear Barney*	Display the big book.	Develops ability to use text clues to make predictions and construct meaning.
	Tell children that as you reread the book they will find that parts of words have been covered—only the beginning consonant *b* will be showing. Encourage them to predict what the word is as they read.	
	Reread the book as in previous readings, inviting children to chime in. Stop at each masked word and have children predict the word. Remove mask to check for accuracy.	By this time many children will be able to read the book. Shows how children are able to use context and the consonant *b*.
Making a word wall of *b* words	Have children go back through the book and find *b* words to put on a word wall. (Accept *brother* or *brown*, even though they are consonant blends.) Encourage use in later writing.	

*Literacy
Lesson
continued*

ACTIVITY	PROCEDURE	NOTES

> **Extending**
> ***My Brown Bear Barney***
> **(These activities were used
> selectively after various
> rereadings of the story.)**

ACTIVITY	PROCEDURE	NOTES
Independently reading *My Brown Bear Barney*	Let children use the big book or little book version to reread the story alone or in small groups.	Reinforces constructing meaning.
Making a mural about favorite things	Encourage children to draw and write about the favorite things in their lives that they always take with them. Have them place their drawings and writings on a class mural. Children may use what they wrote in response to the story as a basis for their drawing (page 304).	Helps children relate what they have read to their lives. Illustrates that different things become "security blankets" for different children.
Reading aloud *The Velveteen Rabbit*	Use as a class read-aloud throughout the unit.	Provides background and interest for the theme.

After Reading the Plan

1. Meet with a friend who has studied the plan to talk about other ways you would have developed it.
2. Use this shared reading plan and the suggested daily schedule on page 303 to write out the daily schedules you would follow. You will have to think about other activities you would add.
3. Locate a teacher who is using shared reading and observe the class for several days. Then meet with the teacher to discuss how the shared reading works.
4. Select a book and develop a shared reading plan alone or with a friend.

SUMMARY

This chapter has stressed that effective constructors of meaning must know how to decode words automatically and efficiently, but that the ability to do this is not learned as a prerequisite to or separate from meaning construction. In order to identify words, children develop some concepts about print, develop a sight vocabulary, and learn to analyze and decode words. They learn these things in stages.

Five principles were given for guiding the development of word identification:

1. Begin all instruction with meaningful text experiences.
2. Children's needs and the texts being read should determine the word identification element being supported or emphasized.
3. Model the element of word identification being emphasized using the texts children are reading.
4. Practice in word identification comes through repeated reading and writing.
5. Allow and encourage children to take risks as they read, trying words before you tell them what they are.

Four ways were suggested for supporting children in learning to identify words—shared reading, minilessons, practice through reading and writing, and helping students develop strategies leading to independence. Guidelines were given for pulling all of these ideas together. A sample shared reading lesson for *My Brown Bear Barney* was presented.

Children's Books

Adams, P. (1973). *There was an old lady who swallowed a fly.* Singapore: Child's Play International.

Ahlberg, J., & Ahlberg, A. (1978). *Each peach pear plum.* New York: Scholastic.

Bennett, J. (1986). *Teeny tiny.* New York: G. P. Putnam.

Butler, D. (1988). *My brown bear Barney.* New York: Greenwillow Books.

Butler, D. (1991). *My brown bear Barney* (Big Book). Boston: Houghton Mifflin.

Carle, E. (1977). *The grouchy ladybug.* New York: Crowell.

Christelow, E. (1989). *Five little monkeys jumping on the bed.* New York: Clarion.

Cowley, J. (1987). *Noise.* Bothell, WA: The Wright Group.

Cummings, P. (1991). *Clean your room, Harvey Moon!* New York: Bradbury Press.

Emberley, B. (1967). *Drummer Hoff.* Englewood Cliffs, NJ: Prentice-Hall.

Geisert, A. (1991). *Oink.* Boston: Houghton Mifflin.

Gilman, P. (1985). *Jillian Jiggs.* New York: Scholastic.

Goldstein, B. S. (1989). *Bear in mind: A book of bear poems.* New York: Viking Kestrel.

Gross, T. F. (1990). *Everyone asked about you.* New York: Philomel.

Hayes, S. (1988). *This is the bear and the picnic lunch.* Boston: Joy Street Books/Little, Brown.

Jones, C. (1990). *This old man.* Boston: Houghton Mifflin.

Martin, B., Jr. (1967). *Brown Bear, Brown Bear*. New York: Henry Holt.

Martin, B. (1970). *Fire! Fire! Said Mrs. McGuire*. New York: Holt, Rinehart and Winston.

Munsch, R. (1989). *Pigs*. Toronto: Annick Press.

Numeroff, L. J. (1985). *If you give a mouse a cookie*. New York: Harper and Row.

Numeroff, L. J. (1991). *If you give a moose a muffin*. New York: HarperCollins.

Peek, M. (1985). *Mary wore her red dress and Henry wore his green sneakers*. New York: Clarion

Raffi. (1980). Willoughby, wallaby, woo. In *The Raffi singable song book* (p. 92). New York: Crown.

Seuss, Dr. (1950). *Yertle the turtle and other stories*. New York: Random House.

Seuss, Dr. (1960). *Green eggs and ham*. New York: Beginner Books, A division of Random House.

Seuss, Dr. (1963). *Hop on Pop*. New York: Beginner Books, A division of Random House.

Shaw, N. (1986). *Sheep in a jeep*. Boston: Houghton Mifflin.

Shaw, N. (1989). *Sheep on a ship*. Boston: Houghton Mifflin.

Shaw, N. (1991). *Sheep in a shop*. Boston: Houghton Mifflin.

Van Laan, N. (1990). *Possum come a-knockin'*. New York: Knopf.

Waber, B. (1972). *Ira sleeps over*. Boston: Houghton Mifflin.

Westcott, N. B. (1988). *The lady with the alligator purse*. Boston: Little, Brown.

Williams, M. (1983). *The velveteen rabbit*. New York: Simon & Schuster.

Bibliography of Favorite Books for Shared Reading

Aardema, V. (1975). *Why mosquitoes buzz in people's ears*. New York: E. P. Dutton

Aardema, V. (1981). *Bringing the rain to Kapiti Plain*. New York: Dial.

Adams, P. (1973). *There was an old lady who swallowed a fly*. England: Child's Play International.

Adams, P. (1974). *This old man*. New York: Grossett and Dunlap.

Ahlberg, J., & Ahlberg, A. (1978). *Each peach pear plum*. New York: Scholastic.

Alain. (1964). *One, two, three going to sea*. New York: Scholastic.

Aliki. (1974). *Go tell Aunt Rhody*. New York: Macmillan.

Anderson, M. D. (1985). *Hungry as a lion*. Worthington, OH: Willowisp Press.

Argent, K., & Trinca, R. (1985). *One woolly wombat*. Brooklyn: Kane/Miller.

Asch, F. (1977). *Monkey face*. New York: Parents' Magazine Press.

Balaian, L. (1972). *The animal*. Nashville: Abingdon Press.

Balaian, L. (1972). *Where in the world is Henry?* Scarsdale, NY: Bradbury Press.

Barohas, S. E. (1975). *I was walking down the road*. New York: Scholastic.

Becker, J. (1973). *Seven little rabbits*. New York: Scholastic.

Beckman, K. (1969). *Lisa cannot sleep*. New York: Franklin Watts.

Bellah, M. (1963). *A first book of sounds*. Racine, WI: Golden Press.

Bowes, C. (1985). *The hogboggit*. Wellington, New Zealand: V. R. Ward, Government Printer.

Boynton, S. (1985). *Good night, good night*. New York: Random House.

Brandenberg, F. (1970). *I once knew a man*. New York: Macmillan.

Brett, J. (1986). *The twelve days of Christmas.* New York: Dodd, Mead.

Brown, M. W. (1947). *Goodnight moon.* New York: Harper.

Brown, M. W. (1949). *The important book.* New York: Harper & Row.

Brown, M. W. (1956). *Home for a bunny.* Racine, WI: Golden Press.

Brown, M. W. (1957). *The three billy goats gruff.* New York: Harcourt Brace Jovanovich.

Brown, M. W. (1975). *Goodnight moon.* New York: Harper & Row.

Brown, M. W. (1987). *Play rhymes.* New York: E. P. Dutton.

Brown, R. (1981). *A dark dark tale.* New York: Dial Books for Young Readers.

Bucknall, C. (1985). *One bear all alone: A counting book.* London: Macmillan Children's Books.

Burningham, J. (1970). *Mr. Gumpy's outing.* London: Henry Holt.

Burningham, J. (1987). *John Patrick Norman McHennessy: The boy who was always late.* New York: Crown

Butler, D. (1988). *My brown bear Barney.* New York: Greenwillow Books.

Cachemaille, C. (1982). *Nick's glasses.* Wellington, New Zealand: V. R. Ward, Government Printer.

Carle, E. (1975). *The mixed up chameleon.* New York: Crowell.

Carle, E. (1977). *The grouchy ladybug.* New York: Crowell.

Carle, E. (1983). *The very hungry caterpillar.* New York: Philomel.

Carle, E. (1990). *The very quiet cricket.* New York: Philomel.

Charlip, R. (1969). *Fortunately.* New York: Parents' Magazine Press.

Charlip, R. (1969). *What good luck! What bad luck!* New York: Scholastic.

Cook, B. (1976). *The little fish that got away.* Reading, MA: Addison-Wesley.

Corney, E. (1983). *T shirts.* Wellington, New Zealand: V. R. Ward, Government Printer.

Cory's counting game. (1979). Los Angeles: Intervisual Communications.

Cowley, J. (1983). *The biggest cake in the world.* Wellington, New Zealand: V. R. Ward, Government Printer.

Cowley, J. (1983). *Greedy cat.* Wellington, New Zealand: V. R. Ward, Government Printer.

Cowley, J. (1983). *Rain, rain.* Wellington, New Zealand: V. R. Ward, Government Printer.

Cowley, J. (1984). *Rosie at the zoo.* Wellington, New Zealand: V. R. Ward, Government Printer.

Cowley, J. (1987). *Did you say, "Fire"?* Wellington, New Zealand: V. R. Ward, Government Printer.

Cowley, J. (1987). *The smile.* Wellington, New Zealand: V. R. Ward, Government Printer.

Cowley, J. (1987). *Where is Miss Pool?* Wellington, New Zealand: V. R. Ward, Government Printer

Cowley, J. (1988). *Greedy cat is hungry.* Wellington, New Zealand: V. R. Ward, Government Printer.

Cummings, P. (1991). *Clean your room, Harvey Moon!* New York: Bradbury Press.

de Regniers, B. S. (1968). *Willie O'Dwyer jumped in the fire.* New York: Atheneum.

Domanska, J. (1971). *If all the seas were one sea.* New York: Macmillan

Duff, M. (1978). *Rum pum pum.* New York: Macmillan.

Emberley, B. (1967). *Drummer Hoff.* Englewood Cliffs, NJ: Prentice-Hall.

Emberley, B. (1969). *Simon's song.* Englewood Cliffs, NJ: Prentice-Hall.

Emberley, B. (1974). *Klippity Klop.* Boston: Little, Brown.

Ets, M. H. (1955). *Play with me*. New York: Viking.

Ets, M. H. (1972). *Elephant in a well*. New York: Viking.

Flack, M. (1932). *Ask Mr. Bear*. New York: Macmillan.

Gag, W. (1977). *Millions of cats*. New York: Coward-McCann.

Galdone, P. (1968). *Henny Penny*. New York: Clarion.

Galdone, P. (1972). *The three bears*. New York: Clarion.

Galdone, P. (1973). *Ask Little Red Hen*. New York: Scholastic.

Galdone, P. (1973). *The three billy goats gruff*. New York: Clarion.

Galdone, P. (1973). *The three little pigs*. New York: Seabury.

Galdone, P. (1984). *The teeny-tiny woman*. Boston: Houghton Mifflin.

Gilman, P. (1985). *Jillian Jiggs*. New York: Scholastic.

Gilman, P. (1988). *The wonderful pigs of Jillian Jiggs*. New York: Scholastic.

Ginsburg, M. (1972). *The chick and the duckling*. New York: Macmillan.

Goss, J., & Harste, J. (1981). *It didn't frighten me!* New York: Scholastic.

Greene, C. (1983). *The thirteen days of Halloween*. Chicago: Childrens Press.

Grimm Brothers. (1983). *The fisherman and his wife*. Mankato, MN: Creative Education.

Guarino, D. (1989). *Is your mama a llama?* New York: Scholastic.

Guilfoile, E. (1957). *Nobody listens to Andrew*. Cleveland: Modern Curriculum Press.

Hawkins, C., & Hawkins, J. (1983). *Pat the cat*. New York: G. P. Putnam.

Hill, B. (1984). *The wind*. Wellington, New Zealand: Government Printing Office.

Hill, E. (1980). *Where's Spot?* New York: G. P. Putnam.

Hoberman, M. A. (1987). *A house is a house for me*. New York: Penguin.

Hoffman, H. (1968). *The green grass grows all around*. New York: Macmillan.

Hoguet, S. R. (1983). *I unpacked my grandmother's trunk*. New York: E. P. Dutton.

Hutchins, P. (1968). *Rosie's walk*. New York: Macmillan.

Hutchins, P. (1971). *Titch*. New York: Collier.

Hutchins, P. (1972). *Goodnight owl*. New York: Macmillan.

Hutchins, P. (1982). *One hunter*. New York: Greenwillow Books.

Hutchins, P. (1986). *The doorbell rang*. New York: Greenwillow Books.

Jones, C. (1989). *Old MacDonald had a farm*. Boston: Houghton Mifflin.

Jones, C. (1990). *This old man*. Boston: Houghton Mifflin.

Joslin, S. (1974). *What do you say dear?* New York: Scholastic.

Kalan, R. (1978). *Rain*. New York: Greenwillow Books.

Kalan, R. (1981). *Jump, frog, jump!* New York: Greenwillow Books.

Keats, E. J. (1971). *Over in the meadow*. New York: Scholastic.

Kent, J. (1971). *The fat cat: A Danish folktale*. New York: Scholastic.

Kovalski, M. (1987). *The wheels on the bus*. Boston: Joy Street Books, Little, Brown.

Kraus, R. (1970). *Whose mouse are you?* New York: Collier.

Langstaff, J. (1974). *Oh, a-hunting we will go*. New York: Atheneum.

Laurence, E. (1974). *We're off to catch a dragon*. Nashville: Abingdon Press.

Leondas, S. N. (1965). *Always room for one more*. New York: Henry Holt.

Lobel, A. (1975). *King rooster, queen hen*. New York: Greenwillow Books.

Lobel, A. (1979). *A treeful of pigs*. New York: Scholastic.

MacDonald, A. (1990). *Rachel Fister's sister*. Boston: Houghton Mifflin.

McGovern, A. (1967). *Too much noise*. New York: Scholastic.

Mack, S. (1974). *10 Bears in my bed*. New York: Pantheon.

Martin, B., Jr. (1967). *Brown Bear, Brown Bear*. New York: Henry Holt.

Martin, B., Jr. (1970). *Fire! Fire! Said Mrs. McGuire*. New York: Holt, Rinehart and Winston.

Martin, B., Jr. (1970). *Monday, Monday I like Monday.* New York: Holt, Rinehart and Winston.

Martin, B., Jr. (1991). *Polar Bear, Polar Bear, what do you hear?* New York: Henry Holt.

Martin, B., Jr., & Archambault, J. (1989). *Chicka chicka boom boom.* New York: Simon & Schuster.

Martin, C. (1982). *My bike.* Wellington, New Zealand: V. R. Ward, Government Printer.

Mayer, M. (1968). *If I had . . .* New York: Dial.

Mayer, M. (1968). *Just for you.* New York: Golden Press.

Memling, C. (1961). *Ten little animals.* Racine, WI: Golden Press.

Moerbeek, K., & Dijs, C. (1987). *Hot pursuit.* Los Angeles: Intervisual Communications.

Moffett, M. (1972). *A flower pot is not a hat.* New York: E. P. Dutton.

Moncure, T. (Ed.). (1987). *Susie Moriar.* Allen, TX: DLM Teaching Resources.

Munsch, R. (1986). *Love you forever.* Scarborough, Ontario: Firefly Books.

Muntean, M. (1980). *I like school.* Racine, WI: Western Publishing.

Nickl, P., & Schroeder, B. (1976). *Crocodile, crocodile.* New York: Crocodile Books, U.S.A.

Nodset, J. L. (1963). *Who took the farmer's hat?* New York: Scholastic.

Numeroff, L. J., & Bond, F. (1985). *If you give a mouse a cookie.* New York: Harper & Row.

Oppenheim, J. (1986). *Have you seen birds?* New York: Scholastic.

Peek, M. (Illus.). (1969). *Roll over!* New York: Clarion.

Peek, M. (1985). *Mary wore her red dress and Henry wore his green sneakers.* New York: Clarion.

Peppe, R. (1970). *The house that Jack built.* New York: Delacorte.

Pienkowski, J. (1984). *Dinner time.* Los Angeles: Intervisual Communications.

Pienkowski, J. (1986). *Little monsters.* Los Angeles: Intervisual Communications.

Polushkin, M. (1978). *Mother, Mother, I want another.* New York: Crown.

Prelutsky, J. (1984). *The new kid on the block.* New York: Greenwillow Books.

Prelutsky, J. (1986). *Ride a purple pelican.* New York: Greenwillow Books.

Prelutsky, J. (1988). *Tyrannosaurus was a beast.* New York: Greenwillow Books.

Prelutsky, J. (1989). *Poems of A. Nonny Mouse.* New York: Knopf.

Prelutsky, J. (1990). *Beneath a blue umbrella.* New York: Greenwillow Books.

Prelutsky, J. (1990). *Something big has been here.* New York: Greenwillow Books.

Purviance, S., & O'Shell, M. (1988). *Alphabet Annie announces an all-American album.* Boston: Houghton Mifflin.

Quackenbush, R. (1973). *She'll be coming 'round the mountain.* Philadelphia: Lippincott.

Rose, G. (1975). *Trouble in the ark.* London: Bodley Head.

Sendak, M. (1962). *Chicken soup with rice.* New York: Scholastic.

Seuss, Dr. (1963). *Dr. Seuss's A B C.* New York: Random House.

Seuss, Dr. (1974). *There's a wocket in my pocket.* New York: Random House.

Seuss, Dr. (1978). *I can read with my eyes shut!* New York: Random House.

Seuss, Dr. (1990). *Oh, the places you'll go!* New York: Random House.

Shaw, C. B. (1947). *It looked like spilt milk.* New York: Harper and Row.

Shaw, N. (1986). *Sheep in a jeep.* Boston: Houghton Mifflin.

Shaw, N. (1989). *Sheep on a ship.* Boston: Houghton Mifflin.

Shaw, N. (1991). *Sheep in a shop*. Boston: Houghton Mifflin.

Shulevitz, U. (1967). *One Monday Morning*. New York: Scribner's.

Stevens, J. (Illus.). (1985). *The house that Jack built: A Mother Goose nursery rhyme*. New York: Holiday House.

Stevenson, J. (1977). *"Could be worse!"* New York: Greenwillow Books.

Stobbs, W., & Bonne, R. (1987). *I know an old lady who swallowed a fly*. Oxford: Oxford University Press.

Stover, J. (1960). *If everybody did*. New York: David McKay.

Strauss, B. (1987). *See you later alligator . . .* Los Angeles: Price/Stein/Sloan.

Tolstoy, A. (1968). *The great big enormous turnip*. New York: Franklin Watts.

Underhill, L. (1987). *The house that Jack built*. New York: Henry Holt.

Van Allsburg, C. (1987). *The Z was zapped*. Boston: Houghton Mifflin.

Vaughn, M. K. (1984). *Wombat stew*. Morristown, NJ: Silver Burdett.

Viorst, J. (1972). *Alexander and the terrible, horrible, no good, very bad day*. Hartford, CT: Atheneum.

Welber, R. (1974). *Goodbye, hello*. New York: Pantheon.

Westcott, N. B. (1988). *The lady with the alligator purse*. Boston: Little, Brown.

Westcott, N. B. (1989). *Skip to my Lou*. Boston: Little, Brown.

Who's your furry friend? (1981). Los Angeles: Intervisual Communications.

Williams, S. (1990). *Mommy doesn't know my name*. Boston: Houghton Mifflin.

Winthrop, E. (1986). *Shoes*. New York: Harper & Row.

Wolkstein, D. (1977). *The visit*. New York: Knopf.

Wondriska, W. (1970). *All the animals were angry*. New York: Rinehart and Winston.

Wood, A. (1984). *The napping house*. San Diego: Harcourt Brace Jovanovich.

Yeoman, J., & Blake, Q. (1990). *Old Mother Hubbard's dog dresses up*. Boston: Houghton Mifflin.

Yeoman, J., & Blake, Q. (1990). *Old Mother Hubbard's dog learns to play*. Boston: Houghton Mifflin.

Yeoman, J., & Blake, Q. (1990). *Old Mother Hubbard's dog needs a doctor*. Boston: Houghton Mifflin.

Yeoman, J., & Blake, Q. (1990). *Old Mother Hubbard's dog takes up sport*. Boston: Houghton Mifflin.

Zemach, M. (1976). *Hush, little baby*. New York: E. P. Dutton.

Zemach, H., & Zemach, M. (1969). *The judge*. New York: Farrar, Straus and Giroux.

Zolotow, C. (1958). *Do you know what I'll do?* New York: Harper & Row.

For Additional Reading

Barrett, F. L. (1982). *A teacher's guide to shared reading*. Ontario: Scholastic.

Bullock, C., & Bullock, C. (1988). *A little book about big books*. Lakewood: Link.

Griffith, P. L., & Olson, M. W. (1992). Phonemic awareness helps beginning readers break the code. *Reading Teacher, 45,* 516–523.

McCracken, R. A., & McCracken, M. J. (1986). *Stories, songs and poetry to teach reading and writing: Literacy through language*. Chicago: American Library Association.

Mason, J. M., & Au, K. H. (1990). Teaching word identification skills. In J. M. Mason & K. H. Au, *Reading instruction for today* (2nd ed.) (pp. 260–300). Glenview, IL: Scott, Foresman/Little, Brown Higher Education.

Mills, H., O'Keefe, T., & Stephens, D. (1992). *Looking closely.* Urbana, IL: National Council of Teachers of English.

Peetoom, A. (1986). *Shared reading: Safe risk with whole books.* Ontario, Canada: Scholastic TAB Publications.

Stahl, S. A., Osborn, J. & Lehr, F. (1990). *Beginning to read: Thinking and learning about print, by M. Adams, A Summary.* Champaign: University of Illinois at Urbana-Champaign, Center for the Study of Reading.

References

Adams, M. J. (1990). *Thinking and learning about print.* Cambridge, MA: MIT Press.

Anderson, R. C., Hiebert, E. H., Scott, J. A., & Wilkinson, I. A. G. (1985). *Becoming a nation of readers: The report of the Commission on Reading.* Washington, DC: National Institute of Education.

Au, K. H. (1991). Speech delivered at the Notre Dame Reading Conference, South Bend, IN, June 25, 1991, sponsored by Houghton Mifflin Company, Boston.

Baghban, M. (1984). *Our daughter learns to read and write: A case study from birth to three.* Newark, DE: International Reading Association.

Ball, E. W., & Blachman, B. A. (1991). Does phoneme segmentation training make a difference in early word recognition and development spelling? *Reading Research Quarterly, 26,* 49–66.

Beck, I., & Juel, C. (1992). The role of decoding in learning to read. In S. J. Samuels & A. Farstrup (Eds.), *What research has to say about reading instruction* (2nd ed.) (pp. 101–123). Newark, DE: International Reading Association.

Bissex, G. L. (1980). *Gnys at wrk: A child learns to read and write.* Cambridge, MA: Harvard University Press.

Bridge, C. A. (1986). Predictable books for beginning readers and writers. In M. L. Sampson (Ed.), *The pursuit of literacy: Early reading and writing* (pp. 81–96). Dubuque, IA: Kendall/Hunt.

Bridge, C. (1989). Beyond the basal in beginning reading. In P. N. Winograd, K. K. Wixson, & M. Y. Lipson (Eds.), *Improving basal reading instruction* (pp. 177–209). New York: Teachers College Press.

Bridge, C., Winograd, P. N., & Haley, D. (1983). Using predictable materials vs. preprimers to teach beginning sight words. *Reading Teacher, 36* (9), 884–891.

Cambourne, B. (1988). *The whole story: Natural learning and the acquisition of literacy in the classroom.* New York: Aston-Scholastic.

Cazden, C. (1972). *Child language and education.* New York: Holt, Rinehart and Winston.

Chall, J. S. (1967). *Learning to read: The great debate.* New York: McGraw-Hill.

Chall, J. S. (1983). *Learning to read: The great debate* (rev. ed.). New York: McGraw-Hill.

Clarke, L. K. (1988). Invented versus traditional spelling in first graders' writings: Effects on learning to spell and read. *Research in the Teaching of English, 22,* 281–309.

Clay, M. M. (1985, 2nd ed., 1979). *The early detection of reading difficulties* (3rd ed.). Auckland, New Zealand: Heinemann.

Clay, M. M. (1991). *Becoming literate: The construction of inner control.* Portsmouth, NH: Heinemann.

Dolch, E. W. (1936). A basic sight vocabulary. *Elementary School Journal, 36* 456–460.

Ehri, L. C., & Robbins, C. (1992). Beginners need some decoding skill to read words by analogy. *Reading Research Quarterly, 27* 13–26.

Gaskins, I. W., Downer, M. A., Anderson, R. C., Cunningham, P. M., Gaskins, R. W., Schommer, M., & The Teachers of the Benchmark School. (1988). A metacognitive approach to phonics: Using what you know to decode what you don't know. *Remedial and Special Education* 36–41.

Gentry, J. R. (1987). *SPEL . . . Is a four-letter word*. Portsmouth, NH: Heinemann.

Halliday, M. A. K. (1975). *Learning how to mean*. New York: Elsevier North-Holland.

Harlin, R. P. (1990). *Effects of whole language on low SES children*. Paper presented at the National Reading Conference, Austin, TX, December, 1990.

Harris, T. L., & Hodges, R. E. (1981). *A dictionary of reading and related terms*. Newark, DE: International Reading Association.

Hodges, R. (1991). The conventions of writing. In J. Flood, J. M. Jensen, D. Lapp, & J. R. Squire (Eds.), *Handbook of research on teaching the English languarge arts* (pp. 775–786). New York: Macmillan.

Holdaway, D. (1979). *The foundations of literacy*. Sydney: Ashton Scholastic, distributed by Heinemann, Portsmouth, NH.

Holdaway, D. (1986). The structure of natural language as a basis for literacy instruction. In M. L. Sampson (Ed.), *The pursuit of literacy: Early reading and writing* (pp. 56–72). Dubuque, IA: Kendall/Hunt.

Johnson, D. D. (1971). A basic vocabulary for beginning readers. *Elementary School Journal, 72*, 29–34.

Johnson, D. D., & Baumann, J. F. (1984). Word identification. In P. D. Pearson (Ed.), *Handbook of reading research* (pp. 583–608). White Plains, NY: Longman.

Juel, C., Griffith, P. L., & Gough, P. B. (1986). Acquisition of literacy: A longitudinal study of children in first and second grade. *Journal of Educational Psychology, 78*, 243–255.

Juel, C. (1988). Learning to read and write: A longitudinal study of 54 children from first through fourth grades. *Journal of Educational Psychology, 89*, 437–447.

Juel, C. (1991). Beginning reading. In R. Barr, M. L. Kamil, P. Mosenthal & P. D. Pearson (Eds.), *Handbook of reading research* (Vol. 2, pp. 759–788). New York: Longman.

LaBerge, D., & Samuels, S. J. (1976). Toward a theory of automatic information processing in reading. In H. Singer & R. Ruddell (Eds), *Theoretical models and processes of reading* (pp. 548–579). Newark DE: International Reading Association.

Lomax, R. G., & McGee, L. M. (1987). Young children's concepts about print and meaning: Toward a model of word reading acquisition. *Reading Research Quarterly, 22*, 237–256.

Lundberg, I., Frost, J., & Petersen, O. (1988). Effects of an extensive program for stimulating phonological awareness in preschool children. *Reading Research Quarterly, 23*, 263–284.

Malstrom, J. (1977). *Understanding language: A primer for language arts teachers*. New York: St. Martin's.

Mason, J. M., & Au, K. H. (1990). *Reading instruction for today* (2nd ed.). Glenview, IL: Scott, Foresman.

Mason, J. M., Herman, P. A., & Au, K. H. (1991). Children's developing knowledge of words. In J. Flood, J. M. Jensen, D. Lapp & J. R. Squire (Eds.), *Handbook of research on teaching the English language arts* (pp. 721–731). New York: Macmillan.

Morell, R. (1992, February 23). Sound words out or get them from context? *Charlotte Observer*, p. 8A.

Perfetti, C. (1985). *Reading ability.* New York: Oxford University Press.

Rhodes, L. K. (1981). I can read! Predictable books as resources for reading and writing instruction. *Reading Teacher, 34,* 511–518.

Ribowsky, H. (1985). *The effects of a code emphasis approach and a whole language approach upon emergent literacy of kindergarten children.* Unpublished paper presented at the National Reading Conference.

Samuels, S. J., Schermer, N., & Reinking, D. (1992). Reading fluency: Techniques for making decoding automatic. In S. J. Samuels & A. E. Farstrup (Eds.), *What research has to say about reading instruction* (pp. 124–144). Newark, DE: International Reading Association.

Teale, W. H., & Sulzby, E. (1986). *Emergent literacy: Writing and reading.* Norwood, NJ: Ablex.

Tompkins, G. E., & Webeler, M. (1983). What will happen next? Using predictable books with young children. *Reading Teacher, 36* 498–502.

Trachtenburg, P. (1990). Using children's literature to enhance phonics instruction. *Reading Teacher, 43,* 648–654.

Yaden, D. (1988). Understanding stories through repeated read-alouds: How many does it take? *Reading Teacher, 41,* 556–560.

Responding and the Construction of Meaning

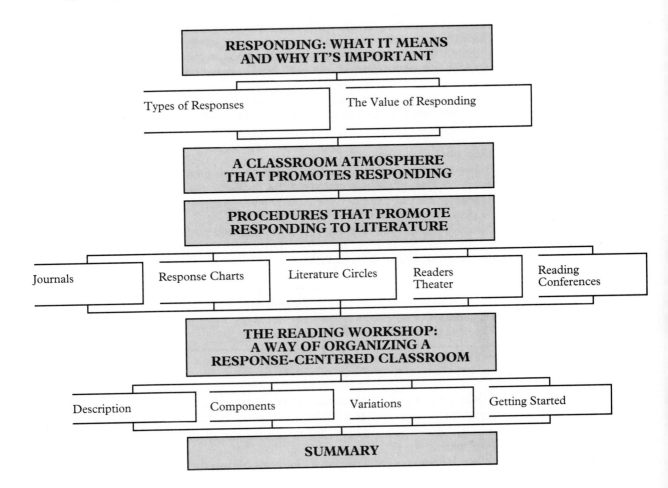

L et's begin by looking in on a third-grade classroom. Many different activities were taking place in the third-grade classroom where Melissa and several other students were sitting at their desks reading Mississippi Bridge (Taylor, 1990). Melissa leaned over to one of her classmates and pointed out an illustration; they chatted for a few minutes and then returned to their reading.

Other students in the class worked with the book James and the Giant Peach (Dahl, 1961). Some students were reading the book, some made notes in their journals, and one very excited young man, Mark, worked on a project. I stopped to talk to him.

"This looks like an interesting project," I said. "Tell me about it."

He showed me the cover of his book. "Have you ever read it?" he asked.

"Yes, I have."

"Did you like it?"

"Yes! Did you like it?"

"I sure did; I loved when the peach started to roll away and the things that happened. I'm making a movie box about this book with my favorite parts."

In another area of the room, the teacher and a group of students sat around a table discussing How Many Days to America? (Bunting, 1988). Joe said that it would be really tough to leave everything you had and go off to a new country. Maria said, "Yes, but it would be better; they might have more things and they wouldn't be afraid of the soldiers; I'd go."

The teacher, Mrs. Eggars, added, "You know, I don't know how I would feel; I've never had to leave my home like the people in our story. Do you know of anyone who has ever had this kind of experience?"

Lisa said, "Our neighbors came from Vietnam."

The discussion continued in this manner.

NOTICE WHAT WE saw in this classroom:

- While Melissa and her classmates were reading a book, it was very natural for them to stop and talk about some point in the book. This type of activity shows that students are taking control of and monitoring their own reading.
- Other students were writing in journals about their books while one student was working on a movie box, a nonverbal response, about the same book.
- Some students and the teacher were a part of a discussion group. Each participated in the discussion, no right or wrong answers were expected, and the teacher was an active participant.
- The teacher's role in this class was very important. Mrs. Eggars had planned the experiences that allowed and encouraged children to read, respond, and monitor their own learning. At the same time, she participated in groups, modeling for students and prompting them as needed.

As all of the students in this class and their teacher showed, active responding is an important element in learning to construct meaning and become literate (Hansen, 1987).

RESPONDING: WHAT IT MEANS AND WHY IT'S IMPORTANT

Responding is what one does as a result of and/or as a part of reading, writing, or listening. The children in our third-grade classroom scene took different actions both during and after reading. You do it all the time, too. You respond to a textbook chapter you are reading by discussing it with a peer (it was easy or too difficult), or you respond to a newspaper article on hunger and the homeless by finding out how to make food donations to a local mission. Responding is a part of the natural process of constructing meaning.

When you respond to a piece of literature or your writing, you are using prior knowledge to construct meaning. Therefore, each person's construction is individual and personal, the result of the transaction between the reader and the text (Rosenblatt, 1938/1976, 1991). Recall from your own college experience when you were asked to read a short story or poem and write your interpretation of it. When your paper came back, you saw you had received a "C" because your interpretation did not agree with that of the person giving the grade. What we know about the construction of meaning leads us to conclude that there are many acceptable interpretations and responses from reading a single piece of literature. There is the generally accepted response, which we have always expected students to give, and there is the more personal response, which varies greatly from student to student. Even within the generally accepted responses, there are often different interpretations. Therefore, as the teacher you must be prepared to *expect*, *respect*, and *accept* a variety of responses from students (Martinez & Roser, 1991). These responses will help you decide what types of additional support students need.

Types of Responses

Students respond to literature in a variety of ways. Applebee (1978) describes four responses that they make, each reflecting a different level of their thought processes:

1. • *Retelling:* This is a simple recall of title, beginning and ending situations, and some dialogue with no relative importance given to any of the events.
2. • *Summary:* Events are retold in order of importance. Summaries are usually shorter than retellings.
3. • *Analysis:* The response to the story is personal and subjective; for example, a student responding to *Annabelle Swift, Kindergartner* (Schwartz, 1988) might say, "This story is like what happened to me in kindergarten," and then relate a similar experience.
4. • *Generalization:* This looks into the theme or "meaning" of the story; for example, a generalization of *Annabelle Swift, Kindergartner* (Schwartz,

1988) might focus on the idea that you should trust yourself and not depend on the advice of others.

Applebee (1978) concludes that these responses are hierarchial in terms of age, suggesting, for example, that younger children can only do retelling. This conclusion, however, has not been found to be true; even younger children can often make limited generalizations or analyze a story to some degree (Many, 1991). Fourth graders can actively construct meaning by analyzing and evaluating literature (Kelly & Farnan, 1991).

Other researchers have also studied the literary responses of elementary children and their relationship to comprehension (Cullinan, Harwood, & Galda, 1983; Eeds, 1989; Galda, 1982, 1983; Gambrell, 1986; Hickman, 1983; Morrow, 1985; Purves, 1972). These studies indicate that encouraging personal responses is important in helping students learn to construct meaning. As Kelly (1990) says, "Allowing students to respond to what they read or heard from a read-aloud provided the framework for what Piaget (in Gallagher and Reid, 1983) referred to as the active involvement in learning through the construction of meaning" (p. 470).

Essentially, students' responses to literature can be divided into two categories, verbal and nonverbal. Both types of responses were seen in the third-grade class scene that opened this chapter. There are many possible responses within these categories. Harste, Short, and Burke (1988) maintain that "readers deepen and extend their interpretations of literature when they respond to that literature in a variety of ways" (p. 305). As responses take place and are encouraged over time, students develop more complex responses that help them become more adept at constructing meaning.

The Value of Responding

When children are given opportunities to function in a response-centered classroom, they develop a sense of ownership, pride, and respect for learning (Hansen, 1987). Because they respond to the same piece of literature as their classmates, they know that their responses will be valued and accepted as much as anyone else's. In addition, when gifted students and at-risk students respond to the same piece of literature together, each responds in a manner consistent with his or her functioning level. Students learn that the teacher values their responses, and they in turn learn to value the responses of their peers. This type of respect leads to a sense of community and ownership.

Responding also helps students learn to monitor their own reading and writing. By being continuously encouraged to think about and react to what they are reading and writing, students develop their metacognitive processes, which are important in constructing meaning (Palincsar & Brown, 1986; Paris, Wasik & Turner, 1991).

A CLASSROOM ATMOSPHERE THAT PROMOTES RESPONDING

If you want students to respond to literature, you must begin by creating a classroom environment that supports and promotes responding (Harste, Short & Burke, 1988). Of course, you must create a literate environment, as discussed in Chapter 2, and include extensive opportunities for students to read and write. But the response-centered classroom has many other characteristics as well.

As the teacher in this classroom, you must believe that all students have reactions and feelings that are important and valid, and students must have this belief about each other and about you. This sense of community may begin with the physical arrangement of the room, but it also includes how you treat students; if they learn that you always expect right answers or that you only reward thinking that you agree with, then they will treat each other in that manner and strive to give only the responses that they think you expect. If, on the other hand, they learn that you accept many possible answers and interpretations of what they have read, they will, in turn, become more tolerant and accepting of one another's ideas.

This classroom attitude is partly developed by the way that you ask and respond to students' questions. Typically, it has been the teacher's role to ask a series of questions to determine whether students have comprehended what they have read. For example, if students have just finished reading *The True Story of the 3 Little Pigs* (Scieszka, 1989), the teacher "checks" their comprehension by asking them a series of questions such as these:

1. Who told this story?
2. What caused the wolf to go to the house of the first little pig?
3. What happened at the house of the second little pig?
4. What made the wolf angry at the third little pig's house?
5. How did you feel about the wolf's story?

Notice that only the last question begins to move students toward thinking more openly and relating what they have learned to their own experiences. Contrast these questions with the following:

1. What was different about this story and the one you already know about the three pigs?
2. Why do you suppose the wolf would choose to tell his story?
3. If you had been in the wolf's place, how would you have approached this situation?

These questions seek varied responses and say to students that it is entirely appropriate for each person to have a different response. The final difference in this second group of questions comes in the way in which *you* respond to the students. If a student answers question 2 by telling you that the wolf probably told this story because he just wanted to tell another story and you say or imply that the answer is wrong, then that student and others who heard your response will begin to get the message that you *are* looking for a correct answer, despite what you say. If, on the other hand, you say, "That is certainly a possibility; let's hear some other thoughts," students will get a totally different message from you.

There is, indeed, a time and place to ask questions like those in the first group, such as when students need support in understanding a story during teacher-guided reading. However, when you want to prompt children's responses to reading, you should ask more open-ended, suppositional questions and then show that you accept and value a variety of responses. Table 6.1 gives some examples of questions that may be helpful.

Table 6.1   Sample Open-Ended Questions That Promote Responses to Literature

Group I

1. Where and when does the story take place? How do you know? If the story took place somewhere else or in a different time, how would it be changed?
2. What incident, problem, conflict, or situation does the author use to get the story started?
3. What does the author do to create suspense, to make you want to read on to find out what happens?
4. Trace the main events of the story. Could you change their order or leave any of them out? Why or why not?
5. Think of a different ending to the story. How would the rest of the story have to be changed to fit the new ending?
6. Did the story end the way you expected it to? What clues did the author offer to prepare you to expect this ending? Did you recognize these clues as important to the story as you were first reading/hearing it?
7. Who is the main character of the story? What kind of person is the character? How did you know?
8. Are any characters changed during the story? If they are, how are they different? What changed them? Did it seem believable?
9. Some characters play small but important roles in a story. Name such a character. Why is this character necessary for the story?
10. Who is the teller of the story? How would the story change if someone else in the book or an outside narrator told the story?
11. Does the story as a whole create a certain mood or feeling? What is the mood? How is it created?
12. Did you have strong feelings as you read the story? What did the author do to make you feel strongly?
13. What are the main ideas behind the story? What makes you think of them as you read the story?
14. Is this story like any other story you have read or watched?
15. Think about the characters in the story. Are any of them the same type of character that you have met in other stories?

Table 6.1, continued

Group II

1. What idea or ideas does this story make you think about? How does the author get you to think about this?
2. Do any particular feelings come across in this story? Does the story actually make you feel in a certain way or does it make you think about what it's like to feel that way? How does the author do this?
3. Is there one character that you know more about than any of the others? Who is this character and what kind of person is he/she? How does the author reveal the character to you?
4. Are there other characters important to the story? Who are they? Why are they important?
5. Is there anything that seems to make this particular author's work unique? If so, what?
6. Did you notice any particular patterns in the form of this book? If you are reading this book in more than one sitting, are there natural points at which to break off your reading? If so, what are these?
7. Were there clues that the author built into the story that helped you to anticipate the outcome? If so, what were they? Did you think these clues were important when you read them?
8. Does the story language seem natural for the intent of the story and for the various speakers?
9. Every writer creates a make-believe work and peoples it with characters. Even where the world is far different from your own, how does the author make the story seem possible or probable?
10. What questions would you ask if the author were here? Which would be the most important question? How might the author answer it?

Source: Reprinted by permission of the author and publisher from Glenna Davis Sloan, *The Child as Critic: Teaching Literature in Elementary and Middle Schools*, 2d ed., pp. 104–106. (New York: Teachers College Press, 1984). Copyright © 1984 by Teachers College, Columbia University. All rights reserved. Also from *Child and Story* by Kay Vandergrift (New York: Neal-Schuman Publishers, Inc., 1980). Reprinted by permission. Both cited by Harste et al. (1988).

Opportunities for students to respond to literature will come primarily in two ways: through self-selected books and materials and through those assigned by the teacher. Self-selected literature may be what the student is reading as a part of independent reading, or you may have reached a point where you encourage self-selected reading for instructional purposes.

Many times you will want the entire class to read the same piece of literature. Obviously, students of differing abilities will approach the literature differently: some will read it independently, some cooperatively, and some supported by you through directed reading or read-alouds (see Chapter 2 for a discussion of modes of reading). In all instances, they will respond to the literature according to their own ability. The literature that you have students read as an entire class will usually be the material that is used for your literacy lessons, which are designed to promote responding. (Recall that the parts of that lesson are introducing, reading and responding, and extending; see Chapter 2 for a detailed discussion.)

PROCEDURES THAT PROMOTE RESPONDING TO LITERATURE

There are many different ways to encourage and support students as they respond to literature, and each procedure has a special function. Five procedures are discussed here: journals, response charts, literature circles, readers theater, and conferences.

Journals

Journals are booklets, notebooks, or folders where students keep personal reflections about their reading and writing. They can range from a simple student-made booklet with a cover and pages to a spiral notebook or binder with loose-leaf pages.

Many educators talk about the use of journals for reading and writing (Atwell, 1987; Harste et al., 1988; Parsons, 1990; Tierney, Readence, & Dishner, 1990; Weaver, 1990). Students who are involved in a writing workshop (see Chapter 7) using process writing develop fluency and confidence in their writing, and using journals extends, reinforces, and supports these skills. Journals help to tie together reading and writing and give students opportunities to construct their own personal meanings.

Basically, journals can be divided into five categories: diaries, response journals, dialogue journals, double-entry journals, and learning logs. Although these forms are similar in many ways, there are significant differences.

- *Diaries* are private records of personal observations, random jottings, or a daily record of thoughts and feelings. These are shared *only* if the student agrees.
- *Response journals* are used by students to keep a record of their personal reactions to, questions about, and reflections on what they read, view, write, or listen to. Response journals are sometimes called reading journals or literature logs. They might include lists of words students want to learn, goals for reading (number of pages to be completed), predictions made before and during reading, notes or comments made during reading, and reactions, thoughts, or feelings recorded after reading. If you just want students to keep track of their independent reading for themselves, you may not read these journals, but if you want them to respond to

Figure 6.1   Page from a Fourth Grader's Response Journal

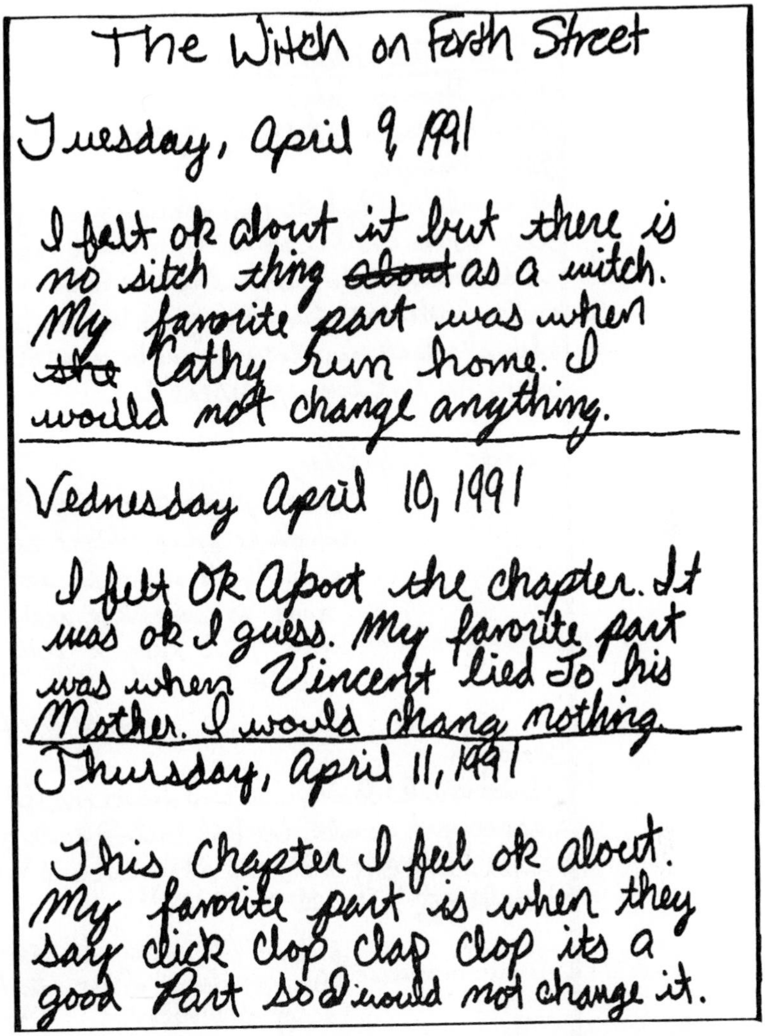

> The Witch on Forth Street
>
> Tuesday, April 9 1991
>
> I felt ok about it but there is no such thing ~~about~~ as a witch. My favorite part was when ~~the~~ Cathy run home. I would not change anything.
>
> _____
>
> Vednusday April 10, 1991
>
> I felt ok apoot the chapter. It was ok I guess. My favorite part was when Vincent lied to his Mother. I would chang nothing.
>
> Thursday, April 11, 1991
>
> This Chapter I feel ok about. My favorite part is when they say click clop clap clop its a good Part so I would not change it.

literature they have read or to pieces they have written, you probably do read them. Figure 6.1 shows a sample page from a fourth grader's response journal.

- *Dialogue journals* have the same basic purpose as the response journals except that the teacher (and sometimes peers) reads and responds in writing to the student's responses. "The major characteristic that distinguishes Dialogue Journals from other forms is the importance given to communications between the student and the teacher" (Tierney, Readence & Dishner,

Figure 6.2   Page from a Dialogue Journal

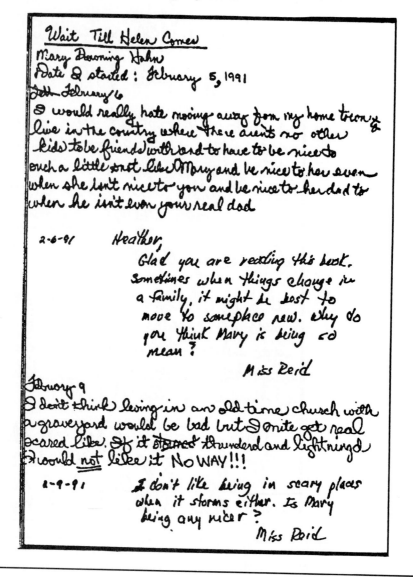

1990, p. 97). In this form of journal, the student may have a dialogue with himself or herself, with peers, and/or with the teacher. The input from others helps the student construct meaning more effectively. Figure 6.2 presents a sample page from a dialogue journal. Notice how the teacher's responses help the student think and construct meaning.

Figure 6.3   Double Entry Journal of a Seventh Grader

May 8
The Summer of the Swans

by Betsy Byars

Predictions

Sara is going to
have a good summer
because swans are
beautifull.

Sara is really bored.
She is not having a
good summer. It is
hard to be a teenager.
Summers are tough.
Sara loves Charlie
even if he is a pain.

Sara and Charlie
are going to do
something good
together.

Sara has been sort
of nice to Charlie.
She is still feeling
sorry for her self.
I think she is
really going to grow
up this summer. Last
summer I was a lot
like Sara.

- *Double-entry journals* have pages that are divided into two parts. On the left-hand two-thirds of the page students make notes, list predictions, and draw diagrams before and during reading. On the right-hand side, they write a response to their reading. If the double-entry journal is also being treated as a dialogue journal, the teacher replies on the right-hand side of the page. These journals have been recommended for use with all students, including at-risk learners (Coley & Hoffman, 1990). Figure 6.3 shows a

Figure 6.4   Sample Entry from a Learning Log, Third Grade

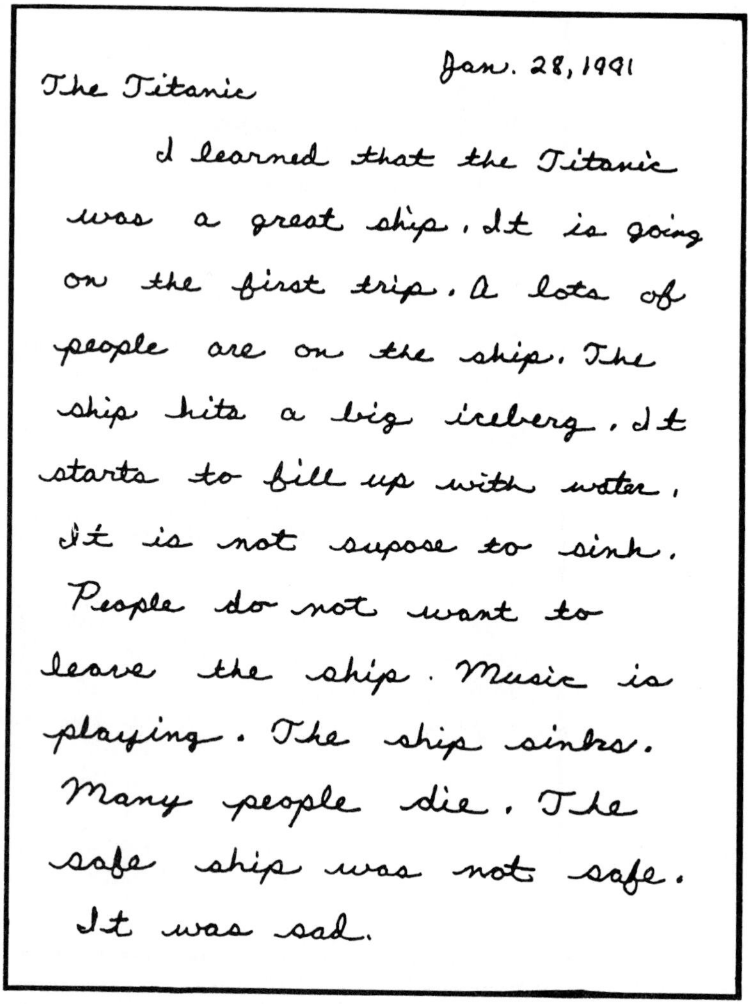

The Titanic   Jan. 28, 1991

    I learned that the Titanic was a great ship. It is going on the first trip. A lots of people are on the ship. The ship hits a big iceberg. It starts to fill up with water. It is not supose to sink. People do not want to leave the ship. Music is playing. The ship sinks. Many people die. The safe ship was not safe. It was sad.

double-entry journal completed by a seventh grader reading *The Summer of the Swans* (Byars, 1970).

- *Learning logs* are daily records of what students have learned (Harste, Short & Burke, 1988; Thompson, 1990). Figure 6.4 shows a sample entry from a third grader's learning log; this is simply a daily account of what this student has learned with little response to the book. Sometimes, however, the learning log may focus on the learning that has taken place

Table 6.2 Types of Journals

Journal Type	Description	Features
Diary	Private records of personal observations and thoughts	Not read by anyone unless student requests
Response journal (literature log or reading journal)	Reactions, questions, and reflections about what has been read	Sometimes a personal record and sometimes read by the teacher
Dialogue journal	A conversation between the student and teacher about what has been read	Read by the teacher and sometimes peers; comments written by the reader
Double-entry journal	A split page where students jot down ideas before and during reading on one side and give reactions after reading on the other side	May or may not be read by the teacher and/or peers
Learning log	A listing of what has been learned	May be treated as a dialogue journal or as a response journal

in a particular content area such as math, science, or social studies. Learning logs may be treated as response journals with no teacher response or as dialogue journals between the teacher and students.

Deciding Which Journal Type to Use

As you can see, there are many similarities between these various types of journals. Table 6.2 summarizes their features. You must decide which of the types you want to use, and you may find that you want to use a combination. The important thing is to know why you are having students keep a journal; is it for

- prompting students to reflect on their personal thoughts and feelings?
- encouraging students to keep a personal record of independent reading?
- encouraging students to respond to literature and/or their writing?
- carrying on a dialogue with students to help them learn to construct meaning?
- having students summarize what has been learned?

Once you have determined your purpose for using journals, you can decide on the type or combination of types that you want to try.

Keep in mind as you begin to make decisions that students do not have to write in their journals every day or after every piece of literature they read. Making such stringent requirements makes journal writing a laborious task and defeats its purpose. At first you may have to nudge some students to write in their journals; however, as they become comfortable with their journals, students will write in them more readily.

Getting Started Using Journals

Once you have decided which type of journal you are going to be using, you are ready to introduce the idea to your class. Journals can be used with students at any grade level, though beginning learners are not expected to write as much or to use their journals in the same ways as older students. The generalized procedures and suggestions given here should be adapted to your students: there are no firm or absolute rules that must be followed.

Begin by making a journal of your own with some entries in it. Show your journal to the students and discuss how all of you will keep journals in which you will write about what you have read. If you plan to read and respond to your students' journals, you should give them the same opportunity to read and respond to yours. It is important for you to model this for students as well as experience what they are going through.

Explain the idea of journal writing to your class. Tell students that the purpose of journal writing is to encourage them all to think about what they are reading and to share their thoughts. Point out that this is a way for you to talk to each of them and for them to talk to you.

Talk with students about what types of entries they might make in their journals. Tell them that they may write about what they have read, draw about it, make notes indicating that they have shared their book in some way with another person, or perhaps decide on some idea of their own. The main thing is that they respond in some way to their reading. Stress that there is no right or wrong way to respond. Obviously, responses will vary in quality, but you will help students improve through the responses that you make to their writing. Urge students to suggest how they might respond to a piece of literature, such as by telling about a character, writing about what they would have done in that situation, constructing a diorama, or relating events to their own lives.

Have students work in cooperative groups to write some journal entries. Cooperative groups support students as they begin journal writing without necessitating the use of models or samples. When I give samples of journal writing, students tend to copy the samples and be hampered by them. However, collaborative writing lets students see that they can create their own types of responses. Encourage students to share their responses with the class.

Talk with students about the format of their journals and how often they should write in them.   Give them a simple format (or several formats) for recording such information as the date of entry, book title, author, and copyright. Then have them write whatever they want to say. If you give students some type of formula to follow or a specific outline, you will inhibit their writing. Hansen (1987) writes about a teacher who used a mimeographed form with specific elements to be covered for each entry during her first year of journal writing. The year was not successful. When the teacher dropped the form, she got much better responses from her students and became more excited about journal writing with them. If you give students several formats from which to choose, you will want to evaluate with them the one they selected. Make modifications, if needed.

If students' journal entries are going to be read by others, encourage them to write so that others can read what they have written. However, do not focus on correct spelling yet. During the writing workshop (see Chapter 7) they will be learning about the common courtesy of writing and spelling to communicate with others. Since some journal entries are just personal notes, words, or predictions, accuracy is not as important as meaning. Moreover, if you tell students that their journal entries are not going to be evaluated for mechanics and spelling, you will begin to free them from some of the hang-ups that might discourage writing.

Atwell (1987) tells how she uses a letter to introduce journal writing to her middle-school students. A copy of a similar letter used by a third-grade teacher is presented in Figure 6.5. This idea could be adapted for use with students at any grade level.

Use a response chart or some other device to prompt and support students who need it.   Response charts were used in the literacy lessons of Chapters 2, 3, and 4 and will be discussed in detail on pages 365–366. These charts are designed to help students think of how to respond to their reading.

Plan with students a system for using and storing journals.   Choose a place for storing the journals alphabetically, such as in boxes, a file drawer, or a crate. Atwell (1987) suggests having students write their names on the fronts of their journals and then arranging them alphabetically. They can then be numbered for easy return to the storage area.

During the initial stages of journal writing, evaluate with students how the procedure is progressing.   Whenever students try something new or different, there are apt to be some details that need to be worked out. Therefore, it is a

Figure 6.5   Letter for Introducing Journals to Third Graders

Michael D. Robinson   Third Grade Teacher   ☺

Dear Girls and Boys,   August, 1990

This year you will be using your Reading Journal to write me letters about the books you are reading. I will write letters back to you as I read your letters. This will be one of the ways we talk about your books. I will also tell you about the books I am reading.

As you write each letter, tell me about your book — how you feel about it, what you like and don't like, what it makes you think about, your favorite parts, etc.... Draw pictures if you want to. I may even draw some pictures for you!

These letters will help you and me decide how you are doing with your reading and writing. We will discuss them during conferences. Here are some things for you to remember:

- date all your letters
- be sure to give the title <u>and</u> author
- write at <u>least</u> two letters each week
- tape this letter in the front of your journal

I'm excited about getting your letters. We'll learn a lot about each other.

Happy Reading,
Mr. Robinson

good idea to take time periodically to talk about how things are going and list ways to improve them.

For more detailed discussions about journal use, see "For Additional Reading" at the conclusion of this chapter.

What to Expect When Students Begin to Use Journals

Students just beginning to use journals may exhibit a number of different behaviors, all of which are normal. Some will show none of these behaviors, and others will exhibit many of them. You can be comfortable in knowing, however, that they will all fade away with continued practice and support from you.

One likely response is "I don't know what to do." These students are probably insecure with their own literacy and are having difficulty constructing meaning. Some who say this may just not be comfortable with the process but will become more so as they gain experience. They may also respond this way if they have had many experiences in which a right or wrong answer was expected. Writing journal responses may be totally new for students; in a sense they are redefining reading for themselves because they are learning that there are multiple interpretations of a text. For students who exhibit these behaviors, make some suggestions for possible responses. (See the discussion of response charts, pages 365–366.)

Some students will be very concerned about accuracy in spelling and usage. These are likely to be those who are uncertain about the language and who may have been in environments where correctness was stressed. Simply keep reassuring them that you are not concerned about correctness in their journals: you are only concerned about their thinking and their reactions.

Another behavior is that of simply retelling what one has read (recall page 347). This is a normal occurrence. Students will progress beyond retelling as they gain more experience in responding, and your responses in their journals should consist, in part, of questions that focus their attention beyond this point. For example, you might write, "How would you have reacted in this situation?" or "What lesson do you think we can learn from this book?"

Some teachers encourage students to retell or summarize as *one way* to respond to literature. This is an effective way to help children construct meaning (Gambrell, Pfeiffer & Wilson, 1985; Marshall, 1983; Morrow, 1985, 1989), and such responses are also easy for teachers to evaluate. Retellings and evaluation of responses will be discussed more in Chapter 10.

Some students will immediately become comfortable with a particular mode of response and "latch onto it," using it again and again. In these situations, your responses are important in moving this student forward. A simple "Have you ever thought about the characters [or other suggestions] in the stories you are reading?" will help them think of alternatives.

Finally, if you are using dialogue journals, some students may be really anxious about what you are going to write in their journals and what you are going to think of their ideas. In these instances, you need to respond with very positive, upbeat comments that will allay these fears.

Journals are an excellent tool to use with all of your students (Hayes & Bayruth, 1985; Peyton & Seyoum, 1989; Sutton, 1989). As Barone (1990) has noted, even young children begin responding by focusing on explicit story elements, but soon they become more interpretive, which indicates that they are working through the text they are reading, focusing on more than literal comprehension, and understanding the story more completely.

Responding to Students' Journals

In a response-centered classroom, both the students and the teacher are responsible for responding (Hansen, 1987). The students respond to their reading and writing and to each other's journals, including the teacher's. The teacher, in turn, responds to the students' journals, especially when dialogue journals are being used.

Teachers who use journals or want to use journals often raise two major questions: (1) "When do I find time to read all the journals?" and (2) "What exactly do I write in response to students' journal entries?" Both are fair questions and deserve serious consideration.

Time to Read Journals.   You do not have to read every journal entry that students make, since many entries are completely private, as with diaries. Response journals are often an individual record for the students' own use and thus require no reading or responding by the teacher. Even when students are using journals that require you to respond, you do not have to do it every day for every entry. Dialogue journals require the most consistent form of response by the teacher because this is a major means of "talking" *with* students and helping them learn.

Finding the time to read journals is not nearly as difficult as it seems at first. Teachers often think that they are going to have to read all the journals plus grade all the papers they normally have. But journals replace many of the papers that have been used to try to engage students in learning and provide a much more meaningful learning task. One fourth-grade teacher said, "I read some of my students' journals during conference period if there is no one ready to talk with me. If there are any journals that I need to see on any day and haven't, I read them right after school. I rarely carry any of them home."

Journals may be read at various times during the day. If you have conferences with your students, you can read some of their journals when you have no appointments. Some teachers use some of silent reading time to read students' journals. Others find that they like to read journals just before or right after school. However you decide to proceed, your plan must fit your teaching style and needs. Again, there is no one best way or best time to read journals; you will find that it becomes a very natural thing to do.

How to Write Responses.   When you write responses in students' journals, keep in mind that you want to encourage students, guide them, refocus their responses, and make helpful suggestions.

Encouragement is your number one goal. You want to encourage students to continue to read and think about what they are reading, as well as to feel good about themselves and what they are writing in their journals. Here are some examples of encouraging types of responses:

Dear Jeri,

You are doing a very good job telling about the characters in *Now One Foot, Now the Other*. Which character do you think is most important in this story? Why? I'm looking forward to your next entry.

Mr. C

Source: Now One Foot, Now the Other, de Paola (1980).

Dear Sam,

The way you are retelling this story, I can tell that you are enjoying it !! Have you ever had an adventure like April's? If you have, why don't you compare your adventure to hers. Keep going! I can't wait to see what you think later in this book.

Mr. C

Source: The Egypt Game, Snyder (1976).

Notice that each of these responses provides a different type of encouragement in different situations. Even though you will do more than encourage with your comments, *encouragement is critical.*

Sometimes, as you are reading a student's journal, you will find that more *guidance* is needed in helping the student see important points or the big message that an author is trying to deliver. This may happen frequently when you are having the entire class read the same book. For example, suppose your third graders are all reading *Fly Away Home* (Bunting, 1991) and you notice that some students are not understanding why it is important for the father and little boy not to be noticed in the airport. (This is a story about a homeless father and son who make their home in a large airport, moving from terminal to terminal to keep from getting caught.) One student wrote:

> The boy in this story did not talk to people. He was not a friend.

The teacher might respond:

> I thought the little boy really wanted to be friends. He was friends with Mrs. Medina and her family. He just couldn't be friends with everyone in the airport. Look back through the book and see if you can find places that show why he can't be friends with everyone.

At other times, students will just need to be *refocused* in their journals and in their reading. If a student always responds by drawing a picture and labeling it "My Favorite Part," you might ask the student to try a different response. For example:

Your pictures of favorite parts are great. For your next entry, draw three pictures that show the three main events in the next chapter. Write a sentence or two about each picture.

This type of response shows how instruction and the student's growth work together. It helps the student use drawing but begins to move toward looking at important events in the story. Refocusing might also be needed when students get so caught up in minute story details that they miss the real message or story line.

At other times, your responses may need to include various other kinds of *suggestions*—for other books to read, responses to try, or things to consider or think about as reading continues. Your response in the journals and the students' responses to you are a part of the running dialogue that lets you know how they are growing and gives you another way to guide them individually. Thus the journal is both a teaching tool and a diagnostic tool. (See Chapter 10 on using students' responses for assessment.)

You may also want to have students read and respond to each other's journals so that they will learn from each other. In "buddy journals" (Bromley, 1989), two students write back and forth to each other. At first, take time to model appropriate responses, showing that the focus should not be on rightness or wrongness but rather on ideas and feelings. It is best to delay this type of journal until after students have used dialogue journals with the teacher.

Response Charts

As students read a variety of literature, you may find that they need support in learning how to respond. In such cases you can use response charts, which are simply charts with suggestions on how to respond to a given piece of literature. These devices were used in the lessons presented at the conclusion of Chapters 2, 3, and 4. Figure 6.6 presents a response chart from a sixth-grade classroom. You will notice that it is much more complex than those presented earlier. The teacher used it to get students back into journal writing at the beginning of the year after the summer break.

Since the response to literature is personal, the goal of response activities is to get students to construct meaning by interacting with the text. It is through this interaction, or transaction, that students become better comprehenders.

Figure 6.6   Sample Response Chart from a Sixth-Grade Classroom

Response Suggestions

Before reading

- List the title and author of the book in your journal. Give the date you started the book.

During reading

- Note words of interest in your journal.
- Think about the story you are reading. Does it make sense? Write any questions you have in your journal.

After reading (select one or more)

- Write a short summary of the story.
- Select your favorite character and describe his or her role in the story.
- Meet with a friend to talk about the story.
- *Other*—You decide what you would like to do.

There are several times when response charts should be useful. First, they accustom students to the concept of responding. By giving students suggestions, you will be "priming" their thinking and helping them learn how to select their own modes of response. Beginning learners or those experiencing difficulty in learning often need this type of support.

Another time for using response charts is when you observe that students are not clearly understanding what they have read or are missing the entire point that an author is trying to make. You can make this judgment by reading students' written responses or listening to or observing their oral or other creative responses. For example, suppose you have a group of fifth graders who have just read *The Scarebird* (Fleischman, 1987), and several students have decided to give a skit based on the book. If they portray Lonesome John as crazy instead of just lonely, you can tell they have missed the point and need support in identifying the story's problems. Therefore, you might model (see Chapter 8) how you would identify the problem in this story. For the next few stories that students read, you might suggest one or two ways for them to respond that would focus their attention more directly on identifying story problems, such as by constructing a group story map or writing a paragraph describing the story problem.

Constructing Response Charts

Response charts are not necessary for every piece of literature that students read. *Ultimately, you want students to be able to decide on their own modes of response*. However, even the best readers in a class still need some response chart support from time to time. One way to meet the individual needs of your students is by directing them to different types of response activities and still allowing choices. Therefore, to construct effective response charts you need a variety of ideas about how students might respond to literature. In all cases, the activities on a response chart should be things students would normally do after reading a book; in other words, they should be "authentic activities."

When constructing response charts, you need to consider two factors: the type of text being read and the needs of your students. Sometimes the same response activity might work for both narrative and expository texts, but in most instances it will not. Students' needs will range from having to focus on the basic ideas in the text to having to become more inferential and evaluative in their responses. In the first case a structured response such as a story map might be helpful, and in the second case students could perhaps think about and be ready to discuss why, for instance, the main character behaved as he or she did.

All response charts should contain one response option that says, "Other— You decide how you want to respond." This is for students who don't need support to come up with their own responses. When students effectively use the "other" option, it's a good sign that they no longer need response charts.

The number of options to include on a response chart should be kept small: usually three to five. For example, a new response chart might have five options, whereas one that you are adding to regularly might only get three new response options at once.

Tables 6.3 and 6.4 list response options that should be helpful in constructing your own response charts for narrative and expository texts. They were developed from a variety of sources, including the works of Spritzer (1988) and Parsons (1990) and the ideas that I and other teachers have found to be effective. As you work with your students, you will develop other options that are appropriate for them.

Sometimes the response chart may include questions that cue students to respond in different ways. Parsons (1990) suggests that some students really need these aids to get them started, and he recommends the following questions for narrative texts:

- What surprised you about the section you read today? How does this change affect what might happen next in the story?
- What startling, unusual, or effective words, phrases, expressions, or images did you come across in your reading today that you would like to have explained or clarified? Which ones would you like to use in your own writing?
- How much do you personally agree or disagree with the way various characters think and act and the kinds of beliefs and values they hold? Where do you differ and why?

Table 6.3   Response Options for Narrative Texts

Response Option	*Description*
Story mapping	Make a story map following the pattern presented earlier in this text.
Rewriting	Rewrite a part of the story illustrating how you would have solved the problem.
Retelling	Retell the story to a friend or small group of friends.
Illustrating	Illustrate your favorite part of important scenes from the story. Write a sentence or two about each illustration.
Sharing	Read your favorite part to a friend or group of friends. Be ready to tell why this is your favorite part. OR read your book to students in a grade lower than yours.
Puppetry	Use puppets to share your story with other classmates or students in another class.
Posters	Make a poster to sell other students in your class on reading this book. Remember to make it exciting so they will want to buy it.
Other books by the author	Select another book by this author. Read and compare the two stories.
Book talk	Give a short (3–5 minutes) book talk focusing on what you feel is most exciting about your book.
Dress-up	Dress like a character from your book and act out a favorite scene for your class.
Play	Work with other students who have read the book to present a play or a reader's theater presentation.
Topical study	Use the topic of your story as the basis for an informational study. (For example, if a child is reading the book *Nine-in-One Grr! Grr!* [Xiong/Spagnoli, 1989], he or she might do a study about the Hmong people of Laos.)
Mobile	Make a mobile of important characters or events in the story.
Movie	Work with others who have read the book to make a movie using a video camera. Have a movie party to share your work with others.

- What issues in this story are similar to real-life issues that you've thought about or had some kind of experience with? How has the story clarified or confused or changed your views on any of these issues?

Figure 6.7 presents a sample response chart with cuing questions.

For expository texts, cuing questions also need to be open-ended. Some *suggested* questions for expository texts are as follows:

- After reading this far in this text, what do you think you will learn about next?

Table 6.4   Response Options for Expository Texts

Response Option	*Description*
Graphic presentation	Share the important ideas you have learned through some type of graphic device such as a chart, timeline, diagram, or graphic organizer.
Speech	Give a persuasive talk using the information you have gained on the topic of your book.
Display	Create a display related to the book you read.
Newspaper article	Write a newspaper article expressing your point of view about the book.
Book	Use the information from the book you read to make a book of your own on the topic. Include text, charts, illustrations, and diagrams if appropriate.
Debate	Have a debate with others who have read the book. Each group debating must take a different point of view.
Bibliography	Read other books on the same topic and compile an annotated bibliography to share with others.
Written report	Write a report about your book focusing on what you learned and how it might be helpful in the world.
Map	Make a map to show important information you have learned. Focus on products, cities, recreation areas, and so forth.
Experiment	Use what you have learned to conduct an experiment. Write your results.
Newsreel	Use a video camera to make a newsreel using the information you and others have gained from their books. Write a script including facts and opinions.

- How would you feel if you were the scientist who made the discovery you just read about? Why?
- How do you feel the information in this text will be helpful in your life?
- How does the information you have just learned compare to what you already know about this topic?

Figure 6.7   Response Chart Using Cuing Questions

Responding to Independent Reading

Directions

As you read, you think about what's happening in your book in many different ways. Sometimes, questions come to your mind about some of the characters and how they are behaving. At other times, you might be impressed by the way someone or something was described. You might even be reminded of something similar that happened to you or to someone you know.

After reading independently today, try to describe the kinds of impressions and/ or questions that your reading has inspired. Some people have found the following kinds of questions useful in guiding their responses. They are only suggestions. Please respond to your reading as you see fit.

- After reading this far, what more do you hope to learn about what these characters plan to do, what they think, feel, and believe, or what happens to them?
- As you think ahead to your next day's reading, what possible directions might the story take? How do you hope the story will unfold?
- If the setting and characters were changed to reflect your own neighborhood and friends and acquaintances, how would the events of the story have to change and why would that be so?
- Do you wish that your own life or the people you know were more like the ones in the story you're reading? In what ways would you like the real world to be more like the world of your book?

Source: Reprinted with permission from *Response Journals* by Les Parsons, p. 14. Copyright © Pembroke Publishers, 528 Hood Road, Markham, Ontario L3R 3K9 Canada, (416) 477-0650. Available in the U.S. from Heinemann Educational Books.

You will find that you will develop your own bank of questions as you work with your students.

Two other forms of response can also be included on your response charts: Literature Circles and Readers Theater. These will be discussed in the next two sections of this chapter.

Literature Circles

Another very useful procedure for promoting responses to literature is the literature circle (Harste et al., 1988). These sometimes are called literature groups (Calkins, 1986; Weaver, 1990) or literature discussion groups or circles. Regardless of the name(s) one uses to designate this procedure, they all have a common purpose—to get students to read and respond to literature. Having students discuss what they have read is critical to developing their ability to construct meaning.

In literature circles, children who have read the same book get together to discuss it and react to it. Initially, the teacher may start the discussion, but as students learn to function in the literature circle, they often take over this role.

The procedures for using literature circles have been described in detail by Harste et al. (1988). The guidelines given here are based on their ideas and my own experiences of working with children and teachers.

Guidelines for Using Literature Circles

Selecting Literature.   You will need multiple copies of whatever students will read. Sometimes you want everyone to read the same book or selection, and at other times you may encourage students to select from among three or four books. If several students have read or are reading the same book or selection as a part of their independent reading, these students may form a literature circle of their own.

Organizing Literature Circles.   If everyone in the class is reading the same book, establish how many circles you need to have four or five members in each and then have students sign up for one of the groups. Allowing students to select the discussion group they want to join gives them some control over their own learning. Many times students will sign up to be with their friends; there is nothing wrong with this. If behavior problems arise, you may have to adjust the groups, but this is usually not necessary.

If you are having the class select their reading from several different books, you can give a bit of information about each as a teaser to spark students' interest and to help them make their selection. Then list the titles on a chart or the chalkboard and have students sign up for the book they want to read. If one book has more than four or five students who want to read it, form several circles for the same book.

The entire class need not be in literature circles at the same time. Those not involved may be doing independent reading or writing or other reading and writing activities.

Starting the Circles.   Students begin by reading. If they are reading a short book or selection, they should read the entire book before coming to the circle. If they are reading a longer book, one with several chapters, they can read chapter by chapter and meet in their literature circle at the conclusion of each chapter and at the end of the book. As the circle meets to discuss each chapter, the groups may decide on reading goals to be completed before the next meeting and should record these in their journals.

Sometimes literature discussion groups may divide into several smaller groups according to interests and/or abilities. When this occurs, the groups should always be encouraged to return to the original literature circle for a culminating discussion and sharing or a culminating activity.

Figure 6.8   Literature Circle Discussion Chart

Literature Circle Discussions

1. Begin by telling the title and author of your book.
2. Talk about what you read.

   • What was your favorite part? Why?
   • How does this book relate to your life?

3. Make a list of things to discuss at your next meeting.

If you are working with beginning readers or students having problems reading, you can read aloud the book to that literature circle. So that students do not feel any stigma to being a part of the read-aloud group, you can announce before students sign up for their circles that a certain book will be read aloud and then invite all students to be part of this circle. Most will want to be in the listening circle from time to time. You can also provide a tape of the book to be placed in the listening center for later use.

Promoting Discussions.   Each literature circle meeting will usually last from 10 to 20 minutes, depending on the book or selection being discussed and the students' experience in working in circles. Since the primary focus of the discussion is to bring the students and literature together and to allow students to construct their own meanings in an authentic way, the discussion must be open-ended.

Many teachers find that using a literature circle discussion chart like the one shown in Figure 6.8 helps get the groups started and keeps the discussion moving. Present the chart to students and explain it. As they become more comfortable, you will find that they will start their own discussions, using the chart as a prompt. You will need to change the chart from time to time, and you can use some of the open-ended questions for cuing presented on pages 368 and 369. After students have learned to work in circles, discontinue the use of charts.

As each group carries out its discussion, move from circle to circle to monitor what is taking place. In many cases, you will want to become a member of the group and add to or stimulate the discussion with questions. For example, suppose a literature circle is discussing *Regina's Big Mistake* (Moss, 1990) and you notice that the discussion seems to be lagging. You might join the group by saying, "You know, when I was in school, I often felt just like Regina. I was afraid of making mistakes. What problems like that have you had in school?" In this way, you are becoming a part of the group by modeling and prompting other things to think about.

In the initial stages of using literature circles, you will need to model and demonstrate good questioning and discussion behaviors. One way is by modeling for the entire class using a small group. Then discuss with the class what happened and any problems they might see. You may also want to create a discussion guidelines chart like the one presented in Chapter 3 to help students carry out their discussions.

Concluding Literature Circles.   When students have completed a book, they can then decide whether they want to share it with the entire class or respond to it some other way. *It is neither necessary nor advisable for students always to complete additional activities.* The literature circle discussions will be sufficient response for most students. *Only when they are really excited about a book should they be encouraged to respond further.*

Tips on Using Literature Circles

There is no one correct way to use literature circles; they are a flexible tool and should be used accordingly. When you are first beginning, proceed slowly and carefully. There are two ways that teachers have found very successful in moving themselves and their classes into literature circle work.

One teacher starts her class by inviting students to help select a book for the entire class. She then introduces and explains the concept of literature circles. After the circles are established, the class reads the book (or first chapter in a longer book) and the teacher presents a literature circle discussion chart like the one shown earlier in Figure 6.8 (page 372). She poses one open-ended question to get all the groups started. As they work, she moves from circle to circle to see what is taking place, joining groups as needed. She repeats this pattern several times using different books until she is comfortable that her students understand literature circles and are working effectively in them. Then she expands to two or more books, letting the children choose which books they want to read.

A second procedure for getting literature circles started is to use a small group and follow the same basic procedure as described above. When one circle is working smoothly, you can add a second and then a third until all students are comfortable.

Again, regardless of the pattern you select, you will want to move slowly. When students have not had the experiences of such open discussions and have been accustomed to giving the teacher the "correct answer," they are often reluctant to talk. You may need to model open discussions several times before students are able to accept the idea that there are no absolute or correct answers.

As you and your students become more comfortable with literature circles, you will find that there are a variety of ways to organize them. For example, you may use them with the whole class reading different books from the same genre (fairy tales or mysteries), in which case you should focus on discussing and comparing a genre, not a book. For further reading on literature circles, see Harste et al. (1988) under "For Additional Reading."

Readers Theater

The Readers Theater is a form of response in which children turn a story into a play.

> *Readers Theatre is an interpretive reading activity for all children in the classroom. Readers bring characters to life through their voices and gestures. Listeners are captivated by the vitalized stories and complete the activity by imagining the details of a scene or action. . . . Readers Theatre becomes an integrated language event centering upon oral interpretation of literature. The children adapt and present the material of their choice. A story, a poem, a scene from a play, even a song lyric, provide the ingredients for the script. As a thinking, reading, writing, speaking, and listening experience, Readers Theatre makes a unique contribution to our language arts curriculum. (Sloyer, 1982, p. 3)*

With this form of response, *all* children are able to take part in the creative interpretation of a story. Even second-language or at-risk learners can succeed in this activity (Werthemer, 1974).

The following procedures for using the readers theater have been developed from numerous sources and my own experiences of working with children and teachers (Coger & White, 1982; Harste, Short & Burke, 1988; Sloyer, 1982).

Select the Literature.   As you begin using the readers theater, you will need to help students select the literature. The stories must have lots of dialogue, strong story lines, suspense, humor, or surprise. Discuss with students the characteristics of a good piece to use.

Read or Reread the Literature.   After reading, students should discuss the story, focusing on the characters, setting, problem, action, and outcome. Many teachers have students develop a story map (see Chapters 2 and 3). This will help students know what needs to be included in the readers theater script and what is not essential.

Develop a Script.   A good way to do this is through shared writing; use a chart or an overhead projector and develop the script with students. This is also a good place to refer students to the story map. Talk about the types of things that can be left out, such as "said _____" and lengthy descriptions that are not essential to the story. Generate a list of story characters and help students see how to identify the parts that must be read by a narrator. Figure 6.9 shows a partial script developed by some second graders and their teacher. Eventually, children can do this on their own.

It is possible to purchase readers theater scripts for many pieces of literature (write to Readers Theatre Script Service, P.O. Box 178333, San Diego, CA 92117). However, one of the values of using this activity comes in developing the script. Therefore, even if you decide to purchase some scripts,

Figure 6.9 Partial Readers Theater Script for *Tye May and the Magic Brush* (Bang, 1981) Developed by Second Graders and Their Teacher

---

TYE MAY AND THE MAGIC BRUSH

NARRATOR: Many years ago a cruel and greedy emperor ruled over China. His people were very poor. One of the poorest was Tye May. Her mother and father were dead and she lived alone. Every day she gathered firewood and cut reeds to sell in the marketplace. One day Tye May passed the school and saw the teacher painting. She knew right then what she wanted to do.

TYE MAY: "Please, sir, I would like to learn how to paint, but I have no money to buy a brush. Would you lend me one?"

TEACHER: (Angry) "Beggar girls don't paint. Get out of here!"

NARRATOR: But Tye May did not give up. She had an iron will. She drew pictures in the dirt when she collected wood. Her pictures looked real but she still didn't have a brush. One night when she was very tired she fell into a deep sleep.

WOMAN: "This is a magic brush. Use it carefully."

TYE MAY: "Thank you! Thank you!"

NARRATOR: The woman was gone and Tye May woke up.

---

you should also have students develop some of their own in order to give them the experience of translating a story into a script. You will need multiple copies of the script.

Discuss Props. Only a few simple props are to be used in a readers theater presentation. These might include chairs, a stool, a yardstick for a sword, paper faces, hats, and so forth. There is no scenery. Talk with students to identify the props to be used.

Prepare and Rehearse for the Presentation. Select students to be the characters in the presentation. If you are working with the whole class, you might want to divide the class into groups so that everyone can participate in this first production; each group could give its own performance of the same program.

Discuss with students how and where to stand and make hand, body, or facial gestures to convey parts of the story to their audience. Give students time to rehearse their program.

Present the Program. When students have had ample time to rehearse, have them perform for the class. After all performances are completed, discuss with the students what was successful and what could be improved in future productions. Focus on all aspects, from selecting the literature to giving the program.

There is no one right way to use the readers theater in your class. Feel free to experiment, following your own ideas and those of your students.

Reading Conferences

Conferences are occasions when two or more people have a discussion for a given purpose. In the literacy-centered classroom, conferences may take place between students or between the teacher and students.

Reading conferences, as discussed here, are when the teacher and student(s) engage in a conversation about a book or books. The concept of a reading conference in the classroom is not new; nearly thirty years ago Veatch (1966/1978) recommended their use with individualized reading. In the literacy program, conferences play an important role in all aspects of literacy learning (Calkins, 1986; Graves, 1983; Graves, 1991). Graves (1991) maintains that "the conference—the listening stance—is the heart of good teaching" (p. 89).

Conferences may be formal, planned events or informal ones that take place any number of times during the day—in the hallway, in the lunchroom, on the playground, or during any part of the daily classroom routine. Some educators refer to informal conferences as miniconferences or on-the-spot conferences (Tompkins & Hoskisson, 1991). These conferences are really nothing more than times when you stop to chat and listen carefully to what students are saying; good teachers do this all the time.

During informal miniconferences you might ask children such questions as "What are you reading?" "How do you like this book?" and "Tell me about what you've been reading lately." For example, a fourth-grade teacher stopped by the desk of one student:

Teacher: What have you been reading lately?

Student: I'm still reading the same book I got last week.

Teacher: How do you like it?

Student: I don't.

Teacher: Why don't you stop reading this book and select another one?

Student: I don't know.

Teacher: Don't you like dinosaurs?

Student: Yes!

Teacher: I saw a great dinosaur book in the reading center this morning. You'll love it! It's called *Tyrannosaurus Was a Beast* (Prelutsky, 1988). Try that one.

In this brief encounter, the teacher was able to determine that his student was bogged down with a book he didn't like and then direct him to an area of interest that she knew was his. Even though informal conferences may last only a minute or two, they yield valuable information about how students are doing and enable the teacher to provide on-the-spot support.

After this brief encounter, the teacher wrote a note about this miniconference on the student's page in her notebook. If it is not always possible to go immediately to her desk, she relies on memory and makes notes later. However, it is not always necessary to make notes about a miniconference. The one presented here just happened to be one where the teacher gathered some valuable information about the student that she felt needed to be recorded. Sometimes teachers carry adhesive notes or labels that they write on and date; later they stick them on the students' pages in their notebook.

Purposes of Formal Reading Conferences

Formal reading conferences may have several different purposes. First, they may be held for *sharing and discussing a book*. The teacher and student(s) talk about a book that is being read or has been completed, and the student(s) may read favorite parts. The teacher might share thoughts or feelings about the book or make suggestions for other books the student(s) might want to consider. If the students are keeping journals, responses might be shared and discussed or questions about the book or words of concern to the students might be reviewed.

A second purpose for the reading conference may be to *provide a minilesson on a particular strategy or skill* that seems to be causing the student(s) difficulty, perhaps a problem with phonics, structural analysis, or comprehension. During this conference, the teacher would use the minilesson concept and model the particular strategy or skill needed. (See Chapters 2 and 8 on minilessons and modeling.)

Finally, reading conferences may be held to *assess students' progress*. By having students share their responses to a piece of literature, the teacher can tell how well they are able to comprehend or construct meaning. Oral reading

Figure 6.10   Conference Sign-up Chart

READING CONFERENCES

	Student Requested	Teacher Requested
Monday	Leo Susan Lisa Joan Jeff	
Wednesday	Terri Frank Joey Sid	Tim mike
Friday		Sara Mary Anne Bill

gives clues to the students' decoding abilities, and written responses in journals provide evidence about spelling, grammar and usage, and comprehension.

One conference might have several purposes. For example, students might be sharing a book at the same time that the teacher is assessing progress. It is not necessary to hold separate conferences for each purpose.

Scheduling Conferences

Reading conferences seldom last more than 5 to 10 minutes. It is best to keep conferences as short as possible and focused on your purpose.

Students should sign up for their conferences on a sign-up sheet or a section of the chalkboard. (Sometimes you will also request to see a student.) Figure 6.10 shows a conference sign-up chart used by a second-grade teacher. Notice that on Friday no one requested a conference, so the teacher had extra time to meet with those she has not seen recently. A good rule of thumb is to

Figure 6.11   Chart Showing Students What to Do While the Teacher Is in Conference

THINGS TO DO DURING
CONFERENCES

- Read your book or selection
- Write in your journal
- Work on your writing project
- Meet with a Literature Circle
- OTHER– You decide on something
        worthwhile to do
- Work in the Listening Center
- Prepare for your conference

hold conferences with students at least once a week for first, second, and third grades and once every other week for fourth grade and above. However, students' needs should be the major determining factor in deciding frequency of conferences.

Each teacher must work out the best time during the daily schedule to hold conferences. Some prefer to schedule a few each day, and others schedule on designated days such as Monday, Wednesday, and Friday.

Preparing for Conferences

To ensure successful conferences, you must be certain that both you and the students are prepared and understand how and why conferences take place. The best way to do this is to role-play and model a conference period so that students see what happens and know how it occurs.

When teachers are first beginning to use conferences, they are often concerned about what the "rest of the class" does while one or two children are in conference. This can be solved very easily by using a chart like the one shown in Figure 6.11 that lists options students have during the conference

Figure 6.12   Chart for Helping Students Prepare for a Conference

BEFORE YOUR READING CONFERENCE

1.   Have your book.

2.   Be sure your journal is up to date.

3.   Make a list of things you want to discuss. Put them in your journal.

period. Once students become comfortable with conference times, a chart is usually not needed.

Students also have to prepare themselves for the conference. Figure 6.12 shows a conference chart that many teachers find helpful in directing students in this process. After a week or so of conferencing, *you and the class* should evaluate how things are going and make adjustments as needed.

Finally, you must prepare yourself for the conferences. You will need some type of loose-leaf notebook with a section for each student. On the first page write the student's name, age, and grade, and also list the student's interests and any pertinent information about his or her reading and writing strengths. One of these pages might look like Figure 6.13. Following the opening page, you will need several blank pages on which to record your observations and comments from the conference and any goals you and the student agree upon to be accomplished before the next conference. Keep the page simple, like that shown in Figure 6.14.

Have some ideas about questions or statements you might use to prompt students to discuss the book they are reading (you can consult the lists of open-ended questions presented earlier, pages 368–369). In addition, Veatch

Figure 6.13   Partial Teacher's Notebook Page for Each Student

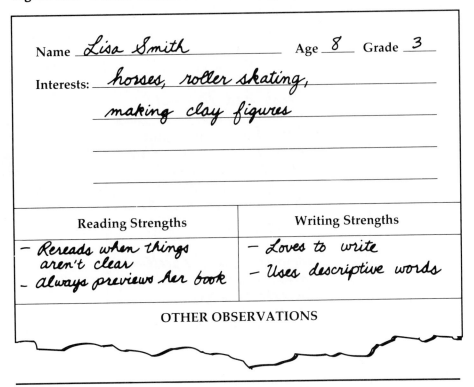

Name *Lisa Smith*   Age *8* Grade *3*

Interests: *horses, roller skating,*
making clay figures

Reading Strengths	Writing Strengths
– *Rereads when things aren't clear* – *always previews her book*	– *Loves to write* – *Uses descriptive words*

OTHER OBSERVATIONS

(1966/1978) suggests that individual conferences should explore four areas with students—personal involvement of the child with the book, ability to read and understand, sheer mechanical reading ability, and oral reading. As Veatch (1966/1978) said many years ago, there are hundreds of questions that can be asked under each of these areas. Here are some of her samples:

1. Area of Personal Involvement

     Teacher: *Why did you choose this story? Do you know anyone else in this class that would like it also?*

     Why do you think you are more interested in this kind of story than others in this class?

     Would you like to be this character? Why?

2. Area of Critical Reading or General Comprehension

     Teacher: *What kind of a story is this? Real?*

     or—

     Could this story have happened? Why? Or why not?

     Tell me the story rapidly.

Figure 6.14   Sample Conference Page from Notebook

Date	Comments	Goals for Next Conference
9/7	Terri had finished reading *Jam*. She loved the story and said her uncle was like Mr. Castle. She thought it was OK for dads to stay home. No problems with vocabulary or comprehension. Excellent oral reading. Needs to select more challenging book.	1. Select a more challenging book. 2. Use different responses in journal other than drawing.

If this character did so and so, would you think he would get in trouble? At the time this story was supposed to have happened, what was going on in our country that was very important?

3. Area of Mechanical Skills

   Teacher: *What words did you have trouble with?*
   or
   Here are two words that look very much alike. Tell me how you know the difference.
   or
   Let me point to several words in your story. Tell me what they are and what they mean.

4. Area of Oral Reading

   Teacher: *Which part of the book have you chosen to read aloud to me?*
   Remember to read so well that you will have people in the rest of the room stopping what they are doing to listen.

Make your voice go up and down.
Make your voice spooky, or scary, or sad, or mean, or whatever the story calls for. (p. 69)

Many of the ideas discussed in Chapter 10 on assessment can easily be incorporated into conference sessions.

Conducting Conferences

During reading conferences, you will be talking with students about books they have selected to read independently or have chosen for instructional purposes. Conferences may also be held for books that you have assigned for the whole class to read, but these are usually dealt with through literature circles or whole-class discussions.

The conference time with each student should be a relaxed, pleasant experience. You can just let the conference evolve naturally, but it may also be a good idea to have a plan in mind. Here is *one* possible sequence for a conference:

- What would you like to talk about today?
- Tell me about your book.
- What have you written in your journal that you would like to share?
- Read aloud the part that you liked best.
- Let's talk about what you think our goals should be for next time.

Every conference will be different, but having such a plan as this in mind will be helpful in the beginning. As you and your students have more experiences with conferences, you will devise a plan that works best for you.

Many teachers are afraid to try conferences because they haven't read every book in the library. The solution is to just tell students if you don't know the book they are reading—they'll enjoy sharing something new with you. It is easier to talk about a book if you have read it, but you can talk about any book by using very general questions:

- Tell me about your book.
- Who are the characters?
- Where does it take place?
- What happened?
- How did the story end?

You will notice that this line of questioning follows the story map concept discussed earlier in this text. You can also develop very general questions for expository texts:

- What is the topic of your book?
- What are the big ideas the author tells you?
- Find me a place to read aloud that supports one of the author's big ideas.

Sometimes you will find that it is good to have conferences with two students at the same time. This is always possible when you have assigned a book for the entire class to read or when students have read the same book or are reading books that are closely related. With two students, you can encourage higher-level thinking by comparing and contrasting books.

Evaluating Conferences

As you work with conferences, you and your students should take time to evaluate them. Together, you should talk about such things as the following:

1. How are our conferences working?
2. What is especially good about our conferences?
3. What problems do we have?
4. What can we do to improve our conferences?

If your students are new to conferences, you will probably need to do this several times during the beginning of the year until everything is running smoothly.

You must also evaluate your own ability to handle conferences. The more experience you have, the better you will be at this activity. Here is a list of questions to ask yourself:

1. How are my conferences going overall?
2. Are they too long or too brief?
3. Am I asking questions that prompt children to think?
4. Is the conference truly a discussion or a time for me to "interrogate" the students?
5. Am I getting good information about my students' ability to construct meaning?
6. Are the other students in the class engaged in productive activities while I am conferencing?

A good way to evaluate your conferences is to tape-record one or two and listen to them. This will help you see how you can improve and will suggest many more questions than those I have raised here. Each year may be different, because new circumstances arise with each new class.

This section of the chapter has discussed five different procedures for promoting students' responses to literature—journals, response charts, literature circles, readers theater, and conferences. Now the big question on your mind is probably "How do I put all of this together with everything else I have learned in this book and make it work?" The remainder of the chapter will help you begin to see how to organize and manage the literacy program in your classroom using a concept known as the reading workshop.

THE READING WORKSHOP: A WAY OF ORGANIZING A RESPONSE-CENTERED CLASSROOM

For many years, teachers in elementary school have used patterns of ability grouping as a means of meeting students' individual needs (Barr & Dreeben, 1991). You can probably recall being in a reading group when you were in school. However, this concept has come under considerable criticism during recent years (Allington, 1983; Dawson, 1987; Harp, 1989; Hiebert, 1983; Slavin, 1986, 1988; Sorensen & Hallinan, 1986). Some of the more significant problems cited for ability grouping and the general concept of reading groups are as follows:

- Students often develop a poor self-image and negative self-concept as a result of being placed in ability groups.
- There is no research evidence showing a *clear, consistent advantage* to any students being placed in ability groups (Dawson, 1987; Slavin, 1986).
- When reading groups are used along with the *traditional basal reader concept*, students actually spend little time reading; they devote most of their time to completing workbook pages or doing worksheets.

Throughout this text, I have stressed the importance of children spending their time reading and writing in order to learn to construct meaning. Therefore, to make this happen in classrooms, we must consider alternative ways of approaching classroom organization for reading instruction.

The concept of the literacy program as discussed in Chapter 2 and referred to in subsequent chapters places the emphasis on developing reading and writing together as children grow into literacy. There is no *one* best way to organize for literacy instruction. Research evidence (Peterson, Wilkinson, & Hallinan, 1984) supports a flexible approach that uses the whole group, small groups, and sometimes no groups.

The reading workshop has been suggested as one way to organize the classroom for reading in a flexible manner. Its companion is the writing workshop, which will be discussed in Chapter 7 along with suggestions on how these two workshops can be combined.

As you develop your literacy-centered, literature-centered classroom, you will find many ways to organize and direct your day. The reading workshop, as discussed here, is only one way to do this, but it can be used as a basic framework on which to build. It will also help you see how to pull together the ideas discussed in this chapter and throughout the text.

Description

Atwell (1987) discusses the reading workshop as a way of approaching reading in her middle-school classes. For her, the workshop is a time when the entire class is engaged in reading, responding, and sharing books with the teacher and with peers. Although there is time for the teacher to help students improve their meaning construction, the heart of the reading workshop is simply time for reading.

Reutzel and Cooter (1991), who have adapted the reading workshop as proposed by Atwell for use in elementary grades 2 through 5, suggest four important criteria that must be considered in organizing for effective reading instruction (p. 549):

- Students should have ownership of their time; that is, they should be allowed to choose how they will spend their time reading.
- The classroom environment and daily routine must encourage reading as a primary activity integrated with the other language modes of writing, speaking, and listening.
- The teacher must communicate the importance of reading by setting an example.
- There must be opportunities for regular demonstrations of reading strategies, for sharing in the reading process (including responding to books), and for evaluating individual reading progress.

The reading workshop meets these criteria. The following discussion of this organizational pattern is based on the suggestions and ideas of Atwell (1987), Heller (1991), and Reutzel and Cooter (1991), as well as my experiences of working with teachers throughout the country.

Components

The reading workshop consists of five main components: teacher sharing time, minilesson, state-of-the-class conference, self-selected reading and responding, and student sharing time.

Teacher Sharing Time

This initial sharing is a time the teacher uses to motivate or excite children about literature. For example, you might use a short story such as *Hemi's Pet* (de Hamel, 1985) to introduce children to a series of books on pets or one of Jack Prelutsky's poems from *Tyrannosaurus Was a Beast* (Prelutsky, 1988) to excite children about the study of dinosaurs. This sharing takes from 5 to 10 minutes and serves to warm up the class; Holdaway (1979) describes this process for kindergarten and first grade. Many teachers also allow students to share a poem they have read or written or to tell a story. You can use this sharing as a way to lead into your minilesson.

Minilesson

The concept of the minilesson was introduced in Chapter 2 and will be discussed in more detail in Chapter 8. This brief lesson on a strategy or skill is designed to meet a need based on students' responses to reading or to provide prereading support such as background or vocabulary for a particular piece of literature that students are going to read. This lesson always incorporates the skill or strategy within the context of a piece of literature students have read or listened to. It may be done with the whole class or a small group.

Minilessons may be drawn from resources such as the basal reader or literature resource book or developed by the teacher. However, skills from a published curriculum guide or teacher's manual should be taught *only* if a real need for it exists. As the term *mini* implies, this lesson is short, usually only 5 to 10 minutes.

State-of-the-Class Conference

During this brief period (5 minutes), you will take stock of what students are doing or planning to do during the remainder of the day's workshop. Reutzel and Cooter (1991) suggest using a chart similar to that shown in Figure 6.15 as a way of keeping track of what each student is doing. Initially, many teachers keep this chart on a clipboard and simply ask each student what he or she is doing on that day. They complete the chart using the code at the bottom. As you and the students become more confortable with the reading workshop, the students can assume responsibility for completing the chart themselves. A large version can be posted each week. Figure 6.15 shows how a teacher has partially completed the chart.

The information from this assessment keeps you in touch with what students are doing and lets you know which students may need a conference or other teacher support. For example, if you notice that a student has been reading the same book for several days without any response group activity, you know that you may need a special meeting with the student to find out what progress has been made and to set new goals or change existing ones.

Self-Selected Reading and Responding

This is the core of the reading workshop, the time when students read and respond to books. Three different types of activities may take place: self-selected reading, literature responses, and individual reading conferences.

Figure 6.15   State-of-the-Class Chart

STATE-OF-THE-CLASS

Name	M	Tu	W	Th	F
Ann	SSR	J			
Beth	LC-D	SSR			
Bill	SSR	LC-D			
Carl	J	SSR			
Cathy	LC-DNR	SSR			
Darin	R	SSR			
David	SSR	SSR			

CODE   SSR - Self-Selected Reading   LC - Literature Circle Meeting
J   - Journal   D   - Discussing
R   - Response Activity   G   - Setting Goals
RK - Record Keeping   DNR - Determining New
                                                      Response

Usually this portion of the workshop lasts from about 40 to 60 minutes, depending on the age level of your students.

Self-selected reading usually lasts from 10 to 25 minutes, depending on the grade level. During this time, the students read. You should also read for some portion of the time to serve as a model, but you should also circulate to hold individual miniconferences, to keep students motivated and encouraged, and to do on-the-spot, incidental teaching. Throughout this time, students may also make entries into their journals.

Literature responses can involve a number of activities, such as writing in journals or meeting with a literature circle. During this time you continue to circulate and confer with individuals, or you meet with a literature circle to participate in the discussion or serve as a recorder. Some students may continue their silent reading while others are meeting in literature circles, working in journals, or doing some other response activity. If students have not chosen to meet with a literature circle, they should always be encouraged to respond in some other way, such as by sharing with a friend or completing a project about the book they have read.

The third type of activity that takes place during self-selected reading and response time is *individual reading conferences*. The last 10 minutes of the period are devoted to conferring with students who are not in literature circles. While this is going on, other students may be completing a literature circle or continuing with self-selected reading. Usually two or three conferences are held each day.

Student Sharing Time

The last 5 to 10 minutes of the reading workshop are devoted to students sharing books they have read and reporting their progress on literature projects or other response activities. Sharing time advertises and promotes the excitement of literacy learning and helps to promote the class as a community of readers. During this time students may ask each other for ideas to improve what they are doing. Some teachers often divide the class into small sharing groups (three to five students) to allow for greater student involvement. The teacher then circulates among the groups, commenting or just listening. Longer sharing times may be scheduled when certain literature circles have a special activity or project to share, such as a readers theater performance or a puppet play.

Reutzel and Cooter (1991) suggest that these five components occupy approximately 70 minutes per day. However, you will notice that the times suggested here put the time range roughly from an hour to an hour and a half per day. The exact amount of time depends on your grade level and class. Atwell's (1987) concept of the reading workshop includes these same basic components except for the initial teacher sharing. However, even many middle-school teachers find this brief initial sharing a good way to open their class, and Atwell does something like this within the framework of her minilesson. Figure 6.16 summarizes the components of a reading workshop.

Variations

The reading workshop is a very flexible organizational structure that allows you to meet your teaching needs and the needs of your students. If you are just beginning to do literature-centered instruction or if you have been doing it for a long time and this plan is new to you, you should find it helpful in your classroom.

If you want the whole class or a selected group of students to read the same book, you can assign the book and provide the needed activities for a

Figure 6.16   Reading Workshop

Reading Workshop (55–95 minutes)

1. Teacher sharing time (5–10 minutes)
2. Minilesson (5–10 minutes)
3. State-of-the-class conference (5 minutes)
4. Self-selected reading and responding (35–60 minutes)
   - Self-selected reading (10–25 minutes):
     Reading of self-selected books
     Responding activities
     Record keeping
   - Literature responses (15–20 minutes):
     Literature circles
     Individual responses
     Journal work
   - Individual reading conferences (10–15 minutes):
     Two or three per day
     Evaluation

5. Student sharing time (5–10 minutes)

literacy lesson. You then include both assigned and self-selected reading in the self-selected reading time, and you adjust the code for the state-of-the-class chart to RT—Reading Time, SS—Self-Selected, AR—Assigned Reading. You can adjust the times for the other activities according to need.

If you decide to move into the reading workshop gradually, you can schedule two days for the workshop and use the remaining days for other reading activities. Then you can gradually expand the reading workshop to your full program.

You may find yourself in a school that requires the use of a traditional basal reader. In this case you can use the reading workshop by having assigned reading groups read their selections during reading time and by using *selected* skill lesson resources for parts of the minilessons. You will have to adjust the code for your state-of-the-class chart to go with the activities within your basal. As you progress in using the reading workshop with a basal reader, the reader can serve as a collection of stories and articles from which students make self-selected choices for reading. If you find yourself in this situation, you should *always* incorporate self-selected reading as a part of your reading workshop activities. Refer back to Chapter 2 for a discussion of the research on independent reading.

Publishers are now producing materials that are truly literature based, that is, incorporating "real literature" that has not been adapted. The focus of these materials is on reading, writing, and responding, and the teachers' materials are viewed as resources from which to pick and choose. Skill work grows directly out of the literature and should be done *only when the need arises*. These materials may also be used for developing reading workshops.

Getting Started

The following suggestions should help you get started using the reading workshop in your classroom.

Work Out a Beginning Plan

After you have read about the reading workshop and/or visited a classroom where it is in use, work out an initial plan for your class. Then post this plan for the class to see and discuss it with them so that they can take ownership of the plan. Ask them for suggestions. This activity should take place over several days as you get your class ready for the workshop. Be sure to convey your excitement and enthusiasm for the plan.

Develop Guidelines with Students for Behavior During the Workshop

Students at all levels need to know what is expected of them during any activity, and the reading workshop is no different. Atwell (1987) suggests that the teachers clarify the rules for reading workshop time. You will have to develop rules to fit your needs and the level you are teaching, but it is best to develop these in conjunction with your students. Figure 6.17 shows a chart developed with second-grade students for their reading workshop behavior.

Try the Reading Workshop

Some teachers worry about how to get started. Once you have a plan and have worked it through with your class, just start. See how things go. Use your own instincts and good judgment to make decisions.

Evaluate and Adjust Your Plan

After each day, think about how things have gone. What did you like? What didn't you like? After a few days, talk with the class about how the reading workshop is going and ask them for their suggestions. They will have many

Figure 6.17   Reading Workshop Rules from a Second-Grade Class

Our Reading Workshop Rules

1. Read your book or story.

2. Do not bother others.

3. If you need to talk to the teacher, write your name on the board.

4. Be ready to meet with your Literature Circle at the end of each day.

excellent ideas. One third-grade teacher reported that after she had tried the workshop for a few days, one young man said, "Just relax and stop worrying about us. We're gonna be OK." This is an important message to remember.

The reading workshop is no panacea. It is, however, a good framework to use for helping you find out how you should organize your literacy-centered classroom. The only way we grow and learn is by trying.

Example 6.1

Planning Response Activities

Now that you have a better sense of what is involved in responding to literature, it is time for you to begin to think about how you might use this information in teaching. Look back at the three pieces of literature and sample literacy lessons presented at the conclusion of Chapters 2, 3, and 4. Review them; then complete one or more of the following activities with a friend:

- Select one literacy lesson and decide how you might change the response suggestions given. Discuss your rationale for the changes.
- Assume that you are in a school where you are required to use a basal reader. Work out a reading workshop plan for using it following the guidelines discussed in this chapter.
- Find a classroom of the grade level of your choice. If the reading workshop is being used, observe for a day or two to see what ideas might help you implement this concept successfully. If the reading workshop is not being used, observe to see how you might begin to incorporate this idea into this room. Discuss it with your friend.

SUMMARY

Responding is the action one takes during or after reading, writing, or listening. This chapter has focused on the importance of responding to literature in the process of constructing meaning. Students can do this in a number of verbal and nonverbal ways. The atmosphere of the classroom sets the tone that promotes and supports students' responding activities. Journals, response charts, literature circles, readers theater, and reading conferences promote responding to literature. Organizing and managing a response-centered literacy classroom is an important task for the teacher, and the reading workshop is a plan that can be used as a starting point for this purpose.

Children's Books

Bang, M. G. (1981). *Tye May and the magic brush*. New York: Greenwillow Books.
Bunting, E. (1988). *How many days to America?* New York: Clarion.
Bunting, E. (1991). *Fly away home*. New York: Clarion.
Byars, B. (1970). *The summer of the swans*. New York: Viking Penguin.
Dahl, R. (1961). *James and the giant peach*. New York: Viking Penguin.
de Hamel, J. (1985). *Hemi's pet*. Auckland: Reed Methuen.
de Paola, T. (1980). *Now one foot, now the other*. New York: G. P. Putnam.
Fleischman, S. (1987). *The scarebird*. New York: Greenwillow Books.

Hahn, M. D. (1986). *Wait til Helen Comes*. New York: Clarion.

Moss, M. (1990). *Regina's big mistake*. Boston: Houghton Mifflin.

Prelutsky, J. (1988). *Tyrannosaurus was a beast*. New York: Greenwillow Books.

Schwartz, A. (1988). *Annabelle Swift, kindergartner*. New York: Orchard Books.

Scieszka, J. (1989). *The true story of the 3 little pigs*. New York: Viking Kestrel.

Snyder, Z. K. (1976). *The Egypt game*. New York: Atheneum.

Taylor, M. D. (1990). *Mississippi bridge*. New York: Dial.

Xiong, B. (told by) & Spagnoli, C. (adapted by). (1989). *Nine-in-one. Grr! Grr!* San Francisco, CA: Children's Book Press.

For Additional Reading

Atwell, N. (1987). *In the middle*. Portsmouth, NH: Heinemann.

Fox, M. (1984). *Teaching drama to young children*. Portsmouth, NH: Heinemann.

Harste, J. C., Short, K. G., & Burke, C. (1988). Literature circles. In *Creating classrooms for authors* (pp. 293–304). Portsmouth, NH: Heinemann.

Parsons, L. (1990). *Response journals*. Portsmouth, NH: Heinemann.

Reutzel, D. R., & Cooter, R. B., Jr. (1991). Organizing for effective instruction: The reading workshop. *The Reading Teacher, 44*, 548–554.

Wollman-Bonilla, J. E. (1989). Reading journals: Invitations to participate in literature. *The Reading Teacher, 43*, 112–120.

References

Allington, R. L. (1983). The reading instruction provided readers of differing reading abilities. *Elementary School Journal, 83*, 548–559.

Applebee, A. N. (1978). *The child's concept of a story: Ages two to seventeen*. Chicago: University of Chicago Press.

Atwell, N. (1987). *In the middle*. Portsmouth, NH: Heinemann.

Barone, D. (1990). The written responses of young children: Beyond comprehension to story understanding. *New Advocate, 3*, 49–56.

Barr, R., & Dreeben, R. (1991). Grouping students for reading instruction. In R. Barr, M. L. Kamil, P. Mosenthal, & P. D. Pearson (Eds.), *Handbook of reading research* (Vol. 2, pp. 885–910). New York: Longman.

Bromley, K. D. (1989). Buddy journals make the reading writing connection. *Reading Teacher, 43*, 122–129.

Calkins, L. M. (1986). *The art of teaching writing*. Portsmouth, NH: Heinemann.

Coger, L. E., & White, M. R. (1982). *Readers theatre handbook: A dramatic approach to literature*. Glenview, IL: Scott, Foresman.

Coley, J. D., & Hoffman, D. M. (1990). Overcoming learned helplessness in at-risk readers. *Journal of Reading, 33*, 497–502.

Cullinan, B., Harwood, K., & Galda, L. (1983). The reader and the story: Comprehension and response. *Journal of Research and Development in Education, 16*, 29–38.

Dawson, M. M. (1987). Beyond ability grouping: A review of ability grouping and its alternatives. *School Reading Review, 16*, 348–369.

Eeds, M. (1989). Grand conversations: An exploration of meaning construction in study groups. *Research in the Teaching of English, 23,* 4–29.

Flood, J., & Lapp, D. (1991). Reading comprehension instruction. In J. Flood, J. M. Jensen, D. Lapp & J. R. Squire (Eds.), *Handbook on the teaching of the English language arts* (pp. 732–742). New York: Macmillan.

Galda, L. (1982). Assuming the spectator stance: An examination of the responses of three young readers. *Research in the Teaching of English, 16,* 1–20.

Galda, L. (1983). Research in response to literature. *Journal of Research and Development in Education, 16,* 1–7.

Gallagher, J. M., & Reid, D. K. (1983). *The learning theory of Piaget and Inhelder.* Austin, TX: Pro-Ed.

Gambrell, L., Pfeiffer, W., & Wilson, R. (1985). The effects of retelling upon reading comprehension and recall of text information. *Journal of Educational Research, 78,* 216–220.

Gambrell, T. (1986). Growth in response to literature. *English Quarterly, 19,* 130–141.

Graves, D. H. (1983). *Writing: Teachers and children at work.* Exeter, NH: Heinemann.

Graves, D. H. (1991). *Build a literate classroom.* Portsmouth, NH: Heinemann.

Hansen, J. (1987). *When writers read.* Portsmouth, NH: Heinemann.

Harp, B. (1989). What do we know about ability grouping? *Reading Teacher, 42,* 430–431.

Harste, J. C., Short, K. G., & Burke, C. (1988). *Creating classrooms for authors.* Portsmouth, NH: Heinemann.

Hayes, C., & Bayruth, R. (1985). Querer es poder. In J. Hansen, T. Newkirk, & D. Graves (Eds.), *Breaking ground: Teachers relate reading and writing in the elementary school* (pp. 97–110). Portsmouth, NH: Heinemann.

Heller, M. F. (1991). *Reading-writing connections: From theory to practice.* New York: Longman.

Hickman, J. (1983). Everything considered: Response to literature in an elementary school setting. *Journal of Research and Development in Education, 16,* 8–13.

Hiebert, E. H. (1983). An examination of ability grouping for reading instruction. *Reading Research Quarterly, 28,* 231–255.

Holdaway, D. (1979). *The foundations of literacy.* Sydney: Ashton Scholastic, distributed by Heinemann, Portsmouth, NH.

Kelly, P. R. (1990). Guiding young students' response to literature. *Reading Teacher, 43,* 464–470.

Kelly, P. R., & Farnan, N. (1991). Promoting critical thinking through response logs: A reader response approach with fourth graders. In S. McCormick & J. Zutell (Eds.), *Learner factors/teacher factors: Issues in literacy research and instruction,* 40th Yearbook of the National Reading Conference (pp. 277–284). Chicago: National Reading Conference.

Many, J. E. (1991). The effects of stance and age level on children's literary responses. *Journal of Reading Behavior, 23,* 61–85.

Marshall, N. (1983). Using story grammar to assess reading comprehension. *Reading Teacher, 36,* 616–620.

Martinez, M. G., & Roser, N. L. (1991). Children's responses to literature. In J. Flood, J. M. Jensen, D. Lapp & J. R. Squire (Eds.), *Handbook of research on teaching the English language arts* (pp. 643–654). New York: Macmillan.

Morrow, L. (1985). Retelling stories: A strategy for improving children's comprehension, concept of story structure, and oral language complexity. *Elementary School Journal, 85,* 647–661.

Morrow, L. M. (1989). Using story retelling to develop comprehension. In K. D. Muth (Ed.), *Children's comprehension of text: Research into practice* (pp. 37–58). Newark, DE: International Reading Association.

Palincsar, A. S., & Brown, A. (1986). Interactive teaching to promote independent learning from text. *Reading Teacher, 39*(8), 771–777.

Paris, S. G., Wasik, B. A., & Turner, J. C. (1991). The development of strategic readers. In R. Barr, M. L. Kamil, P. Mosenthal, & P. D. Pearson (Eds.), *Handbook of reading research* (Vol. 2, pp. 609–640). New York: Longman.

Parsons, L. (1990). *Response journals.* Portsmouth, NH: Heinemann.

Peterson, P., Wilkinson, L., & Hallinan, M. (1984). *The social contexts of instruction: Group organization and group processes.* Orlando, FL: Academic.

Peyton, J., & Seyoum, M. (1989). The effect of teacher strategies on students' interactive writing: The case of dialogue journals. *Research in the Teaching of English, 23,* 310–334.

Purves, A. C. (1972). *How porcupines make love: Notes on a response-centered curriculum.* New York: Wiley.

Reutzel, D. R., & Cooter, R. B., Jr. (1991). Organizing for effective instruction: The reading workshop. *The Reading Teacher, 44,* 548–554.

Rosenblatt, L. (1938/1976). *Literature as exploration.* New York: Modern Language Association.

Rosenblatt, L. M. (1991). Literary theory. In J. Flood, J. M. Jensen, D. Lapp & J. R. Squire (Eds.), *Handbook of research on teaching the English language arts* (pp. 57–62). New York: Macmillan.

Slavin, R. E. (1986). *Ability grouping and student achievement in elementary schools: A best evidence synthesis.* Report No. 1. Baltimore, MD: Johns Hopkins University, Center for Research on Elementary and Middle Schools.

Slavin, R. E. (1988). Synthesis of research on grouping in elementary and secondary schools. *Educational Leadership, 46*(1), 67–77.

Sloan, G. D. (1984). *The child as critic,* 2nd ed. New York: Teachers College Press.

Sloyer, S. (1982). *Readers theatre: Story dramatization in the classroom.* Urbana, IL: National Council of Teachers of English.

Sorensen, A., & Hallinan, M. (1986). Effects of ability grouping on growth in academic achievement. *American Educational Research Journal, 23,* 519–542.

Spritzer, D. R. (1988). Integrating the language arts in the elementary classroom using fairy tales, fables, and traditional literature. *Oregon English, 11,* 23–26.

Sutton, C. (1989). Helping the nonnative English speaker with reading. *Reading Teacher, 42,* 684–688.

Thompson, A. (1990). Thinking and writing with learning logs. In N. Atwell (Ed.), *Coming to know: Writing to learn in the intermediate grades* (pp. 35–51). Portsmouth, NH: Heinemann.

Tierney, R. J., Readence, J. E., & Dishner, E. K. (1990). Reader's theater. In *Reading strategies and practices: A compendium* (3rd ed.) (pp. 190–195). Boston: Allyn and Bacon.

Tompkins, G. E., & Hoskisson, K. (1991). *Language arts: Content and teaching strategies.* New York: Merrill, an imprint of Macmillan.

Vandergrift, K. (1980). *Child and story*. New York: Neil-Schuman.

Vaughn, C. L. (1990). Knitting writing: The double-entry journal. In N. Atwell (Ed.), *Coming to know: Writing to learn in the middle grades* (pp. 69–75). Portsmouth, NH: Heinemann.

Veatch, J. (1966/1978). *Reading in the elementary school*. New York: Wiley.

Weaver, C. (1990). *Understanding whole language*. Portsmouth, NH: Heinemann.

Werthemer, A. (1974). Story dramatization in the reading center. *English Journal, 64*, 85–87.

Writing and the Construction of Meaning

7

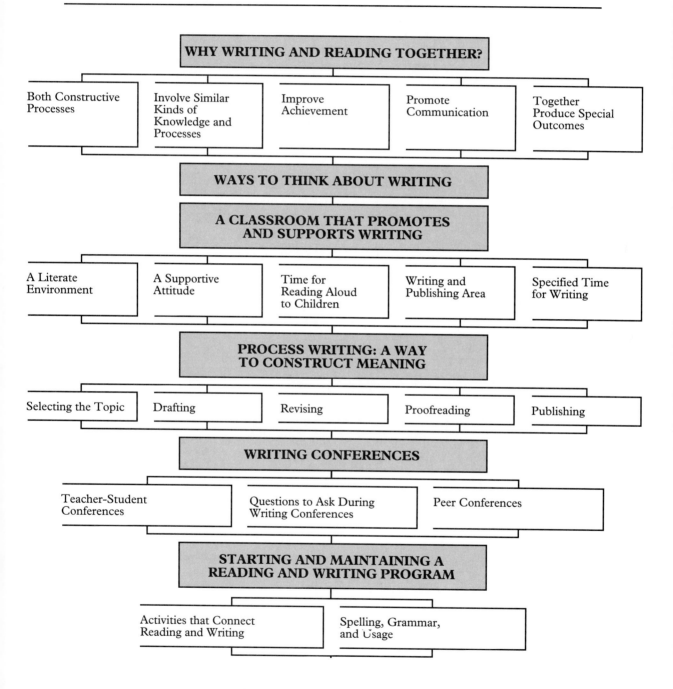

WHY WRITING AND READING TOGETHER?

Both Constructive Processes

Involve Similar Kinds of Knowledge and Processes

Improve Achievement

Promote Communication

Together Produce Special Outcomes

WAYS TO THINK ABOUT WRITING

A CLASSROOM THAT PROMOTES AND SUPPORTS WRITING

A Literate Environment

A Supportive Attitude

Time for Reading Aloud to Children

Writing and Publishing Area

Specified Time for Writing

PROCESS WRITING: A WAY TO CONSTRUCT MEANING

Selecting the Topic

Drafting

Revising

Proofreading

Publishing

WRITING CONFERENCES

Teacher-Student Conferences

Questions to Ask During Writing Conferences

Peer Conferences

STARTING AND MAINTAINING A READING AND WRITING PROGRAM

Activities that Connect Reading and Writing

Spelling, Grammar, and Usage

EXPOSITORY WRITING AS AN AID
TO CONSTRUCTING MEANING

THE WRITING WORKSHOP: A PLAN FOR
ORGANIZING AND MANAGING WRITING

| Elements of the Writing Workshop | Getting Started | Blending Reading and Writing Workshops into One |

A FINAL WORD ABOUT WRITING

SUMMARY

Ryan, a fourth grader, wrote the following first draft of his story:

Ryan

The Haunted Mansion Mystery

Once upon a time, there were two boys. Their names were Scott and Jimmy. One day Scott convinced Jimmy to go into the 100 year old mansion. The mansion was boarded up, the windows were broken, rats were in the window sills, and there were spider webs all over. The boys went inside. Inside it was so dusty every time they breathed, dust blew all over. "Come on, Jimmy," Scott said. So they went into the next room. It was the bedroom. The boys saw a lump under the blankets, Scott brought down the covers. There was nothing there. Then they heard something. It came from a door. It was the basement door. "Come on. Let's go," said Scott. They went down the stairs. They heard a crash. Jimmy asked "What was that?" "It was nothing" said Scott. After they explored the basement, they went back upstairs. Right when they opened the door, a bat flew in their face. They went along and suddenly they saw a shadow.

> figure on the wall. Then they heard a deep laugh.
> Then after that they heard a cat hiss. They went
> into the bedroom. They saw some blood drops.
> Scott saw the doorknob on the door turn. Then it
> stopped. He heard a door creak and then shut.
> Jimmy saw a shadow on the wall. It raced
> across the wall and then it disappeared.
> Everything that happened scared both Scott
> and Jimmy. They decided that they
> were going to leave. Then they heard a BOO!
> and two of Scott's friends grabbed them.
> So the house wasn't haunted after all.

Even though he needed to revise and proofread it, Ryan had already created a story that he wanted to share with others. His tale of the haunted mansion certainly incorporated the suspense and excitement that he wanted to convey. Through the process of writing, he was constructing meaning, and each person reading his story would also construct their own personal meaning from their prior knowledge and experiences. Reading and writing, as this text has stressed, are not separate entities. Although it is possible to think of writing as the core experience from which all of the other language arts develop (Graves, 1978), these two processes actually develop together in literacy learning.

RECENTLY, A THIRD-GRADE teacher and I discussed literacy and reading and writing. I asked him, "What do you think it means to develop reading and writing together?" His answer was very clear:

Children often read books that are related to the topics they are using in writing. At the same time, they often write about what they are reading. For example, a child in my last class was reading the personal narrative Little House in the Big Woods *[Wilder, 1932]; it was very natural for her to extend personal narrative into her writing. Another boy was writing a story about dinosaurs. His writing experience became the catalyst for him to read other books on dinosaurs. So you see, I can't just think of reading or writing. I think of a literacy experience or event. By giving my children support in the event they are experiencing, I am able to help them become better comprehenders; it doesn't really matter whether it is a reading focus or writing focus. They use both of these things together.*

This chapter will take a more detailed look at the relationships between writing and reading and how these processes develop together. The focus will be on *moving toward* a broad instructional perspective rather than on separate lessons for writing and reading.

WHY WRITING AND READING TOGETHER?

Educators have supported the integration of language arts for many years (Durkin, 1989; Loban, 1963; Moffett & Wagner, 1983). More recent research has given us a better understanding of these processes and has helped us to know more about how and why they develop together (Tierney & Shanahan, 1991). In response to the question "Why writing and reading together?" several researchers have helped us to formulate a clearer (although not final) answer (Pearson & Tierney, 1984; Shanahan, 1990; Tierney & Leys, 1984; Tierney & Shanahan, 1991). There are at least five major reasons for teaching writing and reading together:

- Both writing and reading are constructive processes.
- Reading and writing share similar processes and kinds of knowledge.
- Writing and reading, when taught together, improve achievement.
- Reading and writing together foster communication.
- Combining reading and writing leads to outcomes not attributable to either process alone.

Both Constructive Processes

That reading and writing are both constructive processes is obvious from Pearson and Tierney's (1984) description of readers as composers. They describe thoughtful readers as ones who plan reading around a given purpose; with this purpose in mind, they think about the text and begin to activate background relating to the topic. Writers go through a very similar process. They have some purpose for writing and begin to think about what they know or need to know about the topic before beginning to write.

Next readers begin to read and construct or compose meaning in light of their purposes and background. The cues in the text help them compose these meanings. In the same way, writers begin to write and construct meaning; their task is to compose meaning so it can be conveyed to a reader. As they write, they think about the topic and develop it; they may have a general idea when they start to write, but they really develop it only as they think more about it.

As the reading process continues, readers reread and change meaning as necessary. Again, writers do the same: they think about what has been written, reread it, and rewrite it to make it clearer. Finally, readers reach a point where they finalize the meaning they've composed as being the best possibility for that given point in time. Writers do the same in their final copy.

Pearson and Tierney refer to each of these four phases as planner, composer, editor, and monitor stages. The similarities between the reader and writer as composers (or constructors) of meaning are summarized in Table

Table 7.1   Readers and Writers as Composers of Meaning

Processes	Reader	Writer
Planner	Have purpose for reading Generate background	Have purpose for writing Generate background
Composer	Read and compose meaning	Write and compose meaning
Editor	Reread, reflect, and revise meaning	Reread, relect, and revise
Monitor	Finalize meaning	Finalize copy

7.1. Of course, readers and writers do not proceed through these stages one after another; they go back and forth between them as they perform the overall process (Graves, 1984; Murray, 1985; Pearson & Tierney, 1984).

As proficient readers and writers work, they tend to use the two processes simultaneously. Think about your own experiences in writing. As you write your ideas, you reread them to see if they make sense. Often you turn to books or other sources to get more information to include in your writing or to make your meaning clearer. The processes of proficient reading and writing not only function in similar ways, but they also tend to be used together.

Teaching students to write helps them construct meaning by making them more aware of how authors organize their ideas. As they learn to write and organize their own ideas, they will have a greater appreciation and understanding of how other authors do the same.

Involve Similar Kinds of Knowledge and Processes

There are other reasons why reading and writing should be taught together: they naturally develop together (Baghban, 1984; Bissex, 1980; Calkins, 1983; Sulzby & Teale, 1991), and they share many of the same processes and types of knowledge (Tierney & Shanahan, 1991). Researchers have consistently found reading and writing to be highly related (Applebee, 1977; Loban, 1963; Shanahan, 1988; Shanahan & Lomax, 1988), and recently they have been able to identify some specific similarities such as use of similar cognitive processes (Birnbaum, 1982; Langer, 1986; Martin, 1987). But even this type of research is in its infancy and cannot be used to identify the exact elements shared by the two processes (Tierney & Shanahan, 1991); there are still differences that we need to understand more thoroughly (Langer, 1986).

Improve Achievement

One area that researchers have studied is the effect that the teaching of reading and writing together has on overall achievement. The classic U.S. Office of Education study of first-grade reading concluded that programs that incorporated writing were generally more effective in improving reading than those that did not (Bond & Dykstra, 1967). In a review of more recent research on the effects of teaching writing and reading together, Tierney and Shanahan (1991) conclude that "studies have shown that writing led to improved reading achievement, reading led to better writing performance, and combined instruction in both led to improvements in both reading and writing" (p. 258). Caution must be exercised, however; we cannot say that simply providing instruction in one area will automatically lead to improvements in another area; it depends on how the instruction is provided. All we know is that reading and writing together have benefits that neither taught alone will have. Also, by teaching writing and reading together, we are able to help students recognize and understand the connections between the two processes.

Promote Communication

Reading and writing are not just skills to be learned to score better on achievement tests—they are processes that help us more effectively understand and communicate with each other. It is through this communication that we are able to improve our world, to prosper and enjoy it. Since both communication and learning are social processes, developing reading and writing together has many social benefits. As Shanahan (1990) states: "The fusion of reading and writing in the classroom offers children the possibility of participating in both sides of the communication process and, consequently, provides them with a more elaborate grasp of the true meaning of literacy" (p. 4).

Together Produce Special Outcomes

An underlying element of all literacy learning and learning in general is "thinking." In combining writing and reading instruction, learners are engaged in a greater variety of experiences that lead to better reasoning and higher-level thinking than is achieved with either process alone (McGinley, 1988). Since thinking is a critical part of meaning construction, classrooms that actively foster meaning construction through reading and writing will produce better thinkers (Tierney & Shanahan, 1991).

In conclusion, let's return to the original question posed at the beginning of this section—why writing and reading together? Reading and writing are both constructive processes that share common knowledges; while they are similar, they are not absolutely the same. Teaching reading and writing together fosters a broad perspective of literacy as a social process that results in better achievement in both and leads to better thinking. As Tierney and Shanahan (1991) conclude: "We believe strongly that in our society, at this point in history, reading and writing, to be understood and appreciated fully, should be viewed together, learned together, and used together" (p. 275).

Even though many classrooms still focus on reading and writing as separate entities, it is clear from the state of current research that we must view them more as a single entity called *literacy*. For more detailed discussion of the research on writing and reading, see "For Additional Reading." The remainder of this chapter focuses on how to build the reading-writing connection.

WAYS TO THINK ABOUT WRITING

Chapter 2 discussed two different types of texts and their relationship to meaning construction: narrative and expository. Writing can also be seen in terms of broad categories, called domains, that somewhat parallel the types of texts students read. There are four basic domains for writing (McHugh, 1987): sensory/descriptive, imaginative/narrative, practical/informative, and analytical/expository. Each domain represents a specific purpose for writing. Being aware of the domain and its purpose helps students clearly develop their own purposes for writing, and knowledge about domains also helps you as a teacher in planning a variety of literacy experiences. Within each domain, there are many possible projects for students to do that represent many of the functions and uses of literacy as identified by Heath (1983). As you will see, many projects may cut across several domains.

- *Sensory/descriptive domain:* The sensory/descriptive domain focuses on describing something in such rich and clear detail that the reader or listener can almost see or feel it. Description also incorporates the feelings of the writer.
- *Imaginative/narrative domain:* This domain focuses on telling a real or imaginary story. Incorporating some of the descriptive domain, the writer learns to use the elements of a story, including setting, problem, action, and outcome or resolution.
- *Practical/informative domain:* The purpose of this domain is to present basic information clearly. The author is writing the information without analyzing it.
- *Analytical/expository domain:* In this final domain, the writer's primary purpose is to explain, analyze, and persuade. This most abstract form of writing uses elements of all the others. The difference between a report written in this domain and one written in the practical/informative domain is that this report focuses more on "why."

Figure 7.1   Collaborative Story by a Group of Fourth Graders

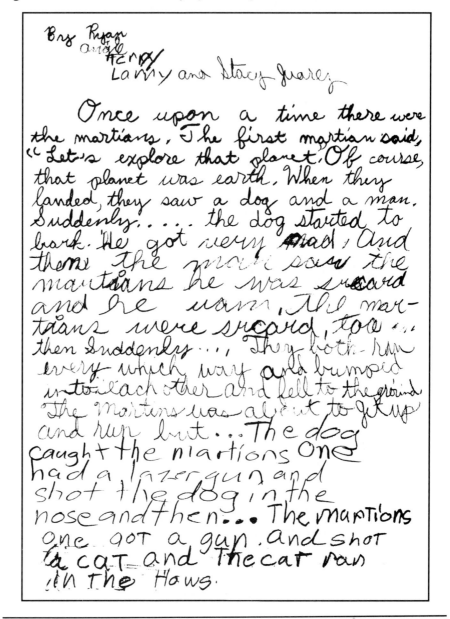

Another way to think about writing is in terms of *modes* of writing (introduced in Chapter 2). There are three such modes: *independent, collaborative* (partners or a small group work together on a single writing product), and *shared* (group with the teacher; this parallels shared reading [see Chapters 2 and 5]). Figure 7.1 shows an example of a collaborative story written by a

Table 7.2 Domains and Modes of Writing with Sample Products or Projects

| | Domain | | | |
Mode	Sensory/ Descriptive	Imaginative/ Narative	Practical/ Informative	Analytical/ Expository
Independent writing	Diary Journal Letters Class notes Poems	Letters Short stories Poems	Lists Reports Letters Directions Class notes Invitations	Reports Letters to the editor Reviews Poems
Collaborative writing	Diary Journal Letters Poems	Letters Short stories Poems	Lists Reports Letters Directions Class notes Invitations	Reports Letters to the editor Reviews Poems
Shared writing	Diary Journal Letters Poems	Letters Short stories Poems	Lists Reports Letters Directions Class notes Invitations	Reports Letters to the editor Reviews Poems

group of fourth graders. Any one of the domains may be handled as independent, collaborative, or shared writing. As has already been noted, the products or projects produced within one domain may also be developed in another domain. Table 7.2 shows sample products that might be developed in each; notice how some products appear in several domains and modes.

A CLASSROOM THAT PROMOTES AND SUPPORTS WRITING

Writing is a constructive process; therefore, literacy experiences that focus on writing develop students' ability to construct meaning. The research-based concept of process writing (Calkins, 1986; Graves, 1983, 1991; Hillocks, 1987a, 1987b) was introduced in Chapter 2 and discussed in relation to the literacy program, whose elements, as you recall, include motivation, independent reading and writing, and instruction in reading and writing. Thus voluntary, independent reading and writing must be balanced with instruction in writing and reading, and one of the major forms of this instruction is process writing. Let's begin by looking at how to create a classroom environment that promotes and supports literacy with more focus on writing. We will then look at ways to develop and use process writing.

A Literate Environment

One of the major elements discussed as a part of motivation in Chapter 2 was the creation of a literate environment. It was strongly suggested that the classroom needed to become an exciting, stimulating laboratory for literacy experiences. The areas or centers suggested for inclusion were a library area, a writing and publishing area, a listening and viewing area, a sharing area, a creative arts area, a group meeting area, and a display area. All of these areas are essential to the overall literate environment and play a significant role in promoting and supporting writing. The creation of physical areas that support literacy is not sufficient, however, to create the overall literate environment. Within the classroom you must also develop an attitude that supports and promotes literacy.

A Supportive Attitude

A writing attitude begins with a teacher who is willing to accept the ideas students express in their writing and who shows sincere pleasure and satisfaction in what students have accomplished no matter how small the amount or insignificant the topic. Too often, students are made to feel that their ideas just aren't good enough. Even if a child writes only a single sentence, it is a beginning, and the effort should be supported.

Students also need many opportunities to see the teacher write and know that the teacher writes regularly. This can be accomplished by writing notes to students, sharing some of your personal writing such as a poem or a letter, or writing responses in students' journals (see Chapter 6 and later in this chapter). When students see you write, they have models for writing and develop a positive attitude about it.

Another important aspect in developing a writing and literacy attitude is letting students know that they are partners with you in learning—"We are all learning together." Students should be encouraged to make their own decisions and choices about what to write about as well as about what type of writing to use.

Finally, a writing attitude develops when there are authentic reasons to write. Just as students must have authentic reading experiences (using real literature the way real readers use it), so they must also have authentic writing experiences that revolve around *real reasons to write,* not contrived ones. Some examples include the following:

- Writing a list of supplies needed for a project
- Writing an invitation to another class to see a play
- Writing a story to be published in the class newspaper
- Writing a mystery to be published
- Writing a letter to a friend

A "writing and literacy attitude" is clearly evident to visitors as soon as they walk through the door. They will see children writing, reading, talking, and sharing. The teacher may be hard to find; he or she may be working with a group, conferencing with an individual, or writing. Evidence of students' writing will be everywhere.

Time for Reading Aloud to Children

The importance of reading aloud was discussed in detail in Chapter 2, and all writing classrooms must incorporate read-aloud time. When children have numerous opportunities at all grade levels to hear good literature, they generally write better (Dressel, 1990). Refer to Chapter 2 for suggestions on reading aloud.

Writing and Publishing Area

As already mentioned, every classroom needs a writing and publishing area or center. In this center, you should have the following items to support students in their writing:

- Tables and chairs
- Paper (unlined for beginners)
- Pencils, pens, markers, crayons
- Scissors
- Tape and glue
- Construction paper and cardboard
- Old wallpaper sample books
- Yarn, brads, and staplers
- A typewriter, new or old
- A computer (see Chapter 2 for software)
- A place to display writing
- A storage area for writing folders

The writing center can be the place where students write, meet for conferences with peers or the teacher, or do the final work on a piece of writing they wish

Figure 7.2 Form for Recording Writing Topics

to publish. By having this area or center in your classroom, you give significance to writing.

All students need a writing folder containing such things as a list of possible topics for writing (see Figure 7.2 for a sample form), pieces of writing in progress, and a list of pieces of completed writing (see Figure 7.3 for a sample form). Students may also choose to keep a list of words from their writing that cause them spelling problems, and many teachers encourage students to do this.

Some teachers also encourage students to keep a record of the conferences they have had with peers (discussed later in this chapter). Such a record helps students prepare for their conferences with the teacher. Figure 7.4 shows a sample form that can be used for this purpose.

The writing folder is basically the student's working folder. It is brought to conferences with the teacher but is primarily for the student's use. Both it and the reading journal (see Chapter 6) are places where students keep their work. They are not the same thing as the literacy portfolio, which is discussed in Chapter 10.

Another record that students might keep in their writing folder is a list of goals established with the teacher during a conference. These may range from general goals such as "Complete my story" and "Try a different ending" to goals that are very specific, such as "Make more use of descriptive words" and "Pay attention to capital letters and periods." After goals are set, the

Figure 7.3   Form for Recording Completed Writing Projects

WRITING RECORD

Name _____

P=Published

Date Started	Type of Writing	Title of Piece	Date Completed or Dropped

Figure 7.4   Peer Conference Record

PEER CONFERENCE RECORD

DATE	CONFERENCE WITH	WRITING PIECE	SUGGESTIONS

student and the teacher discuss the progress that has been made and establish new goals. Figure 7.5 shows a goal sheet from a sixth grader's writing folder.

When you first begin to use writing folders with your students, keep them simple. Many students have difficulty keeping records and need help in learning their importance (Graves, 1991). Don't have students put in so many pieces that the folders lose their real purpose—as *a place to keep writing in progress.*

Figure 7.5   Goal Sheet from a Sixth Grader's Writing Folder

WRITING GOALS

Name _____

✔ = Completed   CW = Continuing work

Date	Goal	Progress
2-5-90	*Finish my story*	2-8-90
2-8-90	*Make sentences more interesting by using descriptive words*	CW

Specified Time for Writing

Finally, a classroom that promotes and supports writing must have identified times for writing. On the basis of his research, Graves (1983) recommends that children write every day, and more recently (1991) he has recommended that this writing time should be 35 to 40 minutes per day for a minimum of four days a week. If you really believe that children and young adults learn to read and write by reading and writing, there is no way to accept anything less than a plan that calls for *writing every day*.

The time provided for writing means the time for students to actually write, not the time for minilessons and other modeling or demonstrations of writing. The writing workshop plan discussed later in this chapter is a very effective way to build in times for both student writing and needed instruction. Once you become comfortable with both reading and writing workshops, you can integrate them into a literacy workshop; such a plan would be similar to the concept of integrated language arts that many teachers have tried to achieve in their classrooms (Templeton, 1991).

Creating a classroom that promotes and supports writing is critical to the success of the literacy program. Regardless of the age or grade level you are teaching, your classroom must be one that empowers students to take charge of their literacy. Figure 7.6 presents a checklist for evaluating your classroom's writing atmosphere.

Figure 7.6   Checklist for Evaluating the Writing Atmosphere in Your Classroom

Checklist for Evaluating Your Writing Atmosphere

	Yes	No
1. Do you have areas or centers to promote literacy?		
Library?		
Writing and publishing?		
Listening and viewing?		
Sharing?		
Creative arts?		
Group meeting?		
Display?		
2. Does your classroom promote a writing attitude?		
Accept students' ideas?		
Students see you write?		
You write notes to students?		
Students know they are partners in learning?		
Authentic reasons for writing?		
3. Do you read aloud to your class?		
4. Is there a well-developed writing and publishing area or center?		
Appropriate supplies?		
Student writing folders?		
Storage for writing folders?		
Places to display writing?		
5. Do you have an identified time for uninterrupted student writing?		

Daily _____

If not, how often? _____

35–40 minutes _____

If not, how long? _____

Areas where I need to improve:

_____

_____

_____

PROCESS WRITING: A WAY TO CONSTRUCT MEANING

Process writing (Calkins, 1986; Graves, 1983, 1991; Hillocks, 1987a, 1987b) is an approach to teaching writing that allows students to take charge of their own writing and learning. It involves five steps that were introduced in Chapter 2—selecting the topic (sometimes called planning or previewing), drafting (sometimes called composing), revising, proofreading (sometimes called editing), and publishing. A good way to help students become accustomed to using these steps is to display them on a classroom poster like the one shown in Figure 7.7.

As students are introduced to process writing, each step should be modeled, guided, and supported by the teacher until students take charge of their own writing. Gradually the need for modeling will diminish; however, the teacher will always be a partner in learning with the students, interacting with them through individual and group conferences, discussing their writing ideas, sharing his or her own writing, and providing minilesson support as needed. Through this continuous, scaffolded support, students grow into writers and come to think of themselves as authors, a process that further develops their ability to construct meaning.

Process writing should begin in kindergarten. At this earliest level students will be at various developmental phases in their writing. Some will be at the *picture-writing* level, where they will simply draw a picture for their story as the student in Figure 7.8 has done. Other students will be at the *scribble-writing* phase (Figure 7.9). As students progress, they will move into the *random letter* phase (Figure 7.10) and then into the *invented spelling* phase (Figure 7.11), in which they begin to associate some letters and sounds. Finally, they will reach the *conventional writing* phase, in which they will spell most words correctly. It is normal for children in any grade to be at varying points in these stages. Beginning or less experienced writers are more likely to be at the picture, scribble, or invented spelling phases, and more experienced writers are closer to the conventional writing phase; in other words, it is normal to see some degree of invented spelling all the way through the elementary grades. (For more discussion of spelling, see "For Additional Reading" at the conclusion of this chapter.)

The following discussion focuses on one way to introduce process writing. As students become comfortable using the steps, the teacher modeling can gradually be dropped. Adjust your suggestions to fit the grade level you are teaching. To begin, have a brief discussion about writing with students. Then show them a chart like the one presented earlier in Figure 7.7 and talk briefly about each step in process writing, using the name of the step.

Figure 7.7   Poster for Process Writing

Figure 7.8   Picture-Writing Phase

Story: Next Friday I'm going to Disneyland (Told orally.)

Selecting the Topic

As students learn the process of writing, they should begin to *select their own topics.* The teacher's role in this process is that of guide and facilitator. From the start, students must know that they really can select their own topics. Take time to allow and encourage them to think of ideas on their own. The following steps can be used to help students learn this process:

1. Give each student a blank sheet of paper and ask the students to list anything that they might like to write about. If you are focusing on the domains of writing at this point, identify the domain or product you want them to produce; for example—"Think of all the topics you would want to write a story about." As students are making their lists, you do the same, making clear that that is what you are doing. After finishing your list, move around the room, trying to spot those who are having trouble. Stop and ask these students such questions as "What have you read that you would like to write about?" or "What topics are you thinking of?" Be careful not to sound critical or insulting. The object is to nudge students to think for themselves and to generate their own ideas.

   After a few minutes, stop the class and share your list, commenting on the topics you selected. Next, ask for volunteers who are willing to

Figure 7.9   Scribble-Writing Phase

Figure 7.10   Random Letter Phase

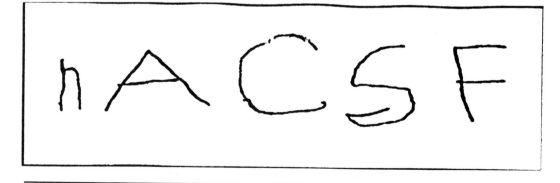

Figure 7.11   Invented Spelling Phase

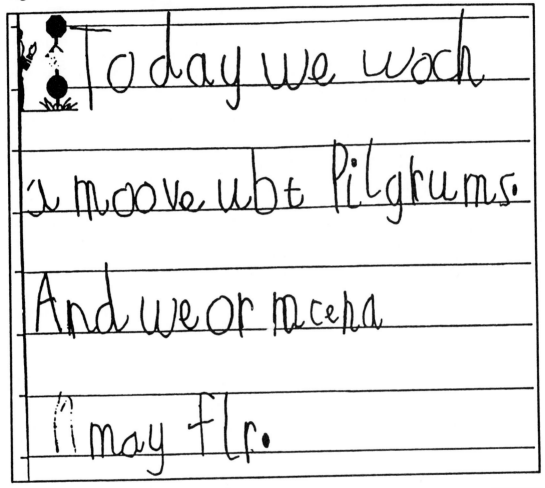

share their lists. As students read, encourage them to comment on any of their own topics and on each other's. Model positive comments about their topics with such remarks as "Those are all exciting topics" "It sounds like you have good ideas" and "You have so many topics you are going to have to really think about which one you want to write on."

Be certain that your comments are supportive and encouraging for all students, not just for those with long lists. After several students have shared their lists, help them see that it doesn't matter whether their list is long or short—all they need is one idea to begin writing.

2. Have students look over their lists to decide if they want to add any topics. You can model the process with your own list, perhaps by adding a topic similar to one a student has selected. This lets students know that it is all right for them to get ideas from others.

3. Have students look over their lists to select a topic for their first piece of writing. Suggest that they consider the following points as they make their decisions: (1) Which topic is the most interesting to you? (2) Which topic do you feel that you know the most about? and (3) Which topic do you think others might enjoy reading the most? Have students circle their choices. Then share your choice with the group and have volunteers do the same.

By following these steps, the teachers help students select their first topic for writing. It doesn't really matter what the topics are so long as the choices are the students' and the students want to write about them.

Students should keep their lists of topics in their writing folders and should be encouraged to add to them when they think of new ideas. They should not be made to feel that they will have to write on every topic on their lists. Their ideas change; therefore, the lists can be changed.

There are many other ways to have students select topics for writing. These should also be tried from time to time throughout the year:

- *Partners:* Have each student work with a partner to develop lists of possible topics. This is using the brainstorming strategy as suggested for activating prior knowledge in Chapter 3. It is a good strategy to use for the student who appears to have few ideas or who doesn't want to write.

- *Clustering:* "Clustering is a nonlinear brainstorming process akin to free association" (Rico, 1983, p. 28). Working alone, with partners, or with the teacher, students start with a topic or idea that forms the core or nucleus for the cluster. They then add all of the things they can think of that are related to it and select the specific topic from the cluster that they wish to write about or use the ideas to develop their writing. Figure 7.13 presents a cluster on animals developed by a second-grade teacher and his class to get ideas for writing. Teachers report that clustering is a successful technique to use with all students, including at-risk and second-language learners (Carr, 1987; Martinez, 1987; Pierce, 1987). For more on clustering, see "For Additional Reading" at the end of the chapter.

- *Looking for ideas away from school:* Encourage students to look for and jot down writing ideas on the way home from school, at home, or in places that they visit.

- *Camera ideas:* Let students use cameras to take pictures of possible topics. If possible, have them take pictures away from school as well. You can also encourage them to bring to class photographs from home that could be topics for their writing.

- *TV topics:* Encourage students to look for interesting topics as they watch their favorite TV shows.

Figure 7.12 Cluster on Animals Developed by Second Graders

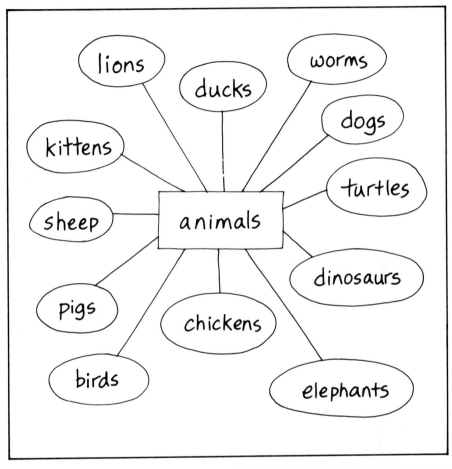

Selecting topics for writing is not always easy for students. Some of the problems they encounter and suggestions for overcoming these problems include the following:

- *No ideas:* Some students will say that they have no ideas to use for writing. One way to help these students is to get them to talk about things they do away from school. As they talk, suggest that each of these could be a topic for writing. Another tactic is to ask the students to think about places they'd like to go or something special they'd like to do, pointing out that these can also be ideas for writing. The teacher might serve as the student's secretary.

- *Too many ideas:* Some students will have so many ideas that they won't know which one to select for writing. In these cases teachers can help students focus by discussing the ideas with them. If discussion doesn't work, the teacher can select one of the topics for the student. One teacher, who had tried other strategies to no avail, finally said to a student, "Close you eyes and point to a topic. Since you like them all, write about the one you point to." That was enough encouragement to get the child started.
- *Don't like to write:* This problem is tougher to deal with, and there are really no easy solutions. Some students simply don't like to write and don't want to write, for a number of reasons. (Likewise, some teachers don't like to write and don't want to teach writing.) These students need to be encouraged to write and to see some of the fun of writing. The teacher can begin by serving as the student's secretary and recording not only the topics but the first draft of the writing. Another tactic is to allow the student to dictate his or her list of topics onto a tape recorder or put them on a computer or word processor; then, write the first draft on the word processor. Shared and collaborative writing are also good ways to get students started.

Selecting the topic for writing is an important part of the writing process, and students need to see that they can use their own ideas. Although there are times when students must write on assigned topics, they must be allowed to choose their own topics when they are learning "how" to write. Even in classes such as social studies, in which students are required to write reports, teachers are likely to get better products if they let students have some choice of the topic.

Drafting

Once students have selected their topics, they are ready to begin to write. The teacher and students have already modeled the process of selecting topics; now the teacher must show students how to write. Drafting includes two stages: planning and composing, both of which should be modeled as students are learning to use process writing.

Planning

Good writers think about what they are going to write and organize their ideas. To do this they consider the purpose for their writing and the audience for whom they are writing. Teachers should model this process using their own topic and the following steps:

1. Tell the class a little about your topic and what you want to write about it. Mention your audience and purpose for writing, and allow students to

ask questions. Next, on the chalkboard, overhead projector, or large sheets of paper, jot down some of the ideas you have about the topic. Group ideas that go together, but don't be concerned about getting all of them organized at this point. Tell students that you now have a general plan of what you want to include in your writing and you know how you want to begin. Figure 7.13 shows the notes one teacher made while planning to write about her family's camping trip.

2. Have students work in pairs, telling each other about their topics. Afterwards, have each student jot down some ideas or words about his or her topic on a sheet of paper. Volunteers should share their ideas with the class and talk about what they want to include in their writing. Help students understand that this is a beginning plan for their writing and that it will probably change as they actually write.

As students mature in their writing abilities, you can introduce outlining and include it in modeling when focusing on expository writing. Students will find outlining a useful planning tool for such activities as report writing. They may also use clustering (discussed earlier in this chapter) or semantic mapping (discussed in Chapter 3) to help them organize their ideas.

The more students mature in their writing, the less they will need to go through the planning phase as a group. However, students should be given enough teacher modeling and support to see how planning is done and how it can help them in their own writing. The more students write, the more automatically they will carry out the process of writing.

Composing

The next phase in the drafting stage is the actual composing. Students should be told to write on lined paper (unlined for beginners) using every other line to leave room for revisions. This practice helps them develop a positive attitude toward revision; it lets them know that changes can and will be made and that it is all right to make changes in their writing.

You must model this activity as well because it is important that the students see the teacher write. Although the teacher and students can write independently and share their results later, this works best with older, more mature writers and it is not as satisfactory for beginning writers since it does not really let students see all of the process of writing. For most students, the following procedure will be most effective:

1. Using the chalkboard, overhead projector, or large sheets or paper, begin to develop the topic you selected, discussing what you are doing as you go. Note the mechanics of starting a sentence and paragraph and show students how to organize ideas into sentences and paragraphs, asking them to suggest words or make changes in your writing. As you write, cross out some words to show students how to make changes without erasing, which often becomes a big problem for students. Don't be afraid to tell

Figure 7.13   Teacher's Notes for Planning Writing

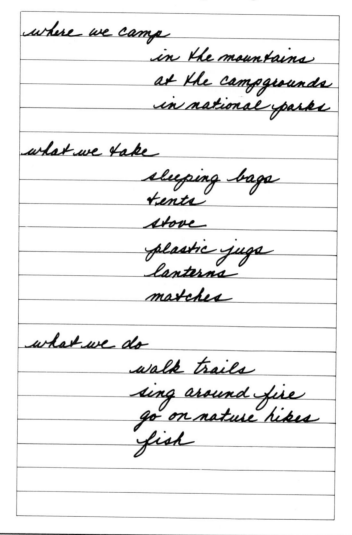

where we camp
    in the mountains
    at the campgrounds
    in national parks

what we take
    sleeping bags
    tents
    stove
    plastic jugs
    lanterns
    matches

what we do
    walk trails
    sing around fire
    go on nature hikes
    fish

students that you don't know what to say next and that you need some help. Figure 7.14 shows a sample of the teacher's draft for modeling the family camping trip story.

2. After the initial teacher modeling, have students start their own writing. Encourage them to use the notes they made as a part of their planning. While students are writing, move about the room offering guidance, assistance, and encouragement to those who need it. If there are students

Figure 7.14   Teacher's Draft for Modeling Writing

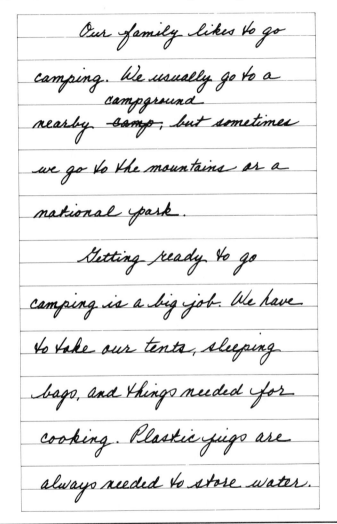

Our family likes to go
camping. We usually go to a
    campground
nearby. ~~camp;~~ but sometimes
we go to the mountains or a
national park.
    Getting ready to go
camping is a big job. We have
to take our tents, sleeping
bags, and things needed for
cooking. Plastic jugs are
always needed to store water.

who are not writing, offer to be their secretary for the beginning few sentences of their draft.

If the writing is going smoothly, continue to move about the room offering assistance and support. A few minutes of talking about the topic or a few questions from the teacher are often enough to keep students writing. Give students as much time to write as the schedule will allow and as much time as they can use productively. If you see that the writing time is producing little or nothing, it is probably best to resume modeling or to stop the writing at this time.

3. If you find it necessary to resume modeling, return to your story and continue to write, explaining as you go. Continue to encourage students to help you. As you model your writing, you can note different elements of good writing; however, during the initial introduction of writing do not overemphasize isolated mechanics.

Composing is the phase of drafting in which students develop their topic. Usually, they will have been given enough direction up to this point that they can proceed with their own writing without additional instruction. During this part of the writing program, students should be given uninterrupted writing time to develop their ideas. Modeling occurs as the teacher moves about the room offering assistance.

In this phase of writing, the object is for students to express their ideas freely and creatively; they should not be hampered by worrying about spelling. The best way to deal with the spelling issue is to encourage students to spell words the way they think they sound (invented spellings). This will allow them to be free to write, realizing that they can take care of any spelling problems during their revision. For those students who are overly concerned about having words spelled correctly or are unable to use invented spelling, provide the correct spellings by writing the words in question on a sheet of paper or the chalkboard or tell them to pretend they are alone on an island with no one to ask. Other techniques can be used, such as having one student serve as a spelling helper or having a list of troublesome words on the board or a chart, but *nothing works as well to develop a sense of spelling as having students try to spell words the way they think they sound and then make corrections during revision and proofreading.*

The amount of time allowed for the composing phase depends on the students, their writing abilities, the nature of the piece being written, and the length of time allocated to writing in the classroom. Usually the composing phase will extend over several days or writing periods. Students can place their writing in their writing folders and return to it at the next writing period or when they have some extra time during the day. The writing, especially in the beginning stages, should be done at school.

Throughout the composing phase, the teacher should continue to be available to help students with their writing. If students get stuck, they should be encouraged to ask the teacher or a peer for suggestions. For example, if a student can't think of a good word to describe his or her old dog, the teacher might give several suggestions and let the student select the one he or she wants to use. Asking questions and offering suggestions as the students are writing is an extension of modeling and is also a "quick conference."

Revising

Revision, the third stage in the writing process, is the step in which the students begin to look at their work to examine content—ideas, choice of words, and so forth. Revision may involve modeling by the teacher, conferences between student and teacher or student and student, and individual student work. It is not a natural step for students to employ (Graves, 1984), and most beginning writers, especially kindergartners and first graders, are not ready for much revision—they think that everything they have written is wonderful. Therefore, teachers must help students learn to appreciate the importance of revision by systematically working through this stage with them.

You can model revision by using your own writing as an example. You and your students should first discuss what to look for when revising content:

1. Have I expressed my ideas clearly so that my audience will understand what I am saying?
2. Are there other ideas that I should add to my writing?
3. Are there other words that I can use to make my writing more exciting and interesting?
4. Are there better ways that I can express my ideas?

The questions generated can be posted for students to think about as they work on their revisions. The items considered in content revision will vary according to the students' level and degree of sophistication.

After you and your students have developed guidelines for revision, show them how to go about revising their writing. Check each of the points listed on the revision checklist and discuss problem areas with them, making changes with their help. Have them try better ways of expressing their ideas. Throughout the revision step, you should stress the importance of expressing oneself clearly because the writing is going to be read by someone else. Figure 7.15 shows a copy of the teacher's story about the family camping trip after the teacher and students revised the content.

Students are now ready to begin to work on their own revisions. At this point they should begin to have revision conferences with each other and with you (for a discussion of writing conferences, see page 431). During these conferences students talk about their writing and look for places where they might make changes, with you and/or other students taking on the role of an editor who asks questions and points out areas of possible improvement. Many students will already know where some of these areas are. The teacher and peers should not become the "fixers" of the student's writing; rather, they should help students note places where work is needed, discuss ideas with students, and have the writer try to make the changes.

Figure 7.15   Teacher's Story Used for Modeling Revision

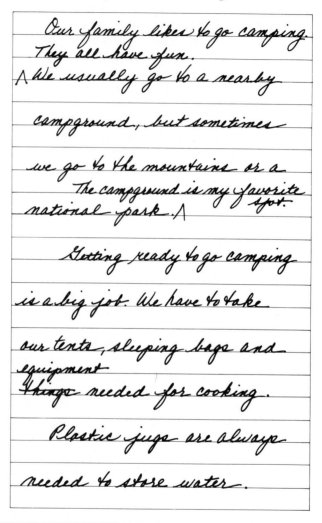

Proofreading

The fourth step in process writing is proofreading, or editing, which should take place after students have made all the content changes they feel are necessary. In proofreading, students get their writing in order for final copy, checking spelling, writing mechanics, and sentence structure. The teacher and students should work together to develop a list of things to look for in proofreading, and the list should be posted in the room so that students can

Figure 7.16   Proofreading Checklist Developed by a Fifth-Grade Class

Proofreading Checklist

	Author	*Editor*
1. Sentences and questions begin with capital letters.	☐	☐
2. Sentences and questions have the correct end marks.	☐	☐
3. Paragraphs are indented.	☐	☐
4. Possible misspellings have been circled and checked.	☐	☐

Author _____

Editor _____

refer to it as they work. In addition to spelling, the list should reflect the writing mechanics that were modeled throughout the writing. Figure 7.16 shows a proofreading checklist developed by a fifth-grade class and their teacher for use at the beginning of the year. This generic checklist can be used by the author (writer) or someone who edits such as a peer or the teacher for any domain of writing. As you become more comfortable with process writing, you will want to develop more specific checklists for each domain, varying the items according to the level and sophistication of the students.

Publishing

The final stage of the writing process is publishing, which has two parts: (1) making a final copy of the writing and (2) putting the writing in form to be shared with others. Although most students will make a final copy of their writing, if they are not making progress with a piece of writing they may select to drop it. This may occur at *any point* in the writing process. Indeed, not all writing should be published. The student together with the teacher should make this decision after considering both the quality of the writing and how the student feels about it. In a conference, you might ask the student such questions as "How do you think others will feel about this piece of writing?" and "Do you think it is a good idea to publish this one?" Sometimes it is appropriate for the teacher to say, "I don't think this is one of your best pieces of writing. Maybe you should just stop on this piece or make a final copy for your file and start work on something new." If a student feels strongly about the piece being published, it is probably best to proceed, but you must always weigh the consequences of having a student publish a piece that is really inappropriate.

Publishing is important for all students, not just a special few. This phase of the writing creates a sense of the reason for writing and gives students pride and enjoyment in their own work. The more students publish their writing, the more they will develop a sense of themselves as authors and grow in the writing process. One precaution: A few students will not want to create final copies or publish. You must support and guide these students until they experience the satisfaction of seeing their work published because this will motivate them to write more.

When the decision is to make final copy only, the copy can be put in the student's writing folder. Even writing that is not published may be used for later review and placed in the literacy portfolio (see Chapter 10).

Producing Final Copy

After students have completed their revision and held their initial publishing conference with the teacher, they are ready to make a final copy of their writing. In making their final copy, they should be encouraged to be as neat and accurate as possible.

One way to get students to produce a good final copy is to use a computer and word processor, since even very young children experience success with this approach.

You and your students should work together to develop a list of guidelines to follow in making final copies, and the list should be kept where students can refer to it easily. Points such as those given below can be included, but each list must reflect the needs, abilities, and level of the students:

Final Copy Guidelines
_____

Be neat.
Indent each new paragraph.
Keep margins at the top, bottom, and sides of the paper straight.
Check punctuation.
Check spelling.
Reread your final copy to be sure it is correct.

The manner in which the final copy is prepared will depend on whether it is to be published or simply filed.

Ideas for Publishing

Publishing is a very important part of the writing process (Calkins, 1986; Graves, 1983). Students need this aspect of the writing to help them develop a sense of importance for their writing, a sense of understanding why one must learn to write, and a sense of their audience.

The most common way for students to publish their writing is in book form. Individual students can produce their own books or several students can collaborate on one. The excitement and pleasure on the face of students after producing their first book is almost indescribable. Publishing brings closure to the students' writing experience.

Books can be produced in many forms:

- Construction paper covers over paper.
- Folder books made from manila folders and paper.
- Shape books cut to show the topic. For example, a snowman shape for a winter topic.
- Hardcover books made from cardboard and cloth. (For directions, see Tompkins and Hoskisson, 1991, under "For Additional Reading.")

Students can move from simple types of books to more complex procedures as they become more practiced. They should be encouraged to include a cover page that presents their name, the illustrator's name, and the date. Then, at the end of the book, they should place a page entitled "About the Author" where they tell about themselves and other books they have written. Also, when books are being published to be shared with other classmates, it is good to include a sheet in the back where students can indicate that they have read the book and make comments about how they felt about it.

There are many other ways for students to share their writing without producing a book. Some of the following ideas broaden the concept of publishing to any form of sharing:

- *Bulletin boards:* Use a bulletin board with a catchy title and attractive background for students to display final copies that have not been made into a book. Titles can be "Great Writing from Great Kids," "Writing We Are Proud Of," "Great Writers Are Blossoming," "Award Winners," and so on. Sometimes you can attach a clothesline to the bulletin board and students can hang their writing out for others to read.
- *Author's chair:* The concept of the author's chair (Graves & Hansen, 1983) was introduced in Chapter 2. This is a special chair labeled "Author's Chair." The student who has a piece of writing to share sits in the chair and reads it to the group, and a discussion of the writing follows. Usually the piece that is shared is the final copy.
- *Class or school newspaper:* A class or school newspaper is an excellent way to create authentic reasons for students to write. Because of the nature of a newspaper, students can get experiences with many domains of writing and numerous products—articles, stories, letters to the editor, and so forth. The newspaper can have a staff, and students can publish it using a computer and word processor.
- *Magazines of student-written works:* Students may also choose to submit their writing to a magazine that publishes student-written works. Table 7.3 presents a list of magazines that publish student writing.
- *Writing circles:* The concept of the literature circle was introduced in Chapter 6. You can also have a writing circle where students get together to share and discuss their writing. Also referred to as RAGs (Read Around

Table 7.3 Magazines That Publish Student Writings

Magazine	Address	Ages	Types of Writing Accepted
American Girl	830 Third Avenue New York, NY 10022	12–14	Short stories, poems, and letters to the editor
Boys' Life	1325 Walnut Hill Lane Irving, TX 75602	all	Short stories, poems, and nonfiction
The Children's Album	P.O. Box 262 Manchester, CA 95459	all	Short stories, poems, and nonfiction
Children's Digest	P.O. Box 567 Indianapolis, IN 46206	8–10	Poetry, short stories, riddles, and jokes
Child Life	P.O. Box 567 Indianapolis, IN 46206	7–9	Short stories, poetry, riddles, jokes, and letters to the editor
Cricket	1058 8th Street LaSalle, IL 61301	6–12	Letters and Cricket League monthly; short story and poetry contests
FLIP Magazine (Future Literature in Progress)	The Art Center of Battle Creek 265 East Emmett Street Battle Creek, MI 49107	all	Poetry and short stories
Highlights for Children	803 Church Street Honesdale, PA 18431	5–10	Poetry, short stories, jokes, riddles, and letters to the editor
Jack and Jill	P.O. Box 567 Indianapolis, IN 46206	5–10	Short stories, poems, riddles, and letters to the editor
Kids Magazine	P.O. Box 3041 Grand Central Station New York, NY 10017	all	Short stories, reports, poems, cartoons, puzzles, and most other forms of writing
The McGuffey Writer	400A McGuffey Hall Miami University Oxford, OH 45056	all	Poetry, short stories, essays, and cartoons
Merlyn's Pen	P.O. Box 716 East Greenwich, RI 12818	12–14	Essays, poems, and short stories
Prism Magazine	1040 Bayview Drive, Suite 223 Ft. Lauderdale, FL 33304	10–14	Poetry, short stories
Scholastic Scope	50 West 44th Street New York, NY 10036	13–14	Poems, stories, plays
Scholastic Voice	50 West 44th Street New York NY 10036	13–14	Short stories and poems; also writing contests
Spinoff (for gifted children)	P.O. Box 115 Sewell, NJ 08080	all	Stories, poems, essays, and word games

Table 7.3, continued

Magazine	Address	Ages	Types of Writing Accepted
Stone Soup	Children's Art Foundation P.O. Box 83 Santa Cruz, CA 95063	all	Poetry, short stories, and book reports (books to be reviewed are provided by the magazine)
Wombat	365 Ashton Drive Athens, GA 30606	all	Short stories, poems, essays, puzzles, cartoons, and book reports
Young Author's Magazine	3015 Woodsdale Blvd. Lincoln, NE 68502	all	Short stories, essays, other nonfiction, poetry, and drama
Young World	P.O. Box 567 Indianapolis, IN 46206	10–14	Poetry, short stories, jokes, and letters to the editor

Source: Reprinted with the permission of Merrill Publishing Company, an imprint of Macmillan Publishing Company, Inc. from *Language Arts: Content and Teaching Strategies* by Gail E. Tompkins and Kenneth Hoskisson, pp. 252–253. Copyright © 1987 by Merrill Publishing Company.

Groups—Olson, 1987), the writing circle consists of five or six students who sit together to read and talk about (not critique) their writing. Several writing circles may be in operation at the same time. (They may also be used for selecting and discussing a topic, revising, and proofreading. To ensure that students know the real purpose of the circle, it might be best to use the title "Writing Circle" for sharing and "RAGs" when the idea is used for other purposes.)

It does not matter how children publish and share their writing as long as they do it, since it is through sharing that they develop their sense of authorship and show how they have constructed meaning by conveying their ideas to others. No matter what grade level, sharing is an essential part of constructing meaning through writing.

WRITING CONFERENCES

Guidelines for holding reading conferences were presented in Chapter 6, and many of those same suggestions apply to writing conferences. These conferences may be held between the teacher and one student or several students at a time, or by two or more students. Conferences may focus on any aspect of the writing process—selecting a topic, actual writing, revision, proofreading, or publishing.

Teacher-Student Conferences

The writing conference is *not* a time to "evaluate" the students' writing. Rather, it is a time for the teacher and student(s) to discuss some aspect of the students' writing and for the teacher to ask probing or guiding questions that will help the students formulate their ideas. Conferences are the core of the process of teaching writing (Calkins, 1986; Graves, 1983). The following suggestions should be helpful in planning your conferences:

- *When you begin to use conferences, explain their purpose and procedures to students.* Role-play several conferences to establish routines and guidelines for behavior.
- *Keep conferences short and focused.* Graves (1991) has noted that conferences need to be brief and focused. If students don't need a conference, don't have one—their time would be better spent writing. Conferences usually last 5 to 10 minutes, though many are much shorter.
- *Maintain a positive, interactive environment.* Use probing questions and statements that encourage students to think about their writing and talk about it. (See the section on conference questions that follows.)
- *From time to time have group conferences during which you talk with several students about their writing.* This is an especially useful procedure if students are doing similar types of writing or appear to have similar needs for support.
- *Keep a simple record sheet for each student such as the one shown in Figure 7.17.* This will tell you what students are doing and what needs they seem to have.
- *Have a plan in mind for the conference.* Although each conference will be different, depending upon the purpose and who called for it, you need to have a basic plan in mind. If the student asked for the conference, begin by having him or her tell what he or she wants to discuss. Then proceed from there. A simple basic plan that works well for many teachers is as follows (Calkins, 1986; Graves, 1983; Millett, 1986).

  1. *Opening:* Students read their draft. You listen or read along as the student reads.
  2. *Discussion:* Talk about the content and sequence of ideas unless the student has some other specific purpose. Ask questions that get the student to talk about the piece of writing.
  3. *Closing:* Help the student focus attention on *one* thing to do to improve the writing. This will help the student see quick success.

Figure 7.17   Record Sheet for Keeping Track of Student's Writing

Name _____ **Grade** _____

Date	Writing Piece	Suggestions	Mini-Lesson Needs	Goals/Comments

Questions to Ask During Writing Conferences

The questions that you ask during a writing conference should help students reflect on their writing (think about it critically), expand their writing, and select ways to improve their writing (Millett, 1986). The following questions are from Millett (1986, pp. 27–29):

Reflecting Questions

- What part is most interesting to you?
- What feeling do you want your reader to have?
- Is this the idea that you wanted me to get?

Expanding Questions

- That's interesting—would you like your reader to know about that?
- Can you tell more about . . . ?
- Is that important to add?

Selecting Questions

Phrase questions that relate to *focus* and *order:*

- Which part is *most* important?
- Where could this new idea go?
- Which parts talk about the same thing?
- How might you put these parts together?

Ask questions about *beginnings* and *endings:*

- Which of three or four titles did your partner like best? Why?
- Can you turn your topic sentence beginning into a more interesting lead?
- Do you end with the most important thing you want your readers to know or feel?
- Does your ending repeat what you said in the beginning, or does it say the same thing in a different way? Which kind of ending is better for this piece? Why?

Ask questions about *sentences:*

- How many of your sentences begin the same way?
- How else could you start two or three of these sentences?
- Could you break this long sentence into shorter ones?
- How might you combine two or three short sentences?

Ask about *wording* and *phrasing:*

- Which sentences do the best job of showing, not just telling?
- Where else could you use words that show instead of tell?

Peer Conferences

Peer conferences are another good way for students to have a conversation with someone about their writing (Dahl, 1988). As with student-teacher conferences, students need to know the purposes of the conference. However, they also need to know what is expected of them and what they should do during the conference. Peer conferences are often held in preparation for a teacher conference.

An effective way to get peer conferences started is to develop with the class a set of guidelines to follow like those from a third-grade class shown in Figure 7.18. Again, these guidelines would need to be adjusted to the particular

Figure 7.18 Peer Conference Guidelines from a Third-Grade Class

> ### Our Peer Conference Guidelines
>
> - Remember that your friend's writing is his/her own work. Don't try to rewrite it.
> - Let the writer read the piece of writing aloud.
> - Talk about the things you like.
> - Ask questions about things you don't understand.
> - Make one or two suggestions for improving the writing.
> - If you are proofreading, also read it silently.

grade level you are teaching. Teacher conferences can serve as models for peer conferences. It is also a good idea to role-play peer conferences and talk with students about how to improve them.

STARTING AND MAINTAINING A READING AND WRITING PROGRAM

The discussion in the preceding pages describes only one way to get a writing program started. You may choose to introduce process writing by having a shared writing experience with the entire class first, demonstrating each of the steps before having the students begin their own work. Some teachers, particularly in the upper grades, simply begin with a little talk about the writing steps and then have students begin, using this initial writing experience diagnostically to determine where their students are and the type of support they need. However, if you are sure that students have little or no experience with process writing, it is better to begin with a procedure like the one suggested here to ensure student comfort and success.

In maintaining a writing program that connects writing and reading, you should also consider activities that connect reading and writing and how to develop grammar, usage, and spelling. Both of these will be discussed in the sections that follow.

Activities That Connect Reading and Writing

Throughout your literacy program you must continually help students see the connections between reading and writing and think about how each carries over to the other. The following suggestions are only a few ways to help students begin to make this explicit connection (Shanahan, 1988):

Reading Specific Types of Writing

Students need to use their writing as a springboard to reading just as they use their reading as a springboard to writing. If you have a student who has written (or is writing) a mystery, encourage her to read some other mysteries such as *Encyclopedia Brown: Boy Detective* (Sobol, 1963) or *The Mysterious Disappearance of Leon (I Mean Noel)* (Raskin, 1971) to see how these authors developed their ideas.

Reading Student-Written Materials

As students begin to publish books, they can read each other's books; they enjoy seeing what their peers have written. These books should be displayed in both the classroom and school library, and should be used as a part of the reading material for the literacy program. In many schools where this is done the student-written books are among those most frequently selected and checked out.

Developing a collection of student-written books is a simple procedure. Begin the school year by telling students that there will be a special section in the school library for books or magazines they have written. Explain that there will be a classroom library of their books and that throughout the year selected books will be placed in the school library. You and your students should develop criteria such as the following for selecting books:

1. Best written
2. Favorite topic or story
3. Topic others would most likely enjoy
4. Book student would like others to read

The student-written book collection for the library can become a school-wide project. At the conclusion of each school year, students may donate a

Figure 7.19   Bulletin Board for Publicizing Student Books in the School Library

certain number of their books to the library and copies should then be made so that authors can also have a copy.

As student-written books are added to the school library, special announcements should be made so that everyone in the school can see them. This can be done through a school newspaper or a bulletin-board display similar to that in Figure 7.19.

Finally, a special time may be designated in the reading program for students to read the books that have been written by their peers. For example, teachers can designate an hour every other week for this purpose and can increase the time to an hour or longer each week as more books are available. Students should use the time to read the books and talk about them with their classmates. These discussions can be handled in small groups or as class discussions, but they should focus on telling about the books, not evaluating them.

Having a time in the literacy program for students to read books written by their peers gives a special importance to both reading and writing. It helps to show students that these processes are related and also gives them incentive for reading and writing.

Summaries

Another way to help students make the connection between reading and writing is to have them write a summary of a text they have just read (Hill, 1991). This is a skill that must be taught. The following steps for summarizing expository texts are based on research by Brown and Day (1983):

1. Determine the topic of the paragraph or text. Identify unnecessary information or trivia, and delete this information; it should not be included in the summary.
2. Look for information that is repeated; it should only be included in the summary once.
3. Note places where ideas or terms can be grouped together. For example, if the paragraph or text being summarized discusses travel by plane, ship, train, and car, all of these can be referred to as "transportation."
4. Identify a main-idea sentence for each paragraph, if possible.
5. If no main-idea sentence exists, formulate one of your own.
6. Formulate your final summary, rechecking to be sure that you have followed each guideline. Keep your summary short.

The process of writing a summary should be modeled for students using procedures similar to those suggested for teaching the writing process.

Writing summaries after reading can be handled in many creative ways. For example, teachers can give students such writing assignments as the following:

• Pretend to be newspaper reporters or TV newscasters who must present a summary of what they have read. First write the summary and then distribute it to other students in newspaper form or give the summary as a part of a TV news report.
• Maintain a log or journal that reports a summary of your readings. Write the log entries after reading your favorite selections. (Students can also be instructed to write log entries for particular selections assigned by the teacher.)

Summaries may also be written for narrative texts in which case the same type of guidelines should be followed focusing on the parts of a story map (see Chapters 2 and 3) instead of main ideas.

Figure 7.20   Sample Story Frame Focusing on a Character

This story is about _____.

_____ is an important character.

_____ tried to _____

_____.

The story ends when _____

_____.

Story Frames

Story frames are another way to build the connection between reading and writing (Fowler, 1982). A story frame is a basic outline for a story that is designed to help readers organize their ideas about what has been read. It consists of a series of spaces hooked together by transition words; each story frame usually follows a single line of thought or aspect of a selection. Figure 7.20 presents a story frame that focuses on a particular character from a selection.

After students read a selection, the teacher can use the story frame as an oral discussion starter. Students should be encouraged to fill in the slots in the frame, basing their responses on their reading; however, they should also be encouraged to express the ideas creatively in their own words. When students have become familiar with the concept of using story frames, the teacher can use story frames in written activities following reading.

Although story frames can be written for specific selections, some of the basic patterns can be used repeatedly. Figure 7.21 presents three additional story frames focusing on setting, plot, and character comparison.

Spelling, Grammar, and Usage

The importance of writing in helping children learn to spell was discussed in Chapter 5. Writing is also important in helping students learn the various conventions of our language.

Formal grammar teaching as a way to promote meaning construction through writing is not considered a useful activity for students. As Hillocks and Smith (1991) state, "Why does grammar retain such glamour when research over the past 90 years reveals not only that students are hostile toward it, but that the study of grammar has no impact on writing quality?" (p. 600).

Figure 7.21   Sample Story Frames

Setting Frame

This story takes place _____

_____. I can tell this because the

author uses such words as _____

_____ to tell

where this story happens.

Plot Frame

This story begins when _____

_____. Next,

_____.

Then _____

_____. The story ends when

_____

_____.

Character Comparison Frame

_____ and _____ are

two characters in our story. _____ is

_____ whereas _____ is

_____. For instance, _____

tries to _____ and

_____ learns a lesson when _____

_____.

They also state that "the grammar sections of a textbook should be treated as a reference tool that might provide some insights into conventions of mechanics and usage" (p. 600).

The basic premise that children learn to read and write by reading and writing with support as needed is also true about grammar, usage, and spelling. Repeated authentic opportunities to write help children learn the conventions of writing and also help them construct meaning through reading. Very brief minilessons held during conferences are sufficient for supporting most students in learning mechanics, usage, and spelling, and these lessons can be built around a demonstrated need in the student's writing.

EXPOSITORY WRITING AS AN AID TO CONSTRUCTING MEANING

An ongoing concern of teachers has been how to help students more effectively comprehend informational texts (Konopak, Martin, & Martin, 1990). This is an especially serious concern as students reach the upper elementary grades and middle school, where they begin to encounter more expository texts in a variety of content areas. Researchers have demonstrated that the incorporation of a writing strategy with reading can improve students' ability to do expository writing, can help them understand different text structures (see Chapter 3 for a discussion of text structures), and can improve their ability to construct meaning (Konopak et al., 1990; Raphael, Kirschner & Englert, 1988). By carefully planning writing experiences across the curriculum, it is possible to improve both students' writing and their ability to construct meaning (Rosaen, 1990).

Helping students learn to do expository writing involves the same basic steps of process writing that were discussed in detail earlier. One program that has proven to be effective is the cognitive strategy instruction in writing (CSIW) program (Raphael & Englert, 1990). CSIW is not a separate reading and writing program; it is an ongoing teaching strategy that complements the literacy program.

Cognitive Strategy Instruction in Writing (CSIW)

CSIW has been used with fourth and fifth graders to help them develop their ability to write and read informational texts. It begins by having students analyze writing to see how authors select their topics and present information so that it will be clearly understood by a reader. As the strategy proceeds, students *write* and *read* informational texts. The strategy is based on a set of "think sheets" and follows four steps:

1. *Text analysis:* Begin by modeling with students how to analyze a piece of writing in terms of the type of text structure you want students to write: *description*, *collection* (sequence), *cause-effect*, *problem-solution*, or *comparison*. You can use writing from previous students, your own writing, or writing selected from a text.
2. *Modeling the writing process:* Select a topic that fits with the type of text analyzed in step 1. Model the process you would go through by showing how you would plan and organize your writing. Use think sheets similar to those shown in Figures 7.22 and 7.23 to show students the process.

Figure 7.22   Plan Think Sheet

Plan **Think Sheet**

Author's name _____ Date _____

Topic: _____

WHO: Who am I writing for?

WHY: Why am I writing this?

WHAT: What do I already know about my topics? (Brainstorm)

1. _____

2. _____

3. _____

4. _____

HOW: How do I group my ideas?

1. Materials I'll need

   _____

   _____

2. Steps

   _____

   _____

3. Things that happened when we made it

   _____

   _____

4. Beginning and ending ideas

   _____

   _____

Figure 7.23 Organize Think Sheet

Organize **Think Sheet**

What is being explained?

Who or what is needed?

Setting?

What are the steps?

First,

Next,

Third,

Then,

Fifth,

Finally,

3. *Guided writing:* Have students use the think sheets modeled in step 2, select their own topic, and write their paper. Offer guidance during all steps of the process.
4. *Independent writing:* Finally, have students write following the models developed in steps 1 to 3. After they have learned to use several structures, give them the opportunity to combine them as writers normally do.

Raphael and Englert (1990) offer detailed guidelines for using this strategy (see "For Additional Reading").

CSIW is an excellent teaching strategy for helping students learn to do expository writing, especially in the practical/informative and analytical/expository domains. It is based on the premises of process writing and uses the same basic procedures. Moreover, it typifies the type of instruction that provides gradual release of responsibility to students. Most important, it is flexible. However, it is only *one* strategy that may be incorporated into the literacy program (Pardo & Raphael, 1991).

Raphael and Englert (1990) report success in using this strategy with students who had serious writing and comprehension problems as well as with higher-achieving students. "It is a program designed to complement, enhance, and guide ongoing writing and reading instruction" (Raphael & Englert, 1990, p. 400). In a follow-up study, researchers found that this strategy helped fourth- and fifth-grade learning-disabled and nonlearning-disabled students in three ways (Englert, Raphael, Anderson, Anthony, & Stevens, 1991): (1) it improved the quality of their expository writing on the trained structures; (2) it transferred to untrained structures; and (3) it made writers more sensitive to their audience. However, it did not affect the students' reading, possibly because of the heavy emphasis on writing. Further study is needed to determine its effects on reading, but it is safe to conclude that CSIW is effective in improving students' expository writing.

THE WRITING WORKSHOP: A PLAN FOR ORGANIZING AND MANAGING WRITING

The concept of the reading workshop was introduced in Chapter 6 as a way of effectively meeting individual needs for reading instruction. The writing workshop is a very similar plan and in fact was the source concept for the reading workshop.

The writing workshop has been recommended by numerous researchers and writing teachers (Atwell, 1987; Calkins, 1986; Hansen, 1987). It is a very flexible plan that places the students and teacher in a partnership for learning. Graves (reported in Atwell, 1987) compares a classroom organized as a writing workshop to an artist's studio: just as the studio is planned, organized, and arranged for the convenience of the artist, so the classroom, as already discussed, is organized for the writer to promote and support writing.

Elements of the Writing Workshop

The writing workshop consists of four basic parts: minilessons, state-of-the-class conferences, writing and conferring, and group sharing. Each part flows into the next to make up the block of time allocated for writing. The ideas and suggestions given here are based on the work of Atwell (1987), Calkins (1986), and Hansen (1987) and my own experience of working with children and teachers.

Minilesson

The minilesson, developed by Calkins (1986), is a short lesson done with the whole class that usually lasts from 5 to 10 minutes. The content of the minilesson is determined by student needs as evidenced during a previous writing workshop. The guidelines presented in Chapter 2 also apply here.

Since the minilesson content is based on student needs, the topics covered may range from how to select a topic to how to write a business letter. However, *be careful not to let the minilesson become an isolated grammar or usage lesson.* You may use some portions of an English textbook as a reference source for certain minilessons if the models provided in the text and the examples help you formulate your lessons, but you should not use the practice exercises that focus on isolated skills. All practice should come through shared or collaborative writing or through the students' own writings. Following is a list of possible topics for minilessons:

- Procedures for the writing workshop
- Writing an opening paragraph
- Punctuating items in a series
- Selecting words to show fear, suspense, bravery, or other characteristics
- Selecting topics
- How to write a friendly letter
- Examples of humor from a piece of literature
- Correct use of paragraph form
- Outlining for a report
- Writing description
- Punctuating dialogue

There is no end to the possible topics for minilessons. If on some days no minilesson is needed, this time may be used for more sharing time or may be added to the writing time.

State-of-the-Class Conference

The state-of-the-class conference, a very brief activity, is a way to be sure that you know exactly what all students are doing during each writing workshop. Atwell (1987) uses a clipboard and chart similar to the one shown in Figure 7.24 to keep track of students each day.

After you have completed the minilesson, take 5 minutes to ask students to identify what they are going to be doing during the day's workshop. Use a code like the one shown in Figure 7.24 to record what each student says. By examining your chart, you can tell who might need some extra conference time or just a quick visit from your during writing. As you become more comfortable with this procedure, you might choose to make a large state-of-the-class chart and have students complete it each day as the writing workshop begins.

The state-of-the-class conference builds in a "comfort factor" for you. It lets you know what students are doing and gives you a way to know what is happening over the week. Teachers who use the writing workshop indicate repeatedly that this portion of the workshop gives them the control they feel they need but still encourages student independence.

Writing and Conferring

Writing and conferring is the core of the writing workshop and usually lasts from 30 to 40 minutes, depending on the grade level you are teaching. During this block of time, students are writing; you may be writing yourself or holding conferences with students.

Since students will be at various stages in developing their writing piece, you will need to do a variety of things, depending on their needs. Some of the time you will simply be seated in your area or at your desk working on some writing of your own, thus modeling adult writing and expressing that you value this activity. This should not be just a time for you to catch up on school work, even though some may be done as a legitimate part of writing.

At other times, you will be circulating through the class talking with individual students, reading portions of what they have written, prompting and encouraging them, and offering whatever support they need. These brief encounters may be viewed as miniconferences or just times to talk with, guide, and support students. During this time you will gain valuable information that will help you plan minilessons and assess and evaluate students' progress. You will want to carry note cards, a pad, or adhesive labels so that you can make notes for future use in planning and/or for insertion into your notebook page for each student.

Some students may be holding a peer conference during this time, working on revision, editing, planning a new piece, or just getting topics for writing.

Figure 7.24   Partial State-of-the-Class Chart

State of Class Chart					
Names	M	T	W	Th	F
Lisa	①	©	②	RV	PR
Ted	①	①	©	②	②
Larry	②	©	RV	PR	P
Susan	©	P	⑤ ①	①	©
Mike	②	PR	P	⑤	①

Code

① — First Draft
② — Second Draft
© — Conference
RV — Revising
PR — Proofing
P — Publishing
⑤ — Shaving

You might stop to visit, but remember that these are peer conferences. You will have a time later to meet with students.

During writing and conferring you will also be holding formal group and/ or individual conferences with students. Using a sign-up chart or place on the chalkboard, students should sign up in advance of conference time to meet with you, either at the beginning of each day's writing workshop or the day before you announce that you are going to hold conferences. You need to be flexible about this.

As you can see, writing and conferring is a significant part of the writing workshop, and there are many different types of activities that can take place. Some days only one thing may be happening, and other days may be filled with several activities. Flexibility and decision making based on students' needs are the key concepts to remember.

Group Sharing

Group sharing is just like an individual or peer conference except that the whole group reacts to a piece of writing. This portion of the writing workshop usually lasts 5 minutes or longer, depending on your schedule and what needs to take place. During this time you might incorporate the concept of the author's chair discussed in Chapter 2.

Group sharing is not just a show-and-tell time; it is a time for students to talk about their writing with peers and get some additional reactions as well as a time to celebrate their successes by sharing finished products. All this sharing helps to promote the classroom as a community of writers, a place where writers discover how well they have constructed meaning. For example, if a student gives a report on dinosaurs, other students might ask questions about things they don't understand or think are incorrect, or even suggest another book on dinosaurs that the author should read before finishing the piece.

Some teachers find that it is often good to divide the class into two or three sharing groups so that more individuals can share at one time. There is a tendency on the part of some teachers to skip sharing time or cut it short. However, you should avoid this, because sharing time

- provides students with authentic reasons for their writing; it gives them the audience that writers need.
- brings closure to the construction of meaning by having both readers and writers discover whether they have successfully accomplished their purpose.
- helps students grow in both their writing and reading by getting feedback from peers and having to respond to that feedback.
- is another point in the process of developing literacy where reading and writing are integrated into one process within the community of learners.

The writing workshop is a very flexible, manageable plan that allows you to meet individual needs. Table 7.4 summarizes the four components of the workshop. Notice that times allotted for each part are flexible, so that some days you may spend more time in one part and less in another. The workshop is your teaching tool; you should use your best professional judgments and make the needed decisions in using it.

Table 7.4 Summary of the writing workshop

Writing Workshop

Component	Time	Purpose
Minilesson	5–10 minutes	Provide students needed support for the process of writing and/or the conventions of writing based on student needs
State-of-the-class conference	5 minutes	Get a sense of what the class is doing daily
Writing and conferring	30–40 minutes	Allow students and teacher to write and confer with each other
Group sharing	5 minutes or longer	Make literacy public; get reactions to constructed meanings and celebrate successes

Getting Started

The writing workshop may be used from the beginning of kindergarten, though obviously at this earliest level it would be used in its simplest form. Getting started using the workshop is really quite easy. Teachers with whom I have worked at various grade levels have found the following procedures very helpful.

1. *Familiarize yourself with the writing workshop plan.* Think about how you will use it in your classroom.
2. *Think through procedures* that you will want to use. The state-of-the-class chart, conference scheduling, and simple record keeping for your conferences are enough to get started. Gradually add other procedures that you have learned from this text and other sources.
3. *Talk with your students* about the workshop. Make a chart showing the parts of the plan and use this as a guide for you and your students.
4. *Designate a day to begin.* This may take place at the beginning of the year or at any point during the year. Students may have pieces of writing that they have in progress, or you may want everyone to start with a new piece of writing. Teachers find both ways successful.

5. *Use your first few minilessons to establish basic routines.* After the first day you will begin to know what types of support your students need with procedures and routines. There really aren't many to be concerned about.
6. *Evaluate what is happening with your students.* Talk about the writing workshop. Ask students for suggestions that would make things better.
7. *Trust your judgment.* You are a professional and know how to make decisions. If something feels right, do it; if it feels wrong, don't do it. However, give things time to work—don't just drop something after one attempt.

Blending Reading and Writing Workshops into One

The goal of the reading workshop (Chapter 6) and the writing workshop is to support students as they grow into literacy and develop their ability to construct meaning. Most teachers find it best to begin with one or the other of the two workshops, depending on where they are in developing their ability to support students in literacy learning. Other teachers start them both at once, but this is not usually as successful. Once one workshop is running fairly smoothly, the other can be added.

You will be able to blend the two workshops into one literacy workshop as you and your students become comfortable with the procedures and with the fact that you are really doing reading and writing all the time. Some teachers never blend the two workshops together, and others blend them almost immediately. Several teachers with whom I work say repeatedly, "One day you just know that these two things go together. You see it. The kids see it. They just fit." When this blending takes place, you might find that the following type of plan works for you:

- *Teacher sharing:* This is a time for getting students excited with a read-aloud book or something you have written.
- *State-of-the-class conference:* Take stock of what students are doing. Adapt the charts suggested earlier.
- *Reading-writing-conferring:* During this time students concentrate on a project that involves both reading and writing, though the focus may be on one more than the other. They should *always* use some time for independent, self-selected reading. Reading and writing conferences also take place.
- *Group sharing:* Students share, talk about, and get reactions to their reading and writing projects.

The time for each of these components would be based on the grade level you are teaching. Use previous time suggestions for the separate workshops and combine to fit your needs. Remember, combining the writing and reading workshops is a long-term goal.

Example
7.1

> **Thinking About and Planning for Writing, Reading, and Literacy**
>
> Now that you have studied more about writing and meaning construction, it is time to think more about how you will use this information in your classroom. Select one of the following activities to carry out alone or with a peer:
>
> 1. Locate a classroom with the grade level of your choice and schedule two observation periods on different days. As you observe, look for ways in which the teacher connects writing and reading. Think about other ways that you would make the reading-writing connection in this class. Discuss this with your peers.
> 2. Identify a class or group within a class where you could introduce students to process writing. Over a period of five or more days, introduce process writing using what you have learned from this chapter and other sources. Keep copies of all students' work and discuss the results with a peer.
> 3. Locate a classroom where the teacher uses a writing workshop. Observe the class for one or two workshop blocks, looking for how the teacher has used or adapted the concept. Talk with the teacher about what was done.

A FINAL WORD ABOUT WRITING

There is so much that has been written about writing, and this chapter has presented only a basic framework on how writing and reading work together to help students learn to construct meaning. I would encourage you to read more extensively about writing using some of the suggestions under "For Additional Reading."

SUMMARY

This chapter has stressed that writing and reading should be taught together because they are both constructive processes, share common knowledges, improve achievement in both areas, foster communication, and together produce outcomes that are not achieved by either alone. The importance of establishing a classroom that promotes and supports writing was discussed, along with suggestions for creating such a classroom. Process writing was developed as a major procedure for helping students learn to construct meaning through writing, and was extended into expository writing with the cognitive strategy instruction in writing procedure. The importance of authentic writing as a means of developing grammar, usage, and spelling was developed. Finally, the writing workshop was presented as a way of organizing for effective writing instruction.

Children's Books

Raskin, E. (1971). *The mysterious disappearance of Leon (I mean Noel)*. New York: E. P. Dutton

Sobol, D. J. (1963). *Encyclopedia Brown: Boy detective*. New York: Lodestar Books, an affiliate of E. P. Dutton Children's Books, a division of Penguin.

Wilder, L. I. (1932). *Little house in the big woods*. New York: Harper.

For Additional Reading

Calkins, L. M. (1986). *The art of teaching writing*. Portsmouth, NH: Heinemann.

Gentry, J. R. (1987). *Spel . . . is a four-letter word*. Portsmouth, NH: Heinemann.

Graves, D. H. (1983). *Writing: Teachers and children at work*. Exeter, NH: Heinemann.

Graves, D. H. (1991). *Build a literate classroom*. Portsmouth, NH: Heinemann.

Raphael, T. E., & Englert, C. S. (1990). Writing and reading: Partners in constructing meaning. *Reading Teacher, 43*, 388–400.

Rico, G. L. (1983). *Writing the natural way*. Los Angeles: J. P. Tracher, Inc. Distributed by Houghton Mifflin Company, Boston.

Shanahan, T. (Ed.). (1990). *Reading and writing together: New perspectives for the classroom*. Norwood, MA: Christopher-Gordon.

Tierney, R. J. & Shanahan, T. (1991). Research on the reading-writing relationship: Interactions, transactions, and outcomes. In R. Barr, M. L. Kamil, P. Mosenthal, & P. D. Pearson (Eds.), *Handbook of reading research* (Vol. 2, pp. 246–280). White Plains, NY: Longman.

Tompkins, G. E., & Hoskisson, K. (1991). Directions for making hardcover books. In G. E. Tompkins & K. Hoskisson (Authors), *Language Arts* (p. 251). New York: Merrill, an imprint of Macmillan.

References

Applebee, A. N. (1977). Writing and reading. *Journal of Reading, 20*, 534–537.

Atwell, N. (1987). *In the middle*. Portsmouth, NH: Heinemann.

Baghban, M. (1984). *Our daughter learns to read and write: A case study from birth to three*. Newark, DE: International Reading Association.

Birnbaum, J. C. (1982). The reading and composing behavior of selected fourth- and seventh-grade students. *Research in the Teaching of English, 16,* 241–260.

Bissex, G. L. (1980). *Gnys at wrk: A child learns to read and write.* Cambridge, MA: Harvard University Press.

Bond, G. L., & Dykstra, R. (1967). The cooperative research program in first-grade reading instruction. *Reading Research Quarterly,* entire issue.

Brown, A. L., & Day, J. D. (1983). Macrorules for summarizing texts: The development of expertise. *Journal of Verbal Learning and Verbal Behavior, 22*(1), 1–14.

Calkins, L. M. (1983). *Lessons from a child on the teaching and learning of writing.* Exeter, NH: Heinemann.

Calkins, L. M. (1986). *The art of teaching writing.* Portsmouth, NH: Heinemann.

Carr, M. (1987). Clustering with nonreaders/writers. In C. B. Olson (Ed.), *Practical ideas for teaching writing as a process* (pp. 20–21). Sacramento, CA: California State Department of Education.

Dahl, K. L. (1988). Peer conferences as social contexts for learning about revision. In J. E. Readence & R. S. Baldwin (Eds.), *Dialogues in literacy research* (pp. 307–315), Thirty-seventh Yearbook of the National Reading Conference. Chicago: National Reading Conference.

Dressel, J. H. (1990). The effects of listening to and discussing different qualities of children's literature on the narrative writing of fifth graders. *Research in the Teaching of English, 24,* 397–414.

Durkin, D. (1989). *Teaching them to read* (5th ed.). Boston: Allyn and Bacon.

Englert, C. S., Raphael, T. E., Anderson, L. M., Anthony, H. M., & Stevens, D. D. (1991). Making strategies and self-talk visible: Writing instruction in regular and special education classrooms. *American Educational Research Journal, 28,* 337–372.

Fowler, G. L. (1982). Developing comprehension skills in primary grades through the use of story frames. *Reading Teacher, 36*(2), 176–179.

Graves, D. H. (1978). *Balance the basics: Let them write.* New York: Ford Foundation.

Graves, D. H. (1983). *Writing: Teachers and children at work.* Exeter, NH: Heinemann.

Graves, D. H. (1984). *A researcher learns to write.* Exeter, NH: Heinemann.

Graves, D. H. (1991). *Build a literate classroom.* Portsmouth, NH: Heinemann.

Graves, D., & Hansen, J. (1983). The author's chair. *Language Arts, 60,* 176–182.

Hansen, J. (1987). *When writers read.* Portsmouth, NH: Heinemann.

Heath, S. B. (1983). *Ways with words.* Cambridge: Cambridge University Press.

Hill, M. (1991). Writing summaries promotes thinking and learning across the curriculum—but why are they so difficult to write? *Journal of Reading, 34,* 536–539.

Hillocks, G., Jr. (1987a). What works in teaching composition: A meta-analysis of experimental treatment studies. *American Journal of Education, 93,* 133–170.

Hillocks, G., Jr. (1987b). Synthesis of research on teaching writing. *Educational Leadership, 44,* 71–82.

Hillocks, G., Jr., & Smith, M. W. (1991). Grammar and usage. In J. Flood, J. M. Jensen, D. Lapp & J. R. Squire (Eds.), *Handbook of research on teaching the English language arts* (pp. 591–603). New york: Macmillan.

Konopak, B. C., Martin, S. H., & Martin, M. A. (1990). Using a writing strategy to enhance sixth-grade students' comprehension of material. *Journal of Reading Behavior, 22,* 19–37.

Langer, J. A. (1986). Reading, writing and understanding: An analysis of the construction of meaning. *Written Communication, 3,* 219–267.

Loban, W. D. (1963). *The language of elemenary school children.* Champaign, IL: National Council of Teachers of English.

McGinley, W. (1988). *The role of reading and writing in the acquisition of knowledge: A study of college students' reading and writing engagements in the development of a persuasive argument.* Unpublished doctoral thesis, University of Illinois at Urbana-Champaign.

McHugh, N. (1987). Teaching the domains of writing. In C. B. Olson (Ed.), *Practical ideas for teaching writing as a process* (pp. 81–87). Sacramento, CA: California State Department of Education.

Martin, S. (1987, December). *The meaning-making strategies reported by provident readers and writers.* Paper presented at the National Reading Conference, St. Petersburg, FL.

Martinez, E. B. (1987). It works! In C. B. Olson (Ed.), *Practical ideas for teaching writing as a process* (p. 23). Sacramento, CA: California State Department of Education.

Millett, N. C. (1986). *Teaching the writing process: A guide for teachers and supervisors.* Boston: Houghton Mifflin.

Moffett, J., & Wagner, B. J. (1983). *Student-centered language arts and reading, K–13* (3rd ed.). Boston: Houghton Mifflin.

Murray, D. M. (1985). *A writer teaches writing* (2nd ed.). Boston: Houghton Mifflin.

Olson, C. B. (1987). *Practical ideas for teaching writing as a process.* Sacramento, CA: California State Department of Education.;

Pardo, L. S., & Raphael, T. E. (1991). Classroom organization for instruction in content areas. *The Reading Teacher, 44,* 556–565.

Pearson, P. D., & Tierney, R. J. (1984). On becoming a thoughtful reader: Learning to read like a writer. In A. C. Purves & O. Niles (Eds.), *Becoming readers in a complex society,* Eighty-third Yearbook of the National Society of the Study of Education (pp. 144–173). Chicago: University of Chicago Press.

Pierce, K. (1987). Clustering in first grade. In C. B. Olson (Ed.), *Practical ideas for teaching writing as a process* (pp. 22–23). Sacramento, CA: California State Department of Education.

Raphael, T. E., & Englert, C. S. (1990). Writing and reading: Partners in constructing meaning. *Reading Teacher, 43,* 388–400.

Raphael, T. E., Kirschner, B. W. & Englert, C. S. (1988). Expository writing program: Making connections between reading and writing. *Reading Teacher, 41,* 790–795.

Rico, G. L. (1983). *Writing the natural way.* Los Angeles: J. P. Tracher, Inc. Distributed by Houghton Mifflin.

Rosaen, C. L. (1990). Improving writing opportunities in elementary classrooms. *The Elementary School Journal, 90,* 419–434.

Shanahan, T. (1988). The reading writing relationship: Seven instructional principles. *Reading Teacher, 41,* 636–647.

Shanahan, T. (1990). Reading and writing together: What does it really mean? In T. Shanahan (Ed.), *Reading and writing together* (pp. 1–18). Norwood, MA: Christopher-Gordon.

Shanahan, T., & Lomax, R. (1988). A developmental comparison of three theoretical models of the reading-writing relationship. *Research in Teaching English, 22,* 196–212.

Sulzby, E., & Teale, W. (1991). Emergent literacy. In R. Barr, M. L. Kamil, P. Mosenthal & P. D. Pearson (Eds.), *Handbook of reading research* (Vol. 2, pp. 727–757). New York: Longman.

Templeton, S. (1991). *Teaching the integrated language arts.* Boston: Houghton Mifflin.

Tierney, R. J., & Leys, M. (1984). *What is the value of connecting reading and writing?* Reading Education Report No. 55. University of Illinois at Urbana-Champaign.

Tierney, R. J., & Shanahan, T. (1991). Research on the reading-writing relationship: Interactions, transactions, and outcomes. In R. Barr, M. L. Kamil, P. Mosenthal, & P. D. Pearson (Eds.), *Handbook of reading research* (Vol. 2, pp. 246–280). New York: Longman.

Tompkins, G. E., & Hoskisson, K. (1991). *Language arts: Content and teaching strategies.* New York: Merrill, an imprint of Macmillan.

Modeling Strategies for Constructing Meaning

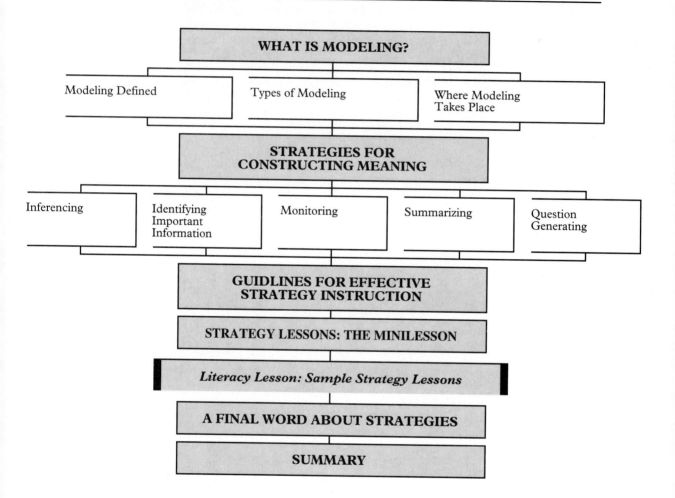

WHAT IS MODELING?

Modeling Defined

Types of Modeling

Where Modeling Takes Place

STRATEGIES FOR CONSTRUCTING MEANING

Inferencing

Identifying Important Information

Monitoring

Summarizing

Question Generating

GUIDLINES FOR EFFECTIVE STRATEGY INSTRUCTION

STRATEGY LESSONS: THE MINILESSON

Literacy Lesson: Sample Strategy Lessons

A FINAL WORD ABOUT STRATEGIES

SUMMARY

*L*et's walk through Brownsville Elementary School to see what is happening in three different classrooms.

Mr. Robinson was reading the big book Pretend You're a Cat *(Marzollo, 1990) with his first graders. As he read aloud each page, he invited children to join in when they felt comfortable doing so. After reading the entire book aloud once, he briefly discussed with the children what they liked in the story. Then he immediately read aloud each page of the book again, stopping to have children read the page with him.*

Farther down the hall, Ms. Garza's third-grade class was finishing story time. She had just read aloud Princess Furball *(Huck, 1989), after which the students had all returned to their seats and immediately started uninterrupted silent reading time. Ms. Garza stayed in the library area and read a section in her own book entitled* Complete Guide to Gardening *(Better Homes and Gardens, 1979). Everyone in the room was actively engaged in reading his or her own book.*

Upstairs, Mr. Lee was showing his fifth graders a strategy poster for previewing and self-questioning. The class was looking at the book Lurkers of the Deep: Life Within the Ocean Depths *(Robison, 1978). Mr. Lee was saying, "As I look through this book, I can see from the section headings and photographs that it is going to give me a lot of information about light in the ocean. One question I would like to answer as I read this book is, 'How does the light in the ocean affect life there?' What question might you want to answer?" Terri volunteered that she would like to know how plants and animals grow in the dark.*

IN EACH OF these Brownsville Elementary School classrooms a different activity was taking place, but one thing was common to all of them—the teacher was modeling some aspect of reading for the students.

- Mr. Robinson was modeling the full process of reading by reading and rereading a big book story. He was showing how words are decoded and how language cues are used to construct meaning.
- Ms. Garza had just completed a read-aloud period, which is also a form of modeling. During uninterrupted reading time she also modeled reading as she read her own book. Finally, the students modeled reading for each other as they read their own books.
- Mr. Lee was modeling a particular strategy, preview and self-question, to help students do what expert readers do—determine their purpose for reading. By sharing his thinking as he used this strategy, Mr. Lee was making his mental processes public to help the students think about this strategy.

These three classroom scenes show the variability in the process of modeling. Sometimes teachers serve as models for students by simply providing day-to-day opportunities where students see them read and write and have natural language interactions. Through these experiences teachers create more than a model to imitate: they become persons whom students admire and respect and whose actions students will then want to imitate (Bruner, 1966). Ms. Garza was providing this type of modeling. At other times, modeling is used as an instructional technique to show students a process or strategy, as Mr. Robinson and Mr. Lee were doing.

If you have been reading the chapters in this text in the sequence presented, you have already encountered both concepts of modeling. Shared reading, an important modeling strategy, was discussed in Chapter 5. Modeling is also a scaffolding technique that supports children as they develop literacy. This scaffolding has been discussed throughout this text in terms of

- different ways to activate and develop prior knowledge, including vocabulary.
- alternative modes of reading to make it possible for students to learn to construct meaning through reading (teacher read-alouds and shared, cooperative, teacher-guided, and independent reading).
- alternative modes of writing to help students learn to construct meaning through writing (shared, collaborative, independent).

As you recall, Chapter 7 explored the use of modeling in developing students' abilities to write. In this chapter, we will explore the concept of modeling in detail, with emphasis on its use with reading strategies.

WHAT IS MODELING?

Literacy learning is an interactive, constructive process. In essence, children develop literacy (writing, reading, speaking, listening, thinking) by having real literacy experiences. However, as they have these experiences, they need carefully scaffolded support (Dole, Duffy, Roehler & Pearson, 1991). Modeling is an important form of such support.

Modeling Defined

Modeling is the process of showing or demonstrating for someone how to use or do something they do not know how to do; most human behaviors are acquired in this way (Bandura, 1986). Modeling can also be described as the process of an expert showing students (nonexperts) how to perform a task so that they can build their own understanding of how to complete that task (Collins, Brown & Newman, 1986). With literacy learning, this expert may be an adult outside of school, an adult in school (usually the teacher), or a peer. When a child sees a parent writing a letter or reading a book, modeling is taking place. When Mr. Lee talked aloud using previewing and self-questioning, he was modeling. When a child sees one of his friends successfully complete a piece of writing and share it, modeling has occurred.

Types of Modeling

As you can see from the examples already presented, modeling can be implicit or explicit (Roehler & Duffy, 1991). *Implicit* modeling takes place when the processes or ideas being modeled occur as a part of an experience and are *not directly* identified or stated. Reading aloud to students and letting students see you write a letter are examples. Implicit modeling always occurs within the context of the complete process of reading and writing. *Explicit* modeling, on the other hand, involves directly showing and talking with students about what is being modeled. Two types of explicit modeling have been identified by Roehler and Duffy (1991)—talk-alouds and think-alouds.

In *talk-alouds*, the teacher presents students with a series of steps for completing a task or a process and then asks questions to guide them through the process. For example, Baumann and Schmitt (1986) describe using a *talk-aloud* approach to teach students how to locate main ideas. A portion of that procedure follows:

> "Here are three steps we will use to figure out unstated paragraph main ideas." [Teacher displays these on a chart or a transparency.]
>
> 1. First, decide what the topic of the paragraph is. The topic is like a short title and is usually one or two words that tell what the whole paragraph is about.
> 2. Next, decide what is said about the topic. Read through the paragraph to see what the rest of the sentences tell you about the topic. Then write a sentence that includes the topic and what is said about the topic. This will be the main idea.
> 3. Then, check yourself. Go through each of the sentences in the paragraph. Ask yourself for each sentence "Does this sentence go with or support the main idea?" If it does, it is a detail that supports the main idea. If you find several sentences that do not support or go with your main idea, go back to Step 1 and start over. (p. 642)

As the steps are presented, the teacher talks the students through them to determine the main idea. The emphasis is on the procedural steps and not on any thinking that takes place in using the steps.

Think-alouds are a second type of explicit modeling (Clark, 1984; Meichenbaum, 1985). In this approach, teachers actually share with students the cognitive processes or thinking that they go through. Compare the following partial *think-aloud* for learning to infer main ideas with the *talk-aloud* presented earlier:

> "As I read through this paragraph I can immediately tell that the topic of it is space travel because it mentions outer space, rockets, and planets. Even though mention is made of early pioneers, I can see that this is only a point of comparison. I notice that all of the points compared show me how early pioneer travel and space travel have been similar."

Notice that the teacher is sharing his thinking in order to reveal the process that one goes through in formulating or inferring a main idea. This *think-aloud* process would also be used with such procedures as the cognitive strategy instruction in writing (CSIW; Raphael & Englert, 1990) as discussed in Chapter 7.

An inherent danger in explicit modeling is that the activities will become nothing more than the modeling of an isolated skill, which is not effective in helping students construct meaning (Pearson, Roehler, Dole & Duffy, 1990). *Explicit modeling must be done within the context of a specific text* (Duffy et al., 1987; Roehler & Duffy, 1991). All examples of modeling presented in this chapter and throughout this text adhere to this important guideline. Table 8.1 summarizes different types of modeling.

Where Modeling Takes Place

Modeling can occur at numerous places throughout the literacy program.

- *During daily activities:* Although the daily activities of the literacy program will afford many opportunities for both implicit and explicit modeling, most of the modeling will be *implicit*. Read-aloud times, shared writing experiences, periods for independent, self-initiated reading and writing, and cooperative reading are just a few examples. Because the literacy-centered classroom operates on the premise that children learn to read and write by reading and writing, all of the activities associated with real reading and writing play a significant role in the modeling of reading and writing.

- *Process writing:* This is another important place where modeling will occur. The process of writing, shared writing, and writing conferences present many opportunities for both implicit and explicit modeling (see Chapter 7).

- *Literacy lessons:* The literacy lesson consists of three parts (see Chapter 2)—introducing, reading and responding, and extending. Within introducing and reading and responding there will be opportunities for explicit modeling of prior knowledge, vocabulary, and particular strategies that students need to construct meaning. Implicit modeling by the teacher and peers will occur in all three parts of the lesson, including extending.

- *Minilessons:* Minilessons, developed on the basis of students' needs, afford the most opportunities for explicit modeling of strategies for both reading and writing. These lessons can be developed around the framework presened in Chapter 2. They may take place during your reading workshop (see Chapter 6) or your writing workshop (see Chapter 7). Later in this chapter we will look at specific strategies for reading and how to model them.

Modeling helps students become more expert readers and writers and gives them better control over their metacognitive processes (Paris, Wasik, &

Table 8.1   Summary of Types of Modeling

Type	Description	Example	Comments
Implicit modeling	Takes place as part of an experience; not directly identified	Reading aloud to a child Writing a group story Shared reading	Has the advantage of always being in the context of the actual process
Explicit modeling	Directly showing or talking students through a process; two types		Should always be done within the context of the process; has inherent danger of becoming an isolated skill
Talk-alouds	Presents a series of steps for completing a process or task	Demonstrating the steps in using a dictionary	
Think-alouds	Presents the thinking one goes through in performing a process or task	Presenting the thinking involved in inferring from text	

Turner, 1991). However, the teacher must effectively balance implicit and explicit modeling. The remainder of this chapter will focus on how to model strategies that help students construct meaning.

STRATEGIES FOR CONSTRUCTING MEANING

For more than three decades, educators and researchers have thought that the way to help readers learn to comprehend was to teach them a set of discrete skills (Smith, 1965). However, research during the last decade and a half has clearly shown that reading (comprehension) is a constructive process in which individuals construct meaning by interacting with the text (Pearson et al., 1990). This constructive interaction involves the individual's prior knowledge, the text, and the reading situation or context (Lipson & Wixson, 1986). As discussed in Chapter 7, this constructive process also takes place through writing. Pearson et al. (1990) conclude the following:

> *Reading is not best learned as a set of isolated skills, picked up one-by-one*
> *along an "assembly line" offered by the teacher and/or the reading program.*

Instead there is a single central goal, building meaning, that recurs from one situation to the next. What changes over time is the level of sophistication of the student's expertise and the amount of conceptual and contextual support teachers need to provide. Teachers would be better off to regard their role as journeymen readers working with knowledgeable and purposeful apprentices rather than purveyors of truth. (p. 25)

Expert readers have strategies or plans to help them solve problems and construct meaning before, during, and after reading (Paris et al., 1991). Although the number of these strategies is small, they should be thoroughly developed (Pearson et al., 1990). Even though there are still many unanswered questions and much research to be done in this area (Dole et al., 1991), there are two major questions that you must address as a teacher: (1) What strategies do my students need as they become expert constructors of meaning? and (2) How are these strategies best developed in the literacy program? We will examine both of these questions in the remaining portion of this chapter.

Volumes of research have attempted to identify the strategies used by expert constructors of meaning (Baker & Brown, 1984a, 1984b; Dole et al., 1991; Paris, Wasik & Turner, 1991; Pressley, Johnson, Symons, McGoldrick & Kurita, 1989). When these studies are examined as a group, five important strategies emerge:

1. Inferencing, including prediction
2. Identifying important information (story line in narrative texts and main ideas in expository texts)
3. Monitoring
4. Summarizing
5. Question generating

Although many other strategies are discussed in the research, these five appear to have the greatest support for inclusion within the literacy program.

Inferencing

Inferencing, the process of judging, concluding, or reasoning from some given information, is the heart of meaning construction for learners of all ages (Anderson & Pearson, 1984). Even very young readers and readers performing a simple task such as reading a sentence use inferencing to supply information that is not given (Kail, Chi, Ingram & Danner, 1977). When students make predictions before or during reading, they are inferencing: using available information and prior knowledge to construct meaning (recall the preview and predict strategy discussed in Chapter 3). Current evidence indicates that inferencing is a significant strategy that can and should be developed as a part of the literacy program (Hansen, 1981; Hansen & Pearson, 1980, 1983; Raphael & Wonnacott, 1985). A strategy poster like the one shown in Figure 8.1 can be used to help students think about this process as they are reading.

Figure 8.1   Strategy Poster for Inferencing

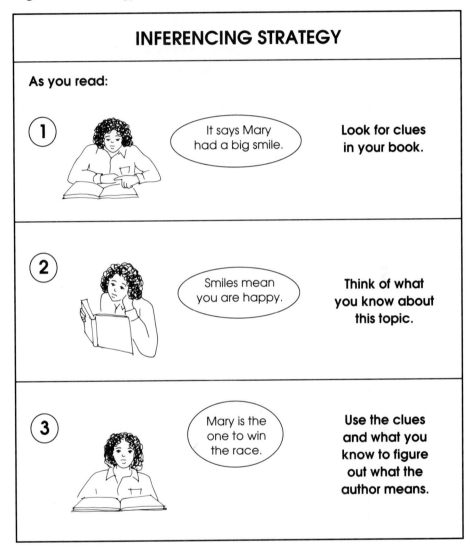

INFERENCING STRATEGY

As you read:

(1)   It says Mary had a big smile.   **Look for clues in your book.**

(2)   Smiles mean you are happy.   **Think of what you know about this topic.**

(3)   Mary is the one to win the race.   **Use the clues and what you know to figure out what the author means.**

Identifying Important Information

Strategic readers identify the important information in what they are reading. In narrative texts or stories, they identify or infer the story line or story grammar (see Chapters 2 and 3; also Mandler, 1984); in expository texts, they identify or infer the main ideas (Baumann, 1986). Although identification in

Figure 8.2 Strategy Poster for Identifying Important Information in Narrative Text

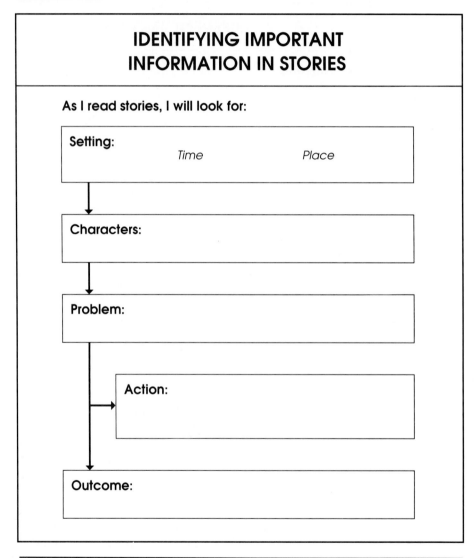

both texts is similar, the task differs because the structures of the texts are different. Whatever terminology is used to describe this process (Winograd & Bridge, 1986), we know that meaning construction can be improved when students learn a strategy for identifying important information in each type of text (Baumann, 1984; Short & Ryan, 1984). Figures 8.2 and 8.3 present

Figure 8.3 Strategy Poster for Identifying Important Information in Expository Text

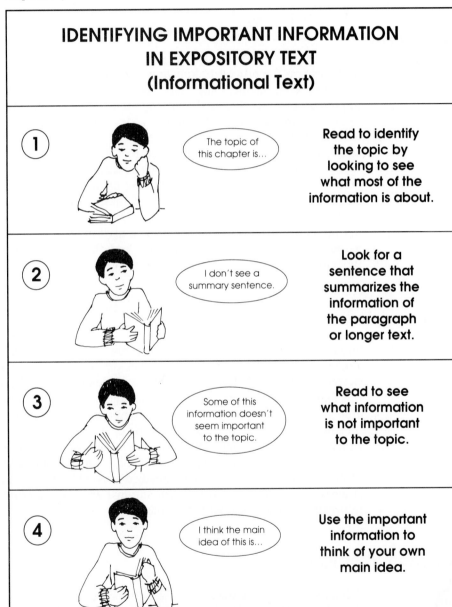

IDENTIFYING IMPORTANT INFORMATION
IN EXPOSITORY TEXT
(Informational Text)

1 The topic of this chapter is... **Read to identify the topic by looking to see what most of the information is about.**

2 I don't see a summary sentence. **Look for a sentence that summarizes the information of the paragraph or longer text.**

3 Some of this information doesn't seem important to the topic. **Read to see what information is not important to the topic.**

4 I think the main idea of this is... **Use the important information to think of your own main idea.**

strategy posters that can be used to help students learn this important strategy for narrative and expository texts, and a sample minilesson for modeling this strategy for narrative text is presented on page 475.

Monitoring

Monitoring is the process of knowing that what you are reading is not making sense and then having some plans for overcoming this problem. This is an important part of students' metacognitive development (Baker & Brown, 1984a, 1984b; Brown, 1980) and is a developmental process that improves with age (Paris et al., 1991). Expert constructors of meaning are able to anticipate problems in reading and correct them as they occur. This "fix-up" process may involve rereading, reading ahead, raising new questions, changing predictions or making new ones, looking up words, or seeking help from an outside source. The value of many of these corrective processes has been verified in the research of Palincsar and Brown (1984a, 1984b, 1986). Figure 8.4 presents a strategy poster that can be used in teaching students how to use a monitoring strategy known as stop and think, and a sample lesson for modeling this strategy is presented on page 482.

Summarizing

Summarizing is the process of pulling together the essential elements in a longer passage of text. Effective constructors of meaning are able to use this strategy; research has shown that certain guidelines can help students develop this skill (Brown & Day, 1983; see Chapter 7 on writing summaries). These guidelines have improved students' ability to construct meaning (Bean & Steenwyk, 1984; Rinehart, Stahl & Erickson, 1986; Taylor, 1982; Taylor & Beach, 1984). Although much of this training research has focused on expository texts, the same types of guidelines can be applied to narrative texts using the story grammar concept already discussed. Figures 8.5 and 8.6 present strategy posters to be used to teach summarizing, and a sample lesson using informational text is presented on page 485.

Question Generating

A final strategy that readers can use to improve their meaning construction is that of generating their own questions to be answered from reading (Singer & Donlan, 1982; Davey & McBride, 1986). This process involves teaching students how to generate questions that require them to integrate information

Figure 8.4 Strategy Poster for Stop and Think

as they read. The Brown and Palincsar (1985) training studies show how effective student-generated questions can be in helping students construct meaning. Figure 8.7 presents a poster for this strategy.

Ongoing research should add to our understanding of how various strategies are used by the literacy learner. However, the current level of our knowledge supports helping readers learn to use the five strategies just discussed. Question generating may have little value unless it is taught thoroughly (Pressley et al., 1990; Denner & Richards, 1987). However, if well

Figure 8.5   Strategy Poster for Summarizing Narrative Text

SUMMARIZING STORIES

1. Read your story to find the important parts:
   - Setting
   - Characters
   - Problem
   - Action
   - Outcome
   Make notes.

2. Look over your notes and decide what can be left out.

3. First I will tell the title and author. Then I'll tell...

   Think about how you will tell or write your summary to make it clear.

4. Tell or write your summary.

Figure 8.6 Strategy Poster for Summarizing Expository Text

Figure 8.7   Strategy Poster for Question Generating

QUESTION GENERATING STRATEGY

1. **Preview the text:**
   - Read titles and subheads.
   - Look at pictures or illustrations.
   - Read first paragraph.

2. **Ask yourself a "think" question.**
   - Write down your question.

3. **Read to find important information to answer your question.**
   - Write the answer.
   - Think about whether your question was a good "think question."

4. **Ask another think question.**
   - If you answered your first one write down your question.

5. **Read to answer your question. Continue to ask and answer questions as you read.**

6. **Look back to see if you have other questions to answer.**

Table 8.2   Points When Strategies May Help Students Construct Meaning

	Reading		
Strategies	*Before*	*During*	*After*
Inferencing (including predicting)	X	X	
Identifying important information	X	X	X
Monitoring		X	
Summarizing		X	X
Question generating	X	X	X

taught, it may be the most useful in promoting meaning construction before, during, and after reading (though all five strategies do this in some way). Table 8.2 shows when each strategy would fit into an individual's reading.

GUIDELINES FOR EFFECTIVE STRATEGY INSTRUCTION

Modeling is *one way* in which children can be supported in their learning. Much of the time this modeling may be *implicit*, but in many circumstances it should be *explicit*. If reading or writing performance indicates need for support in a given strategy, a lesson involving explicit modeling should be provided. Again, we are assuming that much learning, including some strategy learning, will take place through the reading and writing experiences, though research simply does not indicate exactly how much (Dole et al., 1991).

A great deal is known about effective strategy instruction (Pressley & Harris, 1990). The following guidelines should be helpful in developing this instruction within your classroom:

Determine the need for strategy instruction on the basis of student performance.   Students will learn some strategies through their reading and writing experiences. When you observe that their meaning construction would be enhanced by a formal lesson involving modeling, provide it. Do not base the need for lessons on some preset curriculum or published set of materials. *Students' needs should be the primary determining factor in using explicit modeling.*

Introduce only one or two strategies at a time.   This allows you to thoroughly teach the strategy by making certain that students have *repeated* opportunities to use it in real reading situations. At first students may seem uncomfortable or uncertain with the strategy, but this uncertainty will fade away.

Model and practice the strategy in the meaningful context of a real reading experience.   This is a critical issue because an inherent danger in strategy instruction is that the strategies will remain isolated skills. When strategies fail, it is often because they have been taught and practiced as isolated elements. A real reading experience means that students will (1) work with a complete text where the strategy would be useful, (2) use that text as the basis for having the strategy modeled by the teacher, and (3) use additional real texts for practicing the strategy. No fill-in-the-blank, mark, circle, or underline types of exercises should be used because these types of activities isolate the strategy.

Model each strategy at the point when it's most useful.   Make the modeling of a strategy as authentic as possible by doing it when it is most likely to be used in reading. For example, preview and predict should be modeled before reading a text and then followed up after reading.

Be sure that modeling and practicing are interactive and collaborative activities. Strategy learning and use is most effective when students are active participants and work alongside their peers. For example, students learning to summarize may first work together to help the teacher construct a summary and later work with a partner to write a collaborative summary chart of a story they have read.

Gradually transfer modeling from yourself to the students. This is the scaffolding of instruction. Once you have modeled a strategy enough times for students to begin to use it comfortably, have students model it for each other and use it on their own. If you see that more modeling is needed, provide it and then begin to release responsibility to the students again.

Help students experience immediate success with each strategy. Nothing encourages students more than success. Have them explain how the strategy helped them, and point out successes you have seen. If you find that a particular strategy is not working for a student, discontinue using it and move on to another one.

Encourage the use of a strategy across the curriculum. Once students have started to use a strategy, encourage them to use it in areas such as science or social studies. This will help them see the value of the strategy and will interest them in learning additional strategies.

These guidelines will be applied in the sample strategy lessons in the following section.

STRATEGY LESSONS: THE MINILESSON

As noted earlier in this chapter, explicit modeling may take place within the literacy lesson or through minilessons. For example, if, as part of a literacy lesson, you see the need to help students summarize stories, the most logical place to do this would be at the conclusion of the lesson, after a story has been read. They would then practice using the strategy in the meaningful context of reading the next selection.

This section will present three sample strategy lessons organized around the minilesson concept. These lessons may be taught before or after the literacy lesson or as part of it, depending on the particular strategy and where it needs to be placed. First the minilesson concept (introduced in Chapter 2) will be discussed in detail, and then three sample strategy lessons will be given.

The minilesson is a very flexible plan for developing strategy lessons based on the principles for effective instruction using explicit, or direct, teaching (Duffy et al., 1987; Rosenshine, 1986; Rosenshine & Stevens, 1984) and effective strategy learning. The parts of the plan should flow into an interactive dialogue that makes up the entire lesson. As the name *minilesson* implies, the lesson is short and focused, lasting from 5 to 10 minutes and rarely longer than 15 minutes. Some lessons may need to be taught several times, depending on the students and how they respond, and some lessons may not work for certain students and should be discontinued as you move on to more effective experiences. The four parts of the minilesson are (1) introduction, (2) teacher modeling, (3) student modeling and guided practice, and (4) summarizing and reflecting. The three parts of the followup to the minilesson are (1) independent practice, (2) application, and (3) reflection. The first four parts constitute the brief minilesson. The remaining three parts can take place over several days or more.

1. *Introduction:* During this portion of the lesson you let students know what they are going to learn and relate it to reading or writing and their prior knowledge. You may talk directly with them and point out relationships, or you may draw information from them through an interactive discussion. For example, when teaching a lesson on inferencing, you might say:

   > *"Tell me some examples in the last book we read where the author gave clues about something but didn't tell you directly what was intended."* [Students respond.] *"This happens many times in books. When you figured out information from the clues, you were using a strategy called inferencing. Today, we are going to think more about inferencing.*

   This *very focused* introduction should take just a few minutes.

2. *Teacher modeling:* During this part of the lesson you show students how to *use* and how to *think about* the strategy being taught by "thinking aloud" with them. As you do this, you want to make certain that students have the concept of the strategy. For example, with inferencing you might start with something concrete like a text illustration and talk about what it shows and what you can infer from clues such as facial expression or objects pictured. You should always use complete, real texts (as opposed to isolated passages) as the basis of your modeling, and you should make this part of the lesson interactive by drawing students into the modeling. After you have modeled for students, gradually transfer the modeling to them and help them "think aloud" about how they are using the strategy as they read the text. This process flows naturally into the next part of the lesson.

3. *Student modeling and guided practice:* Students are now using the strategy under your guidance, usually within the same text where the strategy was originally modeled. For example, if you are using a short story to model inferencing, you might have students continue through the story to find other places to use inferencing, all the while encouraging them to think aloud as they work. In some cases, you will need to prompt students with questions, examples, or additional modeling. Throughout, give students feedback about how they are doing in using the strategy. The teacher modeling, student modeling, and guided practice flow together so much

that it is often difficult to tell where one begins and the other ends. The purpose of this portion of the lesson is to make certain that students are able to use the strategy before releasing them to practice it independently.

4. *Summarizing and reflecting:* Finally, prompt students to summarize what they have learned and get them to reflect on how and where they might use the strategy. Use prompts such as the following:

  • How did we make inferences in this story?
  • What did we use besides story information?
  • Where do you think you will use this strategy?

Remember that *students* need to verbalize what they have learned and where and how they might use it.

The follow-up to the minilesson consists of opportunities to practice, apply, and think about how the strategy has been useful to the student. This consists of (1) independent practice, (2) application, and (3) reflection.

1. *Independent practice:* This is the time when students use the strategy in authentic reading or writing situations that are very similar to those in which the strategy was developed and taught. For example, if you have modeled inferencing in a mystery, you can have students read additional mysteries and ask them to write solutions to the mysteries in their journals to show how they have used this strategy. Since each strategy must be thoroughly taught, many students will need repeated practice before they are comfortable applying it on their own. Keep in mind, however, that students have been using inferencing throughout their lives. Therefore, they are just transferring something they already know how to do to reading.

2. *Application:* Now students are going to use their newly learned strategy in a totally different situation from the one in which they have learned it. For example, for the inferencing strategy they might self-select mysteries to read or they might write a mystery in which they would provide clues, leaving the solution up to their readers. You may check application during conferences or group discussions. The application phase creates conditions that encourage transfer of the strategy to other areas.

3. *Reflection:* As students are practicing and applying the strategy, encourage them to look back and think about how they have used it. Encourage them to talk about ways to improve and other times and places where they might use the strategy. This activity helps students make the strategy their own and also helps them see how they have succeeded.

The minilesson with follow-up affords a flexible plan for helping students learn to use strategies for constructing meaning. These procedures must be viewed as basic; that is, they may need to be adapted and adjusted to fit the strategy being taught. Table 8.3 summarizes the parts of the minilesson and follow-up.

Table 8.3 Summary of Minilesson and Follow-up Plan for Developing Constructing Meaning Strategies

	Purpose	*Possible Activities*
Minilesson:		
Introduction	Let students know what they will learn. Relate it to prior knowledge and reading and writing.	Interactive discussion led by teacher
Teacher modeling	Show students how to use and think about the strategy.	Teacher-led "think-alouds" Student "think-alouds"
Student modeling and guided practice	Student gradually takes charge of the strategy. Students try the strategy under teacher direction.	Student "think-alouds" Cooperative groups
Summarizing and reflecting	Pull together what has been learned. Think about when it might be useful.	Teacher-prompted discussion Cooperative groups
Follow-up:		
Independent practice	Try the strategy.	Reading in text similar to type used in modeling Writing
Application	Use the strategy in a new situation.	Self-selected books Writing Content-area work
Reflection	Think about how the strategy has been useful.	Student-teacher discussion

Literacy Lesson

Sample Strategy Lessons

The following sections present minilessons dealing with three of the strategies suggested for helping students construct meaning—identifying important information in narrative text, monitoring, and summarizing expository text. Each lesson should be viewed as a *generic model* to help you plan lessons of your own. Although parts of the lessons are scripted to show you the types of things you might say, they are *only examples* to help you plan. The lessons may be read as a group or selectively to meet your needs. The follow-up portions are merely suggestive of the direction you might take and are not presented in their entirety.

*Literacy
Lesson
continued*

Before Reading the Lessons

1. **Review this chapter to clarify any questions you have on modeling or minilessons.**
2. **Read the introduction and text on which each lesson is based. All of these texts were presented at earlier points in this book.**

While Reading the Lessons

1. **Think about how each element of the minilesson was developed.**
2. **Think about how you might change the lesson.**

**Identifying Important Information
in Narrative Text**

Introduction

Purpose: To identify the important information in a story using a story map

Level: Primary (first or second grade)

Text: Jamaica Tag-Along (Havill, 1989; text located on page 72)
Students will have read and responded to this story before the lesson is taught. If the story map prediction strategy discussed in Chapter 3 was used when introducing the story, the reading of the story and this lesson can be closely tied together.

ACTIVITY	PROCEDURE	NOTES
Introduction	Tell students that in order to understand stories they need to be able to identify the important information in them.	Lets students know what they will learn.
	Ask students to recall the story they have just read, *Jamaica Tag-Along.* Discuss it briefly.	Relates lesson to a story students already know.

	ACTIVITY	PROCEDURE	NOTES
Literacy Lesson continued	Teacher modeling	Display the strategy poster in Figure 8.2 (page 464) and tell students that these are the main parts to *all* stories. Briefly discuss each part.	Identifies story parts. If story map prediction was used, it should be related here. Teacher shares thinking.
		Show students how to identify the setting using the following think-aloud:	

> **Teacher Think-Aloud**
>
> "First I want to think about the setting. This includes the time and place of our story. Starting on pages 1–2, I can tell that this story takes place in Jamaica's neighborhood because it says that Ossie wants to play basketball with his friends. You usually play in your own neighborhood. After reading pages 6–9, I am sure this story is taking place in Jamaica and Ossie's neighborhood. It is also taking place during warm weather because you don't play outside without jackets during winter."

	ACTIVITY	PROCEDURE	NOTES
		Record the time and setting on the chart.	
	Student modeling and guided practice	Ask students to go through the remainder of the text, identifying other places that would help them identify the setting. Each time they identify a place, ask them to share how this helped them determine the setting.	Gives students a chance to practice and "think aloud" about what they have just learned.
	Teacher modeling	Tell students that another part of the story is the characters—the people or animals in the story.	Focuses students on the next part. Teacher continues to share thinking with students.

Literacy Lesson continued

ACTIVITY	PROCEDURE	NOTES
	Tell them that a story may have several characters, some more important than others.	
	Use the following "think-aloud" to show students how you would identify the main character:	

> **Teacher Think-Aloud**
>
> "The title of the story tells me right away that Jamaica must be an important in the story. When I read pages 1, 2, and 5, I see that Ossie is important because Jamaica wants to tag along with her brother."

ACTIVITY	PROCEDURE	NOTES
	Record Jamaica and Ossie on the chart.	
Student modeling and guided practice	Ask students to continue looking through the story to identify other important characters. As they identify each, ask them to read the page or pages that made them think this character was important. Prompt and guide students with such questions as the following: Who else took an active part in the story besides Jamaica and Ossie? Were there other characters who were just in there but really didn't do much?	Students try out what they just learned. Teacher prompting may be needed.
		Some students may need help recognizing why Berto is important to the story.
	Record students' responses on the chart.	

Literacy Lesson continued

ACTIVITY	PROCEDURE	NOTES
Teacher modeling	Tell children that the next part of the story to consider is the problem. Talk with them about the problem, explaining that it is the big question or situation that runs through the story.	Focuses students' attention on the next element.
	Tell children that you will show them how to figure out the problem. Have them use their books as you "think aloud" to show how to figure out the problem:	

> **Teacher Think-Aloud**
>
> "On pages 1 and 2 I can tell that Jamaica wants to go with her brother. On page 5 Jamaica says that she doesn't want to tag along. She wants to play. I can tell that Ossie doesn't want to be bothered because she is younger. The problem is that Jamaica wants to play with her older brother but he doesn't want her to. I know that this is the way older boys and girls are about their younger brothers and sisters."

ACTIVITY	PROCEDURE	NOTES
	Record the problem on the chart.	
Student modeling and guided practice	Ask students to find other places in the story that show the problem, sharing their thinking as they proceed.	
Teacher modeling	Tell students that the next part of the story to consider is the action or events that take place as a result of the problem and that lead to the solution. Point out that only the most important things need to be noticed.	

Literacy
Lesson
continued

ACTIVITY	PROCEDURE	NOTES
	Use the following "think-aloud" to show students how to identify the action:	

> *Teacher Think-Aloud*
>
> "After Jamaica knew that Ossie wasn't going to let her play, she followed him to the playground on her bike. She didn't want him to know she was there. On pages 6–7 I can tell this because of words like *hide* and *crept*." (Record the event on the chart under "Action.") "On page 8, I learn that Jamaica tries to get in the game." (Record the second event on the chart.)

ACTIVITY	PROCEDURE	NOTES
Student modeling and guided practice	Ask students to continue finding important events and telling why they selected each one. Help them select the following events: The boys still won't let Jamaica play (page 11). Jamaica goes to the sandlot to play by herself (page 13). As Jamaica swings, a little boy (Berto) gets in her way and she doesn't like it (page 15). Berto tries to help Jamaica build her sandcastle but she doesn't like it (pages 16–17). Berto's mother tells him to leave Jamaica alone and Jamaica realizes that's how her brother Ossie hurts her feelings (pages 18–21). Jamaica lets Berto help her build the sandcastle (page 23).	Students will want to identify every little detail. Encourage them to focus only on the important things.

Literacy Lesson continued

ACTIVITY	PROCEDURE	NOTES
Teacher modeling and student modeling	Record students' responses on the chart. Tell students that the final important part of the story is the outcome. Tell them that they know how this story ends and that you want them to help you "think aloud" to tell how you could identify the outcome. Talk students through the outcome and record it on the chart. (Ossie joins Jamaica and Berto; Jamaica doesn't even mind if Ossie tags along.)	By this time students will all know the story. Therefore, let them help identify the outcome.
Reviewing the story	Use the completed story map and have children retell the story. Point out each part of the story as they retell it.	Pulls the story together for the students.
Summarizing and reflecting	Ask students to explain what they should look for to identify the important information in stories. Ask them when they will be able to use this strategy. Remind them that the strategy poster will be available to help them recall the important parts of a story.	

Discussion

This minilesson would be followed by many opportunities to read other stories. There are many possibilities. Before each reading, it is always good to remind students to think about the story parts by referring them to the strategy poster.

Literacy
Lesson
continued

There are many ways to develop this lesson. For some students, it might be good to focus on one story element at a time. However, I have found that children learn this strategy much more readily if you introduce the whole concept at once and then focus on each element in detail as needed. Also, notice in this lesson how the teacher modeling was alternated with the student modeling and guided practice. This shows the flexibility of this plan to fit students' needs and the strategy being taught.

As subsequent stories are read, you will want the modeling to become more student directed and less teacher directed. Even young children can begin to verbalize their thinking as they identify story elements. Research has shown that teaching students to identify the important information in stories does help them construct meaning (Pressley et al., 1989).

It is important to keep in mind that strategy instruction should not destroy the story. Keep the learning light and fun; even though you focus on the strategy, the content of the story is what will be of most interest to the children.

As mentioned earlier, this strategy could be combined with story map prediction (see Chapter 3), which could be started before reading and used after reading as a way of teaching the strategy for identifying important information. After reading, you would return to the predictions made by students as a way of helping them identify the important information in stories. These two strategies flow nicely into teaching students to summarize stories.

**Monitoring
(Self-Monitoring)**

Introduction

Purpose: To use the monitoring strategy of stop and think to improve meaning construction

Level: Third or fourth grade

Text: The Bicycle Man (Say, 1982; text located on page 243)

Monitoring is the heart of the meaning construction process because it brings together many strategies and processes. It is a strategy that develops in students gradually and will need to be taught or at least reviewed and expanded numerous times. One version that I like to use is stop and think. Figure 8.4 (page 467) presents a basic poster for this strategy. When using stop and think, students periodically stop and say, "Does this make sense to me?" If it does not, they try a number of "fix-up" techniques such as rereading, reading ahead, looking up words, or seeking help from another source.

This strategy is best taught by introducing it before reading and then modeling it during teacher-directed reading with teacher and students taking turns modeling. (This type of instruction is similar to the process used in reciprocal teaching; see Palincsar and Brown, 1984a, 1984b.)

Literacy Lesson continued

ACTIVITY	PROCEDURE	NOTES
Introduction	Display the strategy poster in Figure 8.4 (page 467). Explain to students that good readers "stop and think" about their reading to be sure it is making sense. Explain each step on the poster and tell them that they will learn to use this strategy as they are reading the book *The Bicycle Man*.	Lets students know what they are going to learn.
	Introduce the book using some of the procedures suggested earlier in this text. Have students predict what they think will happen in the story.	
Teacher modeling	Read aloud the first three pages (two with text, one with picture); then stop and use the following "think-aloud":	You have to create a problem so you can model the process.

> **Teacher Think-Aloud**
>
> "This is a good place for me to stop and ask myself, *Does this make sense?* I understand that the author is telling this story and it takes place in a school in Japan. I'm not sure if I know what a sportsday is. I think I'll reread page 3." (Reread page 3 aloud.) "A sportsday must be like our field day where we have different events. So far I haven't learned much about my prediction about the bicycle man."

ACTIVITY	PROCEDURE	NOTES
Student modeling and guided practice	Direct students to silently read the next two pages to see if they make sense. Tell them you will call on one of them to be teacher and talk about what she or he did when she or he stopped to think.	The first few times students do this, you may need to prompt them. They will become comfortable with this procedure over time.

*Literacy
Lesson
continued*

ACTIVITY	PROCEDURE	NOTES
	If needed, prompt students as they play the role of teacher: Were there any words you didn't know? What parts would you reread? What did you learn about your predictions from these two pages?	
Teacher modeling	Direct students to continue silently reading the next three pages to see what they learned about their predictions. Then use the following "think-aloud":	Teacher models another "fix-up" strategy.

Teacher Think-Aloud

"The story is making sense to me but there was one word I didn't know. Do any of you know this word?" (Write *lacquered box* on the board. Ask students for help. After they respond, continue.) "When I stop and think about this word, the clues in the text tell me it is some type of box. The exact type of box seems unimportant, so I wouldn't look this word up in the dictionary. I still haven't learned much about my prediction and the bicycle man. So, I'll read on."

	Continue alternating with teacher modeling and student modeling and guided practice until the story has been completed.	
Discussing the story	Encourage students to respond to the story by telling how they felt about it and what they learned.	Pulls the story together.

Literacy Lesson continued

ACTIVITY	PROCEDURE	NOTES
Summarizing and reflecting	Display the strategy poster and ask students to tell what they learned about stop and think and talk about how and when they could use this strategy.	Helps students make the strategy their own.

Discussion

Students will practice and apply this strategy as they read other books. Most children require several modeling experiences before they learn to use stop and think. For younger students, it is often good to model only one "fix-up" procedure at a time.

Once you have introduced the strategy, you should concentrate on it over a block of days to allow students to become comfortable with it. The procedure of alternating modeling between yourself and the students is a very effective way to make the strategy a natural part of students' reading. Another approach is to have them use cooperative reading and take turns being the teacher. If the entire class is doing this, you can move through the class to monitor student progress and provide additional support by joining a pair of students who might need more help.

Summarizing Expository Text

Introduction

Purpose: To summarize informational (expository) text

Level: Intermediate and higher

Text: "The First Egyptian Mummies," from *Mummies, Tombs, and Treasure* (Perl, 1987; text located on page 170)

Summarizing informational or expository text requires students to focus on different elements than narrative text. The strategy presented here is based on rules developed by Brown and Day (1983) and successfully researched by others (Bean & Steenwyk, 1984). The rules are as follows:

1. Delete trivial information.
2. Delete redundant information.
3. Substitute superordinate terms for lists of terms.
4. Integrate a series of events with a superordinate action term.
5. Select a topic sentence.
6. Invent a topic sentence if there isn't one.

*Literacy
Lesson
continued*

It is best to teach this strategy after students have learned to use it to identify important information in expository text. Your first lessons would focus on summarizing paragraphs; later lessons would be extended to longer texts. This lesson would be taught after students had read "The First Egyptian Mummies"; it is assumed that they already know how to summarize paragraphs.

ACTIVITY	PROCEDURE	NOTES
Introduction	Ask students to recall the strategy they have learned for summarizing paragraphs.	Relates what is to be learned to what is already known.
	Tell them that they are going to learn to apply this to longer texts.	
Teacher Modeling	Display the strategy poster shown in Figure 8.6 (page 469). Review each step with students.	Focuses students' attention on what is to be learned.
	Ask students to recall the chapter they have just read, "The First Egyptian Mummies," and briefly discuss it.	
	Tell students that you are going to show them how to apply the summarizing informational text strategy to more than a paragraph. Use the following "think-aloud" along with a transparency of the text. As you use the "think-aloud," mark out the text and make notes in the margin. Figure 8.8 shows how one page would look.	Shows students how to think through the steps of the strategy.

*Literacy
Lesson
continued*

Figure 8.8   Marked Page for Modeling Summarizing

sues of once-living things, returning them to nature in other forms.

Shows that these mummies were not planned

But sometimes nature springs a surprise or two on us. One such surprise took place long ago in the vast North African desert country of Egypt. Before the beginning of recorded history — perhaps seven or eight thousand years ago — people began to settle on the banks of the Nile River, which runs through the Egyptian desert. The ribbons of well-watered land that bordered the Nile provided precious soil for growing food crops. So, in selecting a place to bury their dead, the Egyptian farming people avoided the river shore. They chose instead the hot, barren sands that lay beyond it.

The people dug small shallow graves. Usually they buried their dead in a crouched position. They placed them on their sides with their knees drawn up to their chests. That way their bodies took up as little space as possible.

The Egyptians hoped that in some magical way the dead were not really dead. Perhaps their spirits lay beneath the sand along with their limp, unclothed bodies. Perhaps a spirit might wish to eat or drink just as the living did. So the families of the dead included some clay pots of food and jars of water in the shallow pit graves. And sometimes they added a man's favorite tool or spear of sharpened stone, a woman's beads of shell or bone, or a child's toy.

Interesting but not important to our summary

Then the family covered the grave with sand and piled some rocks on top of it. The rocks helped to mark the grave. They also made it difficult for jackals and other wild animals of the desert to reach the body inside it.

Delete for summary

Most of this page not important to our summary

Literacy
Lesson
continued

ACTIVITY	PROCEDURE	NOTES

Teacher Think-Aloud

"First, when we read this chapter we determined that the topic was mummies. We decided that there were three parts to the topic: (1) mummies, (2) combining upper and lower Egypt, and (3) man's attempt to improve mummies. The test related to the first topic ends at the top of page 6. So we have completed the first part of step 1—identify the topic. Now we need to delete the trivial information and use stepts 2 and 3.

"It seems to me that most of pages 1 and 2 are additional explanations of details that can be grouped together; they relate to the definition of a mummy:

A mummy is a dead body that has been preserved.

"Pages 3 and 5 have many ideas relating to how the first mummies came to be. These can be grouped together; also, there is additional information about the Nile that could be deleted. We could list these ideas for our summary:

Egyptians buried people in hot sands.

Hot sands preserved the bodies by taking out the moisture.

Dry cold also preserved bodies of the Incas in the Andes Mountains of South America.

*Literacy
Lesson
continued*

ACTIVITY	PROCEDURE	NOTES

"In step 4, we need to look for a main-idea statement. The closest thing we have to one is the first sentence in paragraph 2 on page 5, but this doesn't really give the main idea. It only tells part of the information presented. We will have to go to step 5 and formulate our own main-idea sentence. Based on the important information we have, I think this is the best statement for this part of our text:

> The first mummies were accidents of nature.

"Now we are ready to put our summary together using the ideas we have identified with this strategy:"

> A mummy is a dead body that has been preserved. Egyptians buried bodies in hot sand. The sands preserved the body by taking out moisture. Dry cold also preserved the bodies of the Incas in the Andes Mountains of South America. The first mummies were accidents of nature.

	ACTIVITY	PROCEDURE	NOTES
Literacy Lesson continued		Discuss the summary paragraph. Point out that the summary for this chapter should probably have three paragraphs since there were three parts to the topic identified.	Pulls together ideas modeled.
	Teacher-student modeling and guided practice	In using the strategy, direct students to summarize pages 6–8, which is the text related to the secnd part of the topic.	Begins to release responsibility to students.
		Use a transparency of the pages and have students mark out information and make notes as they "think aloud" about the process.	
		Prompt them as needed: What happened to bring Egypt together? What information can be deleted or grouped? Combining upper and lower Egypt created the need for what?	
		Assist students in writing their summary.	
	Student modeling and guided practice	Using a transparency of pages 8, 9, 10, and 11, have students mark out material and make notes as they "think aloud" to summarize this last part of the chapter.	Lets students try the strategy with teacher support if needed.
		Have students work with a partner to develop the summary for the last part.	

Literacy
Lesson
continued

ACTIVITY	PROCEDURE	NOTES
Creating a final summary	Put all three parts of the summary together and have students check to see if changes need to be made.	Pulls all parts of the summary together.
Summarizing and reflecting	Prompt students to summarize the parts of the strategy and talk about its uses: What steps do you follow when summarizing longer text? What is different when summarizing longer text instead of paragraphs? How and when do you think you might use this strategy?	Helps students see what they have learned and why it is important.

Discussion

This lesson would be followed by having students read the next chapter, "Why the Egyptians Made Mummies," and practice using the summarizing informational text strategy. Most students will need repeated teacher modeling and guided practice. They could begin summarizing Chapter 2 in cooperative pairs; this would allow you to observe what they have learned and how they are using the strategy.

Since summarizing is difficult for students to learn, lessons are much more effective if they are kept short and focused, with emphasis on meaning construction; in other words, the most important thing is to respond to and understand the text. They will learn to use the strategy best through repeated meaningful experiences with the text along with modeling support from the teacher.

You should use the poster for this and other strategies to keep students aware of the strategies, displaying the posters where they can be easily seen and used. Periodically, invite students to reflect about how they are using the strategy and talk about how they can use it better.

After Reading the Plans

1. **Select any strategy lesson plan presented in this chapter. Working with a friend, develop several more "think-alouds" that you would use to model the strategy.**

Literacy
Lesson
continued

2. **Working with a friend, select any strategy that you would like to teach and prepare a lesson on it. Teach the lesson to a small group, and discuss the results with your friend.**
3. **Select a grade level of your choice, and observe for an hour or two, looking for evidence of students using the strategies mentioned in this chapter. Talk with the teacher to see how the children learned them. Were they taught? Did the students learn them through their literacy experiences?**

A FINAL WORD ABOUT STRATEGIES

The strategy lessons just described should serve as models to help your develop your own lessons. Although research supports the inclusion of the five strategies discussed here, it must be remembered that this is not the last word. *Many students may do just as well by reading, writing, and interacting with their peers and you about their reading and writing.* Children are only going to get better at reading and writing if we allow them to read and write. Teaching strategies *may be* a helpful form of support for some students, but not for others. Only the wise, informed, observant teacher can decide if students are profiting from strategy instruction. You must be that teacher!

SUMMARY

This chapter has focused on modeling as one aspect of scaffolded instruction. Modeling is the process of showing someone how to use or do something he or she does not know. It may be *implicit* or *explicit*. Explicit modeling may involve "talk-alouds" where steps are described or "think-alouds" where cognitive processes are shared.

Five strategies were suggested for helping students improve their meaning construction: inferencing, identifying important information, monitoring, summarizing, and question generating. Guidelines and three sample lessons were presented.

Children's Books

Havill, J. (1989). *Jamaica tag-along.* Boston: Houghton Mifflin.
Huck, C. (1989). *Princess Furball.* New York: Greenwillow Books.
Marzollo, J. (1990). *Pretend you're a cat.* New York: Dial.
Perl, L. (1987). *Mummies, tombs, and treasure.* New York: Clarion.
Robison, B. H. (1978). *Lurkers of the deep: Life within the ocean depths.* New York: David McKay.
Say, A. (1982). *The bicycle man.* Boston: Houghton Mifflin.

For Additional Reading

Pressley, M., Burkell, J., Cariglia-Bull, T., Lysynchuck, L., McGoldrick, J. A., Schneider, B., Snyder, B. L., Symons, S., & Woloshyn, V. E. (1990). *Cognitive strategy instruction that really improves children's academic performance*. Cambridge, MA: Brookline.

Pressley, M., & Harris, K. R. (1990). What we really know about strategy instruction. *Educational Leadership, 48*, 31–34.

References

Anderson, R. C., & Pearson, P. D. (1984). A schema-theoretic view of basic processes in reading comprehension. In P. D. Pearson (Ed.), *Handbook of reading research* (pp. 255–291). New York: Longman.

Baker, L., & Brown, A. L. (1984a). Cognitive monitoring in reading. In J. Flood (Ed.), *Understanding reading comprehension* (pp. 21–44). Newark, DE: International Reading Association.

Baker, L., & Brown, A. L. (1984b). Metacognitive skills in reading. In P. D. Pearson (Ed.), *Handbook of reading research* (pp. 353–394). New York: Longman.

Bandura. A. (1986). *Psychological modeling: Conflicting theories*. Chicago: Aldine-Atherton.

Baumann, J. F. (1984). The effectiveness of a direct instruction paradigm for teaching main idea comprehension. *Reading Research Quarterly, 20*(1), 93–115.

Baumann, J. F. (1986). *Teaching main idea comprehension*. Newark, DE: International Reading Association.

Baumann, J. F., & Schmitt, M. C. (1986). The what, why, how, and when of comprehension instruction. *Reading Teacher, 39*, 640–647.

Bean, T. W., & Steenwyk, F. L. (1984). The effect of three forms of summarization instruction on sixth graders' summary writing and comprehension. *Journal of Reading Behavior, 16*, 297–306.

Better Homes and Gardens. (1979). *Complete guide to gardening*. Des Moines, IA: Meredith Corporation.

Brown, A. L. (1980). Metacognitive development and reading. In R. J. Spiro, B. C. Bruce & W. F. Brewer (Eds.), *Theoretical issues in reading comprehension* (pp. 453–481). Hillsdale, NJ: Lawrence Erlbaum.

Brown, A. L., & Day, J. D. (1983). Macrorules for summarizing texts: The development of expertise. *Journal of Verbal Learning and Verbal Behavior, 22*(1), 1–14.

Brown, A. L., & Palincsar, A. S. (1985). *Reciprocal teaching of comprehension strategies: A natural history of one program to enhance learning*. Technical Report No. 334. Urbana: University of Illinois, Center for the Study of Reading.

Bruner, J. S. (1966). *Toward a theory of instruction*. Cambridge: Harvard University Press.

Clark, C. M. (1984). Teacher planning and reading comprehension. In G. G. Duffy, L. K. Roehler & J. Mason (Eds.), *Comprehension instruction: Perspectives and suggestions* (pp. 58–70). New York: Longman.

Collins, A., Brown, J. S., & Newman, S. E. (1986). *Cognitive apprenticeship: Teaching the craft of reading, writing and mathematics*. Report No. 6459. Cambridge, MA: BNN Laboratories.

Davey, B., & McBride, S. (1986). Effects of question generating training on reading comprehension. *Journal of Educational Psychology, 78*(4), 256–262.

Denner, P. R., & Rickards, J. P. (1987). A developmental comparison of the effects of provided and generated questions on text recall. *Contemporary Educational Psychology, 12*, 135–146.

Dole, J. A., Duffy, G. G., Roehler, L. R., & Pearson, P. D. (1991). Moving from the old to the new: Research on reading comprehension instruction. *Review of Educational Research, 61*, 239–264.

Duffy, G., Roehler, L., Sivan, E., Rackliffe, G., Book, C., Meloth, M., Vavrus, L., Wesselman, R., Putnam, J., & Bassiri, D. (1987). Effects of explaining the reasoning associated with using reading strategies. *Reading Research Quarterly, 22*, 347–368.

Hansen, J. (1981). Inferential comprehension strategy for use with primary grade children. *Reading Teacher, 34*, 665–669.

Hansen, J., & Pearson, P. D. (1980). *The effects of inference training and practice on young children's comprehension.* Arlington, VA. (ERIC Document Reproduction Service No. ED 186 839).

Hansen, J., & Pearson, P. D. (1983). An instructional study: Improving the inferential comprehension of fourth grade good and poor readers. *Journal of Educational Psychology, 75*(6), 821–829.

Kail, R. V., Chi, M. T. H., Ingram, A. L., & Danner, F. W. (1977). Constructive aspects of children's reading comprehension. *Child Development, 48*, 684–688.

Lipson, M. Y., & Wixson, K. K. (1986). Reading disability research: An interactionist perspective. *Review of Educational Research, 56*, 111–136.

Mandler, J. M. (1984). *Stories, scripts and scenes: Aspects of schema theory.* Hillsdale, NJ: Lawrence Erlbaum.

Meichenbaum, D. (1985). Teaching thinking: A cognitive behavioral perspective. In S. Chapman, J. Segal, & R. Glaser (Eds.), *Thinking and learning skills: Current research and open questions* (Vol. 2, pp. 407–426). Hillsdale, NJ: Lawrence Erlbaum.

Palincsar, A. S., & Brown, A. L. (1984a). *A means to a meaningful end: Recommendations for the instruction of poor comprehenders.* Champaign, IL: Center for the Study of Reading, reprint.

Palincsar, A. S., & Brown, A. L. (1984b). Reciprocal teaching of comprehension-fostering and comprehension-monitoring activities. *Cognition and Instruction, 2*, 117–175.

Palincsar, A. S., & Brown, A. L. (1986). Interactive teaching to promote independent learning from text. *Reading Teacher, 39*(8), 771–777.

Paris, S. G., Wasik, B. A., & Turner, J. C. (1991). The development of strategic readers. In R. Barr, M. L. Kamil, P. Mosenthal & P. D. Pearson (Eds.), *Handbook of reading research* (Vol. 2, pp. 609–640). New York: Longman.

Pearson, P. D., Roehler, L. R., Dole, J. A., & Duffy, G. G. (1990). *Developing expertise in reading comprehension: What should be taught? How should it be taught?* Technical Report No. 512. Champaign, IL: Center for the Study of Reading.

Pressley, M., Burkell, J., Cariglia-Bull, T., Lysynchuck, L., McGoldrick, J. A., Schneider, B., Snyder, B. L., Symons, S., & Woloshyn, V. E. (1990). *Cognitive strategy instruction that really improves children's academic performance.* Cambridge, MA: Brookline.

Pressley, M., & Harris, K. R. (1990). What we really know about strategy instruction. *Educational Leadership, 48*, 31–34.

Pressley, M., Johnson, C. J., Symons, S., McGoldrick, J. S., & Kurita, J. A. (1989). Strategies that improve children's memory and comprehension of text. *Elementary School Journal, 90,* 3–32.

Raphael, T. E., & Englert, C. S. (1990). Writing and reading: Partners in constructing meaning. *Reading Teacher, 43,* 388–400.

Raphael, T. E., & Wonnacott, C. A. (1985). Heightening fourth-grade students' sensitivity to sources of information for answering questions. *Reading Research Quarterly, 20,* 282–296.

Rinehart, S. D., Stahl, S. A., & Erickson, L. G. (1986). Some effects of summarization training on reading and studying. *Reading Research Quarterly, 21,* 422–438.

Roehler, L. R., & Duffy, G. G. (1991). Teacher's instructional actions. In R. Barr, M. L. Kamil, P. Mosenthal, & P. D. Pearson (Eds.), *Handbook of reading research* (Vol. 2, pp. 861–883). New York: Longman.

Rosenshine, B. V. (1986). Synthesis of research on explicit teaching. *Educational Leadership, 43*(7), 60–69.

Rosenshine, B. V., & Stevens, R. (1984). Classroom instruction in reading. In P. D. Pearson (Ed.), *Handbook of reading research* (pp. 745–798). New York: Longman.

Short, E. J., & Ryan, E. B. (1984). Metacognitive differences between skilled and less skilled readers: Remediating deficits through story grammar and attribution training. *Journal of Educational Psychology, 76,* 225–235.

Singer, H., & Donlan, D. (1982). Active comprehension: Problem-solving schema with question generation for comprehension of complex short stories. *Reading Research Quarterly, 17,* 166–186.

Smith, N. B. (1965). *American reading instruction.* Newark, DE: International Reading Association.

Taylor, B. M. (1982). Text structure and children comprehension and memory for expository material. *Journal of Educational Psychology, 74,* 323–340.

Taylor, B. M., & Beach, R. W. (1984). Effects of text structure instruction on middle-grade students' comprehension and production of expository text. *Reading Research Quarterly, 19*(2), 147–161.

Winograd, P. N., & Bridge, C. A. (1986). The comprehension of important information in written prose. In J. B. Baumann (Ed.), *Teaching main idea comprehension* (pp. 18–48). Newark, DE: International Reading Association.

Constructing Meaning Across the Curriculum

9

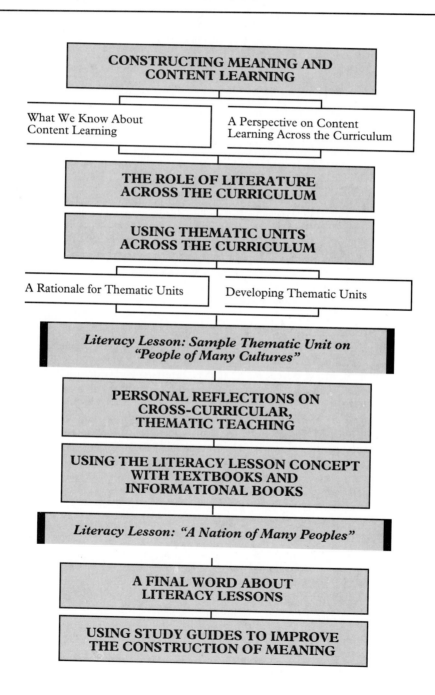

CONSTRUCTING MEANING AND CONTENT LEARNING

What We Know About Content Learning

A Perspective on Content Learning Across the Curriculum

THE ROLE OF LITERATURE ACROSS THE CURRICULUM

USING THEMATIC UNITS ACROSS THE CURRICULUM

A Rationale for Thematic Units

Developing Thematic Units

Literacy Lesson: Sample Thematic Unit on "People of Many Cultures"

PERSONAL REFLECTIONS ON CROSS-CURRICULAR, THEMATIC TEACHING

USING THE LITERACY LESSON CONCEPT WITH TEXTBOOKS AND INFORMATIONAL BOOKS

Literacy Lesson: "A Nation of Many Peoples"

A FINAL WORD ABOUT LITERACY LESSONS

USING STUDY GUIDES TO IMPROVE THE CONSTRUCTION OF MEANING

**STUDY TECHNIQUES FOR IMPROVING
THE CONSTRUCTION OF MEANING**

SUMMARY

*H*ow do students construct meaning across the curriculum? A visit to Mrs. Kimbrough's combination fifth and sixth grade classroom will give us a sense of how she helps her students accomplish this task.

Upon entering the classroom we saw a large bulletin board like the one shown in Figure 9.1 indicating that the theme for the month was "how people began to live and learn." The theme goals and activities were designated and outlined for the four major areas of the curriculum: language arts and reading, science, social studies, and math. We noticed immediately that many students had a goal sheet on a folder at their work areas that was a duplicate of the bulletin board. As we walked around the class, we saw that each student had checked off certain activities under each goal.

The room was alive with activity. Two small groups of students and several pairs were working on different tasks, and other students were working alone in their work areas.

One group of students was working with a collection of artifacts that they had collected from their study of early pioneer history. They were preparing a display labeled "How Early Pioneers Began to Live and Learn," using encyclopedias, brochures from museums, and other books to identify each artifact and write a few sentences about it on cards for the display.

Students working with partners were developing a number of different activities. Some were having peer conferences where they were discussing and revising reports on a variety of topics, such as "The Life of Prehistoric Man" and "Life in the Old World and the New." Others were estimating the populations of different countries in the Old World at selected points in time and comparing them on a graph.

The students who were working alone were reading books such as The People Could Fly (Hamilton, 1985) and Lincoln: A Photobiography (Freedman, 1987). Some students were recording in their learning logs.

Mrs. Kimbrough was meeting with a group of students in the reading center. They were discussing a chapter students had read from a social studies textbook. One student was recording information using a graphic organizer on the chalkboard to show the important ideas from the chapter. As the group carried out its discussion, Mrs. Kimbrough participated as a group member, answering and asking questions like any other member of the group.

Near the end of our time in the room, Mrs. Kimbrough called the class together to have them take stock of what they had done and where they were with their unit activities. She and the class together worked out a plan for completing the day's activities and set up a plan for the next day.

Figure 9.1 Bulletin Board from Mrs. Kimbrough's Class

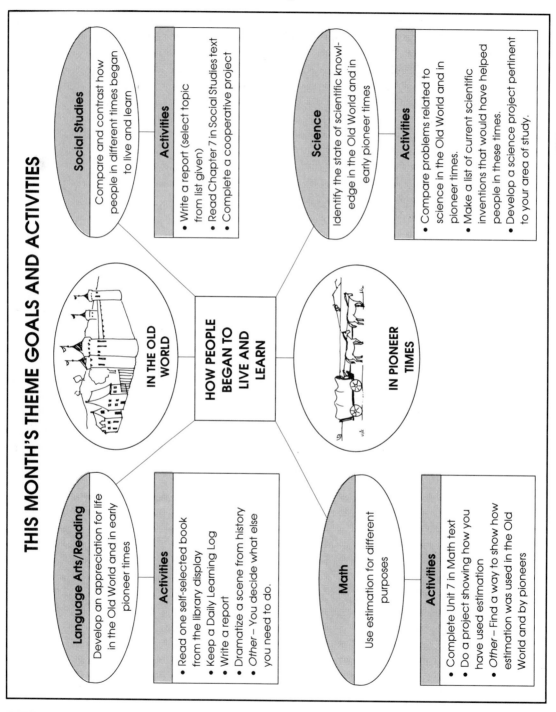

THIS MONTH'S THEME GOALS AND ACTIVITIES

HOW PEOPLE BEGAN TO LIVE AND LEARN

IN THE OLD WORLD

IN PIONEER TIMES

Social Studies

Compare and contrast how people in different times began to live and learn

Activities

- Write a report (select topic from list given)
- Read Chapter 7 in Social Studies text
- Complete a cooperative project

Science

Identify the state of scientific knowledge in the Old World and in early pioneer times

Activities

- Compare problems related to science in the Old World and in pioneer times.
- Make a list of current scientific inventions that would have helped people in these times.
- Develop a science project pertinent to your area of study.

Language Arts/Reading

Develop an appreciation for life in the Old World and in early pioneer times

Activities

- Read one self-selected book from the library display
- Keep a Daily Learning Log
- Write a report
- Dramatize a scene from history
- *Other* – You decide what else you need to do.

Math

Use estimation for different purposes

Activities

- Complete Unit 7 in Math text
- Do a project showing how you have used estimation
- *Other* – Find a way to show how estimation was used in the Old World and by pioneers

IN THIS BRIEF visit to Mrs. Kimbrough's fifth- and sixth-grade class we were able to see a teacher who believed in integrated learning using cross-curricular themes. There are a number of things that we should notice about this classroom:

- The monthly theme, "How People Began to Live and Learn," was selected by Mrs. Kimbrough to help students focus on living and learning in pioneer times and in the "Old World" (Europe). These were required curricular areas for fifth and sixth graders in her school.
- The theme incorporated various types of activities that focused on four different curricular areas.
- Students knew what the goal and activities were for each curricular area and were encouraged to select some of the activities that they did.
- Various types of literature were used as a *part* of the learning experiences in the classroom, including informational books, novels, short stories, and textbooks.
- Learning was interactive. Students did projects and activities that required them to solve problems cooperatively and independently.
- Students were constructing meaning that was focused on the theme topic. They used writing, reading, listening, speaking, thinking, and viewing in a variety of authentic learning tasks.

Mrs. Kimbrough's classroom was designed to help children construct meaning through an integrated, cross-curricular approach that focused on thematic units in which students generated and tested many of their own hypotheses under her guidance. Although there is strong support for this type of learning (Pappas, Kiefer, & Levstik, 1990), few classrooms in the elementary, middle, junior, or senior high school use this approach. Most still focus on separate subject teaching such as science or social studies. However, there is much that we know about helping students construct meaning across the curriculum. First, let's examine this information.

CONSTRUCTING MEANING AND CONTENT LEARNING

Traditionally, educators have first thought about reading instruction and language arts instruction and then, at some other time, instruction in math, science, social studies, and so forth. It has been typical to hear educators say that first children "learn to read" and then they are able to "read to learn." This line of thinking led us to talk and think about an area known as *content reading* (Herber, 1978, 1984). Though there is, indeed, a time when students are more focused on "learning to read," which gradually gives way to "reading to learn," the two tasks are neither mutually exclusive nor entirely sequential.

Children develop literacy and use literacy to learn simultaneously (Wells, 1986).

All of the ideas and principles presented in earlier chapters of this text apply as we begin to think about constructing meaning across the curriculum in different content areas. In fact, it is the various content areas of the school curriculum that are the basis for the authentic experiences that students need to become effective constructors of meaning. For example, in Mrs. Kimbrough's thematic unit, "How People Began to Live and Learn," the different curricular areas helped to provide the vehicles for developing many cross-curricular learnings. However, even when you are teaching a single content area using a single textbook, students are actually learning to construct meaning.

What We Know About Content Learning

The process of constructing meaning has many of the same features in various content areas (Dupuis, 1984):

- Students construct meaning by having authentic experiences within the content areas.
- These experiences involve and integrate all aspects of the language arts— writing, speaking, listening, reading, and thinking.
- When using *any* text, students construct meaning by activating their prior knowledge and interacting with the text.
- As students construct meaning, they build relationships between old knowledge and new knowledge. Learning in one curricular area is enhanced when relationships can be built between that area and others.
- When learning in any curricular area, students need scaffolded support from the teacher and peers to help them construct meaning.

Although all content areas share these features, they also have their differences, such as different text structures that students must understand (see Chapter 3 on text structure) and terminology peculiar to the discipline that students must deal with.

Armbruster (1991) makes six recommendations for improving learning in content areas as well as the ability of students' to construct meaning:

1. Integrate reading (and all aspects of literacy) with content instruction. This integration should take place across disciplines and should focus on more holistic learning as opposed to the learning of isolated facts. This type of learning is in line with what we know about schema theory (see Chapter 3) and how students construct meaning. It helps students build relationships and leads to greater transfer of knowledge and skill from one discipline to another.

2. Increase opportunities for students to read informational texts throughout *all levels of schooling*. Students are very interested in such books but need more experience with reading and meaning construction in these different text structures.
3. Provide students with the experiences that will help them become strategic readers by scaffolding instruction and gradually releasing them to be responsible for their own reading. Model strategies using informational texts.
4. Keep students actively learning by helping them focus on what to do before reading, during reading, and after reading. Help them learn to monitor their reading, build connections with old knowledge, and use writing to improve their construction of meaning.
5. Increase opportunities for collaborative learning.
6. Change teacher education to ensure that *all* teachers gain the knowledge and techniques needed to make these five things happen.

The remainder of this chapter focuses on how to improve students' ability to construct meaning in all content areas across the curriculum. No attempt will be made to cover all aspects of learning. Rather, the emphasis will be twofold:

1. Using thematic, cross-curricular units as a way of planning and organizing for literacy learning and content learning
2. Applying principles and techniques for successful meaning construction by focusing on how to use textbooks more effectively

A Perspective on Content Learning Across the Curriculum

In far too many classrooms, content knowledge is isolated into separate disciplines that really do not promote broad understandings and relationships. Learning is assumed to take place through primarily one avenue—the textbook—and even this is frequently not read by the students (Armbruster, 1991); the information is told or read aloud by the teacher. In contrast, learning across the curriculum is interactive, allowing students to construct meaning through a variety of problem-solving experiences that use many types of literature and other resources such as films, resource persons, and hands-on projects and experiments. For example, the concept to be learned in science and math are *not* most effectively learned by reading a book or article, which is only *one* source of information. Authentic learning in science and math takes place through hands-on experimentation and problem solving.

The point of view taken in this text is that the ability to both construct meaning and to gain content knowledge is enhanced by thinking about and engaging in cross-curricular learning. Even if you are in a teaching situation focusing on a separate subject, you can enhance learning by building connections between the subject you are teaching and other disciplines.

THE ROLE OF LITERATURE ACROSS THE CURRICULUM

The textbook has been assumed to be the centerpiece for learning throughout our educational system, particularly in content areas such as math, science, and social studies (Elliott, 1990). There are two major problems with this situation. First, as already noted, the textbook is only one source of information; and second, textbooks have numerous problems that often hinder meaning construction:

- *Textbooks are often unappealing to students* (Elliott, 1990). Many textbooks, in an effort to avoid controversy, do not present material that is of interest to students.
- *Textbooks are often too difficult for the grade level for which they are assigned* (Chall & Conrad, 1990). Even though many have been improved, there are still problems with the complexity and structure of many textbooks.
- *Textbooks are often inconsiderate* (Anderson & Armbruster, 1984a). They are often written with an organization and style that does not help students construct meaning. One problem is difficulty, as mentioned.
- *Textbooks often cover many topics in a cursory manner* (Tyson & Woodward, 1989). As a result, students cannot study a topic in depth. Many authors and publishers have tried to correct this problem.
- *Textbooks used in schools are often dated* (Tyson & Woodward, 1989). When schools are unable to buy new textbooks often enough to keep them up to date, students have to use textbooks that contain dated or inaccurate information.
- *Textbooks are developed by publishers for a national marketplace* (Elliott & Woodward, 1990). This situation means that schools who depend solely on textbooks are unable to focus on the specific concerns of their curriculum. They are bound to this "national curriculum."

Even though textbook publishers have made strides in improving their products and facing many of these concerns (Elliott & Woodward, 1990), they are unable to totally overcome some of these problems. Therefore, one very good way for schools to deal with this dilemma is to use the textbook as only *one resource* and to build their curriculum around a variety of quality literature.

Research has shown that literature has educational value for content-area learning (Hickman & Cullinan, 1989). Students can "read, hear, and discuss biographies, myths, fairy tales, and historical tales to fire their imagination

and to whet their appetite for understanding how the
is" (History-Social Science Curriculum Framework ar
1988, p. 5). Therefore, the use of all types of lite
textbooks has been strongly recommended as a wa
learning and meaning construction (History-Social Scie
work and Criteria Committee, 1988; Moss, 1991).

The literature to be used across the curriculum can be b.....
nonfiction. Some topics lend themselves to both types because they help
students understand the culture and characteristics of the times, whereas other
topics may lend themselves only to nonfiction. For example, an upper-grade
or middle-school class studying medieval times might read historical fiction
pieces like *Knight Prisoner: The Tale of Sir Thomas Malory and His King Arthur*
(Hodges, 1976) or *A Connecticut Yankee in King Arthur's Court* (Twain, 1987)
as well as such nonfiction pieces as *Age of Chivalry* (Wright, 1988), *Luttrell
Village: Country Life in the Middle Ages* (Sancha, 1983), and *Castle* (Macaulay,
1977). All of these books, both historical fiction and nonfiction, could be used
to support and extend the chapters on medieval times provided in the social
studies text. By doing this, we broaden students sources of information and
enliven their study by bringing the period to life.

Nonfiction books (autobiographies, biographies, and informational books)
are available on a great many topics. Norton (1991) says that "books of
nonfiction encourage children to look at the world in new ways, to discover
laws of nature and society, and to identify with people different from
themselves" (p. 608). "Trade books serendipitous to a curricular topic can
make the difference between a passive reader who quits when the bell rings
and an active life-long, self-motivated reader/learner" (Sebesta, 1989, p. 114).

From the kindergarten level with books like *Box Turtle at Long Pond*
(George, 1989) to the upper grades with such a book as *Pompeii: Exploring a
Roman Ghost Town* (Goor & Goor, 1986), literature can be a vital part of the
materials that students use to construct meaning. It will serve to motivate
students, extend textbooks, and make learning more authentic and exciting.

The next section will focus on how to develop a thematic unit using both
textbook resources and literature. This will be followed by a section showing
how to use all types of text resources to further develop students' abilities to
construct meaning using the literacy lesson concept.

USING THEMATIC UNITS ACROSS THE CURRICULUM

Thematic units (see Chapter 2) are frameworks for planning and organizing
learning experiences around common bodies of knowledge, thinking, or
concepts that cut across many curricular lines, such as language arts, science,

art, or music. They provide an organization and structure that create communities of learners who continue to construct meaning and knowledge (Pappas, Kiefer & Levstik, 1990).

Even when thematic units are used only to integrate the language arts, many other curricular areas come to play. These cross-curricular or interdisciplinary connections are "real" only when they are meaningful and are relevant to the curriculum and students' lives (Routman, 1991). Thus although you may begin using thematic units as a way of integrating the language arts, you will soon begin to see how the important curricular concepts from many disciplines can be developed through these units.

A Rationale for Thematic Units

From the beginning, every chapter in this text has helped to develop a rationale that supports the use of thematic units as a way of organizing for effective learning. Since this type of learning experience differs from the way most of us were taught, it is important that we keep thinking about the basis on which this instruction rests. This rationale can be summarized in four major points:

1. The research in schema theory has shown us that individuals' prior knowledge and background play a significant role in constructing meaning (Anderson & Pearson, 1984; see Chapter 1). Since this knowledge consists of interrelated concepts, any plan for effective learning must capitalize on these interrelationships.

2. Comprehending is the process of constructing meaning by interacting with the text (or other source of learning, such as a film or an experiment). This interaction involves relating one's prior knowledge to new ideas to build new relationships and concepts and to expand old ones (see Chapters 1, 2, and 3). An effective learning plan must not only encourage this interaction but must also build relationships between areas of knowledge.

3. Learning to read and write (like learning to do anything) takes place through authentic experiences. Thus all learning plans must allow for authentic experiences in which students can try things out.

4. As students have authentic learning experiences they often need the support of a more knowledgeable individual who can provide them models and feedback about what they are learning (Wells, 1986; see Chapters 2–7). Gradually, the support must be removed to help students develop independence (scaffolded instruction).

Thematic units are a framework for learning that accounts for these four points. These units build on students' interests and prior knowledge by focusing on topics that are relevant to students' lives. They build relationships among knowledge and allow for authentic learning by encouraging problem solving that cuts across curricular lines. They also support students in a variety of interactive and collaborative ways.

Developing Thematic Units

Many suggestions have been given for developing thematic units (Pappas, Kiefer & Levstik, 1990; Routman, 1991). The process is not really complicated and should be kept as simple as possible, especially in the beginning stages. It can be divided into three stages: planning, implementing, and culminating. Figure 9.2 shows these three stages with the activities that take place within each. There is no one correct way to carry out this process.

Planning the Theme

Planning a thematic unit involves four activities: (1) choosing the theme, (2) identifying what students might learn, (3) selecting resources, and (4) selecting activities and developing a timeline. The planning process is interactive; as you think about a particular theme or consider certain resources, you get other ideas about themes or other activities that you might add.

Many teachers carry out the planning process alone, especially as they begin to use thematic units. However, it is possible and more authentic to involve students whenever appropriate. Sometimes all teachers at a grade level collaborate, and sometimes collaborations are schoolwide.

Choosing the Theme.   You may think about such things as student interests, what you want students to learn, what is developmentally appropriate, or topics you are responsible for within the curriculum. The theme should be broad enough to allow you to involve several different curricular areas but not so broad that students will lose sight of it and fail to make the connections. Also, selecting a topic that is too broad or unmanageable will discourage you and cause students to lose interest. Recall that although the theme Mrs. Kimbrough used in the chapter opening scene, "How People Began to Live and Learn," was broad, she limited it to the early pioneer period and the "old world.". At the same time, the theme was broad enough to allow her to involve several different curricular areas in meaningful ways.

As you begin to use themes more extensively in your classroom, you may become concerned about how to keep track of the various concepts you have developed across the curriculum. Some teachers find a form like the one shown in Figure 9.3 helpful. Notice that not all themes cover all curricular areas. Figure 9.4 presents some sample themes that might be used at various grade levels. However, any one of these themes could be covered at any grade level.

Identifying What Students Might Learn.   While you are selecting a topic or right after you have selected it, you need to think in general terms about what students might learn during the unit. Recall from Chapter 2 the major outcomes related to attitudes and habits and constructing meaning (see page 63). These

Figure 9.2 Developing a Thematic Unit

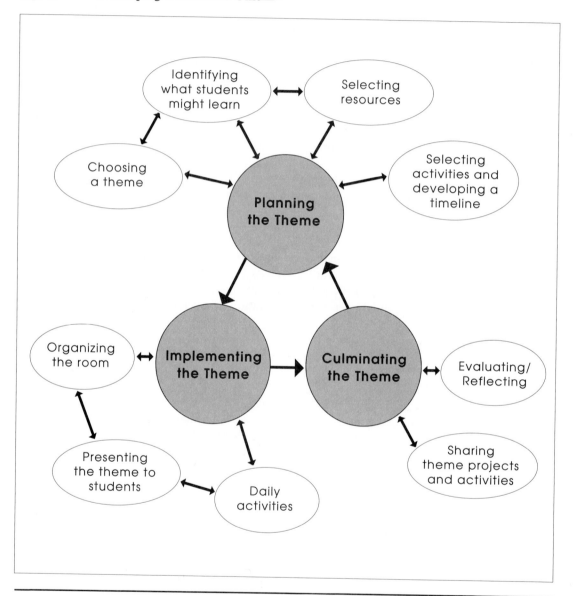

Figure 9.3 Form for Keeping Track of Themes and Curricular Areas

Curricular Area Theme	Language Arts	Social Studies	Science	Math	Health	Art Music Drama PE	Other
Helping Out	•Decodes words independently •Retells stories	•Has a concept of helper		•Uses addition to keep simple records		•Art – Uses form and color	
Baby Animals	•Identifies important information •Writes simple reports		•Understands the importance of animals	•Keeps records and compares growth – weight	•Good food important to animals and people		

same two categories can be used for cross-curricular units. Following are examples of the outcomes developed for a unit on foods:

- *Attitudes and habits*
    1. Develops an improved attitude about proper foods to eat
    2. Appreciates the planning and preparation required to prepare a healthy meal

Figure 9.4 Sample Themes at Various Grade Levels

K   Colors of the seasons
1   Preparing for winter
2   A favorite author or illustrator
     (choose any author or illustrator)
3   Fairy tales
4   Prehistoric animals
5   Space travel
6   Science fiction
7   Understanding the environment
8   The cost of pollution

- *Constructing meaning*
  1. Knows the four food groups and can choose a balanced daily diet
  2. Identifies the procedures in planning a basic meal
  3. Understands the processes required in growing food for a country

In addition to major outcomes, you may also identify specific strategies and skills that students might develop within the unit. For example, for the foods unit, you might choose to focus on such strategies and skills as the following:

- Selects appropriate book sources for a report
- Identifies important information in text
- Takes notes
- Writes a report
- Uses simple addition

Of course, many other skills and strategies will also develop as a result of the unit experiences, but these are the ones you plan to focus on. Identifying what students might learn forms part of the foundation for assessment and evaluation, both throughout and at the conclusion of the thematic unit.

Selecting Resources.   These can include print resources, hands-on resources, community resources, and the arts (Pappas, Kiefer & Levstik, 1990). Again, there is no one right set or type of resource to use. Your decision depends on the thematic unit and the level for which you are developing it. Table 9.1 presents various examples.

When making your selection, remember to maintain a balance of types of resources. You will nearly always use print resources, but other resources may not be available for all themes. Try to think about which ones will create the

Table 9.1 Categories of Theme Resources

Resource	Examples
Print resources	Literature
	Textbooks
	Newspapers and magazines
	Encyclopedias and reference books
	Primary source materials (notes from observations, interviews, letters, etc.)
Hands-on resources	Old pottery
	Tools
	Appliances
	Clothing
	Masks
	Toys
Community resources	People
	Museums
	Libraries
	Parks
	Chambers of commerce
Arts	Paintings
	Samples of architecture
	Sculpture
	Graphic and decorative arts and crafts
	Music
	Theater
	Television, videos, film
	Records, tapes, compact discs

most authentic learning experiences and provide the greatest motivation as students continue to develop their abilities to construct meaning.

Selecting Activities and Developing a Timeline.   This is the last part of your planning process. Remember that your purpose is to help students understand the theme and continue to learn to construct meaning. You will need three categories of activities—for initiating the theme, developing the theme, and culminating the theme. Although you may preplan certain activities, you will add or change others as the unit progresses and as you assess students' progress. Figure 9.5 presents a form with categories of activities.

Activities for the theme should involve such things as problem solving; reading; writing reports; making charts, graphs, or timelines; projects; art; music; drama; and so forth. Your role as the teacher will be to direct some groups, monitor others, and participate in others. Sometimes you will be working with small groups or having individual conferences, and at other times you may be conducting a whole-class activity. Several different books

Figure 9.5   Form for Planning Thematic Unit Activities

Activities	Independent/ Individual	Cooperative/ Small Group	Whole Class	Self-Selected	Teacher Assigned	Teacher Directed
Initiating activities						
Developing activities						
Culminating activities						

listed under "For Additional Reading" provide many ideas, including Ward (1988) and Moore, Readence, and Rickelman (1989). You may also choose to use strategies like K-W-L, which was discussed in Chapter 3.

In planning and selecting activities for a theme, give special attention to those used to initiate the theme. These should be very interactive and should do three very important things for students:

1. Motivate students and get them excited about the theme.
2. Activate prior knowledge and develop background needed for the theme.
3. Set the tone for the theme by helping students take ownership in their learning during the theme.

Since a great variety of initiating activities are possible for any theme, you must select ones that best meet your students' needs and the theme you are developing. Initiating activities should include such things as drama, group discussions, displays of artifacts or other items to motivate interest, reading aloud a good piece of literature, music (good source books are *The Raffi Singable Songbook* (Raffi, 1980) and *Go In and Out the Window* (Fox & Marks, 1987), and art. Sometimes you will use several initiating activities; at other times you will only need one. Just be sure to get the unit off to an exciting start.

As you proceed, you can enhance your planning by using a technique known as webbing, which was recommended by Norton (1982) and further developed by Pappas, Kiefer & Levstik (1990) (see Chapter 4). Once you have selected the thematic unit you want to develop, you proceed as follows:

1. Make a list of ideas that you think of in relation to your chosen theme and the outcomes you desire.
2. Begin to group the ideas into categories and create a web like the one shown in Figure 9.6.
3. Think specifically about what students might accomplish in the thematic unit.
4. Make lists of resources and activities you might use.
5. Group ideas, resources, and activities and continue to add them to your web.

The web in Figure 9.6 shows the results of initial teacher planning and thinking. This planning process is a dynamic one, with ideas and thoughts constantly changing. A sample thematic unit is provided later in this chapter to illustrate the complete process, and you may wish to refer to that theme at this point (see page 518). Culminating activities should pull together the ideas and concepts developed in the unit, as well as give students a time to share what they have done and to use what they have learned. Culminating a unit should be fun and should be looked forward to. It should also include some time for reflecting on the unit and on each student's individual goals and activities.

Finally, you must develop a timeline for your thematic unit. Units may last for a few days or several weeks, and in some classes with upper-grade students they may last up to a month. Relevant factors to consider in determining the length of the unit include the scope of the theme, your instructional objectives, student interests and motivation, and how involved students become in certain activities. As you become comfortable in using thematic units, you will find it easier and easier to adjust your time schedule. An initial timeline for a unit might be just a simple daily listing of the major activities you plan to accomplish. For example, the theme on foods discussed earlier might be planned for two weeks, and the rough timeline might look as follows:

September 23	Introduce theme and brainstorm with students
September 24	Select project and begin individual work
September 25	Begin literacy lesson using textbook chapter with whole class
September 26	Have discussion circles to review what has been learned; conduct individual project work
September 27	Begin small-group projects

Figure 9.6 Initial Planning Web for a "Time" Theme

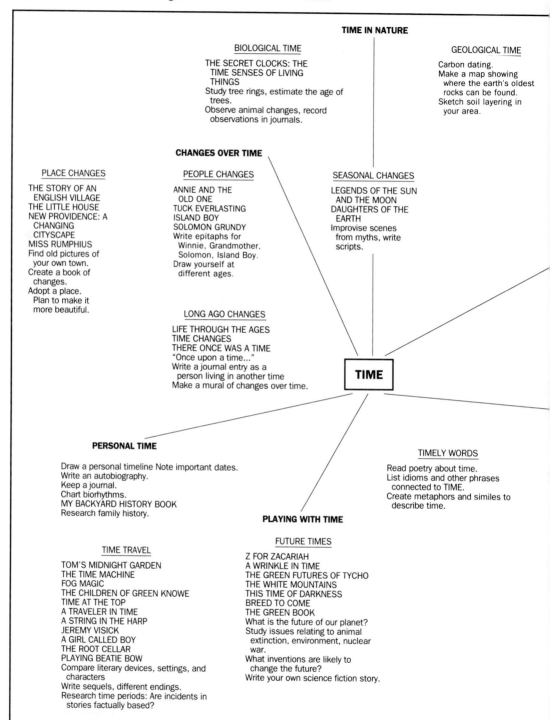

TIME IN NATURE

BIOLOGICAL TIME

THE SECRET CLOCKS: THE
TIME SENSES OF LIVING
THINGS
Study tree rings, estimate the age of
trees.
Observe animal changes, record
observations in journals.

GEOLOGICAL TIME

Carbon dating.
Make a map showing
where the earth's oldest
rocks can be found.
Sketch soil layering in
your area.

CHANGES OVER TIME

PLACE CHANGES

THE STORY OF AN
ENGLISH VILLAGE
THE LITTLE HOUSE
NEW PROVIDENCE: A
CHANGING
CITYSCAPE
MISS RUMPHIUS
Find old pictures of
your own town.
Create a book of
changes.
Adopt a place.
 Plan to make it
more beautiful.

PEOPLE CHANGES

ANNIE AND THE
OLD ONE
TUCK EVERLASTING
ISLAND BOY
SOLOMON GRUNDY
Write epitaphs for
Winnie, Grandmother,
Solomon, Island Boy.
Draw yourself at
different ages.

SEASONAL CHANGES

LEGENDS OF THE SUN
AND THE MOON
DAUGHTERS OF THE
EARTH
Improvise scenes
from myths, write
scripts.

LONG AGO CHANGES

LIFE THROUGH THE AGES
TIME CHANGES
THERE ONCE WAS A TIME
"Once upon a time..."
Write a journal entry as a
person living in another time
Make a mural of changes over time.

TIME

PERSONAL TIME

Draw a personal timeline Note important dates.
Write an autobiography.
Keep a journal.
Chart biorhythms.
MY BACKYARD HISTORY BOOK
Research family history.

TIMELY WORDS

Read poetry about time.
List idioms and other phrases
connected to TIME.
Create metaphors and similes to
describe time.

PLAYING WITH TIME

TIME TRAVEL

TOM'S MIDNIGHT GARDEN
THE TIME MACHINE
FOG MAGIC
THE CHILDREN OF GREEN KNOWE
TIME AT THE TOP
A TRAVELER IN TIME
A STRING IN THE HARP
JEREMY VISICK
A GIRL CALLED BOY
THE ROOT CELLAR
PLAYING BEATIE BOW
Compare literary devices, settings, and
characters
Write sequels, different endings.
Research time periods: Are incidents in
stories factually based?

FUTURE TIMES

Z FOR ZACARIAH
A WRINKLE IN TIME
THE GREEN FUTURES OF TYCHO
THE WHITE MOUNTAINS
THIS TIME OF DARKNESS
BREED TO COME
THE GREEN BOOK
What is the future of our planet?
Study issues relating to animal
extinction, environment, nuclear
war.
What inventions are likely to
change the future?
Write your own science fiction story.

Source: From *An Integrated Language Perspective in the Elementary School: Theory into Action* by Christine C. Pappas, Barbara Z. Kiefer, and Linda S. Levstik, pp. 54–55. Copyright © 1990 by Longman Publishing Group.

TIME PASSING

FROM DAY TO DAY

WHAT MAKES DAY AND NIGHT
Compare and contrast the use of time in
  these books.
Make a cartoon or filmstrip to show the
  passage of time.
THE HOUSE FROM MORNING TO NIGHT
MORNING, NOON, AND NIGHTTIME
  TOO
DAWN
FOG DRIFT MORNING
DUSK TO DAWN
NIGHT IN THE COUNTRY
Sketch or paint your favorite time
  of day. Choose music to capture your
  mood.

THE WAY TO START THE DAY
WHEN THE SKY WAS LIKE LACE
Write rules for your favorite time
  of day.
PORCUPINE STEW
HILDILID'S NIGHT
GRANDFATHER TWILIGHT
Write about a magical event.

OPENING NIGHT
NIGHT GHOSTS AND HERMITS
NIGHT MARKETS
Interview someone who works at
  night.
View night creatures at the zoo.

FROM SEASON TO SEASON

THE REASONS FOR SEASONS
MY FAVORITE TIME OF YEAR
SUGARING TIME
TIME OF WONDER
OX-CART MAN
Survey peoples' favorite times of year.
Compare hours of daylight and dark at
  different times of year.

TIME IN MUSIC

Grofé, "Sunset" and "Sunrise" from
  Grand Canyon Suite
Ravel, "Daybreak" from Daphnis
  et Chloe
Prokofiev, "Midnight Waltz"
  from Cinderella
Vivaldi, The Four Seasons

TIME IN ART

French Impressionists
  Monet
  Sunset Impressions, Haystacks
Sisley, June Morning
American Luminists—Heade, Twilight,
  Spouting Rock Beach
Church, Morning in the Tropics

Other Artists—
  Van Gogh, Starry Night
  Turner, Norham Castle, Sunset
  Constable, Clouds
  Hopper, Night Hawks, Night
  Shadows

MEASURING TIME

MUSICAL CLOCKS

Metronomes
Notation system

SIMPLE CLOCKS

Make sundials,
  sand clocks,
  water clocks.
13 CLOCKS
MS. GLEE WAS WAITING
CLOCKS
THIS BOOK IS ABOUT TIME
CLOCKS AND MORE CLOCKS
CLOCKS AND HOW THEY GO

Make a graffiti wall of time words.
Compose accompaniment for TIME poems.

THE IDEAS OF EINSTEIN
IT'S ALL RELATIVE
Study the theory of relativity.

MECHANICAL CLOCKS

Bring time places
  from home, sketch
  and describe them.

October 1	Work on individual projects and reports and conferences
October 2	Work on individual projects and reports and conferences
October 3	Work on individual projects and reports and conferences
October 4	Culminate the unit and share projects

Implementing the Theme

Implementing the theme involves organizing the room, presenting the theme to students, and carrying out daily activities. This phase will cover most of the time allotted for the theme.

Organizing the Room.   This involves planning and setting up appropriate centers and areas to support the theme. Chapter 2 discussed setting up a literate environment in detail (page 31); you may want to reread that section now. It is important to create the atmosphere for the unit because this helps get students motivated and excited. Moreover, the various areas and centers provide the vehicles for managing the daily schedule as the theme develops.

Presenting the Theme.   This involves motivating students and getting them excited with an initiating activity or activities and sharing the theme plans, helping students decide which activities they will do. It is by presenting the theme that you activate prior knowledge and develop background for the overall subject, which is vital to the construction of meaning. The types of activities to use here were discussed in the previous section.

During this time, you must also help students begin deciding and planning what they are going to do. As you share the theme activities with them, point out where they have choices to make. Some teachers use a bulletin board as Mrs. Kimbrough did in the opening scene for this chapter, some post charts in the room, and some give a printed outline to each student. Some teachers also like to use a form like the one shown in Figure 9.7 to help students make decisions and keep track of their work. This form may become a part of their literacy portfolio (see Chapter 10).

Carrying Out Daily Activities.   This final portion of implementing the theme requires that you work out a daily and weekly time schedule that allows you to get in your theme activities. You may choose to build in the concepts of the reading workshop or writing workshop as discussed in Chapters 6 and 7. Figures 9.8 and 9.9 show two different daily and weekly time schedules for teachers who use cross-curricular thematic units.

Figure 9.7 Student Record Sheet for a Theme Plan

THEME PLAN

Name _____ Theme _____

Date started _____ Date completed _____

THEME GOALS	
What I Want to Accomplish	How I Did
1.	
2.	
3.	

MY OWN PROJECT(S)			
Focus	Started	Completed	Comments

OTHER ACTIVITIES				
Activity	Done With	Started	Completed	Comments

Figure 9.8   Second- and Third-Grade Time Schedule

Weekly Schedule, Estella Esquivel's Second- and Third-Grade Family Grouping Classroom

Time	Monday	Tuesday	Wednesday	Thursday	Friday
7:30	Teacher preparation time				
8:00	Children arrive, put away coats, prepare lunch count, and take attendance.				
8:10	Group time. Teacher reads poetry, story, or information book. Plans for the day are discussed.				
8:30	Integrated work time. Children work in small groups or individually. Teacher works with small groups or has individual conferences.				
10:00	Recess				
10:15	Art	Music	Health	Art	Music
10:45	Math				
11:45	Group meeting. Teacher and students discuss morning's work. Several students share their writing or other projects.				
12:00	Lunch and outdoor play				
1:00	Sustained silent reading				
1:20	Book talk. Several children talk about the books they have been reading.				
1:30	Integrated work time. Children continue work time, or teacher works with whole class.				
2:15	Physical education				
2:35	Clean-up				
2:45	Read-aloud. Teacher reads or asks children to read from their work.				
3:00	Dismissal				

Source: From *An Integrated Language Perspective in the Elementary School: Theory into Action* by Christine C. Pappas, Barbara Z. Kiefer, and Linda S. Levstik, pp. 132. Copyright © 1990 by Longman Publishing Group.

Culminating the Theme

In this final stage, you will use the culminating activities you developed as you planned your theme. Students will share theme projects and activities and evaluate and reflect on the results of the theme.

Sharing Projects and Activities.   Sharing is critical to helping students construct meaning and feel a sense of community and ownership. During this

Figure 9.9 Sixth-Grade Time Schedule

Weekly Schedule, Caitlin Cooper's Sixth-Grade Classroom

Time	Monday	Tuesday	Wednesday	Thursday	Friday
8:00	Opening exercises				
8:10	Forum. Children gather to share work, group plan, and learn about activity choices for the day.				
8:30	Integrated work time. Children sign up to work in various areas, participate in special projects (i.e., digs). Opportunity for problem solving, creative thinking, self-expression, communication, and content engagement.				
9:50	Special classes: art, music, physical education, library				
10:30	Recess				
10:45	Integrated work time				
12:00	Lunch				
12:45	Sustained silent reading				
1:00	Forum. Whole-group experiences that include introducing new material, guest speakers, writing and editing workshops, math reviews, and the like.				
2:00	Integrated work time				
2:30	Clean-up, announcements, dismissal				

Source: From *An Integrated Language Perspective in the Elementary School: Theory into Action* by Christine C. Pappas, Barbara Z. Kiefer, and Linda S. Levstik, pp. 157. Copyright © 1990 by Longman Publishing Group.

time students give talks, show their work, and talk with each other about the theme activities. Sharing may take the form of a special day, event, or activity devoted to pulling together what has been learned, having a play or fair, putting on some type of display, inviting students from other classes, and so forth. An entire day or more may be devoted to culminating the theme if there are enough activities to make it worthwhile.

Evaluating and Reflecting. This is also an important culminating activity. Throughout the theme, you and your students will have been assessing progress, and at this point you want them to return to their theme plan and talk about how they have done on the theme activities. You may use small-group discussions and circulate to talk with each group, or you may use individual conferences. Students should talk about how they have done in relation to the theme goals, focusing on what they have done well and what they might do better in the next unit. This should not become a "heavy time" for "grading." Rather, it should be a natural time where you and the students reflect and take stock of how things have gone. From the kindergarten level on, this can be a positive, constructive time that helps all students grow in their own literacy abilities.

As the teacher, you will also want to reflect on the unit. Was the length of time appropriate? How has it gone? What would you change? How have your students grown? How have you grown? These and many other questions will help you get better at using cross-curricular thematic units.

In summary, developing a theme involves planning, implementing, and culminating the theme. Each of these stages is very fluid and interactive and should be adjusted to fit your needs and the needs of your students. The following section presents a sample cross-curricular theme entitled "People of Many Cultures."

Literacy Lesson

Sample Thematic Unit on "People of Many Cultures"

The sample theme presented in this section was developed for use in a fifth-grade class with a wide range of abilities. Both the planning process and theme outline are presented.

Before Reading the Thematic Unit
1. **Review the portion of this chapter focusing on developing thematic units.**
2. **Discuss any questions that you have with a peer or your instructor.**
3. **Read the planning process for the theme.**

While Reading the Thematic Unit
1. **Think about why certain activities might have been selected.**
2. **Think of other ways you might have developed the theme.**
3. **Keep in mind that there is no "right way" to develop a theme. There are many alternatives.**

Planning Process for the Theme

Basically, I planned this theme using the process described in this chapter.

1. I considered many different topics by brainstorming a list of ideas. I finally settled on "People of Many Cultures" because with this idea I could make many connections across the curriculum. This is also a theme that could go in many different directions or could be the focus of study for an entire year.
2. Next, I began to brainstorm learning goals, resources, and activities. The rough web shown in Figure 9.10 helped me focus and limit the theme.

Figure 9.10   Rough Planning Web for Thematic Unit "People of Many Cultures"

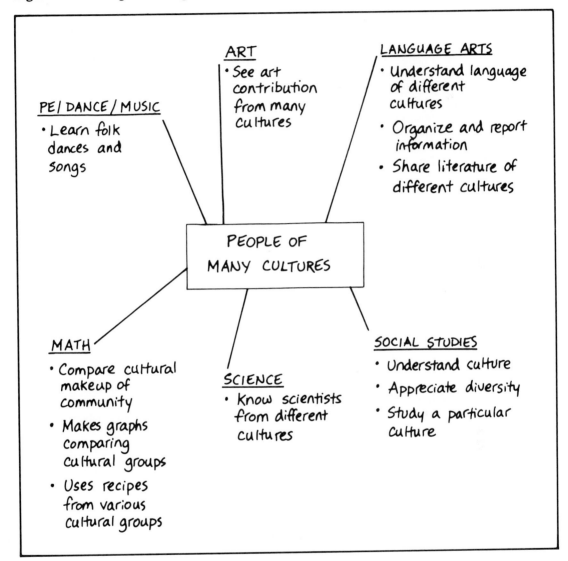

*Literacy
Lesson
continued*

3. I decided to focus first on my major outcomes: attitudes and habits and constructing meaning. Since I could use this theme early in the year, I wanted to develop the idea that America's strength comes from its diversity of cultures. More in-depth study would come in later themes.

In terms of skills, I wanted to stress things that would be basic throughout the year—gathering information, presenting information, and measuring and understanding proportions.

Literacy Lesson continued

4. I identified many resources, including all types of literature, reference sources, and a social studies text, *America Will Be* (Armento, Nash, Salter, & Wixson, 1991); the first chapter in this book was appropriate. The literature selected represented a wide range of cultures, interests, and difficulty levels. I also identified some community resources. The focus of my outcomes helped me keep the number of resources reasonable.

5. I generated possible activities that were appropriate for a three-week theme, which was the amount of time I planned for the unit. I focused on initiating, developing, and culminating activities. I also thought about possibilities for assessment and evaluation.

6. After completing my basic plans, I worked out a timeline and pacing chart and a daily schedule. I knew that daily plans would change as students carried out their activities.

7. Finally, I analyzed my unit in terms of cross-curricular learning.

> ### Thematic Unit: People of Many Cultures

Major Outcomes, Strategies, and Skills

Attitudes and Habits
- Appreciate the cultural diversity of America
- Relate cultural diversity to one's own life

Constructing Meaning
- Understand culture and diversity of cultures
- Understand how different cultures have contributed to America
- Know that the strength of America lies in diversity
- Begin to understand the challenges of living in a culturally diverse society

Strategies and Skills
- Gathering information (reference books, literature, and textbooks; interviews)
- Presenting information (reports, oral and written; charts and graphs; timelines)
- Math (percentage and proportion, measuring)

Resources

Possible Theme Literature: These books will be used for self-selected reading, group projects, and individual activities. Other books may also be located in the library.

Nonfiction:
Ashabranner, B. (1984). *To live in two worlds*. New York: Dodd, Mead.
Dolphin, L. (1991). *Georgia to Georgia: Making friends in the U.S.S.R.* New York: Tambourine Books.
Feelings, M. (1971). *Moja means one: Swahili counting book*. New York: Dial.
Feelings, M. (1974). *Jambo means hello: Swahili alphabet book*. New York: Dial.

*Literacy
Lesson
continued*

Freedman, R. (1980). *Immigrant kids*. New York: E. P. Dutton.
Garza, C. L. (1990). *Family pictures*. San Francisco: Children's Book Press.
Jacobs, W. J. (1990). *Ellis Island: New hope in a new land*. New York: Scribner's.
Perl, L. (1989). *The great ancestor hunt: The fun of finding out who you are*. New York: Clarion.

Biography:
Mitchell, B. (1987). *Raggin': A story about Scott Joplin*. Minneapolis: Carolrhoda Books.
Roberts, M. (1986). *Henry Cisneros: Mexican American mayor*. Chicago: Childrens Press.
Say, A. (1990). *El Chino*. Boston: Houghton Mifflin.
Walker, A. (1974). *Langston Hughes, American poet*. New York: Crowell.

Poetry:
Adoff, A. (1982). *All the colors of the race*. New York: Lothrop, Lee & Shepard.
Katz, J. B. (1980). *This song remembers*. Boston: Houghton Mifflin.
Schon, I. (Ed.) (1983). *Doña Blanca and other nursery rhymes and games*. Denison.

Folktales:
Griego, Y., Maestas, J., & Auaya, R. A. (1980). *Cuentas: Tales from the Hispanic southwest*. Santa Fe: The Museum of New Mexico.
Hamilton, V. (1985). *The people could fly*. New York: Knopf.
Mendez, P. (1989). *The black snowman*. New York: Scholastic.
Young, E. (1989). *Lon Po Po*. New York: Philomel.

Realistic Fiction:
Baylor, B. (1976). *Hawk, I'm your brother*. New York: Scribner's.
Bunting, E. (1988). *How many days to America? A Thanksgiving story*. New York: Clarion.
Galarza, E. (1971). *Barrio boy*. Notre Dame, IN: University of Notre Dame Press.
Haugaard, E. C. (1991). *The boy and the samurai*. Boston: Houghton Mifflin.
Hurwitz, J. (1990). *Class president*. New York: Morrow Junior Books.
Lord, B. B. (1984). *In the year of the boar and Jackie Robinson*. New York: Harper & Row.
Lowry, L. (1989). *Number the stars*. Boston: Houghton Mifflin.
Politi, L. (1949). *The song of the swallows*. New York: Scribner's.
Say, A. (1982). *The bicycle man*. Boston: Houghton Mifflin.
Taylor, M. D. (1990). *Mississippi bridge*. New York: Dial Books for Young Readers.

   Textbooks and Reference Books
   • *America Will Be*, Chapter 1, by Armento, Nash, Salter, and Wixson (1991), pp. 2–27 (Note: A literacy lesson for this textbook chapter is presented on page 529.)
   • *The World Book Encyclopedia*
   • *The World Almanac*
   • Daily newspapers
   • Weekly news magazines

*Literacy
Lesson
continued*

Community Resources
- Persons from different cultural groups
- Chamber of commerce
- Local cultural centers

Theme Activities

ACTIVITIES	INDEPENDENT/ INDIVIDUAL	COOPERATIVE/ SMALL GROUP	WHOLE CLASS	SELF-SELECTED	TEACHER ASSIGNED	TEACHER DIRECTED
Initiating activities:						
Teacher read-aloud *How Many Days to America?*, Bunting			X			X
Small-group discussions using K-W-L *Focus:* What we know about different cultures in America		X			X	
Start a family tree (complete throughout unit)	X				X	
Complete theme goal sheet *Focus:* • Unit options • What I want to learn	X					
Developing activities:						
Write a make-believe personal journal *Topic:* My trip to America	X				X	
Read books reflecting the literature of different cultural groups	X			X		
Literature circles *Focus:* • Discussing literature of various cultures • Comparing literature of various cultures		X		X		

*Literacy
Lesson
continued*

ACTIVITIES	INDEPENDENT/ INDIVIDUAL	COOPERATIVE/ SMALL GROUP	WHOLE CLASS	SELF- SELECTED	TEACHER ASSIGNED	TEACHER DIRECTED
Keep a daily learning log	X				X	
Study a cultural group and write a report *Focus:* • Language • Important people • Foods • Customs • Architecture	X			X		
Develop timeline of cultural growth in *our* community *Focus:* • Events • Causes			X			X
Read Chapter 1 in *America Will Be*			X			X
Make graphs showing cultural diversity in our • country • state • city or town • school • classroom		X		X		
Math lessons on • percentage • proportion			X			X
Make posters about famous American scientists from other cultures	X *OR* X			X		
Make a recipe collection *Focus:* Recipes of different cultural groups		X		X		
Learn authentic folk dances			X			X

Literacy Lesson continued

ACTIVITIES	INDEPENDENT/ INDIVIDUAL	COOPERATIVE/ SMALL GROUP	WHOLE CLASS	SELF- SELECTED	TEACHER ASSIGNED	TEACHER DIRECTED
Make a cultural map of the country *Focus:* • Where various groups settled • Where groups came from and why • Where groups have moved within the country		X				X
Interview a person from another culture	X			X		
Culminating activities: Share reports and projects	X ....*OR*.... X					
Festival of our culture *Focus:* • Literature (drama, storytelling) • Foods • Dances, songs, games			X			
Panel discussion and interviews *Focus:* How different cultural groups have contributed to America's strength		X				
Complete and discuss K-W-L chart		X			X	
Reflect on the unit *Focus:* • Self-evaluation • Ways to improve			X			X

Literacy Lesson continued

Plan for Implementing the Unit

Timeline and Pacing

Total days: 15
Days 1 and 2:   Initiating activities
Days 3–13:   Developing activities
Days 14 and 15:   Culminating activities

Daily Schedule

8:30   Opening activities (teacher read-aloud, song, or student sharing)
8:50   Reading workshop
    8:50   Minilesson
    9:00   State-of-the-class conference
    9:05   Teacher-assigned reading and responding
    9:30   Self-selected reading and responding
    10:05 Sharing
    10:15 Morning break
    10:40 Writing workshop
        10:40   Minilesson
        10:50   State-of-the-class conference
        10:55   Writing and conferring
        11:30   Sharing
    11:45 Lunch and recess
    12:30 Teacher read-aloud
    12:45 Small-group and independent project time
    1:30   Whole-group progress report
    1:40   Whole-class instruction *or* small-group instruction and independent work
    2:25   Review the day
    2:35   Prepare for dismissal
    2:45   Dismissal

Evaluation

Self-Evaluation
- Using K-W-L chart
- Theme goal sheet

Daily Observations
- Teacher's log on individual students

Portfolios (discussed in Chapter 10)
- Work samples (teacher selected and student selected)
- Records of independent reading
- Teacher-developed unit test

Literacy
Lesson
continued

Theme Analysis

THEME	LANGUAGE ARTS	SOCIAL STUDIES	SCIENCE	MATH	ART	MUSIC/PE
People of Many Cultures	Gather information: Reference Books Interviews Textbooks Literature Present information: Reports Charts and graphs Oral reports	Culture Diversity Maps Population	Famous inventors and their inventions	Percentages Proportion Measurement	Art forms of different cultures	Songs and dances from different cultures

---

After Reading the Thematic Unit

1. Work with a partner and discuss how you would have changed this theme.
2. Select a topic and develop a theme of your own.

PERSONAL REFLECTIONS ON CROSS-CURRICULAR THEMATIC TEACHING

Many years ago, when I was a beginning teacher, I was assigned a combination fifth- and sixth-grade class, and I approached it as I had been taught to do in college. In the process of trying to teach separate subjects to each grade level, I almost decided that I didn't want to teach. However, I had a wonderful supervisor named Dr. Grace Champion who suggested that I forget the subjects and plan a unit in which my students could study different problems.

Under Dr. Champion's direction I planned my first integrated unit. As best I can recall, it had a "living things" focus, which I chose because it was a topic in the curriculum common to both fifth and sixth grade. My students read many books about living things, and I had many basal readers from which to choose. We found all the stories that related to our theme and read them,

I brought in books from the public library, we planned and completed projects, we wrote reports, we created many displays, and we used materials from our science texts, from encyclopedias, and from any other available sources.

When students needed special help on something, I pulled together small groups and taught them what they needed, whether it was how to locate information, how to write a paragraph, how to use a certain math concept needed to make a graph, or just how to read and discuss certain chapters in a book that was causing them difficulty.

From this point on I taught my combination class in thematic units. There were many things I didn't know (and still don't know), but I stumbled forward. Each unit got better and better. At the end of the year, my students *all* made substantial gains on their achievement tests, despite my (then) rather unorthodox way of teaching.

Over the next few years of my teaching, I used cross-curricular units in every grade I taught. Students went to the library. They read; they wrote; they solved problems. My classes always scored very high on their achievement tests.

Over the years, as I became a reading specialist and went to graduate school, I got further and further away from my thematic teaching. Only through further study, research, and working in classrooms over the past ten years have I come to realize what I had and what I left behind. Dr. Champion, who had also been my first-grade teacher and college professor in children's literature, had started me in a positive direction that I now know was important.

Cross-curricular teaching is not easy at first, but it is possible for all teachers. It is a matter of good planning and letting go of preconceived ideas about what classrooms ought to be. The rewards come in seeing children who are excited, who want to learn, and *who do learn*!!

Each person grows into this ability to do integrated, cross-curricular teaching in many different ways. No one ever completely integrates everything, and each teacher must handle it differently. However, if you want to help students at all grade levels and in all subject areas learn to construct meaning more effectively, take the ideas about integrated, cross-curricular teaching to heart. It has taken me nearly thirty years to get these ideas together, and I am still learning every day.

USING THE LITERACY LESSON CONCEPT WITH TEXTBOOKS AND INFORMATIONAL BOOKS

One of the problems regarding content-area teaching is how students and teachers use textbooks (Armbruster, 1991). In order to improve this situation, scaffolded support should be provided for students who need it before, during, and after reading. The literacy lesson concept that you have learned to use throughout this text can be applied to help students become more active constructors of meaning in content classes and in cross-curricular learning situations. As you recall, it consists of three parts: introducing, reading and responding, and extending.

When *introducing* a textbook or informational book chapter, you activate students' prior knowledge and background for the chapter. Sometimes this may include developing a *few* key concept terms before the chapter is read (see Chapter 4). At the same time students must develop purposes for their reading.

In a *well-written* informational text, the key concepts and main ideas are clearly evident and it is therefore often easier to identify the key background concepts and key terms than it is in a story or narrative selection. If you develop key terms when introducing a chapter, follow the guidelines and suggestions given in Chapter 4.

Reading and responding to the text means that students must read the chapter and *actively* respond to it by doing something with what they have learned. Depending on the grade level, students' abilities, and the text they are reading, many students will be able to read the textbook or other text resource independently, but some will need more support provided by cooperative reading, shared reading, teacher-guided reading, or teacher read-alouds.

A variation of teacher-guided reading that is often used with textbooks is a study guide, which gives students a set of questions or activities to help them through the text. The guide serves as a partial replacement for the teacher and supports students as they work independently or with a partner. Study guides are discussed in more detail later in this chapter.

Responding should involve students in a variety of authentic activities, including discussion, retelling, summarizing, and writing about what was read (see Chapter 6). Doing the end-of-chapter questions provided in most textbooks is *not* appropriate responding, although questions may be used to focus a discussion group.

Another part of responding should be completely individual and personal. Students might use a learning log or some other device or activity to respond to the textbook chapter or informational book that is the focus of the literacy lesson (see Chapter 6).

Extending is the final part of the literacy lesson, the time when students take the meanings they have constructed and use them in some way. For example, if students have just learned some information about how to perform an experiment in science, a natural way to extend their learning would be to have them perform an experiment. If the literacy lesson is a part of a thematic unit, extending should always tie back to the unit.

Since textbooks contain a variety of text structures (see Chapter 3), it is often necessary to vary the literacy lesson to accommodate text differences and student needs. For example, students reading a social studies text may need to focus on the sequential or cause-effect development of historical events, and students reading a science text may need to focus on major ideas and the cause-effect relationships in nature.

The following section presents a literacy lesson for the chapter "A Nation of Many Peoples" from *America Will Be* (Armento, Nash, Salter & Wixson, 1991). This is the social studies text used in the thematic unit "People of Many Cultures" presented earlier in this chapter.

Literacy Lesson

"A Nation of Many Peoples"

America Will Be (Armento, Nash, Salter & Wixson, 1991) is a social studies text that incorporates primary sources and literature to develop social studies content. This lesson uses the literacy lesson concept and is considered a part of the thematic unit presented earlier.

Before Reading the Lesson

1. **Review the portions of this chapter focusing on the literacy lesson. If you need more information, return to Chapter 2.**
2. **Read the lesson preparation to help you understand how and why the lesson was developed as it was.**

While Reading the Lesson

1. **Think about why the lesson activities were carried out as they were.**
2. **Look for places where you might have conducted the lesson differently.**

Lesson Preparation

The following steps illustrate the preparation that was done for this lesson:

1. I read the chapter to determine its key concepts and overall structure:
   - The chapter was divided into three lessons.
   - Each lesson developed one concept:

     Lesson 1: New Orleans has a pluralistic culture where many different cultures live together. It is an example of the culture of the United States.

     Lesson 2: People immigrating from other countries have made America a pluralistic culture.

     Lesson 3: A pluralistic culture has many benefits and challenges.

   - The chapter has many graphs, photographs, and charts. Unless they already know, students will need to learn how to use these resources since the chapter contains much more than expository text.

Literacy
Lesson
continued

- The chapter has six key terms—*culture, pluralism* (lesson 1), *immigrant, descendant* (lesson 2), *ethnic custom, prejudice* (lesson 3). Since these terms are developed as part of the text, *I will not preteach them.*
- The chapter also contains resources for helping students use the encyclopedia and for interviewing. Since both of these activities are important in our theme, "People of Many Cultures," I will use them as minilessons in the reading workshop or during whole-class instruction time. Since it is the beginning of the year, I feel that most students need to review and refine their use of encyclopedias and interviewing.

2. Because the chapter has three lessons, I will plan three separate literacy lessons. (Only one is presented here.) The first lesson will focus on learning to use the resources in the book and on reading lesson 1, "A Tale of One City." Lessons 2 and 3 will build on this first lesson. All three lessons will be tied to our thematic unit.

3. Since this is the beginning of the school year, I am going to concentrate on getting students to use two important strategies for constructing meaning—preview and predict (see Chapter 3) and summarizing informational text (see Chapter 7). Lesson 1 will concentrate on preview and predict.

> ### Introducing the Textbook and
> ### "A Tale of One City"

ACTIVITY	PROCEDURE	NOTES
Previewing *America Will Be*—cooperative activity	Divide class into teams of three. Direct each team to preview the text to compile a list of things they find (charts, maps, stories, and so forth).	Since the book is new to students, this is a good interactive way for them to learn its features.
	Have each group report. Compile a class list of things found in the text and discuss their uses.	
Using the preview and predict strategy with a partner	Ask students to tell what they know about the preview and predict strategy.	Students will already have prior knowledge for this chapter because of initiating theme activities. Therefore, this strategy focuses directly on the text to be read and will activate prior knowledge directly for the text.
	Display the strategy poster (Chapter 3, page 125).	

Literacy Lesson continued

ACTIVITY	PROCEDURE	NOTES
	If students need assistance, model previewing and predicting, showing them how to use headings, photographs, illustrations, and so on.	
	Have students preview the chapter (pages 2–8) and predict what they think they will learn.	
	Discuss responses, relating ideas to the overall theme.	
Using learning logs	Have students record predictions in their learning logs.	By writing predictions, students will keep their purposes for reading in mind. They can also use their learning logs to take notes or change their predictions as they read.

Reading and Responding to "A Tale of One City"

ACTIVITY	PROCEDURE	NOTES
Cooperative reading	Divide students into partner teams or groups of three to cooperatively read the chapter, keeping their individual predictions in mind. (See Chapter 2 on cooperative reading.)	Cooperative reading will free me to move around the room to see how different students read. I can use this as a diagnostic time to find out what type of support students need.
Responding in learning logs	After students complete the reading, they can each return to their learning log to comment about their predictions and identify and react to what they learned.	Promotes personal response to the chapter.

Literacy Lesson continued

ACTIVITY	PROCEDURE	NOTES
Discussion circles	After reading is completed, have students form discussion circles to discuss the text, focusing on their predictions, what they learned, and how they felt about this chapter.	Further promotes personal response to text. Helps foster meaning construction.
Making a class chart of key points learned	After discussion circles are completed, work with students to compile a class chart of key points learned. Use section questions to guide selection of points: Where is New Orleans? Who lives in New Orleans? How is the United States like New Orleans?	Pulls chapter section together. Good preparation for introducing summarizing in next section of chapter.

Extending "A Tale of One City"

ACTIVITY	PROCEDURE	NOTES
Making a timeline of cultural growth in our community	Have students work on a timeline showing cultural changes in their community.	This theme activity is a good extension of this section of the chapter.
Putting key terms in learning logs	Have students work with a partner to identify terms that they learned in this section of the chapter. Have them put the terms in learning logs with an example for each.	Gets students actively involved in learning new vocabulary.

After Reading the Lesson

1. **Working with a partner, think of other ways you might have carried out this lesson.**
2. **Select a textbook or informational book and develop a literacy lesson of your own.**

A FINAL WORD ABOUT LITERACY LESSONS

The literacy lesson format is very flexible and can be used with any textbook or informational text to help students learn to construct meaning. Within a thematic unit, it is not necessary to have a literacy lesson for all texts students read: they will receive much of the support they need through other theme activities and the use of self-selected books and materials. In the next section we will look at how to use study guides as a part of the literacy lesson.

USING STUDY GUIDES TO IMPROVE MEANING CONSTRUCTION

As noted earlier, a study guide may be used as an alternative to teacher-guided reading in the literacy lesson. Researchers have found that study guides help students set purposes as they read content text (Armbruster, Anderson & Osterlag, 1989). A study guide, as its name implies, is a guide for studying, similar to the monitoring guide discussed in Chapter 2. It is a set of activities and questions that direct students through the reading of a textbook or other informational text.

Study guides can fulfill at least three different purposes:

1. They can provide support for students who need help in constructing meaning in textbooks and informational texts. The more structured and directive the guides, the more support they will provide.
2. They can stimulate thinking by providing thought-provoking questions and/or activities.
3. By changing the design and construction of the study guide, you can meet a broad range of literacy needs within your classroom.

Research has shown that the use of study guides does help students construct meaning (Alvermann & Moore, 1991). They may be used in very simple forms in grades 2 and 3, but are usually most effective in grade 4 and above.

Designing and Constructing Study Guides

There are eight guidelines you should consider when constructing a study guide:

Determine your purpose.   Is your purpose to give students the scaffolding they need to more effectively construct meaning, to stimulate thinking, or to do both?

Decide on the amount of support you want to provide.   Once you have determined your purpose for the guide, this decision usually follows rather readily. For students who are having difficulty constructing meaning, you need to provide a lot of support. For example, you may use activities like the following:

- (p. 398, paragraphs 3 and 4) Identify the two main causes of air pollution.

  _____

  _____

- List three factors that contribute to lung disease:

  1. _____

  2. _____

  3. _____

When putting the study guide together, follow the flow of the chapter.   Since the activities and questions should help students actively construct meaning, it is important to focus on ideas in the order that they appear.

Include opportunities for students to write.   An important part of constructing meaning is expressing what has been learned in your own words. Activities such as the following can help accomplish this task:

- Write one or two sentences telling why insects are helpful to people.

  _____

  _____

  _____

  _____

Incorporate opportunities for students to make predictions and to monitor their reading.   Activities such as the following will help with both of these processes:

- _Previewing and predicting:_ After looking through this chapter, what do you think you will learn? List two things.

  _____

  _____

- _Stop and think:_ How do pulleys help people?

  _____

  _____

  _____

_or_

Have your predictions changed? Why?

_____

_____

_____

Provide questions and activities that bring out key concepts or main ideas. Too often, study guide questions or activities focus on trivial information and don't lead students to big ideas and/or concepts developed in the text. Questions or activities like the following are more likely to help students construct meaning:

- Complete the following graphic organizer showing how the discovery of the atom has helped people:

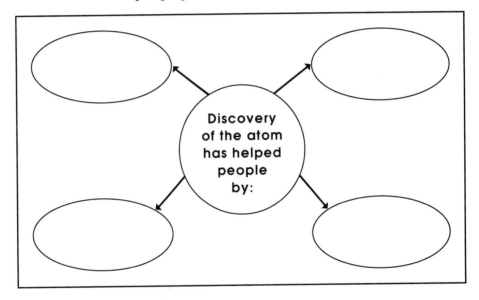

- Write a sentence or two telling how the Mayflower's voyage changed the world.

_____

_____

_____

_____

_____

Include activities and questions on all study guides that require students to "think" and make use of what they have read. Even students who are having difficulty constructing meaning are able to think and need to think. Activities like the following are good ones to incorporate into a study guide.

- Complete the following chart:

Three Ideas for Good Health	
Ideas	*How I Feel About These Ideas*
1.	
2.	
3.	

- How will the information in this text help you in your lifetime?

_____

_____

_____

_____

Provide activities and questions that help students pull together or summarize the text.   By providing questions or activities that follow the flow of the chapter and bring out key ideas, you are leading students to a summary. A final activity on the study guide should require students to do some type of summarizing. Here are some examples:

- Look back at the first three guidelines. Now, write a sentence or two telling the big ideas you have learned in this text.

_____

_____

_____

_____

These eight principles can serve as a basis for developing a study guide. Figure 9.11 shows an example of a partial study guide written to go with the informational book *Voyager to the Planets* (Apfel, 1991).

Figure 9.11   Partial Study Guide That Provides Heavy Support for Students

---

STUDY GUIDE
FOR
VOYAGER TO THE PLANETS

Name _____ Date _____

① *Preview and predict:* Look through the book at the photographs. Read the captions. Predict two or three things you think you will learn in this book; write them below.

_____

_____

_____

_____

_____

② pages 7–9
   What was the purpose for Voyager I and Voyager II?

   Voyager I _____

   _____

   Voyager II _____

   _____

Figure 9.11   cont.

③ pages 10–11
  Describe how Voyager looked.

  _____

  _____

  _____

  _____

  Now you think: Why did Voyager look this way?

  _____

  _____

  _____

  _____

  What problem did Voyager have?

  _____

  _____

  _____

  _____

  Now you think: Why was it important to correct this problem?

  _____

  _____

  _____

  _____

Figure 9.11 cont.

④ pages 12–15
Complete this chart showing what Voyager learned about Jupiter.

Things Learned About Jupiter
Temperature
Clouds
Jupiter's Solar System

STUDY TECHNIQUES FOR IMPROVING THE CONSTRUCTION OF MEANING

As students learn to construct meaning across the curriculum, they must develop techniques that will help them study, think about, and remember information. Teachers in many curricular areas have frequently encouraged students to use a number of techniques, such as underlining, note taking, summarizing, outlining, mapping or making some type of graphic organizer to show information that was learned, and student questioning. The value of summarizing and student questioning was already discussed in detail in Chapter 8. Now, let's examine what we know about these other techniques.

The conclusions discussed here are based on the very thorough and critical reviews of research by Anderson and Armbruster (1984b) and Alvermann and Moore (1991).

- *Underlining:* With this technique, students underline information that they feel is important or should be remembered. In fact, you are probably doing this as you are reading this chapter. Research tends to show that underlining is no more effective than any other study technique in helping students learn and remember information (Anderson & Armbruster, 1984). In fact, Alvermann and Moore (1991) conclude that it is no better than just having students read for understanding and recall. It must be remembered, however, that the number of studies focusing on underlining is small because students are discouraged from marking in their textbooks. The real value in underlining is most likely to come from the process of deciding what information is important in the text, not the underlining itself. Therefore, the strategies for identifying important information in Chapter 8 are probably more important for students than underlining.
- *Note taking:* This is the technique of writing down ideas or information that one feels is important. The research in this area (Alvermann & Moore, 1991; Anderson & Armbruster, 1984b) shows that note taking is an effective study technique if it involves thinking about the text as opposed to just writing down isolated facts or insignificant information. The value in note taking, as with underlining, comes in the process of thinking and deciding what is important. Here we see again the importance of the strategies discussed in Chapter 8.
- *Outlining:* Outlining involves writing a verbal sketch showing the main points and supporting information in a text. For this technique to help students construct meaning, it must be thoroughly taught (Anderson & Armbruster, 1984b; Alvermann & Moore, 1991). Students must not only learn the various forms of outlining, but they must also learn how to identify the information that is important and know what ideas support this information. Again, this goes back to the strategies developed in Chapter 8.

- *Mapping or graphic organizers:* This technique involves showing the information gained from a text in some type of visual way. (See Chapter 3 for examples.) Again, research shows that for this technique to be helpful it must be thoroughly taught over the long term. Students must be able to identify the important information in a text and the relationships among pieces of information. The process of deciding what information is important and how to construct the graphic organizer is the type of active involvement that students must have to ensure that they construct meaning. Research also suggests that it is better for students to construct the organizer themselves than to have the teacher supply a prepared organizer.

In conclusion, what can be said about teaching students various techniques for studying? All the techniques reviewed here revolve around the strategy of identifying important information discussed in Chapter 8. In order for students to use any of these techniques, they must know how to use that strategy.

All the techniques must be thoroughly taught and modeled. No one technique appears to be significantly better than another for helping students construct meaning. Rather, each person finds his or her own best way of studying and remembering information. Some persons use one technique, some use another, and still others combine techniques or create their own. Therefore, it is best to give students experiences with all these techniques and allow them to find the one (or ones) that works for them.

SUMMARY

This chapter has focused on how students construct meaning across the curriculum. It was stressed that this process is one whereby students learn to build relationships between and among various curricular areas, each of which provides the basis for the content that students actually use for constructing meaning. Textbooks are only one resource. A variety of types of literature used in conjunction with the textbook create many more authentic and exciting opportunities for learning.

It was suggested that using cross-curricular thematic units is an effective way to improve students' meaning construction and overall learning. The process of developing a thematic unit was discussed and illustrated, as well as the use of the literacy lesson concept for textbooks and informational text. Study guides were suggested as a strategy to incorporate into the literacy lesson.

Reviews of research on various techniques for studying were summarized. Basically, all techniques for studying involve the strategy of identifying important information in texts. No one technique for studying appears to be better than another.

Children's Books

Apfel, N. H. (1991). *Voyager to the planets*. New York: Clarion.

Fox, D., & Marks, C. (1987). *Go in and out the window: An illustrated songbook for young people*. New York: Henry Holt.

Freedman, R. (1987). *Lincoln: A photobiography*. New York: Clarion.

George, W. T. (1989). *Box turtle at Long Pond*. New York: Greenwillow Books.

Goor, R., & Goor, N. (1986). *Pompeii: Exploring a Roman ghost town*. New York: Crowell.

Hamilton, V. (1985). *The people could fly*. New York: Knopf.

Hodges, M. (1976). *Knight prisoner: The tale of Sir Thomas Malory and his King Arthur*. New York: Farrar, Straus and Giroux.

Macaulay, D. (1977). *Castle*. Boston: Houghton Mifflin.

Raffi. (1980). *The Raffi singable songbook*. New York: Crown.

Sancha, S. (1983). *Luttrell Village: Country life in the Middle Ages*. New York: HarperCollins.

Twain, M. (1987). *A Connecticut Yankee in King Arthur's court*. New York: Morrow.

Wright, S. (1988). *Age of chivalry*. New York: Watts.

For Additional Reading

Moore, D. W., Readence, J. E., & Rickelman, R. J. (1989). *Prereading activities for content area reading and learning* (2nd ed.). Newark, DE: International Reading Association.

Norton, D. E. (1991). Nonfiction: Biographies and informational books. In D. E. Norton (Ed.), *Through the eyes of a child: An introduction to children's literature* (3rd ed.) (pp. 607–677). New York: Macmillan.

Pappas, C. C., Kiefer, B. Z., & Levstik, L. S. (1990). *An integrated language perspective in the elementary school: Theory into action*. New York: Longman.

Ward, G. (1988). *I've got a project on . . .* Australia Primary English Teaching Association, distributed by Heinemann, Portsmouth, NH.

References

Alvermann, D. E., & Moore, D. W. (1991). *Secondary schools*. In R. Barr, M. L. Kamil, P. B. Mosenthal & P. D. Pearson (Eds.), *Handbook of reading research* (Vol. 2, pp. 951–983). New York: Longman.

Anderson, R. C., & Pearson, P. D. (1984). A schema-theoretic view of basic processes in reading comprehension. In P. D. Pearson (Ed.), *Handbook of reading research* (pp. 255–291). New York: Longman.

Anderson, T. H., & Armbruster, B. B. (1984a). Content area textbooks. In R. C. Anderson, J. Osborn, & R. J. Tierney (Eds.), *Learning to read in American schools* (pp. 193–226). Hillsdale, NJ: Lawrence Erlbaum.

Anderson, T. H., & Armbruster, B. B. (1984b). Studying. In P. D. Pearson (Ed.), *Handbook of reading research* (pp. 657–679). New York: Longman.

Armbruster, B. (1991, May 5). *Content area reading instruction*. A presentation given at the Conference on Reading Research, CORR, Las Vegas, NV.

Armbruster, B. B., Anderson, T. H., & Osterlag, J. (1989). Teaching text structure to improve reading and writing. *Reading Teacher, 43,* 130–137.

Armento, B. J., Nash, G. B., Salter, C. L., & Wixson, K. (1991). *America will be.* Boston: Houghton Mifflin.

Chall, J. S., & Conrad, S. S. (1990). Textbooks and challenge: The influence of educational research. In D. L. Elliott & A. Woodward (Eds.), *Textbooks and schooling in the United States* (pp. 42–55). Chicago: National Society for the Study of Education.

Dupuis, M. M. (Ed.). (1984). *Reading in the content areas: Research for teachers.* Newark, DE: International Reading Association.

Elliott, D. L. (1990). Textbooks and the curriculum in the postwar era: 1950–1980. In D. L. Elliott & A. Woodward (Eds.), *Textbooks and schooling in the United States* (pp. 42–55). Chicago: National Society for the Study of Education.

Elliott, D. L., & Woodward, A. (1990). Textbooks, curriculum and school improvement. In D. L. Elliott & A. Woodward (Eds.), *Textbooks and schooling in the United States* (pp. 222–232). Chicago: National Society for the Study of Education.

Herber, H. L. (1978). *Teaching reading in content areas* (2nd ed.). Englewood Cliffs, NJ: Prentice-Hall.

Herber, H. L. (1984). Subject matter texts—Reading to learn: Response to a paper by Thomas H. Anderson and Bonnie B. Armbruster. In R. C. Anderson, J. Osborn, & R. J. Tierney (Eds.), *Learning to read in American Schools: Basal readers and content texts* (pp. 227–234). Hillsdale, NJ: Lawrence Erlbaum.

Hickman, J., & Cullinan, B. E. (1989). A point of view on literature and learning. In J. Hickman & B. E. Cullinan (Eds.), *Children's literature in the classroom: Weaving Charlotte's web* (pp. 3–12). Needham Heights, MA: Christopher-Gordon.

History-Social Science Curriculum Framework and Criteria Committee. (1988). *History-social science framework.* Sacramento, CA: California State Board of Education.

Moss, B. (1991). Children's nonfiction trade books: A complement to content area texts. *Reading Teacher, 45,* 26–32.

Norton, D. E. (1982). Using a webbing process to develop children's literature units. *Language Arts, 59,* 348–356.

Norton, D. E. (1991). *Through the eyes of a child—An introduction to children's literature* (3rd ed.). New York: Macmillan.

Pappas, C. C., Kiefer, B. Z., & Levstik, L. S. (1990). *An integrated language perspective in the elementary school: Theory into action.* New York: Longman.

Routman, R. (1991). *Invitations.* Portsmouth, NH: Heinemann.

Sebesta, S. L. (1989). Literature across the curriculum. In J. W. Stewig & S. L. Sebesta (Eds.), *Using literature in the elementary classroom* (pp. 110–128). Urbana, IL: National Council of Teachers of English.

Tyson, H., & Woodward, A. (1989). Why students aren't learning very much from textbooks. *Educational Leadership, 47,* 14–17.

Wells, G. (1986). *The meaning makers: Children learning language and using language to learn.* Portsmouth, NH: Heinemann.

Assessment and Evaluation in the Literacy-Centered Classroom

10

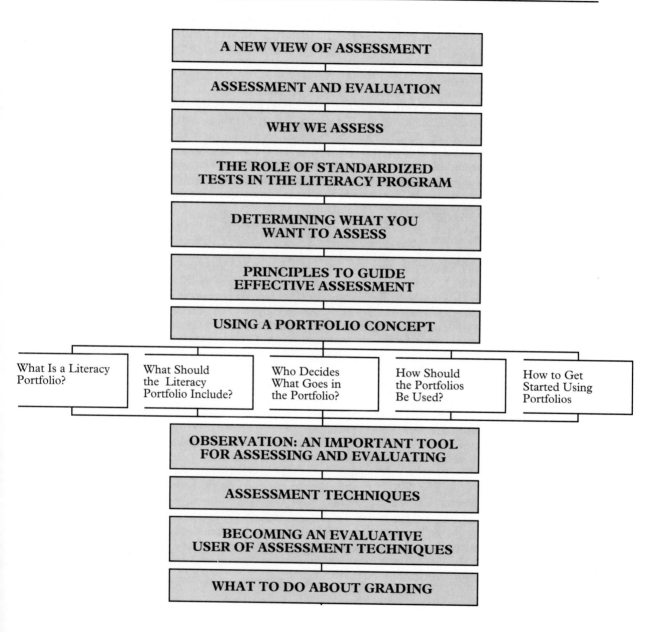

A NEW VIEW OF ASSESSMENT

ASSESSMENT AND EVALUATION

WHY WE ASSESS

THE ROLE OF STANDARDIZED TESTS IN THE LITERACY PROGRAM

DETERMINING WHAT YOU WANT TO ASSESS

PRINCIPLES TO GUIDE EFFECTIVE ASSESSMENT

USING A PORTFOLIO CONCEPT

What Is a Literacy Portfolio?

What Should the Literacy Portfolio Include?

Who Decides What Goes in the Portfolio?

How Should the Portfolios Be Used?

How to Get Started Using Portfolios

OBSERVATION: AN IMPORTANT TOOL FOR ASSESSING AND EVALUATING

ASSESSMENT TECHNIQUES

BECOMING AN EVALUATIVE USER OF ASSESSMENT TECHNIQUES

WHAT TO DO ABOUT GRADING

SUMMARY

*M*r. Ryan is a second-grade teacher who is very concerned about the growth his students are showing in learning to construct meaning. A look at some of the activities that take place in his classroom will begin to give us a sense of how Mr. Ryan assesses student progress in literacy.

As we entered Mr. Ryan's second-grade classroom, we saw that the class was divided into four small literature discussion circles, each group discussing the same book, Ira Says Goodbye (Waber, 1988). Three discussion points were listed on the chalkboard:

1. Why Reggie acted as he did
2. Your favorite part
3. How you would feel

Mr. Ryan was seated with one of the groups, listening. At one point he joined in by saying, "When my best friend moved away, I wouldn't talk to anyone about it. How would you act if you had been in Ira's place, Lisette?"

Mr. Ryan was carrying a clipboard and a pad of adhesive papers. As he moved from one circle to the other, he jotted down notes on the adhesive papers and stuck them on sheets on the clipboard.

After the literature circles were completed, the class began self-selected, independent reading time. When it was over, some students went to a box marked "Reading and Writing Portfolios" and recorded the book they had just read.

At the end of the day, Mr. Ryan looked over the notes he had placed on the clipboard throughout the day. He had a notebook with a section for each student, and he placed some of the adhesive notes on students' pages, reading and discarding others. Then he looked through the portfolios to see how much independent reading students had done and to see if they had added any other pieces of writing to their portfolios.

From his notes and his examination of the portfolios, Mr. Ryan saw that all students except for one were doing a lot of independent reading, so he made a note to have a conference with her as soon as possible. After seeing that several students did not seem to understand the story Ira Says Goodbye, he listed their names so he could form a group that would reread and discuss the story.

THINK ABOUT THIS classroom in terms of assessment, and list all the places where you thought assessment was taking place. Then compare your list to the following discussion.

Some observers might not see any evidence of assessment in Mr. Ryan's classroom: what you "see" depends on your perspective on assessment and literacy learning. However, Mr. Ryan obviously believed that children learn to read and write by reading and writing, and assessment in his classroom was an integral part of the instructional activities. Look at all the places where this was evident:

- Mr. Ryan was participating in the literature circles and so was able to observe students' actual responses to *Ira Says Goodbye* (Waber, 1988).
- Mr. Ryan made notes as he observed various aspects of students' reading. Later he reviewed those notes and placed some of them in his notebook for use in planning future instructional activities.
- Students participated in their own assessment by recording books in their reading and writing portfolios that they had completed during independent reading time. Independent reading is an important part of literacy learning and assessment.
- Mr. Ryan reviewed his notes at the end of the day and reviewed students' portfolios as a way of assessing their progress and planning future activities.
- Mr. Ryan was assessing students against their previous performance, comparing performance on current work to what was already in their portfolios.

Although this was only a small part of the overall assessment plan in Mr. Ryan's room, we begin to get a picture of how he viewed and approached assessment. His approach is very different from that used in most classrooms over the last two decades. This chapter will focus on some basic ideas about how to develop assessment that is in line with the overall concept of the literacy program stressed throughout this text. Emphasis will be placed on the classroom, with only minor attention being given to the overall school literacy program. *The material in this chapter should be viewed as a basic framework for thinking about assessment in the literacy-centered classroom. You will want to read extensively and explore this topic in much more detail as you develop your classroom literacy program.*

A NEW VIEW OF ASSESSMENT

For the last twenty to thirty years, assessment in reading has focused on measuring students' performance on isolated skill elements. For example, it has been (and still is in many schools) the normal practice to give students tests to determine whether they have mastered certain skills. These practices were based on the belief that students learned to read and write by learning a collection of skills that were viewed as integral parts of reading and writing and that could be taught and tested as separate elements. Furthermore, it was assumed that one taught reading and writing by imparting information to students and then testing to see whether or not they had mastered it.

The constructive, interactive view of literacy learning has given us new views on assessment. Clearly, practices in literacy assessment have not kept pace with what we know about literacy learning (Cambourne & Turbill, 1990; Pikulski, 1989; Valencia & Pearson, 1987). Because of Mr. Ryan's view of literacy learning, he was developing this new view perspective.

ASSESSMENT AND EVALUATION

Although the terms *assessment* and *evaluation* are often used interchangeably within the field of education and especially within the field of literacy, they really do represent different aspects of related processes (Bertrand, 1991). *Assessment* is the process of gathering information about something (getting students to respond), and *evaluation* is the process of judging that information (judging students' responses) to determine how well individuals are achieving or have achieved what they or someone else expects them to achieve. For example, asking a student to retell a story is assessment; you are asking him to respond. Then, when you judge the accuracy of the retelling and give it a score or a grade, you are evaluating the response.

In the literacy-centered classroom, procedures for assessment and evaluation are not going to be as "cut and dried" as they were in the skills-centered classroom, where we often gave students a test and expected them to achieve at least a score of 80 percent. If they achieved the score, we assumed they knew whatever the test was supposed to be measuring. If they came short, we simply retaught what the test said it was measuring and then retested the students. However, often teachers saw students who could pass the skills tests and yet could not read or write and vice versa. What was being assessed and evaluated in the skills-centered classroom clearly was not reflecting the processes that were of greatest concern—reading and writing.

Assessment and evaluation must go together in the literacy-centered classroom: there is really no value to one without the other. A beginning step in planning for assessment in your classroom is to think about why you are assessing students.

WHY WE ASSESS

Many educators have strong negative feelings about many or all aspects of assessment and evaluation. They are concerned about such things as

- procedures not assessing what is being taught.
- assessment being separate from instruction.
- misuses of assessment data.
- cultural biases of tests.

Even in light of these and other issues, there are still some strong reasons why we must have assessment and evaluation procedures in all classrooms and especially the literacy-centered classroom.

First, all teachers need ways to determine students' progress. This information provides the basis for making decisions and planning instructional activities and experiences, and for distinguishing effective from ineffective procedures. Second, good assessment helps students take ownership of their learning, seeing and planning ways to foster their own literacy growth. When students think about and reflect on their learning, they become a more active part of it. Finally, it is important to have good assessment procedures to prove to our communities that we are doing an effective job of helping children learn to read and write. We must remember that nearly every person in every community is a "self-proclaimed" expert on teaching because he or she has been through the system. Therefore, when schools begin to do new things, they must keep the community members informed and to show them evidence of successes.

THE ROLE OF STANDARDIZED TESTS IN THE LITERACY PROGRAM

Standardized tests contain specified tasks and procedures so that comparable measurements may be made by testers working in different geographic areas; specific norms allow for comparison from one group to another (Harris & Hodges, 1981). These types of tests, which have become more and more widely used in recent years, include various achievement tests, state competency tests, and tests used for the National Assessment of Educational Progress (NAEP, 1990a, 1990b). They have been widely criticized for a number of reasons (Tyler & White in Farr & Carey, 1986):

1. Tests do not reflect the full range of student cultural backgrounds and thus lead to decisions that are unfair to minority students.
2. Current standardized tests have only limited value for holding teachers, schools, and school systems accountable for the quality of education.
3. Tests exercise a limiting effect on classroom teaching.
4. Tests are too narrow in scope to provide fair evaluation of new approaches to teaching. (p. 11)

Although these criticisms were made about standardized tests in general, they also apply to tests that have been used for assessing and evaluating literacy learning and construction of meaning. The problems with existing standardized testing, combined with what has been learned about how children actually develop literacy, have led some educators to conclude that norm-referenced tests are of no value to teachers (Harp, 1991).

Even in light of these criticisms, many educators recognize that school districts will probably continue to use norm-referenced, standardized tests to evaluate literacy programs (Pikulski, 1990b). However, these tests are being changed to better match what we know about learning (Pikulski, 1990b). Changes are occurring in state competency tests (Wixson, Peters & Weber, 1987) and will occur in the National Assessment of Educational Progress in 1992 (NAEP, 1990a, 1990b). They include such points as the following:

- Not testing isolated skills
- Using full-length, authentic texts for assessing meaning construction
- Accounting for students' prior knowledge before reading
- Incorporating a broader concept of assessment by collecting samples of student work
- Including some type of student self-assessment

Although these changes will not make the various tests used throughout our educational systems perfect, they will begin to move assessment closer to what we know about literacy learning and effective literacy instruction. At some point in the not too distant future, it may even be possible for teachers to use the new norm-referenced tests to help them plan instruction.

It is critical that we prove to our communities that our programs are successfully helping students develop literacy, especially as we try new instructional techniques. Failure to do this will result in a return to practices that we have learned are not as valuable to students as we once thought. The only way to prevent this return to a past is to "move assessment activities closer to the actual work of teachers and children; we must make classrooms the starting points for linking learning to large educational and social purposes" (Perrone, 1991, p. 164).

DETERMINING WHAT YOU WANT TO ASSESS

Assessment must be based on goals. What do we want students to do? How will we know if they are learning to do it? What is the overall goal of the literacy-centered classroom? We want students to develop their abilities to construct meaning through reading and writing and to assume responsibility for their own learning. Therefore, this is what we want to assess.

Since students in the literacy-centered classroom are writing and reading every day, it should be easy to assess this activity. Assessment can be an integral and natural part of instruction (what Cambourne and Turbill [1990] call a "Natural" Theory of Assessment) in which the routine daily activities of reading and writing also serve as the assessment activities.

Au, Scheu, Kawakami, and Herman (1990) have taken the idea of what to assess in a literacy-centered classroom one step further. Maintaining that the overall goal of the literacy program is effective construction of meaning

Figure 10.1   Six Aspects of Literacy

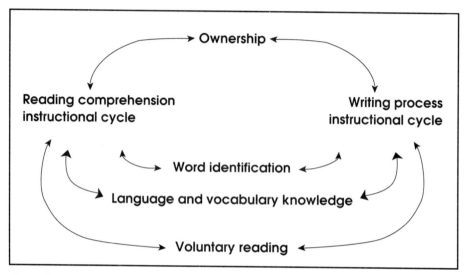

Source: From Kathryn H. Au, Judith A. Scheu, Alice J. Kawakami, and Patricia Herman, Assessment accountability in a whole literacy curriculum, *Reading Teacher* (April 1990), p. 575. Reprinted with permission of Kathryn H. Au and the International Reading Association.

through reading and writing, they have identified a literacy curriculum framework that contains six aspects: (1) ownership, (2) reading comprehension, (3) writing process, (4) word identification, (5) language and vocabulary knowledge, and (6) voluntary reading. They feel that "students' ownership of literacy is the overarching goal in the framework, and its position highlights the affective dimension of literacy development" (Au, Scheu, Kawakami & Herman, 1990, p. 575). See Figure 10.1.

On the basis of these aspects of literacy, Au and her colleagues identify everyday instructional experiences that can serve as assessment tasks. Designated tasks become a part of each student's literacy portfolio (discussed later in this chapter) and are used by the teacher to determine each student's growth in literacy development.

Another concern is deciding what is expected of students each year in school. These yearly expectations, referred to as "benchmarks" (Cambourne & Turbill, 1990), serve as guideposts to help the teacher determine the progress students are making in literacy development. Table 10.1 presents some sample benchmarks for three different grade levels. It is important for each school or school district to determine its own benchmarks in light of its overall literacy goals and student population. Figures 10.2 and 10.3 present some checklists developed for this purpose that Cambourne and Turbill (1990) have found effective. You may find these useful in planning your own benchmarks and assessment procedures, even if these are predetermined for your school.

Table 10.1 Sample Literacy Benchmarks for Three Grades

First grade:

Retells a simple story, noting important details

Expresses ideas in own words (orally and written)

Reads for enjoyment and fun

Third grade:

Summarizes stories in own words

Expresses ideas clearly in writing

Shares self-selected books with peers

Sixth grade:

Critically reacts to texts read

Continues to use reference sources as a part of writing

Continues to participate in literature circles, sharing self-selected books

Figure 10.2 Sample Language Evaluation Sheets for Writing and Reading

Language Evaluation Sheet: Writing

Name _____

☐ Displays a willing attitude toward writing
☐ Willingly seeks and accepts advice
☐ Attempts a variety of genres
☐ Is able to gather and brainstorm for information
☐ Can select a topic
☐ Makes a positive attempt to edit to the limit of his or her maturity
☐ Shows organization toward a story form (beginning, middle and end)
☐ Consults a variety of sources in search of information
☐ Writes leads that arouse interest
☐ Writes descriptively and gives details
☐ Reveals a growing vocabulary
☐ Sequences ideas logically
☐ Writes satisfactory endings
☐ Shows improved control of spelling
☐ Displays word attack skills
☐ Structures sentences correctly:
    ☐ a. Simple punctuation
    ☐ b. Commas
    ☐ c. Question sentence
    ☐ d. Speech marks
☐ Structures a paragraph using a topic sentence

Figure 10.2   continued

Language Evaluation Sheet: Reading

Name _____

- ☐ Shows obvious enjoyment and displays a willing attitude toward reading
- ☐ Borrows books regularly from the school library
- ☐ Can talk about reading and the reading process
- ☐ Reads for a sustained period of time
- ☐ Knows how to choose a book suited to his or her needs and interests
- ☐ Applies strategies to overcome reader's block
- ☐ Recognizes good and bad miscues
- ☐ Predicts meanings in texts by appropriate use of cues (graphophonic, semantic, syntactic)
- ☐ Selects literature appropriate to his or her reading ability
- ☐ Understands the value of rereading parts for information
- ☐ Can skim to obtain information
- ☐ Can handle longer texts
- ☐ Shows developing reference skills
- ☐ Can summarize, including all major points
- ☐ Selects reading material appropriate to his or her reading ability
- ☐ Selects a range of literature to read
- ☐ Can describe story line development in particular novels: setting, problem, climax, ending in order
- ☐ Can identify characters and character traits
- ☐ Can classify books—fiction, nonfiction, fantasy, and so on

Source: B. Cambourne and J. Turbill, Assessment in whole language classrooms: Theory to practice, *Elementary School Journal, 90* (1990), pp. 347–348. Used by permission of the University of Chicago Press.

PRINCIPLES TO GUIDE EFFECTIVE ASSESSMENT

As you begin to plan for assessment in your classroom, there are eight principles that you should consider. Numerous researchers and educators have developed guidelines for literacy-centered assessment (Harp, 1991; Valencia 1990a, 1990b). The principles presented here are based, in part, on their ideas and my own interpretation of this research as I have worked with teachers.

Assessment should be a continuous, ongoing process.   Reading assessment is not a test given at the end of a unit or a block of study, separate and apart from the ongoing daily activities of instruction. Instead, assessment should take place every time a child reads or writes. When assessment is viewed as an integral part of instruction, it becomes natural and expected.

Figure 10.3 More Generalized Checklist of Teacher's Expectations for Literacy

Revised Language Checklist

- ☐ Shows positive attitudes toward learning
- ☐ Seeks and accepts advice willingly
- ☐ Accepts responsibility for learning and organization
- ☐ Accepts mistakes as a natural part of learning
- ☐ Has confidence to discuss learning
- ☐ Accepts the necessity for justifications in discussion and argument
- ☐ Has control of a variety of genres in reading, writing, speaking
- ☐ Makes considered decisions with regard to reading, writing, and speaking
- ☐ Understands the need for preparedness and correctness when going public
- ☐ Consults a variety of sources in search of information
- ☐ Reads for a sustained period of time
- ☐ Recognizes good and bad miscues
- ☐ Has strategies to overcome blocks in reading and writing
- ☐ Understands the value of rereading for information
- ☐ Makes a positive attempt to edit
- ☐ Displays a developing vocabulary
- ☐ Controls the conventions of writing
- ☐ Understands the elements of various forms of writing
- ☐ Applys knowledge

Source: B. Cambourne and J. Turbill, Assessment in whole language classrooms: Theory to practice, *Elementary School Journal, 90* (1990), pp. 348. Used by permission of the University of Chicago Press.
This second checklist was developed as the teacher became more informed about language and literacy.

Effective assessment is an integral part of instruction. The best forms of assessment are the routine daily activities of instruction, which tell us exactly how our students are performing. By comparing the work of individual students over time, we can determine patterns of growth. When a student writes a story about her trip to visit friends, you can assess her ability to organize ideas, express herself, and use the various conventions of language. Overall, you are getting a picture of how effectively she constructs meaning through writing. Throughout my years of teaching and working with teachers, many teachers have said, "There was no reason to give that test. I already knew what my kids could do from their daily activities." In other words, we must learn to trust our judgments.

Assessment must be authentic, reflecting "real" reading and writing. For years, I have asked teachers in workshops and classes, "If you want to know how well children read and write, what do you need to have them do?" They have always replied in unison—"Have them read and write." Even at the height of the isolated skill assessment practices, teachers knew for years that "marking, circling, and underlining" did not reflect authentic reading and writing. The tasks of assessment in a literacy-centered classroom must reflect and honor the "wholeness" of language (Harp, 1991). It is possible for learners to be very effective readers and writers and not do well on a test covering an isolated piece of the process. But when a student reads the wonderful Roald Dahl book *Esio Trot* (1990) and writes a response to it, I can authentically assess his ability to construct meaning.

Assessment should be a collaborative, reflective process.   It should not be viewed as something that the teacher does *to* the students. We know that learning is a collaborative process; we learn alongside and with our teachers and our peers (Collins, Brown & Newman, 1986). If this is true for learning, it is also true for assessment. As students collaborate with their teacher on assessment, they are reflecting and asking themselves, "How have I done?" "What can I do to improve?" Thus students should help you assess and evaluate their own progress in reading and writing. I learned this the hard way many years ago from a fifth-grade student named Paul. Paul was an excellent student. He could read and critically discuss anything I put in his hands. However, I often asked Paul to read aloud because he wasn't a good oral reader. I then decided he needed to be placed in a lower-level book, but he still couldn't read aloud. Finally, I asked Paul what he thought his problem was. He was not only very intelligent, but also very outspoken. He said, "I don't have a problem. When are you going to learn that I don't like to read out loud?" Needless to say, I learned pretty fast. It turned out that Paul could construct meaning better than any fifth grader I had that year.

Collaboration means that students sometimes help select *what* they want evaluated. This becomes a joint effort where teacher and students work and think together, and it should also involve parents (Dillon, 1990). When students, teacher, and parents collaborate on evaluation, the responsibility is shared, as it should be.

Effective assessment is multidimensional.   Quality assessment should use several different tasks, such as samples of writing, student retellings, records of independent reading, self-evaluations, and checklists. In making these choices you need to trust your own intuition based on your knowledge and observations about students. More formal types of assessments have proclaimed their validity and reliability using various statistical procedures. Although many of the techniques being suggested today are more informal, we must still know that they are *trustworthy* (Valencia, 1990a), and one way to determine this is to use multiple tasks to get a consistent pattern of performance. Cambourne and Turbill (1990) argue that data generated from multiple sources using teacher observation and judgments are just as trustworthy and "scientific" as those generated by what have been called measurement-based approaches to assessment.

Assessment should be developmentally and culturally appropriate. We know that children develop literacy and their abilities to construct meaning by "trying out" their reading and writing and by making approximations. Therefore, tests or procedures that require absolute mastery at a given level or complete mastery of a given set of words before moving to a new book are *completely contrary* to how we know children learn. We must select assessment tasks that honor children's developmental levels of learning.

At the same time, we must also consider the cultural diversity of our classrooms. Children from different cultures have not only different language bases but also different patterns and styles of learning (Au, in press). We must take these into consideration as we plan our assessment procedures.

Effective assessment identifies students' strengths. Children learn to construct meaning by doing what they already know how to do and by getting support in gaining new strategies and techniques. This is using what Vygotsky (1978) calls the "zone of proximal development." Effective assessment, therefore, must help us identify what our students do well. For many years, we have given students tests to find out what they do *not* know; then we proceeded to plan lessons totally around these weaknesses. This is contrary to how students acquire language and contrary to how they learn to construct meaning.

Assessment must be based on what we know about how students learn to read and write. This entire text has focused on how students learn to read and write and construct meaning. Clearly, we know that assessment has not kept pace with our knowledge about reading and writing (Pikulski, 1989; Valencia & Pearson, 1987). We know that the two processes are similar but different. We also know that they develop together and produce benefits that are attainable by neither one alone (Tierney & Shanahan, 1991). And we know that reading and writing are both constructive processes. As we plan assessment tasks, we must keep this knowledge in mind, incorporating new knowledge as it becomes available.

These eight principles should guide us as we plan for assessment within our literacy-centered classrooms. We should always remember that we are a part of our students' learning processes. We are working *with* them, not *on* them. The remainder of this chapter will focus on ideas and techniques for applying these eight principles to the literacy-centered classroom.

USING A PORTFOLIO CONCEPT

During the last few years, a new concept for dealing with assessment and evaluation has appeared on the education scene—the portfolio (Wolf, 1989). Artists, architects, advertising specialists, and authors have always maintained portfolios of their best work to allow future employers or potential clients to assess and evaluate their skills and abilities, and this concept has now found its way into the field of education. The portfolio presents a viable alternative for dealing with assessment and evaluation that is in line with the eight principles discussed in the previous section. It has also been called an evaluation portfolio, an assessment portfolio, a literacy portfolio, and a reading/writing portfolio. (I will use the term *literacy portfolio* in the remainder of this chapter.) Regardless of its title, it is a useful and reasonable way to assess and evaluate students' abilities to construct meaning. We are beginning to see literacy portfolios used widely and are learning more about them all the time. They have been hailed as one of the more promising practices for making authentic judgments about students' achievement (Valencia, in press).

What Is a Literacy Portfolio?

A literacy portfolio is "a purposeful collection of student work and records of progress and achievement collected over time" (Valencia, in press, p. 3). It is usually kept in a folder, sometimes an accordion type with compartments or sections. However, a literacy portfolio is much more than a folder: it is a vehicle for reflection, self-assessment, and goal setting on the part of both the students and the teacher (Au, 1991). When a student and teacher look at, talk about, and reflect on the contents of the portfolio, they have a way to determine progress, identify strengths, and set realistic goals for the future.

Portfolios should be accessible to the students and teacher at all times. They are used throughout daily instructional activities, referred to as students work independently, and used during student-teacher and student-student conferences.

What Should the Literacy Portfolio Include?

Since literacy portfolios should reflect the needs of the students, the teacher's goals, and the school's goals, each teacher and/or school must decide what should be included in them. Many different suggestions and recommendations have been made (Au, 1991; Au, Scheu, Kawakami & Herman, 1990; Cambourne & Turbill, 1990; Church, 1991; Flood & Lapp, 1989; Mathews, 1990; Tierney, Carter & Desai, 1991; Valencia, 1990a), but the main point is that the portfolio must not become a random collection of materials that will overwhelm both the student and the teacher.

The following six categories should help you decide how to develop a framework for your literacy portfolio. They are presented only as suggestions.

As you work with portfolios, you may find some of them much more valuable than others, and you may also identify new ones.

Work Samples

One of the most valuable items to include in portfolios is samples of students' work.

- Writing such as stories, reports, letters, and so forth. By analyzing the writing and comparing it over time, you can get a picture of how students construct meaning through writing.
- Written responses to the literature they have read. These indicate students' abilities to construct meaning through both reading and writing. Samples may come from journals, learning logs, or papers students have written.

All work samples should be dated.

Records of Independent Reading and Writing

An important aspect of assessment and evaluation in the literacy-centered classroom is the amount of independent reading and writing that is being done. This record may include nothing more than a listing of books with title, author, and date completed and a listing of writing pieces completed or in process. Ideas for these records will be presented later in this chapter.

Checklists and Surveys

These may include reading development checklists, writing development checklists, ownership development checklists, and general attitude and interests surveys. Specific ideas for these items will be presented later in this chapter.

Self-Assessments

Since an important part of portfolio assessment is students' self-evaluations, you may want to have forms that students complete periodically to show how they feel they are doing in reading and writing. These may be very simple, like those shown in Figure 10.4.

Figure 10.4   Sample Forms for Self-Evaluation

Name _____ Date _____

At this time, I feel my strengths in reading are _____

_____

_____

_____

To improve my reading, I should _____

_____

_____

_____

Name _____ Date _____

My writing is _____

_____

_____

_____

To improve my writing, I need to _____

_____

_____

_____

Notes

Many teachers are finding it helpful to simply write notes about their observations or about student progress. For example, a third-grade teacher wrote the following and placed it in the student's evaluation portfolio:

> 11-20-90
>
> Randy is improving in his ability to summarize informational text. This can be observed in his oral responses and his written summaries.

Students may also be encouraged to write notes about their own reading and writing. Sara wrote the following and placed it in her portfolio:

> 1-12-90
>
> *I am making my writing more interesting but I need other ideas to help me improve.*

These notes may be placed on sheets like the one shown in Figure 10.5 and used during conferences to evaluate student progress and set goals.

Formal Tests

Some teachers in some schools want to include records of standardized tests. Others want to include tests such as those that accompany published materials that they are using. Some of the more formal tests may include such things as running records (Clay, 1985), informal reading inventories, or a reading miscue inventory (Goodman & Burke, 1972). More will be said about some of these procedures later in this chapter.

As you plan your literacy portfolios, you will want to select the categories of information to be included in light of your students' needs and your program goals (see Figure 10.6). Because the portfolio is, in part, a showcase for students' work, it is also important to involve them in this process. When students collaborate with you in making this decision, they immediately begin to take more ownership of their literary learning.

Once you have identified the categories to be included in the portfolios, you will need to work out a plan for organizing them. If materials are just randomly placed in a folder, they often become difficult to use. Therefore, it is wise to use folders with multiple pockets or sections that can hold the raw data or supporting pieces. You will also need a cover or summary sheet so that you can review the contents at a glance. Figure 10.7 shows a summary sheet used by some teachers just beginning to use portfolios. As you work with these folders, you will find that you need to continuously revise your plan and forms such as the summary sheet.

Figure 10.5   Sample Pages for Recording Notes in the Portfolio

Notes About Reading and Writing

Name _____

Name _____

Date _____

Name _____

Date _____

Name _____

Date _____

Name _____

Date _____

Who Decides What Goes in the Portfolio?

You must also decide who will select the pieces to be placed in the portfolio. Some educators seem to think the teacher should make this decision (Au, Scheu, Kawakami & Herman, 1990; Mathews, 1990), and others lean more toward a combination approach, having the student and the teacher both select pieces to include (Tierney, Carter & Desai, 1991; Valencia, 1990a, in press).

Figure 10.6 Suggested Categories of Information to Be Included in a Literacy Portfolio

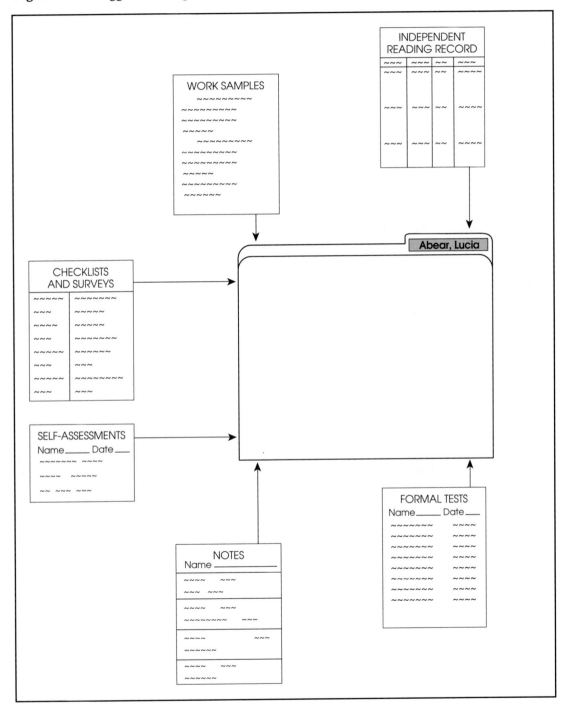

Figure 10.7 Portfolio Summary Sheet

Student Literacy Summary Sheet

Last name	First name	Middle initial	Date of birth

Grade	Retention	Chapter I	Other

Independent Reading Record

Sept.	Oct.	Nov.	Dec.	Jan.	Feb.	March	April	May	Total

Periodic Reading Survey Scores

	1	2
Constructing meaning		
Self-evaluation/attitudes		
Overall		
Comments		

Theme Tests

	1	2	3	1	2	3
Constructing Meaning						
Phonics decoding						
Overall						
Comments						

Interests/Attitudes _____

IRI

Form	Date	Independent	Instructional	Frustration

Comments:_____

Comments:_____

Figure 10.7   cont.

Taped Oral Sample
Date   *Text*   *Comments/Observations*

_____   _____   _____
                                                _____
| Fluent | Adequate | Labored | _____

_____   _____   _____
                                                _____
| Fluent | Adequate | Labored | _____

Retelling
Date   *Text*   *Score*   *Comments*

_____   _____   _____   _____
                                             _____

_____   _____   _____   _____
                                             _____

Standardized Test Scores

Writing

Date	Product	Holistic Finding	Comments

Figure 10.7 cont.

Other Writing Products

Title	Comments

Comments/Observations

Date   Entry

Simmons (1990) suggests an approach termed theirs-mine-ours in which some pieces are selected by the student, some pieces by the teacher, and some by the student and teacher together.

I have found that placement of items in the portfolio should be a collaborative decision because this further establishes student ownership in the overall literacy learning process. In the beginning, many teachers are more comfortable having students select one piece each week with the teacher designating the other pieces. As both student and teacher become comfortable with this process, they can have more student-selected pieces and collaboratively selected pieces that are chosen during conferences.

When students select pieces, it has been recommended that they attach a slip, often called an "entry slip," telling why they have made their selection (Tierney et al., 1991; Valencia, in press). Figure 10.8 shows an entry slip used by a second-grade teacher.

Since the contents of a portfolio can become overwhelming, it is very important that you be selective. The categories of information you identify for creating the portfolio will help with this process, but even so, you and your students will have to decide which writing papers, which drafts of papers, which journal responses, and so forth you want to include. A good rule of thumb is to *select pieces that tell the most about the student*. Sometimes, however, pieces will be selected by the student and/or the teacher because they are unusual, are special accomplishments, or represent a certain pride on the part of the student or the teacher.

Periodically, it is important that you and the student meet and review the portfolio's contents to decide what should remain and what should be discarded. Information of a permanent nature may be noted or recorded on the summary sheet and passed on to the next teacher. At the conclusion of her first year of using portfolios, one fifth-grade teacher met with each student and discussed what should be left in the portfolio for the next teacher to see. Many students wanted some of their first and last pieces of work kept together to show how they had improved. Others wanted only their last pieces of work. The teacher and students negotiated on some pieces of work, and then each selected others of their own. Each student then wrote a letter to the upcoming teacher explaining what he or she thought the teacher should know.

How Should Portfolios Be Used?

You will recall that earlier in this chapter we briefly looked at three primary reasons why assessment is needed: (1) to determine student progress and plan instruction, (2) to help students take ownership and responsibility for their own learning, and (3) to account for our programs to those outside the classroom. Literacy portfolios help in all of these ways because they show students' strengths and progress in learning to construct meaning.

Figure 10.8 Entry Slip for Placing Items in a Portfolio

Name _____ Date _____

I included this in my portfolio because _____

_____

_____

_____

_____

_____

_____

The portfolio can be used as the centerpiece for conferences with students, parents, and school administrators (see Chapter 6 on conferencing). Although individual conferences may be held with each of these groups periodically, in many situations a group conference including student, parents, and an administrator may be of value.

Student-teacher conferences should be held periodically to

- review the student's progress.
- discuss areas of strength.
- set goals and make plans for future learning activities.
- evaluate what is in the portfolio and discuss items to be removed or added.

Portfolio conferences should be conducted like other reading or writing conferences and should focus on a few key points. Sometimes students take the lead by discussing items that are on their minds based on what is in the portfolio. At other times, you take the lead. The conference should be a flexible give-and-take process resulting in positive conclusions that let students know their strong points. At the end of each conference you should identify a specific goal or task to be accomplished.

Portfolio conferences can usually take place once a month or every six weeks. Remember, assessment and evaluation are an integral part of instruction and are taking place all the time, so the conference is just a review and discussion of what has been taking place in the student's literacy experiences. Conferences usually last from 10 to 15 minutes depending on the grade level and focus. Each teacher must determine the pattern that is best for his or her classroom.

Some teachers are finding that student-student portfolio conferences are also very effective. Before holding a student-teacher conference, students meet with a partner or in a small group of three to review their portfolios. Teachers who use these conferences usually give students one or two things to focus on in their discussions, such as

- what has been read independently.
- types of writing that have been done.
- strengths in reading.
- strengths in writing.
- ways to improve in reading or writing.

It is always good to model this process with the whole class before having students hold their conferences.

The literacy portfolio can also be used in parent conferences. Flood and Lapp (1989) report that this is an effective way to show parents the progress a child is making. It can be done by comparing work samples or by comparing samples of oral reading that have been tape-recorded, comparing the scores on an informal comprehension measure that have been taken over time. Figure 10.9 shows a comprehension graph that a sixth-grade teacher had students keep showing the percentage of correct comprehension responses they attained on three samples of reading taken at intervals throughout the year. Notice that this teacher planned to take additional samples later in the year. (Informal measures of comprehension will be discussed later in this chapter.) By using a graph like this, you can help parents see how their students are performing in reading and writing.

One big advantage of having parent-teacher portfolio conferences is that parents become partners in the evaluation process and you do not have to assume all of the responsibility. This truly makes assessment "collaborative." By viewing and comparing work samples, tapes, and so forth, parents learn to draw their own conclusions about how their child is performing and about what they can do to help.

Students should also be a part of the parent-teacher conference. Some teachers like to have the parents and the student present all the time; others like to start with the parents and the student and conclude with just the parents. Use the pattern that is best for your particular situation.

Finally, literacy portfolios should be used for conferences with administrators—principals, supervisors, and consultants. In these conferences, you may find that you rely more on the summary sheets than on all of the individual samples of work. You will focus on various things—overall student growth, specific student growth, unusual strengths, areas where programmatic changes might be needed, and so forth. Some schools are also finding that small-group student-teacher-administrator portfolio conferences are effective ways to support the literacy program. Although it is often impossible for one administrator to meet with every student individually, in many schools some type of pattern can be worked out that makes this student-teacher-administrator conference a very important part of the literacy program.

Figure 10.9 Sixth Grader's Comprehension Responses for Three Stories over Time

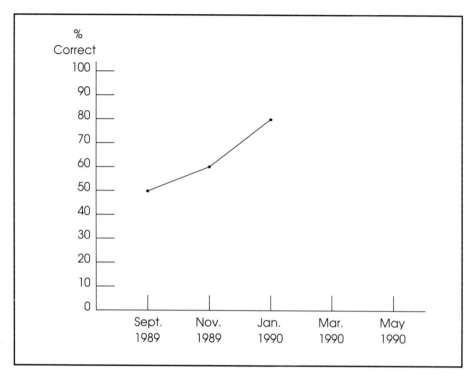

Using portfolios, just like designing them, requires continuous evaluation and revision. As you begin to work with portfolios, you will want to be constantly looking for new and better ways to make use of them.

How to Get Started Using Portfolios

Getting started using portfolios is not difficult. Many suggestions have been made (and continue to be made) for initiating this process in schools and classrooms (Au, Scheu, Kawakami & Herman, 1990; Mathews, 1990; Tierney, Carter & Desai, 1991; Valencia, 1990a). Once you have decided to use literacy portfolios in your classroom, you should find the following suggested steps helpful. Of course, you will need to adjust them to the grade level and maturity of your students.

Introduce the literacy portfolio concept to students.   Begin by discussing the concept of a portfolio and how it can help you and them improve literacy learning. Engage students in a conversation about why the literacy portfolio will be an effective way to improve learning and teaching in your classroom, drawing out their thoughts and ideas. Explain that you will all be working more closely together to assess and evaluate progress and plan for instruction. This *immediately* establishes the literacy portfolio as a collaborative process and begins to help students take ownership in using the literacy portfolio.

Identify categories of information to include in the portfolio.   Generate a list of categories and discuss this with students, asking them for their suggestions. Point out that they will each have some ideas and that together you will reach some conclusions. This is not just turning decisions over to students, but is establishing and making ownership authentic. *It is important to begin small with just a few categories;* others can be added over time.

Plan procedures with students for using the portfolios.   Identify a location for keeping the portfolios that will make them easily accessible to the students and you. Establish initial guidelines for such things as the following:

- Selecting materials for the portfolio
- Placing materials in the portfolios
- Using entry slips
- How and when to use the portfolios
- Holding portfolio conferences
- Periodic review and evaluation of the entire process

Inform parents about the use of portfolios.   It is important to make them an active, collaborative part of the portfolio process. For example, you can hold parent meetings at school or write parents a letter (see Figure 10.10). Involving parents helps everyone understand what is involved in literacy and learning.

Hold literacy portfolio conferences.   Once you have the physical concept of the literacy portfolio organized and basic routines established, you need to plan your conferences. Start the conferences after the first couple of weeks of keeping portfolios. In the beginning, most teachers hold more frequent conferences so they can have a better sense of how things are progressing. You may want to have small-group conferences at first just to get a sense of what is being put in the portfolios and then move on to individual conferences.

One of the major problems at the outset is a tendency to place *too much* material in the portfolio. This happens primarily because both the student and teacher are afraid that they will miss something important. Through the conferencing process, reference to the categories of information to include,

Figure 10.10 Sample Parent Letter Explaining Portfolios

February 16, 1990
Portfolios

Normandy School

Dear Parent(s),

At open house I discussed our use of portfolios for the year. First, I would like to refamiliarize you with what we have been doing. The children collected their work done in reading and writing in a storage bin (accessible to them) in the room. Throughout the first nine weeks they shared the work with classmates. Toward the end of the first nine weeks each child chose three pieces that were special to him or her in some way. Finally, I met with each child. In the conference we spoke about why each of the three pieces was special, and I used this opportunity to help the student verbalize why one particular piece might be stronger than another. Weaknesses in areas were also noted and discussed. I believe strongly that these are critical opportunities for the children to evaluate their own finished pieces and to begin to verbalize their strengths and weaknesses.

We are all in a learning curve with this project, and as we repeat this process each nine weeks I am sure the benefits will increase.

A next important step with the portfolio is to share them at home. You are receiving two separate units with this letter. The larger set of items were those completed in the first nine weeks but not chosen by the children for their portfolio. These you may keep. The second set of items are the three special pieces.

I would ask that you allow your child to share his or her special pieces with you. I have attached a sheet on which I would encourage you to comment. It is imperative to a portfolio project such as this that you give your child lots of praise. If you see problems, realize these are being addressed in class. If you are concerned please feel free to contact me. Most important, I ask that you find only positive things to say about your child's work.

We will be repeating this process after each nine weeks and I feel sure that as concerned and involved parents I can count on your support.

The three special pieces must be returned by __________ so that we may keep them in our portfolio and compare our work as we grow throughout the year.

Thank you again.

Miss Fritschle

Source: Tierney et al. (1991), p. 76. Copyright © 1991 Christopher-Gordon Publishers Inc. Reprinted by permission from Robert J. Tierney, Mark A. Carter, and Laura E. Desai, *Portfolio Assessment in the Reading-Writing Classroom,* and by permission of the author, Darice D. Fritschle.

and procedures that you have established, you will easily overcome this problem. As you begin to hold the conferences with individual students, remember that these are to be *reflective, collaborative* conferences focusing on such things as the following:

- How does the student feel about what he or she is doing?
- What strengths can you and the student identify?
- What does the student think he or she needs to do to improve?
- What goals would the student and you like to establish?

After you have student portfolio conferences going, you will want to begin to think about parent and administrator conferences.

Review, evaluate, and revise the portfolio process.   Using portfolios is a continuous, ongoing process, so periodically talk with the entire class about how it is working and what might be done to improve it. Reflect on the use of the portfolios yourself, and discuss and share ideas with other teachers who are trying this process.

These six steps will help you get started using portfolios. However, since there is a great deal more to learn and think about in using this collaborative, reflective process of evaluation, you should read further in this area. The "For Additional Reading" section of this chapter provides very good suggestions, and current journals frequently have articles on literacy portfolio assessment.

The focus in this chapter has been primarily on using the literacy portfolio for student assessment and evaluation. However, it is also a very good tool to help you reflect on and evaluate your own teaching by looking at how your students are progressing.

Portfolios are not panaceas (Valencia, in press), although they do offer what appears to be a better way to focus on assessment and evaluation. However, we must also commit some time to studying and thinking about the most effective ways to use them. As Valencia warns, "Without a commitment to sufficient time and careful study of the potential advantages and problems of portfolios, they are destined to fail. Once again, we will find ourselves back under the bonds from which we have so desperately fought to be free" (p. 21).

OBSERVATION: AN IMPORTANT TOOL FOR ASSESSING AND EVALUATING

One of the most important instructional techniques is observation. In literacy-centered classrooms assessment and evaluation need to be based on a combination of techniques both formal and informal, and many of these techniques are highly dependent upon observing students as they are reading and writing. "Kid watching" (Goodman, 1986), as it is frequently described, is the process of watching students as they perform authentic literacy tasks or looking at the results of those tasks.

You learn to be an observer of children first by realizing that it is a powerful and reliable part of your assessment and evaluation process (Farr & Carey, 1986). Far too many teachers assume that their own observations about students' reading and writing are not as valuable or reliable as more formal pencil-and-paper tasks or formal tests. However, researchers (Farr & Carey, 1986; Cambourne & Turbill, 1990) strongly refute this belief.

Quality, reliable observations must be based on what you know about how children learn to read and write. Therefore, you need to understand what responses are expected and normal and what responses might indicate a need for more or different support. For example, the student who writes a sentence about his *dg* is not misspelling the word *dog;* rather, he is making an approximation that shows that he is learning the spelling pattern in the word *dog.* Therefore, this student would profit from more shared reading experiences with natural, repetitive language and words following the type of spelling pattern found in the word *dog,* as well as many opportunities to continue to write his own stories.

"Kid-watchers" must develop the habit of always looking, thinking, and asking, "What does this mean?" Opportunities to observe students are unlimited:

- Listening to a student read aloud
- Watching students give a play
- Reading and noting how a student has written a response to a story
- Analyzing a student's written report
- Listening to and studying what students say as they give oral reports
- Listening to dialogue between two students waiting in line for lunch

Nearly every classroom activity can be used for some form of observation of literacy learning, and all these observations can become the data on a checklist or a note placed in a literacy portfolio.

When you are using observations, you must keep in mind that good assessment must be multidimensional. Therefore, one observation is not sufficient: you must look at several observations over time, watching for patterns of performance. It is from these patterns that you can assess and evaluate students' abilities to construct meaning. "Observation can be very powerful in developing a complete picture of a child's literacy development" (Cockrum & Castillo, 1991).

There are many techniques that can be combined with observation or used in addition to observation to help you become an effective "kid-watcher." As you develop this stance in your teaching and gain more experience with it, you will become more and more comfortable in using a more authentic process for assessment. You will soon realize that instruction and assessment are really one ongoing process. The next section will focus on specific techniques that enhance or support observation.

ASSESSMENT TECHNIQUES

Assessment as discussed in this chapter is a dynamic and interactive process that is an integral part of instruction. Instruction and assessment blend into one ongoing activity that is supported by the literacy portfolio and by effective use of observations. There are many different techniques that you can use as a part of this process. Many blend naturally into instruction; others give you a somewhat more formal way to assess student progress informally.

Since the overall goal of literacy learning is meaning construction, the techniques suggested here either look at that process as a whole or look at an important aspect of the process. Most of them can be easily used on the basis of the information given here; appropriate references are given for those that require more detailed study. As you study and review these techniques, you should be thinking about those that will be most advantageous to you in your classroom and those you need to learn more about. *You do not need to use them all.*

Checklists

Checklists are an excellent tool for observing various aspects of your students' abilities to construct meaning. They may be developed in general areas related to meaning construction, such as reading, writing, speaking, and listening, or they may be developed for specific aspects of literacy learning, such as concepts of print or story retelling.

Each checklist should contain the particular qualities or traits that you are looking for accompanied by some procedure for recording what you observe about them. Sometimes the checklists can be developmental (Cockrum & Castillo, 1991) in that they focus on certain stages of development, particularly if they are language-related checklists. Other checklists simply help you look for the presence or absence of the traits under consideration.

You will recall that we discussed the idea of student ownership being the overarching goal in the Au, Scheu, Kawakami, and Herman (1990) approach to literacy assessment. These educators view ownership as being the students' attitudes toward literacy and their habits in using literacy. The checklist shown in Figure 10.11 for assessing ownership can be used at any grade level. The teacher indicates the presence of a particular trait and comments on it or on

Figure 10.11   Checklist for Ownership of Reading

CHECKLIST FOR OWNERSHIP OF READING

Teacher _____   Grade _____

Names	Date	Enjoys Reading	Shows confidence, pride	Shares books with others	Is developing preferences	Reads outside school	Reads for own purposes	Recommends books	Learns from reading	Obtains books (nonclassroom)	
Comments											
Comments											
Comments											

Source: Kathryn H. Au, Judith A. Scheu, Alice J. Kawakami, and Patricia Herman, Assessment of students' ownership of literacy, *Reading Teacher* (October 1990), p. 155. Reprinted with permission of Kathryn H. Au and the International Reading Association.

the student's overall development of ownership. Checklists may be compared over time to see how the student's ownership or attitudes and habits change.

More general checklists such as that shown in Figure 10.12 may also be used. This list, which would be included in the literacy portfolio, has four places to record observations during the school year. It can be completed by the teacher, the student, or both.

You will often find that you will want to develop your own checklists for the particular thing(s) that you want to observe. There are many sources of checklists—curriculum guides, textbooks, journal articles, and so forth. You

Figure 10.12   Checklist for Meaning Construction

Construction of Meaning

Name _____

Date	1	2	3	4
Retells stories and text accurately				
Gives responses to stories and text that show understanding				
Conveys meaning through written stories and reports				
Conveys meaning through spoken language				
Comments:				

CODE:
+ = very effectively
√ = effectively
− = needs improvement
NO = Not Observed

Figure 10.13   Independent Reading Record

Independent Reading Record

Name _____

Date Completed	Title and Author	Comments

can take an existing checklist and adapt it to fit your needs. Some checklists can be developed for group observations (Figure 10.11), and others for individual observations (Figure 10.12).

Records of Independent Reading and Writing

An important factor to consider in assessing students' meaning construction is the amount of self-selected, independent reading and writing that they do. These records may be kept in journals or learning logs where students record their independent reading or do their writing. However, it is often good to have a form that summarizes this information to place in the student's literacy portfolio. Figure 10.13 presents a simple form that can be used for recording independent reading, and more detailed responses may be made in journals or in other individual activities. Figure 10.14 shows a more creative form that

Figure 10.14   More Elaborate Form for Recording Independent Reading

INDEPENDENT READING RECORD

BOOKS THAT CARRY ME AWAY

might be used for this same purpose. Chapter 7 contains forms that can be used to summarize writing pieces that have been started, completed, and published.

Retellings

Retellings are powerful tools because they are one of the most authentic techniques that can be used for both instructional and assessment purposes (Gambrell, Pfeiffer & Wilson, 1985; Marshall, 1983; Morrow, 1989). Though retellings integrate instruction and assessment, in this chapter, we will focus only on using them as assessment tools.

"Retellings are postreading or postlistening recalls in which readers or listeners tell what they remember either orally or in writing" (Morrow, 1989, p. 40). By studying the students' retellings, you can gain insights into their thinking, organization, and general understanding of what they have read or listened to. For instance, you can learn how they identify important informa-tion, make inferences, and summarize information. This is one of the most effective techniques for holistically assessing the process of meaning construction.

Retellings can be used with both narrative and expository texts. By comparing a student's retellings over time, you can determine their progress in learning to construct meaning. In addition, each retelling can be used diagnostically to help you develop support activities.

Morrow (1989) has given very complete guidelines for using retellings as assessment tools. The following guidelines are based on her suggestions as well as on my own experiences in working with children and teachers.

Guidelines for Using Retellings for Assessment

Selecting the Text.   Select the story or informational text (expository text) that students are to read or have students make the selection. If you are comparing students' retellings over time, use the same type of texts each time—for example, compare narrative with narrative, expository with expository. As texts are selected, look at them to be sure that their conceptual difficulty is not drastically different. In other words, don't compare retellings from a simple text like *Cranberries* (Jaspersohn, 1991) with a more complex text like *Franklin Delano Roosevelt* (Freedman, 1990). This decision is made by informal inspection.

Preparing the Text.   Read the text. For stories, identify the setting (place and time if important), characters, problem, action (events leading to outcome), and outcome or resolution. For informational texts, identify the topic, purpose, and main ideas. List this information on a sheet.

Reading and Retelling the Text.   Have the student read the text silently. (If you are using this as a listening experience, read the text to the students.) This should be treated as a routine instructional activity. Immediately following the reading, ask the student to retell the story or text. Do not prompt initial retellings, though you can use generic types of prompts such as "Tell me more" or "Keep going; you're doing a nice job."

As students give their retellings, check off the ideas given on the sheet you prepared earlier. After they have completed their unprompted retellings, you may then prompt them with questions about specific parts of the story or text that they did not include in their unprompted retelling.

Summarizing and Evaluating the Retelling.   Figures 10.15 and 10.16 present sheets that can be used for summarizing each student's retelling. Each retelling has a possible score of 10, and the guidelines for scoring each retelling are basically the same. One point is given for correct responses, and exceptions to this rule are given on the summary sheets. In scoring retellings, use your own judgment and your observations.

After scoring each retelling, you can examine it to determine whether the student understands the story or text, has ideas well organized, or has used various strategies. You will then want to discuss and review the retelling with the student. This information can help you develop instructional experiences. As Morrow (1989) notes, retellings can develop essentially the same skills and processes as they assess.

PREP: A Plan for Assessing Prior Knowledge

Langer (1981, 1982, 1984) has developed and researched a procedure called the prereading plan, or PREP, for assessing students' prior knowledge. This word-association technique can be used as a strategy in its own right or combined with other strategies like preview and predict or K-W-L (see Chapter 3). PREP can be used at the beginning of a theme or before a selection is read to determine how much prior knowledge support students need. The following suggestions for using this group procedure are based on Langer's ideas.

1. Review the text to identify several key concepts covered (*examples:* friendship, exploration).
2. Direct a group discussion using the following types of questions:

   - What comes to mind when you hear or read _____ ?
   - Given what we have just discussed, can you add any new words about _____ ?

Figure 10.15   Retelling Summary Sheet for Narrative Text

Story Retelling Summary Sheet

Name _____ Date _____

Title _____

Student selected _____   Teacher selected _____

	Unprompted	Prompted
Setting:		
Begins with introduction (1 pt.)	_____	_____
Gives time and place (1 pt.)	_____	_____
Characters:		
Names main character (1 pt.)	_____	_____
Identifies other characters (1 pt.)	_____	_____
Gives names _____		
Gives number _____		
Actual number _____		
Number given _____		
Problem:		
Identifies primary story problem (1 pt.)	_____	_____
Action:		
Recalls major events (1 pt.)	_____	_____
Outcome:		
Identifies how problem was solved (1 pt.)	_____	_____
Gives story ending (1 pt.)	_____	_____
Sequence:		
Retells story in order (2 pts. = correct; 1 pt. = partial, 0 = no evidence of sequence)	_____	_____
TOTAL SCORE (10 pts. possible)	_____	_____

Observations/comments:

Analysis:

Source: Adapted from L. M. Morrow, Using story retelling to develop comprehension, in K. D. Muth, ed., *Children's comprehension of text: Research into practice*, pp. 37–58 (Newark, DE: International Reading Association, 1989).

Figure 10.16   Retelling Summary Sheet for Informational Text

Informational Text Retelling Summary Sheet

Name _____ Date _____

Title _____

Student selected _____   Teacher selected _____

	Scores	
	Unprompted	Prompted

Introduction:
   Identifies topic (1 pt.)   _____   _____
   Gives some purpose or focus (1 pt.)   _____   _____

Main ideas:
   Number given _____
   Actual number _____   _____   _____
   (6 pts. = all correct; 4 pts. = 2/3 correct;
   2 pts. = 1/3 correct; 0 pts. = none correct)

Sequence of ideas:
   Gives ideas in order appropriate to text (2 pts. =   _____   _____
   correct; 1 pt. = partial; 0 pts. = none correct)

                           TOTAL SCORE   _____   _____
                           (10 pts. possible)

Observations/comments:

Analysis:

Record students' responses on the chalkboard or overhead with names written beside their responses.

3. Ask students to look at the information they have given and try to group it into some meaningful patterns or categories (*example:* friendship):

    qualities

    "caring"
    "kindness"
    "takes you as you are"

Figure 10.17   Sheet for Evaluating Prior Knowledge Using PREP

PREP Evaluation Sheet

Topic: _____

Names	Much Prior Knowledge	Some Prior Knowledge	Little Prior Knowledge

examples of friends

Bob
Susan
Martha
Terry

4. Have a sheet like the one shown in Figure 10.17 prepared to evaluate each student's prior knowledge. Those with *much prior knowledge* show accurate understandings of concepts, give precise definitions, and make accurate connections among concepts. Those with *some prior knowledge* give examples and characteristics of concepts but make no connections. Those with *little prior knowledge* show little or no understanding of the concept; they might give some related experiences but cannot make meaningful relationships.

Responses to Literature

The importance of students' responding to literature was discussed in Chapter 6. The type of response given *may* help to indicate how the student has constructed meaning. For example, the student who continuously says or writes such things as "I liked it," "It was funny," or "The best part was _____" may not be processing or understanding what was read, or perhaps has not learned to respond to literature and needs more support and prompting from the teacher (see Chapter 6). The student who gave the following response to *Where the Red Fern Grows* (Rawls, 1974) demonstrated in her journal that she had constructed very appropriate meaning from this book:

> Billy's love for his dogs is like my love for my cat Prince. I had to work hard to get Prince. I love him so much. Billy learned how important love was. I did to. Everybody needs somebody to love.

As you encourage students to respond to literature, you will need to develop some criteria for evaluating those responses. The following questions should be helpful:

1. Does the response show that the student knows the story line (narrative) or main ideas (expository) of the text?
2. Did the student simply retell the text or relate it to his or her own experiences?
3. Does the response show that the student is thinking clearly and logically?
4. Does the response show that the student is making connections to other pieces of literature?

How would you evaluate the response given to *Where the Red Fern Grows* using these questions?

Many teachers use a simple form like the one shown in Figure 10.18 to evaluate students' responses to literature. They then attach the evaluations to the response and place it in the portfolio. Teachers also use this evaluation for grading purposes.

Student Self-Evaluations

Student self-evaluations have been recommended as a vital part of assessing and evaluating meaning construction (Flood & Lapp, 1989; Tierney, Carter & Desai, 1991). You can promote these evaluations very easily by asking

Figure 10.18   Form for Evaluating Responses to Literature

Constructing Meaning Evaluation

Name _____ Date _____

Title _____

Circle one:

$\boxed{+}$	$\boxed{\sqrt{}}$	$\boxed{0}$
Shows thorough understanding	Shows some understanding	Needs support in developing understanding

Comments:

students to write in their journals about the progress they are making in reading and writing. Self-evaluation can be prompted by such questions as the following:

- How do you feel you are doing in reading/writing?
- What are your strengths in reading/writing?
- What do you enjoy the most about reading/writing?
- What do you feel you need to do to improve your reading/writing?

Another way to get students to evaluate their construction of meaning is by giving them a form like the one shown in Figure 10.19 to evaluate their understanding of what they read. The form can be completed periodically and placed in the literacy portfolio. Similar types of self-evaluation forms may also be completed for writing.

Self-evaluation is important in helping students learn to monitor their own reading and writing. For example, they can use a checklist like the one presented in Figure 10.20 to evaluate how they have used various strategies as they read a text. This type of checklist can be shortened to include only those strategies students have learned.

Figure 10.19   Form for Self-Evaluation of Reading

Self-Evaluation of Reading

Name _____ Date _____

Book read _____

Mark the scale below:

|———————————————|———————————————|———————————————|

I feel that   I don't
I thoroughly   feel that
understood   I understood
this book.   this book.

Why I marked the scale as I did:

_____

_____

_____

_____

_____

Process Interviews

Learning more about students' metacognitive development, or how they "think about their reading," is important in helping them learn to construct meaning (Baker & Brown, 1984; Brown, 1980). To determine students' thinking about their reading, Paratore and Indrisano (1987) developed a procedure known as the process interview, sometimes called a reading interview. It consists of the following questions:

How do you choose something to read?
How do you get ready to read?
When you come to a word you can't read, what do you do?
When you have a question you can't answer, what do you do?
What do you do to help remember what you've read?
How do you check your reading?
If a young child asked you how to read, what would you tell him or her to do?
(Paratore & Indrisano, 1987, p. 782)

Figure 10.20   Student Self-Monitoring Checklist

THINKING ABOUT MY READING

HOW DID I DO?

	Yes	No

BEFORE READING

- Did I preview the text?
- Did I make predictions?

DURING READING

- Did I STOP AND THINK about what I was reading?
- Did I change my predictions?

AFTER READING

- Did I think back about my predictions?
- Did I summarize in my head?

To improve my reading, I need to: _____

_____

_____

After a student orally answers the questions and these responses are recorded, you analyze them to see what type of support the student needs. For example, a student who answers question 6 even after prompting by saying that she "looks for pictures" does not have a good set of monitoring strategies. It might be helpful to teach this student to use a strategy like stop and think, focusing on rereading, reading ahead, and other techniques for monitoring reading.

A process interview for writing may be done using questions that follow a pattern similar to those used for reading. Since this is an informal procedure, questions for either the reading or writing interview can be rephrased or changed to make sure that students understand them. Interviews of this type can be conducted with students of all ages as long as the questions are worded appropriately.

Teacher-Selected Reading Samples

One of the most important criteria for assessing and evaluating students' progress is that the materials used must be books and texts that students read every day. It is no longer a viable option to give students short passages taken out of context or created for a test.

Select a book, chapter of a book, or short story or text that you want students to read, and introduce the material as you would in a literacy lesson (see Chapter 2). Have students read the text silently, and then ask them to complete a task appropriate to their grade level that would let you see how effectively they have constructed meaning. These tasks could include the following:

- Completing a story map
- Listing the most important or main ideas in the text
- Writing a summary (this is a very sophisticated process and should be reserved for the upper elementary and middle-school levels)
- Answering questions that focus on the story elements
- Answering questions that draw out the main ideas of the text

All tasks except the summary can be scored by determining the percentage of items correct. The summary has to be scored more holistically by giving it a rating like the following:

1 = All major ideas included
2 = Most major ideas included
3 = Many major ideas missing

Samples of reading can be taken over time and compared to determine student progress.

Many teachers also find it very helpful to use teacher-selected or student-selected samples for oral reading. After students practice their passages, they read them aloud onto a tape recorder. The teacher takes several passages over time and compares them to show student development in decoding; effective constructors of meaning know how to automatically decode words (see Chapter 5). This technique is different from the miscue analysis (discussed later) because in miscue analysis students do not prepare their passages. This procedure would let you compare a student's "best" performances over time.

These taped passages can be analyzed by looking at the patterns of students' responses to determine students' abilities to decode words. Many teachers find it useful to make the tape recordings a part of the student's portfolio. In this way students can compare their passages to determine their own growth in decoding; the tapes can also be used during parent conferences to help parents determine the progress their child is making. Figure 10.21 shows a passage that a first grader read from *Fix-It* (McPhail, 1984). The teacher's markings and notes show what the student read and how the teacher judged the student's decoding abilities.

Figure 10.21   First Grader's Marked Oral Passage

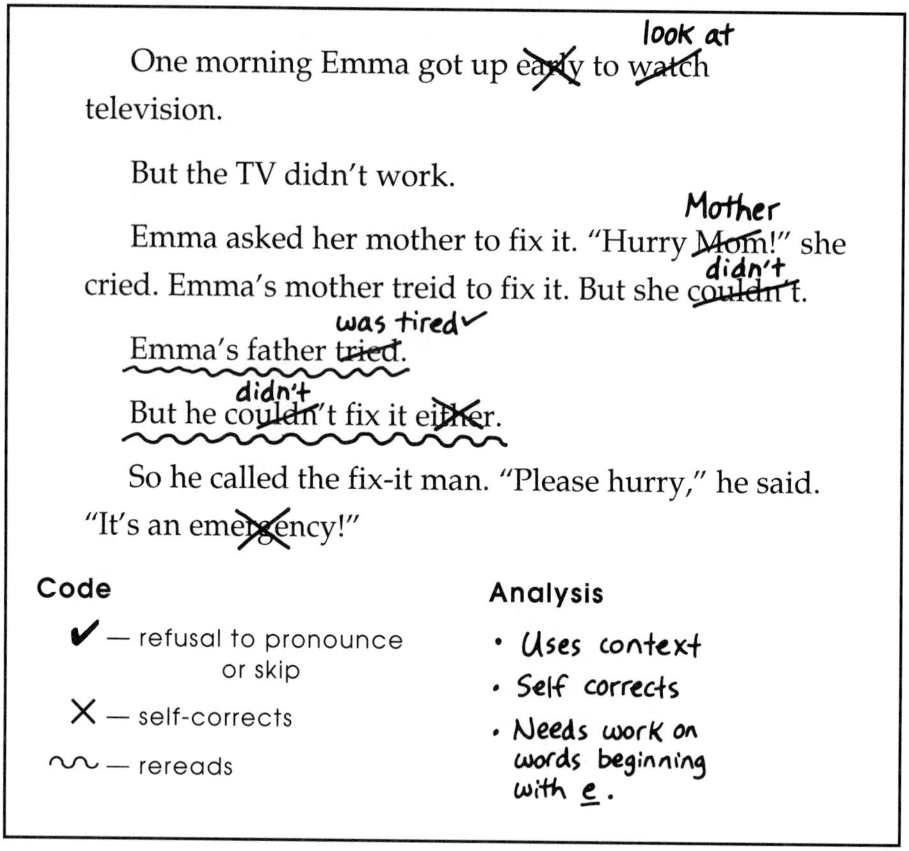

One morning Emma got up ~~early~~ to ~~watch~~ **look at** television.

But the TV didn't work.

Emma asked her mother to fix it. "Hurry ~~Mom~~ **Mother**!" she cried. Emma's mother treid to fix it. But she ~~couldn't~~ **didn't**.

Emma's father ~~tried~~ **was tired**✔.

But he ~~couldn't~~ **didn't** fix it ~~either~~.

So he called the fix-it man. "Please hurry," he said. "It's an eme~~r~~gency!"

Code

✔ — refusal to pronounce or skip

✗ — self-corrects

〰 — rereads

Analysis

- Uses context
- Self corrects
- Needs work on words beginning with e.

Literature Circles

The literature circle (see Chapter 6) presents a good opportunity to observe students' abilities to construct meaning in an authentic literacy experience. Wood's (1988) procedure for assessing and evaluating comprehension during a group discussion involves looking at nine behaviors related to meaning construction as students discuss what they have read: making predictions, participating in discussion, answering questions on a variety of levels, determining word meaning through context, reading smoothly and fluently, retelling selections in own words, comprehending after silent reading, reading between the lines, and having a broad background knowledge. A grid is used to record students' responses using a simple code: Often = +, Sometimes = S, Seldom = −, and Not Observed = N.

Researchers (Paradis, Chatton, Boswell, Smith & Yovich, 1991) who tried to employ this procedure found that they ended up looking for each of the nine aspects of comprehension much like they would observe students' use of specific skills. However, when the teachers involved in the project identified what they wanted to observe during discussion, they were much more effective in focusing on the full process of meaning construction than when they tried to use a predetermined list. Paradis et al. (1991) concluded, "We learned we could not implement a procedure developed by someone else. Only the teachers knew what children should do in their classrooms to demonstrate comprehension. Each teacher had to decide the specific indicators for that classroom" (p. 17). When the teachers in this project were asked to list their own indicators of comprehension (constructing meaning), they all listed different traits. However, three indicators were common to all teachers—predicting, inferencing, and summarizing. This is certainly consistent with what was discussed in Chapter 8 on strategies for constructing meaning.

I have found that teachers are able to use the literature circle to assess and evaluate meaning construction. However, like Paradis et al. (1991), I have also found that teachers need to develop (or adapt from some other source) their own specific procedure and indicators. The following general guidelines should help you accomplish this purpose:

Guidelines for Developing Procedures for Observing Literature Circles

Select indicators for meaning construction.   Use the information in this text and other sources to help you decide what indicators you should look for to tell you that your students are effectively constructing meaning. In the beginning, keep the number small, remembering the importance of strategies such as predicting, confirming and/or changing predictions, inferencing, and summarizing. Following are examples of indicators you might use:

general indicators

- Participates in discussion
- Listens to responses of others
- Builds own response on ideas of others

narrative texts

- Identifies important parts of story (setting, characters, and so forth)
- Relates story to own experiences
- Compares to other stories

expository texts

- Identifies topic
- Identifies main ideas
- Sees relationships in text
- Shows signs of using knowledge gained

Figure 10.22 Grid for Observing Construction of Meaning During a Literature Circle

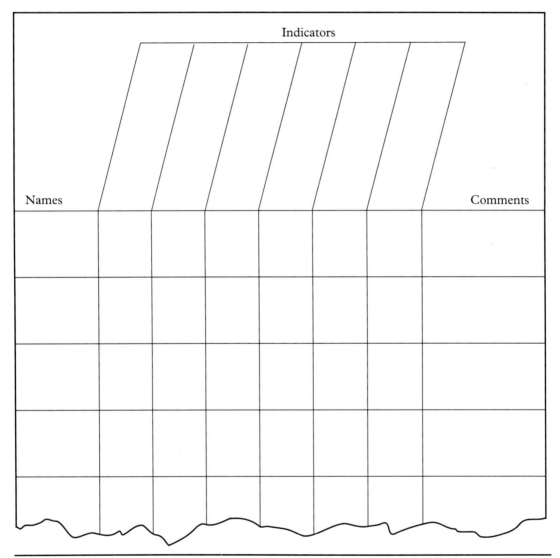

Develop a procedure for recording information. A simple grid like the one shown in Figure 10.22 can be used with a code similar to the one developed by Wood (1988), discussed earlier. This grid even contains a space for comments or observations.

Designate a time for observation. It is not necessary to observe every literature circle for assessment purposes—use selected ones. You may either participate in the discussion or sit off to the side to observe. Teachers who become accustomed to this procedure report that they find themselves always observing even when they are just participating in the circles. This activity becomes a natural part of teaching.

Review the data for yourself and with students.   After you have completed your observation, study the data you have collected to see what your students' strengths are. Think about ways to use these strengths and also provide ongoing support. For example, if you observe that several students are very good at predicting but have difficulty summarizing, have them make predictions using story map prediction. Then use their story map predictions to lead into the summarizing stories strategy (see Chapters 3 and 8). Take time to review and discuss your observations with students, asking them for their perceptions and reactions.

Interest Inventories

Another important assessment and evaluation technique is the interest inventory. The information obtained may be useful to you in a number of ways:

- Choosing book collections from the library to bring into the classroom
- Ordering books
- Planning thematic unit topics
- Creating study groups
- Conferring with individual students or groups of students

There are many different forms of interest inventories, but they generally consist of a number of statements that students respond to orally (during conferences or interviews) or in writing. Often these are incomplete statements that students are asked to complete (see Figure 10.23 for examples).

Holistic Scoring of Writing

Holistic scoring is a widely used procedure to assess and evaluate a student's ability to construct meaning through writing. It involves looking at a piece of writing in its entirety and assigning it a score (Cockrum & Castillo, 1991); it is generally used on process writing assignments given by the teacher rather than on self-initiated writing or written responses to literature. Holistic scoring assumes that all aspects of writing are related and must be viewed in their entirety (Patchell, 1986).

When using the holistic procedure, the teacher reads the piece of writing and assigns it a score from 0 to 4. Although a detailed discussion of holistic scoring is beyond the scope of this text, the following scale from Millett (1986) may help you get a sense of how this procedure is used.

Figure 10.23 Completion Statements for an Interest Inventory

Directions: Use these statements to develop an interest inventory. Add your own ideas.

Read the statements aloud and ask the student to complete them orally or have students read and complete them in writing.

1. I enjoy _____.

2. My favorite subject in school is _____.

3. When I read, I like to read _____.

4. My favorite thing in the world is _____.

5. I like to spend time _____.

6. My hobbies are _____.

7. I like to write about _____.

8. When I finish school, I want to be _____.

9. My favorite television shows are _____.

10. I would like to learn more about _____.

11. I would like to spend more time in school _____

_____.

---

0 *Papers in this category cannot be scored for one reason or another. Papers that are blank, that respond to an assignment different from the one given, that merely comment on the assignment ("This topic is silly"), that only copy or rephrase the assignment, or that are illegible would all be included in this category.*

1 *Papers in this category attempt to deal with the assignment, but they fail to do so adequately. These papers are too general, abrupt, or refer to the assignment only indirectly.*

2 *Papers in this category respond to the task set up in the assignment, but they do so in a way that is sketchy, inconsistent, and incomplete. There are gaps or other problems in the organization. Vocabulary may be too general and the paper lacking in the detail necessary to convey the purpose clearly and exactly. The reader has a basic idea of what the writer is trying to say but has to make many inferences.*

3 *Papers in this category fulfill the requirements of the assignment although the reader might encounter a little confusion from time to time. The paper is generally well organized so that the reader does not need to make a lot of*

inferences. These papers include sufficient details so that the reader under-stands the writer's message.

4   *Papers that merit this highest score are well organized, complete, and explicit. These papers include all of the strengths of the 3 category, but they are more clearly and consistently presented. The reader grasps the writer's message easily without having to make inferences. The writer uses a varied and exact vocabulary that enhances as well as clarifies the message. (pp. 51–52)*

Miscue Analysis

Miscue analysis is a procedure that lets the teacher "get a window on the reading process" (Goodman, 1965). A miscue is an oral response that is different from the text that is being read. For example, if the text reads, "Billy rode his horse around the ranch," and a child reading this says, "Billy rode his pony around the ranch," this miscue shows that the child has constructed the appropriate meaning for this sentence even though she didn't say the exact words. Sometimes miscues are referred to as unexpected responses or errors.

Goodman (1965) concluded from his research that by studying a student's miscues from an oral reading sample the teacher could determine the cues and strategies the student was using or not using in constructing meaning. This procedure attempts to look at the process of reading holistically.

On the basis of the Goodman (1965) research, the reading miscue inventory (Goodman & Burke, 1972) was developed. Although this analysis is normally reserved for students who are having difficulty constructing meaning, the classroom reading miscue assessment (CRMA), a simplified version of miscue analysis (Rhodes & Shanklin, 1990), can be used with all students in a classroom. The CRMA takes from 10 to 15 minutes per student. Rhodes and Shanklin indicate that it "helps teachers gather important instructional information by providing a framework for observing students' oral reading and their ability to construct meaning" (1990, p. 254).

All of the variations of miscue analysis require additional study on your part as a teacher. See "For Additional Reading" for suggestions.

Informal Reading Inventories

The informal reading inventory (IRI) consists of a series of samples of text organized in increasing difficulty; students individually read the texts orally and/or silently. By studying their oral reading patterns and their responses to comprehension questions, the teacher can get a picture of how they analyze words in context, how they construct meaning, and what their approximate level of reading is. This procedure has been used in assessing and evaluating reading since the 1920s (Beldin, 1970). IRIs usually consist of four types:

1. *Teacher constructed* using materials from which students will be reading.
2. *Publisher constructed* to match series of texts to be used for reading instruction.
3. *Generic IRIs* using samples of a variety of types of texts.
4. *Group IRIs* that have been adapted from the individual IRI concept.

One of the major advantages of using IRIs has always been that students' reading was actually being used as the basis for seeing how well they could read. Their ability to analyze words was being determined by looking at how they actually carried out this process in context. Applying some of the concepts of miscue analysis to the analysis of oral reading improved the process. Even when there is much controversy about reading assessment, the use of IRIs remains a very popular procedure (Pikulski, 1990a).

A full explanation of the procedures for using IRIs is beyond the scope of this text, but there are many sources to consult. One of the more complete discussions is by Johnson, Kress, and Pikulski (1987), listed in "For Additional Reading." As you learn to use this widely used procedure, keep the following questions in mind:

1. Does the reading of samples or portions of text give you the same picture of students' ability to construct meaning as does the reading of complete texts?
2. Is it really possible to identify precise levels of text and determine a students' reading levels using these texts?
3. In general, are the procedures used in administering, scoring, and interpreting the IRI consistent with what we know about how children develop literacy?

These are presented to help you be a more critical (evaluative) user of the IRI. Obviously, I question whether the IRI is as valuable as even I once thought it was. Therefore, I believe that it should be used judiciously.

Running Records

Another procedure for analyzing a student's reading is the running record (Clay, 1985), which is similar to miscue analysis. In this procedure, students read three samples of text ranging from easy to difficult. By looking at the students' responses, you are able to see their strengths and weaknesses in using various reading strategies. Running records are an important part of the assessment and evaluation used in the Reading Recovery Program in New Zealand and the United States (Clay, 1985; Pinnell, Fried, & Estice, 1990), and they are generally used with beginning literacy learners. For more information, see *The Early Detection of Reading Difficulties* (Clay, 1985).

Assessment Procedures
Accompanying Published Materials

For many years, the publishers of basal readers have produced different types of tests to accompany their materials. Many publishers are moving more and more toward authentic literature and real books as resources for literacy development and are including in their packages a variety of suggestions and procedures for more authentic assessment and evaluation. If you are using one of these published resources, you should keep in mind what you have learned about effective literacy learning and assessment and select only those procedures that fit your needs and the needs of your students.

BECOMING AN EVALUATIVE USER OF ASSESSMENT TECHNIQUES

Figure 10.24 summarizes the assessment techniques discussed in the previous section in a reference guide for your use. All of these techniques are sound possibilities that can be used in the literacy-centered classroom and reflect some of the best that we know about literacy learning and assessment at this time. *No classroom needs all of these techniques all of the time.* You must become a selective user of the various techniques. Consider the following points as you decide which techniques to use:

- *How children develop literacy:* This is paramount to everything that has been discussed in this text. Any assessment technique used should be in line with what we know about how children learn and develop literacy.
- *Principles for effective assessment:* Continuously refer to these principles and ask yourself whether the techniques you are using are consistent with them (see page 552).
- *Trust your judgment:* If you know and feel that a technique is inappropriate, question it—maybe it shouldn't be used. Consider another alternative.
- *Start small:* Select one or two techniques to use, and try them out. Add others if necessary.
- *Evaluate techniques:* As you use various assessment techniques, evaluate them. Are they assessing what you want to assess? *If they don't help you and your students improve literacy learning, they shouldn't be used.* Talk with your colleagues to come up with alternative techniques.

Figure 10.24   Reference Guide to Assessment Techniques

Technique	Purpose	Comments
Checklists (p. 573)	Guide observations	May be used to guide observations in many areas related to literacy learning
Records of independent reading and writing (p. 576)	Keep track of independent reading and writing	Should be used at all levels; gives insights about students' attitudes and habits
Retellings (p. 578)	Assess meaning construction	One of the best procedures to assessing construction of meaning
Prep (p. 579)	Assess prior knowledge	Helps you plan type of support students need
Responses to literature (p. 582)	Assess meaning construction, levels of reading, and use of word recognition strategies	Shows how students use what they have read and integrate ideas into their own experiences
Student self-evaluations (p. 583)	Determine student's perception of own reading and writing	Helps students take ownership of learning
Process interviews (p. 585)	Gain insight into student's metacognition processes	Individual procedure that should be used selectively
Teacher-selected reading samples (p. 587)	Assess meaning construction Assess decoding, if done orally	Good informal procedure; may be collected and compared over time
Literature circles (p. 588)	Assess meaning construction	Integrates instruction and assessment
Interest inventories (p. 591)	Determine student's interests	Provides a basis for planning learning activities
Holistic scoring of writing (p. 591)	Evaluate meaning construction through writing	Provides a way of judging writing by looking at the entire piece
Miscue analysis (p. 593)	Assess decoding and use of strategies	Procedure requires detailed training (see "For Additional Reading")
Informal reading inventories (p. 593)	Assess meaning construction	Procedure requires detailed training (see "For Additional Reading") Use judiciously
Running records (p. 594)	Assess use of decoding strategies	Procedure requires detailed training (see "For Additional Reading")
Assessment procedures accompanying published materials (p. 595)	Varies according to publisher	Should be used selectively

WHAT TO DO ABOUT GRADING

Even with a new concept of assessment, one issue continues to frustrate many teachers—grading. Nearly all schools continue to give grades after they have adopted a portfolio concept, and in most instances the report card system does not match the assessment plan they have started. One point needs to be kept in mind: *grading has always been an issue* in reading instruction. Why, however, does it appear to be a more significant issue with this new concept of assessment?

Under the old concept of assessment, teachers could easily take numerical grades from worksheets, workbooks, and tests, place them in a grade book, total them, and average them for a grade. They could then show the students, parents, and administrators "their proof" for the grades given without feeling that they had to judge or evaluate what the students had actually done. This was a very comfortable position, but it did not really reflect what the students were doing.

The report card systems in place in many schools (A-B-C letter grading) simply do not match the new view of assessment developed in this chapter (Cockrum & Castillo, 1991; Tierney et al., 1991). Therefore, most schools need to rethink and evaluate the report card system. Figure 10.25 shows a portion of a new report card designed by the Exeter Township Schools in Pennsylvania. Letter grades of A-B-C and so forth are given on this card.

If letter grades must be given in a literacy-centered classroom, evaluation must be viewed as being more subjective. Therefore, there are a number of factors to consider:

- Written descriptions for each letter grade should be developed that vary by grade level and school and that are based on the overall school objectives. The descriptions could include some of the benchmarks discussed earlier. For example, an "A" at grade 3 might read as follows: "A = Reads many self-selected books with understanding. Is able to compare books and draw conclusions. Shows a thorough understanding of what has been read." These letter descriptions would guide the assessment.
- If you must record letter grades, use a rating scale to evaluate written and/or oral responses to literature. For example, "A = Response indicates *thorough* understanding of what was read; B = Response shows *some* understanding of what was read," and so forth.
- Involve students in their own grading. After discussing your grading criteria with them, ask them to determine their own grade and place this in their portfolio with written justification.

You will find that establishing your own criteria for grading will make the job of grading far less difficult than most people make it out to be. Use the principles for assessment discussed earlier in this chapter. These, along with

Figure 10.25 New Report Card Focusing on Integrated Language Arts

INTEGRATED LANGUAGE ARTS	Semesters				
	1	2	3	4	Ave.
Reading:					
Demonstrates an understanding of text					
Reads silently for a sustained period					
Reads a variety of materials					
Reads independently					
Incorporates vocabulary skills meaningfully					
Applies vocabulary skills					
Writing:					
Writes on a regular basis					
Experiments with skills, topics, and formats					
Demonstrates correct use of writing process					
Demonstrates knowledge of proper mechanics					
Speaking:					
Maintains the subject line in conversation					
Expresses his or her ideas appropriately					
Asks appropriate questions					
Uses appropriate speaking skills					
Listening:					
Attends to peers and adults					
Responds appropriately to information					

Source: From Exeter Township Schools, Pennsylvania, 1991–1992. Used by permission.

your criteria for grading, should help to make this difficult task easier. Finally, keep in mind that grading is subjective and is generally in conflict with the overall concept of a literacy-centered classroom (Cockrum & Castillo, 1991).

DEALING WITH PROBLEMS IN CONSTRUCTING MEANING

When you use various instructional and assessment techniques, you will find that some students are encountering problems in meaning construction. Years ago, teachers looked at these students and asked, "What skills are they lacking?" or "What types of comprehension questions are they unable to answer?" What we have learned about the process of constructing meaning and literacy learning leads us to look at these problems in other ways: to ask different questions and to use different techniques to support students in this situation. The following six questions should be helpful in thinking about and analyzing students who are having problems with meaning construction:

Does the student's behavior indicate a "real problem" with meaning construction, or is it a normal expectation or specific to one situation? Often young readers will exhibit reading behaviors that are normal parts of their literacy development and do not reflect problems at all. For example, a first or second grader reading books like *Jillian Jiggs* (Gilman, 1985) or *The Lady with the Alligator Purse* (Westcott, 1988) may not recognize every word but may have a thorough understanding of the stories. It is normal to expect that students at the early levels of literacy learning will not know by sight all of the words in every story they read. A sixth grader reading an informational book about prehistoric animals may miss an important point because he does not know one or two unusual key-concept words in the text. This is a specific situation and does not indicate a major problem in constructing meaning.

To determine whether students are having "real problems" in learning to construct meaning, look for *patterns* of behaviors. Ask whether these patterns are normal occurrences in literacy learning, are specific to one type of situation, or are "real" problems for the student.

Is the problem one of understanding the text or of decoding individual words? Sometimes students will read a text and will not be able to respond to it personally, retell it, or answer questions posed by the teacher. When you examine the situation further, you might find that this student is unable to read the text aloud—in other words, to decode the words. Perhaps the student has not learned the letter-sound relationships of the language and does not know phonics and the other cueing systems that would help develop this ability. This student should receive support such as the following:

- *Shared and repeated readings:* Engage the student in shared and repeated readings using texts that have strong, rhythmic patterns; this is also appropriate for older students. Use the texts to point out decoding clues such as context, structural elements, and phonic elements (see Chapter 5).
- *Make lists of patterned words to be used in writing:* Brainstorm *with students* to create a list of words that follows a particular phonic or structural element, and encourage them to use these in their writing.

    examples:

    cat   cap
    map   nap
    bat   lap

    unsafe
    unhappy
    untied

- *Involve students in writing:* Have students do shared, collaborative, and independent writing, encouraging them to spell words as they think they sound (see Chapters 2 and 7).
- *Teach students a strategy for inferring word meanings:* A strategy like the word detective strategy discussed in Chapters 4 and 5 helps students relate decoding and meaning.

There are many other techniques that you might use in this situation. These are the types of support that are consistent with what we know about how students learn to decode words in a meaningful way (see Chapter 5).

If you determine that the student's problem is one of constructing meaning, continue to ask the following questions before deciding on a plan of support.

Does the reader have the prior knowledge (schema, background) for the text being read?   Because this is so important to successful meaning construction, you should examine the status of the student in these areas. You may want to use a plan like PREP (discussed earlier in this chapter) or other observation techniques. Some students often need more detailed activation of prior knowledge and background to gain a framework for meaning construction, and many teachers report that more thorough development of background is helpful. See the strategies and techniques discussed in Chapter 3.

Is the text clearly written?   Sometimes readers have the needed background to read and understand a text, but the text may not be clearly written or the author may not have given enough information or background to get the ideas across. In these cases the text must be carefully examined to see if it is part of the difficulty. For example, a reader may have trouble understanding a particular author's writing style or a particular type of text.

If the text to be read is a major part of the problem, there are several different ways to provide support for the student:

- Change the text.
- Use a mode of reading that is more structured, such as teacher-guided reading (see Chapter 2).
- Use graphic organizers before and after reading to help students identify the important information in the text (see Chapters 3 and 8).

Does the reader know the key-concept vocabulary to construct meaning from the text? In some instances, particularly with expository texts, readers may have difficulty because they do not understand key-concept words. Many of the suggestions presented in Chapter 4 may be helpful in these situations.

Can the reader use strategies like predicting, monitoring, and summarizing? These three strategies are important to constructing meaning (see Chapter 8). If you are able to tell through observing students' responses to reading that they cannot use these strategies, you may need to provide more support for them. Ideas discussed in Chapters 3 and 8 should be helpful to you in developing a stronger strategic support system for students.

Monitoring is often a problem for students who are having difficulty constructing meaning. A good way to tell whether readers are able to monitor their own comprehension is to have them read and answer questions about the text and then ask them to tell whether they think their answers are correct. Good comprehension monitors know when their answers are correct but may think some of their answers are wrong when they are actually correct. Poor comprehension monitors will think that their answers are right when they are really wrong (Palincsar & Brown, 1984).

Analyzing a student's problems is not a simple task, but as we continue to learn more about the process of constructing meaning we can become more effective in locating the possible causes for problems and find better ways to provide support for students.

SUMMARY

This chapter has focused on a new concept of assessment for the literacy-centered classroom. Eight principles for effective assessment were suggested:

1. Assessment should be a continuous, ongoing process.
2. Effective assessment is an integral part of instruction.
3. Assessment must be authentic, reflecting "real" reading and writing.

4. Assessment should be a collaborative, reflective process.
5. Effective assessment is multidimensional.
6. Assessment should be developmentally and culturally appropriate.
7. Effective assessment identifies students' strengths.
8. Assessment must be based on what we know about how students learn to read and write.

The portfolio concept was discussed, and observation was stressed as an important aspect of assessment.

A variety of assessment techniques consistent with these principles was presented and discussed. They include checklists, records of independent reading and writing, retellings, PREP, responses to literature, student self-evaluations, process interviews, teacher-selected reading samples, literature circles, interest inventories, holistic scoring of writing, miscue analysis, informal reading inventories, running records, and assessment procedures accompanying published materials. The need to become a selective user of these techniques was stressed. Grading was briefly discussed, and a series of six questions was suggested as a way of thinking about and analyzing problems in the construction of meaning.

Children's Books

Dahl, R. (1990). *Esio trot.* New York: Viking.

Freedman, R. (1990). *Franklin Delano Roosevelt.* New York: Clarion.

Gilman, P. (1985). *Jillian Jiggs.* New York: Scholastic.

Jaspersohn, W. (1991). *Cranberries.* Boston: Houghton Mifflin.

McPhail, D. (1984). *Fix-it.* New York: Dutton Children's Books, a Division of Penguin.

Rawls, W. (1974). *Where the red fern grows.* New York: Bantam.

Waber, B. (1988). *Ira says goodbye.* Boston: Houghton Mifflin.

Westcott, N. B. (1988). *The lady with the alligator purse.* Boston: Little, Brown.

For Additional Reading

Au, K. H., Scheu, J. A., Kawakami, A. J., & Herman, P. A. (1990). Assessment and accountability in a whole literacy curriculum. *Reading Teacher, 33,* 574–578.

Clay, M. M. (1985, 2nd ed., 1979). *The early detection of reading difficulties* (3rd ed.). Auckland, New Zealand: Heinemann.

Goodman, Y., Watson, D., & Burke, C. (1987). *Reading miscue inventory: Alternative procedures.* New York: Richard C. Owen.

Johnson, M. S., Kress, R. A., & Pikulski, J. J. (1987). *Informal reading inventories* (2nd ed.). Newark, DE: International Reading Association.

Millett, N. C. (1986). *Teaching the writing process: A guide for teachers and supervisors.* Boston: Houghton Mifflin.

Tierney, R. J., Carter, M. A., & Desai, L. E. (1991). *Portfolio assessment in the reading-writing classroom.* Norwood, MA: Christopher-Gordon.

References

Au, K. H. (1991). *Assessment*. Speech given in Phoenix, AZ, September 19, 1991.

Au, K. H. (in press, to be released in 1993). *Literacy instruction in multicultural settings*. Orlando, FL: Harcourt, Brace, Jovanovich.

Au, K. H., Scheu, J., & Kawakami, A. J. (1990). Assessment of students' ownership of literacy. *Reading Teacher, 44*, 154–156.

Au, K. H., Scheu, J. A., Kawakami, A. J., & Herman, P. A. (1990). Assessment and accountability in a whole literacy curriculum. *Reading Teacher, 43*, 574–578.

Baker, L., & Brown, A. L. (1984). Metacognitive skills in reading. In P. D. Pearson (Ed.), *Handbook of reading research* (pp. 353–394). New York: Longman.

Beldin, H. O. (1970). Informal reading testing: Historical review and review of the research. In W. K. Durr (Ed.), *Reading difficulties: Diagnosis, correction, and remediation* (pp. 67–84). Newark, DE: International Reading Association.

Bertrand, J. E. (1991). Student assessment and evaluation. In B. Harp (Ed.), *Assessment and evaluation in whole language programs* (pp. 17–33). Norwood, MA: Christopher-Gordon.

Brown, A. L. (1980). Metacognitive development and reading. In R. J. Spiro, B. C. Bruce, & W. F. Brewer (Eds.), *Theoretical issues in reading comprehension* (pp. 453–481). Hillsdale, NJ: Lawrence Erlbaum.

Cambourne, B., & Turbill, J. (1990). Assessment in whole language classrooms: Theory into practice. *Elementary School Journal, 90*, 337–349.

Church, C. J. (1991). Record keeping in the whole language classroom. In B. Harp (Ed.), *Assessment and evaluation in whole language programs* (pp. 177–200). Norwood, MA: Christopher-Gordon.

Clay, M. M. (1985). *The early detection of reading difficulties* (3rd ed.). Auckland, New Zealand: Heinemann.

Cockrum, W. A., & Castillo, M. (1991). Whole language assessment and evaluation strategies. In B. Harp (Ed.), *Assessment and evaluation in whole language programs* (pp. 73–86). Norwood, MA: Christopher-Gordon.

Collins, A., Brown, J. S., & Newman, S. E. (1986). *Cognitive apprenticeship: Teaching the craft of reading, writing and mathematics*. Report No. 6459. Cambridge, MA: BNN Laboratories.

Dillon, D. (1990). Editorial. *Language Arts, 67*, 237–239.

Farr, R., & Carey, R. F. (1986). *Reading: What can be measured?* (2nd ed.). Newark, DE: International Reading Association.

Flood, J., & Lapp, D. (1989). Reporting reading progress: A comparison portfolio for parents. *Reading Teacher, 42*(7), 508–514.

Gambrell, L., Pfeiffer, W., & Wilson, R. (1985). The effects of retelling upon reading comprehension and recall of text information. *Journal of Educational Research, 78*, 216–220.

Goodman, K. S. (1965). A linguistic study of cues and miscues in reading. *Elementary English, 42*, 639–643.

Goodman, K. (1986). *What's whole in whole language*. Portsmouth, NH: Heinemann.

Goodman, Y., & Burke, C. (1972). *Reading miscue inventory manual: Procedures for diagnosis and evaluation*. New York: Richard C. Owen.

Harp, B. (1991). Principles of assessment in whole language classrooms. In B. Harp (Ed.), *Assessment and evaluation in whole language programs* (pp. 35–50). Norwood, MA: Christopher-Gordon.

Harris, T. L., & Hodges, R. E. (1981). *A dictionary of reading and related terms.* Newark, DE: International Reading Association.

Langer, J. (1981). From theory to practice: A prereading plan. *Journal of Reading, 25,* 152–156a.

Langer, J. (1982). Facilitating text processing: The elaboration of prior knowledge. In J. Langer & M. T. Smith-Burke (Eds.), *Reader meets author/bridging the gap* (pp. 149–162). Newark, DE: International Reading Association.

Langer, J. (1984). Examining background knowledge and text comprehension. *Reading Research Quarterly, 19,* 468–481.

Marshall, N. (1983). Using story grammar to assess reading comprehension. *Reading Teacher, 36,* 616–620.

Mathews, J. K. (1990). From computer management to portfolio assessment. *Reading Teacher, 43,* 420–421.

Millett, N. C. (1986). *Teaching the writing process: A guide for teachers and supervisors.* Boston: Houghton Mifflin.

Morrow, L. M. (1989). Using story retelling to develop comprehension. In K. D. Muth (Ed.), *Children's comprehension of text: Research into practice* (pp. 37–58). Newark, DE: International Reading Association.

NAEP. (1990a). *Assessment and exercise specifications.* 1992 National Assessment of Educational Progress in Reading, March 28, 1990. [mimeographed document]

NAEP. (1990b). *Reading framework: 1992 National assessment of educational progress reading assessment.* 1992 NAEP Consensus Planning Project, March 28, 1990. [mimeographed document]

Palincsar, A. S., & Brown, A. L. (1984). Reciprocal teaching of comprehension-fostering and comprehension-monitoring activities. *Cognition and Instruction, 2,* 117–175.

Paradis, E. E., Chatton, B., Boswell, A., Smith, M., & Yovich, S. (1991). Accountability: Assessing comprehension during literature discussion. *Reading Teacher, 45,* 8–17.

Paratore, J. R., & Indrisano, R. (1987). Intervention assessment of reading comprehension. *Reading Teacher, 40,* 778–783.

Patchell, G. (1986). Holistic scoring in the classroom. In C. B. Olson (Ed.), *Practical ideas for teaching writing as a process* (pp. 185–187). Sacramento, CA: California State Department of Education.

Perrone, V. (1991). Toward more powerful assessment. In V. Perrone (Ed.), *Expanding student assessment* (pp. 164–166). Alexandria, VA: Association for Supervision and Curriculum Development.

Pikulski, J. J. (1989). The assessment of reading: A time for a change? *Reading Teacher, 43,* 80–81.

Pikulski, J. J. (1990a). Informal reading inventories. *Reading Teacher, 43,* 514–516.

Pikulski, J. J. (1990b). The role of tests in a literacy assessment program. *Reading Teacher, 43,* 686–688.

Pinnell, G. S., Fried, M. D., & Estice, R. M. (1990). Reading recovery: Learning how to make a difference. *Reading Teacher, 43,* 282–295.

Rhodes, L. K., & Shanklin, N. L. (1990). Miscue analysis in the classroom. *Reading Teacher, 44,* 252–254.

Simmons, J. (1990). Portfolios as large-scale assessment. *Language Arts, 67,* 262–268.

Tierney, R. J., Carter, M. A., & Desai, L. E. (1991). *Portfolio assessment in the reading-writing classroom.* Norwood, MA: Christopher-Gordon.

Tierney, R. J., & Shanahan, T. (1991). Research on the reading-writing relationship: Interactions, transactions, and outcomes. In R. Barr, M. L. Kamil, P. Mosenthal & P. D. Pearson (Eds.), *Handbook of reading research* (Vol. 2, pp. 246–280). New York: Longman.

Valencia, S. (1990a). A portfolio approach to classroom reading assessment: The whys, whats and hows. *Reading Teacher, 43,* 338–340.

Valencia, S. (1990b). Alternative assessment: Separating the wheat from the chaff. *Reading Teacher, 44,* 60–61.

Valencia, S., & Pearson, P. D. (1987). Reading assessment: Time for a change. *Reading Teacher, 40*(8), 726–732.

Valencia, S. W. (in press). Portfolios: Panacea or Pandora's box. To appear in F. Finch (Ed.), *Educational performance testing.* Chicago, IL: Riverside Publishing.

Vygotsky, L. S. (1978). *Mind in society.* Cambridge, MA: Harvard University Press.

Wixson, K. K., Peters, C. W., & Weber, E. M. (1987). New directions in statewide reading assessment. *Reading Teacher, 40*(8), 749–754.

Wolf, D. P. (1989). Portfolio assessment: Sampling student work. *Educational Leadership, 46,* 35–39.

Wood, K. D. (1988). Techniques for assessing students' potential for learning. *Reading Teacher, 41,* 440–447.

Epilogue: A Celebration of Literacy

Every day in every classroom should be a celebration of literacy and learning for students and their teachers. The thrill and joy of learning should be a part of every classroom community.

Throughout this text we have looked at ideas, strategies, and procedures that can help us support children as they learn to construct meaning. No single strategy or procedure mentioned will solve all literacy problems. We must begin by accepting the idea that *all* students *are* constructors of meaning, and that our job is to support and encourage them in this process. We must celebrate all successes no matter how large or small, continuing to seek new ideas and improve our understanding of how children learn and how we can support them in doing this. We cannot afford to get trapped into one point of view or one set of procedures. Our task is to continuously help students achieve new horizons in what they do.

Recently, I conducted a series of workshops for a group of teachers in a major city. On the first day I worked with first- and second-grade teachers on how to use one piece of literature with students and change the mode of reading to meet their individual needs. I challenged them to return to their classrooms the next day and try some of these procedures.

On the second day of the workshops, I worked with third- and fourth-grade teachers. Before the workshop began, a teacher came up and said, "I have a message for you from Mrs. _____. She was here yesterday." Needless to say, I was a bit concerned about what I was going to hear. She said, "Mrs. _____ tried some of the ideas this morning that you discussed yesterday. She said to thank you for telling her it was okay to do these things. She sends you a hug and so do twenty-eight first graders." This type of response shows that teachers and students need to be supported in making their classrooms exciting environments for constructing meaning.

Author/Source Index

Subject Index